George Giffard

Sermons upon the Whole Book of the Revelation

George Giffard

Sermons upon the Whole Book of the Revelation

ISBN/EAN: 9783337827267

Printed in Europe, USA, Canada, Australia, Japan

Cover: Foto ©Lupo / pixelio.de

More available books at **www.hansebooks.com**

SERMONS VPON
THE WHOLE BOOKE OF
THE REVELATION.

Set forth by GEORGE GIFFARD, Preacher of the
Word at Mauldin in Essex.

REVEL. 18.2.

And he cried out mightily with a lowd voyce, saying: It is fallen, it is fallen, Babylon the great citie, and is become the habitation of diuels, and the hold of all foule spirites, and a cage of every vncleane and hatefull bird.

LONDON,
Printed for Thomas Man.
1599.

TO THE RIGHT NOBLE
EARLE OF ESSEX, HIS VERIE GOOD LORD.

That famous Captaine Iehosua (vnder whose conduct the kings of Canaan, & their armies were destroyed, and the tribes of Israell seated and planted in that land of promise) was straightly cōmanded by the Lord, Iehos. 1. that the booke of the law should not depart out of his mouth, but that he should meditate therein day and night. A cōmandemēt not peculiar to him alone, but necessarie for all mightie warriours. For doubtlesse if there were any man that doth stand in deede to be wholly directed by the counsell and ayde of the Lord God in all his affaires, it is the noble warriour. And that for sundry causes: first, for that the true fortitude it selfe, wherewith he is to performe his valiant and noble actes, is not a vertue (as I may say) humane, or which any man hath in his owne nature, or can attaine vnto by the powers of his owne minde: but a diuine gift, a worke of grace, which is to be learned, and attained, onely by the holy Scriptures: for the Lord doth not decke the minde of man with true vertue, but by his sacred word. Then further it is requisite for him that warreth, to see and to know assuredly, that the cause and quarrell in which he fighteth, is good, iust, and warrantable by that written

THE EPISTLE DEDICATORIE.

word of God: otherwise, how sauage, how foule, and how cruell a thing, is the shedding of bloud? Finally, he is wholly to depend vpon the mouth of God, to be guided by his wisedome, counsell and direction in all his affaires, that so his battels may be the battels of the Lord, that if he stand and conquer, he conquereth to the Lord, if he be wounded and fall, he falleth & dieth in the Lord. This is a most cleare case, and without all doubt or controuersie. Of such worthies so guided by God, the Church for her defence had plentie in old time, according as her need required, being (as the holy histories do shew) beset on euerie side, with so many and so fierce enemies, that the prophet in the Psalme reporteth, saying: Except the Lord had beene on our side, now may Israell say, except the Lord had bene on our side, when men rose vp against vs, they had swallowed vs vp quicke, when their wrath was kindled against vs. Of such also she standeth in great need in these daies, being in the middest of those fierce and terrible warres, which this Reuelation so long since hath prophesied of, and foreshewed. The time is now past, in which the fift angell, as we reade chap. 16. hath powred forth his vial vpō the throne of the beast, and that bloudy kingdome of Antichrist waxeth dark, their brightnesse & glorie is diminished, wherfore they be so vexed, that they gnaw their tongues for sorrow. The sixt Angell also (as it is said in the same chapter) hath powred forth his viall vpon the great riuer Euphrates, & the water thereof is dried vp, that is to say, the riches, the strength, the fortification and munition of great Babell doth so decaie, that the way for the kings of the earth is in preparing. The dragon, the beast, and the false prophet, haue sent forth their

messengers

THE EPISTLE DEDICATORIE.

messengers, euen their vncleane spirites which are like frogges, into all lands vnto the kings of the earth to stirre them vp vnto battaile. The Iesuites, the Seminarie Priestes, are dispersed in all countries. The armies of Gog and Magog, which compasse about the tents of the Saints, and the beloued citie, Reuel. 20. are yet but in part destroyed. The beast and the kings of the earth, and their armies are yet assembled to war against the Lord, Reuel. 19. All these things come to passe in the daies that we liue in: Now of late yeares there entred (as they call it) into the holy League, Kings & Princes, binding themselues with solemne vow to do their vttermost to destroy and to roote out all that professe the holy gospell of Iesus Christ: here is great conspiracy against the Church. And by the singular blessing of God, our noble Queene hath bene, and is the greatest defender and protector of the holy worship, & true worshippers that is vnder heauen. The Churches in other countries haue by her aide bene much supported & releeued in their distresses. The Romish beast & his companie haue espied so much and do make full account, that all their wars & enterprises against the Church are to small purpose, vnlesse they could first supplant and destroy her Maiestie. And to effect this their wicked desire, they haue inuented all the waies and meanes which possibly they can. Their Pope (who is the standerd-bearer in that apostacie) did long since excommunicate her Highnesse. He hath frō time to time sent forth his Iesuite Priests & others, to worke all maner of trecheries, and traiterously to murther her royall Person: wherein the Lord God hath oftē preuented them miraculously, for which we are bound most deepely to giue him thanks. The

King of Spaine, who hath giuen his power to the beaft, fent his forces Anno 88. for to inuade her land, & to throw down her excellent Highneffe, from that facred authoritie & power in which almighty God hath placed her, & miraculoufly protected her, fighting from heauen againft her enemies, euen to the wonderment of the whole world. And what fhall we thinke, that they haue now done? Nay, looke how long that great fierie dragon, Sathan, that prince of darkenes doth burne in hatred againft God & his truth, fo long Antichrift and his adherents moued by his inftigation, will be reftles in feeking the fubuerfion of our religion, Queen, and countrie. Then do we efpecially and aboue many others, ftand in neede of noble warriors & mighty men, who in fo great and waighty caufes are to be guided by the moft high God, euen by the light of his moft facred word, that through his bleffing they may profper and haue good fucceffe. Among other bookes of the holy Scripture, this Reuelation doth giue both fpeciall inftruction and direction, and alfo incouragement vnto thefe warres. For it doth not only prophefie of them and defcribe them, and fhew what fhall be the iffue of the, but alfo fetteth forth how the Lord himfelfe doth as it were found the trumpet vnto this battaile againft Babell, faying: Reward her euen as fhe hath rewarded you, and giue her double according to her workes, and in the cup that fhe hath filled vnto you, fill her the double. In as much as fhe glorified her felfe and liued in pleafure, fo much giue ye to her torment and forrow, chap. 18. This prophefie then is moft fit for the warriers of our time, that defire to warre in the Lord, and for his truth. I haue according to my fmall abilitie expounded it in publike auditory,

THE EPISTLE DEDICATORIE.

torie, as a matter very profitable for the daies that we liue in: and I do present and offer it to your H. not that my simple exposition is worthy to come into the hands of so Honorable & so learned a person, where it can adde very small or rather no instruction: but I commend the prophesie it selfe as a book most fit for your H. to be exerciced in. And if it be requisite for all true christians to be instructed in it, then much more is it necessarie for your H. aboue others, to be euen throughly acquainted with it, for which I can easily render great and apparant reason. The enemies prepare themselues with mightie forces, threatning great terror vnto this land, euen as the waues of the sea, readie to ouerwhelme vs. If such wars and troubles do come, there is on the other part, and that generally through this Realme, among all that loue the safetie and good of their countrey, a rare expectation of great things to be performed by your Honor. This expectation is as a great aduersarie opposed, which your H. shall neuer be able to satisfie without the singular power, direction, and blessing of God. And if your H. with an vpright heart, shall firmely cleaue vnto the Lord God of Heauen, that power of his, that direction and blessing shall not be wanting. It may be some will object, that manie haue done exceeding great things, and to their great honour and commendation which haue had no true knowledge nor feare of God, but led with vaine glorie, and with the fiercenes of nature. I answere that it hath bene so, but yet to their small good: for some of them hauing gotten great praise and honor, haue in their life time seene the buriall of the same. Other some haue left behind them a fame among men: but to what purpose? Can the breath of men

which

THE EPISTLE DEDICATORIE.

which vttreth their praise here vpon earth, any thing coole or mitigate the heate of those torments which they sustaine in hell? Looke vpon the valiant men of Israell, and behold what course they tooke, how they prospered, & how their honor doth stand both with God and men. King Dauid in the name of the Lord slue that great Giant Goliah. And he saith: Blessed be the Lord my rocke, which teacheth my hands to warre, and my fingers to the battaile. King Asa hauing throwne downe idolatry in his kingdome, and caused the people to worship the true God, there came an armie out of Ethiopia to inuade his land, an armie of a thousand thousands, he made his prayer to the Lord, resting vpon his power, and ouerthrew them, 2. Chron. 14. The Moabites & Ammonites gathered an exceeding multitude, & came against that godly king Iehosaphat: he assembled his people to fast and pray, & in the assembly vttered a prayer himselfe vnto the Lord God of heauen, and so obtained a glorious victory, 2. Chron. 20. VVhat should I speak of king Ezechias, who after he had restored the true worship of the Lord, had the enemies entring so neare, that they compassed Ierusalem with a mightie armie, where Rabsaka blasphemed the God of heauen: but the king and the Prophet Esay lift vp their prayer vnto God, & the Angel of the Lord went fort that night, and slue in the armie of the Assirians, an hundreth fourescore and fiue thousand, 2. king. 19. and 2. Chron. 32. He is the same God still vnto all that with vprightnes of hart cleaue vnto him, & rest vpon his mightie power: and whosoeuer they be, that cast away his feare, & dishonor him, vndoubtedly they shall not alwaies prosper. In the booke of the Iudges there be also sundrie valiant

THE EPISTLE DEDICATORIE.

ant men of warre spoken of, and likewise in other bookes of the holy scripture: and their worthie actes be set forth, I omit them, let your H. looke vpon the description of the war and the warriours against Antichrist in these times, which is in the 19. chapter of this booke. For there is described both our great captaine the Lord Iesus, comming forth to battaile against the enemies of his Church, and also the noble warriors and worthy souldiers which fight vnder his banner. I saw heauen open (saith S. Iohn) and behold there was a white horse, and he that sate vpon him was called faithfull and true, and he iudgeth and fighteth righteously. His eyes were as a flame of fire: and vpon his head are many crownes: & he had a name written which no man knoweth but himselfe. And he was clothed in a garment dipped in bloud: and his name is called the word of God. The armies also in heauen followed him vpon white horses, clothed in fine white linnen & pure. Out of his mouth went a sharpe sword, that with it he might strike the heathen; for he shall rule them with a rod of Iron: and it is he that shall tread the wine-presse of the fiercenesse and wrath of God almightie. And he had in his garment and in his thigh a name written, the king of kings, and Lord of Lords. And a little after it followeth: and I saw the beast, and the kinges of the earth, and their armies gathered together to war with him which sate vpon the horse, and with his armie. This battaile is fought vpon the earth, otherwise how do the beast, and the kings of the earth and their armies fight? Moreouer, the armies of Christ are men vpon the earth, euen the godly kings, Princes, Nobles, & worthie captaines, which with the materiall sword defend the Gospell, and the ministers

and

THE EPISTLE DEDICATORIE.

and preachers of the truth, which with the spirituall sword fight against Antichrist. Against these the armies of the beast and of the Kings do fight. These are said to bee the armies in heauen, because their cause for which they fight, is from heauen, and also the power with which they fight. These ride vpon white horses, and are clothed in fine white linnen and pure. They come strongly, swiftly, and cheerefully to this battaile. They come in sinceritie, integrity, & puritie of faith, of loue, and of other affections. For all is pure white about them. The warriours of this world, which warre according to the lustes of their flesh in ambition, in pride and crueltie: may be said to ride vpon red horses, and to be clothed in bloudie garmenrs. Put on that fine white linnen and pure, ride vpon that white horse among this blessed company, and follow this high captaine: and then shall your H. performe right worthy things to the glorie of God, to the good of his people, and to your owne eternall praise and felicitie.

Your Honours most dutifull to commaund:

GEORGE GIFFARD.

The argument of the booke, vnto the Christian Reader.

IT shall not be amisse (good reader) to set downe briefly the matters which are handled in this prophecie: seeing the booke seemeth dark vnto many, yea so darke, that it cannot be made cleere to their vnderstanding. True it is, that if a man light vpon some peece of it, & take it by it selfe, he shall find it dark: but if he look vpon the whole course of the matters throughout the booke, and see how things be iterated, he shall find no such darknes as he feareth, & for that respect I suppose that a briefe opening is necessarie, I vvill not stād vpon an exquisite diuision of this prophecy into the maine parts, & so into subdiuisions: but in a more plaine or rude course I will proceed, euen as the matters do lye in order. First, therefore we are to knovv, that this booke is a prophecie which openeth the state of things to come in the world from the time that it was giuen to Iohn, euen to the great day of the generall iudgement. The three first chapters are to be ioyned together, because in them there is no opening or foreshewing of things to come, but of matters that were then present. For in the first chapter after the generall title of the booke in three verses, & the salutation of Iohn to the seuen churches in fiue verses, ye haue the first vision, in which the Lord appeareth vnto Iohn, calleth him & authoriseth him, to receiue this prophecy, to write it, & to send it to the Churches, where the mysterie of the seuen stars, & of the seuen candlesticks is opened. In the second chapter, & in the third, there is opened by seuen seuerall Epistles sent frō the Lord, the state of euery one of the 7. churches of Asia, vnto which this prophecy was to be sent: so that by thē we may see in what estate the vniuersal church militant was at that time: for as some of these sēnē as yet stood firme, & other some had much declined, so was it with other churches. There be many right excellent instructiōs in these three chapters, both for the pastors & for their flocks & nothing dark or difficult, because the Lord himself expoūded that mystery of the 7. stars, & of the 7. golden candlesticks. Then next there be eyght chapters to be ioyned together, beginning at the fourth, & so continuing to the end of the eleuenth. In these eyght chapters there are set out very briefly & darkly, the summe of all the whole prophecy, for it reacheth to the generall iudgement which these chapters containe, as it is most euident by the oath of the Angel chap. 10. who sweareth that there shal be no more time but in the dayes of the voyce of the seuenth Angel vvhen he shall begin to blovv the trūpet: vvhich trūpet is blovvne in the end of the eleuenth chapter, vvhere there is also a description of the last iudgemēt. And now for the particulars in these eyght chapters. In the fourth chapter there is a glorious vision, which setteth forth the maiestie, the glorie & praise of the most high God, that raigneth & ruleth ouer all with his infinit povver, vvisedome, prouidence, & iustice, frō vvhom this reuelatiō cōmeth. For it is called the reuelatiō of Iesus Christ, vvhich God gaue him cha. 1. And vve reade in the beginning of the next chap, that the book sealed with seuen seales (vvhich is this reuelatiō) vvas in the right hād of him that sate vpō the throne. Then further in this fift chapter, there is none found worthy to ope the seales of this booke but the Lamb, euen the Lord Iesus alone, vvhose praise both mē & An-

gels

TO THE REEADER.

gels, and all creatures do sound forth. Then the summe of these two chapters is, from how high, how mighty, how wise, how iust & how glorious a God this prophecie commeth, & also frō how worthy a mediator: who receiueth it, & openeth the seuē seales thereof. In the sixt chapter we come to the reuealing of the mysteries, when the Lamb openeth fiue of the seuen seales. Vnder the first of them is figured the conquest vvhich Christ maketh ouer the natiōs of the world by this Gospel. Vnder the secōd, the third & the fourth, are resembled the plagues & iudgements which the Lord sendeth vpō the wicked world for despising and abusing the same his holy and precious Gospel. For when the graces & rich treasures of God are published & offered vnto men, and they set light by them, blaspheme & impugne them, he sendeth bloudie wars, famines, pestilences and such like in all ages. Vnder the opening of the fift seale, there is shewed the happie rest of the soules of those which were murthered by the tyrants, and cruell rage of the people for the testimony of Iesus: And how their bloud crieth alowd in the eares of the Lord for vengeance vpō those wicked mē which so cruelly slue thē. Wherupon vnder the opening of the sixt seale, there follovv vvonderfull terrible signes of Gods wrath, & cōmotions, euen to the horror of the most wicked. Also vnder the same sixt seale is set forth a spirituall plague of God vpon the world, euen the staying of the course of the holy Gospel, which is figured by foure vvicked Angels or diuels, holding the foure vvinds that they shold not blow. This in the seuenth chapter, where also it is shewed how the Lord yet prouideth for his elect both of Iewes & Gentiles, which triumph & glorifie God for their saluatiō together with al the heauēly company of blessed Angels. In the opening of the seuenth seale, are figured out the greatest plagues of all, for the Lord cōmeth to battell in hostile maner against the wicked vvorld, wherefore 7. Angels do sound 7. trūpets, and ye knovv that trūpets are sounded vnto war. In the midst of these horrible plagues the Lord God still preserueth his church, & to declare so much, before the sounding of the trumpets, the Lord Iesus appeareth in visiō standing at the altar with a goldē censer & sweet odors. In the soūding of the first, the secōd, the third and the fourth trumpet, the haile and fire mingled with bloud, are cast into the earth, the great mountaine burning with fire is cast into the sea, a great star falleth into the fountaines of waters & maketh thē bitter, & the third part of the sun, of the moone, & of the stars is strikē & darkened. By al which is meāt such an vniuersall plague in all parts of the world in corrupting & deprauing the pure religiō, as shold lay wast, poysō & darkē, euen to the finall destruction of many. We may not think it strange that one plague is set forth vnder diuers figures, which is because the vniuersality of it is described by reaching to the heauēs, to the earth, to the sea, & to the riuers of waters. To the earth a vvasting & corrupting tēpest, to the sea a burning moūtaine, to the fresh waters a bitter star, & to the sunne, moone & stars, that which doth darkē. After these 4. trūpets sounded, S. Iohn seeth an Angel flying in the midst of heauen, whom also he heard pronouncing, Wo, wo, wo, to the inhabitants of the earth, & declaring that these three vvoes shoļd be at the sounding of the three trūpets that remayned. For the plagues vvhich come at the sounding of these three trūpets are exceeding great, yea the greatest of all other. The first of thē, vvhich is at the sounding of the fift trūpet, set forth in the ninth chapter, frō the beginning of it vnto

the

TO THE READER.

the 13. verse, is the plague of the great Antichrist. This horrible plague is described vnder a great star that droppeth downe from heauen, to whom is giuen the key of the bottomlesse pit, euen the key of hell. Starres in this booke (as the Lord sheweth in the first Chap.) do signifie the Ministers of the Gospell. So that this plague which is the kingdome of the great Antichrist, cōmeth by a Minister which falleth frō heauenly doctrine, to that which is of the earth, yea of the diuell: for he openeth the pit of hell, & bringeth in the smoke of ignorance, & darknesse, & errors, which darkneth the ayre & the sunne. Out of which smoke breed the swarmes of Locusts, which like Scorpiōs do sting men. Then at the sounding of the sixt trūpet, which beginneth at the 13. ver. of the 9. chap. there are foure diuels let loose at Euphrates, & thē followeth the descriptiō of the sauage kingdome of the Turkes: whose armies do wast & destroy mē in the Popish Antichristiā kingdome, euen those vvhich worship images of gold, of siluer, of brasse, of wood, & of stone, which yet repēt not at that plague. The 10. chap. cōtaineth matter of great comfort: for after that darke kingdome of Antichrist, and that cruell kingdome of the Turkes, the Lord commeth downe with brightnesse frō heauen, with the booke of Gods word open, to expell that smoke of Antichrist. He standeth vpō the earth & the sea, he denounceth by seuē thunders horrible iudgemēts against his enemies, he sweareth that the last day shall be at the sounding of the next trumpet, and Iohn in the person of the Ministers which should liue whē this should come, is willed to take the litle booke & to eate it, & to prophecie to the kingdomes & nations. This thing is come to passe in our dayes, for after the great darkening, the Lord is come downe with light, the holy Bible is againe opened, & the seruants of God haue vvith great studie, euē as it were eaten it vp, & haue preached it vnto great kingdomes & nations. This matter is continued in the 11. chap. where Iohn is willed to measure the tēple, &c. For the Church is measured & built vp by the preaching of the word. And by this occasion here is annexed the historie of the builders, that is to say, of the faithfull Ministers of the Gospel, vvhom the Lord calleth his two witnesses. It is in the Law, that to testifie any matter, there must be at the least two witnesses: & therefore that nūber is here chosen, to shew that the Lord will neuer be without a sufficient nūber of witnesses to his truth, whē the Church was persecuted by the heathen Emperors of Rome, & afterward by the secōd beast, which is the great Antichrist. Their dignity & spirituall power is set forth to be very great, but the beast shal kill their bodies, & the seruāts of Antichrist shall vse very sauage crueltie towards thē, but God giueth them glory. For when others do succeed them endued with the same spirit, and do set forth the same truth, & maintaine the same cause that they did, they may vvell be said to be raised vp againe to life, to the great wonderment of the wicked enemies, vvho are amazed to see thē lifted vp to heauen with honor, whom they had condēned vnto hell as heretikes: & this commeth vvith great commotion & diuision of the people. And then cōmeth the third wo of the three which the Angel proclaimed, vvhich is the last & the greatest, euen the euerlasting wo, which beginneth with great terror, at the sounding of the seuenth trūpet, which is the last. And thus haue we the vvhole matter of this reuelatiō layd open in the opening of the seuē seales. All matters, as ye may see, are opened, but briefly and darkely. And it was behoueful to the seruants of

God,

TO THE READER.

God, to haue them more fully and more clearely opened, and for that cause, the Lord of his great goodnes, doth set forth the chiefe and principal matters more at large, & far more cleerely. For now from the beginning of the twelfth chapter, vnto the end of this booke, ye shall finde large and plaine descriptions, vvhich open the former things more clearely. Let vs then come vnto them.

In the beginning of the twelft Chapter, the Church militant is shewed in visiō, vnder the forme of a woman decked vvith heauēly ornaments, & trauelling vvith faith and hope, to bring forth her Sauiour, the promised Messias. Thē appeareth also in vision, her chiefe enemie, a most ugly monster the diuell, vvaiting to destroy the blessed seede so soone as he should be borne. He faileth of his purpose, and is ouercome in battel by Christ, and cast downe from heauen, so that he can no longer assaile the Church to plucke her downe from her heauenly inheritance, at vvhich there is the voyce of triumph, of ioy and gladnesse. Then Sathan being conquered by Christ, he seeketh vtterly to destroy the vvoman at once out of the earth, the Church being then in a narrow compasse, and failing therein, he maketh vvar vvith the remnant of her seede. In the 13. Chapter there are shewed in vision the chiefe instruments that the dragon vseth in vvarring against the faithfull, in persecuting and afflicting of thē: of vvhich the first is the beast with seuen heads & ten hornes. A beast most monstrous, sauage & cruell, & of so great power that the world wōdereth after him, & worshippeth him. The sixt head of this beast euen the heathen persecuting Emperours of Rome, vttered great blasphemies against God and his Church, and made vvar against the saints, & ouercame them, and slue thousand thousands of them, in those ten first persecutions vvhich histories of old do report. And what power vnder heauē can be shewed, that so murdered the saints, since Christ, but the Empire of Rome? The other is the beast with two hornes like the Lambe, which speaketh like the dragō. This is the great Antichrist (as the Papists themselues are forced to confesse) & therefore it is set forth, how he seduceth the inhabitants of the earth with signes & wonders. He is both the seuēth head of the former beast, and a beast by himselfe, exercising double power, and therefore the Angell, chapter 17. calleth him both the seuēth head of the beast, & saith also that he is the eight. He erecteth the verie patterne or image of the heathen Empire that former beast, and causeth the inhabitants of the earth to worship and to obey the same. He causeth all to receiue his marke, and none may buy and sell, except he haue his marke, or his name, or the number of his name, vvhere the number of his name is expressed. In the 14. Chapter there is first a vision of the Lambe vpon mount Sion, vvith his holy and pure companie of true and sincere vvorshippers, vvhich sing laude and prayse to God. For the Lambe preserueth them as his holy Church militant vpon earth in the dayes of that kingdome of Antichrist.

Then followeth the fall of great Babell, vvhich is that tyrannous kingdome of Antichrist. And her fall is by the preaching of the Gospell, vvhich the Angell representing the Ministers, doth publish, calling vpon all nations, kindreds, tongues, and people to vvorship the true God, & so the vvorship erected by Antichrist, being the worship of creatures, down it falleth, this is come to passe in our dayes: and there is vengeance denounced against all those which will not forsake that wicked idolatrous kingdome.

Then

TO THE READER.

Then followeth in the last part of the 14. Chapter, a description of the last iudgement vnder two figures, the one of harues̈t, the other of the vintage. The latter indeed which is of the vintage, doth represent only the cutting downe of the wicked, & casting them like clusters of grapes into hell, which is as the great wine presse of the wrath of God. In the 15. and 16. Chapters there followeth another vision of seuen Angels with the seuen last plagues. They be the plagues which are powred forth vpō the kingdome and subiectes of the great Antichrist, six of them in this world, least it might be thought, shall they escape here vntill the last day? And the seuenth which is at the day of iudgement, the last and the greatest, euen that eternall plague. And before these plagues are powred forth, the vision doth shew, how the faithfull do escape being set in safetie in the middest of them, passing through the sea of this world, which is called glassie and mingled with fire, euen as the children of Israell did escape from Pharaoh, when he pursued them in the red sea. Moses and the children of Israel did sing a song to the Lord, whē they were passed through: And so they that passe through this gulfe of the world and get the victory ouer Antichrist, are said to sing the song of Moses and the song of the Lambe. The Angels powre forth their vials, and there is a grieuous sore, and bloudshed by wars, there is famine and pestilence through immoderate heate at foure of them. And then at the fift the kingdome of the beast waxeth darke by the preaching of the Gospell, which is an exceeding sorrow vnto the Idolaters, and at the sixt the great riuer Euphrates, which is the fortification of Babell drieth vp, so that the way is in preparing for those that shall destroy her. And hereupō the dragon, the beast & the false Prophet do bestir them, & send forth their Ambassadors into all lands to get forces vnto battell against those which destroy their kingdome. Which war is now at the hottest in our dayes. And thē followeth the powring out of the last vial, which containeth together with the last vengeance of eternall iudgement, great & horrible plagues going immediatly before the last day. The there followeth the 17. Chapter, where the Angell sheweth vnto Iohn great Babell borne vp with the beast with seuen heads, and interpreteth vnto him the mystery of euery part. As what the beast is, what is signified by the seuen heads, & also by the ten hornes, and what they should do: and last of all, who that woman is which sitteth vpon the beast, & saith it is the great Citie which ruleth ouer the kings of the earth. Rome is the great Citie, Rome is great Babell, Rome of necessitie is the seat of the great Antichrist: for what other Citie in the world is builded vpon seuē hils beside Rome, which the Angell saith is meant by seuen heads? What other Citie in the world beside Rome, had those seuē seuerall gouernements? of which fiue were fallen when Iohn receiued this prophesie, one was, euen the Empire, & one to come, that is the Papacie. What other Citie hath shed the bloud of the Martyrs but Rome, let the Papistes shew if they can. Then is Rome Babel, euē the woman drunken with the bloud of the saints. In the 18. chapter the fall of Babel is set forth more at large, She falleth by the light of the Gospell, for as chapter 10. the Angell commeth downe with the little booke open, so here againe he commeth with great light, & downe falleth Babel, & becōmeth the habitation of diuels. She hath cōmitted horrible things, and aboundeth in sinne, and the people of God are called vpon to depart from her, and

not

not only that, but also to execute vengeance vpon her, and to recompence her for all the mischiefe that she hath wrought. And at her great fall and destruction, there are brought in her louers & friends, wayling and lamenting verie dolefully, euen all such as haue comitted whoredome and liued in pleasure with her, and gayned by her: for their pleasure and their gaine is gone, for she commeth to vtter desolation. Then in Chapter 19. there is first the voyce of the heauenly companies praysing the Lord for her fall and destruction. Then is there also a very great ioy and reuycing, and prayse, for the celebration of the mariage of the Lambe, which is the mariage of Christ to his Church, and the blessednesse of those which come to that feast. And lastly there is in that Chapter a glorious description of the Lord Iesus comming forth vnto battell with his armies, against the Beast and his adherents, with the victorie which he hath ouer them. And this is the full ouerthrow of Antichrist. But there hath as yet bene no mention of the destruction of the chiefe enemy of all, that is to say, of the dragon himselfe the diuell, in the 20. Chapter therefore his iudgement and destruction is set forth. And because he hath bin a more generall worker, & his mischiefe hath extended larger then the kingdome of Antichrist, there is in that 20. Chapter an historie of him set forth by it selfe: he seduced the nations before the comming of Christ, who at his coming bindeth him by the light of his Gospell from seducing the nations, and so holdeth him shut vp for the space of a thousand yeares, in which the Church doth florish greatly, and many are raised in the spirituall life. But when the thousand yeares are expired, Sathan is loosed and goeth forth againe to seduce, and by the great Antichrist, and by the Turke, gathereth innumerable multitudes into his armies to fight against the Church, which armies are called God & Magog, but they are all ouercome and destroyed and that old serpent himselfe is caught, and together with his instruments the Beast and the false Prophet, is cast into eternall fire to be tormented. After this we haue in that 20. Chapter a goodly description of the generall iudgement, with the execution of vengeance vpon the wicked. And then in the two last Chapters, that is, in the 21. and 22. there is described the eternall felicitie & blessed estate of the Church, and that in such goodly manner, that he is euen a verie blocke or a stone, that is not moued therewith. There be the greatest riches, and glorie, and ioyes shadowed out that euer were heard of. After this in the latter part of the 22. Chapter from the tenth verse, followeth the generall conclusion of this booke, where the authoritie of it is ratified with sundry ratifications. If men do but obserue this generall course of this Prophecie, and studiously obserue the handling of matters, they shall finde no such darknesse as is feared, much lesse shall it be found so obscure as the Papistes do beare in hand, when they would driue men from the reading and studie of it, because it painteth out great Babell, that Romish harlot. Farewell in Christ.

THE I. SERMON.
CHAP. I.

1. *The Reuelation of Iesus Christ, which God gaue vnto him to shew to his seruants things which must shortly be done: and he signified sending by his Angel, vnto his seruant Iohn,*
2. *Who bare record of the word of God, and of the testimony of Iesus Christ, whatsoeuer things he hath seene.*
3. *Blessed is he that readeth, and they that heare the words of this prophecy, and keepe the things which are written therein, for the time is at hand.*

IT is not many yeares past (as yee know) since I did expound this booke euen in this place, and vnto this auditorie: and therefore least any should maruaile, why I vndertake to expound it againe, I let ye vnderstand, that there is great reason to moue me hereunto, as namely, that the booke is a most excellent and a most precious iewell, which God hath bestowed vpon his Church, and great pitie it is, that all Gods seruants are not throughly acquainted with it, especially in these times. The holy Ghost saith, *Blessed is he that readeth, and they that heare the words of this prophecy, and keepe the things which are written therein, &c.* which sufficiently proueth it to be most precious, and most excellent, and the vse of it right necessary for all good Christians, and especially (as I sayd before) in these times. If any will say, why especially in these dayes? let him marke a litle. This booke (at least one great part of it) doth describe & paint out as it were in liuely colours, the tyranous kingdome of Antichrist, euen great Babylon, the mother of whoredomes & abominations of the earth. It hath pleased God, of his great goodnesse, & abundant mercy towards his people, a little before our dayes, and in our dayes, to powre forth a viall of his wrath vpon the very throne of that babylonicall beast, and to make his kingdome waxe darke. The pure light of Gods word hath displayed & disclosed al their filthines. Their power, their estimation, their glory, their riches & their dignity are much come downe and decayed. They gnaw their tongues for sorrow, they be vexed in mind. They be studious now in learning, and ransacke all corners, in what writers soeuer to find any thing which may make some shew of defence for themselues. They be both subtle, and full of cruell practises: and all, if it were possible, is to re-

SERMONS VPON

couer their ancient glorie, and to repaire the breaches which are made in the walles of their great citie. Is it not then good that men should be armed against them with the things reuealed in this booke? Is not now in these dayes, the very heate of the battaile betweene them and vs? and this prophecie leaueth them open, whereby ye may well perceiue, that there is great reason to expound it againe and againe, that it may arme the seruants of God. But here will be obiections and shew of reasons brought forth, to proue that this Reuelation is not to be medled withall, nor in any wise to be expounded among the common people. The Papists indeed cannot abide, that the people should haue any part of the holy Scriptures in a knowne language, nor that they should haue any skill or vnderstanding in them: because all sacred Scriptures detect and bewray their treacheries: but of all others, they cannot abide that this prophecie should be made knowne, or expounded publikely. The ancient Fathers (say they) the greatest and learnedest Doctors of the Church since the Apostles times, confesse that this prophecie is so mysticall and so darke, that they could not vnderstand it. And our English Iesuites of Rhemes, alledge for this purpose a saying of *Hierome*, that the Reuelation hath as many mysteries as words, and that in euery word there is hidden manifold and sundry senses. Also they alledge *Denis* Bishop of Corinth speaking to like purpose. The matter commeth to this in effect: If the great learned Fathers could not vnderstand it, how can any man of lesse learning take vpon him to expound it? is it not great arrogancie to say we do vnderstād it better then they did? Or shal the vnlearned people be made to vnderstand that which those learned Fathers could not attaine vnto? Where there is such mysticall sense and ambiguitie, what certaintie can there be in the exposition? And if the interpretation be not certaine, but that one will say this is the sense, an other will differ from him, and say that is the sense, and a third from them both, to what purpose should it be interpreted?

Let not this trouble any man, or cause him to thinke it in vaine to seeke for the interpretation of this prophecie, for all is but a blind cauill, and very easie to be refelled, which also I will now partly answer, and partly when we come to the handling of the words in the text which I haue read. I doe, and I may boldly affirme, that a man of meane learning in comparison, may now in these dayes more easily vnderstand, & expound this booke far more perfectly, then the learnedst Doctors could, and Fathers in ancient times. And further I say, and can proue that it is no arrogancie to speake thus, because there is great reason for it, as one of the ancientest Fathers, *Irenæus* I meane, in his fourth booke, chap. 43. doth shew. For he vpon a saying in Daniel 12. of sealing vp the booke vntill the time determined: and from a saying out of the Prophet *Ieremias*, that in the last dayes men should vnderstand those things: inferreth, that euery prophecy before it take effect, is darke riddles and ambiguitie vnto men. But when the time came (saith he) and it commeth to passe which was prophecied, then the prophecies haue a cleare and an vndoubted exposition. If this saying of his be true, (as none that hath sense can deny it) then this Reuelation hath many things in it, which vnto the same *Irenæus*, vnto *Denis*, vnto *Hierome*, vnto *Augustine*, and vnto the rest of the Fathers were, as *Irenæus* sayth,

Ænigmata,

THE REVELATION.

Enigmata, darke riddles, and ambiguitie, and might be taken diuerse wayes, because they liued before the times in which they should be fulfilled, which now vnto vs that haue seene them come to passe, haue a cleere and vndoubted exposition. I will open this more particularly thus: Some things in this booke were fulfilled before the dayes of these Fathers, and some in the dayes in which they liued, these they did vnderstand. Some things were figured out which should come to passe after their dayes, as the comming of the great Antichrist, and all that he should do. They vnderstood that such a wicked dominion should be set vp, yea some of them saw plainly, and so they testifie in their writings, that this monster, the man of sinne should haue his throne in Rome: but that the Bishop of Rome should so farre degenerate, as to become the head and the standard-bearer in this Apostasie, to set vp idolatrie and all blasphemous abhominations, and to persecute the holy Gospell of Iesus Christ, they did not see. Hereof it came, that many things darke vnto them, are now so cleere vnto vs being fulfilled, that all which are not wilfully blind by despising the light, cannot but see them, yea euen vnlearned men and women. And thus you may see that this obiection of the Iesuites is but a meere cauill. We haue a cleere and vndoubted exposition of the chiefest and almost of all things in this prophecy: because they be come to passe, and agree in all respects with the things which haue fallen out.

There is another obiection, and that seemeth to carry greater waight: That is this, there be many great learned men, Bishops, Doctors, and wise Princes, which do take the Pope to be the Pastor ouer Christs Church, and in no wise to be Antichrist. If it be cleere by the Reuelation, if it haue so certaine & so vndoubted an exposition vpon the fulfilling of prophecies, that Rome is Babylon, the papacy the apostasie, the Pope the man of sinne, their religion the worship of diuels: how commeth it to passe, that all these learned and wise men should not see it, no not any one of them? Do not they read the Scriptures? do not they vnderstand the Scriptures, as well as others? Is it like that so many of them should be blind in that which a few others of lesse account should see? Nay, shall we say that all they cannot know that, which vnlearned men and women do take vpon them to see and to know? Shall we thinke these of the common people can be right and the other wrong? Shall these talke of the reuelation, & say thus & thus it is to be vnderstood, the Popery is the kingdome of the beast, the Pope is Antichrist, and so teach them that be learned? What man of wisedome will thinke that plow men and artificers know such misteries, and great wise Doctors know them not?

Thus they rattle, & make a noise to trouble weake men: and indeed vnto mans wisedome, it seemeth an hundreth to one, that all those great Cardinals, Bishops, Doctors, and wise Princes should rather see the truth, then a few despised persons: but looke into the holy word of God, go into his sanctuary, as the Prophet speaketh Psalme.73. and you shall find it nothing at all which they obiect. For in very deede it is the same argument, or rather I may say, the same blind cauill that the Priests and Pharisies made against our Sauiour Christ, and against those that followed him, Ioh.7. They gathered a councell, they sent their officers to apprehend

B 2   Christ,

Chrift, and to bring him before them. They fate and expected their comming, and the officers returned without him. Why haue you not (faid they) brought him? Neuer man (fayd the officers) fpake like this man. Then the Pharifies anfwered: Are ye alfo deceiued? do any of the Princes, or of the Pharifies beleeue in him? but this multitude that knoweth not the law is accurfed. Is not this vnto mans wifedome in all likelihood a very ftrong argument? Compare both fides together and fee. Here are the high Priefts, the Pharifies, the Doctors, the Princes, and the ftudied men in the Scriptures: all thefe cry out with one voice, and condemne Chrift to be a feducer, a deftroyer of Gods holy worfhip, a falfe Prophet. On the other fide, who follow Chrift, who imbrace his doctrine, & beleeue in him? his chiefe difciples are a few fifhermen. Then certaine women, and fome of them that had bene great finners, as *Mary Magdalene*, and fhe that wafhed his feete with teares, and wiped thē with the haires of her head. Then next the Publicanes, and many both men & women of the common fort. Here is great oddes, if we looke vpon men: How commeth it to paffe that thefe latter haue their eies opened to fee the light, & the other haue not? *Mofes* and the Prophets foretold of Chrift, defcribed him, fet foorth his death and paffion, and refurrection, the place where he fhould be borne, and the time when he fhould fuffer, alfo that the chiefe rulers in the Church called the builders, fhould refufe him being the head corner ftone. All thefe learned Priefts, Pharifies, and Princes, did read and ftudy the Scriptures, and yet as Saint *Paul* faith, Act. 13. they fulfilled the voyces of the Prophets, by putting him to death. What is the reafon? They did fwell in pride and ambition, and were puffed vp in opinion of their owne knowledge. They had corrupted the truth with their own deuifes. They had in their blind imagination framed to themfelues fuch a Chrift, that when the true Chrift was come they could not know him, but fulfilled all things that were written of him. The Scriptures of the new Teftament in like manner forefhew the comming of the great Antichrift: They paint him out in his colours, what manner of one he fhould be, what he fhould do, and where he fhould raigne. The Pope, his Cardinals, his great Prelates, and Doctors of all forts, ftudie and reade thefe Scriptures: they fpeake much of the comming of this monfter: they play all the parts in this tragedie, and fulfil all that is written of him, & yet do not know him: & why fo? They be as proud as the Pharifies, they haue corrupted the holy Scriptures with the leauen of their owne doctrine, more then they did farre and by many degrees. They haue their fabulous inuentions touching Antichrift, fo that they cannot know him. Why then fhould any thinke it ftrange, that they cannot fee that which poore men and women do fee touching Antichrift, when poore Publicans knew Chrift, and the Pharifies could not? Thus hauing anfwered thefe obiections, wherby they would driue vs from this booke, let vs now come to words of the text which I did reade.

The Reuelation of Iefus Chrift, &c. Before Saint *Iohn* doth come to declare the vifions that were fhewed him, he vfeth a preface, which is contained in eight verfes. This preface confifteth of two parts: The one is the infcription, or generall title of the booke, in the three verfes that I haue read vnto you; The other his falutatio or greeting

greeting which he sendeth to the seuen Churches, contained in the fiue verses next following. In this first part of the preface, which is the title, there be two things chiefly intended: the one is the high authoritie of this prophecie, the other is the singular fruite and benefite which the Church shall receiue by it. And both these are expressed in the first entrance, to prepare the minds of the hearers, to make them attentiue, readie to heare and to learne, and to carrie a good will and liking to the things. For that which commeth from the most high God, with so great authoritie & for such singular good of the whole Church, must needs moue our minds, with all due reuerence and submission to heare it. It must needs stirre vp our hearts to be willing to learne, yea to loue and to delight in the things which we shall learne in the same, if we regard either the authoritie of our soueraigne Lord, or our owne felicitie. But let vs come more particularly: the holy Prophets of God in old time, when they came to the people to vtter any message, least it should be set light by, and despised as the word of man, vsed commonly this preface: *Thus sayth Iehoua: And heare the vvord of the Lord.* In like manner Saint *Iohn* being to deliuer this heauenly prophecy, to the ende we should not esteeme basely of it, calleth it the Reuelation of Iesus Christ, which God gaue vnto him, &c. Our Lord Iesus the eternall wisedome which the Father possessed in the beginning of his way, before his works, before there was any time: which was begotten before there were any deepes, and before the Mountaines were fixed. Prouerb. 8. who is made vnto vs of God wisedome, 1. Cor. 1. is he through whose mediation all the counsels of God, euen from the beginning, haue bene reuealed to the Church: as it is written: *No man hath seene God at any time, the onely begotten Sonne vvhich is in the bosome of the Father, he hath declared him,* Ioh. 1. He then in old time sent the Prophets, furnishing them with his spirite: hee was afterward in the fulnesse of times manifested in the flesh, and taught all things: he being ascended into his glorie, sent downe the holy Ghost vpon his Apostles, which tooke of his, and shewed vnto them, Iohn. 16. We may see then that all trueth, euen all the holy counsels of God, haue bene giuen and opened to the Church through the mediation of Christ: but because he was not then manifested in the flesh, the Prophets speake not so clearely of his mediation in the deliuerie of the word, as Saint *Iohn* doth here. They say, heare the word of God, and thus saith the Lord, and Iehoua hath sent vs vnto you with this message: But *Iohn* telleth that this prophecie which he bringeth is the Reuelation of Iesus Christ, which God gaue vnto him, to shew to his seruants things which must shortly be done. Behold then all mysteries come from the most high God, through Iesus Christ the mediator in our flesh. They be giuen vnto him, that he may shew them, as we see in the fourth Chapter of this booke, the lambe taketh the sealed booke (which is this Reuelation) out of the right hand of him that sitteth vpon the throne, and openeth the seales thereof. God the Father of our Lord Iesus Christ so louing his Church, that he gaue his only begotten sonne to redeeme and to reconcile it vnto himself, through his crosse, giueth all things with him. Whatsoeuer things then are good and conuenient for the Church to know, he giueth them: wherefore it is said, that God gaue this Reuelation to Iesus

sus Christ, to shew to his seruants things which must shortly be done. The Lord Iesus, who hath loued his spouse, and washed her in his owne bloud, hath so tender a care ouer her, that what may do her good, and be for her safety while she is here vpon earth in her pilgrimage in the middest of her foes, he cannot withhold it from her: wherefore receiuing this Reuelation, he sendeth his Angell, and signifieth to his seruant *Iohn*, the disciple whom he loued, that he might receiue and publish the same. Behold then the loue of the Father, behold the loue of the Sonne in giuing this prophecy, to open to his seruants the things that should be done, before they come to passe. But still for the authority of the booke, it commeth from the high God, it is from Iesus the mediator, it is sent by an Angell, here is no blemish: but it commeth also from a man. Indeede it commeth from a man, but from such a man, and in such sort, that the authority is nothing at all diminished, for the holy Apostles and Prophets were but the instruments of the holy Ghost, and deliuered nothing of their owne, but whatsoeuer the spirit by them vttered: as it is written: *For the prophecy came not in olde time by the will of man: but holy men of God spake as they were moued by the holy Ghost.* 2. Pet. 1. This Saint *Iohn* respecteth when he sayth here of himselfe: *which bare record of the word of God, and of the testimony of Iesus Christ, and of all things that he saw.* He doth not here vtter any thing but as a faithfull witnesse, euen as the tongue and penne of the holy Ghost. Then is it our part humbly to stoope downe with all reuerence, to hearken to God, and to our Lord Iesus Christ, who in singular loue hath sent this Reuelatiõ vnto al his seruants. We must take heede that we despise not things comming from so great and so glorious a mediator, sending them vnto vs for our speciall good. Thus much for the high authority of this booke.

    Now come to the second part, which expresseth the singular fruit and commoditie which the faithfull shall receiue thereby: *Blessed is he that heareth, and they that read the words of this Prophecy, and keepe the things which are written therein: for the time is at hand.* What can be said more to stirre vs vp to reade, to heare and to imbrace with all good wil and gladnesse, the things which are sent vnto vs, and vttered in this booke? They be no trifles, they be not things onely for a shew, to moue wonderment, or to delight the curious mind of man: but such as indeede, do giue true blessednesse vnto all those which are well instructed in them. What is greater, then to be blessed for euermore with all heauenly and spirituall blessings? And if we be not wonderfull dull, yea euen like stones and blockes, it must needes stirre vs vp. If it were sayd, he that heareth, and they that reade the words of this prophecy, and keepe the things that are written therein, shall find plenty of riches, and rise vnto honour and dignity here in the world, thousands would hearken vnto it: and shall we not set much more by true blessednesse, in which we shall be made rich with the true treasure, and lifted vp into honour and glory in the kingdome of God? Let not your blessednesse be taken from you: learne and keepe the things which are vttered in this prophecy: for otherwise it shall not make you blessed. For with reading and hearing he ioyneth the keeping of the things which are here written: as our Sauiour saith in the Gospell: *Blessed are they that heare the*

word

THE REVELATION.

word of God, and keepe it. If we heare and reade, and do not vnderstand, or if we vnderstand and carelesly forget, what are we the better? If euer you loue the blessing of God vpon your soules and bodies, learne and keepe the things which are written in this Reuelation.

It may be sayd, was not this Reuelation giuen many yeres after the ascension of Christ? The Church was without it in all that time, and yet was blessed. That doctrine which the Church had, which maketh me blessed, we haue in the other writings of the Prophets and Apostles. Why may we not then aswell as they be without this booke? Did they want any of that doctrine which should make them blessed? Then the booke being hard to be vnderstood, what should we trouble our selues for to vnderstand it? To this I answere, that ancient writers do report, that Saint *Iohn* was banished by *Domitian* the persecuting Emperour, into the Ile called *Patmos*, about the yeare of our Lord, 96. and then receiued this Reuelation. It must needs be granted, that in all this time the Church had it not, and yet was blessed. We haue also all the doctrine in the other bookes of the Scriptures, by which they became blessed: but yet all this doth not take away the necessary vse of this booke, whereby the seruants of God shall be made blessed. There is in deede but one God, one redeemer, one faith, and one Church. The state of this Church according to the diuersities of times is diuerse, being diuersly assaulted. She is blessed by standing in the faith: then that is sayd to make her and her children blessed, which doth arme them in all their particular assaults, and make them to stand in the faith. Great dangers were now at hand, most grieuous things to behold raised vp by Sathan should follow the Gospell euen to disgrace it: the time of false Prophets which should seduce and deceiue, if it were possible euen the elect, Math. 24. was now comming: Sathan was to be loosed, and to come with strong delusion to make men beleeue lies. The dayes of the great Antichrist did now approch: the man of sinne, the aduersary which should exalt himselfe, and sit in the Temple of God, 2. Thess. 2. he commeth as Christs vicar, chalenging to himselfe the power of Christ, as if none could be saued but by him, and so draweth vnder the shew of Christs power, the world to worship himselfe, and to worship the Dragon. Here be speciall assaultes and trials comming, and therefore there is neede of speciall armour: and that is the cause why our Sauiour giueth this Reuelation, and sayth, the time is at hand. For some things were euen then shortly to be fulfilled, it was time for men to looke to this prophecy, and by it to put on armour. The Church in the time of the Apostles had her conflicts, but not these which now are to follow: They heard and were taught by the Apostles, that such things should come, but yet this prophecy which painteth out, and describeth things more cleerely and particularly, was not giuen to them, because they did but heare of the dangers, and not endure the assault of them. Such as haue their eyes opened through the cleere light of the Gospell of Iesus Christ, looking into things past, may behold, besides other plagues described in this prophecy, the popery, that is the kingdome of the beast, that confused Babel, ful of idolatries, blasphemies and cruell murthers, euen like a darke cloude and huge tempest passed ouer, not yet vtterly spent, but the remnants

B 4 and

and the tayle of it remayning. They may also behold the grimme and terrible army of the Turkes, which like a whirle wind hath spred it selfe farre and neere, and laide all waste, as it were with a tempest of mighty hayle. They may behold a goodly part of this prophecy fulfilled in our dayes, and things to fall out fitly in all respects as they be in this prophecy described: they may see there are things yet behind, whereof some be darke, but when they come to passe, they will be cleere. Then blessed is he that readeth, and they that heare the words of this prophecy, & keepe the things which are written therein: for he shall be able to stand in the truth, and to ouercome all daungers. Thus we see what authority this booke is of, comming from the high God through the mediation of our great Prophet Iesus Christ, and also what fruit euen vnto true blessednesse we may receiue thereby: that we may with all dutifull reuerence be attentiue to learne, and then to loue as precious treasure that which we are here taught.

Hauing thus shewed you the summe of this title of the booke for the two maine parts of it: I will now come to stand vpon some collection, wherein we are to argue against the Papists: for here is strong matter against them. First you see it is called a Reuelation, which is as much as to say, an vncouering of things that did lie secret, for it is peculiar to God to know all his works from the beginning, his counsels and decrees are secret to himselfe, vntill he open them. What his Church should here vpon earth passe through, what combats and afflictions she should sustaine, what victory and glory she shal at the last obtaine, he hath before in his high wisedome and secret counsell decreed. What monstrous huge enemies should rise vp against her, what they shall deuise and practise, and how far they shall preuaile: also what ouerthrow and destruction shall come vpon them, he hath likewise in the same his secret counsell appointed. All these being most secret with God, are reuealed to the man Iesus Christ, who also reuealed them to his seruant *Iohn*, and he by his commandement vnto the whole vniuersall Church. If it be a Reuelation, then how say the Papists, that it is so darke, that very litle in respect can be noted in it? Are the things so vncouered, that they be still not to be vnderstood?? How should it then be called a Reuelation? All and euery part of this booke is a Reuelation: Shall we say that the holy Ghost, the spirit of truth, hath giuen a wrong, yea a false title vnto it? For if it hide matters, or so set forth that they cannot be vnderstood, then is it not rightly called a Reuelation. It may be they will then say, and are the matters indeed so cleere and euident? Is there no hardnesse in them? I haue already shewed, that this Reuelation serueth the Church in her seuerall estate as the times fall out. Wherefore such things as were fulfilled in the dayes of the learned fathers were cleare vnto them, the things to come they could not vnderstãd for the most part, but did grope at them. These are now fulfilled in our eyes, and are manifest, at the least the most of them: and the rest which remaine (vnlesse it be some few) the tenor of the former things leading vs to see. Some thinges which yet remaine vnfulfilled, must needes be darke vntill the time come: but to haue this opinion, that all or the most part of it is darke, is contrary to the nature of a Reuelation. The slouthfulnesse, the negligence and the contempt of holy things, that are in men,

THE REVELATION.

men, do make it hard. The Lord himselfe expoundeth some mysteries in the first Chapter, which giue cleere light especially to the first vision. The Angell expoundeth other, and especially in Chap. 17. The writings of Moses and the Prophets, vnto which there be sundry allusions, and from which sundry things are drawne, do manifest many things. So that indeed to be ignorant in it, is either wilfully, or negligently to despise that which we may, and ought to know vnto our happines. Then remember when thou hearest any go about by the hardnes of the booke to disswade from the reading and hearing of it, I say remember, the Lord saith it is a Reuelation: be not so easily driuen away from it.

Moreouer, if any be ready to cauill further, and to say, it is a Reuelation, but not vnto all. It was giuen to *Iohn*, it might be giuen likewise to some speciall men, which could tell how to vse it, but not for the vnlearned. Indeed the Papists reason after such sort: but the next words do quite put them downe, when he sayth, *To shew to his seruants things which must shortly be done*. That is, vnto all Gods seruants, men and women, young and olde, and therefore *Iohn* is commaunded to write all in a booke, and to send it to the seuen Churches of Asia. Marke well that he sayth, that this Reuelation is giuen to Iesus Christ, to shew to his seruants, &c. If it cannot be interpreted, nor vnderstood, how doth it, or how can it shew things? And if thou regard not or canst not vnderstand it, take heede, looke to thy selfe, least thou be found none of Gods seruants, for it sheweth to the seruants of Christ things that must be done. When the seruants of God which with all humility submit themselues, and depend vpon him to be taught, shall haue their eyes opened to see, the wicked proud world, and children of the world shall be blind, yea so blind and so farre from vnderstanding this prophecy, that they shall fulfill the things which are prophecied in it. The Popish Cleargy, the Cardinals, the Bishops, Abbots, and Iesuite Priests confesse, they do not nor cannot vnderstand it: whereby it is most euident, that they be not the seruants of Christ. Let none draw thee away with their cauils, desire the Lord to open thine eyes, that among the number of his seruants, the things may be shewed vnto thee which this booke reuealeth. Lastly, if this booke be so darke and so mysticall, that it cannot be vnderstood: if the interpretation of it be vncertaine: or if the common people cannot be taught to vnderstand it, & therefore are not to meddle with it, how should the holy Ghost say, *Blessed is he that readeth, and they that heare the words of this prophecy, and keepe the things which are written therein?* Let any man iudge that hath common sense, shall a man euer become blessed by reading or hearing those things which he cannot vnderstand, or which he is not to meddle withall? Iudge also in this, whether part are we to beleeue? The Pope (who chalengeth to be the vicar of Christ, and so guided by the spirit of truth, that iudicially from his chaire he cannot erre) sayth this is a booke dangerous for the people to meddle withall. The Cardinals, the Prelates in that kingdome, the Iesuites and other, beare men in hand that it is euen so, and that the safest way for the people is, neuer to deale with it. The holy Ghost by the penne of Saint *Iohn* proclaimeth aloude, that they be blessed which reade, heare, and keepe the matters here written. Who sayth the

truth?

truth? for they cannot both speake truth, their sayings be so flat contrary. Are yee not sure the holy Ghost doth speake the truth? then doubt not but be as sure that the Pope and Papists do speake by a lying spirite, euen by the spirite of the diuell. Thus haue we in this first part of the preface, the high authority of this booke comming from the God of glory, through the mediation of Iesus Christ, and the singular fruit which we shall receiue thereby. Let it moue vs with reuerence to be attentiue to the things vttered, to learne them, and to loue them, that we may be blessed for euermore. *Amen.*

THE II. SERMON.

4. *Iohn to the seuen Churches which are in Asia, grace be with yee, and peace, from him which is, and which was, and which is to come, and from the seuen spirits which are before his throne.*
5. *And from Iesus Christ, which is that faithfull witnesse, and that first begotten of the dead, and that Prince of the kings of the earth, vnto him that loued vs, and washed vs from our sinnes, in his blond,*
6. *And made vs kings and Priests to God euen his father, to him I say, be glory and dominion, for euermore. Amen.*
7. *Behold he commeth with clouds, & euery eye shall see him, yea euen they which pierced him through, and all the kindreds of the earth shall waile before him, euen so, Amen.*
8. *I am Alpha, and Omega, the beginning and the ending, saith the Lord which is, and which was, and which is to come, euen the Almighty.*

WE had in the three former verses, the title of this booke, being the first part of the preface: and here we haue in these fiue verses the second part, that is the salutation, or greeting, which *Iohn* sendeth to the seuen Churches. It was the vsuall manner of the Apostles, when they did write vnto any, to begin with salutation, testifying thereby how vehemently they did loue them to whom they wrote, how well they did wish vnto them, praying for their saluation through the high blessing of God. *Iohn* was willed (as ye see afterwards in this Chapter) to write this Reuelation, & to send it to seuen Churches of Asia, which are named vnto him, that they might receiue this prophecy, and deliuer forth true copies of it vnto other Churches, And before
he

he will declare the visions which were shewed vnto him, he greeteth them louingly. If we compare his salutatiō with that which *Paul* & the rest vse in their Epistles, we shall find in substance of matter no difference at all, but in the manner and order he differeth, vsing such a style, and such descriptions, as are agreeing to the Maiesty of this booke.

Consider the things in particular, as they be set downe. Touching the matter wished in the salutations vnto those to whom they write, Saint *Paule* wisheth grace and peace, to the Romaines, to the Corinthians, Galathians, Ephesians, &c. and sometime, grace, mercy, and peace, as to *Timothy*, and vnto *Titus*. Saint *Iohn* craueth the same things for the Churches to which he sendeth: as ye see, *Iohn to the seuen Churches which are in Asia, grace be with ye, and peace, &c.* If ye will demand what is meant by grace and peace, they signifie the free fauour and good will of God towards men, and all good things which flow from the same. In a word, when the Apostles wish for grace and peace, they pray for all spirituall blessings in heauenly things, as Saint *Paul* speaketh, Ephes.1. they pray for all the rich and precious treasures which are giuen vs in Christ, & manifested by the glorious Gospell. Whereupon I may here by the way note one thing briefly, touching the true ministers of Christ, what property they haue: For we all confesse that the blessed Apostles were faithfull Ministers indeed, and great patterns for all other to follow. They spent their strength in labouring, they passed through all daungers and perils, to display & to manifest vnto the people the riches of the grace of God in Christ Iesus. It was loue onely that constrained them, both the loue they bare to Christ, to his truth and glory, and the loue and pity which they bare vnto men. Wherefore as they did preach the grace of God which bringeth saluation, so did they instantly pray, that the people might be partakers of the same, vnto their eternall blessednesse. The Ministers which follow these steps, are in the right way: but if they preach and labour for filthy luker, in respect of worldly benefits; if they preach to magnifie themselues, to seeke their owne glory, they be not then true seruants of Christ, although they should preach the truth. For if they seeke their owne, and not the things which are Christs, is not their belly their God? as Saint *Paule* speaketh, Philip.3. Let all that labour in the ministerie, not onely studie to find out the truth, and to lay it open, but also pray and wish that the people may imbrace the same vnto their eternall blessednesse. S. *Paule* wisheth grace and peace from God the Father, and from our Lord Iesus Christ, not mentioning the holy Ghost: but *Iohn* here craueth grace & peace from all the three persons in the most blessed Trinity, which may seeme to be some difference, but verily in effect there is no difference at all. For when the holy Ghost is not expresly named in the salutation of the Apostles, yet he is not excluded, seeing he is the worker of all in the hearts of men: and therefore indeed there is no difference but only in the expresse mention, betweene *Iohn* and the other Apostles. Also this may be noted, that the vsuall placing of the persons is in this order, the Father, the Sonne, and the holy Ghost: but *Iohn* beginneth with the Father, then next the holy Ghost, and so commeth to the Sonne in the third place. This may not seeme strange, seeing there is no degree of dignitie in one perſon aboue another: the Father is not greater then the Sonne, the Sonne is not greater then the holy Ghoſt. They be all of the ſame power, maieſtie, and glory, none is before or after other. And it was more conuenient that Saint *Iohn* ſhould here ſet out our Sauiour in the third place, becauſe he maketh a large deſcription of him, and in the ſame ſpeaketh of the laſt iudgement, and ſo from thence commeth fitly to conclude his ſalutation in that high and magnificall maner which he doth.

Now let vs ſee the deſcription of euery perſon in the Deitie. He ſpeaketh of the Father thus, *Grace and peace from him which is, and which was, and which is to come*. That is as much as to ſay, from him that is eternall, immortall, and vnchangeable, who hath his being of him ſelfe, and giueth vnto all creatures their being. Saint *Iohn* (as it ſeemeth) by theſe three words which he writeth in the Greeke, would expreſſe the force of the name of God *Iehoua* in the Hebrew, or of *Eheie*, Exodus the third. Whom (ſaith *Moſes*) ſhall I ſay hath ſent me? Anſwer is made, ſay *Eheie* hath ſent me vnto ye: that is, I wil be, or as they ſay, the future tenſe may haue all times included in it, and ſo it is as much as to ſay, I am, I was, and I will be, hath ſent me vnto yee. It may here be obiected, is not the Sonne *Iehoua*, or *Eheie*, he that is, and he that was, and he that is to come? Is not the holy Ghoſt alſo *Iehoua*? I anſwer, that reſpecting the eſſence, the Father, the Sonne, and the holy Ghoſt, are but one and the ſelfe ſame eternall, immortall, and vnchangeable God: but *Iohn* ſpeaketh here diſtinguiſhing the perſons. And the Sonne being begotten of the Father, the holy Ghoſt proceeding from the Father and the Sonne, the Father in this diſtinguiſhing of the perſons, is propoūded as the fountaine of the Deitie, and the fountaine of all being, of life, of grace, and peace. According to this we ſhall find ſundrie places of ſcripture, as when he ſaith, *God ſo loued the world, that he gaue his onely begotten Sonne, that whoſoeuer beleeueth in him ſhould not periſh, but haue life euerlaſting*, Iohn. 3. *God was in Chriſt reconciling the vvorld to himſelfe, not imputing their ſinnes*, 2. Cor. 5. *Becauſe ye are ſonnes, God hath ſent the ſpirite of his ſonne into your hearts, which crieth Abba, Father*, Galath. 4.

Then next he wiſheth grace and peace from the holy Ghoſt, the worker of all grace in the faithfull, ſaying: And frō the ſeuen ſpirits which are before his throne. There be ſundry gifts, and ſundry operations, and yet but one holy Ghoſt, how doth Saint *Iohn* then call him ſeuen ſpirits? This hath cauſed ſome to take it of the Angels, not that Saint *Iohn* ſhould wiſh grace and peace from them, as from the authors of grace and peace, but as they ſtand as miniſtring ſpirits before the throne. And vpon this the Ieſuites of Rhemes lay hold, ſaying, that the holy Ghoſt may be here meant, and ſo called for his manifold graces. But they ſay, it ſeemeth more probable, that he ſpeaketh this of the holy Angels: and ſo they conclude, it muſt needs be confeſſed, that grace and peace is wiſhed by the Apoſtle, not onely from God, but alſo from his Angels. And hereupon they inferre, that it is not ſuperſtitious, but an Apoſtolicall ſpeech, to ſay, God and our Ladie bleſſe vs, God and his Angels, or God and any of his Saints helpe vs, or bleſſe vs. But there are reaſons in deed ſufficient to proue, that theſe ſeuen ſpirits be the holy Ghoſt, and not the

miniſtring

ministring Angels. Let it be a light reason that these seuen spirits are placed betweene the Father and the Sonne, as proceeding from them both, and of equall Maiesty and authority: yea we must note that grace and peace is wished from these seuen spirites, euen with the same manner of speech, that they be wished from the Father and the Sonne, the coniunction coupling them all in one. Againe, Saint *Iohn* speaketh of the holy Ghost, as he appeareth vnto him in visiō in this Reuelation. Here are seuen Churches, which represent all Churches. The holy Ghost did worke so fully and perfectly in euery one of these seuen, as if he had bene in euery one a seuerall spirit (as also in all and euery one through the whole world) and for that cause is shewed in vision chap. 4. as seuen lampes burning before the throne, called there the seuen spirites of God. The holy Angels be the Lords Ministers, but neuer I thinke in the Scriptures called the spirites of God. Euery Angell indeed is in some sense a spirite of God, but when the Scripture sayth the spirit of God, it is the holy Ghost. Moreouer, the Angels are before the throne, and about the throne, but proceede not out of the throne: but the holy Ghost sent and proceeding from the Father and the Sonne, commeth forth of the throne. For it is sayd, there proceeded out of the throne, lightnings, and thundrings, and voices, and seuen lampes of fire, burning before the throne. Doth not the construction carry it plainely, that these lampes which burne before the throne proceeded out of the throne? Also the holy Angels, although they be employed in the seruice of Christ, exercising his power and prouidence, yet the holy Ghost is in a most high and peculiar manner the eyes and hornes of the Lambe, that is, his absolute wisedome & power: as in the sixt Chapter these seuen spirites of God are called the eyes and hornes of the Lambe: by these the Lambe openeth the seales of the booke. These seuen lampes, seuen eyes, & seuen hornes, do not worship before the throne, as the other: wherefore we may take it for certaine, that Saint *Iohn* here doth wish grace and peace, as from the Father in the first place, so from the holy Ghost in the next, who is the worker of all grace and peace in the harts of men.

  In the third place, he wisheth grace and peace from Iesus Christ: he is the mediatour betweene God and man: he alone hath wrought the reconciliation: he is our peace-maker, that hath brought vs into fauour with God: worthily therefore doth he wish grace & peace from him. He doth not, as ye see in bare tearmes, according to the visuall manner, wish grace and peace from Iesus Christ, but setteth him foorth with a goodly description, full of excellent glory, touching euery part of his office, and the communicating the same with vs. The parts of his office are in these, that he is the great Prophet, the mighty Prince, and mercifull high Priest. The first is expressed in these words, *That faithfull witnesse.* He as the Prince of all Prophets, brought all the counsels of God, and reuealed them vnto men: as it is written, *No man hath seene God at any time, the onely begotten Sonne which is in the bosome of the Father, he hath declared him,* Iohn. 1. verse. 18. He did beare record to the truth euery way: for being apprehended, brought before *Pilate,* and accused, he asked him, *Art thou a King? He aunswered, for this cause was I borne, & for this cause came I into the world, that I might beare witnes to the truth.*
Iohn. 18.

Ioh. 18. verf. 37. Wherefore Saint *Paul* faith, *He witneſſed vnder Pontius Pilate, a good confeſſion,* 1. Timoth. 6. he opened all truth, & fealed it vp with his bloud. But it may be demanded, Did not all the Prophets fet forth the truth, and beare record to the fame as faithfull witneſſes? Did not the holy Apoſtles the fame? Haue not the Martyrs alfo fealed it in fome fort, with their bloud? What is here then afcribed vnto Chriſt, which is not common with him vnto them? What matter of excellent glory is here giuen vnto him? True it is, that the Prophets and Apoſtles fet forth the found truth, & bare record vnto it, & are of right to be called faithful witneſſes: but yet our Lord Ieſus Chriſt is here by an excellency farre aboue them al, fet in a peculiar glory to himſelfe alone, when he fayth, *That faithfull witneſſe.* For he is not here called a faithfull witneſſe, as one among the reſt: but as the Prince & head of all Prophets and witneſſes, from whom they all receiued their light, & the truth vnto which they bare record. For he being the eternall wiſedome of the Father, as *Salomon* bringeth in wifedome fpeaking, Prouerb. 8. faying, *God poſſeſſed me in the beginning of his way, before his workes, before there was any time. Before the world was I annoynted, before the beginning, before the beginnings of the earth. When there were no deepes was I begotten, when there were no fountaines abounding with waters. Before the mountaines were fixed, before the hilles was I begotten. He had not yet made the earth, &c.* He is alfo as Saint *Paule* fayth, *made vnto vs of God, wiſedome.* 1. Cor. 1. ver. 30. *In him are all the treafures of wiſedome, and knowledge hidden.* Coloſſ. 2. ver. 3. All the Prophets from the beginning of the world had their doctrine from him. He gaue them his fpirit to inftruct them in his counfels. He hauing with his owne mouth vttered & preached the whole Gofpel when he walked vpon the earth, after his refurrection afcended into heauen, and according to his promife fent downe the holy Ghoſt vpō his Apoſtles, *Which* (as he fayth) *ſhould teach them all things, and bring to their remembrance all things which he had fayd,* Ioh. 14. ver. 26. This fpirit he faith ſhould glorifie him, becauſe he ſhould take of his, and ſhew vnto them. Then ye fee his glory, when he faith, *That faithfull witneſſe*: namely, that he is the Prince of al Prophets, hauing a fingular glory herein aboue all the reſt. Woe be vnto them which wil not giue credit to his teſtimony, but defpife the words of his mouth.

Then next he defcribeth him as the moſt mighty king, in thefe words, *That firſt begotten of the dead, and Prince of the kings of the earth.* Here be two parts in this glorious and kingly eſtate of Chriſt. The one is touching his victory and conqueſt ouer all the mighty enemies: and the other is in his exaltation in glory, and princely maieſty at the right hand of God, in which he ſhall raigne for euer and euer. The former of thefe is expreſſed thus, *That firſt begotten of the dead.* The conqueſt ouer death and ouer Satan, was by dying and rifing againe from the dead. Satan preuailed againſt our firſt parents, caſt them downe into thraldome with all their children. Now as man was ouercome by Satan, and brought into captiuity, fo the Lord God wil haue a man to triumph ouer Satan, and to deliuer the captiues from vnder his tyrannie. The eternall wiſedome of the Father tooke our nature, as it is fayd, *The word was made fleſh,* Iohn. 1. *And God fent his ſonne made of a woman.*

Galath

THE REVELATION. 15

Galath.4.and in the same nature of ours as a most mighty king triumphed ouer Satan, and ouer death it selfe. *By a man came death, and by a man came the resurrection from the dead.*1.Cor.15. Also the Lord had decreed, not onely that the seede of the woman should breake the Serpents head, but also that it should be brought to passe, euen by that ouer which Satan hath his dominion and Lordship, that is, by death. He tooke the humane nature that he might taste of death, and by death ouercome the diuell and death it selfe. The holy Ghost setteth forth these things, saying, *Because therefore the children were partakers of flesh and bloud, he also in like manner tooke part of the same, that by death, he might abolish him that hath the Lordship ouer death, that is the diuell* Hebr.2.vers.14. *This is the king of glory, the Lord strong and mighty, the Lord mighty in battaile.* Psalme.24. He encountred by his death, with Sathan and with death, rising againe victoriously, and so is *That first begotten of the dead.* In his crosse, *He spoyled principalities and powers, and led them in shew openly triumphing ouer them.* Coloss.2.vers.15. *He is ascended vp on high, and hath led captiuity captiue:* Ephes.4.verse.8. He is called the first begotten from the dead, because all his brethren, euen all, he redeemed, shall in their time through the vertue of this his mighty conquest be raised vp, and set free from the bondage of corruption. He must raigne vntill all his enemies be made his footstoole. *He shall put downe all rule, and all authority: and death shall be swallowed vp into victory:* 1.Cor.15. This is the glorious victory of our king, expressed in these words, *That first begotten of the dead.*

The other part touching the glorious maiesty, in which he doth raigne and in which he shall raigne for euermore, is vttered in these words, *That Prince of the kings of the earth.* He to whom all power is giuen in heauen and earth, as he sayth, Math.28. He that is exalted at the right hand of God, as the Apostle sayth, *Farre aboue all principality, and power, and might, and Lordship, and euery name that is named, not onely in this world, but also in that to come.* Ephes.1.vers.21. *He to whom all knees shall bowe, of things in heauen, of things in earth, and of things vnder the earth.* Philip.2.verse.10. *He that is ascended farre aboue all heauens, that he might fill all things.* Epes.4. verse.10. Euen he, must needes be the Prince of all the kings of the earth : for his kingdome being ouer the heauenly mights and dominations, and hauing subdued the infernall powers, it is much more ouer the kings of the earth. Thus ye see the glorious triumphant king, the man Iesus which was raised from the dead.

Now in the third place he describeth him, as our most mercifull high Priest, in this sort: *To him that hath loued vs, and washed vs from our sinnes in his bloud.* Here are two members in this part of the description, his loue, as he sayth, *To him that hath loued vs,* and the effectuall declaration of the same, in this, *and hath washed vs from our sinnes in his bloud* What greater proofe of his loue can there be then this? We were all of vs vncleane sinners, most vgly, foule, the children of wrath, heires of destruction. That he might reconcile vs to his Father, he tooke our burthen vpon him, *He bare our sinnes in his body vpon the tree:* 1.Pet.2.verse 24. *He was made sinne for vs, that we in him might be made the righteousnesse of God.*2.Cor.5.ver.21.

To deliuer vs frō the curſe of the law, *He was made the curſe*, Galath. 3. ver. 13. And was it not a wonderfull loue, that he ſhould giue vp himſelfe to death, euen to endure all torments and ſorrowes for vncleane ſinners? If when we were enemies, and deſerued nothing but hatred and curſe, he loued vs, and gaue vp himſelfe to be a ranſome for vs, how ſhould we now doubt of his loue, when his bloud hath purged vs from our ſinnes? The Prieſtes vnder the law of *Moſes*, did offer ſacrifices of ſlaine beaſts, whoſe bloud did not waſh a way ſinne, but was a figure and a ſhadow of the bloud of this vnſpotted Lambe of God, which purgeth away all our ſinne: as we may reade in the Epiſtle to the Hebrewes. The holy word doth teach vs, that there is no other purging away of any ſinne, but only in this bloud of the Lambe: as it is written, *If we walke in the light, as he is in the light, we haue fellowſhip one with another: and the bloud of Ieſus Chriſt his ſonne cleanſeth vs from all ſinne*. 1. Iohn. 1. ver. 7. The Papiſts aſcribe to the bloud of Chriſt the waſhing away of originall ſinne: but actuall ſinnes, if they be after Baptiſme, they will haue to be taken away and diſcharged, by ſatisfactions of our owne. Yea they haue ſo many kinds of ſatisfactions, indulgences, merites, bloud of Martyrs, and purgatory, that it is very little which they leaue to the bloud of Chriſt. This wicked blaſphemous ſacriledge againſt the glory of the croſſe of Chriſt they do ſtill maintaine: not conſidering that they make many things equall in power and dignity with his death and precious bloud: For if any thing can purge away ſinne, where is the glory of his paſſion, that hath companions in that worke of purging ſins? Is that great glory, which doth but that which many other things doe? The falſe Apoſtles which taught that men ſhould be iuſtified and ſaued, partly by Chriſt, and partly by the workes of the lawe, are therefore by Saint *Paule* called the enemies of the croſſe of Chriſt: and are not then the Papiſts which will not aſcribe the purging of al ſinnes, only to the bloud of the Lambe, to be reputed and tearmed blaſphemous aduerſaries to his paſſion? We do confeſſe, that of tender compaſſion and loue towards vs, as a moſt mercifull high Prieſt, he offered vp himſelfe in ſacrifice, euen a ſlaine ſacrifice for the ſinnes of the world, and ſo with his bloud hath waſhed away al our ſinnes, and reconciled vs to his Father. Thus we ſee the deſcription of our Sauiour in euery part of his office: now next in that he communicateth the ſame to vs.

And made vs Kings and Prieſts to God euen his Father. He is not annoynted King and Prieſt to himſelfe alone, but we are alſo through him annoynted Kings and Prieſts, euen to the moſt high God. They be great benefites, and great dignities which are here ſpoken of, and ſhall ſo appeare vnto vs, if we conſider the top of the glory vnto which we are aduanced in them, and the bottome of our baſe eſtate, out of which we are drawne. We were in bondage vnto our luſtes, and ſeruants vnto ſinne: a vile ſlauery. Being annoynted with his ſpirite, our olde man is crucified with the luſtes and concupiſcences, ſo that they raigne not ouer vs, but as mighty kings, through his mighty grace we bring them vnder and ſubdue them. A Prince in the world ouer men, that is bond to his luſtes and ſerueth them, is a baſe ſeruant: and a poore nſā that through the worke of grace ſubdueth thē, is a mighty Prince. This *Salomon* reſpecteth in his booke called Eccleſiaſtes, when he ſayth:

THE REVELATION.

I sawe seruants vpon horses: and princes walking vpon the ground like seruantes. chap. 10. verf. 7. We were in bondage vnto Satan the prince of darkenes, obeying him and doing his will: but being annointed with the spirite of Christ, we treade him downe as mightie princes, vnder our feet, & as a pray are deliuered from him, and as captiues are set free from the hands of such cruell power. We were captiues, in bondage vnto death, vnto eternall shame and misery: but being annointed with the holy Ghost, we shalbe raised vp from death in great triumph and glorie, to raigne for euer & euer with our head Iesus Christ. We were the children of wrath, through our vncleannes; he hath washed vs in his bloud, and made vs the sonnes of God, and that is, he hath made vs great kings. For the children of Emperours and kings here in the world inherit riches and glorie, and are borne princes. All the kings of the earth are but beggers, being compared vnto him; then must his children of necessity all of them, be great kings and princes: and who is able to expresse with any words, the riches and the glorie which they shall inherit? He bestoweth many good things in this world vpon all, but how great are the thinges which they shall enioy, whom he maketh kings? This is a blessing doubled vpon vs; for to be deliuered from the miserie and basenesse is much: but then to be aduanced so high is more. How vehemently ought we to pray, *Let thy kingdome come?* It is a blessed kingdome. How well is it with those that are made kings to God? It may be said, if the beleeuers be lifted vp by Christ into such a dignitie; how commeth it to passe that they be so base and so despised in the world? If a man come into the presence of a kings sonne, by and by he is moued with a reuerence, and sheweth that he doth regard and honour him. But they that professe the Gospell, and to be the sonnes of God, are base and contemptible in the eies of men. Saint *Iohn* answereth this in another place, saying, *See what loue the Father hath giuen vs, that we should be called the sonnes of God. Therfore the world knoweth vs not, becau se it knoweth not him. Beloued, we are now the sonnes of God, but it doth not appeare what we shall be: we know that when he shall be made manifest, we shall be like vnto him: because we shall see him as he is:* 1. Ioh. 3. verf. 1.2. To the same purpose it may be cited, which Saint *Paul* speaketh, Rom. 8. verf. 19. of the reuealing of the sonnes of God. We must then not looke vpon the present estate of the faithfull, but what it shall be; for here the sonnes of God which shall shine in glorie as kings, do lye subiect vnto contempt, vnto basenesse, vnto reproches, & vnto manifold miseries. Being washed then in the bloud of the Lambe, and cleansed from all our sins we are alreadie the sons of God, we are kings, but we may not looke to come to the glorie in this world.

Now for the other, that he hath made vs priests to God euen his Father: this may seeme to be but a small matter, vntill we consider what it is to be priestes to God. Nothing that is polluted and prophane can haue accesse vnto God to abide in his presence. A Priest to God is sanctified and priuiledged to come vnto him euen with fauour. As euery prophane thing is abhominable to God, so euery gift & oblation offered vnto him by such prophane ones is reiected: but a sanctified priest to God offering vp giftes and sacrifices, the same are delightsome and acceptable

C vnto

vnto him. We are all of vs by nature vncleane, prophane and abhominable to him, and quite shut out from hauing any accesse into his presence. There were priests of old time that did approch and offer gifts and sacrifices which were accepted, but they were figures of Christ, and offered vp all in his mediation: for he alone is our priest that hath sanctified vs with his own bloud, and made the way for vs to enter euen vnto the throne of grace, and as holy priestes to offer vp such sacrifices as do please him. We are not made priests as in the law to offer carnall sacrifices, according to the law of the carnall commandement, (as the holy Ghost speaketh, Hebr. 7. verf. 16.) but we are priests to offer spirituall sacrifices. We are made *An holy Priesthood, to offer vp spirituall sacrifices acceptable to God through Iesus Christ*: 1. Pet. 2. verf. 5. We are to consecrate our bodies a sacrifice liuing, holy & acceptable to God, Rom. 12. verf. 1. And as it is written, *We must almaies by him* (that is euen by Christ) *offer to God the sacrifice of praise, that is the fruit of the lippes which confesse his name. To do good and to distribute forget not, for with such sacrifices God is pleased*. Heb. 13. verf. 15. 16. These be spirituall sacrifices, therefore all true Christians may be called spirituall priests, and no one man is more a priest then an other, no not euen the holy Apostles, *Peter*, or *Paul*, or *Iohn*, or any other; neither is there any other priesthood remaining among men, but this spirituall priesthood. The Iesuit Papists in their annotations do grant that all true Christians be spirituall priests to God: but to say that all be priests alike, or that there ought to be none but such spirituall priests, they cry out vpon, and say it is the seditious voice of *Core*, who said to *Moses* & *Aaron*, Are not all the Lords people holy? They vse this argument, that as he should be a seditious heretike, that would reasō thus, all Gods children are kings, therefore there ought to be no other earthly powers or kings to gouerne in worldly affaires ouer Christians: so are they seditious heretikes that vpon this place or the like would inferre, that euery one in a proper signification is a priest, or that all be priests alike, or that there ought to be none but such spirituall priests. We do not reason so, they leaue out that vpon which we stand. The holy scripture doth teach that all true Christians be spirituall kings, and yet that there be other kings also to gouerne ouer Christians, and ouer all other. The scripture saith, all are priests to offer vp spirituall sacrifice; we say that the scripture doth not teach that there be any other priests, but these spirituall priests. They affirme, that there be other priests so properly called, which offer vp in sacrifice the Lord Iesus to his Father. This is wicked blasphemie, and as they cannot shew by the word of God that any such sacrifice remaineth to be offered for the quicke and the dead: so can they not shew that the holy Apostles or any other ministers of the gospel were called priests. When I say they be not any of them called priests in a proper signification restrained to a ministery, I meane such priests as offer sacrifice: for the word Priest is vsed confusedly in our tongue, for if our english word priest come of *Presbiter*, then in that sence *Peter* may be called a priest, seeing he was *Presbiter*, as he calleth himselfe, 1. Pet. 5. verf. 1. and so are all ministers of the Gospell priests. For Bishoppes, Pastors, and Teachers, are all called *Presbiteri*, that is elders, euen for their office and ministery. But when priest is vsed for a sacrificer, then shall we find

that

THE REVELATION.

that neither *Peter* nor any other is called a priest, that is a sacrificer, otherwise then all Christians are called priests or sacrificers. All Christians are not *Presbyteri*, for that is proper to the ministery and Church gouernors: but all Christians be sacrificers alike, there is no sacrifice which some offer, and not other some.

Vpon this mention of the benefite of Christ, S. *Iohn* breaketh forth into his praise, saying, *To him be glorie and dominion for euermore, Amen*. He that is the faithfull witnesse, euen the prince of all Prophets: he that is our mighty king hath ouercome for vs death and the diuell, and is exalted at the right hand of God: He that is our mercifull high priest hath loued vs and washed vs in his bloud from our sinnes: He that hath made vs kings and priests to God euen his father: is not he worthy of all glorie and dominion for euermore? Whosoeuer he be that feeleth that he is thus deliuered by Christ from destruction, and aduanced to such dignity and glorie: how can he stay, but breake forth with S. *Iohn* into praising and glorifying of Christ? In deed if we feele not our selues partakers of his glorie, our hearts are still shut vp, and our tongues are tyed from glorifying him with ioy & delight. It may be said, hath he made vs only kings and priests? Hath he not also made vs Prophets? Yes, he hath also made vs Prophets: though S. *Iohn* doth not mention that, he hath giuen vs knowledge of heauenly mysteries: *I will powre out of my spirit (saith he) vpon all flesh, and your sonnes and your daughters shall prophecie &c.* Act. 2. 17. Reioice then in the Lord Iesus, and praise him with gladnesse of hart, that hath done so great things for vs. Let not this vaine world, nor the transitory things which be in it, that are in deed in comparison but beggerly trash, so bewitch and besotte our minds, as to set light by these heauenly treasures and dignities. For doubtlesse such as set their harts vpon the lusts of this world, neuer regard these heauenly dignities.

He addeth one thing further vnto this description of Christ, and that is his glorious comming to iudge the quicke and the dead. *Behold he commeth with cloudes, and euery eye shall see him, yea euen they which pierced him through: and all the kindreds of the earth, shall waile before him, euen so, Amen*. Why is this his comming to Iudgement here described? Because all this glorie and dignitie shall then be made manifest, not onely to the children of God which shall inherite the same, but also euen to the wicked. The glorie of Christ is now published, & how he doth communicate the same with his redeemed: but all this glorie, both in his person, and in his chosen, is seene of vs only by faith. It is farre remoued from our bodily sences. We see not him, & we feele our selues subiect vnto great basenesse, and vnto a thousand calamities. Saint *Iohn* lifteth vp our mindes vnto this day, saying, *behold he commeth with cloudes, &c*. The kings and great Iudges of this world haue a pompe and maiestie when they sit in iudgement, but nothing comparable to this that he shall come with cloudes, to sit vpon the throne of his glory. And then euery eye shall see him. Not onely the godly shall behold the king in his glorie, but also all the wicked, euen the worst that euer haue bene; yea his aduersaries that did so cruelly murder him, shall be constrained to their shame & endlesse sorrow to looke vpon him, & vpon the glorie of his Saints, whom they so hated & despised.

despised. Then shal all the prophane people, euen al the kindreds of the earth waile before him: their sorrow shall then come vpon them, but all too late to find any place for mercy at his hands whom they haue so despised. They now hate and despise his word, they raile vpon those which professe it: then shal come their punishment: for then shall they giue account for all their wicked deeds, when he commeth with cloudes; and when euery eye shall see him, euen the eyes that now are the eyes of the dead, as well as the eyes of the liuing. Ye see there shall be two sorts of people: the one sort shall lift vp their heads and reioyce, for the day of their redemption is come: the other sort shall lament and mourne, and crie out dolefully with bitter griefe and sorrow, because the day of wrath and vengeance is come vpon them. I pray you thinke well of this, and walke so carefully now, and so wisely, that when that day commeth, ye may not be of that company which shall houle and lament, but of those which with great ioy shal be crowned with glory to raigne with Christ. He that doth not studie now to know the wayes of God, and to walke in them, that he may at this second comming of the Lord be blessed, he is more then a foole, yea is more then madde. All our whole life ought to tend to this, that we may be accepted in that day: and marke how Saint *Iohn* doth confirme this with a double affirmation, the one in a Greeke word, and the other in an hebrew word, which is, Amē, which is, So be it. By this he doth not only set downe the certainty of his comming, but declareth his vehement desire for the same: and thereby he giueth vs an example euen to long for it. For then the kingdom of Sathan shall be quite put downe, Sathan and the wicked shall be shut vp in the prison of hell: the glory of Christ shall shine forth in full perfection, and his Saints shal be glorified with him. For both these respects, we haue cause to long and to pray for the comming of this great day.

Now remaineth the conclusion or shutting vp of this salutation, and it is a confirmation of this grace and peace to come from God alone, who is (as he saith) *Alpha* and *Omega*, that is the beginning and the ending, for *Alpha* it the first of the Greeke letters, and *Omega* is the last: he was before all, and gaue to euery creature the being, he continueth for euer, and supporteth all. He is eternall and vnchangeable, that is, that was, and that is to come: he is that Almighty, exercising his power and prouidence ouer all. And here we may note, that whereas before in the distinguishidg of the persons in the Trinity, *he that is, he that was, and he that is to come*, is spoken of the Father, here to declare the vnity of substance, it is spoken of the whole three persons. Thus much for the salutation of *S. Iohn* to the Churches.

THE

THE III. SERMON.

9. *I Iohn euen your brother, and companion in tribulation, and in the Kingdome and patience of Iesus Christ, was in the Ile called Patmos, for the word of God, and for the witnessing of Iesus Christ.*

10. *And I was in the spirit vpon the Lords day, and heard behind me, a great voice, as it had bene of a trumpet,*

11. *Saying: I am Alpha, and Omega, that first, and that last, that which thou seest write in a booke, & send it to the seuen Churches which are in Asia, vnto Ephesus, and vnto Smyrna, and vnto Pergamus, and vnto Thyatira, and vnto Sardis, and vnto Philadelphia, and vnto Laodicea.*

12. *Then I turned backe to see the voyce that spake with me: & when I was turned, I saw seuen golden candlestickes,*

13. *And in the middest of the candlestickes, one like vnto the Sonne of man, clothed with a garment downe to the feete, and girded about the pappes with a golden girdle.*

14. *His head and haires were white, as white wooll, and as snow, & his eyes were as a flame of fire.*

15. *And his feet like vnto fine brasse, burning as in a fornace, and his voice like vnto the sound of many waters.*

16. *And hee had in his right hand seuen starres: and out of his mouth went a sharpe two edged sword, and his face shone as the Sunne shineth in his strength.*

17. *And when I saw him, I fell at his feet as dead: then he layd his right hand vpon me, saying vnto me, feare not, I am that first, and that last.*

18. *And am aliue, but I was dead, and behold I am aliue for euermore, Amen. And I haue the keyes of hell and of death.*

19. *Write the things which thou hast seene, and the things which are, and the things vvhich shall come hereafter.*

20. *The mistery of the seuen Stars which thou sawest in my right hand, and the seuen golden candlestickes is this: the seuen Stars are the Angels of the seuen Churches: and the seuen candlestickes, are the seuen Churches.*

Fter the preface consisting of the title of this booke, & of the salutation to the Churches, Saint *Iohn* commeth now to his narration, and declareth the first vision which was shewed vnto him, contained in three Chapters. It shall not be amisse to lay open vnto you in the first place to what end and purpose this vision serued, which is three fold: for first it was to cal

SERMONS VPON

and authorise S. *Iohn* to write: secondly, to set vp the authority of this prophecy: & thirdly, to declare in what estate the Church then present vpon the earth was.

Touching the calling and authorising of S. *Iohn*, it may be said, was he not one of the Lambes twelue Apostles, and had now many yeares executed the office of the Apostleship right faithfully? What needed he, being an Apostle, to be called againe, or to be authorised? It may be answered, that this is a new and a speciall worke, and therefore requireth a new and a speciall calling. Againe, it is as God dealt with the old Prophets: for when he would foreshew great and speciall matters, he called diuerse of them by very glorious visions: as yee may reade what a goodly vision *Esay* had, Chap. 6. what a vision ful of heauenly glory *Ezechiel* had, Chap. 1. and what a vision the Prophet *Daniel* had, Chap. 10. euen in maiestie like vnto this which *S. Iohn* hath here. Thus it is then to be considered: *Iohn* is as the old Prophets to foreshew things to come, therefore the Lord appeareth vnto him in vision; and calleth him, and authoriseth him thereunto, as he appeared vnto them & called them. Thus much for the first end, to which this first vision serued.

The second is (as I sayd) to set vp the authority of the booke it selfe: which thing is to be drawne from the high maiesty, and glory, and power of him that appeareth in the vision, vpon which I need not to stay.

The third thing is, that this first vision is to declare in what estate the vniuersall Church vpon the earth was at that present time. For when the Lord wold reueale in what case his Church should be euen to the worlds end, he first declareth the present estate thereof. In deed there are but seuen Churhes named, the seuerall estate of euery one of which is opened in the two next Chapters: but vnder these seuen, among which some were in better or more perfect case then other, the state of the whole vniuersall Church militant is laid open. It had bene a matter infinite to recken vp all the particular Churches that were then in the world, & to haue opened their estate. Therefore as this prophecy, which is for all the seruants of God in what Church soeuer, is sent but to those seuen by name: so vnder those seuen, all other Churches are comprised.

These three things thus in generall obserued, now let vs come to the vision, to euery branch of the words in order as they lie, in which there be many particulars which concerne the person that is called, the person that calleth, and the Churches whose estate is layd open. He beginneth with himselfe, who was called by this vision, saying, *I Iohn, euen your brother and companion in affliction, and in the Kingdome, and patience of Iesu Christ, &c.* Let it not seeme strange that he nameth himselfe againe, for this is at his calling, as ye shall reade in the Prophet, when he expresseth those great visions, how often he repeateth, *I Daniel*. But I may here againe speake a litle touching the former obiection. Was not the office of the Apostleship, the highest degree of authority among the ministers of the Church? And was not Saint *Iohn* an Apostle? And did not the Apostles prophecy of things to come? Yea, but this prophecy which Saint *Iohn* receiueth here goeth further then that which the Apostles had, it is a speciall Reuelation, and therefore he hath a new calling vnto it, which he doth not in vaine mention, saying, *I Iohn*. In the

next

THE REVELATION.

next place he giueth himselfe certaine titles, but not such as are swelling or pompous, no not euē such as he might, as the title of an Apostle or Prophet, but of a brother to all the faithfull, and of a companion with all those which were afflicted & persecuted for the Gospell of Christ, vnder hope of the glory to come. But why may some say, did he not here take the title of an Apostle or of a Prophet, seeing he is to commend the authority of the booke? Was it not lawfull for the Apostles and Prophets to take those titles? Yes, but here was a particular respect, for which *Iohn* setteth himselfe so low? for surely, I suppose that Saint *Iohn* hath the same mind here that Saint *Paul* telleth of himselfe, 2. Cor. 12. He (I meane *Paule*) was highly exalted with visions, and reuelations, and being forced to glory & boast againft the false Apostles and euill men, he durst not enter into the glorying and boasting in those visions and reuelations in his owne name, or vnder his owne person, for feare least he might in some sort be puft'ed vp, carying still in him the remnants of the old man: but chose more gladly as he saith, to glory of those things wherein he was humbled and abased: for he did glory in his infirmities, and that most gladly. *Iohn*, as yee see through this booke is admitted to see great things, goodly visions and reuelations are shewed him: but he will not glory in them, he will not lift vp himselfe on high by them, but of purpose commeth downe, and sitteth among the poore distressed and persecuted, saying, your brother and companion in affliction, &c. O worthy example of two so noble instruments: how farre the proud and vaine nature of man is from this which they haue shewed, may euidently appeare by many: who if they can skill in some art, and do excell others, or can vtter a few sillables in learned tongues, and speake rhetorically, though these be nothing in comparison to that which is giuen to *Iohn*, or to *Paule*, yet they flie vp and mount aloft, and looke with disdaine ouer simple men, not as companions, but as if in comparison of them they were petty Gods. The Lord giue vs grace, euen the grace of his spirit, to frame our harts to follow these great Apostles in true humility.

And now further it is not to be omitted, that with affliction he ioyneth the Kingdome and patience of Christ: seeing it is added as a sweete and comfortable thing, to mitigate the bitternesse of persecutions and afflictions. For they that patiently endure and suffer affliction for his names sake, ye know how it is written, that they shall raigne with him. Saint *Iohn* therefore is not ashamed to be a companion in those afflictions, where he hath Christ himselfe a companion: with whom also hee shall be crowned with euerlasting glory. Let vs alwayes consider this, and we shal not be so much afraid to suffer afflictiō for the gospel. It doth indeed make mē base and miserable in outward appearance to the world, when their persecutiōs and afflictions be sore and grieuous: but how full of glory is it to be cōpanions with the blessed Apostles and Martyrs, yea euen with the Lord Iesus himselfe? Moreouer what a goodly thing is it to passe through these light & momentany afflictiōs into the euerlasting & most glorious kingdom of heauen? these are speciall things to be thought vpō. In the next words he sheweth the place where he receiued this reuelation, and that was the Ile called Patmos. It pleased the holy Ghost to make this cir-

C 4 cumstance

cumstance knowne touching the place, & therefore it is not in vaine to be noted. Ancient histories do report, that Saint *Iohn* was by the Emperour *Domitian* banished into that Iland, about the yeare of our Lord 96, and there receiued this Reuelation: and the next words do seeme manifestly to expresse so much, I meane that he was banished thither for the Gospell, when he saith, *For the word of God, and for the witnessing of Iesus Christ.* It may be sayd that he was there to preach the word of God; but the phrase seemeth rather to expresse the former sense. The next circumstance is, that he was rauished in the spirit, for thus he is made fit and capable of these heauenly visions: For the spirit which he here speaketh of, saying: *I was in the spirit*, is the holy Ghost. If ye read the Prophet *Ezechiel*, ye shal find how he saith he was taken vp by the spirit in the visions of God, and caried to Ierusalem. Saint *Paul* was by the spirit taken vp into the third heauen, euen into Paradise, and saw things which could not be vttered, & could not tell whether he were taken vp thither in the body, or whether he were only in soule taken vp out of the body. And so whether the bodily senses of *Iohn* did cease, his soule rapt for the time, I do not take vpō me to determine, it is sufficiēt for vs to know, that he was after a more thē ordinary maner rapt in the spirit, & made capable of so heauēly visiōs. Then in the next words the time is noted, when he saith it was vpon the Lords day. It is the day which Saint *Paul* to the Corinths calleth the first day of the weeke, 1. Cor. 16. in which the assemblies did meet for the holy exercises in religion: which is also euident because he saith, They came together that day to breake bread, Acts. 20. God created the world and all things therein in sixe dayes, and rested the seuenth, wherfore he blessed the seuenth day & hallowed it. He appointed the seuenth day for the holy exercises in the publike assemblies. There was somewhat in that Sabbath ceremoniall, as it appeareth plainly by the words of the Prophet *Ezechiell*, where the Lord saith, *I gaue you my Sabbaths, to be a signe betweene you & me, that I the Lord do sanctifie you:* and also by the words of Saint *Paule*, which saith, *The Sabbaths and festiuall dayes were shadowes of things to come.* The holy Apostles therefore euen by the Scriptures, & by the direction of the holy Ghost, did change the day, & chose for the holy assemblies the next day vnto it following, vpō which day our Sauiour rose from the dead. The cauill of the Papists here is vaine and friuolous, affirming that the Apostles had no scripture to warrant this, nor any commandement we reade of, but did change the day, not only otherwise then was obserued, but plainly otherwise then was prescribed by God himselfe in the commandement, seeing God commanded precisely that the seuenth day, and not the eight should be kept holy. How wickedly would they draw from hence a power in the Church to abrogate things that are commanded by God in the Scriptures, and to establish things not commaunded by the same? for they faile in these two things: the first, that they see not how the obseruation of the Sabbath so farre as it was ceremoniall, was by the Scriptures to be abrogated. The second, that the holy Apostles were led by the holy Ghost to deliuer all doctrine to the Church: and the Church since hath the holie Ghost not in such measure, to haue power to abrogate any ordinance set to be perpetuall, nor to teach any new things, but to know

and

THE REVELATION. 25

and to continue in the doctrine of the Apostles. For as our Sauiour preached all the whole Gospell, as he saith, *All things that I haue heard of my father, haue I made knowne vnto you.* Iohn 15. verse 15. so he sent downe the holy Ghost vpon the Apostles, which led them into all truth, Iohn 16. verse 13. This Comforter did bring al things to their remembrance whatsoeuer he had said vnto them, Ioh. 14. 26. And so the holy Apostles, euen as Saint *Paule* witnesseth of himselfe, Acts 20. vttered all the whole counsels of God. In so much that he is bold, and saith, If an Angell from heauen preach any other Gospell vnto you beside that we haue preached, let him be accursed, Galath. 1. If he had not preached all the doctrine of the Gospell, how should he say, If any preach beside that we haue preached? If he had said, against that we haue preached, it had not bene so much as to say, beside that we haue preached: for they may say and cauill, that their doctrine is not against or contrarie to that which the Apostles preached, but if it be added, is it not beside? and it is to be knowne that the Papists of Rhemes do themselues translate it, beside that I haue preached.

Further that they say, this day is called the Lords day, and frō ancient time, yea euen from the Apostles, and that to call it Sunday is an heathenish calling, they say right: but then why do not they consider that the calling it Sunday was not only taken vp in Poperie, as the rest of the dayes of the weeke, (in which for my part I am not scrupulous) but also if any that professe the Gospell call it the Lords day, the Popish sort among vs haue them by and by in derision. I trust they will do it no longer, if they know that the Iesuits say it is an heathenish calling, to call it Sunday. Thus much for the time.

Now followeth the calling of Saint *Iohn*, & authorising of him by commandement vnto this speciall businesse. He is indeed first called vpon, and receiueth commandement by a voyce, not seeing any thing. For he heard (as he saith) behind him a great voyce, as it had bin of a trumpet: no doubt there was some cause why this goodly loud voyce it vttered behind him, to stir him vp before he saw any vision, but I will not stand about coniectures. Then he telleth what the voyce spake, *I am Alpha and Omega, that first, and that last.* This is to let him vnderstand, of what authoritie he is that calleth him, and appointeth him to this worke: for that is a chiefe point, & a thing necessary for him to know. He is indeed the eternall God, the second person in the Trinity, euen the Lord of all Lords: for who but eternall God is *Alpha* & *Omega*, the beginning and the ending? And the great God alone hath authoritie to call ministers of his word, and to deliuer matters vnto them, for the instruction and saluation of his people. If they be not called by his appointment, and to bring his word, what authority haue they? who need to care for thē, or what they say? This is a strong place against the most damnable heresie of the wicked Arrians, which affirme that our Sauior is God, but not eternall God. They ascribe vnto him a secundarie Godhead which tooke beginning. We see it most euident by that which followeth, that it is Iesus which here appeareth: for he saith, *I am* . . . *and was dead*. Iesus as a man died, and as eternall God he saith, *I am Alpha and* . . . *ga, that first, and that last.* If he were not the same God with the

Father

Father and the holy Ghost, how should he be the first and the last? Do not doubt then of his eternall Deitie. Let vs proceed.

Here followeth what commandement the voice vttered, which consisteth of two parts. The first willeth him to write in a booke that which he seeth: then the other is, that he should send it to the Churches: because the Lord wold haue it remajne in perfect record vnto the vse of the whole Church, euē to the worlds end; he willeth it should be written in a booke. The Papists to vphold their kingdome, because the written word is against them, boast of vnwritten verities, and traditions, which they say are things so mysticall, that the Apostles would not commit them to writing, nor make them cōmon to all the people, but deliuered them vnto some few chiefe persons, that they from one to one might deliuer them to others which should succeed. Here they must bring in their hallowing of Altars, baptizing of bels, and a thousand such like trumperies. But if any thing had bene to be kept secret indeed from the common sort, and therfore not to be deliuered in writing, it might seeme to be the mysticall things vttered in this prophecie: but the Lord will haue them written in a booke: and not onely that, but the other part of the commandement is, that he should send it to the seuen Churches which are in Asia, vnto Ephesus, and vnto Smyrna, and vnto, &c. He doth not will him, when he hath written it, to keepe it close, or to send it vnto the Bishop of Rome, that he might haue the custodie therof, to deliuer to his Cleargie: but he must send it to the whole Church, and to all the members of the vniuersall Church, which is represented by these seuen, and which from these seuen was for all particular Churches to receiue the true copies thereof, to the end that whosoeuer would be blessed, might reade and heare the words of this Prophecie, and keepe the things which are written herein.

Now he commeth to set forth the vision, which consisteth of the description, partly of him that appeareth, and giueth him charge for this worke: and partly in the resemblance of the Churches and their ministers. Here is indeed a wonderfull goodly description of Christ Iesus, our high Priest and chiefe Pastor and king, exercising at the right hand of God his kingly and pastorall office, with great glory, wisdome and power, to the good of his chosen, & to the subduing & vtter destructiō of his enemies. We see how the Gospell by the foure Euangelists describeth him while he was vpon the earth, both before and after his resurrection, euen vnto the day that he ascended vp into the heauens: but how he is in the heauens is not there set forth, but here is shewed in vision vnto *Iohn*. It may delight vs to haue his glorie in some maner resembled, though we be not able to comprehend the same, no not by manie degrees, as it is in the fulnesse. Then in this place behold such a representation thereof shewed to *Iohn* in view, and vttered to vs in words as no colours can serue to paint out. He did not appeare thus while he preached vpon earth, but tooke vpon him the shape of a seruant, Philip. 2. yet in his second comming at the last day to iudge the quicke and the dead, he will come indeed in this glorie. The enemies that then despised him, because he was base in shew, and which now despise him, because they see him not, shal at that day, when this glorie shal appeare, not despise him. But let vs examine the particulars: *Iohn* saith, he turned him to see the

the voyce. And when he was turned, he saw seuen golden candlestickes, and in the middest of them one like to the sonne of man. Then the first thing is this, our Lord Iesus appeareth in the midst of the seuen golden cādlestickes. The golden candle-stickes are expounded by the Lord himselfe, that we may haue a certainty in the exposition, to be Churches: and I will speake more of them whē we come to that exposition. Here we are to note thus much by them, that our Lord Iesus is continually in the middest of his Church here vpon earth. Indeed he hath but one Church, or one spouse, but there be many particular Churches, as members of the same: and to shew that he is indeed with the vniuersall, and with all the members thereof, he appeareth in the middest of the seuen here named, which represent all other particular assemblies and faithfull members. ¶He is indeed touching his man-hood ascended vp aboue the heauens, and the heauens must containe him vntill the time of the restoring of all things, Act 2. and he must come downe euen as he went vp, Acts 1. He is not now by his bodily presence in the earth, no not inuisibly as the Papists would haue it in the Sacrament, for that destroyeth the truth of his humanitie, and maketh the properties of the humane nature, and of the Deitie to be all one, as to be inuisible or insensible, & to be in all places both of heauen and earth at once. And if men receiue the verie flesh or humane nature of Christ o-therwise then after a spirituall maner, they must needes also receiue the verie es-sence of the diuine nature with the same, which draweth with it horrible and most execrable blasphemies. For will they separate the Godhead and the manhood in Christ? will they be so blasphemous as to say, a man may receiue his manhood e-uen corporally, and not together therewith his Godhead, as being but one person? or will they be so absurd as to say, that a man may receiue with the manhood the verie essence of the Deitie, and not be deified, which is the diuellish blasphemie of those that be of the Family of loue? For they say men be deified. Wel, although we receiue the verie flesh and bloud of our Sauiour in the Sacrament, but mystically, and after a spirituall and heauenly maner, which is aboue our capacitie to compre-hend; and so touching his bodily presence he is remoued farre from the earth: yet after another sort he is always present here below. And so he sayd to his Apostles, *Behold I am with you alway, euen to the end of the world,* Math. 28. He defendeth, he cōforteth, he feedeth his Church: he performeth all things which belong to the office of the great shepheard. In verie deed all other shepheards are but his instru-ments by which he worketh, he himselfe doth all in all: he seeketh vp that which goeth astray, he feedeth the hungrie, he comforteth and supporteth the feeble and weake, he bridleth the froward, he repelleth the wolfe, and euerie rauening beast that wold deuoure the tender lambes of his flocke: For as we shall see by this vision, he is in the middest of his flocke, not weake, nor idle. How then doth the Pope of Rome boast as though Christ were absent, and had left him in his stead, as his Vi-car, committing his whole office and authoritie into his hands? and looke what he saith, it must be taken as equall in authoritie with that which Christ hath said. He saith, he is the head of the Church in Christs absence: but we see here that our Lord Iesus raigning in glory at the right hand of his father, is so present with his Church,

that

that he worketh all, and needeth not to haue a vicar. The Pope indeede is a vicar, but as we shall see afterward in this booke, and that most manifest, not by humane coniecture, but by cleare testimonie of Gods spirite, he is not the vicar of Christ, but the vicar of the diuell: the dragon giueth him his throne, &c. For albeit the diuell is not absent, yet he hath a vicar, becauſe he cannot worke well without one, vnto whom he may giue his place, his throne and his authoritie.

Then next he noteth his attire, which is a garment downe to the feete, and girded about the breasts with a golden girdle: the Kings vſe large and royall robes, and the Priests alſo at Gods appointment by *Moſes* in the time of the Law. This figure then doth represent that he is among the candlesticks, as our King & Priest: and when they that wore large garments did execute any office (as we may reade of the Priests in the Law) least their garments should hinder, they were girded to them with a girdle. The garment is here girded to Christ with a golden girdle: which doth not onely represent, that he is in the midst of his Church not idle, but executing his Kingly and Priestly office, but alſo that this his worke, is most precious and acceptable to God, as we ſee the fine gold is vnto men. Looke vp then beloued, our King and great high Priest, is entred into the most holy place in heauen, and is at the right hand of God in glorie, but yet he is preſent here below, and executeth his office to our ſaluation; for behold he is in his robes girded vnto him.

Then next he ſaith that his head and haires were white, as white wooll, and as ſnow: the white colour in the Scripture doth ſometime repreſent innocencie and puritie: ſometime heauenly glorie, light and ioy. And ſo we ſee that the holy Angels haue appeared in white raiment, Matth. 28. Alſo Chriſt transfigured vpon the mount, hath his garments white, Matth. 17. But here it is ſpoken of the head and haires, and therefore doth rather repreſent his full and ripe knowledge and wiſdome to performe all things in his Church: for the auncient in dayes haue wiſdome and knowledge, and their haires & heads grow whiter, as they waxe older. The Lord God appearing in viſion vnto *Daniel*, chap. 7. verſe 9. the haires of his head were as pure wol. The figure in this place doth repreſent the ſame thing with that in *Daniel*. 7. Indeed touching this figure, we muſt not extend it further then vnto one point: for old men by the multitude of dayes gather wiſedome: they be white headed if they waxe exceeding old; now to repreſent a full ripeneſſe of wiſdome, the viſion is with head and haires as white as white wooll, and as ſnow. But thus it holdeth not, that as by the number of dayes, naturall heate decaying in men, they grow feeble, and their haires waxe white, ſo God ſhould alſo waxe old: for there is no chaunge or waxing old in God, nor in Ieſus Chriſt, nor no increaſe of wiſedome in the deitie by any experience.

Then further he ſaith, his eyes were as a flame of fire: the fire (as we knowe) is verie quicke and piercing to paſſe through all things, and alſo goeth with cleare light, which expelleth darkeneſſe, and diſcouereth things that lye hid: and for that cauſe is here vſed to repreſent the piercing ſight of our Lord Ieſus Chriſt, from which nothing can lye hid, no not euen in the darkeſt corners in the world, nor in the deepeſt ſecrets of mens hearts. His eyes behold all things, both in the good and

in

in the bad: all things are naked and open vnto his eyes, with whom we haue to do, Heb.4.verſ.13. The ſincere godly man is often accuſed and condemned to be an hypocrite, by the corrupt malice of men which are blind: but his eyes be as a flame of fire, he ſeeth the intents of the hart, & knoweth the deſires of his ſeruants, not caried awrie with the ſiniſter opinion that the world hath of them. The glorying and gloſing hypocrite, making outwardly a notable ſhew, and highly commended of men, being but as a painted ſepulcher, faire and beautifull without, & within full of rottenneſſe and dead bones, cannot lye hid from his eyes. The craftie enemies in their ſecret counſels, which they take againſt the poore innocent lambes of Chriſt, and in their deepe diſſembled pollicies how to entrap and deſtroy them, are indeed often farre remoued from the ſight of the wiſeſt men: but his eyes are as a flame of fire, he ſeeth thẽ all well enough. The deuils in hell can deuiſe nothing againſt his ſeruants, but it is euident to his ſight. As this may terrifie all tyrants and hypocrites, ſo may it comfort all the godly exceedingly, and encourage them to fly vnto him, and to depend vpon him in all diſtreſſes.

Then followeth that his feet are like vnto fine braſſe burning in a furnace. This declareth not only the perfection of his wayes, but alſo his mightie and inuincible power to tread downe all his enemies: for the kind of braſſe which his feete are likened vnto, is of a maruellous ſhining colour, eſpecially when it is burning in a fornace: ſuch is the excellent puritie and brightneſſe of his wayes. But why then is not this repreſented by the fineſt and pureſt gold, which of all mettals doth excell? The cauſe here, as alſo in Daniell 10. is euident, that ſuch a mettall is choſen, as beſides the brightneſſe, is alſo verie hard and ſtrong, to repreſent as I ſaid, the power which he hath to tread downe all his enemies: for he ſhall make all his enemies his footſtoole, Pſalme 110. If the moſt fine gold were equall in ſhining colour with this kind of braſſe, yet gold is a ſoft bowing mettall, and not ſo fit to repreſent his inuincible ſtrength. He is of might indeed to ouerthrow all the mightieſt, and to deliuer his. It alſo ſetteth forth his might, that he ſaith his voice is like to the ſound of many waters. How the great nations haue bene called and ſubdued vnto him by his mightie voyce, I will not ſtand to rehearſe. Here are yet ſome parts of this goodly deſcription remaining: as firſt, that he had in his right hand ſeuen ſtarres. The ſtarres are the Angels of the Churches, for ſo the Lord himſelfe expoundeth it in the laſt verſe of this chapter, where we will ſpeake more of them: but here we may note, that Chriſt in feeding & guiding his Church, vſeth the miniſtery of men. For leaſt any ſhould gather by this viſion, vpon this, that Chriſt as King and Prophet is preſent, & worketh all in his Church, that the miniſterie ſhould be in vaine, this figure is ſet forth, that indeed he worketh all, but he worketh by the miniſtery of men. And how readily men deſpiſe the miniſtery of the Goſpell, imagining a ſafetie without the ſame, we haue too much experience: but if thou wilt haue the right hand of the Lord Ieſus to worke vpon thee, to frame thee vnto an holy temple, or to faſhion thee to be a liuing ſtone in the temple, or if thou wilt be defended by him from all ſpirituall euill, ſubmit thy ſelfe vnto the miniſterie of the Goſpell, for thou ſeeſt the ſtarres be in his right hand, he worketh by them. To the ſame

purpoſe

purpose also it is set downe, *That out of his mouth went a two edged sword.* The word of God is called the spirituall sword, Ephes. 6. and it is sharper then any two edged sword, Hebrew. 4. he worketh with this, the starres and this sword are wel set together: for the ministers of the Church are to do all, both in feeding and gouerning only by that word which proceedeth out of his mouth. They can do nothing without it, they are to meddle with none other word in the work of the ministery, there is none other word that hath power and authority. The Church of Rome boasteth much of the power aud authority of her word: but if it come not out of Christs mouth, it hath no power, neither are they his ministers which deale by a word which is not his. Whose word it is, or whose doctrine, his ministers they be that teach it: if it be the doctrine of Antichrist, euen the doctrine of diuels, then are they the ministers of Antichrist, and the seruants of the diuell that teach it; as they be Christs ministers which faithfully vse this two edged sword that commeth out of his mouth. I know the Pope and all Papists do boast, that their word is the word of Christ: but when they can shew that it came out of his mouth, that it is to be found in the writings of the holy Apostles and Prophets (which haue vttered all that came out of his mouth) we will beleeue them. We know that whatsoeuer doctrine commeth not from his mouth, (as all that is not contained in the holy Scriptures) it commeth out of the mouth of the dragon. Lastly, Saint *Iohn* expresseth the wonderfull brightnesse of his face, for he saith it did shine as the sunne shineth in his strength, that is, when the sunne shineth cleareft: for when the sunne riseth, commonly the thicke vapours which are neare the earth, betweene vs and it while it is low, do dimme the beames thereof, and so when it goeth downe, then our eyes can in some sort stedfastly behold and looke vpon it. Sometime also the aire being ouercast with some thicke mist, we may looke vpon the sunne, euen at noone when it is at the highest. But when it is at the highest, euen at midday, and the aire cleare indeed, then doth it shine in the full strength, and then is no mortall eye able to behold it stedfastly: such is the brightnesse of his face. The Prophet *Dauid* prayeth, Psalm. 4. Lord lift vp the light of thy counteuance vpon vs: the whole Church also in the Psalme prayeth, Shew vs the light of thy countenance, and we shall be safe. The light of his countenance is with ioy and comfort, expelling all darkenesse and sorow: this bright countenance of Christ comforteth and lighteneth the whole Church.

Thus we see what a glorious, mighty, and most wise King, and high Priest the Church hath, who is alwayes present with her, working effectually her saluation by his liuely word and ministers, treading downe her enemies, & shining most comfortably vpon her. Now it followeth, how *Iohn* could not endure the sight of this vision, vntill he was strengthened by the Lord: for when he saw him, he fell at his feet as dead: there was as it were no spirit left in him. The Prophet *Daniell* was in the like case at the sight of the vision which he had, chap. 10. This glorie of Christ doth not lift vp Saint *Iohn* into any pride, that he is admitted to see his Lord in such maiestie, but contrariwise it doth humble him euen to the ground, in as much as by it he findeth his owne weaknesse and imperfection, not capable of

such

such a sight so farre as to endure it.

It was no doubt profitable, or as I may say, needful, that the holy seruãt of Christ should thus be humbled and made fit to receiue this reuelation with the greater reuerence from his great Lord & maister: but yet it was chiefly for vs, as it appeareth in that euery part of this vision is rehearsed in the Epistles to the Churches. We see not Christ with bodily eyes, we cannot conceiue the greatnes of his glory, and that boldeneth vs to despise and to disobey the words that come from him. Such a shew thereof, and representation of his glory, is needfull for vs. Now he cõfortteh & cõfirmeth him, partly by signe, & partly by words, that he might not be afraid. The sign is this, whẽ he saith, *He laid his right hand vpõ me.* The laying on his right hand signifieth that he is his protector: yea all this power & maiesty is for the good of the Church. Woe be to the diuels, and to all the wicked tyrants, that Christ Iesus is so mighty, they shall tremble and quake at it. indeede: but let the Church reioyce, for with his right hand and strong arme, he is her defender. And let it not dismay vs that *Iohn* is so terrified at the sight of Christ, for he was not yet fully perfected: *For when this mortall hath put on immortality,* 1. Cor. 15. and wee shall bee quite rid of all infection and diseases both in body and soule, then shall the beholding of the king in his glory be most comfortable vnto vs, which was yet thus terrible vnto *Iohn.* Then follow his words, *Feare not, I am that first, and that last, &c.* Shall *Iohn* feare, or shall the Church feare at this high maiesty? nay it is that which must comfort and deliuer vs from all dread, that our redeemer is so mighty, as both the vision, and his words here do set foorth. Iesus Christ is not only God, but God euerlasting, and before all eternity, for he saith, *I am that first and that last*. With this eternall Deitie, the manhood is also in such sort vnited, that together they make but one person: For the same which saith, *I am that first, and that last*: saith also, *I am aliue, but I was dead, &c.* The diuine nature could not suffer nor die; the humane nature had beginning, & was not that first, but yet being so vnited, he that is first and last, is aliue and was dead. All power is from the godhead, (it is the spirit that quickneth, the flesh profiteth nothing, Iohn. 6. and the second man is the Lord from heauen, 1. Cor. 15.) but because the children are partakers of flesh & bloud, he also tooke part with them, that he might destroy through death, him that had the power of death, that is the diuell, Hebr. 2. ver. 14. he tooke our nature then that he might die, and by death ouercome the diuell and all the power of death and hell, and deliuer his captiues. In that he was dead and is aliue, yea liueth for euermore, death is swallowed vp into victory, 1. Cor. 15. In that he died (as the same Apostle saith) he died once to sinne; but in that he liueth, he liueth to God, Rom. 6. ver. 10. *Behold* (saith the Lord Iesus here) *I am aliue for euermore, Amen.* He willeth vs to behold, as a very speciall thing, and then ratifieth it with this word, *Amen.* For in that he liueth for euermore, his kingdome and priesthood are eternall, as it is written, *Thou art a Priest for euer, after the order of Melchisedech:* Psalm. 110. This is necessary, and comfortable to be knowne, as a thing most surely confirmed and ratified vnto vs: because vpon it dependeth the perfect saluation of the whole Church. For thus sayth the holy Ghost, *This man because*

SERMONS VPON

he endureth euer, hath a priesthood which cannot passe from one to another. Wherefore he is able also perfectly to saue them that come vnto God by him, seeing he euer liueth to make intercession for them. Heb.7.ver.24.& 25. This setteth forth the great glory of his eternall priesthood, and for the power of his kingdome, marke what he sayth in the next words: *And I haue the keyes of hell and of death*. The keyes in the holy Scripture are put for the rule, and power, and authority, which he hath that is made high steward in an house, or in a kingdome, to order and dispose all things as he shall see good. Looke in Isay chap. 22. where the Lord threatneth *Sebna*, that he would remoue him, and that he would set *Eliachim* in his place to haue the rule ouer the house of the king of Iuda, and ye shall find it expressed in this maner: *I wil put the key of the house of Dauid vpon his shoulder, he shall open, and none shall shut, he shall shut, and no man shall open*. The Lord Iesus Christ is set at the right hand of God the Father Almighty, all rule and power is committed into his hand in heauē and earth, Math. 28. and therefore he saith in the third Chapter of this booke, speaking of himselfe, that he hath the key of *Dauid*, that he openeth and no mā shutteth, that he shutteth & no mā openeth. This expresseth his Soueraignty ouer the whole Church which is the house of *Dauid*, into which they be receiued in, & they be shut out, whom he will. He saueth, and he punisheth, & none can resist him: he commādeth, and he forbiddeth, and none may gainsay. In this place to take away all feare not only from *Iohn*, but from all his chosen, he saith, *I haue the keyes of hel and of death*. For if he haue the Lordship ouer hel it selfe, and ouer death, they can hurt vs no longer, we need not to feare. As he that winneth a defenced city, taketh the keyes, openeth and shutteth: so Christ hauing vanquished death and hell, euen all the infernall powers, in their strong hold, keepeth the keyes, and none of his shall be hurt: and as for his enemies, euen Satan and all his Angels, and all the wicked, he will shut them vp in hell, and punish them for euer. Thus hauing confirmed and comforted *Iohn*, both by laying his right hand vpon him, and by his speech, he cōmandeth him againe to write this Reuelation. And we may nowe, that he deuideth it into these three parts, *The things which thou hast seene, the things which are, and things which shall come hereafter*. He had then seene that glorious vision of the mighty sonne of God appearing in the middest of the seuen golden candlestickes, which he according as he was commanded, committed to writing, euen euery particular: for the vision was not for him alone, but for the whole Church, that we may know what manner of one he is from whom this Reuelation doth come. This is the first branch.

Then the second is, the things which are: and those bee contained in the two next Chapters, the second & the third. For there is the state of the seuen Churches of Asia layd open, in which they were at that present, that by them (as I sayd before) we may vnderstand in what estate the whole Church militant was at that time. S. Iohn, according to this commaundement, hath written vnto euery one of them seuerally, that message which the Lord committed vnto him. Then ye may see the second branch, which is, the things that are.

Now the third is, the things which shall come hereafter: and that is all things opened

THE REVELATION. 33

pened in this booke forefhewed to come, and to be fulfilled euen to the end of the world. He left out nothing of that was fhewed him: he added nothing more then was fhewed him: he was a right faithfull feruant of the Lord. And for our part we muft receiue euery thing writtē in this book, as from the mouth of our great Lord and maifter, neither adding thereunto, nor taking therefro. We muft receiue this booke, will fome fay, but how can we vnderftand it? Is not the interpretation of it doubtfull? becaufe things darke and myfticall may be taken diuerfe waies, and men follow fome one fenfe, and fome another, as feemeth moft like vnto them. Nay if we haue not an vndoubted certaintie for the fenfe & meaning of this book, we are neuer the nearer. That is it which the Papifts would driue vs vnto: but behold the great goodneffe, the great kindneffe of the Lord, which will not haue vs follow coniectures or reafons of men, & therfore himfelf expoundeth the darkeft and the moft myfticall things, at the leaft fo many of them, and fo farre, as the reft are thereby laid open and made manifeft: As here he expoundeth the myfterie of the feuen ftarres, and of the feuen golden candlefickes: whereby we vnderftand the vifion, & all that is written in the two next chapters to the feuen Angels of the feuen Churches. Can any man then doubt any longer, or call it into queftion, when the Lord himfelfe hath giuen the fignification? Let vs fee then what is fignified by the figure of the feuen ftars in his right hand, and by the feuen golden candlefticks. *The myfterie of the feuen ftarres which thou faweft in my right hand, and thefeuen golden cendleftickes is this: The feuen ftarres are the Angels of the feuen Churches, and the feuen candleftickes are the feuen Churches.* Is not this euident enough, that the ftarres do reprefent and fignifie the Paftours and Teachers of the Churches, which teach the Gofpell of Chrift? and the candleftickes are the Churches? Indeed Angels are moft vfually taken for heauenly fpirites which are about the throne of God, but as the prieft is called the Angell of the Lord of hoftes, Malach. 2. fo the minifters of the Gofpel are called Angels here. If any man fhall fay, how is that out of all controuerfie? I anfwere, it is fo euident and paft all doubt, that the Iefuites which would faine fet vp the patronage of Angels, are conftrained to confeffe, that in this place the Angels of the Churches are not the heauenly fpirits, as it is manifeft, fay they, and therefore muft needs fignifie the Priefts or Bifhops, &c. But fhall we take it from them to be manifeft, becaufe they fay fo? Nay, I alleage them to this purpofe, that they feeking to depraue all things, this is fo manifeft to be the paftors of the Churches, that they cannot depraue it, or wreft it. For reade the two next chapters, and ye fhal fee that almoft euerie one of thefe feuen Angels is reproued for fome fault or other, which cannot be in the heauenly Angels, for they be without all fault. Ye fee thefe are willed to repent, and threatned if they do not, and therefore they be men.

Ye may fee alfo that the vertues commended in them, and the vices rebuked, do indeed concerne the worke of the minifterie. Then why are the minifters of the Gofpell called ftarres? becaufe as the ftarres do fhine from heauen, fo the minifters of Chrift, the true minifters of the Gofpell, do fhine and giue light vnto men by heauenly doctrine, and godly conuerfation of life. The Popifh prelates chalenge

D   to

to be these stars, being indeed nothing lesse, teaching their owne inuentions, and resisting the true heauenly light of the Gospell. Why do these stars in this vision appeare in Christs right hand? becaufe he worketh, he buildeth, and he preserueth his Church by them: for howsoeuer the worke of the ministery seemeth a base & contemptible thing vnto the blind world; yet is it a thing most precious, seeing the ministers bee the instruments of Christs right hand, by which hee bringeth his Church vnto eternall glory. Woe be to them that degenerate from so high a dignity, and from so precious a worke, but blessed are they which be found faithfull: for though the proud worlings despise them, their honour is with God, and with our Lord Iesus Christ.

And now for the Churches, why are they resembled by golden candlestickes? Touching the mettall gold is precious, so that we are hereby giuen to vnderstand how precious the Churches be before the Lord. There be indeed many infirmities, yea deformities in the true members of the Church, and we are base in sundry respects, which causeth many euen to loath and despise vs: but we must learne to esteeme the Church as the Lord esteemeth it, euen precious as gold, not looking vpon the present estate which it is in here vpon the earth, but whē he shal make it to himselfe a glorious Church, not hauing spot or wrinkle, Ephes.5.vers. 27. maruell not then that the candlestickes be of gold: for how precious and deare is that vnto him, which he bought and purchased with his owne bloud? Some esteeme true Christian people, especially if they be poore, euen as much as they do ragges: I would they did vnderstand this vision of the golden candlestickes.

Then further, why are the Churches resembled by candlesticks? Becaufe as the candlesticke doth not giue the light, but the light is put vpon it, and it beareth vp the light: so the Church receiueth all her light put vpon her from Christ, she shineth with light, but not her owne, the whole doctrine is from God, and not of men, the heauenly light doth remaine in her and vpon her onely. This is the cause why Saint *Paul* calleth the Church, the pillar and ground of truth, 1.Timoth.3.vers.15. No man can be partaker of the true heauenly light, except he abide in the Church. There is the onely candlesticke which beareth the light: seeke therefore to be of the true Church. And that Church which taketh vpō her not to be a candlesticke, but to giue light of her owne, yea to make her owne decrees equall or aboue the word of God (as the Church of Rome) flie from it, it is the Synagogue of Sathan. Thus much for these words of this first vision.

THE

THE REVELATION. S. 4

THE IIII. SERMON.
CHAP. 2.

1. *To the Angell of the Church which is at Ephesus write, these things saith he that holdeth the seuen starres in his right hand, and that walketh in the middest of the seuen golden candlestickes:*
2. *I know thy workes, and thy labour, and thy patience, and how thou canst not beare with them that are euill, and hast examined them which say they are Apostles and are not, and hast found them liers.*
3. *And thou wast burthened, and hast patience, and for my name sake hast laboured, and hast not fainted.*
4. *Neuerthelesse I haue somewhat against thee, because thou hast left thy first loue.*
5. *Remember therefore from whence thou art fallen, and repent, and do the first workes, or else I will come against thee shortly, and will remoue thy candlesticke out of his place, except thou amend.*
6. *But this thou hast, because thou hatest the works of the Nicholaitans, which I also hate.*
7. *Let him that hath an eare, heare what the spirit saith to the Churches: to him that ouercommeth will I giue to eate of the tree of life, which is in the middest of the Paradise of God.*

Aint *Iohn* (as we haue seene in the former Chapter) was commaunded by the Lord, to write that he saw, and to send it to the seuen Churches of Asia, which are there named. And now being to foreshew the state of the Church, he beginneth first with these seuen Churches themselues. For here is to euery one of them seuerally, a seuerall Epistle or message, sent from the Lord, in which their estate which they were then in, is layd open. In these same messages, there be many excellent things set downe for our instruction, which require our diligent obseruation. For there is not onely layd open in what estate the sayd Churches were at that time: but also we shall find what things the Lord praiseth & commendeth in the ministers of his Church, and in all Christians, likewise what he disalloweth and condemneth. Moreouer we shall see admonitions and threatnings, also very great and precious promises.

But let vs handle the words in order as they be set downe: The first message is sent

sent to the Angell of the Church of Ephesus, for that was the chiefe city of Asia, and by all likelihood there was the greatest and the most populous Church of these seuen. But how is it, that where he commaunded him before to write to the seuen Churches, now he willeth him to write but to the Angels, that is, to the pastors and teachers of the same Churches, as here to the Angell of the Church of Ephesus, and so in all the rest? We must know, for to answer this, that writing to the pastors, he excludeth not the Churches, but in very deed in them or vnder them he writeth to the whole Churches. And least any may imagine, that this is but mans interpretation, reade the conclusion of euery message, and yee shall find these words, *Let him that hath an eare heare what the spirit saith to the Churches*. He beginneth with the Angels of the Churches, and endeth with this: let him heare what the spirit saith to the Churches: then that which is spoken to the Angell of the Church, is spoken to the Church. What is the reason of this (may some demaund) that directing the speech but to the Angels of the Churches, yet he writeth to the Churches, or being to write to the Churches, he nameth but the Angels of those Churches?

It may be sayd, that it was requisite, that the pastors should haue the state of their flockes laid open vnto them, to the end that they might apply the doctrine & censures of the Church accordingly. This is true, but not all, there is a further cause: And if ye consider that the pastors are commended, and reproued together with their flocks, so that their owne estate, and the state of their flockes is layd open to be all one, ye may soone gather what it is. Such shepheards, such flockes, such builders such building: the praise of the good, and the blame for the euill, lieth vpon the Pastors. God indeed buildeth his Church, Christ feedeth his flocke, but he doth it by the ministery of me, as the holy Apostle teacheth, Ephe. 4. There is a great matter depending vpon this ministery: for if the builders be wise, if they be expert and carefull, the building goeth vp accordingly, very goodly and faire.

If the shepheards be full of the spirit of God, if they be full of faith, full of loue, ful of zeale, and full of all holy vertues, so that they be patterns in holy doctrine & godly conuersation: then their flockes are well instructed, well fed, and wel guided: there be very excellent sheep for knowledge, for faith, for loue, for zeale, and for all godlinesse. Contrariwise, if the builders be vnskilfull, the building is vnperfect, they do but marre it: If the shepheards be vnwise, if they be negligent, if they be corrupt, either in doctrine or in manners, the sheepe remaine ignorant, the sheep are weake and feeble

And further, as the shepheards increase in graces, the sheepe increase (for God poureth forth his graces vpon the flockes of his ministers,) they bee the vessels in which the treasure is brought, 2. Cor. 4. verse. 7. As the shepheards decay & waxe cold, the sheepe go backward and waxe cold with them, euen as the kettle vpon the fire cooleth as the fire slaketh.

Maruaile not then that the Lord opening the state of the Churches, doth it by opening the state only of their pastors and teachers. Here is a lesson for the ministers of the Gospell; and here is also a lesson for the people; the ministers and pastors

THE REVELATION. 37

stors must consider what a waight lieth vpon their shoulders: if they performe the things which are required at the hands of Christs true ministers, they shall (as Saint *Paul* saith of *Timothie*, chap. 4. v. 14. 15. 16.) saue themselues, and those that shall heare them. So likewise on the contrary part, if the pastors be vnskilfull, corrupt and negligent, they destroy the flockes. Where there be good things in the shepheards, they flow forth vpon the whole flockes; and where there be euill things in them, they infect and destroy the sheepe.

Let no man thinke that this is to ascribe too much on both sides vnto men: but reade what S. *Paul* writeth, 1. Cor, 3. vers. 9. *For we together are Gods laborers, ye are Gods husbandry, and Gods building.* He compareth (as ye see) the Church vnto tillage, as also vnto a building, and the ministers they be the workemen that till and dresse the ground, and that frame & fit the stones, and couple them in the building. Now we must needs confesse, that it is Almighty God alone, that maketh the corne to grow; but yet if the husband man doe not plow, and harrow, and sowe, and weede, what haruest will there follow? The husband man is Gods instrument to bring forth the fruites of the earth. In like manner it is said of the Lords spirituall haruest, *Paule hath planted, Apollo hath watered, but God gaue the increase,* 1. Cor. 3. ver. 6. If there be none to till, to dresse, to plant, to water, what increase, or what haruest shall there be vnto the Lord? If any will say, God is able to saue without the ministery of men: so is he able to make the corne grow without the labours of the plowman. But we are not to looke what he is able, but what he hath ordayned and appointed to be. I may say likewise for the other similitude, it is written: *Except the Lord build the house, their labour is lost that build it.* But yet if the Carpenter, and Mason, do not hew, and square the timber, and the stones, what building shall we haue? Would to God that all that haue the roomes, and occupy the places of Bishops and pastors in the Church, would well and throughly consider this.

And for that lesson which the people are here to learne, it is this: euen to see what a singular blessing of Almighty God it is, to haue godly and skilfull pastors, and wise builders. And what a plague and curse it is on the other side, to haue such as be naught: for be they not left as ground vntilled, and as stones and timber not hewne for the Lords building, where they haue naughty ministers? Are they not as sheepe scattered and deuoured of the wild beastes? Ah poore men how they laugh, and how glad they bee, euen many of them, when they see him that should instruct and guide them, ignorant, and wicked in his wayes? As if the matter did not touch or concerne them at all, they know not that the Lord doth in the state of the shepheards, declare also what the flockes be: they know not that it is their owne plague. Thus much for that he saith to the Angell of the Church which is at Ephesus.

Now to the message which he is willed to write; it consisteth (and so doth euery one of the seuen) of three parts, that is to say, of the exordium or beginning, of the narration, and of the conclusion. The exordium is taken from the person of him that sendeth, and according to the glory of the vision in which he appeared. *These things*

D 3

SERMONS VPON

things saith he, that holdeth the seuen starres in his right hand, and that walketh in the middest of the seuen golden candlestickes. Of what authority, of what power, maiesty and glory he is that holdeth the seuen starres in his right hand, and that walketh in the middest of the seuen golden candlestickes, the vision doth shew: his eyes as a flame of fire, his feete like vnto fine brasse burning in a fornace, his voyce as the sound of many waters, his face as the sunne shineth in his strength, & so of al the rest. For this one part is to put them in mind of the whole, that they might consider from what an high, mighty, and glorious Lord, and most wise, the message did come, and so beware that they did not esteeme light of it. For the more excellent the person is that sendeth, the lesse safe it is for men to despise the message which is sent. It might moue sufficiently to say, thus saith the Lord Iesus sitting at the right hand of God the Father Almighty: but we are dull, and therefore he hath in vision set forth some part of his glory that he raigneth in, and from the maiesty and power, of the same sendeth the message. We see by this that the vision in which Christ, appeared, chap. 1. was not for *Iohn* alone, but for the Churches to whom hee sent, yea euen for vs all. Christ our blessed Lord from his glory, hath sent this booke vnto vs: let vs then receiue and imbrace it with al humblenesse of mind, for so it becometh vs to do, vnlesse we will set light by so mighty a king. Let not this heauenly vision be in vaine or fruitlesse, as set forth vnto blocks or stones, which are nothing moued thereby. This for the beginning.

The narration followeth, which in this Epistle to the Angell of the Church of Ephesus, hath these seueral parts. First, he is commended and praised for sundry good things which are expressed in the second and third verse. Then is he discommended for somewhat wherein he halteth, which is noted in the fourth verse. After that he is admonished to repent, and threatned if he do not, but the threatning is mitigated, verse the fift and sixt. Now before we handle these things, marke how he saith, *I know thy workes*. This is to put him in mind, yea to put vs all in mind, that the Lord Iesus commendeth and discommendeth, vpon a perfect ground and measure of all actions. For that the praise may be iust, neither too much nor too little, and likewise the disprase; it is requisite that he which praiseth and dispraiseth, should know perfectly, how good and how euill all actions or deedes of men be. Wherefore when he commeth to lay open the state of the Angels of the Churches, to commend and to discommend, he beginneth with this vnto euery one of them, *I know thy workes*.

We are ready to nothing more then to praise and dispraise that which we heare and see in our brethren, but for want of perfect knowledge, that we cannot see from what roote euery worke springeth, from what faith, from what loue, from what intent and sincerity of heart, we commend and discommend not onely vnperfectly, but also oftentimes vniustly and rashly. We praise a man for his vertues, or discommend him for his faults, either too much or too little: we commend a man highly for his works, when it may be they are naught before God, as he doth them: and so we disallow and discommend often that which is well done in the sight of God. But our Sauiour Iesus Christ, whose eyes are as a flame of fire, and

pierce

pierce through all things, before whom all things lie naked and open, Hebrewes.4. who seeth the intents and counsels of all harts, and will make them manifest, and will bring into light things hid in darknesse; 1.Cor.4.verse. 5. this Lord, I say, in praising and dispraising, faileth not one iot, or as they say, one haire breadth. All that followeth then touching the praise and dispraise of the Pastors and the Churches, we must take as a most perfect censure proceeding from him that saith, *I know thy workes.*

This is a great comfort vnto all the true and faithfull seruants of Iesus Christ. For howsoeuer their doings are depraued among men, and they be euill rewarded, yet the Prince of Pastors, the Lord Iesus sitting in glory at the right hand of God, is present among them, beholdeth and knoweth most perfectly all their wayes, and will giue them their iust praise and reward. This caused Saint *Paule* to set so light to be iudged by mans iudgement, as he professeth, 1.Cor.4.verse.3. If the negligent, vnskilfull, and vngodly shepheards, which seeke but for lucre or glory, wold marke these words well (*I know thy workes*) it might strike them as a most terrible thunderbolt. For can they thinke they shall escape his iudgement that knoweth all their workes? or do they imagine, it is a light matter to destroy the flocke of Christ? All and euery Christian man ought continually to be mindful of this, that the Lord sitteth in his glory, beholdeth and knoweth all their workes, that so they may indeuour to worke well, to walke vprightly and faithfully before him, & so to fight the good fight of faith, as that by him they may be crowned.

We be souldiers in the Lords army to fight vnder his banner against sinne, the world, and the diuell: when the Emperour in the worldly battailes doth stand and behold them, how valiantly euery coward will then lay on and fight? And shall not we (our Emperor looking vpon vs) fight so in this spirituall battaile, as that he may approue of vs? We shal be rewarded for euery good worke which we do of a sincere faith and loue towards him, Math.10.ver.42. Marke.9.ver.41. How happy a thing is it then to be rich and plenteous in all good works?

Now let vs see what his works were which the Lord saith he did know, and first those for which he did commend him. Here are sixe vertues, which are euen holy ornaments vnto a faithful shepheard rehearsed by the Lord, & ascribed vnto him: Labor, patience, zeale, wisedome, sincerity of heart, and heroicall magnanimity. These be the sixe. I might in some sort haue sayd seuen, because he hath a double commendation for his patience. These vertues do shew that he was a very excellent seruant of Christ, especially before this his blemish, when he blameth him that he was somewhat decayed, and had left his former loue: for if he had wanted other things which are by the rules of the word of God required in a pastor, he should haue bene blamed for them also: but hee is blamed, onely for some decay in loue. Looke now vpon the vertues which our Lord ascribeth vnto him.

The first is labor, for he saith, thy labor. He that in the ministery of the Gospell will follow the steps of Christ the great shepheard, and the steps of the blessed Apostles which follow next vnto him, hee must take great paines and labour, hee must not be idle and negligent. For ye may reade in the Euangelistes how Christ

did

did trauaile from Towne to Towne, and from City to City, preaching the Gospell of the kingdome, Math. 4. verse. 23. We reade of the labours and trauailes of Saint *Paul*, 2. Cor. 11. and what charge he gaue to others, Acts. 20. 1. Timoth. 3. 13. 15. 16. 2. Timoth. 4. verse. 2. Can a man feede, and guide a flocke of sheepe, and not take paines? And saith not Christ vnto *Peter*, Feed my sheep? Iohn. 21. Can the husband-man plow, harrow, sow, dresse and weede his grounds, but it will cost him great labours? The Church, as Saint *Paul* saith, is Gods husbandry, euē his ground that is to be tilled and sowne, 1. Cor. 3. verse. 9. Can the builders build vp an house and not worke vpon it? The Church in the same place is called Gods building. There is no ground so churlish, so vnfit for seede, and so plentifull in euill weedes, as the harts of men are without continuall dressing and tilling, vnfit for heauenly seede, and plentifull in all vices. There is no timber, or stones which aske more labour to hew and to square them, then men doe to bee framed, and made fit to bee coupled in the spirituall building. Such then as haue charge ouer soules, & be idle and negligent, spending away their time in vaine pastimes, follow not the steps of Christ and his Apostles, but destroy and scatter the flocke, lay the Lords husbandry wast and ouergrowne with noysome weedes, and pul downe his Temple, Do these men make account that there is any iudgement seate? do they thinke they shall euer be called to their reckoning? He that will bee a true minister of Iesus Christ, he must make account he hath entred vpon a matter of continuall labour & caresse: vnlesse he regard not what become of the Lords sheepe, of his husbandrie and building.

The second vertue is patience: This is ioyned with labor in the Church, because without it, the labours cannot be continued. Indeed where a man seeth good successe of his trauaile, it carieth him on forward to labour sore, euen willingly. But in the Church some be so dull and slow of capacity, that they must bee taught as the Prophet Isay saith, like children new weaned, *Line vnto line, line vnto line, precept vnto precept, precept vnto precept, a little here, and a little there*: Isay. 28. yea with great labours they seeme to profit nothing. Some are so vnconstant, fickle, & wauering, that when they are taught, the labours seeme to be but lost, they be harder to be kept, then they were to be found. Others there be which are somewhat froward, and if the pastors be not patient, yea very patient towards them, they must needes slacken in their care and labours. For these offer oftentimes so great indignitie, by little esteeming, yea euen by misconstruing and deprauing the labours and trauailes which are taken euen of purpose for their good, that if the seruant of God looke but vpon men, he shall thinke he hath the most thanklesse office that may be. It is certaine that he which looketh but vnto men shal neuer endure, but if he looke vp vnto Christ, he shall then proceed with patience. But why wil the Lord haue his ministers tried with so hard a triall? They seeke to saue mens soules, and they take it scornefully.

It is needfull that all men should be humbled, and their patience manifested, but aboue al others the pastors and teachers, which are to shew themselues as patternes and examples for the flockes to follow. They must be examples in pure doctrine

THE REVELATION. 41

and godly conuersation, yea euen in all vertues, then in patience. And if they haue no difficulties to ouercome, no iniuries, no reproches nor vnkind dealings offered vnto them, how shall they shew theselues examples & patternes of true patience vnto the flocks? It is a great perswasion vnto euerie true Christian to be patient in afflictions, iniuries & hard dealings, that they imitate the Lord Iesus in mecknesse and lowlinesse of mind: but besides this, the pastors and teachers haue this further perswasion to patience, that they therin leade the flocks into the right way, & vnto a verie speciall and heauenly vertue. O how good a thing is it to leade men vnto goodnesse, both by pure doctrine & good example of life and conuersation! Then despise not the triall of patience.

The third vertue is zeale, contained in these words, *And how thou canst not beare with them which are euill*. This is not the least vertue in a godly shepheard to be zealous, seeing the great shepheard himselfe, whose steps we must follow, did abound in feruent zeale. He went to Ierusalem, made a whip with cords, and draue them out that bought and sold in the Temple, and ouerthrew the tables of the money changers, and as the holie Ghost saith, his disciples remembred that it is written, *The zeale of thine house hath eaten me vp*, Iohn 2. vers. 17. The loue he bare to the glorie of his Father, brought forth a feruent zeale, not to endure such pollutions. So it is said here of this Angell of the Church of Ephesus, that he could not beare with them that are euill.

The diuell seeketh to bring all infamie and reproch vpon the Gospell, he endeuoureth to defile and corrupt the Church with false doctrine and wicked maners, and for this cause raiseth vp euill men, sendeth them among the flockes of Christs true sheepe, there to spreade abroad their filthie poyson: Some of these came to Ephesus, & began to vtter their wares: but this Pastor bare such a loue to his flocke, that he could not endure that such euill men should remaine there, but by the censures and power of the Church cast them forth. We may learne by this place how highly it pleaseth our Lord Iesus Christ, that wicked heretikes shold not be borne withall in the Christian congregations, least they seduce with false doctrine, & corrupt with euill maners, and so destroy or defile the Church. Some haue this zeale in derision as a franticke thing, and mocke at it: but in truth where it is wanting, the euill men are suffered and do corrupt all. If the gouernours or pastors ouer the Lords flocke haue not zeale, all goeth to wracke: for then are all sorts of euill men borne withall, which pollute, lay waste, and destroy the Church.

It is therefore a thing most requisite in all true ministers of the Gospell to know that the Church is a verie precious thing, that therfore they may loue it most tenderly, and so be moued with a feruent zeale, not to suffer those things which hurt and corrupt the same. For if they can patiently beare to see the glorie of the Lord troden downe, the Gospell despised, and the precious Temple of God polluted, the loue of Christ is not in them: for if they did loue him, they would be zealous for his sake.

We come now to the fourth vertue for which he is commended, and that is wisdome to discerne, to try & to find out the spirits, which is expressed in these words,

And

And hast examined them which say they are Apostles and are not, and hast found them lyers. Behold then how excellently well qualified this man was, to be a Pastor ouer the sheepe of Christ. He held the sound knowledge of the truth, and by the perfect rules thereof, tried out falſe doctrines. And whereas those euill men, whom he could not beare withall, being the ministers of Satan, had transformed themselues into the likenesse of the ministers of Christ (as S. *Paule* saith) and boasted that they were Apostles sent euen by the Lord himselfe, he trying and examining their doctrine, and behauiour, and purpoſes by the holy Scriptures, found them lyers: a singular good worke.

We see then how this ſhepheard was so wise and skilfull in the word of truth, that he was able to defend & preserue his flock from the wolues, though they came neuer ſo ſubtilly clothed in ſheeps clothing: happie are those flockes that haue such paſtors to watch ouer them. But if the watchman be blind and dumbe, who hath committed ſo precious a charge into his hand, how shall he trie the ſpirits, & driue the wolues from the flocke? Are there no wolues now, or is the diuell dead? If he were ſo bold, & if his inſtruments were ſo bold as to thruſt in themselues into those excellent Churches, which were founded and taught by the Apoſtles themselues, and euen while the Apoſtles were yet liuing, how can we perſwade our ſelues that there is no feare of perill, nor care to be taken in these dayes? Durſt they encounter with *Paule*, & dare they not encounter with any now? there were neuer more ſuttle and bold ſeducers, more impudent corrupters then be now, and the ſheepe of Chriſt had neuer more need of ſkilfull, wiſe, and zealous paſtors to feede them, and to watch ouer them, then in these dayes. The Lord powre forth his ſpirit vpon the miniſterie, guide and defend his poore ſheepe from the iawes of all ſuch rauening wolues.

I noted before, that this man hath a double commendation for his patience: for it followeth, *And thou waſt burdened, and haſt patience*: we may not take this to be but a bare repetition. But as before he needed patience to go through with his labours in reſpect of the Church it ſelfe, for the cauſes I ſhewed touching the dulneſſe, the inconſtancie and frowardneſſe of manie: ſo here is need of a further patience in reſpect of thoſe euill men, the falſe Apoſtles whom he could not beare. O how Satan doth ſtorme and rage where his miniſters haue the repulſe, and how impudent are they againſt thoſe that ſoyle them, in deuiſing and raiſing vp lies and ſlanders, reproches and troubles! This paſtor could not endure them in the Church to ſpreade their poyſon to infect the ſheepe of Chriſt, but he muſt endure, and doth endure the whole load and burthen of all their lies, reproches, ſlanders, and raylings. And the Lord praiſeth him, that he did beare them patiently, for he ſaith, *Thou waſt burthened, and haſt patience.* Then we learne that the ſeruants of God muſt be armed with double patience. Their weake & froward brethren in the Church will trie their patience, the enemies will lay a further load vpon them: they muſt be armed to go through all.

The fift vertue for which he is commended, is the ſinceritie and integritie of his heart in all his labours: theſe words do ſet it forth, *And for my names ſake haſt laboured*

which is the high Iudge of all, who knoweth the secrets of all hearts, euen from his glorie testifieth vnto this his sincerity, saying, *And for my names sake hast laboured.* This is a great praise, what need he care if all the world should condemne him? As on the other side, if a man labour neuer so much, and go through all trauels of studie, of teaching, &c. and that with the highest commendation that may be, what is he the better, if this Prince of pastours shall say vnto him, thou hast thy reward, thou didst seeke thine owne praise and glorie, thy heart was set vpon gaine and preferments, and thou hast found them? Here is then a glasse for all the ministers of the Gospell to looke in, and to behold themselues: for we see what a Iudge we haue to deale withall. There is great difference betweene these two, *for my names sake hast laboured,* & for thy bellies sake thou hast laboured: reade the third chapter of the Epistle to the Philippians, and see what their end is which mind earthly things.

Now there remaineth but the sixt vertue, which is the last for which this man is praised: and that is his heroycall magnanimitie: the words be these: *And hast not fainted.* His burden of labours was great, his troubles many, both in dealing with the flocke, and against the false Apostles (as we haue seene) and yet he stood vnder it with a valiant courage, and neuer fainted. The power of God was in him, or else he could not but haue waxed wearie and haue fainted. Such courage as this doth indeed become the ministers of Christ, and verie necessarily it is required in them: for they shall be set vpon on euerie side. They must pull downe Sathan, he will roare: if they be faint-hearted, if they will be made affraid and terrified at euery blast, they can neuer hold out in the worke. If they will haue peace in the world, they must let alone the building of Ierusalem, nay, they must be at peace with the diuell, and helpe to pull downe Gods truth. Well, Christ commended this man for his courage and fortitude, that nothing could make him faint, or waxe wearie of all the burthen which was layd vpon him: let all the seruants of God looke vpon his praise, for it is written for our instruction, that we may follow the same steps.

Hitherto he hath bene commended; now followeth his dispraise in somewhat: the words are these, *Neuerthelesse I haue somewhat against thee.* Then although he were very excellently qualified for the worke of the ministerie, yet there is some fault which the Lord doth not conceale, but plainely layeth it open: and what was it? Ye see it set downe, euen in these words, *Thou hast left thy former loue.* We may well see by those former vertues, that he had not lost the graces of the holy Ghost (as the Papists would proue from hence that the regenerate may fall from grace) but he was somewhat decayed and gone backward in loue: for by naming

ming his former loue, he attributeth a loue vnto him now, but inferior to the former. For indeed although he that is borne of God (as Saint *Iohn* saith) sinneth not, neither can sin, because his seede remaineth in him, and because he is borne of God, 1. Ioh. 2. verf. 9. Yet the graces of the spirit may for a time decay in him, or lye smothered, not shewing such force: and that we may see in *Dauid*, and other holy persons.

His and their fault being thus laid open, here followeth first an admonition, in these words, *Remember therefore from whence thou art fallen, and repent ; and do the first workes.* This admonition, as ye see, doth consist of diuers branches, all tending to this, that he might be recouered from his decay. First, when he biddeth him remember from whence he is fallen, it sheweth that men do decline in religion by negligence and forgetfulnesse of former graces: and the way to recouer, is to be mindfull in what estate we haue bene, aboue that which we are presently in, if we be declined. It teacheth also (by saying from whence thou art fallen) how high they be lifted vp which loue God and their brethren, how precious a thing loue is before God, that the decay therein, is accounted so great or so foule a fall. For if it were not a thing of very great price, why should it be said, remember from whence thou art fallen? Ye see how highly Saint *Paule* extolleth loue, 1.Cor.13. And where it is not, all is in vaine, and the decay in it is so much the fouler fault, because we are taught that we ought to grow and increase, yea more & more to abound therein. Then he willeth him to repent: he being entred into a dangerous course of declining and going backeward, the Lord Iesus the great shepheard, who seeketh vp that which is gone astraie, and recouereth that which is readie to be lost, seeketh to heale him by repētance. For when we are awrie, there is no way but to alter our course by repentance, & returne againe into the right way: & that we should not imagine that the repentance is but some affection of the mind that resteth within, he addeth, *and do the first workes*. If we repent indeed, with the true and vnfayned repentance, we shall (as *Iohn* Baptist willeth, Matth. 3.) bring forth fruites worthy repentance.

O how ready are we, when our harts accuse vs that we are fallen or declin'd in any godly duties, as in zealous and fruitfull profession of the Gospell, to rest in some inward touch thereof in mind, and some confession in speech, and neuer returne to the actions. We are therefore willed here, in the person of this man, so to repent, that we do the former workes: thou hast beene a zealous man in the profession of the Gospel, thou hast loued tenderly the glorie of God, the Gospel of Christ, & the Church, thou hast bēn reddy in actions to aduance the same: thou art now waxē cold, thou doest both confesse it in words, and seeme to bewaile it, and to be sory for it: take heede thou hold not this enough, but if thou wilt repent indeed, do the former workes: shall wordes or inward motions serue? Nay, bring forth the fruites of repentance; that is loue in deede and in truth, where the workes of loue are wrought. But what shall we say to this that he requireth of him, to do but the former workes, were the former so full and perfect that no more could be required? Saint *Paule* sheweth how he went still forward, Philip.3. verse.12.

This

This is to be answered, that when the Lord requireth that he should do the former workes, it includeth not a perfection in which he might lawfully stay, but a proceeding further, for he was in a race in which he was going forward. If a man be out of the way, and then set into it againe, it is that he may go forward. Do the former workes, thou wert in a good way going forward, now thou goest backeward, repent, returne, and go in the former way. Then here is added the threatning if he repent not, and if he returne not to his former loue, and do the first works: it is in these words, *Or else I will come against thee shortly, & will remoue thy candlesticke out of his place except thou repent.* This is a sore thing, that Iesus Christ will come against him in punishment if he do not repent, it sheweth how highly he was displeased with this fault. If God be on our side, who shall be against vs? And if he come against vs, who shall be able to rescue or deliuer vs out of his hand, or any way to relieue vs? The punishment threatned is, I will remoue thy candlesticke out of his place. This is not darke or hard to be vnderstood, because we haue the Lords owne exposition: *The seuen golden candlesticks, are the seuen Churches.* Here then Christ threatneth the Church at Ephesus, that if there follow not repentance, both in their Pastor and in them, he will remoue his Church from thence, & they shall remaine his Church no longer.

We know the parable of the vineyard let forth to husbandmen, which would not render the fruits of it, as our Sauiour telleth, Math. 21. and how it is said the vineyard should be taken from them, & let to other husbandmen, which will render to him the fruits in due season: and then how he expoundeth it plainely, *The Kingdome of God shall be taken from ye, and giuen to a nation that will bring forth the fruits thereof.* The Lord doth not threaten to breake the candlesticke, but to remoue it vnto another place: for he neuer destroyeth his Church: but when his Gospell is abused in one place, he remoueth it to another; as when the Iewes were obstinate, it was taken from them, and giuen to the Gentiles: and these Churches of Asia here named, and many other famous Churches haue long since bin miserably oppressed, and laid waste by the cruell enemy the Turke. We see then it is a sore threatning, euen to terrifie them from backsliding, and that they might seeke to recouer themselues from decay, vnto their former estate.

Here is indeed a glasse for vs all to looke in: and the Lord of his tender compassion open our eyes, that we may in it behold our selues. First, let the ministers of the Gospell consider what a maruellous waight is laid vpon their shoulders, in that the Angell of this Church hauing left his former loue, the whole flocke is threatned: why is it, but that they with him were gone backe, and had forsaken their former loue? If they in his declining had not declined with him, why shold it be said, I will come against thee shortly, and will remoue thy candlesticke out of his place, except thou repent? Should they all be threatned, if they were not in fault? The pastors then, the teachers, the guides and shepheards ouer the Lords flocke, had need to be carefull, yea verie carefull that they decay not in loue, nor in any spirituall graces; for if they continue and stand firme and faithful to the end, in the holy worke of the ministerie, they saue themselues, and those that heare them. If

their

their loue and zeale waxe colde, and the care ouer the flocke decay, they cast downe themselues by litle and litle, and not only that, but they hazard the flockes. It is no light matter for a man to take such a fall in respect of the waight of his own person: how much more that the destruction of the people is laid to his charge? Is it a small matter to be guiltie of the peoples bloud? O what need haue the ministers of the Gospell to be instant with the Lord to guide them, and to keepe them vpright, that they may stand to the end, and with a feruent loue to Christ and his Church performe all holie duties! We may see by this Angell of the Church of Ephesus, that very notable men be in danger.

And surely all that runne do not obtaine: for couetousnesse, vaine glory, & ambition do vtterly in all ages ouerthrow some. Now for the people, yea for vs all, we are taught in this place, how hainous a thing it is before God to waxe cold in loue. No doubt to feele the loue of Christ through faith, & to be by the same euen constrained to loue him with a feruent loue, and in him and for him tenderly to loue his Church, is a thing in most high price before God, & bringeth forth great fruits. On the contrarie part, for these fruits to diminish, and this loue to be abated and still decaying, prouoketh so farre the displeasure of God, that he threatneth against it grieuously. We haue seene what excellent vertues the Lord commendeth in this shepheard and his flocke, and yet notwithstanding he threatneth for the waut of their first loue, if they do not repent.

Most lamentable is our estate in these dayes: for who can looke vpon any place where the Gospell hath bin preached but euen a few yeares, and not see, I will not say, decay of their first loue, and of their former workes, but euen in verie deed almost an vtter forsaking? yea many there be which at the first hearing of the Gospell, were so inflamed with the loue of it, & had such a tast of the sweetnesse therof, that they could not but acknowledge the great kindnesse of God towards them, & seemed to run zealously from the wayes of wickednesse vnto true godlinesse, and would euen stirre vp others, which now (as it is written, 2. Pet. 2.) *The dog to his vomit, and the sow that was washed, to the wallowing in the mire*. And thinke it not strange, for our Sauiour foretold this, speaking of the last times, Matth. 24. verse. 12. saying, *Because iniquitie shall abound, the loue of many shall waxe cold.* Many neuer come to haue any true loue at all, but despise all goodnesse, and hate bitterly all that with sincere affection imbrace the light, and they raile vpon them, as Saint Peter foretold, 1. Pet. 4. vers. 4.

The mischief doth not rest in these, these haue not left their first loue which they neuer had, these are not of those which haue declined, and are willed to repent & to do the former workes, these are not they that are willed to remember from whence they are fallen: but the backesliding professors of the Gospell: I leaue this thing for them to consider.

Here is yet one thing to be noted, and it is a great thing, and I would to God it were deeply printed and grauen in our harts: for I am perswaded few do obserue it, both of teachers and people, which casteth downe many. It will be said, that to forsake their first loue, is a thing obserued, when it falleth out, either in the ministers

THE REVELATION. 47

sters of the Gospel, or in the common professours. Yea but yet it is not throughly obserued in this point, that some do seeme to themselues and to others to grow vpward, when as indeed they fall downeward, with a grieuous and most dangerous fall. They increase in other gifts, as in experience, knowledge, vnderstanding and such like, which are fit and necessarie for all Christians, and decay in loue.

Thus it is, when men are first lightened, their harts are much inflamed with loue and zeale: but there is often great defect of knowledge, & of discretion, & of other good gifts. Time bringeth on these, and in time their loue waxeth cold: they do espie some errours in their waies (as who doth not?) which they do correct: but herein they faile, yea fall, that they correct loue it selfe, I meane they suffer it to decay, to waxe cold, and to be diminished in them. It is a good thing to correct ignorance, error, and rashnesse, and to grow in knowledge and discretion, but withal we must hold the pure loue, and increase also therein: for if that faile, though we abound in many goodly gifts, let Saint *Paule* tell vs what we be, 1. Corinth. 13. Thou wert a zealous man, full of burning loue to the glorie of Christ, and to his Church, and forward to performe euery good work that might aduance the same, thou art increased in many things: but thy first loue is quenched, thou doest glory as a man lifted vp and beautified: but do not glorie, but remember from whence thou art fallen, & that thou hast lost thy iewell which did most of all beautifie thee. Repent and turne againe, and do the former workes, or else the Lord doth threaten thee. I may say to another, thou hast goodly learning and knowledge, thou doest excell many waies, but thou neuer haddest thine hart inflamed with sincere loue and zeale, but hast sought thy belly, remember (I say not from whence thou art fallen, seing thou diddest neuer clime so high) but what thou commest short of, repent, and let thy latter workes exceed the first.

Let vs all looke vpon this place, let vs labour to abound in spiritual graces, but especially in the holy loue: if we let it be quenched, wo be vnto vs. There remaineth now some mitigation of the threatning, in which the Lord sheweth that this Angell and the Church at Ephesus did one thing highly pleasing vnto him, which is in these wordes, *But this thou hast, that thou hatest the workes of the Nicholaitās, which I also hate.* That which our Lord loueth, it pleaseth him that we loue the same: and on the other side, look what he doth hate, and highly loath, it delighteth him that we hate and loath it. He hated the works of the Nicholaitans, the Church at Ephesus hated them, this was verie well, & for this, much is granted vnto them. The scripture doth not tell of whome these Nicholaitans tooke their name, nor what were their works: but the auncient writers that liued somewhat neare to the times of the Apostles, say they tooke their name of *Nicholas*, one of the seuen Deacons, Act.6. And that they held, men might haue their wiues in common. Saint *Iude* in his Epistle, and Saint *Peter* in his second Epistle chap.2. Do write of very filthy persons which were crept into the Churches, & very like it is they were these Nicholaitans. There haue risen vp filthy monsters in these daies, as Libertines, such as be of the Familie of loue and others, the Lord God graunt that we may hate their workes: pittie the men if they may be any way brought to repentance,

tance, but hate their workes. Thus much for the narration of this Epiftle: now we come to the conclufion.

This conclufion is fet downe in thefe words, *Let him that hath an eare, heare what the fpirit faith to the Churches: to him that ouercommeth vvill I giue to eate of the tree of life, vvhich is in the middeft of the paradife of God.* In this fame conclufion there be two parts: the firft is to moue attention to heare, and the other setteth downe the precious promife which is made. When he faid, *Let him that hath an eare, &c.* it sheweth plainly, that that which is directed in thefe feuen Epiftles to the feuen Angels of the Churches, appertaineth indeed and is directed vnto euerie Chriftian man and woman. Secondly, when he calleth vpon, and ftirreth vp him to heare that hath an eare, it teacheth that none can heare rightly what the Spirit faith, but thofe to whom it is giuen from aboue: for if thefe outward eares could ferue, why should it be faid, *Let him that hath an eare, &c.* Beg of the Lord to haue the eares of our hearts opened: and whereas ye fee many that haue thefe inward eares shut vp, let vs giue moft humble thanks to the Lord: for were it not for his mercie, we should haue continued euen like vnto them. The holy Ghoft is the spirit of truth, the spirit of wifdome, and of all wholfome counfell: and therefore the spirit whom we ought moft reuerently and attentiuely to hearken vnto. And as I faid, when we fee men shut vp their eares, defpife his counfell, and walke on ftubburnly in their owne wicked wayes, we may fee how much we are bound to God that hath opened our eares: and let it moue vs to be fwift to heare what the spirit faith to the Churches.

The other part of this conclufion containeth a great promife, euen the promife of eternall life, vnto euerie one that ouercommeth. There is no ouercomming, or getting victorie where there is no battell to be fought: this therefore putteth vs in mind of the ftate we are here fet in, euen in the fpirituall battell againft finne, the world, and the diuell, as fouldiers vnder the banner of Iefus Chrift: if we fight valiantly, and ftand to the end, we shall be faued: if we put on the whole armour of God, as S. *Paule* willeth, Ephef. 6. If we ftand in the holy faith: for S. *Iohn* faith, *This is the victorie vvich ouercommeth the world, euen our faith,* 1. Iohn 5. verf. 4. feeing then we haue no promife vnleffe we ftand in the faith, and ouercome all the power of the diuell and finne, let vs feeke by all meanes to haue our faith dayly increafed. It is a moft worthy and bleffed fight that is againft fuch deadly enemies: let vs neuer faint, the Lord will vphold vs: hate the diuell and all his wicked wayes, and cleaue faft to that which is good, and ye shall liue for euer. This is the promife which is vttered thus: *I vvill giue vnto him to eat of the tree of life, vvhich is in the midft of the paradife of God.* This promife is made vnder a figuatiue fpeech: for in the earthly paradife wherin *Adam* was placed, there was in the middeft thereof the tree of life, which was a Sacrament vnto *Adam*, and whereof he might eate fo long as he ftood in obedience. But here the heauenly paradife is fpoken of, and in the middeft thereof is the Lord Iefus, who is the tree of life: he is the bread of life, Iohn 6. In him, by him, and through him, all that get the victorie shall liue in the heauenly and ioyfull Paradife of God, for euer and euer. Thus
much

much touching this first message which was sent to the Angell of the Church of Ephesus.

THE V. SERMON

8. *And vnto the Angell of the Church of the Smyrnians write, these things saith he that is first and last, which was dead and is aliue:*
9. *I know thy workes and tribulation, and pouerty (but thou art rich) and I know the blasphemy of them which say they are Iewes, and are not, but are the Synagogue of Sathan.*
10. *Feare none of those things which thou shalt suffer: behold it shall come to passe, that the diuell shall cast some of you into prison, that ye may be tried, & ye shall haue tribulation ten dayes: be thou faithfull vnto the death, and I will giue thee a crowne of life.*
11. *Let him that hath an eare, heare what the spirite saith to the Churches: he that ouercommeth shall not be hurt of the second death.*

THe second Epistle or message is directed to the Angell of the Church of the Smyrnians. They be called the Smyrnians because they dwelled in the citie called Smyrna: as we know it hath bene and is the vsuall manner to call the Citizens by the names of their cities, as of Rome the Romains: of Corinth, the Corinthians, &c. Smyrna (as it is reported by writers) was the chiefe city of Ionia, and had in it a great Church of sincere Christians, both of men & women which professed the holy Gospell. Who planted this Church at the first, whether Saint *Paule*, or Saint *Iohn*, or other of the Apostles and seruants of Christ, it is not expressed in the Acts of the Apostles, neither as I suppose, can it be gathered for certainty. Indeed it is not materiall to enquire: but this one thing we are sure of, that here is a most excellent shepheard, and a right worthy flocke, as it will appeare by the testimony which the Lord himselfe giueth of them. There is indeed but one ministery of the Gospell, and but one Church: but there be many ministers and many particular Churches: and as we may here learne, some ministers far excell others in the heauenly graces, and so is there great difference betweene the particular Churches, which are members of the whole, some being more pure, and some subiect vnto greater spots and deformities.

E The

The exordium or beginning of this message is taken from the person of him that sendeth it, in these words, *These things saith he that is first, and last, which was dead, and is aliue.* These be the words which he pronounced of himselfe vnto *Iohn* in the former chapter, where he appeared vnto him in that glorious vision. Here was no need then to repeate euery part, for he that is the first and the last, &c. is the same which holdeth the seuen starres in his right hand, and walketh in the middest of the seuen golden candlestickes, and that hath his eyes like a flame of fire, &c. It is euen hee which hath all that magnificall power, wisedome, and operation in the Church, in which he is before described. Then is this Angell and the Church at Smyrna, to receiue attentiuely and reuerently this message sent vnto them from their great Lord. That which he saith, I am the first and the last, which was dead and am aliue, we haue handled before.

These three great and high points of our faith are fully and cleerely set forth in the same: the first, that Iesus Christ is eternall God, before all beginning and without ending: *He is the first and the last.* If he had but a secondary Godhead as the Arrians most blasphemously hold, how could he be the first and the last? The second, that he is a very man, how else could he die, and be raised from the dead? as he saith, *I was dead, but am aliue.* The wicked seed suggested vnto some in old time, that he had but a phantasticall body, or a body but in shew, and that he died but in apparance. If he were not a mā in al things tempted like vnto vs, as the holy Ghost saith, sinne excepted, Hebr. 4. ver. 15. how could he say, I was dead, but am aliue? The third, that the two natures of God and man are so vnited, that they make but one person. The manhood is not the first, that is to say, before all eternity, nor the Godhead cannot die: & yet the same that saith, I am the first & the last, saith, I am aliue, but I was dead: because God & mā is but one Christ. For if it were as *Nestorius* maintained, and *Petrus Enaphæus*, that in Christ the humane nature was one person by it selfe, and the Godhead which dwelled in him another, how could he that is the first and the last, say, *I am aliue, but I was dead?* Now to the narration.

I know thy workes, &c. I haue shewed before that he only can giue iust praise, and dispraise, which perfectly knoweth all workes, beholding the deepest secrets, and intents of all harts, and that is Christ Iesus, who hath his eyes as a flame of fire. It is a comfortable thing, as it is writtē, *The Lord knoweth the way of the righteous:* Psalme. 1. for his knowledge is with approbation, yea with supportation: as on the contrary part he doth behold the way of the wicked, disalloweth and condemneth it, and therefore it shall perish, and come vtterly to naught. Here be diuerse parts of this narration (as we shall see in the particular handling) and yet no one vertue named.

We had in the pastor and Church of Ephesus (as we noted) sundry particular vertues expressed by name, of great commendation, and in this Angell and Church not one in particular. Indeed the Lord saith, I know thy works, thy affliction, and pouerty (but thou art rich) and the blasphemy of those which say, they bee Iewes and are not, but are the Synagogue of Sathan. What then, is not the Angell and Church of Smyrna commended? Commended, yes aboue them all, euen as the

most

THE REVELATION. 51

most excellent. For albeit there is no one particular vertue named, yet whē he saith, *thou art rich*, speaking of the spiritual riches, for in the worldly riches he was poore, it includeth all vertues, if we ioyne this, that the Lord reproueth no fault in him. Among many goodly vertues in the Church of Ephesus, there was this blot, that they had declined and forsaken their first loue. Other pastours and Churches also are found fault withal, some for one thing, & some for another: but here is nothing reproued. Here be all Christian vertues both in the shepheards and their flocks, and no grosse vice: For if there had bid any grosse fault, the Lord wold not haue concealed it, no more then he hath in the rest.

If we respect the Angell of the Church at Smyrna, that is, the pastor, or pastors, (for vnder one diuerse pastors may be meant, as well as the whole cōgregation) he was rich in the precious faith of our glorious Lord Iesus Christ, he was rich in knowledge and vnderstanding of the heauenly mysteries, filled with spirituall wisdome, he was rich in loue and zeale, in meeknesse and patience: he was rich in care and diligence to feed and guide the flocke of Christ: for if any of these had bene wanting, how could it be said, thou art rich? how could he haue escaped without rebuke? Then if we respect the Church it selfe, they were excellently well instructed and fed, and builded vp in the truth: they were rich, & enriched in all spirituall graces: they were rich in vertues, and good works: yea their light did so shine before men, that they might see their good works, and glorifie God, as appeareth in that they be not rebuked nor admonished to repent, nor threatned, as the Church of Ephesus. Here is then a worthy example for all to follow, both pastors and people. What a goodly thing is it, to be thus allowed and commended of Christ? It is more comfortable then to enioy all the riches and pleasures vnder heauen. But it may be said, were they so perfect that no fault could be found in them? Is there any so holy, so iust, so pure & vpright in his waies, that he may abide the trial & the sētēce of the high Iudge? Is it not written, who vnderstandeth his errors, Psalm.19.& who can say my hart is cleane? and doth not Saint *Iohn* say, *If we say we haue no sinne we deceiue our selues and the truth is not in vs?* We may not so take it, that this not reprouing him for any fault, doth argue a perfection: but the Lord doth not mention small things, but doth couer them. This Church had her frailties, but was free from grosse offences. Behold herein the great kindnesse of our Lord Iesus Christ, in couering all the frailties of his true seruants. He is the iudge before whom we shall stand, and we haue many imperfections: how much haue we to reioyce, that he dealeth so louingly? If he should neuer approue of vs vntill he should find vs perfect, and in euery respect to be liked, we were vtterly lost and cast away for euer: but in those that in singlenesse of hart do loue and obey him, ye see all imperfections and spots are couered and forgotten. Let it encourage vs, specially such as serue him in the ministery of the Gospell, to be cheerefull in performing all good duties. Let vs not faint nor be discouraged with any troubles, nor with the beholding our frailties, for he will deale most louingly with vs. I will now proceed to the words as they lie.

That he saith, thine affliction and pouerty, it doth import very euidently, that this Church was assailed by enemies, and so far, that it endured no small troubles. For the Lord, if the troubles had bene small, would neuer haue made mention of them. Moreouer, the pouerty which he doth ioyne with the affliction, did grow partly from the same: For the rage of the enemies was such, that they did in some places euen flie vpon the goods of the Christians, and spoile them: as ye may reade how the holy Ghost doth testifie of the beleeuing Iewes in the Church of Iudea; how when they were lightened, they were reproched, aud suffered the spoyling of their goods, Heb. 10 ver. 34.

The Lord did know this affliction which his seruants did indure for his sake: for the profession of his name brought it all vpon thē. If they had suffered as euil doers, it could be no comfort to heare from the Lord in his glory that he did know their affliction: but being for the truth, it might incourage them notably, that their great captaine vnder whose banner they did fight, beheld how valiantly they did acquite themselues, and shewed his great liking & approbation thereof. He taught that they are blessed which suffer persecution for righteousnesse sake, Matth. 5. and here he telleth this Angell and the Church, how he regardeth their sufferings. Let vs learne here then how to arme our selues against temptations: If it fal so out that affliction do come heauy vpon vs, our nature is fraile, and the diuel is ready to suggest, that we are forgotten, and that Christ doth not regard vs: will hee deale so hardly with those whom he loueth? Yea it is no hard dealing, for the holy Scripture in many places as ye know, setteth forth that these afflictions are for the great good of the faithfull: reade the first chapter of the Epistle of *Iames*, the first of the first Epistle of *Peter*, and also the fourth, & the twelfth chapters of the Epistle to the Hebrues, and the latter end of the eleuenth chapter of the first to the Corinthians, and ye shall find how God afflicteth his for their good.

And now further, that the Angell of this Church, and the whole company of the faithfull, were poore touching worldly substance, it sheweth how they despised the riches of this world to gaine Christ, in whom indeed are al the true treasures: As *Moses* is commended, that he refused to be called the son of *Pharaoh*s daughter, and chose rather to suffer affliction with the people of God, then to enioy the pleasures of sin for a season, esteeming the rebuke of Christ, greater riches then the treasures of Egypt, Heb. 11. ver. 24. 25. 26. so were they here in the Church of Smyrna content to suffer the spoyling of their goods, rather then they wold be driuen from the open, bold and constant profession of the Gospell and glorious name of our Lord Iesus Christ.

And ye know how our Sauiour telleth vs plainely, that if we cannot find in our hearts to forsake all that we haue in this world, and to take vp the crosse and follow him, we cannot be his disciples. The Scripture calleth the rich mā a foole that built his barnes greater, & laid vp store, Luk. 12. ver. 20. And our Sauior saith in the next verse there following, so is euery one that heapeth vp treasure, & is not rich toward God. Such then (by the words of Christ) as imbrace the Gospell, although it shold be to their vtter spoile in the world, that they may be rich towards God in the true heauenly treasures, be wise men.

And

THE REVELATION. 53

And on the contrary part, they that are greedy of this world, & heape vp riches and worldly store, not willing to forgoe them for the truthes sake, nor yet desiring to be filled with faith and heauenly vertues that they may be rich to God, be starke fooles. They preferre drosse and trash before fine gold. In this point we may not reason with flesh and bloud: for the world doth account them the ranckest fooles that liue, which for their profession will go so farre as to endure the losse of their goods and dignities, and liue in banishment, in prison, in pouerty, and in contempt: because the worldlings are blind, and cannot see the riches which these do treasure vp. Moreouer, they magnifie them highly as wise fellowes, which can so carry themselues, as to keepe and increase their wealth of what religion soeuer, and to climbe vp in the world.

When we shall suffer affliction and be pressed downe with pouerty and other calamities, let vs call to mind these words of our Sauiour, *I know thine affliction & pouerty, but thou art rich*: and if our affliction come vpon vs for the Gospell, it will comfort vs much. Consider yet one thing further in these words touching the Angell of this Church of Smyrna, for he (whether it be spoken of one or of more) was afflicted, he was poore, and yet he was rich. He was a right excellent shepheard, and tooke great paines in feeding and guiding the flocke of Christ, and yet as ye see his reward in this world was but small, for he liued in pouerty. What, did not the flocke care for him? yes, if they had bene rich, he should not haue bene poore. He doth not repine at it, he is not an hireling that dealt for filthy luker, but dealt euen of loue, and as Saint *Peter* requireth, of a ready mind, 1. Pet. 5. He saw what labours the holy Apostles endured, what daungers they passed through, and how poore they were touching worldly wealth. As Saint *Paule* testifieth of himselfe & his fellowes, we are poore, and yet make many rich, 2. Cor. 6. v. 10. This is a worthy example for vs to follow: If we haue gifts of learning for the ministery, and be imployed, and take paines to the comfort and benefit of the Church, we thinke it so vnworthy a thing to be in pouerty, as that we are ready to be impatient at it, and many thinke that the excellency of the worke of the ministery may warrant them to heape vp worldly treasurs, euen to the detriment of the Church. If the charge be committed vnto vs, and we are to feede the flocke of Christ, and the flocke be in that estate that we cannot haue from them the wealth of the world to aboūd in any plentifull measure, we must be content with that which may suffice euen for necessitie.

We are not better then the holy Apostles were, we are not better then the Angell of the Church of Smyrna, nay well are we if we walke in their steppes, though we come much behind them in regard of their excellency. Then must we looke for the reward of our labors, in the seruice of Christ, and of his Church euen as they did, and that is not in this world, but at the appearing of the great shepheard. If we will needs preach the Gospell, and take paines in study, and labour to get wealth and preferments here vpon earth, it shall be sayd vnto vs, ye laboured, but ye had your wages, there is no further reward remayning as due vnto you. Alas what case shall we be in then? euen turned out with those whom the holy Apostle speaketh

E 3 of

of, whose belly is their God, that mind earthly things, Philip.3. O how much better is it, to treade downe the loue of the world, and to bend all our care and diligence to feede the flocke of Christ, waiting for that crowne of glory that is laid vp for all Christs faithfull seruants and souldiers?

Whatsoeuer become of vs in this world, I meane, if we should bee a as poore as *Lazarus*, which lay at the rich mans gate, let it not discourage vs, if it may be said, I know thy pouerty, but thou art rich. We do all of vs account pouerty in these earthly things an heauy burthen, and indeede it is so, and we are much afraid of it, and labour to shunne and auoid it: O would to God we could as well feele, and iudge of the pouerty in spirituall things, which is a burthen a thousand times more heauy and miserable, for then we wold be as carefull to auoid it, as we are to auoid the other.

There was yet a further affliction layd vpon this pastor and Church of Smyrna, and that is, the reproches, and raylings, wherewith vngodly men did reuile Christ Iesus and the Gospell, and all the faithfull: for he saith further, *And I know the blasphemy of them which say they are Iewes and are not, but are the Synagogue of Sathan*. There be foure things in these words, the first is the blasphemy: the second that the Lord did know it: the third, who they were that did blaspheme: and the fourth, in what accout they were before God, whatsoeuer they boasted themselues to be. To be reuiled, railed vpon and blasphemed by euill men, is a grieuous thing, especially when it is for the holy profession, when the pure doctrine, and the Lord of glory himselfe are with most vile & filthy speeches railed vpon and blasphemed. Now it was maruellous to heare with what tearmes they which were vnbeleeuers did raile vpō the Lord Iesus, as a false Prophet, a decciuer, & one that did al by the power of the diuel. And also to heare how they did tearme the Gospell here sie and falshood, and all that beleeue it heretickes, and cursed people. This is the blasphemy which our Sauior saith he did know.

It is vttered for comfort, that the Lord saith he did know the blasphemy: for he will call the blasphemers to account for it, as Saint *Peter* teacheth, 1. Pet.4.vers.5. they shal not escape free, though the Lord seeme to wink at the matter of their raylings vpon his seruants for a time. And the godly shal haue great reward for suffering such reproch for the name of Christ: For this we haue the plaine words of our Sauiour; saying, *Blessed are ye when men reuile you, and persecute you, and say al maner of euill against you for my sake falsely: reioyce, and be glad, for great is your reward in heauen*. Math.5. Here we see there is great reward layd vp in heauen for such as are rayled vpon, reuiled, and reproched for the glorious Gospell of Christ, yea so great that he willeth them to reioyce, for they are blessed. Saint *Peter* saith, if ye be railed vpon for the name of Christ, *Blessed are ye*: for the spirit of glory and of God resteth vpon you, which on their part is euill spoken of, but on your part is glorified, 1.Pet.4.vers.14. Now lay these together with that Christ saith here to this Church, *I know the blasphemy, &c.* and you may see it is to let them vnderstand, that they wery very highly blessed in suffering such railings for the name of Christ. *Moses* by faith esteemed the rebuke of Christ greater riches then the treasures vse to say, they be full of the spirite, they be precisians, &c. It is a very great honor and glory, let it not discourage vs or make vs ashamed, for what are we that wee should be accounted worthy to beare any rebuke for the glorious sonne of God? We see euen at this day the great weaknesse of many, they beare some loue to the Gospell, but they heare the reproch and railings which are cast foorth vpon those which follow it, and they dare not be seene, least they should be hated and mocked: for a litle thing doth snib them.

Let vs set before vs the example of this blessed Angel of the Church at Smyrna, and of the faithfull Christians there. They were blasphemed and railed vpon exceedingly: and as we see when any notable strumpet is carted, how they which haue filthy things will cast them forth vpon her: so did they cast forth vpon these holy seruants of God, all the most villanous railings and filthy slaunders they could deuise, and they went through, bare it strongly, and neuer shrunke. And now to encourage them and all others that shall come into the battaile thus to fight vnder the banner of Christ against the diuell and his souldiers, the Lord himselfe from his glory in the heauens sendeth word, *I know the blasphemy*: I know how much thou art railed vpon, & what thou doest suffer for my sake. If men come in place where they heare their Prince railed vpon and dishonoured, and they stand bold in the defence of their Princes honour, do they not accouut it a great preferment if therfore they be reproched? and doe not the kings and Princes of this world highly accept of such faithfulnes and loue of their subiects, & are they not ready to aduance them as most trustie? And shall not we then count it an honour very great, where the truth, euen the Gospell of Christ the most glorious king, is of vngodly men, euen vassals of Satan, railed vpon, if we defend it, and magnifie the dignitie of it, and so suffer hatred, reproches, reuilings and slaunders for the same? Or shall we thinke that the Lord Iesus doth not know or regard what we endure for his sake, or will he not highly account of, and reward such faithfulnes? I beseech you think well of this: let it not slip out of your minds, be valiant in the defence of your kings honor.

Now the third thing commeth for to be considered, and that is, who they were that did blaspheme this Church. All the infidels and heathē Idolaters did raile vpō Christ, vpō the Christians, & vpō the Christian religiō: but of al other the obstinate Iewes did excell in blasphemies, & were the most bitter enemies. But he saith here, they say they are Iewes, but are not. It is not meant that they were not Iewes according to the flesh, (for they were the seed of *Abrahā* according to the flesh) but they were not Iewes in that sense in which they boasted, that is to say, they were not the true Church and children of God. For to be right Iewes indeed, was to be the

E 4 true

true children of *Abraham* accordiug to the faith, it was to be indeed regenerate, sanctified, and circumcised in hart. And so Saint *Paule* setteth it forth in his Epistle to the Romains: for he is not a Iew (saith he) which is a Iew outward, neither is that circumcision which is outward in the flesh: but he is a Iew, which is one inwardly, and the circumcision of the hart, which consisteth in the spirit, and not in the letter is circumcision, whose praise is of God, and not of men. Rom. 2. vers. 28. 29. These obstinate blasphemers were Iewes outwardly, and circumcised in the flesh, bearing there the seale of Gods couenant, but as the Prophets complaine euery where of the ancient rebels, their wicked forefathers, that they were vncircumcised in hart, so were these. They boasted most arrogantly that they were the onely true Church of God, and in most shamefull maner railed vpon the Christian Religion. They could make shewes of comming out of the loynes of *Abraham*, and being of that holy people which God had chosen out of all nations, & separated to himselfe as his peculiar, and vnto whom he had granted so many priuiledges and speciall dignities. But now through hardnesse of hart, blindnesse and infidelity, hauing reiected the Sauiour of the worlde, and the worde of life, they are no longer the Church of God, but as the Lord saith here, the very Sinagogue of Sathan, which is the fourth point.

O what a fall is here! How much were they deceiued in their opinion? They came of that blessed stock, they had the couenant, and were the onely people, and visible Church: and now (so many as blasphemed Christ) quite cast down, and become the malignant Church of the diuell. It was very requisite, considering in what glorie the Iewes had bene, and how they gloried still of their fauor with God, that the Lord should testify thus much of them from Heauen, that all their assemblies, in which they reade *Moses* and the Prophets, and seeme to worship the true God, are but blasphemous assemblies, and Sinagogues of Sathan. No man is to be troubled with that which they glorie and bragge of out of *Moses* and the Prophets: they are fallen from their dignitie and glorie, in denying him which was the ende of the Lawe. This is a speciall place to be considered, not onely for the Iewes, but also betweene the Papists and vs: they boast and glorie of the Church of Rome, as the onely true spouse of Christ: and they rayle vpon all that imbrace the heauenly doctrine of the Gospell, terming them heretikes, and schismatikes, & deuising against them most filthie lies and slaunders.

But seeing they haue forsaken the true doctrine, and set vp a doctrine and worship of their owne deuising, maintaining all maner of superstition, lies, and idolatries, shewing themselues the very blasphemous Church of Antichrist that whore of Babilon, why should we stick to pronounce them plainely, to be as they be in deede, not the chast spouse of Christ, but the whorish Church, euen the Sinagogue of Sathan? What priuiledges haue they to boast of more then the Iewes had? Rome in olde time had a famous godly Church in it, of true sincere Christians, it had godly Bishoppes, which gaue their liues for the testimonie of our Lord Iesus Christ: what doth that helpe these which are fallen from that holy faith and godlinesse? The high Priests were the successours of *Aaron*, the Scribes and Pharisies did sit in *Moses* chaire, the Law came out of Sion, and the word of the Lord from Ierusalem: Rome was neuer comparable to that Church for sundrie respects. And now because like the degenerate Iewes they rayle vpon vs, and glorie that they be the only true catholike Christians, shall it moue or trouble vs, seeing that for all their boasting they may be, and indeed are (as we know by cleare testimonies of Gods word) the synagogue of Sathan. Let vs stand firme & bold in the defence of Christs glorie and worship against them, and let them raile, and slaunder, and blaspheme euen their fill: as the Lord sayd to the Angell of the Church of the Smyrnians, I know the blasphemy of those which say they are Iewes, but are not, but are the synagogue of Sathan: so will he say vnto vs, I know the railings, reproches and blasphemies of those which say they be the true Catholike Christians, but are not, but are the limmes of Antichrist, the Church of the diuell. The Romans set forth such glorie of their Church, and boast of priuiledges, as if they were the only floure of the world: but reade after in this booke, and ye shall find their Church is the mother of whoredomes and abhominations.

There is great ods betweene that which they glorie and brag of, & that which the Lord pronounceth them to be: but some man will say, if we could see it as euident, that the Lord calleth the Church of Rome the false malignant Church of Antichrist, as it is here that he calleth the Church of the Iewes, the synagogue of Sathan, it might greatly bolden vs to stand against them, and to endure all their reproches for the Gospell of Christ. But they say they blaspheme the holy Catholike Church, the spouse of Christ, which say the Church of Rome is that whore of Babylon. It is no matter what they say, but what the infallible truth proclaimeth, what the holy Ghost, the spirit of truth saith: the Iewes thinke and say that they be the holy people, beloued of God: the Lord himselfe saith they be of the diuell. The Papists say they be the onely true Christians: the Lord doth not in expresse tearmes say, the Pope or the Popish kingdome is the great Antichrist, Rome is the seat of Antichrist, and that the Papists worship the diuell: but yet all these are so clearely set forth in this booke, that he which is not blinded, euen by the iudgemēt of God vpon him, or that doth not euen obstinately shut his eyes, may see them to be out of all doubt. But this by the grace of God we shall see when we come to those places.

Thus haue we seene the commendation of this Angell and his flocke, and what they endured for the Lords cause. Now he encourageth them against those sufferings which were yet behind: *Feare none of those things* (saith he) *vvhich thou shalt suffer, &c.*

First we may note here, that euen as the Captaines in warre do exhort and stirre vp their souldiers to be valiant, so the great Captaine doth his souldiers in this spirituall battell. Other Captaines can but moue & perswade, they cannot put strength and victorie, and so some of them euermore are ouerthrowne: but this Captaine biddeth feare not, he giueth strength, and cleauing vnto him, and following his direction, they fight not doubtfully, but are sure to get the victorie: when he saith, feare not, let all the diuels of hell come, we are safe enough. Was not this a goodly
con-

consolation, was it not singular fauour and loue, to forewarne them of dangers approching, and to bid them be out of feare? He doth the same to vs all, if we will be directed by him.

Secondly, we are to note, that the troubles which were to come vpon this Church should come in a terrible maner: for they were strong, and had suffered much before, and a litle would not make them affraid. And he saith not in vaine euen to such valiant tried souldiers, Feare none of the things which thou shalt suffer, the enemie will set vpon thee verie fierce and grimme, he will make all the terrour he can, and if thou be not well armed he will put thee in feare, but stand fast in the faith, and thou shalt ouercome.

Then we may note here further, that all their former calamities and afflictions, by which they were brought into pouertie, and so much reuiled and railed vpon, did not free them from further and from greater trials. The diuell had a desire to assaile them yet further, and the Lord giueth him scope. It is a thing greatly to be noted, and whereof we may haue speciall vse: we heare of the crosse, and of afflictions for the Gospell, and manie can stand for a brunt or two verie valiant: but perceiuing that there is none end, but still they may looke for new, and it may be more grieuous, they begin to waxe weary, to faint, and to withdraw themselues by litle and litle out of the dint and edge of the battell. We are readie to thinke if we haue suffered some things, that we haue done enough: whereas indeed we are vnder this Captaine to receiue all assaults and onsets that may be made, euen to our last breath. Say not then, I haue suffered much, I may now take mine ease and be spared, but learne here, that there may be yet far greater things behind, and seeke to be armed against they come. For it is so precious a thing to enter into glorie, and to raigne with Christ, that to attaine vnto it, we ought with Saint *Paule* to account all the sorrowes and afflictions of this life, light and momentane, and not worthie of it.

What fooles are they which will loose such glorie, rather then they will endure hatred and reproch, the losse and spoyling of their goods, pouertie, imprisonment and death? The Lord willing them not to feare anie of the things that they should suffer: now he telleth what should come vpon them, *Behold* (saith he) *it shall come to passe, that the diuell shall cast some of you into prison, &c.* Marke well how the Lord telleth them that the diuell shall do this, he shall cast them into prison. It is a great encouragement to know that the battell is against such an enemie, therfore he is noted as the graund Captaine on the other side, & as the chiefe agent. A thing needfull to be knowne, because the diuell is not seene to worke it.

Persecutions against the Church are raised by Princes and Potentates, as at that time the Church at Smyrna, and other Churches were persecuted by the power of the Romane Emperors. Now we must know, that the powers be of God: & when they persecuted the true Christians, they pretended it was for their disobedience to gouernment, and danger which they brought vnto the common wealth, because they would not do sacrifice to Idols. And least the weake might be troubled and cast downe by thinking it came from Princes, & from the power ordained of God,

the

the Lord taketh away this doubt, and faith: *The diuell shall cast some of you into prison*. The diuell shall put into the heart of the Emperour to persecute the Churches, and the diuell shall inflame the hearts of inferiour gouernours and officers vnder him, with bloudy and cruell hatred of the Christian name, and the diuel shall fill the hearts of the blind multitude with mad furie, and so they as his instruments shal run violently vpon you. In this place we haue a lesson taught vs to iudge of persecutiōs. When the true and faithfull seruants of God are persecuted, there is alwayes a great shew made by the Persecutors, that it is for their misdemeanour. They do it (they will say) euen in the zeale of their dutie towards God, and no doubt many thinke so. But in truth whatsoeuer they pretend, ye see it is the diuell in them that doth all, they do but execute his will, they do but satisfie their owne bloudy desires. The Powers are to punish and roote out euill doers, and godly Princes do punish and imprison heretikes and seducers: but where were euer any persecuted by wicked tyrants for the truth, but they pretend is it for euill? Let vs be wise then, and looke into the cause for which men do suffer, and not what is pretended.

Here is a good lesson for all those which oppose thēselues against the preaching and profession of the Gospell, if it might please God to open anie of their eyes for to see it. They beare themselues in hand oftentimes, that they do well, yea, that they do good seruice to God, when as in verie deed the diuell beareth all the whole sway in their hearts, and setteth them a worke, they do but fulfill his lusts. Their hearts indeed are inflamed with wrath, but the diuel is the bellowes to blow vp, and to make the fire to flame, he moueth the heart, which they do not perceiue. They take craftie counsell, and deuise mischieuous practises, but the subtill diuell doth helpe to suggest the same into their minds. They giue their tongues to lie, to slaunder, to raile, and blaspheme, but the father of lies doth thrust them forward. And to speake in a word, whatsoeuer they do, he hath an oare in it. He being their maister that setteth them a worke, they shal haue their hire with him: then may we learne here in what miserable estate all the enemies of the true seruants of God be, the diuel hateth extremely the children of light, and coueteth to haue them rooted out: because his kingdome is hindred by them. And seeing he hath no way to deale against them of himselfe, but by temptations, which they resist, he is driuen into a rage, and seeketh instruments that haue power, which may execute that crueltie which he desireth. These, like blind men, run in rage & furie, not knowing whose seruants they be, or whose will they execute. He vseth them but homely oftentimes: for when they haue told foule lies, and raised slaunders, and it fall out that the truth commeth to light, and all men see they haue lyed shamefully, so that for a time they be halfe ashamed, yet he thrusteth them on againe, and how often soeuer they be taken tardie, yet they must on forward. Thus much that he saith, the diuell calleth into prison.

The kindnes of our Sauior to his faithful seruants hath appeared euen in this, that he forewarned thē of the dangers to come, & encouraged them not to feare: but he sheweth it yet further by adding most comfortable things. The first of them is in these words, *That thou maist be tried*. This setteth forth the counsel and purpose of

the

the Lord, or to what end he would haue them suffer affliction: and that is, not for any harme towards them, but indeed for their great good. For this trying which he speaketh of is a right worthie thing, and to the singular commoditie of the faithful. Reade the first chapter of the Epistle of S. *Iames*, and ye shal find, that he willeth vs to account it all ioy, when we fall into diuerse temptations, knowing, as he setteth downe, vnto what integritie we are brought through the trying of our faith: and that the man is blessed which indureth temptations, because when he is tryed, he shall receiue the crowne of life, &c.

Likewise ye may reade what Saint *Peter* saith touching the same, Ye are in heauinesse through manifold afflictions, that the triall of your faith (being much more precious then gold that perisheth, though it be tried with fire) might be found, to be to your praise, and honour, and glorie, at the appearing of Iesus Christ, 1.Pet.1. 6.7. Likewise in the fourth chapter of the same Epistle, he exhorteth them not to thinke it a strange matter concerning the fiery trial which was come among them, for to proue them. Then marke this, the diuell in a rage would terrifie and throwe downe all, and stirreth vp cruell and bloudy tyrants to make all the shew of terror that may be: both the diuell and his instruments do all of a most wicked purpose euen with wrath and malice, euen to trie if they can with any feare make them denie and fall from the truth: this is the triall they make. But the high Lord ouer all, which gouerneth and directeth all things according to his good pleasure, will haue his seruants tried to a farre other purpose, and that is, as the gold is put into the fire to be tried, to haue the drosse and mixture burnt out, and so to be fined and made more pure & bright: so the faithfull are cast into the fornace of afflictions, that they also may be fined and become more tried and pure. Is not this a good comfort to make vs cheerfully to beare troubles for the Lords cause? what wise man indeed will not reioyce in that which is for his great good?

The next comfort here ministred, is in the shortnesse of the time which this persecution shall last, vttered in these words: *And ye shall haue affliction ten dayes*. Although we feele and find by experience that afflictions do vs good, yet our frayle nature will hardly endure them long, and in continnance of time we waxe wearie and are readie to faint, if we see no liklihood but that they will continue. For this cause the Prophet proclaimeth in the Psalme, The rod of wickednesse shall not rest vpon the lot of the righteous, that the righteous stretch not forth their hands vnto wickednesse, Psal. 125.

Accordingly, the Lord foresheweth to this Church at Smyrna, that their persecution for the great violent heat and terror of it, should not last euer, nor yet continue long, for he saith it should be but for ten dayes. This is indeed a verie short time, if we take it but for ten of these naturall dayes, whereof euerie one consisteth but of 24 houres: but the holy Scripture sometimes in the Prophets, and namely in *Daniel* vseth so many dayes for so many yeares, as euerie weeke is seuen yeares: & so it seemeth to be in this place, ten dayes, that is, ten yeares. Why shold it not thē as well be said yeares, if it be meant ten yeares? There is reason for that, we be no good measurers of time, we thinke a few yeares to be a wonderfull long time. And

there-

therefore the Lord leadeth vs to confider of yeares rightly, to be indeed as nothing, and which speedily come to an end.

It seemeth that this persecutiō of the Church of the Smyrnians, which is said to be for ten dayes, was that which was raised vp by the Emperour *Traianus*: for he followed very shortly after this message was sent, vnder him (as ancient histories do report) was the Church at Smyrna persecuted, and his persecution did continue ten yeares. Saint *Iohn* receiued this reuelation toward the end of the raigne of *Domitian*. Then next succeeded *Nerua*, whose Empire lasted but one yeare, foure moneths, and nine dayes. After followed *Traianus*, he raigned 19 yeares, he began to persecute at the tenth yeare of his raigne, and continued vnto his end: and so this affliction of ten yeares came to an end, and vanished as if it had bene but for ten dayes.

Now remaineth the last comfort, which is the greatest, expressed thus, *Be thou faithfull vnto the death, and I will giue thee a crowne of life.* This is a precious promise, and full of sweet consolation vnto all the afflicted seruants of Christ. They be sharpe brunts which they endure for the time, but being once broke through them, they enter into the high glorie to be crowned kings, and to raigne in ioy for euer. But see how this promise dependeth vpon a condition: and that is, if we continue faithfull to the end: for he saith, *Be thou faithfull vnto the death, and I vvill giue thee a crowne of life.* If we runne a great part of the race swiftly, and then stay, turne aside, or go backe againe, what shall it auaile vs? If we fight manfully vnder the banner of Christ, against sinne, the world, and the diuell a long time, and then our faith faile, and we cowardly yeeld, be taken captiues, and ouercome, what haue we gained? Our Sauiour saith, He that continueth to the end, he shall be saued, Math. 24. That he saith, *Vnto the death*, it forewarneth that the persecution among them should be vnto bloud. And the histories do shew that *Polycarpus* Disciple of Saint *Iohn*, a verie old man, after he had manie yeares serued the Lord Iesus, as a right faithfull shepheard ouer this flocke of God at Smyrna, did most constantly suffer, and died a glorious Martyr. We haue not yet resisted vnto bloud, striuing against sinne, as the holy Ghost speaketh, Hebr. 12. The battell being against sinne, and the crowne of glorie set before vs, let vs not faint nor giue ouer for the sheading of our bloud: for if we do, if we yeeld vnto the enemies, we are not worthie to be crowned with the crowne of life. The Lord increase our faith, and vphold vs and keepe vs vpright in the battell, as his true and faithfull souldiers, euen to the end. Thus much for the narration of this Epistle, now to the conclusion.

Let him that hath an eare, heare what the spirit saith to the Churches: He that ouercommeth shall not be hurt of the second death. Here is againe as it were a publike proclamation to stirre vp and to moue attention in all that haue eares, to heare what the spirit saith to the Churches. No man can heare except the Lord giue him an eare, let vs beg it of him instantly. O wold to God we could heare throughly well what this is that he saith, he that ouercommeth shall not be hurt of the second death: for then would it stirre vs vp to fight valiantly in the Lords battell,

and

and to stand against all the terrour of death, and torments whatsoeuer. For what though we lie as yet subiect vnto the first death, that is, the separation of the soule from the body, and so our bodies putrifie & turne to dust? yet holding the faith, & being thereby armed with the mighty power of God, we get the victory ouer the world, & ouer the Prince of this world, so that the second death, which is the eternall damnation both of soule and body in hell, shall not hurt vs. Our victorie then which we get through faith, hath a double comodity; the one, that it deliuereth vs from the torment of the second death (which were a great benefit, if we should be after without feeling, either of good or euill, as the beast is after he is dead) and the other, that we shall be crowned with the crowne of life. These two things be so of such waight, that it ought to moue our harts vnto a dayly & cōtinual care aboue all other things to seek to be established in the most holy faith, that we may ouercome

THE VI. SERMON.

12. *And to the Angell of the Church which is in Pergamus, write, these things saith he that hath the sharpe sword with two edges:*

13. *I know thy works, & where thou dwellest, euen where the throne of Sathan is, & thou holdest my name, and hast not denied my faith, euen in those dayes when Antypas my faithfull martyr was slaine among you, where Sathan dwelleth.*

14. *But I haue a few things against thee, because thou hast there them that maintaine the doctrine of Balaam, which taught Balake to put a stumbling blocke before the children of Israell, that they should eate of meat sacrificed to Idols, and commit fornication:*

15. *Euen so hast thou them which maintaine the doctrine of the Nicholaitanes, which thing I hate.*

16. *Repent, or else I will come vnto thee shortly, and will fight against them with the sword of my mouth.*

17. *Let him that hath an eare heare what the spirit saith vnto the Churches, to him that ouercommeth will I giue to eate Manna that is hid, and I will giue him a white stone, & in the stone a new name written, which no man knoweth, but he that receiueth it.*

THe third Epistle is sent to the Angel of the Church in Pergamus. This Pergamus was the chiefe citie of Phrygia, in which Christ had now his faithfull flocke. The Exordium of this message, is frō the description of the most high and mighty sonne of God, described only here with this one part of the vision, that it is he which hath the sharpe sword with two edges: for by this one part they might be induced to thinke vpon

all

THE REVELATION. 63

all the rest of his glorie. This sword is the liuely word which is come out of his mouth. It may right well be said to be a sharpe two edged sword, for it slayeth sin and corruption in the faithfull, and it killeth with eternall destruction all the vnbeleeuers and euill men, and cutteth downe all wicked heresies. And here is mention made of it, becaufe the Lord faith afterward, he would fight with it against those wicked corrupters of that Church: euen those spots & blots that were among the, as S. *Iude* speaketh. The Church and all her true children are armed with this sword against the diuell, and against all other enemies, and it shall slay & destroy them all. Thus much may suffice touching the Exordium or entrance of this Epistle.

Then in the narration he faith, *I know thy works*. And so he telleth them what he did commend in them, and what he did difallow, adding both an admonition for repentance, and a threatning if that did not follow. It doth indeed verie manifestly appeare, that the Pastor of this flocke was also a right worthie feruant of Christ, full of spirituall gifts, and that the flocke also followed his steps: and yet here is but one vertue named for which the commendation is giuen, and that is, their constant, open, and bold profession of the name and faith of Christ, euen in the midst of hot persecution, and in the midst of Sathans gard. This diuine constancie in the truth (as we shall see by circumstances) could not be without manie other precious vertues, though they be not named. And we may confider first, that it is a maruellous thing by which the Lord doth commend vnto all posterities the valiant constancie and fortitude of this Pastor of the Church in Pergamus, and the constancie and boldnesse of the flocke : when he faith, *Thou dwellest where Sathan hath his throne*. The diuell had preuailed in all places of the world, and as a great Lord bare sway, but yet in some places he did carie them deeper into all blindnesse and horrible impieties then in other. And that is meant here when the Lord faith, that Sathan had his throne in Pergamus: he did raigne there in an exceeding high maner, he had men so vnder his dominion, and was so great a commaunder, that he might attempt almost what he would. What a place was this Church of Pergamus then planted in? and what an incommodious habitation had it? They did dwell euen at Sathans court gate, by his royall pallace, and by the seat of his kingdome, & euen in the midst of his gard and garrifons of his souldiers. Here was euen as sweet a dwelling as *Lot* had among the Sodomites, of whom Saint *Peter* reporteth, that from day to day he tormented his righteous soule, in hearing and seeing their vngodly deeds. For here the holy feruants of God, abhorring filthy vncleannesse both in words and deeds, were euen constrained to heare of and to see much, which could not but highly vexe the: feeing this is the custome of Sathans vassals who he thrusteth headlong into all abomination, if they see any vexed at it, to do it the more. What railings, what blafphemies, what reproches against Christ, against his Gospel and Church, were there powred forth, and did euen as flouds runne downe the streets, ye may coniecture. What filthinesse or vncleannesse in all other vices could there be wanting? The holy Gospell of our Lord Iesus Christ is most pure and full of heauenly light, difclosing and condemning all such abhominations. The faithfull Christians which professe the same, walke as the children of the light, and wil haue no fellowship with the vnfruitfull works of darknesse, but reproue them. Oh what a spite was this, and what a disgrace vnto Satan, that such a doctrine, & such a cōpanie must come and be seated euen vnder his nose, and euen at his Court gates? And what a griefe did this strike into the minds of his ministers, that now they must be detected and rebuked, and could not so quietly as before performe their seruice vnto their great Lord with such pleasure as before? For it taketh away some of their delight in the doing, when euill men do perceiue their deeds be discouered and misliked. Then how mad was the diuell? what meanes and wayes would hee leaue vnsought, vtterly for to roote out this Church? And how ready were all his seruants to accomplish his will? Satan their prince sitting in his throne, that is in deed in their heartes which were his vassals, he would kindle all wrath and rage in them, and inflame their hearts with all sauage crueltie. Hereupon was raised bitter persecution euen vnto death.

Then consider all this, and it doth highly magnifie (as I said) the valiant constancy of this Church. For it is added, *And thou keepest my name, and hast not denied my faith, in the daies that Antipas my faithfull Martyr was slaine among you, &c*. It standeth thus for the sense, thou dwellest where Sathan ruleth as king, sitting vpon his throne, and hauing so manye to obeye his will, raiseth vp all mischiefes, terrours, and daungers, euen so farre that some haue beene cruelly murthered among you, and yet thou hast stoode constant, thou hast not beene afraide, nor ashamed to confesse me, and to professe my faith, euen in the middest of all Sathans rout, when thou couldest see nothing but extreme dangers and perils. This praise is great by reason of these circumstances. The gouernour of a ship and the mariners in a calme sea are not tried: it is no maisterie nor praise for them to keepe vpright: but if in boysterous tempestes, and through the raging surges they can keepe vpright, and goe safe through, it is to their great commendation. The captaine in wars and his souldiers, are not said to be valiant vpon no assault of enemies, or for some light skirmish: but if they bee set vpon on euerie side, and compassed round about with fierce and terrible enemies, and are not then abashed, nor shrinke not, but stand valiantly in the fight, and giue the repulse to their enemies, who doth not magnifie their courage? This Captaine ouer the Lordes band at Pergamus, and those Christian souldiers, were wonderfully set vpon by Sathan and his armies, and yet stoode it out to the ende as conquerours. Their ship was tossed exceedingly, and yet they carry her safe vnto the shoare: were they not worthie of high commendation? Yes, and the Lord from heauen giueth them the praise of it. Thus we see the meaning of the words. Now let vs see what is to be gathered more particularly from the same.

That they dwelled where Sathan had his throne, it sheweth first what miserable estate all men are in without Christ, euen vnder the cruell tyrant Sathan, who ruleth in their corrupt lusts, and holdeth them captiue to do his will. For albeit some are led more deepely into thraldome then others, yet all that haue not Christ raigning in them, are the seruants of Sathan, and their case is very wofull.

Secondly, this doth magnifie and extoll the mercie of God, that would send his
Gospell

THE REVELATION.

Gospell into such a place, euen almost as it were into hel, for could it be much better where Sathā had his throne? It may teach vs to offer the gospel, if it be our calling, euen vnto most wicked people, hoping that God may draw at the least some of them out of the iawes of Sathan: the power of the heauenly doctrine is such.

Thirdly, as we may see, it extolleth the might of our Lord Iesus Christ, not only in planting his Church there, but in preseruing it. For, will Sathan make small resistance when that is set vp which casteth him downe, and euen in the place where he dwelleth? Men can better endure that which they mislike, if it be further from them, then if it be iust by them. Then that he saith, thou hast kept my name and not denied my faith, it is a most excellent thing. The diuel laboureth nothing more, then through terror of persecution to driue men from confessing Christ: & Christ himselfe saith, that if we deny him before men, he wil deny vs before his father, and before the holy Angels, yea though it be so that we cannot confesse him but with extreame perill of our liues. For our Lord Iesus is a most honourable king, full of glory, and such as are called to beare his name, & to stand in the defence of his glory, it is the greatest honour that in this word can light vpon any man: and shall men then be ashamed of him when he is blasphemed? What an vnworthy thing is that? how vnworthy are they to be partakers of his so great glory with him? Seeing if we will raigne with him in glory, we must not refuse to beare his crosse, and to be reproched for him. Let vs not shrinke though we be compassed about with neuer so many wicked enemies, but follow the example of this Church of Pergamus. We shal haue the same praise which they had from the Lord, we shall by his power tread downe Sathan, and raigne with him our Lord in his euerlasting kingdom. It is much to be marked, that he putteth both these two together, That they kept his name, and denied not his faith. For this sheweth that a bare confession of Christes name, is not sufficient, but we must hold his doctrine and faith: for the diuell coueteth that men may vnder the bare profession of the name of Christ, deny Christ. If heretickes and wicked men hold of his name, they dishonor him more then such as vtterly deny him. The whole popery is broached vnder the name of Christ, which destroyeth his doctrine and his faith, and setteth vp the doctrines of diuels. Now when they persecute with fagot and sword all that imbrace and confesse the faith of Iesus, many thinke they may deny the doctrine, becaufe they deny not the name of Christ.

But let vs learne out of this place that we must not deny the faith, or the pure doctrine of the gospel, if we wil confesse Christ aright. If the diuel can driue vs frō the doctrine, to deny that, euen any principle of our holy faith, it is enough for him, he doth separate vs from Christ. For we haue no hold nor no part in Christ but by a liuely faith, and the faith is founded vpon the pure doctrine of Gods word. What comfort then can that man haue in professing the name of Christ, which knoweth not the doctrine of faith, despiseth it rather, or he that knoweth it, and for feare of daunger denieth it, still holding a profession of Christs name? These are baptized, and the Church doth swarme full of them, but the Lord in his time will fanne out such chaffe. Learne thou then to know the holy faith, euen all the pure doctrine of

F   our

our Lord, stand fast in it, fight the good fight of faith. Obey and bring foorth fruits agreeable to Gods most holy will: and let Sathan and his instruments vtter all their malice against thee: let them racke and torment thy body, let them shed thy bloud, and take away thy life, it is all they can doe, thou shalt be crowned as a conqueror with the crowne of glory and eternall blessednesse. We are called, and haue giuen our names vnto Christ, to fight vnder his banner against the diuell and against sin. This Church at Pergamus (as ye see) was euen in the edge and dint of the battaile. They stood valiantly vnto it.

If we abide not so sore brunts, nor so bitter assalts, and yet be made to turne our backs and to become cowards, what excuse can be made for vs? No doubt Sathan is a great Prince, and hath a great stroke in all places, wherfoeuer a man be professing Christ he cannot be out of the battaile: yet it is in some place more sore then in other. If the Lord haue set vs as it were in the hindermost part of the campe, where we indure but small assaults in comparison, and yet do faint, what wold we do if we dwelt where Sathan hath his throne? We are at the will of our Emperor to set and place vs in what ranke he will, and if he do appoint vs to encounter with the greatest enemies, and to meet them in the face, the more fierce and strong they be, the more valiantly we must resist: for we are sure of the victory. There is nothing more glorious in this world, then to fight the good fight of faith, to pul down Sathan from his throne, and to destroy sinne. Sathan wil rage and roare at this, they shall haue much trouble, which go about it, euen by as many as he can stirre vp against them. Let no man dreame of a quiet aduancing of the Gospell. I speake the more of this vpon the worthy example of this Church, because there be many which can be content to heare the Gospell, and to speake well of it so long as it bringeth no trouble, but they are weary, & wil professe it no further then they may without rebuke or danger. There be some which betray the Lords cause, and run from his tents to the tents of Sathan. They fought a while, and seemed worthy soldiers, but now shake hands with the enemies, and fight for the diuell, and approue such wicked wayes as they haue before condemned.

Well to conclude this point, thinke not thy selfe vnhappie if thou beest troubled much, and induredst hard things for the name of Christ, but reioyce if thou maiest any way be a meane to breake downe any peece of Sathans kingdome, & to further the kingdome of Christ. It is a blessed worke, & not to be shrunke at for any perill. If the place where thou dwellest, be so full of wicked men and of all wickednesse, that it may be said, that Sathan hath his throne there, faint not, but remember this Church at Pergamus: it is not thy case alone, and the more that the strength of sin increaseth, the more the malice of the enemies aboundeth: resist with the greater courage and strength of Gods spirite, for then is no time to faint, or to bee negligent.

Now followeth the other part, which commmendeth the constancy of this Angell, and of the congregation with him, in professing the name and faith of Christ: and that is, when there was persecution vnto bloud among them, and such cruelty shewed, if it had bin possible to terrifie them, and cause them to deny their profession:

sion: for *Antipas* was murdered by Sathans seruants, euen for the zeale of his wicked throne: and they of the Church, professing the same faith that he died for, what could they looke for but cruell death? euen to be dealt withall as he was, vnlesse they would recant their doctrine, and do as their neighbours about them did: and yet they stood firme and constant: their mind was fully set, if they had beene laid hold of and put to it, to haue giuen vp their liues as *Antipas* did, and to haue endured the shedding of their bloud, rather then so much as in any outward shew to deny their redeemer. The Lord God of his mercy grant vnto vs the like constant boldnesse, if euer we be called vnto any triall, that we may be praised by Christ as they were. They were euen as Martyrs before God, that in mind they were thus setled, and looked for none other but cruell death and torments: so the thing was as done before God. *Abraham* did not slay his sonne *Isaac* at the commandement of God, but before God it was as done, because he meant none other, and was lifting vp his hand to strike, but then was commanded to stay his hand.

The Angell of the Church at Pergamus and the flocke with him, were not all brought to suffer the crueltie vnto death, but they looked for it, and made full account, they went not one haire breadth from the truth to shun any perill, & this pleased God. But here is mention made but of one that was put to death among them, that is *Antipas*: it is not vnlike but that they murthered more besides him, being the place where Sathan had his throne, but he is only mentioned, as a worthy man aboue others. It may be (as writers report) that he was a pastor ouer that flock, euen a captaine to leade the bands, and therefore especially hated and killed: for the diuell doth feele who doth wound him or his kingdome most deeply, and against him he is in the greatest wrath and furie. And his seruants likewise, his courtiers, the more gloriously the light breaketh forth in any, and the power of the truth, the more their madnesse is enflamed, for they will not haue any light come into the Lords hall, but loue darknes rather then light, because their works be euil. For euery one that euil doth (saith the Lord) hateth the light, and commeth not to the light. *Cain* slue his brother *Abel*, and why slue he him? (saith Saint *Iohn*) because his works were euill, and his brothers were good.

Well, whether this one blessed Martyr were slaine alone in that Church, or whether their cruelty extended further, and slue some other, yet here we may behold the great prouidence and protection of God ouer his, in brideling the malice and rage of the diuell, and of the wicked. We may be sure that Sathan doth desire that all the faithfull were rooted out: if he had power to bring it to passe, it should not fayle but be done. Here in the citie Pergamus, he sitteth in his throne as King, the Church is compassed about with his rout of seruantes, and all of them inflamed with wrath and furie by him, and yet but one man, or some few slaine by them: why were they not all beate downe and destroyed? Who bridled this mighty tyrant in the heate of his displeasure? Euen the Lord Iesus, who hath trode downe Sathan, and can preserue his Church, dwelling among a rabblement of as good as may be found in hell.

Let this teach vs, when wee behold the multitude of vngodly enemies, and thinke that by mans reason all will downe, let it I say, teach vs not to despaire, but to remember that the Lord doth so bridle Sathan, that hee will preserue his little flocke euen where Sathans throne is, & neither he nor the proudest seruant he hath, shall touch them further then may be for their triall, and their great good. Ye see fell dogges which are chained vp, how they barke and striue for to breake loose at such as passe by, that they may bite and teare them: euen so the diuels are chayned vp by the prouidence and rule which God hath ouer them, that albeit they rage & fret to haue scope to run vpon all, yet they can reach no further then he doth enlarge their chayne. The vassals of the diuell, whose minds he doth possesse, fume & gnash their teeth, and wish that all were hanged vp out of the way, which with any earnest and sincere affection professe the Gospell; they raile, they lie, they slaunder, they stir what they can: but the Lord hath them chayned vp also: & although at some times he giueth them large scope to afflict his people, yet hee shorteneth their chayne againe, and tieth them vp, when he will refresh with peace his poore seruants. Let vs not doubt of this, seeing they could do no more here, where he saith Sathan did dwell, and where his throne was.

Then further let vs note what honorable mention the Lord maketh of his seruant *Antipas* which was slaine: he calleth him his faithfull Martyr. For it teacheth vs, how deare and precious vnto Christ the glorious Martyrs be: the persecutors do account them the most base and vile things vpon the earth, yea euen the off-scouring, and as it were the scumme, not worthy to liue among men: they curse and reproch them, they raile vpon them, they put vpon them all the torments which they can deuise: but contrariwise (as we be here taught) before God they are as precious pearles among heapes of base stones. They are blessed, & after their paines here ended, they liue with the Lord in glory: they bee honourable among the Angels in heauen: their memory is blessed vpon the earth among all posterities that feare God.

This may teach vs, to search out the holy faith, euen the pure doctrine of Christ, that sound truth, which he himselfe hath deliuered, and as the faithfull witnesse sealed with his bloud. And then it may encourage vs to stand fast in the open profession thereof, and if the multitude of the world rise vp against it and condemne it, yet let vs be faithfull euen vnto death, for there can be no greater honor, then this that he saith, My faithfull Martyr.

Hitherto we haue seene the commendation of the Angell and Church in Pergamus: now followeth their reproofe in the matter for which they are rebuked of the Lord. *But I haue* (saith he) *a few things against thee*. This Angell then and this flocke are not without their faults, yea their grosse blot, albeit they are the faithfull souldiers of Christ: a thing worthy to be noted, least we condemne excellent Churches for some faults.

This is the mercy of the Lord, not to reiect the faithfull for the faults that bee in them. It is not to encourage or bolden any to commit sinnes careleslie, and to continue in the same: for that is a great presumption and contempt: but it is to comfort such as withall their heart studie vnfainedly to please the Lord, and

yet

taught or held the same to remaine in their fellowship. The Angell and Church at Pergamus, stood in their faith and loue, and although they could not but hate the doctrine of Balaam, and the doctrine of the Nicholaitans, yet they negligently suffered those spottes and blottes (I meane the men which held the same) to remaine among them. It seemeth that the doctrine of the Nicholaitanes, and the doctrine of Balaam was all one: but set foorth vnder the name of Balaam for to make it more odious.

Touching this Baalam, ye may reade in the booke of Numbers chap. 22. and so in the chapters following. Balake the King of the Moabites sent for Balaam the soothsayer, and would hire him for to curse Israell for his sake: he was for rewards sake desirous for to curse them, but letted by the Lord, and compelled to blesse them. Yet greedy of rewarde, he tooke the King and taught him how he might procure the ruine of the children of Israel, & that was, if they might be brought to sinne against God: for the subtill wretch did know that they could not be plagued, and brought vnder, vnlesse God were offended with them. Then he taught him how they might be entised vnto sin, and that was, that they should set before the the beautifull women which might allure them to fornication, and so vnto idolatry, euen to feast with them at their idol feastes: which thing came to passe; for the children of Israel did commit whoredome with the daughters of Moab, and went to their sacrifices, and worshipped Baalpeor: and the wrath of the Lord was kindled, and he commanded they should be slaine: and there fell of that plague twentie and foure thousand, Numb. 25.

True it is, this counsell of Balaam vnto Balake is not set downe: but hee told Balake that he would giue him counsell, chap. 24. verse 14. and when the thing was come to passe, Moses saith it was by the counsell or word of Balaam, chapter 13. verse 16. And in this place the Lord saith expresly, that Balaam taught Balake to put a stumbling blocke before the children of Israell, that they might eate of thinges offered vnto idols, and commit fornication. The Nicholaitanes taught, that it was lawfull to commit fornication, and to eate of things offered to idols, and therefore he setteth them forth to be the disciples of Balaam. They taught such filthie doctrine euen for their bellies sake, and through couetousnesse, and therefore Saint Peter and Saint Iude speaking of them, euen of such wicked men crept into the Church, say, woe vnto them, they haue perished in the reward of Balaam. They be Balaamites, they teach filthines, euen to bring plagues vpō the Church. The Lord saith, which thing I hate, which teacheth a lesson, not only to the Nicholaitans, to see how abhominable they were before God, but also to al such as corrupt the Church any way: for there be at this day many filthy Epicures,

which

which like of any thing but true godlines, for that they cannot abide. If a man will not powre forth himselfe vnto all excesse of riot, to gowse and sweare, and to be filthy, they gibe at him by and by, terming him precise and one addicted to singularity, and raile vpon him with other reprochfull tearmes. Nay, if a man make but the least shew of honest conuersation, he shall be sure to heare of it that way.

Most lamentable it is to behold these abusers of the grace of God, turning it into wantonnesse, as the holy Apostle saith, in what multitudes they swarme in the Church. Their very multitude, and custome causeth them euen to prescribe as if the right were on their side. But let them looke well vpon this place, how odious a thing it is to corrupt the Church of God: the Temple of God is holy and pure, and they be blessed which seeke to establish the Christian people in all purenesse, and chastity, both of body and soule: and cursed are they which do corrupt and defile, or be occasions to bring in or to nourish pollutions among Gods people.

Many can discourse gallantly to proue the indifferency of this and that action, and why may not a Christian do it, without all consideration of the most vile and horrible abuses which are nourished and maintained by such meanes. They are very zealous to haue nothing abridged of all that they suppose is graunted for fleshly pleasure; but for the glory of God, and for the soules of the people, they haue no zeale nor care at all: for deale roundly with them, and they will confesse, that indeed manifold euils, euen soule sins do follow in such liberty. But many of them againe haue this plaister for that, for what one thing can we do (say they) but we sin? We know there be many euils committed: yea and ye do laugh and sport your selues at them. The Prophet saith, that riuers of teares did descend from his eyes, because men kept not the Law of God, Psalm.119. but ye laugh. The foole (sayth *Salomon*) maketh a sport of sin: and is it not strange, that among those which professe Christ, there should such monsters be found, as will get in men to make them drunken, that they may laugh to see them either tumble like swine, or heare them raile and vtter all filthy speeches? O wretched dayes, the patience of God is great. These beasts shall one day come to their account: for the Lord doth hate such filthy abominations, euen as he saith he hated the doctrine of the Nicholaitanes. Let as many as feare God, stand fast against them in the way of godlinesse, haue no fellowship with them in their corrupt and corrupting wayes.

Beloued, this admonition is so much the more necessary, that there be not a few, but swarmes of corrupting Nicholaitanes in these dayes. And as ye see a mighty floud beareth downe all that standeth before it, that standeth not very fast: so the generall streame of their carnall impieties carieth all such away, as are not strongly armed with the feare of God.

The Lord hauing set downe the fault which was in this Church, now he calleth for repentance: *Repent* saith he. Then the godly are to repent: yea that they are, for the most godly that liue are but in the way to perfection: and so haue somewhat dayly to amend, & repent for: they are to pray so long as they liue, Forgiue vs our trespasses. Many so soone as euer they haue receiued the profession of the Gospell and left some of their grossest sins, imagine that they be ioly Christians, neuer studying

dying to reforme dayly the euill affections and corrupt lusts of their harts, and so in time they wither away and come to naught. Againe, our nature is ready to swel, and euen to chalenge priuiledges and liberties, if we haue endured any assaults for the Gospell: I was persecuted (saith one) I was imprisoned, I was banished, I was spoyled of all my goods. Now tell him of repentace if he walke in some grosse sins, and he thinketh ye offer him great wrong: as if the former sufferings had giuen euen a full liberty. This Angell of the Church at Pergamus had stood in the battaile, and so had the flocke, there was one fault among them, and the Lord willeth them to repent. And out of all controuersie if we haue stood in time of affliction & persecution raised against the truth, it maketh much against vs, if afterward we be ouercome of the world: for hauing found the strength of God to vphold vs in aduersity, in persecution and terror, if we gaue not ouer our selues in carelesse security of the flesh, should not the same power preserue vs in time of peace and prosperity, from being ouercome with the loue of this world? And being ouercome, what a fall haue we taken? Alas shall we glory in a fall? Shall we glory in that whereof we ought to be much ashamed? O let vs repent, as the Lord here requireth, for that which is amisse in vs, whatsoeuer we are, or whatsoeuer we haue bene.

After this admonition to repentance, here is added a threatning conditional, that is, if thou do not; for if he repented, there should come no harme: but if not, marke what he threatneth, *I will come vnto thee shortly, and will fight against them with the sword of my mouth*. The Lord Iesus is sayd to come diuerse wayes: he is sayd to come to succour his when they be in distresse: but here he sayth he will come vnto battaile, and will fight against that wicked crue, euen with that sharpe two edged sword, which proceedeth out of his mouth. This is his mighty word, by which he will slaie all the wicked. But he telleth the Angell of this Church, that he will fight against them, against those Nicholaitanes, which taught to commit fornication and idolatry, who as Saint *Peter* saith, had eyes full of adulterie, that could not cease to sinne, beguiling vnstable soules: he doth not say he would fight againg him or against the Church: yea but we see this is a threatning against him and the Church, and therefore the Lords fighting against the Nicholaitanes includeth some punishment, also euen against him, and against so many of the flocke, as did not so much shun them as they ought to do. For it is not enough for vs to condemne wicked heresies and vncleane vices, but the men which are guilty in them, ought to be cast foorth and auoyded, the Church must be purged and rid of them. For how can such be suffered without a great sinne against Almighty God? especially when the sufferance is not only a prophanation of most holy things, as the giuing of the, that is, the holy Sacraments vnto dogs and swine: but the weake are seduced and corrupted. Thus much for the narration of this Epistle, now to the conclusion.

Let him that hath an eare, heare what the spirit saith to the Churches. This we haue had in the two former Epistles, and not in vaine repeated, for we are dull of hearing, and neede to bee stirred vp with often admonition. And seeing we shall be conquerors through faith, it behoueth vs for to heare, vnlesse wee will be ouercome.

come. We haue the diuell and all that he can make againſt vs, yea euen our owne corrupt harts, but yet through hearing, we ſhal get the victory, we ſhal ſtand faſt, euen vnto the end, and all finiſhed, we ſhall ſtand. Then ſhal we obtaine the precious promiſes which are made: as here follow ſome. The firſt is, *to him that ouercommeth will I giue to eate Manna that is hid*. We know how the Scripture doth ſet forth, that God fed the children of Iſraell forty yeares in the wilderneſſe with Manna. Whereof it is ſaid in the Pſalme, that man did eate the bread of Angels: for that bread which was brought vnto them by the miniſtry of Angels, is called the bread of Angels, as we call ours the bakers bread. This Manna ſerued vnto a further vſe thē to feed the belly, for it was a Sacramēt, or a figure of the true bread of life the Lord Ieſus, who is that bread of life which came downe from heauen, Iohn.6. That Manna, which the fathers did eate in the wilderneſſe, was viſible vnto all, but this true Manna is hid, none can come nigh it, none can ſee it, none can taſt of it, but ſuch as haue a true and liuely faith. They all indeede which beleeue ſhall receiue ſomewhat of it, euen as it were ſome morſels thereof in this life preſent, (which are ſufficient to make them liue) and in the life to come, they ſhall be moſt plenteouſlie filled, and fed thereof with continuall delight: for it is not as our dainty meates, which when we are full we loath: but the ſweete taſt continueth ſtill for euermore. Bleſſed are they which hunger for this heauenly Manna, as they cannot but long for it, which once do truly taſt it: for all the ſweet dainties in this world are but as draffe vnto it. Let vs then fight to the end that we may come to this heauenly delicate banquet. Souldiers fight to get ſomewhat to liue on, to fare well, and to maintaine a countenance here vpon the earth: and ſhall not we fight to come to this heauenly table?

The other promiſe here made vnto the conquerors: *I will giue him a white ſtone, and in the ſtone a new name written, which no man knoweth but he that receiueth it*. It is out of queſtion that vnder diuers figures the Lord doth promiſe to his faithfull ſouldiers, the ſame reward, the ſame dignity, felicity and glory, according as diuers things may repreſent it vnto vs: as here by the white ſtone & the new name writtē in it, which none knoweth but he which receiueth the ſame, the remiſſiō of ſins, the ſanctification, the iuſtification, the peace of conſcience, & ioy of the holy ghoſt, yea all the ſpiritual graces, & the dignity which followeth with them, ſeeme to be here reſembled. The conquerors were wont to haue ſuch things giuen vnto them as might be apparant figures vnto others of their worthines: but here he ſaith, that the name is knowne to none but to him that receiueth it. This is not ſo to be taken, as though the glory and honor of the faithful ſhal be hid or ſecret from the ſight of others: but the ioy and conſolation, and peace, are felt onely of him that hath them, and none can be partaker with him. Thus much touching the meſſage to the Angell of the Church at Pergamus.

THE

THE REVELATION. 73

THE VII. SERMON.

18 *And vnto the Angell of the Church which is at Thyatira write, these things saith the sonne of God, which hath his eyes like vnto a flame of fire, and his feet like fine brasse.*

19. *I know thy vvorks, and thy loue, and seruice, and faith, and thy patience, and thy vvorkes, and the last are moe then the first.*

20. *Notwithstanding I haue a few things against thee, that thou suffereft the vvoman Iezabel, which calleth her selfe a Prophetesse, to teach, & to deceiue my seruants, to make them commit fornicatiō, and to eate meats sacrificed vnto Idols:*

21. *And I gaue her space to repent of her fornication, and she repented not.*

22. *Behold I will cast her into a bed, and them that commit fornication with her into great affliction, except they repent them of their vvorkes:*

23. *And I will kill her children with death: and all the Churches shall know that I am he vvhich searcheth the reines and hearts: and I vvill giue vnto enerie one of you according to your vvorkes.*

24. *And vnto you I say, the rest of them of Thyatira, as many as haue not this learning, neither haue knowne the deepnesse of Sathan (as they speake) I vvil put vpon ye none other burthen,*

25. *But that which ye haue already, hold fast till I come.*

26. *For he that ouercommeth, and keepeth my workes vnto the end, to him will I giue power ouer nations,*

27. *And he shall rule them with a rod of yron: and as the vessels of a potter shall they be broken.*

28. *Euen as I receiued of my father, so will I giue vnto him the morning starre.*

29. *Let him that hath an eare, heare what the Spirit saith to the Churches.*

The fourth message is sent to the Pastour of the Church at Thyatira, a citie of Lydia. The entrance is as in the former, from the great Lord of glorie, the sonne of God: he noteth himselfe by one part of the vision in which he shewed his glorie in the former chapter, as namely, *That his eyes are as a flame of fire, and his feet like fine brasse.* For (as I haue sundrie times noted) by this one they might consider of all the rest: seeing there is none whose eyes pierce through, & with cleare sight behold all secrets, nor that hath such strength, such stedfast-

nesse

nesse and perfection in his wayes, but onely that mightie Redeemer, our Lord Iesus Christ.

Then he saith in the second part, which is the narration, *I know thy vvorks*. This we see he saith vnto all: and this is peculiar to him, and he can giue due praise, & a iust reproofe, neither more nor lesse then euerie one deserueth. There is no pleading against him, no gainsaying nor colouring of anie matter. He doth first greatly commend this Angell, as his worthie seruant and faithfull shepheard among his flocke, and so together with him the flocke is commended. The vertues which he reporteth to be in him, are generall and large, as loue, seruice, faith, patience, & works, and the same increased: for so many steps there be in his praise.

Touching the loue, whether we vnderstand it the loue he did beare to Christ, or the loue he did beare to the Church, or generally of them both, it is all one in effect: seeing we cannot loue the Lord Iesus, but we must needs loue his Church, neither can we loue his Church, except we loue him first. These go inseparably together: and therefore we must take it that he loued God, he loued Christ, he loued the Gospell, he loued the Church. He was not void (as ye see) of that which Saint *Paule*, 1.*Cor*.13. sheweth, if it be wanting, all other things are but a vaine shew. His faith was the true and liuely faith, which (as the same Apostle saith) worketh by loue. If a man be neuer so full of knowledge, and seeme to haue neuer so much faith, and haue not loue, he knoweth nothing as he ought to know, he is in darknesse, his faith (which in some sence the Scripture calleth faith, as Iam.2.) is not faith properly and indeed, but a dead image and resemblance of faith: therefore still I say, we are put in mind to excell and to abound in loue. Vnto this his loue the Lord ioyneth his seruice, that is, his ministerie, euen all the labours and duties which he performed to the Saints, in teaching & otherwise, & so all the seruice of the Saints, and their labours of loue in their place, following the steps of their Pastor. This is verie well ioyned vnto loue, as the fruit thereof: for as Christ said to *Peter*, *Louest thou me? feed my sheepe, feed my lambes*: and as that chosen vessell *Paule*, taking exceeding great paines, enduring many troubles, and running through manie daungers to feed the Church, seeming vnto some to be as a man either out of his wits, or vainglorious, rendreth the right cause, saying, The loue of Christ constraineth vs, 2.*Cor*.5.

So euerie true minister of Christ beholding what loue the Lord hath shewed towards vs, and how deare his Church is vnto him, with how great a price he hath redeemed it: cannot but louing him, be thrust forward by that loue, to performe (though it be painfull and dangerous) all the duties of their ministerie, in feeding, strengthening, and comforting the weake and tender lambes of Christ. And euerie faithfull man feeling the loue of God, doth loue him againe, and thereupon laboureth to do all the seruice he can. If a man take neuer so much paines and trauell in studie, in teaching, or in whatsoeuer, if it proceed not from this loue, but either to seeke gaine, or glorie, (as I noted also before) all his ministerie to himselfe before God is nothing worth. I say to himselfe, because it may profite the Church,

but

but he shall receiue no reward with God. The sincere seruice doth proceede from loue: and so we see it here commended in this holy Bishop. It is certaine that such as be loose and negligent in seruice of Christ and his Church, it is because they neuer felt the loue of God, and so do not loue him.

Then next his faith is set downe, and with it his patience: here may seeme to be no good order obserued for this. We know that loue is the fruit of faith, and followeth of it, as I noted before, that Saint *Paul* saith, *Faith worketh by loue*. It is so then as faith is to haue the first place: but our Sauiour would commend the ministerie of this his seruant, before he would praise the patience in the same, and therefore setteth loue in the first place. There is no mention of wicked men, as of Iewes or such aduersaries in this citie, but yet you may perceiue the diuell wanted not his instruments, (as indeed he wanteth them no where in the world) for this man was withstood, and so were the people, and endured great troubles, & therefore his patience is commended. If he had not bene troubled, what patience could there be? If his troubles and afflictions had not bene great, what neede there anie mention of his faith by which he bare them? For it is said, *Thy faith and patince.* A man euen by humane courage can beare much: but the afflictions, the troubles, the reproches and dangers of this man were such, as that he could not haue borne them, but being armed with the heauenly power of God through faith. We may not thinke that the diuell being so madde and full of wrath as he is, where his kingdome decayeth, would suffer any such seruant of Christ to passe without great assaults. For doubtlesse he that will serue the Lord Iesus indeed, let him be armed, and that with the power of God through faith, for he shall be assaulted, his patience shall be tried and tried againe. If we haue faith we shall stand as this man stood, and neuer be ouerthrowne: but if we want faith, we cannot but fall in the great assaults.

Now further, this faith and loue of his could not be without many good works, yea many sweet and pleasant fruites, and therefore he againe saith, *and thy workes*. This man was a branch in the vine which bare fruite, Ioh. 15. The Christians taught by him abounding in faith and loue, were fruitfull. And he is commended that he grew more and more fruitfull, and they together with him. For he saith, *The last are moe then the first*. This is a great commendation, and a very rare thing to bee found. For albeit, God require that we should grow vp in Christ dayly, & become better and better, fuller of faith, of loue, and of all good works, as he saith: *As new borne babes couet the sincere milke of the word, that ye may grow thereby*: 1. Pet. 2. yet very few do it, but we shall find many euerie where which with the Angell of the Church of Ephesus forsake their former loue, and do not their first works, & marke what followeth. God did threaten the Church of Ephesus, for the Church did decline and decay with their Bishop in forsaking their former loue. Yea he did threaten them with a sore threatning, that if they did not repent, he would remoue their candlesticke out of the place. Here was also a fault in this Pastor, but yet no such seuere or sharpe threatning against the Church, which did grow better and better: what is the reason? Surely the Lord is so highly pleased where men that be-

lieue

Iceue are going forward though it be flowly, yea euen but creeping, that he beareth with great infirmities. He that is declining and forsaking his former loue, of a forward man may soone come farre behind, and fall into a dangerous estate, (yea many fall quickly, and neuer rise againe) but he that is going forward and doth become better and better, in faith, in loue, and good works, though he be loden & compassed about with infirmities, and some grosse sinne appeare, yet in time hee groweth to be a very good man: For what saith Christ, *Euery branch in mee that beareth fruit, he purgeth it, that it may bring forth more fruit.* Ioh. 15. Let vs then I pray ye for Gods sake, studie to go forward, and take heede of backsliding. Yee see in one Church the going backward, and how it is misliked: and in another the going forward, and how it is commended; no seuere threatning against their fault, for they are growing better.

There is but one vniuersall Church, euen one spouse of Christ, but I pray you marke the varietie of the true members thereof, while they be here in this world not vnburdened of this corrupt flesh. For here ye see one part decaying and waxing worse, and an other growing better. He that seemeth to be aloft and most excellent comming downeward, is in worse case then he that is below climing vpward. Now commeth the reprehension, or the fault which is found in this man and his flocke.

Notwithstanding I haue a few things against thee, &c. I noted before that the Lord findeth nothing to be reproued in the Angell of the Church of Smyrna: not that he was perfect, or free from all faults, (which is not to be found in any that liueth) but he had no grosse offence: So here when he saith, *I haue a few things against thee*: It is not to be vnderstood that the frailties & imperfections of this holy man, & of the faithfull in that Church were few, but that there were a few grosse things in him & in thē. We see the Lord doth testify for him, that he did grow better & better, both he & the people: but yet he had this foule fault in him, that contrary vnto all good order of discipline, he suffered a most vile and wicked woman to teach filthie doctrine in the Church, and therewith to seduce the weake seruants of God. The doctrine which she taught, is the same which before he called the doctrine of *Balaam*, to eate of things offered vnto Idols, and to commit fornication. It is (as we may learne euery where by Saint *Paul*) a great commendation for the Pastor to beare meekely and patiently many infirmities in the flocke, both for differences in some pointes of doctrine, as also in manners; also to beare with froward men, and to suffer patiently: but to suffer such abhominable poison as this to be powred forth and spread among the saints of God, euen to the polluting of the Church, to the reproch of the holy faith, and extreme danger of the weake, was as I said before, a foule fault. The good man and the whole flock, or the most of them, in this thing were ouer gentle and too too patient. The Lord calleth this wicked woman *Iezabell*, (not that her name was so) whether it were but one woman or diuers, but to shew how odious and accursed she was in his sight: whatsoeuer she pretended, she was like *Iezabell*, & euē no better, for *Iezabel* was the wife of *Ahab*, king of Israell. And as she drew on *Ahab* vnto most horrible idolatrie, as she withstood

THE REVELATION.   77

stood and persecuted the Lords holy Prophets; as she kept a table for foure hundred false prophets of *Baal*, and was euen as an head of false prophets, a ringleader and mistresse of all filthinesse, euen cursed *Iezabel*. So this filthy woman called her selfe a Prophetesse, and would be a great doer in the Church, as if she had vttered all her doctrine by the reuelation of the holy Ghost, when as in verie deed she had it from the diuell himselfe. For so the craftie diuell hath at all times (to purchase credite to his abhominable wares, and to make them saleable) set them forth vnder the name and authoritie of the holy Ghost: for if he should offer them as comming out of his owne shop, men wold then take heed of them. She was a Prophetesse of the diuell, but she boasted of the holie Ghost. This hath bin the whole sleight of the Poperie; the Pope cannot erre, he sitteth in *Peters* chaire, looke whatsoeuer he decreeth, it is from the holie Ghost. Thus I say haue all the most filthie dregs of Poperie bene greedily drunke vp of the blind world, because the wicked diuell hath brothed them vnder the name and authoritie of the holy Ghost. And marke a litle the comparison betweene these two. This woman called her selfe a Prophetesse, but Christ tearmeth her *Iezabel*. The Pope of Rome chalengeth to be the head of the Church, but the Scripture tearmeth him Antichrist: so that we must not looke what such seducers tearme themselues, for they will take glorious titles, but what Gods word sheweth them to be.

Now the Lord proceedeth to denounce iudgement, that if she and her followers could not be reclaimed, yet others might therby take warning. First, the Lord doth declare his long suffering, which she abused: *I gaue her space* (saith he) *to repent of her fornication, but she repented not*. This was a great kindnesse of God, to call such horrible sinners to repentance, and to giue them time and space to repent. We see he doth so at this day vnto manie, but they take occasion thereby (as the Lord chargeth them, Psalm. 50.) to be more bold in their wickednesse, euen as if God did allow of their wayes, because he doth not speedily strike them downe with plagues. But his plagues wil be the more grieuous, that his kindnesse is so abused, and that he giueth time to repent, and they waxe worse. For marke what he saith here, *Behold, I will cast her into a bed, and those that commit fornication with her, into great affliction, except they repent them of their vvorks. And I will kill her children with death*. Here is vtter destruction and wrath denounced; the speech indeed being applied according to the matter. For because fornicators delight in beds to commit their sinne, the Lord saith he will cast this woman into a bed, and her louers with her, and this he expoundeth to be great affliction. This is not to be restrained to afflictions in this world, but without repentance, they should haue this bed euen in hell. Which is also to be vnderstood, when he saith, he will slay her children with death. No doubt the second death should deuour these children of fornication. And the execution of this iudgement shall be made so manifest, that (as he saith) *All the Churches shall know, that I am he vvhich searcheth the reines and the hearts: and I vvill giue vnto euerie one of you according to your works*. The Iudge of all the world, which must iudge vprightly, and render to euery one

accor-

according to his works, muſt know the ſecret thoughts and intents of all harts, and that doth Chriſt Ieſus, as he pronounceth here.

And it is to be marked, how he can and will diſtinguiſh and ſeuer thoſe which are mingled together in the Church, while it is in the world. For this wicked *Iezabel* with her children that ſhe brought forth by her abhominable doctrine, were mixed among the Saints: but Chriſt will part them aſunder, and for their wicked works they ſhall be caſt into hell: and the other which haue not cōſented vnto that wicked doctrine, nor bene defiled with thoſe ſoule workes, but haue held the pure doctrine and faith of Chriſt, and brought forth the good fruits of the ſame, ſhall be rewarded with glorie in the heauens.

This is a thing worthie our conſideration. It is indeed a comfortable thing: for as it ſhall not profit the wicked at all, that they haue a place in the Church, & are mixed for a time with the godly (ſeeing they ſhall be plucked out & receiue according to their works) ſo ſhall it be no dammage to the true beleeuers, which keepe thēſelues vndefiled from their filthie pollutions, that ſuch vncleane ſwine remaine with them in the boſome of the Church. True it is, that the Church & the Goſpell are much diſgraced, & lye ſubiect vnto great reproch, when ſuch ſoule mōſters are ſuffered to harbor among the people of God, yea manie are defiled & endangered by thē, & therfore the Paſtors & Church gouernors do ſin a great ſinne (as we ſee by that which is reproued in this Angell) when they be negligent, and do not their beſt to purge and cleanſe the Lords houſe, & keepe it from being defiled with ſuch doing. Shall they not care how the Goſpell be diſhonoured? ſhall they not be grieued to ſee the weake ſeduced? But yet we may alſo learne here, that the godly are not thereby defiled, which conſent not vnto ſuch wickedneſſe: the Lord Ieſus ſpeaketh kindly vnto them, not blaming them that they did not ſeparate thēſelues from that ſociety & cōmunion, where ſo horrible perſons were ſuffered to remaine by the fault of the teachers and gouernors. For he ſaith, *And vnto you I ſay, the reſt of Thyatira, which haue not this learning, neither haue knowne the deepneſſe of Sathan (as they ſpeake) I wil put vpon ye none other burthen.* Theſe whom he calleth the reſt of Thyatira, are they which did abhor that filthie doctrine of that *Iezabel*, & did hold conſtantly the holy faith of Chriſt. He ſaith, he will lay no further burthen vpon them: he doth not charge them as men defiled, for cōmunicating in that Church, in which ſo foule an abuſe was ſuffered: he denounceth no terrour againſt thē: he doth not charge thē to take heed, & hereafter if their Biſhop & guides that then were, or anie other that ſhould ſucceed, did permit ſuch abuſe among them, to depart away & to ſeparate thēſelues, leaſt they ſhold all therby be defiled: he doth not I ſay, lay anie ſuch burthen vpon them: for that would make much for Donatiſme, but he only willeth, whatſoeuer fall out, *that which ye haue already, hold faſt till I come:* ſtand faſt in the holy, and pure, and ſound faith which ye haue receiued.

Beloued in the Lord, marke this ſaying wel, for that which is ſpoken vnto theſe, is ſpoken vnto vs all. It commeth to paſſe, & that not ſeldome in the true Church of Chriſt, where the ſound faith is taught, that there ſpring vp foule hereſies, wicked

ked opinons and abhominable deeds. It falleth out also, that the Gouernours and Paſtors are negligent, and do not caſt them forth, their fault is here rebuked, when he ſaith, *I haue a few things againſt thee, that thou ſuffereſt that vvicked vvoman Iezabel, &c.* But Chriſt layeth no commandement vpon thee to depart out of that companie, neither doth he threaten thee as a man polluted by the open ſinnes of others: but willeth thee to hold faſt to the end the truth, and not to conſent vnto that which is foule, either in doctrine or maners. If (I ſay) he laid no other burthen vpon the reſt of Thyatira, he layeth no other burthen vpon vs, but that we holding the truth, keep our ſelues vnpolluted from ſuch abhominations as are permitted, euen in the Church.

But there is ſome darkeneſſe in theſe words, when he ſaith, *That haue not this learning, neither haue knowne the deepeneſſe of Sathan (as they ſpeake) &c.* The learning which he ſpeaketh of, was the doctrine of that *Iezabel*, that falſe Propheteſſe, which ſhe taught, and whereby ſhe ſeduced ſome to eate of things offered to idols, and to commit fornication: thoſe which reiected it, are ſaid not to haue it. Moreouer, this *Iezabel* which called her ſelfe a Propheteſſe, and the reſt which were the chiefe teachers of that doctrine, boaſted of verie high myſteries and deepe points, reckening them but as dullards, which did not receiue the ſame, and as men of ſo ſhallow capacitie, that they could not reach vnto the deepneſſe of matters. They doubtleſſe, boaſted of a deepneſſe from the ſpirit of God, but the Lord calleth it the deepneſſe of Sathan: and yet ſaith, *as they ſpeake*, euen becauſe they called it a deepneſſe. For ſo ye ſhall find, that when heretiks, or men which come with ſtrange and vaine ſpeculations, if they be not receiued, they ſay it is becauſe of the depth of the diuine matter, which ſuch dull heads cannot reach vnto. But as ye ſee, the Lord doth ſcorne them, and tearmeth it indeed a deepneſſe, but yet the deepneſſe of Sathan. Indeed he is deepe in his kind to deceiue proud lofty minds, which deſpiſe the plaine ſimplicitie of Gods truth, deliuered in the holy Scriptures. And what was the deepneſſe of Sathã in this propheteſſe, to ſeduce to ſuch abhomination? It is not to be doubted, but that the doctrine of the Nicholaitans, the doctrine of *Balaam*, or of this *Iezabel*, was the ſame which thoſe abhominable curſed men held that were crept into the Church, whom Saint *Peter* & Saint *Iude* do ſo paint out, and warne men to take heed of. Ye ſee there were fine wittes among the Corinthes, which could take vpon them to defend the feaſting with idolaters in the idoll Temples, with the meats offred to idols: and though the Apoſtles withſtood them, yet ſome euerie where grew more peruerſe, and increaſed by the helpe of the diuell, euen by his ſuggeſtions, the ſubtill cauils, by which they made, either that eating meates offered to idols, ſeemed lawfull, or the bodily fornication, and ſuch like, for verily all their deepneſſe was, to proue that they were not defiled by their actions in thoſe ſinnes.

This brood continued in the Church, and no doubt in the Valentinians we may ſee what the deepneſſe of Sathan was. For *Ireneus* in his firſt booke and firſt chapter, deſcribeth their maners, and alſo declareth the chiefe reaſons whereby
they

they vttered the deepnesse of Sathan in prouing it lawfull to commit such things. They called themselues (as he reporteth) spirituall, as hauing the perfect knowledge of God. Such in the Church as receiued not their doctrine, they called naturall, and not hauing perfect knowledge. To those than are naturall, they held it of necessitie to saluation, to haue good workes, otherwise vnpossible to be saued: but they themselues as they boasted, being spiritual, they could not (as they said) but be saued, in what actions soeuer they walked: for they held it impossible for that which is spirituall to receiue anie corruption, in or by what workes soeu.r. For proofe they vsed this comparison: that as gold in the mire doth not loose the beautie, but keepeth still the proper nature, the mire doing no harme to the gold: euen so they said, that they in whatsoeuer materiall actions they were conuersant, they were not hurt at all, nor lost their spirituall substance. Hereupon (as *Ireneus* saith) they durst do any thing which is forbidden: they did eate of things offered to idols, making no difference, thinking they were not thereby polluted. And when the Pagans made feasts in honour of their Idols, they were euen of the first that came thither, as he reporteth. Also among other horrible facts, he sheweth of their vncleannesse with women, euen wheresoeuer they lusted, if they could seduce them, to draw them from their husbands: fornication or whoredome could not defile them that had so deepe knowledge, and were become spirituall. This is the deepnesse of Sathan, this is the mysticall diuinitie of that *Iezabel*: carnall men could not, nor cannot vnderstand this learning: these mysteries are aboue the reach of the common sort.

 Now as Sathan laid the foundation of this his deepe diuinitie in the Apostles times, which he afterward did further build vp by the Valentinians and others, so in these last times, so soone as euer the light of the Gospell brake forth, he set it on foot againe by the Anabaptists, Libertines, Family of Loue, and other such monsters: for they boast of such deepnesse of illumined elders, and men deified, that looke whatsoeuer they committed, euen the foulest deeds, yet they sinne not. Many are offended at this day, that such things spring vp with the preaching of the Gospell, and take occasion thereby to slaunder and deface it: but why do they not also condemne the preaching of the Apostles, seeing the holy Scriptures do thus plainely witnesse, that such things followed them? The wicked Papists know right well how it began in the time of the Apostles, and how shortly after the Churches euerie where were grieuously rent and tormented by such monstrous heretikes and most filthie persons, and yet they are not ashamed to obiect it as a most vile reproch against vs, that heretikes do spring vp where the Gospell is preached. But let them consider whom they reproch: euen the holy Churches of old, euen the holy Apostles and the Lord himselfe. We may not take it to be no true Gospell, no right preaching, or no godly Churches, where such horrible and most vile things spring vp, but rather acknowledge and confesse, that it is the same Gospell which is now preached, and the right Catholike Church, which Sathan seeketh to deface, euen as he did in old time.

If

If we thinke the diuell be still like himselfe, why should we not looke for his working and practises against the Gospell to bee the same that they were in olde time? When yee thinke of these things that grew vp in the Churches, and followed the preaching of the Gospell, euen in the times of the blessed Apostles, let it arme you against all the damnable heresies, sects, and schismes, which follow the sincere preaching; and likewise be not seduced nor discouraged, by the blasphemous railings of the Papists, which charge the most holy and heauenly doctrine of the Gospell, to be the seed of all heresies and errors, and tumults. For it is the diuell which soweth all the euill seede, and then setteth them (I meane Papists and Atheists.) a worke, to exclame, as hee did set the heathen a worke in olde time, against Gods truth, and his faithfull people, as if the fault were in the doctrine. This packing of the diuell, many of the Papists do know well enough, and yet are content to gratifie him: for they dare not say the Apostles or their doctrine was the cause of such abhominable things of old. And why should they thinke it the cause now? It is malice, it is malice, which carieth them headlong, let vs stand fast, and despise it.

Now follow the promises to the conquerors, by which we may be encouraged to fight valiantly against the diuell and all his armies: *He that ouercommeth* (saith he) then adding, *and keeping my workes vnto the ende*. The workes of God are holy workes, and here set against the filthy workes of the disciples of that wicked *Iezabel*, which boasted of such deepenesse of knowledge. The diuell labored to draw as many as hee could to follow their workes, whom hee by that false prophetesse of his had seduced: and the Lord promiseth him life, blessednesse, dignity and glory, that shall stand constant in his wayes against them, and against all other euill wayes, euen to the end: for he onely getteth the victory which continueth to the end. If a man be ouercome, though not in the beginning, nor in the middest of his race, but euen towards the latter end, what is he the better that he ranne or fought at all? hath he not lost all his former labour? Let vs therefore take heede, and bee carefull to be stedfast in loue and zeale of the truth to the end. We see many that are but as a morning deaw, or as apples that are blasted so soon as they bee out of the bossome, and so fall downe. Againe we see, that there bee some, that after long time, do wither away and rot, as fruites that hang too long vpon the trees: the warning therefore is very needefull which the Lord giueth in this place.

Then follow the promises to him that ouercommeth, the first in these words, *To him will I giue power ouer nations, and hee shall rule them with a rodde of Iron, and as the vessels of a potter shall they bee broken*. These speeches the holy Ghost vseth to set foorth the rule and power which Christ shall haue ouer nations, by which he shall breake downe all the force of his enemies, and raigne ouer them, Psalme.2. And then that all his chosen which in him and by him get the victory, shall be partakers of his kingdome, and raigne with him: which is meant by these speeches here vttered. The other promise is in these words, *As I receiued of my Father, so will I giue him the morning starre*. Christ in his manhood

hood receiued all things of the Father to communicate with vs: therefore as he is the bright morning ſtar, full of all true and glorious light, ſo all the faithfull in him ſhall be made ſhining ſtarres. Let vs then neuer faint in tribulation for the Goſpell, ſeeing our victory ſhall be with ſo great glory. We are now full of darkneſſe, albeit we haue the Sunne of righteouſneſſe ſhining vpon vs, and giuing vs light: but then all darkneſſe and corruption ſhall be aboliſhed out of vs, and the brightneſſe of God ſhall be vpon vs: therefore he willeth againe, *Let him that hath an eare, heare what the ſpirit ſaith to the Churches.*

THE VIII. SERMON.
CHAP. 3.

1. *And vnto the Angell of the Church which is at Sardis, write, theſe things ſaith he that hath the ſeuen ſpirits of God, and the ſeuen ſtarres, I know thy works: for thou haſt a name that thou liueſt, but thou art dead.*
2. *Be awake, and ſtrengthen the things which remaine, that are ready to die: for I haue not found thy works perfect before God.*
3. *Remember therefore how thou haſt receiued and heard, and hold faſt and repent. If therefore thou wilt not watch, I will come on thee as a theefe, and thou ſhalt not know what hower I will come vpon thee.*
4. *Yet thou haſt a few names in Sardis, which haue not defiled their garments: and they ſhall walke with me in white, for they are worthy.*
5. *He that ouercommeth ſhall be clothed in white aray, and I will not put out his name out of the booke of life, but I wil confeſſe his name before my father, and before his Angels.*
6. *Let him that hath an eare, heare what the Spirit ſaith to the Churches.*

THe fift meſſage, is ſent to the Angell of the Church at Sardis. This Sardis was a very famous city, in which (as writers report) the Kings of Lydia kept their Courts, and in it now the King of Kings had ſet his throne. The entrance of this meſſage, is alſo from the perſon of Chriſt, as, *Thus ſaith hee that hath the ſeuen ſpirites of God, and the ſeuen ſtarres*: that is, he who hath the holy Ghoſt, whoſe manifold gifts he ſent downe vpon the Churches, as he promiſed his Apoſtles, that he would before he aſcended, ſend them the comforter. It is hee which vſeth the miniſtery of men in the building of his Church. The Angell

of

THE REVELATION.

of this Church, and with him the most of his flocke, were in a very weake case touching spirituall life, and needed the quickning of this spirit to put them in mind hereof: he taketh this with some part of the vision, *Thus saith faith he that hath the seuen spirits of God.* Also he that hath the seuen stars in his hand, is that great Lord who buildeth vp his Church by the ministery of men. This was good also for him to consider, that he might remember he had the place of a starre, and indeuour to performe his office.

In the narration he telleth him, *I know thy workes:* but alas how poore were his workes? how poore were the works of the flocke? For here is no commendation giuen vnto him at all. He is dispraised or discommended, he is admonished to a-wake & to repēt, & he is threatned grieuously if he do not amēd, euen with a terrible threatning. Indeed his dispraise is set downe in few words, as thus (*Thou hast a name that thou liuest, but thou art dead:*) But it is a discommendation very great and grieuous: for he was a minister, or ministers of Christ, a shepheard, yea a Christian, rather in some shew, and outward account before men, then in deed and in truth before God: and so were the most of the flocke, as we shall see afterward, but as dead. For when he saith, thou hast a name that thou liuest, what is it, but as if he had sayd, thou hast the roome, and office, and account among the Churches of one that hath receiued the true faith, and so is ingraffed into me, and made partaker of my life, yea of one that is a minister of the same grace of life vnto others, but thou art dead? What a terrible message was this vnto him from heauen? and how farre doth he differ from the Angell of the Church of Smyrna? and with him how farre did the flocke differ from those Smyrneans? For as it was a singular comfort vnto him to haue his ministery so fully approued, and his sheepe so praised by the Lord from his glory, that hee reprehended nothing at all in him and them: so must it needs strike this man as a terrible thunderbolt, that he is so deeply disallowed, as that no one thing is commended in him. These then may stand as contraries. If all the ministers of Christ and all Churches at that time in the world had giuen such sentence against him, it could not haue had such force, nor haue strook so deep, as comming from Christ in his glory. For we see how men can flatter themselues, and take it they haue great wrong offered them, when any thing is vttered against them by men, which is sharpe, though it be from the manifest word of God, such is mans hypocrisie. Yea we shall see them rouse vp themselues as if they were euen of the best and most faithfull ministers of Christ, being nothing lesse, and euen enter into comparison with the best. But here is no gaynsaying, here is no colouring, he knoweth him throughly, both within and without, which sendeth him this message, and telleth him what he is. No doubt this was a great mercy shewed to this

Lord knoweth his works, so in whatsoeuer, either in his heart, or in his outward deeds, they swarue from the holy word, he shall heare the same at the day of iudgment, that this man had sent vnto him, I meane according to the measure of his fault. It were best for vs indeed to heare it now, and repent euen from the bottome of our harts, but as I say, we are all so full of hypocrisie, we can set such a face & so bolster out all matters, that although our works testifie against vs that we be far worse then this man was, yet we beare our selues in hand that all is well. This man did professe the sound doctrine of the Gospell, he taught the people in some sort the way of God, his life was not notoriously euill or spotted with grosse vices. For if any of these had bene wanting, how could it here haue beene omitted? how should he haue had a name that he liued? or how could he haue beene suffered to continue in his place? For shall we think that the Churches euen then exercised no discipline to cleanse the ministerie? It is a cleare case then, that if a man that doth teach, and that cannot be detected of grosse sinnes, but is thought to liue an vpright life, is yet neuerthelesse dead before God, if he haue not the power of the spirit of God in him to do all duties of a sincere zeale and loue of Christ, and not for an outward order & fashion. Then those shall lesse escape iudgement that haue not so much as an outward shew of goodnesse: that be so farre from hauing a name among true Christians that they liue, that euen the ignorantest people can rightly discerne and say, their works be not the works of true ministers of Christ: we see they be whoremongers, drunkards, quarellers, common dicers, and such like.

The Lord Iesus Christ hauing thus layd open vnto him his estate, and so the estate of the people there, now giueth him admonition and warning, & them also to repent. *Be awake* (saith he) *and strengthen the things that remaine which are readie to die*. We see how our Sauiour and his Apostles do teach vs in many places, that it behooueth all Christians to watch, for we are in the midst of cruell enemies which seeke to spoile vs of all heauenly treasures, and to deuour vs. And of all other, the pastors and guides of the Church are called vpon for the same thing, I say to be watchfull. They be after a peculiar sort called watchmen: And this shepheard was fallen fast a sleepe, yea euen into a dead sleepe, and into such securitie that the deuils had almost stript his soule, and bereft him and the greatest part of his flocke, of all graces and life; and that little which was left, was euen dying and withering away. O most miserable condition, could such a man get the place of a Bishop in the primitiue Church? Out of doubt this man had great gifts in him both of knowledge & zeale, at the least of zeale in shew, when he was first chosen into the place, to be the pastor in that Church: for the Churches at that time, when they ordained pastors, had either some Apostle, or Euangelist, or some excellent men to direct them, and so farre as they could deeme, they chose the very best & fittest men. Whereby we may learne not to wonder, when some men of great note, become euen as nothing, and fall almost quite away. Do ye not see an example in this man? we may indeed iudge it most likely he did repent, and was saued: for a man may thinke this message from heauen would awake him; but how neare

the

THE REVELATION. 85

the pits brinke was he before this message was sent? He was euen as the lampe where the oyle is quite spent, sauing a maruellous little in the wicke, which doth (as we speake) winke, and winke, and is ready to go forth, except a new supply of oyle be poured in. Christ doth not shew such fauour vnto euery one, as to send vnto them, and to warne them in this sort from heauen, & therefore many decline, & fall quite away. Indeed there be other speciall meanes, as sharpe affictions whereby he rouseth some out of their sleepe: and some are quickned by admonition & rebuke from godly men. But yet let men beware how they decline neuer so little and continue therein: for it is not in their owne power to recouer themselues, & all that fall do not rise againe. Here the question may be moued, whether this bee spoken of the Angell of this Church alone, or together with his flocke, as being both in one case.

I haue already noted vnto yee, that the state of euery Church is set forth vnder their pastor: for the sheepe follow their shepheard. If he be full of graces, and of the power of the spirit, the sheepe are well fed, and are in good case. If he be barren and dead, they starue also and pine away. So in this Church a few excepted (as ye may see verse. 4.) they were in such a dead sleepe, that the little which remained in them, was euen ready to die. When he is willed therefore to bee awake and to strengthen the things which are ready to die, it is not meant that he should looke to himselfe alone, but as the duty of a shepheard requireth, he is willed to looke among his sheepe. For while he was thus fallen into such a dead sleepe, the sheepe were scattered, the wolfe was broke in among them, & had made hauocke. Some went astray, some it is like were deuoured of the wolfe, many were so bitten and torne, that scarse any life remained in them, the little which remained, was ready to die. If he do not now awake and bestirre him, to gather that which is gone astray, to heale that which is brused and broken, and to support and comfort the feeble, many are euen at the point to be lost. Thus much this admonition giuen vnto him importeth.

Might not the Angell of this Church haue a very heauy heart to heare that so many were endangered, and so extremely, through his security? and that a godly Church was thus fallen into decay? It is not in vaine (which now could not but enter into his mind) that the Lord God threatneth he will require the bloud of his sheep which perish through negligence, at the hands of the shepheard. If the watchman be asleepe when he should giue warning, and the sword come and deuour, it shall be vpon his head. They be in bad case then that haue such watchmen and such shepheards, but the shepheards and watchmen themselues be in worse estates for their reckening will be greater, the bloud of all the rest which perish, shal be required at their hands.

The clause which followeth, doth expresse the whole matter further and more plainely: for it doth as it were argue the causes by the effects. *I haue not* (saith he) *found thy workes perfect before God.* This imperfection of his works, shewerh the imperfection of that in him, from whence good workes do spring: that is, of his faith, and so of his loue, of his zeale, of his care, and of all other spirituall graces, for from these inward graces, doe all good workes spring. What were then the workes which were not full in him? All workes, euen the works which euery Christian is bound vnto, and the workes of his ministery, the workes of a shepheard in his flocke. He did preach (for it were a most absurd thing to thinke otherwise of a pastor in those times) he did admonish and exhort men, he did rebuke, how else could he haue a name that he liued? But how weakely, and how coldly was all this done? not of any feruent loue, but euen for fashion sake. He did build, but how vnperfect was his building? How farre oft were the most in his flocke, from that which should be in true Christians? Alas being fallen into a dead sleepe, what good and perfect worke could he make among them? That he did was euen much like to a dreame. But it will be said, whose workes be full and perfect before God? is there any man that can haue that praise? I answer, that all mens works are indeed imperfect before God; but he speaketh here of a further matter then of the common imperfections which are in the best: for where there is a soundnesse and sincerity of hart, the blemishes and imperfections are not imputed, though they be many: but where that is wanting, though the works may outwardly seeme before men to be many and good, yet before God it is farre otherwise: for God iudgeth mens works to be perfect, not by the number or greatnesse in outward shew, but according to the inward affections of the hart.

Now followeth another admonition, *Remember therefore how thou hast receiued and heard, and hold fast and repent*. It is a great matter which is here spoken. For this pastour and this Church was taught and gathered by some one of those chiefe builders. They came with great power of the holy Ghost, and after an heauenly manner vttered and declared the diuine mysteries. And for this cause they are willed here to call to mind how they had receiued and heard, and to hold fast, and repent. We are then taught in this place, that when we decline, or decay in the holy religion, it is by forgetting, and letting slip out of our minds, the doctrine and the graces which we haue heard and receiued in former times. There bee many things that delight men, and their memory doth hold and keepe them so fast, that they can neuer forget them if they would neuer so faine. The mysteries of God though the glory of them be such as that our minds be euen rauished for the time with ioy at the hearing and receiuing of them, yet how suddenly do they slip away from vs, as if there had neuer bene any such thing. This commeth partly from our owne nature, and partly from the diuell. Vaine and corrupt things do agree with our vaine corrupt nature, and the diuell doth eftsoones suggest them: and they bee very light to carrie with vs, and sticke fast. The heauenly things are so contrary to our affections, that for them to abide in vs is euen like fire and water put together, they be so heauy, that we waxe weary, and the diuell doth what he can continually to quench the light of them in our harts, and so vtterly to remoue them, as that there may not so much as any print of them be left behind. How dangerous a thing it is to be so loose and rechlesse hearers, not onely this example, but also that terrible threatning, Hebr. 2. least at any time ye runne out, may teach vs. And now it is to be obserued, that in calling vpon him to repent, he is willed to cal those former

mer things to mind, and to hold them. Is this the way of repentance? then many go awrie, which haue long since heard and receiued the mysteries of the Gospell, and do heare still, but not delighted, but with some new matter. These are like the mill which is turned about dayly, but yet with new water: for the other passeth away. The Lord willeth vs to keepe that which we heare, and let it be renued daily in vs, and so it shall haue power: for it is not the hearing, the bare vnderstanding, or delight for the present time, but the power of the doctrine remaining in vs which shall saue our soules. Therefore, although this sentence was spoken but to the Angell of one Church, yet let vs keepe it in mind: *Remember how thou hast receiued, and heard, and hold fast, and repent.*

Here followeth now the threatning, if hee shall not repent. It is a maruellous seuere threatning and denouncing of wrath: *If thou wilt not watch, I will come on thee as a theefe, and thou shalt not know what hower I will come vpon thee.* If the good man of the house did know (sayth our Sauiour in another place) what hower the theefe would come, he would watch, and not suffer his house to be broken vp. But the theefe watcheth his time when men be saftest on sleepe, breaketh in, killeth, and stealeth. After this manner the Lord threatneth here, that he will come vpon this Angell of the Church at Sardis, and vpon so many of the flocke as were in his case, if they continue sleeping. Yea and hee will be sure to find them sleeping: for he saith, thou shalt not know at what hower I will come on thee. But for what will hee come vpon him thus suddenly and vnwares? surely euen to cut him off in iudgement.

This doth shew how much Christ Iesus is displeased with men that from care and zeale in the trueth, grow into a drousie security, and so bring ruine vpon his Church. And it is a notable place against those which doe so mocke and dallie, and which can so pleasantly sooth themselues in all irreligious and worldly prophanenesse vpon hope of a good end. I, saith he (in the iolity of his sinne, in which hee is fallen into a sleepe) doe not care so I may haue time to call for mercy and pardon at the last when I am sicke, and perceiue I shall die. What should a man trouble himselfe that way vntill he be ready to die? repentance shall saue a man at all times. Marke here ô foolish man how Christ threatneth that he will come vpon thee like a theefe, euen while thou art a sleepe, and thou shalt not know of his comming. Art thou sure he will wake thee when he commeth? (for none but he can wake thee out of this dead sleepe.) Nay he threatneth to come suddenly vpon thee, when thou shalt be still a sleepe, and shall not know. Is this meant onely of sudden death? We see God cutteth downe euer anon one or other in all places suddenly: which might be a warning vnto euery one of vs to watch and to be in a readinesse. For why may it not come vpon any one of vs as well? But what if a man be so sicke, and that many dayes, that he seeme to be in daunger of death, is he by and by awaked out of his sleepe in sinne? nay we see many sicke, which looke not for death, and on a sudden their vnderstanding is taken away, and they are cut off. And there be also that haue long time and looke for death, but are they euer the better, is it in their owne power to awake, to beleeue, and to repent? God giueth

G 4 these

these gifts, and is it like such men shall haue them which prouoke him to wrath? let not men trust to this: for the Prophet in the name of the Lord willeth to turne vnto him, and not to put off from day to day, because his wrath shal come suddenly, and in time of vengeance he will destroy thee. If we desire the Lord to giue vs warning, and not to come vpon vs suddenly, as he here threatneth, because we are so full of imperfections, yet it may not be a meane to hold vs in security, but wee must as ye see at all times watch. These bee hard things which are spoken against the pastor of this Church together with his flocke: therefore here followeth some mitigation, not towards him, nor towards the multitude of that Church which were in the like case that he was: but towards those which had kept the faith, and the right way without declining. Yet (saith he) *Thou hast a few names at Sardis which haue not defiled their garments: and therefore they shall walke with me in white, for they are worthy*: This not defiling of their garments is but a borrowed speech, and he meaneth that they had not polluted and spotted their soules and bodies with the filthy pollutions of sinne. But alas hee saith there were but a few of these, for the pollutions were spread ouer the body of the Church: as it cannot otherwise be where the pastors and guides bee so dead in their ministerie. This is a great comfort, that where there is such deadnes in the shepherd, yet the lord by some meanes or other preserueth some. There be some godly faithfull men scattered among the multitude: and the Lord is so farre here from threatning them, as defiled with the pollutions of such as they were mixed among, and with whom they did communicate, that he promiseth them life and glory, for that is meant by this that he saith, they shall walke with me in white garments. And that he sayth they are worthy, it is not meant that men can merite eternall life by their workes: but their worthinesse is to be taken of a fitnesse, in that they were iustified in Christ as their sincere godly life did declare.

Also hee promiseth in the words following generally vnto euery one which ouercommeth, the same thing which before, though not in the same words. First, that whosoeuer ouercommeth, he shall be clothed in white garments. Then this is not a thing peculiar vnto those few names in Sardis, which had not defiled their garments: all that by faith are armed with the power of Christ, and so get the victory ouer the diueil, shall be couered ouer with innocency, with heauenly glory and shining brightnesse, euen as it were with a large and precious garment. These garments do most fitly represent that righteousnesse wherwith all the blessed ones shall stand clothed and couered before God: and it is not inherent righteousnesse, it is not from themselues, but giuen vnto them from another, and put vpon them: Blessed are they whose iniquities are forgiuen, and whose sinnes are couered: blessed is the man to whom the Lord imputeth not his sinne, Psalm. 32. Then blessed are all those which haue these white garments put vpon thē, for by them their sins are couered. Woe be to all those that shall bee found naked and vncouered, not hauing these white garments, which stand to be iustified not by free forgiuenes of sins, or by free imputation of Christs righteousnes through faith, but by their own workes: for albeit their deeds seeme to be many, and to be very glorious, yet before

THE REVELATION.

fore God they shall be found nothing else, but euen as a polluted and defiled garment, yea euen like dung.

It is added further, *Neither will I put out his name out of the booke of life; but I will confesse his name before my father, and before his Angels.* These be verie great & high promises: the Lord is said to haue a booke of life, in which all their names are written that shall be saued. It is indeed but a borrowed speech from the common vse among men, applyed vnto our capacitie: for men cannot keepe in their memorie a great multitude of names, and therefore they vse to write the names in a booke: the Lord God needeth no such helpe, but yet to shew vnto vs the stablenesse of this election, and that no one of them whom he hath chosen can be forgotten, it is said, he hath written vp and registred their names in a booke.

But the saying here vsed, may seeme to be superfluous (*I will not put out his name out of the booke of life*) seeing Gods decree is vnchangeable, and no one of Gods elect, whose names are written vp, can be blotted out: when as I say, it is not possible that any one should haue his name blotted, why or how is it said, *Neither will I blot his name out of the booke of life?* Herein also we must learne, that our Sauiour applyeth his speech according vnto that which seemeth to be so in our eyes: for when a man is an earnest professor of the Gospell, and his life to mans sight, framed according to the same, he seemeth to haue his name written in the booke of life, and he for his part taketh it to be so: now when he falleth away, becommeth an heretike, denyeth the truth in time of persecution, or falleth into wicked life, and so continueth to the end, though his name were neuer written, yet he is said to be blotted out, because it is made manifest vnto men, that he is not of that companie of which he seemed to be. They went out from vs (saith S. *Iohn*) because they were not of vs, for if they had bene of vs, they should haue continued with vs. But this is to manifest that all are not of vs, 1. Iohn 2.

In the Church of Sardis, through that deadnesse of their Bishop, a great number that before time seemed to be excellent Christians, and to haue their names written in the booke of life, had defiled their garments, and were fallen away: and that is the cause why this promise is made to the rest, *I will not put out his name out of the booke of life.* And then the cotrary to the putting out, is promised in these words: *But I will confesse his name before my father, and before his Angels.* Then not to be put out, is to be confessed by Christ: and to be denyed by Christ before his father and the Angels, is to be blotted out. It is no small matter to be accounted of, to haue Christ Iesus in his glorie confesse vs before his father, and before the holy Angels: and if we walke worthie of the Gospell, and confesse him indeed before men, he hath promised that he will do it: and so on the contrarie part, what can be more grieuous, then to be denied of him at that day? Depart from me ye workers of iniquitie, I know ye not. Though they haue cast forth diuels, and done other miracles in his name, and so were taken to be registred vp in the booke of life: yet being such as haue defiled their garments, euen workers of iniquitie, Christ will not confesse them, but blot out their names. Therefore let vs which professe the holy Gospel, study to walk in purenesse of life, that Christ may acknowledge vs to

be

be his true disciples. Now followeth the generall conclusion.

Let him that hath an eare, heare what the spirit saith to the Churches. The holy Ghost speaketh nothing in vaine, and therefore we must heare, not what he hath said to one Church, or some things that he saith, but whatsoeuer he saith vnto all the Churches. We see what he hath said to this Church, and what a pitifull case it was in: it ought to warne all the Pastors and their flockes. Would to God there were not at this day, more then one for euerie seuen, both of the pastors & flocks, in as bad a case, or worse then is here described. This man made some shew, he taught the Gospell, otherwise being in that office, how shold he haue a name that he liued? He was not an open grosse sinner. How farre be many from so much? The only comfort and hope is, that the Lord hath a few names among vs, that haue not defiled their garments, and for their sakes doth take pitie vpon vs.

THE IX. SERMON.

7. *And vnto the Angell of the Church which is at Philadelphia, write, these things saith he which is holy and true, which hath the key of Dauid, which openeth, and no man shutteth, which shutteth and no man openeth.*

8. *I know thy workes: behold, I haue set before thee an open doore, and no man can shut it: for thou hast a litle strength, and hast kept my word, and hast not denied my name.*

9. *Behold, I will make them of the Synagogue of Sathan, which call themselues Iewes, and are not, but do lye: behold, I say, I will make them come and worship before thy feete, and shall know that I haue loued thee.*

10. *Because thou hast kept the word of my patience, therefore I will keepe thee from the houre of temptation, which will come vpon all the world, to trie them that dwell vpon the earth.*

11. *Behold, I come shortly, hold that which thou hast, that no mã take thy crowne.*

12. *Him that ouercommeth will I make a pillar in the Temple of my God, and he shall go no more out: and I will write vpon him the name of my God, and the name of the citie of my God, the new Ierusalem, which commeth downe out of heauen from my God, and I will write vpon him my new name.*

13. *Let him that hath an eare, heare what the spirit saith to the Churches.*

THe sixt Epistle is sent to the Angell of the Church of Philadelphia: this Philadelphia was a citie of Lydia, not very famous, nor yet of the meanest. The Angell and Church at Smyrna are highly commended, as we saw in the former chapter, and nothing reprehended: so also here is commendation giuen to

this

this Angell and Church of Philadelphia: goodly promises and comfortable are made vnto them, and nothing reproued, vnlesse we take this as some kind of reproofe, that he saith, *Thou hast a litle strength.* Here was then a worthy Pastor, & a worthy flocke, as we shall see by the particulars.

Here is the Exordium also taken from the person of him frō whom the message is sent: *These things saith he that is holy and true, which hath the key of Dauid, &c.* These things are peculiar only to the glorious son of God, howsoeuer the first of them may seeme to be common. For the Angels in heauen be holy, and no spot of impurity in them at all; they be true, euen without any errour or falshood: but yet not as Christ, for he is not only holy and true in himselfe, but also the fountaine of holinesse & truth vnto all others. Then next he doth mention that which is peculiarly ascribed vnto him euerie where, as namely, the soueraigne authority, the dominion and gouernment ouer the whole house of God, which is committed vnto him. The gouernment is laid vpō his shoulder, the Father hath committed all power into the hands of his Son. He setteth forth this power by the keyes which are to open and to shut: euen as the steward and gouernour ouer an houshold hath the keyes committed vnto him. He calleth them the keyes of *Dauid*, to shew that this dominion and rule is so fit vpon the throne of *Dauid*, and to raigne ouer the house of *Iaakob*, that is, the Church and house of God, for euer & for euer. He said in the first chapter, *I haue the keyes of hell and of death:* for he hath indeed not only the soueraigntie ouer the Church, to dispose and order all things therein, but also he hath all the infernall powers, and all enemies vnder him, so that none of them can hurt or hinder the blessednes of his elect, no not euen of the least of thē. He being then holy and true, and of this full power and dominion ouer all, let vs not doubt to trust vnto him, and to shew our selues euerie way dutifully subiect.

None can come to be of the family of God, but such as he openeth the doore vnto to take them in: all and euerie one of those that be of the same are so kept in by him, that not one of them can be drawne out. All the hypocrites, all the vnbeleeuers, all the workers of iniquity, euen all the vncleane, will he cast forth, and they shall find no helpe to get in: for, *he shutteth and none openeth.* The Pope of Rome challengeth this power, as if Christ had granted it to him, that he may open and shut, that he may saue and destroy, lift vp to heauen and cast downe to hell at his pleasure. He challengeth indeed these keyes at the second hand, as first giuen to *Peter*, to whom Christ said, *To thee I giue the keyes of the kingdome of heauen:* and so from *Peter*, he saith they come to him by succession. But ye see here how the Pope lyeth: Christ saith, he hath them still himselfe, and exerciseth in his owne person the power of them. *Peter* indeed and the other Apostles had power giuen them to bind and to loose, as Ministers vnder him, by whom he wrought: and the power of the keyes is committed vnto all the Ministers of the Gospell, to bind and to loose, to open and to shut, to thrust out, and to receiue in: but not at their pleasure, or for mony, as the Pope vseth: but as ministers to pronounce and to exercise Christs word: and all their doings herein are so far ratified, onely as they agree with his truth. For if anie take vpon them to receiue in those, whom his word pro-

pronounceth to be shut out, what are they the better for retaining a roome and a place in the visible Church vpon earth? here is one holdeth the keyes which will thrust them forth, and shut them out at the last. And againe, if by wicked prelates, any man contrary to the truth be cast forth, what is he the worse? there is one openeth, and none can shut, which will receiue him in. If any had the power of the keyes (as the man of sinne, the great Antichrist boasteth) how could it be said, I open and none shutteth, I shut, and none openeth? Here is the onely gouernour ouer the house of *Dauid*, which is neuer absent from his Church, and therefore needeth no vicar.

Now we come to the narration, *I know thy workes*: That the Lord doth know his workes and approue them, as appeareth by this, that he blameth nothing in him, it might giue great encouragement to proceede. For would not any of vs be glad to heare from the Lord, that the things which we do are pleasing in his sight? He knoweth all our workes, and will bring them all vnto iudgement, let vs therefore endeuour with all our might to serue and please him.

Then he saith: *Behold I haue set before thee an open dore, and no man can shut it*: This doth accord with that he said, I open and none shutteth: he had made a passage for the Gospell, to spreade & to take place in conuerting men vnto God, and no force of enemies could withstand the same. S. *Paul* vseth the same speech. 1.Cor.16. A notable point for vs to consider, that we may behold the worke of God in all times and places. We see how the world is bent against the Gospell, what power Sathan doth raise vp to persecute & expell it: we see also how meane in outward shew the ministers of Christ are, and yet where he hath any elect and chosen people to be called home into his family, he openeth the dore for them to enter, he giueth a passage to his heauenly word: the diuell with all his power, euen with all the bands of his souldiers, strugling and laboring to shut it, are not able. Here we may learne to know how it commeth, that the Gospell is remoued from some places, and continueth in other some. Christ openeth the dore, & none can shut it: he shutteth and none can open it: where they be despisers and abuse his Gospell, it shall be easily remoued: where his kindnesse is embraced, the truth loued, and the fruites therof brought forth, the enemies do rage and fret, they deuise and practise all the waies they can, and yet cannot shut the dore.

Let vs thinke vpon this, *Behold I haue set before thee an open deore, which none can shut*, and labour with all our might to serue Christ while wee feele it is so. Againe, let vs take heede we prouoke him not by our sinnes to shut vp the dore: for as none can take the Gospell away from vs, so long as we deale well with it, and please him, so if he be offended and will remoue it, who shall be able to giue it vnto vs?

Enemies there are very many of all sorts in this our land, which labor to banish the Gospell & which indeed prouoke the Lord to depart away, & (as he threatned the Church at Ephesus) to remoue the candlestick: but if those that fauor the Gospell euery where, would euen stir vp the graces of God in them, and let their loue spring afresh, euen to the glorie of God, and to the magnifying of his truth, those enemies

THE REVELATION.   93

nemies should neuer be able to preuaile against vs: but he that hath opened the doore, will open it still wider, and hold it open, let them do all what they can. If the Lord shut vp the doore, the sinnes of Gospellers do prouoke him to do that: for he will neur to gratifie the vngodly prophane enemies, so plague those which sincerely embrace the truth, and obey him. Would to God this might be well considered in time: for the sinnes of those which professe themselues Gospellers (euen in multitudes of thē) are growne vnto an exceeding height. Shal such as wil be Gospellers condemne and reproch the way of godlinesse? Here is our feare: here is our danger.

If euer any thing ouerthrow, or bring heauy plagues vpō this land, it is this, that many abuse the Gospel vnto their couetousnesse, ambition, & other corrupt lusts. Will the Lord suffer the heauenly doctrine to be made a cloake for sinne, and not be reuenged? Manie do depend vpon the courage and strength of men and munition both by sea and land: but the safetie of our land hath hitherto stood in this, that Christ set a dore wide open, and hath giuen passage to his Gospell, which as yet none could shut: and so long as he holdeth this doore open, so long our safetie shall continue. Whereupon it followeth, that as they be the greatest procurers of Gods wrath to be powred forth vpon vs, which vnder some kind of professing the truth, abuse, prophane, & disgrace it: so they on the contrarie, are the greatest pillars of our peace, which with thankfull hearts embrace the Gospell, euen in such vprightnesse & sinceritie, that they do glorifie God in bringing forth the worthie fruits thereof. Thou desirest to bring some defence to thy country, thou hearest of valiant warriers both by sea & land, in whom great trust is reposed: these may be ouerthrowne when God taketh displeasure: shew thy sincere godlinesse of heart, be faithfull in thy seruice vnto Christ, in magnifying & honoring euery way to the vttermost of thy power, his holy and pure religion, and thou doest more then anie of them. An armie of an hundred thousand of the most valiant Captaines and souldiers in the land are not of so sure defence, as tenne thousand sincere Christians, which with feruent zeale of Gods honour embrace his truth, worship & call vpō him, shewing forth their faith by their holy conuersation, in all the workes of charitie. For these retaine Christ the king of glory still holding open the doore: whose mightie power shall protect vs. If it rise in thy mind, where shall ten thousand such be found? do thy best to adde one to that number thy selfe: and God may blesse thine example to draw on others also.

The next words in the text do confirme this, when he saith to the Angel of this Church, *Thou hast a litle strength, and hast kept my word, and hast not denyed my name.* This Pastor & his flocke stood soundly & vprightly in the faith in the open profession and obedience of Christs holy word: for the keeping of the word was not in word alone (for which they should neuer be praised) but in deed also & in truth. The kingdome of God is not in words but in power: and not euery one that saith, Lord, Lord, shall enter into the kingdome of heauen (saith our Sauiour) but he that doth the will of my father which is in heauen. They standing thus, none can shut the doore which Christ had set opē before them. He saith to this Angell, thou
hast

hast a litle strength. He stood with his litle strength, and did great things, wherein we may behold the maruellous wisedome of God, that by weake instruments would triumph ouer Sathan and all his power. No doubt it is written for our comfort, that when we feele our selus weake, and that we haue but a litle strength, and see great and terrible power of the diuell and the world bent against vs, we should not be dismayed. For if our faith and loue be in sinceritie, though but as a graine of mustard seed, let vs not cease to stay vpon Christ, and continue faithfull in his seruice, we shall vndoubtedly get the the victorie. For when great things are done by feeble instruments, by weake means, the power of God doth more gloriously shine forth. If the instruments be glorious and mightie in shew, mens eyes are turned vnto them, and they often stand in the way to shadow the glorie of the Lord. God giueth exceeding great gifts of learning, of knowledge, and courage vnto such as he raiseth vp to encounter the suttle aduersaries: but neuerthelesse ye shall euer see some great learned men in all knowledge which he passeth by, litle or no good comming to the Church by them, & doth very great things by manie men of lesse learning: he is maruellous in all his wayes. It is certaine, that lesse gifts, and not godly simplicitie, make vnfit: and the greater learning where it puffeth vp, hath not the blessing of God: but employ that litle which thou hast receiued with and vpright and good heart to the glorie of Christ, & he will blesse it exceedinglie. Be faithfull and humble before him, and he wil make thy litle strength (as it is here called) do great things in the aduancement of the Gospel, I meane to the comfort of Gods people. If such as be exceedingly learned (and haue not learned true humilitie) despise thee, thou art yet more blessed then they, thou hast greater vse of thy learning then they: for spirituall gifts serue not for ostentation, or for the glorie of the men which haue them, but for the edification and good of Gods people. If thou hast but a litle strength, as it is said to the Angell of this Church, and doest imploy it well, thy praise is great. Thus farre touching the commendation giuen to this shepheard and his flocke, now follow the promises that Christ maketh vnto them.

The first is vttered in these words: *Behold, I vvill make them of the Synagogue of Sathan, vvhich call themselues Iewes & are not, but ao lye: behold, I say, I wil make the come & worship before thy feet, & shal know that I haue loued thee.* The pastors & teachers, & the Christians in this Church were so sincere & constant in the holy faith and feare of the Lord, shewing forth their godly deeds, that he promiseth not onely to hold open the doore to let in some that were yet without; but also euen of those that were the most bitter enemies, that is, of the vnbeleeuing Iewes: for of all others the Iewes did most wickedly raile vpon & blaspheme Christ, condemne his Gospell, and persecute the Saints of God. They gloried much that they were Iewes, that is, the children of *Abraham*, the chosen people, & the true Church of God, which worshipped him according to his law deliuered vnto the by *Moses*. They said they were *Moses* disciples: but the Lord saith they lie, they be no true Iewes, they be not his Church, but are indeed the Synagogue of Sathan. That he saith, these shall come and worship before his feet, it is not meant that they should

THE REVELATION. 95

come hypocritically, nor compelled by any force against their wils, but indeed with conuerted harts vnto the Lord. As *Saul* of a great persecutor and wolfe, was conuerted & became a most excellēt shepheard: so these of hatefull enemies, should be made friends, and members of the Church.

Here may we note diuers things: as first, in what lamentable state the Iewes are at this day. They take themselues to be the only people whom God loueth, and ye see though they imbrace the writings of *Moses* and the Prophets which they vnderstand not, yet because they reiect Christ and his Gospell, they are indeed become the sinagogue of Sathan. What matter is it what they haue bin of old? They are to be pittied and prayed for: they be the kinsemen of our Sauiour Christ according to the flesh, the Lord take pittie vpon them, and draw them out of the iawes of Sathan. Then that the doore was opened at Philadelphia vnto some of these, it may put vs in mind of that precept which Saint *Paul* giueth, 2. Timoth. 2. vers. 25. In meeknesse to instruct the gainesayers, waiting when God will turne their harts: for he often suffereth sundrie of his chosen to erre and go astray, to hate and raile vpon the truth, and vpon those which professe it, whome afterward he bringth home, whereby the riches of his grace are manifested. There bee euermore some hypocrites in the Church, and some which beleue but for a time: and it is a grieuous thing to the Pastours and teachers when they see them fall away, especially if they haue bene such as haue bene of account for their forwardnesse. But this is as great a comfort, that where the teachers continue their diligent labours, and walke in all godly simplicitie, the Lord doth open the dore, and bring in euen as it were to supplie the places of those that fall away, euen of their deadly enemies, and such as there seemed to be scarce any hope of, that euer they should be turned to the Lord. The Christian people do helpe forward this blessed worke much, if they walke according to the holy rules of the word: for Christ saith: *Let your light so shine before men, that they may see your good workes, and glorifie your father which is in heauen*. They which know not the word (as Saint *Peter* speaketh) are very much moued where they behold all godly vertues in them which professe it, and they will say, it is a good religion: but where they see euill workes proceed from those that professe the Gospell, and especially in those which preach it, this driueth them further off, & openeth their mouth to speake against the heauenly doctrine of God. As he then is blessed which is a meane by his true faith and godlinesse to conuert soules, and to magnifie the holy religion: so is he accursed which layeth a stumbling blocke before the blind, whereby they fall, and which causeth the glorious name of the Lord to be blasphemed.

The Papists at this day do boast that they be the onely true Catholikes, as these Iewes did, but if we examine their doctrine and worship by the holy word of God, which is the only touch-stone of all truth, all (that are not starke blind) may see it is the doctrine and worship of diuels which they hold and maintaine, euen the doctrine and worship of the great Antichrist. They be bitter enemies against all that professe the Gospell. If we would haue them conuerted, this is the way, euen to follow the example of the Angell and Church of Philadelphia, that is,

hold

SERMONS VPON

hold the faith constantly, and bring forth all the good fruits thereof. But as our Sauiour saith, wo to the world because of offences, of necessitie it is that offences do come, but wo to the man by whom the offence doth come: so wo to the Iew, wo to the Turke, wo to the Papists, because many which professe the Gospell, liue wickedly and lay stumbling blockes and offences which driue them backe: and wo to those, euen to those Gospellers, which lay those stumbling blockes in their way: their burthen shall be great in the day of the Lord.

That the Lord saith he would make them of the Sinagogue of Sathan to come & worship before the feet of this Angell, it sheweth their vnfained conuersion: for so long as they tooke the Lord Iesus to be a seducer, and all that beleeued in him to be but heretikes, and children of *Belial*, so long I say, they would neuer be brought to worship at their feet, nor be taught of them, as of true teachers, which preached the faith of Christ. Neither could it euer enter into their thought, that the Lord God loued them, so long as they thinke that they preach heresies and false doctrines, euen blasphemies against God: but he saith here, *They shall know that I loue thee.* Then should they know that the truth was taught in that Church, and God there truly worshipped, for else how could they know that the Lord loued them? The Ministers of the Gospell, and all true Christian people, when they be hated, despised, and railed vpon by the blind world, euen as if they were but scumme and drosse, let them remember this, that standing fast in the way of the truth, and honouring the Lord, as it is written, he will honour them: for he will make euen the enemies to know that he loueth them. And then there followeth a reuerence: for where men perceiue that God hath set his loue, they cannot but giue regard. Doubtlesse the Lord doth make it appeare vnto men, whom he liketh, and whom he misliketh: indeed it cannot be knowne by riches or such like things, but he powreth contempt vpon rich and honorable which are euil, so that their memoriall doth stinke: and he maketh the verie name sweete of those which feare him, euen as the sweet sauour of a precious ointment.

The Prophets in the dayes that they liued in were despised and persecuted: but in the ages following honoured both of good and bad: the Scribes and Pharisies did garnish their sepulchers, Math. 23. The like may be said of the holy Apostles and blessed Martyrs: their fame is precious, and shall be to the last day: for it is knowne God loued them.

The Papists which seeke all corners to find somewhat that may colour and hide their vngodly sacriledge, in giuing diuine worship and adoration vnto creatures, lay hold of this place: for to worship before the feete of this Angell, they will needs haue to be, to worship this Angell, this Pastor of the Church at Philadelphia. All men may see that this is a weake argument to proue such a matter: for who doth not know that men come and worship before the feete of Christs Ministers in the assemblies, and yet worship not them, but God onely? Although this were enough to answere such a slender cauill of theirs in defence of this that Christ speaketh to Sathan, Math. 4. *Thou shalt worship the Lord thy God, and him onely shalt thou serue:* yet there is a further answer: and that is, that the word is vsed

sed in the holy Scriptures indifferently for diuine worship, and for ciuill worship. If the Lord said here, I will make them of the sinagogue of Sathan, come & worship before thy feete, that is, I will make them come and worship thee: yet will it make nothing for the Popish worshipping of creatures, seeing it is then but that ciuill bowing of the body which is done vnto Princes, and reuerend persons.

The other promise which is made vnto this Angell and his Church, is in these words, *Because thou hast kept the word of my patience, therefore I vvill keepe thee from the houre of temptation, which vvil come vpon all the vvorld, to trie them that dwell vpon the earth*. It doth appeare by the first words of this sentence, that the Angell and Church at Philadelphia, had endured troubles and afflictions for the Gospell, for he saith thou hast kept the word of my patience. This commendation could not be giuen, but where patience was shewed in suffering for the truth, and the constant holding of the same: and because they kept the word, and would not by any trouble or danger be driuen from it, the Lord doth promise he would keepe them from being ouercome in the time of temptation which was to come vpon the world. Sathan being in extreame fury desired to tempt, and the Lord for the triall of the inhabitants of the earth giueth him scope. He raiseth vp subtle and pestilent heretikes to seduce and to poyson such as had receiued the liuely word: he raiseth vp also cruel tyrants to persecute with all the terror that may be shewed: he raiseth vp indeed so many euils and mischiefes, as that he setteth all on a broyle & in confusion, many are cast downe, but the Lord promiseth the Angell & Church of Philadelphia, that because they had kept the word of his patience, he would keepe them safe in the middest of all these dangerous temptations. This promise we must know is generall, that all they which stand constant and faithfull in the defence of the Lords quarrell, against all enemies whatsoeuer, their doings are so acceptable vnto him, that he will keepe them euen in the greatest trials that shall fall out vpon the earth. He sayd to keepe them from the houre of temptation, not because the temptation commeth not vpon them, but because being tempted they get the victory.

This is a sweete promise, and full of comfort vnto those that stand in the maintenance of the Lords truth: we know not what grieuous triall will arise, but be faithfull now, and we are sure Christ will keepe vs when the stormes shall be the greatest, and Sathan shall be let loose for a time (for it is called the houre of temptation, to teach that his time is limited) euen to worke his whole will. And marke how Christ calleth the Gospell the word of his patience, it teacheth patience, it sheweth that he which will imbrace it, and desire to haue his part in the same, hee must patiently beare the crosse. If thou wilt not beare rebuke, nor suffer any losse, or be in daunger for thy profession, what doest thou professing the Gospell? He calleth it the word of his patience, and thou wilt hold it and be free from afflictions. What doest thou thinke Christ hath altered it, and that he will not now haue them afflicted and persecuted which professe it, to the end that their faith and patience may be tried? Or doest thou imagine that Sathan is wearied or spent with age, that he will not any longer raise troubles about it? Or is the fire of his wrath

wrath quenched? Doth he no longer hate and enuy the glory of God, and the saluation of the Church? Is he become more gentle, or doth he want instruments to fit his turne? Assure thy selfe that Sathan was neuer in greater rage and fuller of wrath then in these dayes, because he seeth his time is short, and his kingdome doth draw towards an end: and therefore if euer the Gospell might be called the word of Christs patience, it may now. If euer men needed to stand firme, & to be armed against all trials, it is now.

After these promises made, now followeth an admonition, *Behold I come shortly, hold that thou hast, that no man take thy crowne*: Least we might thinke that the promises of Christ should make them secure and negligent, this is added: for it will arise in mans mind, I haue promise made me that I shall be deliuered, what neede I striue and contend any longer? Yea but we are entertained into Christs seruice with this condition, that we must be faithfull and fight euen to the end: and the nature of faith which layeth hold of the promises, that he will make vs get the victory, is not thereby to take occasion to be slicke, but to take courage indeede to fight more valiantly. Christ promised he would deliuer them from the houre of temptation, but yet this goeth withall, hold that thou hast, ye must stand in the faith, ye must not let go the holy doctrine: for if ye do, ye loose your Crowne. None shall be crowned but they that haue layd hold of the trueth, are armed by it with the whole armour of God, and hauing finished all things, do stand. And although a man haue fought long, yet if he let go his hold at the last, he looseth all. It is certaine the power is strong which assaileth vs dayly, to plucke out of our harts the liuely power of the trueth, and it is a very necessary warning which is here giuen, *hold fast that thou hast*. This is not spoken, neither to such as yet haue neuer layd hold of the heauenly doctrine, but neglect & despise it, neither to such as haue professed with zeale and are fallen backe and reuolted, but indeed onely to those which haue receiued the faith, and stand in it. He that hath lost his hold, may bee willed if it be possible to lay hold againe of that which he hath let go. So may they that yet refuse be exhorted to imbrace and loue that which hitherto they haue not: onely to the godly and sincere Christian it is sayd, hold fast that which thou hast, that none take thy crowne from thee. And marke how our Sauior doth encourage his seruant to the battaile, by telling him he shall fight but a litle while, *Behold I come quickly*, saith he. Our nature is fraile, and the Lord knoweth it better then we our selues, & will not suffer vs to be held long vnder afflictions, but most graciously either quickly endeth, or metigateth the fury of the battaile. Againe we are ready to thinke a few daies of trouble very long, he telleth vs that it is but a short time: and if we can indeed come to measure the time, and the waight of them rightly with Saint *Paul* (who calleth them light and momentane) it giueth great encouragement. We wold continue, we care not how long in that which doth delight our flesh, but for griefe and sorrowes, we care not how little they be, or how soone they be ended. Well we are told he will come quickly, let vs beleeue him, let vs not shrinke nor quaile for a little. Thus farre touching the narration, now to the conclusion of this message.

Here

THE REVELATION.

Here are set downe in this conclusion, promises very great to euery one that o-uercommeth. In what particular Church soeuer, of what country, nation or people, man or woman, rich or poore, bond or free, that getteth the victory ouer Sathan, ouer sinne, yea ouer what enemies so euer, these promises belong indifferently vnto them.

The first is, *Him that ouercommeth, will I make a pillar in the Temple of my God, and he shal go no more out.* This is a promise of the perpetuity and stableneste of the glory and felicity which the conquerors shall obtaine and enioy in the presence of the most holy God for euermore. For a man to come to the heauenly glory, and to haue it in such sort as that he may be cast out from it, were but a fickle and an vncertaine estate: but the Lord doth promise and assure, that he shall be euen as a firme pillar in the Temple of God, which shall neuer be remoued. God is eternall & vnchangeable, his Temple euen the habitation of his holinesse standeth for euer. It must needs be so, then he that is a pillar in this Temple, how shall he decay, how shall he be remoued, how shall not he abide in his estate world without end? Indeede to be shut vp in a place, here seemeth to be a bondage, though the place be neuer so delightsome, men loue to looke abroad: how is this figure then fit to represent the endles ioy of the faithfull? It is not meant they shall be pent vp to stand as it were in a corner (for the Teple of God is most large, in which they shal dwell for euer) but this similitude of the pillar is to shew, that they shall neuer be remoued nor displaced. Againe, in the presence of Almighty God is the fulnesse of all ioyes, at his right hand there are comely pleasures for euermore, as the Prophet *Dauid* speaketh, Psalme. 16. To dwell with God there is no straightnes: to dwell with God there is no wearinesse, no desire to see any further variety of all delights, for the infinite fulnesse is in him. Who will not striue & fight against Sathan and al his bands of souldiers, to come to so happy and blessed an estate? Christ calleth his father his God, for he saith, *I will make him a pillar in the Temple of my God*. He is himselfe eternall God, euen the eternall Sonne of the Father, yea the wisdome of the Father, who he was not before, for the Father was neuer any moment without his wisdome, but he is also man. And so when he did hang vpon the crosse, he cried out with a loud voyce, *My God, my God, why hast thou forsaken me?* And when he was risen againe from the dead, and appeared vnto *Marie Magdalene*, he willed her to go tell his disciples, whom he calleth his brethren, *Behold I ascend to my Father, and to your Father, to my God, and to your God*. Foolish is the cauill of the Iewes, which deny that the Messias promised to the fathers should be God, because he should as it is written in the Prophets, make his prayer to God. Shal God, say they, pray vnto God? Nay but the man which is also God, prayed vnto God, and calleth him still his God.

The next promise is, *I will write vpon him the name of my God, and the name of the City of my God, the new Ierusalem, which commeth downe out of heauen from my God, and I will write vpon him my new name*. Here be sundrie things, and euery one of them of great price and dignity. First, he that ouercommeth, shall be as it were marked vp to God, with his name set vpon him: for men wil set their names vpon that which belongeth vnto them. This man shall be sealed vp to be the Lords: which is a most speciall dignity, and glory. Then next hee shall haue the name of the City of God, the new Ierusalem set vpon him: he shall be free of that heauenly City: he shall bee partaker of all the commodities which it doth affoord. Lastly, he shall haue the new name of Christ written vpon him: hee shall raigne with Christ in glory: for the new name of Christ, is his exaltation in glory: for hauing humbled himselfe in obedience, euen vnto the death of the crosse, God exalted him, and gaue him a name aboue euery name, &c. He then is exalted in power, in dignity, in maiesty, and glory; not to himselfe alone, but to lift vs vp also with him.

Then he concludeth with this acclamation, *He that hath an eare, let him heare what the Spirit saith to the Churches*. It is the holy Ghost which vttereth these promises vnto all that shall ouercome. Let vs not through negligence loose so great glory: let vs put on the armour of God, and fight valiantly to get the victory: for we cannot stand by our owne might, but by the mighty power of God. Let vs not mistrust or feare, for hee that hath promised, is most faithfull, and neuer deceiueth any that cleaue vnto him. It is but a little while, euen a few dayes that we stand in the battaile and are tried: but the victory being gotten, we shal stand as pillars for euer in the Temple of God, we shall be consecrated and sealed vp vnto him, and bee partakers of his glory in the heauens for euer, euen world without ende. O beloued faint not, nor shrinke not from so high a calling: but thinke how the time of your pilgrimage doth swiftly draw towards an end.

THE

THE X. SERMON

14. And to the Angel of the Church of Laodicea, write, these things saith Amen, the faithfull and true witnesse, the beginning of the creatures of God:
15. I know thy works, that thou art neither cold nor hote, I would thou wert cold or hote.
16. Therefore because thou art luke warme, and neither cold nor hote, I will spue thee out of my mouth.
17. Because thou saiest I am rich, and enriched, and want nothing, and knowest not that thou art wretched and miserable, and poore and blind, and naked.
18. I counsaile thee to buy of me gold tried in the fire, that thou maiest be rich, & white rayment that thou maiest be clothed, that thy filthy nakednesse do not appeare, and annoynt thine eyes with eye-salue that thou mayst see.
19. As many as I loue I rebuke and chasten, be zealous therefore and repent.
20. Behold I stand at the doore, and knocke: if any heare my voyce, and open the doore, I will come in to him, and will sup with him, and he with me.
21. To him that ouercommeth, will I graunt to sit with me in my throne, as I also haue ouercome and haue sit with my Father in his throne.
22. Let him that hath an eare, heare what the spirit saith to the Churches.

He seuenth or last message is sent to the Angell of the Church of Laodicea: this Laodicea (as some writers report) was the chiefe city of Caria. The exordium of the message is taken from the person of him that sendeth it, that is, from Iesus Christ: *Thus saith Amen, the faithfull and true witnesse.* Christ is a firme and constant truth, and (as Saint *Paul* saith) all the promises of God in him, are yea & Amen, 2. Corinth. 1. He bare record most faithfully, and constantly to the truth. He requireth that all his seruants, euen all his disciples, should follow his steps, and especially the Ministers of the Gospell, who are as guides and examples herein to go before the flocke, which thing the pastor of this Church failed in. It is written of Christ, in standing for and witnessing the truth, *The zeale of thine house hath eaten me*: But this Angell and his Church, had no zeale nor heate of loue in them, as we shall see in the narration. But first we must consider the other part of the description, which is in these wordes, *the beginning of the creatures of God.* He is called the beginning of the workemanship of God, because all was created and had beginning by him.

As Saint *Paule* calleth him the first begotten of euery creature, and then saith, because by him all things were created, which are in heauen, and which are in the earth, things visible, and inuisible, whether they be thrones, or dominations, principalities, or powers, all things were created by him, and for him: and he is before all things, and in him all things consist, Coloss. 1. verse. 15.16.17. And we may note, that there is the first creation, and there is that which is called the new creation, as in the Prophets, Behold I make all things new. And as all things were made by him in the first creation, Iohn. 1. so is the restoring of all things, euen the new creation, by him. He is the beginning of it. Hitherto the exordium, now to the narration.

I know thy workes, &c. It is small comfort to this Angell, and to this Church, that Christ did know their works: for he doth not praise them in any thing, but discommendeth and disalloweth them, layeth open their wretched estate, and giueth them aduise how to deale for their recouery from the same. The Lord doth not tell them that they held false doctrine, nor that they were idolaters, adulterers, or such like, but onely this, *Thou art neither cold nor hote*. They had bene taught in the true doctrine, they had receiued the same and did professe it, they caried themselues in some ciuill course of life, but they wanted the heate of loue and of zeale. If they had not professed the truth, and in some sort walked in it, how could it be sayd, thou art not cold? And if they had bene endewed with loue and zeale, how might it be sayd thou art not hote? So then here is no vtter denying, nor here is no sound professing. And now least this Church or any other might thinke it but a small matter, to be neither cold nor hot: the Lord doth declare and lay open, how loathsome a thing it is vnto him, and in how miserable estate such be, as are neither cold nor hot.

Many do suppose at this day, so they allow and professe the Gospell and name of Christ in any sorte, that they be right Christians, and in most excellent case, though they be voyd of all zeale, being luke warme, neither hot nor cold. Against such, this scripture is most plaine. For I hope they will not gainsay that which our Lord with his owne mouth vttereth from his glory. Then let them, and let vs all hearken what he sayth to the Angell of this Church: *I would thou wert either cold or hot*. Doth the Lord then allow of coldnesse, which is as much as to haue no religion at all, I meane no true religion? Doubtlesse that cannot be: for ye know how it is written, *Be zealous in spirit*. The Lord God requireth feruent loue and zeale in religion. When he saith then: *I wold thou wert either cold or hot*, it is not to shew that there is any goodnesse in being cold, but to set forth the badnesse of being betweene both, as we call it luke warme. To be cold is naught, yea very naught, but to be neither cold nor hot is worse.

And behold how our Sauiour expresseth his detestation of this thing, saying, *It will come to passe that I shall spue thee out of my mouth*. That which men do vomit or spue out at their mouth, the stomacke abhorreth, and they receiue it not againe, but cast it away with detestation and loathing. Such then as the vomit is to the offended stomacke, to the mouth, and to the man that speweth out, such are

luke-

THE REVELATION. 103

lukewarme Gospellers to the Lord Iesus Christ, and shall be cast forth by him as loathsome vomit. A most terrible sentence of iudgemēt, vttered by the Iudge himselfe. It might fray thousands, & ten thousands in our daies, for all is ouerspred with newters and such lukewarme Gospellers, as be here spoken of. Indeed the maner of this denouncing iudgemēt, seemeth to be taken from hence, that water neither hot nor cold, but warme, & as we vse to say lukewarme, doth prouoke the stomacke to vomit. This is then an allegoricall speech, that the stomacke of Christ doth loath such, & he will spue them forth of his mouth. This is no fable, this is not the word of any mortall man, but of the most blessed Lord himselfe, the only fountaine of all truth: I beseech ye let it not passe away without credit, let vs beleeue it assuredly. For the time will come when such haulters as are without zeale, and can ioyne with all companies, and neuer be tormented, vexed nor grieued in their soules, by hearing and seeing the abhominable and filthy words and deeds of vngodly men, shallbe cast forth with loathing and vtter detestation. But it will be said, our time is not without zeale, men are hot, euery sort as they take. I answere, that this is spoken not of euery heate to be wanting, for there is a true zeale with loue and mecknes of spirit, which is from God, and there is a bitter zeale, which is from the flesh. Of this latter, the Lord doth not speake, for it doth abound euerie where. Euery false religion, euery heresie and sect hath those which with great vehemencie and zeale stand to defend it: but this zeale is from the flesh. Onely the Lord Iesus and his truth find few which with pure zeale stand in defence of them. The newters, the lukewarme Gospellers, which are neither cold nor hot, are earnest and zealous, but not for the Gospell: but in defence of their owne waies. In cōdemning those that be feruent in spirit to be fooles, they can shew themselues very vehement. In defending the course which they themselues do follow, if any disallow it, they be very hot and fiery, looke not to haue them lukewarme therein. Be these men in so euill a case? Are they worse then they that be cold? Yea, mark how the Lord layeth them open further: *Because thou sayest I am rich, and enriched, & I want nothing: and knowest not that thou art wretched, and miserable, & poore, and blind, and naked.* It is one step towards blessednesse, for a man to know and to feele his miserie. And he that is in a miserable estate, and thinketh he is in good case, is so much the further off. The lukewarme Gospeller is most wretched, & of all other imagineth his estate to be the best. Therefore the Lord wisheth rather that they were cold, then neither cold nor hot. I beseech ye marke well, and let it be deeply printed and engrauen in your harts which the Lord vttereth here. It may do vs good, for are we not growing lukewarme, euen as the Church to whom this message was sent? Then looke what is said of them and to them, let vs take heed the same come not vpon vs.

The Angell of Laodicea, and the Church consisting of lukewarme Gospellers, tooke themselues to be rich, and enriched, and to want nothing. Writers do report of that citie, that it was verie wealthie in worldly substance through wollen cloath. And where men abound in wealth, and liue in pleasures, hauing all thinges which the flesh desireth, they easily grow secure, & imagine that they be in excel-

H 4

lent good cafe. But alas how farre are they deceiued? What faith he that knoweth indeed what they be? *And knoweſt not* (faith he) *that thou art wretched, and miſerable, and poore, and blind, and naked?* Here is a great difference indeed, from that which they did imagine of themſelues. Here are (as yee ſee) diuers words heaped vp, of miſerable wretchedneſſe, of pouertie, nakedneſſe and blindneſſe, touching ſpirituall things. And why is this heaping vp of words, but to ſet forth the certaintie of a moſt wretched eſtate? And why ſo, but becauſe Goſpellers neither cold nor hote, of all others need to be moſt terribly thundered againſt, that if it be poſſible they may be brought to ſee their miſerie. Let vs obſerue a few things in this place for the vſe of our time.

Chriſt doth not ſend any meſſage now, but this meſſage was ſent once for all, and if euer to any, to a great number of Churches in theſe daies. And then further, what aſſembly is there any where in all the world of ſincere Chriſtians, but there are mingled among them many ſuch lukewarme Goſpellers, haulting profeſſors, and newters? Talke with them, and ye ſhall find that they are perſwaded, & haue this opinion of themſelues, that they be very happie men. They know that there is remiſſion of ſinnes through the bloud of Chriſt. They know and profeſſe all points of doctrine ſet forth in the Goſpell. How ſhould theſe men be in euill caſe? Come then to the touchſtone to try the pure gold: come to the words which the Lord himſelfe hath vttered, and ſearch by them and ſcanne the true Chriſtian. Thou ſaieſt of thy ſelfe, I am a ſinner, I looke for pardon through Ieſus Chriſt. The promiſe is, all that beleeue ſhall be ſaued. I do beleeue. I take my ſelfe to be rich, & enriched, and to want nothing. Wel, but is thine hart enflamed with the loue & zeale of the glorie of God? haſt thou a burning deſire that the name and glorious Goſpell of Chriſt may be magnified? haſt thou an earneſt care of the good of thy brethren? Doth this loue of thine breake forth and ſhew it ſelfe in actions tending to the ſame purpoſe? doth it vexe and torment thee when Gods glorie is troden downe, when the holy truth is deſpiſed and defaced, when the Church goeth to decay and into ruines? If it be thus with thee, thou art well indeed: but if thou doeſt want this loue and zeale, making religion ſo indifferent, and ſo light a matter, being in the cauſes of God neither cold nor hot, thinke while thou wilt that thou art in good caſe, we know the Lord ſayeth true, we muſt giue credite to his words before all vaine opinions which men haue of themſelues, which are theſe: *And knoweſt not that thou art wretched, and miſerable, and poore, & blind, and naked.* I may very well mention here that which Saint *Paul* writeth: *He that thinketh he doth ſtand, let him take heed he do not fall.* 1. Cor. 10. For we ſee it plainely, that ſome thinke they haue faith, and that they be rich, and that they be in very good caſe, when they are not, but indeed are moſt wretched, blind and beggerly. Mens opinion and conceipt doth deceiue them. We muſt examine our ſelues whether we haue the true zeale. Among the Corinths there were ſuch Goſpellers, as could go into the idol temple with the heathen, and feaſt with them, at thoſe feaſts which they made at the worſhip & in the honor of their idols. They could reaſo ſmoothly to proue it lawfull as a thing indifferent, but indeed they wanted loue, they wanted

THE REVELATION. 105

ted zeale against al such horrible abhominations, & therfore the holy Apostle speaking to such, saith, *Let him that thinketh he standeth, take heed he fall not.* Then doubtlesse the lukewarme Gospeller doth thinke he standeth, but doth not. We haue not the Idoll Temples of the heathen among vs: but we haue Papists & such as do rayle vpon the ministers of the Gospell, and vpon all that do professe it. We haue them which be so loose in life, and so giuen ouer to follow the corrupt lusts of the flesh, that they cannot abide any which will not poure forth themselues to the same excesse of ryot, or at the least allow thereof: and there be Gospellers which are so zealous, that they can be familiar with the, & verie merrie euen when they heare them slaunder and reuile the preachers and professors of the Gospell. What halting is this? what newters are these? If there were anie loue of God or true zeale in them, how could they endure such things? Can a man abide to haue those reuiled and slandered which are deare and precious vnto him? The Prophet in the Psalme testifieth thus of himselfe, *Riuers of teares descend forth of mine eyes, because men keepe not thy law.* This was the zeale of the Prophet. And Saint Peter testifieth of *Lot* whe he did dwell in Sodome, that he vexed & tormented his righteous soule fro day to day, in seeing & hearing there their wicked deeds, 2. Pet. 2. And now a dayes we haue some Gospellers which can laugh euen heartily at the committing of great sinnes and enormous offences: it is a sport to make men, or to see them made drunken. If I should enter into all particulars, I should be tedious. Ye may easily see what maner of professing the Gospell hath inuaded our Churches, and how far it hath preuailed: namely vnto this, that they be accounted the wisest and the verie best Christians, they carie away all the commendatio, which be neither cold nor hot: they be the men which are worthy to be magnified, that be lukewarme.

This is the estate now generally, how miserable, let the words of Christ himselfe here testifie. All seemeth now happie, the Gospell, the Gospell, is in euerie mans mouth: but if the Lord will spew out of his mouth all lukewarme Gospellers, all that be neither cold nor hot. If all such thinking themselues to be in happy case, are indeed wretched, & miserable, and poore, and naked, & blind, what shall become of multitudes? Looke vpon many at this day, they haue the Bible, they reade a litle now and then, they bring their bookes to the Church, they open them and looke vpon the text at a Sermon, but yet a man may dwell by them long, and not be able to discerne whether they fauour the Papists or the Protestants. Well, let vs learne to iudge both of our selues & of others, not as the world iudgeth, which can abide no zeale in the Lords causes: but as our Sauiour Christ hath here pronounced: or say and do all what they can, his word shall be found true at the last. Wo be to newters, wo be to the lukewarme Gospellers which are neither cold nor hot. Christ will spew them out, he will reiect them with lothing and detestation. Their soules contrarie to their opinion, are void and destitute of all heauenly ornaments and spirituall graces. If they repent not they must perish, therefore let them heare now what the Lord saith further to the Angell of this Church.

I counsell thee to buy of me gold tried in the fire, that thou maist be rich, & white
raiment

rayment, that thou maist be clothed, that thy filthy nakednesse appeare not, & annoint thine eyes with eye salue, that thou maist see. O bounteous Lord and gracious Sauiour, who giueth counsell to this Pastor and his flocke, how they may come out of their miserie. Was it not great kindnesse that such a pastour & such a Church as this should be chosen for one of the seuen, vnto whom this prophecy was to be sent? Is it not much, that they must stand as one of the seuen golden candlestickes? Is it not more, that he layeth open their estate vnto them plainely? for whom would they haue beleeued among men, that shold haue told them so much? And yet he goeth further, and giueth them most wholsome aduise and counsell, wherby they may become verie blessed in all spirituall & heauenly blessings. The counsell is, to receiue from Christ all good things. He vseth speeches answerable to those by which he layd open their miserie: *Thou sayest I am rich (saith he) and enriched, and knowest not that thou art miserable, and poore.* He that hath plentie of gold is not poore, for gold maketh rich: and so he saith here, *Buy of me gold tried in the fire, that thou maist be rich.* The gold which is tried in the fire, is the more pure without drosse and mixture: and therefore to note the puritie and perfection of the heauenly riches giuen to vs in Christ, they are called gold tried in the fire. There is plentie of fine gold in Christ, to make vs rich vnto God: and we are called vpon to come and buy it of him. Then because he said, *Thou art naked,* he saith, *Buy of me vvhite raiment, that thou maist be cloathed, that thy filthy nakednesse do not appeare.* Clothing is to couer nakednesse: we are not onely naked in our selues, but full of filthinesse & shame which appeareth vnto God, who can not but cast vs forth and loath vs as filthy and abhominable, so long as we stand in it. Christ hath the white raiment to put vpon vs, euen his owne innocencie & pure holines which is without all spot or blemish, & therfore called white raiment. And because we are washed in his blood from our vncleannesse, and his righteousnesse through faith is put vpon vs, it is most fitly compared to a garment. All our pure raiment is in Christ, such as put him on, shall be able to stand in the presence of the most glorious God: for he that is cloathed with the white raiment of Christ, what want can there be? Then where he had said, *Thou art blind,* he saith, *Annoint thine eyes vvith eye salue, that thou mayst see.* In Christ the remedies against all miseries are to be had. He hath this precious eye-salue for to bestow vpon vs: for he hath the spirit of light, the spirit of all true wisdome, which doth open & illuminate the eyes of our soules, which are vtterly blind. O Lord giue vs this precious eye-salue, that we may see.

Thus we see the goodly treasures which are in Christ to make vs happy: but how doth he will vs to buy them of him? are the heauenly graces of Christ sold? or haue we any thing for which we may buy the? For answer vnto this, we are first to note, that this buying is without any price giuen to him, it is to buy for nothing. We may not thinke this strange, for the like saying is in the Prophet: *Oh euery one that thirsteth, come to the waters, & they that haue no mony, come buy & eate: come I say, buy vvithout money, and vvithout price vvine and milke,* Esay 55. Here ye see all are called to buy for nothing: and so is Christ Iesus here to be vnderstood. For

alas

THE REVELATION. 107

alas what haue we to giue for such heauenly treasures? and what wāteth the Lord Iesus? hath he not all fulnesse in himselfe? are not all good things his both in heauen and earth? They be worse then mad which imagine that the heauenly treasures can be bought with any price: but yet notwithstanding we are said to buy them after a sort, as I will lay open vnto you.

Our Sauior saith, *The kingdom of heauē is like to a treasure hid in the field, which when a man hath found he hideth, and for ioy thereof goeth and selleth all that he hath, and buyeth that field.* Also he saith, *The kingdome of heauen is like to a marchant man seeking goodly pearls: which when he had found one pearle of great price, went and sold all that he had and bought it.* How is this to be vnderstood? First, ye see the kingdom of heauen is a most rich thing, but it lyeth hid as treasure couered in the earth, & as a most precious pearle which none cā value but he that hath skil that way. For albeit the riches of the graces of Christ be displayed and laid open by the preaching of the Gospell, yet they lie hid to the world: and therefore the world passeth by them, and esteemeth them not. But such as haue their eyes opened, and do see them indeed, are so rauished with ioy and delight, and do make so precious account of them, that in respect and comparison of the same, they despise and set light by all other things which they possesse here in the world. When they with the eye of faith looke vpon the fine tried gold & pure raiment which Christ offereth, all earthly riches are vile vnto them, and but dung in comparison. When they behold the ioyes and sweet delights which they shall possesse for euer, that shall raigne with Christ in glorie, they contemne all fleshly pleasures, and despise all earthly honours, as vaine and transitorie. When a man (as Christ requireth) doth forsake father and mother, wife and children, lands and houses, yea all that he hath for to take vp the crosse, or when a man is so prepared in his mind, preferring the kingdom of God before them all, this is after a sort to sell all that he hath to buy the precious pearle, and the fine gold & pure raiment. The Church at Laodicea was wealthie in worldly things, and euen drowned in the loue of them, but the heauenly treasures in Christ they did litle esteeme, wherefore this doctrine was necessarie for thē, to sell all, & to buy those things. It was a most fit admonition for them, to pull their affections from the things here below, and to set them vpon heauenly things. Let vs then I pray you, remember some good lessons from this place, and let vs be carefull neuer to forget them: and that is, if we feele our selues dull in religion, neither cold nor hot, and so imagine that we be rich, because we be not as vtter despisers, nor as the worst sort of men, how farre we are wide, how much we be deceiued, seeing the Lord telleth vs, that we be indeed wretched, poore, naked, and blind.

Thē further, let vs know it is the loue of this world that doth beguile vs, we loue riches, and all things which may satisfie the lusts and delights of the flesh: and then that we are admonished to sell all, and to buy the gold tried in the fire, and the white raimēt of Christ. Finally, that we must annoint our eyes with eye-salue, that we may see: for certainly if men were not blind, and so through blindnesse make a blid choise, that is, preferre earthly things before heauenly, they could neuer be

luke-

lukewarme, but for ioy would sell all and buy those precious things of Christ. May we, will some say, hold that some men learned, and able learnedly and deeply to dispute in diuinitie, are yet blind, for there be at all times learned diuines, which are neither hot nor cold? I answer, it is strange that such should be blind, & shold need this eye-salue to annoint their eyes: but yet certainly they are blind. They do take themselues without all comparison to see best, they thinke themselues rich aboue others: but being drowned in the loue of riches and honours of the world, being indeed blinded with the corruptible gold of this earth, they neuer saw the glorie of these treasures which Christ selleth vs, and of which they can so learnedly speake: for if they had, the sight would rauish them with ioy, they should not be lukewarme, but sell all, euen treade downe as dung all earthlie treasures to winne those. Be out of doubt that all and euerie which are neither cold nor hot, though they be neuer so learned, are blind, and miserable, and poore, and naked: and need to be called vpon to sell all, and with ioy, with loue, & with zeale to buy this gold & white raiment. Ye shall hardly perswade anie that are worldly minded, but that they are in good case, if they professe the Gospell, how then shall a man be able to perswade a great diuine, which in his owne opinion is euen a light to all men, that he is wretched, poore, naked, and blind? If he will not be perswaded, let vs beleeue the Lord Iesus, that all lukewarme worldly minded Gospellers be euen no better, though they seeme neuer so learned and wise.

But see how the Lord proceedeth in admonition to this Angell & his Church: *Those whom I loue I chastise, be zealous therfore and amend.* We see how the Lord hath laid open this Angell and this Church euen to their great shame and reproch among all Churches, and to their owne griefe and terror : for they had a very high opinion of themselues, & the Lord setteth thē as low. Now least this sharp rebuke and chastisement should make them desperate, and cast them further off, as taking it that the Lord did abhorre and hate them, he sheweth that it proceeded wholly from loue. The naturall parents that loue their children dearely, and had rather feele smart themselues, then it should light vpon their children, will rather, though it be to their owne griefe, make them feele the smart of sharpe chastisement, then that they shold be vnnurtured, and cast thēselues headlong into miserie. The holy Ghost witnesseth, that our heauenly father dealeth after the same maner. Heb. 12. If instruction and admonition by words will not serue, but that we will runne on vnto our great perill and hazard of eternal destruction, rather then he will haue vs perish, though he delight not in our miseries, yet will he presse vs downe with rebuke and sorrow. The same thing doth our Sauiour here testifie, that of loue he doth chastise. It mixeth a great sweetnesse with a sharpe reprehension, when we know it proceedeth from good will, and from loue, of such as be our friends, and wish vs well. How much more then might this Angell and Church reioyce in the sharpe rebuke and chastisement here laid vpon them, when the Lord Iesus professeth that he doth it of loue? How far doth his loue surmount and excell, to loue them that did not shew anie heate of loue towards him? Might it not make them euen ashamed of themselues, & so moue a wrath and an indignation against their

owne

own ..vant of zeale towardes him? He did it to none other purpose, but that they might repent and be saued: and so he addeth, *Be zealous therefore and amend.* He did not tell them openly to the end he might disgrace them, that they were wretched, poore, naked, and blind, but in verie deed that he might heale them. There be diseases so dangerous, that the Phisition is forced to giue very bitter & violent potions, or els he shall do no good at all: so dealeth the Lord here with him that carieth himselfe aloft vpon the opinion of his wisedome, and that he is rich in all spirituall treasures, and a man very happie, and hunteth after estimation that way, there is no greater cut, nor more grieuous wound, then to lay him open to be a blind foole, naked, poore, and very miserable. The heauenly Phisition must either loose him, or giue him this purgation to emptie his stomacke: and that is the cause it is done in this manner. He disgraceth them openly, and with very sharpe threatning and terror, not delighting in their reproch, but they haue neede of it, that they may be brought to repentance, and enflamed with pure zeale, and so be saued. Let vs obserue here what an excellent thing it is, to be feruent in spirit. Let the worldly lukewarme Gospeller drily laugh and smile at it, yea let him haue it in vtter derision as a mad thing: but let vs remember that Christ saith: *Be zealous therefore and amend.*

Againe, let vs know that the ministers of the Gospel are to imitate the Lord Iesus, euē sharply to rebuke such as stand in need to be so dealt withall, but of a tender loue to saue their soules: and let them know they are to take it well when it is to such an vse, although they seeme to be much disgraced. It is better (saith our Sauiour in the Gospell) to enter into life hauing but one eye, or maymed, then the whole bodie with two eyes should be cast into hell fire: so it is better for a man to be layd open and disgraced, yea euen to his great reproch and shame, and so come to repentance and be saued, then to go in a wrong way euen with estimation and credit vnto destruction.

Behold I stand at the dore and knocke, &c. Here is yet further kindnes declared: the Lord standeth at the doore knocking to be let in. He is the good shepheard, he seeketh vp that which goeth astray, he standeth knocking at the doore of mans heart to enter and to make it his Temple to dwell in. Marke here diuers things: as first that the Lord doth not onely knocke and call at the doore of mans heart, but continueth the same: for he standeth at the doore, and hath stood at the doore, as the word importeth. This is much that he must waite vpon vs, mouing vs to receiue him: but the truth is, we neuer haue anie mind of him but when he doth stand knocking at the doore of our heart. Then further behold how difficult a thing it is for the heart of man to receiue Christ, and to be turned to God. We are so well contented that the power of darknes shall raigne in vs, we take such delight and pleasure in the corrupt lustes of sinne, and we are so fast asleepe, that he may knocke and knocke againe, we regard him not. But let vs take heed, for albeit his kindnes is maruellous, yet he will not alwaies offer himselfe, nor alwaies be found. Ye know how it is written: *To day if ye will heare his voice, harden not your hearts*: and then, *while it is called to day.* Heb. 3. And how terribly he threatneth,

that

that such as regard not, but despise when he calleth, how they shall crie vnto him when their miserie commeth vpon them, but he will not heare, but laugh at their destruction. Be not therfore too bold with him: if he haue by his word and by the motions of his spirit, stood dayly knocking at the doore of thy heart, shewing thy sinnes, and mouing thee to repentance, and thou hast made light thereof, take heed least those knockings of his cease, and thine heart be more hardened, so that there is no feeling of anie godly sorrow vnto repentance. Make much of this knocking, make much of these motions of the spirit, for manie that haue had great remorse & beginnings for to repent, are now hardened and boldened in sin. Most miserable are they which despise his knocking and driue him away. On the contrarie part, they be a thousand times blessed which open vnto him, and so receiue him. For marke what he saith: *If any do heare my voice, and open the doore, I will come in to him, and will sup with him, and he with me.* What more happy guest can be receiued in? what good thing can be wanting where he is? If Christ dwell in the heart by faith, if the graces and power of Christ be receiued in, all euill and miserie is driuen out, and all goodnesse and felicitie do succeed. Darknesse is driuen out, the diuell is expelled, sinne is destroyed, and horror of the dreadfull iudgement doth vanish away. There is light, there is God, there is righteousnesse, and peace, and ioy of the holy Ghost. Full notably doth the Prophet *Dauid* set forth this, Psal. 24. when he saith, *Lift vp your heads ye gates, and be ye lift vp ye euerlasting doores, and the king of glorie shall come in. Who is the king of glorie? the Lord strong & mighty, the Lord mighty in battell.* Our enemies be strong, euen death, and sin, and the diuell, but he hath encountred with them in battell, and subdued them, so that we receiuing in him, we receiue in all heauenly power. We are base and vile in our corruption: he is the king of glorie, and we through him shall be raised vp vnto glorie. He setteth it forth that we shall receiue all good things by him, in these words, that *if any opē the doore, he will come in and sup with him, &c.* He bringeth all the dainties with him, & compareth it vnto a supper, for we shall be fed with them: we shall be euen filled abundantly with all sweet ioyes: this supper shall neuer be ended. But it may be said, seeing all the good things are from him, how is it said he will sup with vs? what haue we to giue him any supper? He taketh ioy and delight in our faith, in our loue, in our obedience, or in all holy vertues which proceed from vs. For these are those sweet things which *Salomon* in his Song of songs, declareth that Christ delighteth in frō his Spouse. But in this place the Papists step in for free will: Christ Iesus (say they) doth knocke, that is, he doth offer grace, and it lyeth in man to giue cōsent by free wil, holpē also by his grace. Likewise that saying in the Psalme, *Lift vp your heads ye gates, and be ye lifted vp ye euerlasting doores, and the king of glory shall come in,* seemeth to ascribe it to mans owne wil to open the doores of the hart to receiue in Christ. We haue the plaine testimonies of the holy scriptures, that there is nothing left in man, no not so much as to think a good thought, Gen. 8. 21. 2. Corinth. 3. 5. Ephes. 2. 1. Moreouer, if a man could thinke a good thought of himselfe, then could he do somewhat without Christ, but Christ saith, *Without me ye can do nothing,* Iohn 15. ver. 5. *It is God* (saith S. *Paule*) *that worketh in you both to will and to accomplish,* Phil.2.ver.13. If a man will say then, how are those former speeches to be construed? Thus you must vnderstand: first, that God worketh vpon the hearts of men, not as men worke vpon blocks or stones, which haue no sense nor vnderstanding: for man hath vnderstanding, he hath a will, he hath affections. Then secondly, that free is opposed to bond, & free is opposed to compelled. In respect of the one, man hath free will, in respect of the other he hath not. Man naturally loueth & delighteth in euill, his will not forced nor copelled, doth choose the same: man despiseth and reiecteth the Gospell of his owne will. In this respect his will is free vnto all euill, that is, he willeth euil not compelled, but caried thereunto with pleasure.

But now touching the other, corruptio is spread ouer al the powers of his soule, so that he is in thraldome and bondage vnto sinne, and hath not the freedome so much as to thinke one good thought. So farre as the grace, the life, and power of Christ crucified is in him, to the killing of this corruption, in which his will is held captiue, so far is his will set free, so far can he will well, and do well: as it is witten, *If the Sonne make ye free, then shall ye be free indeed.* So far shall we consent to that which is good, loue that which is good, and delight in that which is good: so farre shall we hate and abhorre that which is euill: as this grace of Christ increaseth in vs, so we lift vp our heads in freedome more and more. Then marke what Christ saith, *No man commeth vnto me, vnlesse the Father that sent me draw him,* Iohn 6. This drawing is not by force, but God reformeth the will & the affections, so that a man ioyfully receiueth Christ, & therfore is said to open the doores of his heart. Thus much touching this point. Now remaineth the conclusion of this Epistle.

He that ouercommeth I will giue vnto him to sit with me in my throne, as I ouercame, and sit with my father in his throne. This is a great promise vnto euerie one that shall stand in the battell and get the victorie. Christ hath ouercome and raigneth in glorie, and they that ouercome shal raigne with him, though not in equal glory. There can be no greater thing then this, let it therfore put heart and courage into vs, to fight the good fight of faith against the diuell, against sinne, and against all the enemies of God. If this do not moue vs, it is because we haue not an eare to heare: let vs therefore earnestly begge, that our eares may be opened more and more, that we may heare what excellent and most worthy things the spirit speaketh to the Churches. And thus we haue seene what the estate of the seuen Churches was, and so be able to iudge of the state of the vniuersall Church at that time: for by these seuen, ye may see in whate estate all were.

THE

SERMONS VPON

THE XI. SERMON.
CHAP. 4.

1. *After this I looked, & behold, a doore vvas open in heauen, & the first voyce vvhich I heard, vvas as it vvere of a trumpet talking vvith me, saying, come vp hither, and I vvill shew thee things vvhich must be done hereafter.*
2. *And immediatly I vvas rauished in the spirit, and behold, a throne vvas set in heauen, and one sate vpon the throne.*
3. *And he that sate vvas to looke vpon like vnto a Iasper stone, and a Sardine, & there was a rainbowe round about the throne, in sight like vnto an Emeraud.*
4. *And round about the throne vvere foure and twenty seates, and vpon the seates I saw foure and twenie Elders sitting, cloathed in vvhite rayment, and had on their heads crownes of gold.*
5. *And out of the throne proceeded lightenings, and thundrings, and voyces, and there vvere seuen lampes of fire burning before the throne, which are the seuen spirits of God.*
6. *And before the throne there vvas a sea of glasse, like vnto Christall: and in the middest of the throne, and round about the throne were foure beasts full of eyes before and behind.*
7. *And the first beast vvas like a Lion, and the second beast like a Calfe, and the third beast had a face like a Man, and the fourth beast vvas like a flying Eagle.*
8. *And the foure beasts had each one of them sixe wings about him, & they were full of eyes within, and they ceased not day nor night, saying, holy, holy, holy, Lord God Almighty, vvhich was, and vvhich is, and which is to come.*
9. *And vvhen those beasts gaue glorie, and honour, and thanks to him that sate on the throne, vvhich liueth for euer and euer:*
10. *The foure and twentie Elders fell downe before him that sate on the throne, and worshipped him that liueth for euermore, and cast their crownes before the throne, saying,*
11. *Thou art worthie ô Lord to receiue glorie, and honour, and power: for thou hast created all things, and for thy wils sake they are and haue bene created.*

IN the former chapters we haue had the first vision of this booke, by which S. *Iohn* was called, authorised and appointed to receiue this prophecie, and to write it in a booke, and to send it to the seuen Churches of Asia. We haue had also seuen seueral Epistles or messages vnto the seuen Angels of those seuen Churches,

ches. In which we haue seene by those seuen what was the state and condition of the vniuersall Church militant at that time. For some were very excellent pastors, & had excellent flocks, some were commended, and also in some things dispraised, and some were wholly discommended. No doubt if the Lord had gone through all the particular Churches at that time in the world, it would haue fallen out euen so. We haue had also very worthy and precious promises set foorth to all that get the victory in the Christian battaile.

• Now followeth the second vision, which reacheth vnto the twelfth chapter, setting foorth the state of things, euen to the worlds end: in which there is first (as namely in this Chapter & the next) set forth how Christ receiued this Reuelation from the hand of the Father, to giue to his Church, for he calleth it before in the first Chapter, the Reuelation of Iesus Christ, which God gaue him, to shew to his seruants, &c. And here shall we see how it was giuen him. In all this whole Chapter, the glorious maiesty of God Almighty, from whom the Lord Iesus receiueth this Reuelation, is described & set forth euen as Iohn saw the same in vision: now to the words as they lie. The things here reuealed, be all from the secret counsels of God, they be heauenly, and therefore he saith, *I looked, and behold a doore was open in heauen.* Why is this doore opened? This doore is opened for to let him in to see all these things which should come to passe: that is the first circumstance. Then next he is called vp with a loude and glorious voyce: for he saith, *The first voyce which I heard, was as it were of a trumpet talking with me, and saying, come vp hither, and I will shew thee things which must be done hereafter*: for he doth not presume in any thing, but as the heauenly voyce calleth him, and giueth special and direct commandement. *Then he was immediatly rauished in the spirit*: For as the Prophet *Ezechiel* was by the spirit in the visions of God, caried from Chaldea to Ierusalem, so this holy Apostle is caried by the spirit in the visions of God, into Heauen, he is by the spirit made fit, and capable to see, and to receiue all those heauenly visions that should be shewed him. And now he sheweth what hee saw there, for he was not taken vp to see things for his owne priuate vse, or which could not, or might not be vttered. *Behold a throne was set in heauen, and one* (saith he) *sate vpon the throne*. Now beginneth that description of the most high and most glorious diuine maiesty, as it was shewed him in vision. It is set forth in sundry parts: as in the first place by his office, that he sitteth as King, and Iudge of all the world, vpon his glorious throne, for when the Scripture will set God before vs as King and Iudge, it placeth him vpon his throne.

It may here be said, that God is inuisible, incomprehensible, and that as he saith by the Prophet *Esay*, Chap. 66. The whole heauens be his throne, and the earth his footestoole, how then doth he see a throne set in heauen, and one sitting vpon it? The answer vnto this is, that the maiesty of God is here described, not in the fulnes thereof, but as it was shewed to *Iohn* In vision, euen so farre as he and we might be capable thereof. In the next place he shewed, that God the father, first is most glorious of himselfe, and in himselfe, and then that with the same his glory he beautifieth all things: that precious glory of God in himselfe, is resembled by two precious stones: for he saith: *He that sate was to looke vpon like vnto a Iasper stone, & a Sardine.* The other is resembled by the raine-bow round about the throne, in sight like vnto an Emeraud: by this I say, is resembled, how he beautifieth the creatures. For as the Sun casting his beames into the darke rainy cloud, causeth the rain-bow with bright and goodly colours: so God almighty, the fountaine & father of lights, casteth forth his light vpon the darke creatures, and maketh them to shine with glorie.

Then further, this heauēly maiestie of God is set forth in an other part, as namely by that honourable companie which sitting vpon seates, compasse his throne round about. For he saith, *That round about the throne were foure & twenty seats, & vpon the seates were foure and twenty Elders, &c.* We know that great kings, & chiefe Iudges, sitting in their royaltie, and shewing their glorie, are accompanied with their nobles and princes that sit with them. Euen so this king of all kings, and most high iudge, sitteth vpon the throne of his glorie, and raigneth for euermore, in the middest of all those whom he hath exalted vnto that heauenly dignitie to be kings and priests vnto him. By these foure and twentie, then are resembled not only the Patriarks and Prophets of old, & the Apostles of Christ in the new testament, but also the whole Church, euen the whole companie of blessed Saints. The glorie of this companie is resembled in this, or as I may say, in all these, that they be so nigh about the throne of God, that they sit vpon seates, that they be clothed in white, and haue on their heads crownes of gold. For all the sonnes and daughters of the most high (though many of them for a time be base vpon the earth in outward shew) are exceeding glorious Kinges and Queenes, and shall raigne with the Lord for euer. Fourthly, here are operations and effectes to declare this glorious maiestie of God almightie: *For out of the throne proceeded lightninges, and thundrings, and voices, & there were seuen lampes of fire burning before the throne, which are the seuen spirites of God.* These are the effectes of his mightie word, and holy spirit. With his voice and word he striketh, shaketh and terrifieth all things, he lighteneth and quickeneth by his spirit. By the lightnings and thundringes his terrible voice of the law is fitly resembled: for the law giueth light, but such as is with trembling and terror, because it findeth vs sinners. And therefore at the deliuery of it, there were lightnings and thundrings, and the mount Sinay it selfe did tremble and shake. The Gospell giueth a comfortable light, and chearefull, the ministerie thereof, being the ministerie of the spirit, 2. Cor. 3. and therefore is resembled by the seuen lampes, which (he saith) are the seuen spirits of God. There is indeed but one spirit, but because of his manifold operations, and (as I shewed in the first chapter) because *Iohn* writeth vnto seuen Churches, and he may seeme to worke in euerie seuerall Church of those seuen, as a seuerall spirit, he is set forth by seuen lampes, and is called the seuen spirits of God. In the sit place, we haue the prouidence and sight of God into all, & ouer all things here in this world. This is resembled by these words, *And before the throne was a sea of glasse like vnto Christall.* This sea of glasse is the world: for the world is fitly called a sea, because it is full of stormes, and tempestes, and waues that are raised vp. It is full of rockes

ypon

THE REVELATION.

vpon which many do dash, and make shipwracke, and are drowned in destructiō and perdition. And although vnto vs there be many things in it which are secret and hid, many things seeme to happen by chance, yet vnto him of whom the Prophet speaketh (saying, *The darkenesse is no darkenesse vnto thee, but the darkenesse and the light are alike* : Psal. 139.) there is nothing secret. And therefore this sea is sayd to be like vnto chrystall. Ye know that the chrystall is so cleere, and our sight doth so run through it, that if there be but a little spot it appeareth: Euen so for this whole world the sight of God pierceth through it without any let, and seeth euery thing far more cleerely, then we see the spots if any be in a chrystall. For all things lie open and naked vnto his eyes, Heb. 4. The diuell is subtle in the darke, and wicked men haue deepe reaches to practize mischiefe against the Church: but this is a speciall comfort, that they can hide nothing, no not euen their secret thoughts from the eye of God. Remember this I pray ye, that this world is like a chrystall sea before the throne of God. For they that be good may haue great comfort by it, and the euill conscience may be terrified: For God seeth cleerely through the hart and conscience.

And it is not to be omitted that this sea is of glasse, for albeit the reprobate are drowned in it, yet through the fauor of God, though it be a most troublesome sea, yet no one of the elect can be drowned in it: for vnto them it is as glasse. Whensoeuer ye see troubles and turmoiles raised, and all seemeth to be confused as if there were no diuine sight or prouidence: call to mind this place, that this sea of glasse is before the throne of God Almighty, and that vnto him it is in euery part as cleere as chrystall. Consider also, that this high maiesty which reuealeth the things which should fall out in this troublesome world, seeth them perfectly and cleerely afore hand, euen as in a most cleere chrystall.

Thus hauing set forth the heauenly maiesty of God by his sight and prouidence: he commeth in the next place vnto the chiefe & principall ministers of his power, the holy Angels, in whom and by whom he declareth his glory and magnificence. These are ministring spirits: Hebr. 1. Saint *Paule* calleth them thrones, principalities, mights, and dominations, Coloss. 1. for they are about the throne of the most high, and he doth execute his will and decrees by them. Of these he saith here, *That in the middest of the throne, and round about the throne, were foure beasts full of eyes before and behind.* Then about this throne there be most glorious instruments, as we shall see their nature and properties by that description which is giuen. They are most vigilant, being full of eyes before and behind. The first of the foure is like a Lion. And the Lion is the king of beasts: so that here is noblenesse & courage resembled hereby. The heauenly spirits haue nothing base in them, which to vs is resembled by the likenesse of the Lyon. The second is like a calfe : by this there is strength and might signified: for the oxe is strong, they be mights and powers. The third had the face of a man: whereby is signified their vnderstanding and wisdom: for among the creatures below, man only hath wisedome and vnderstanding. The fourth was like a flying Eagle. The Eagle doth mount aloft: whereby may very well be vnderstood that the heauenly spirits do receiue the knowledge of high

I 2   secrets

secrets and counsels. For they are aloft euen about the throne of God, and manie high and great secrets are opened vnto them. The Lord hath had here vpon earth among men excellent worthie instrumentes, circumspect and vigilant to do his worke; noble, valiant, full of courage, strong, expert and wise, vnto whom he hath also communicated high secrets, but yet in all these they haue come farre short of the blessed and glorious Angels in heauen, which are about his throne, which are resembled by these similitudes. Further it is said, that euery one of them had sixe wings about him. The Angels being spirits haue indeed no bodily or visible shape, but for our vnderstanding and capacitie, they are said to haue winges, whereby is represented how swift, how full of readinesse and expedition, they be at all times to execute the will of God. They be sent from the highest heauens into all parts of the world, and do most speedily performe their seruice, and therefore are said to haue winges. Vnto this, *Dauid* had respect, when he said: The Lord rode vpon Cherub, and came flying, Psalm.18. ver.11. The Prophet Esay chapter 6. saw the Lord sitting vpon his high throne, and the Seraphims standing aboue it. He saith they had each of them sixe wings. And moreouer he addeth, that with two of those wings they couered their faces, with two they couered their feete, & with two they did flie. And what did this signifie? The two wings wherewith they co-uer their faces do teach, that albeit the Cherubins, and Seraphims, euen those hea-uenly spirits be very bright and glorious, yet they come so farre short of the Lord God of glorie himselfe, that they be not able to endure the beholding of his infinit brightnesse and maiestie. Ye see we inioy, and walke in the chearefull light of the Sunne, but yet we are not able to looke fully and directly vpon it, when it shineth in the full strength and brightnesse: euen so it may not seeme strange vnto vs, that the Angels themselues, are not able to looke vpon the depth of Gods maiestie. With two they couered their feet, saith the Prophet. They be holy and pure, there is no spot or blemish of sinne in them: but yet their holinesse is not infinite, and so not to be compared with the holinesse of God, their waies are not equall with his waies, and this is testified in that they couer their feete. They stand not to iustifie their waies in comparison of the Almightie. How far from this are prophane hypo-crites which dwell in houses of clay, and which drinke in sinne like water, and ha-uing nothing cleane in them, yet stand to iustifie themselues euen before God? With two they flie. This is to declare (as I said before) how swift and readie they be in the seruice of God. Saint *Iohn* doth not speake here that these couered their faces, and their feet, and therefore I cannot tell whether these sixe wings, to each haue the same signification which I haue shewed of the Seraphims. It is very like, but I do not affirme for certaine.

Then he saith: *They were full of eyes within.* He said before, that they were full of eyes before and behind, to see & behold euery way for to execute their ministery and seruice to God: but this hath a further meaning, and that is, that they do not onely behold things which lie open, but also things hid and secret. True it is, that God alone is the searcher of the hart, but yet withall we must vnderstand, that as great kings do make their secrets knowne vnto them which are next vnto them, so

the

the Lord openeth secrets to his Angels. They are made to see hid and secret things.

Then next he sheweth how these glorious Angels do continually without ceasing, laud and magnifie God. For he saith, *They ceased not day nor night, saying, holy, holy, holy, Lord God Almighty, which was, and which is, and which is to come.* In that they do not cease day nor night, we may not thinke it strange: for though it be a wearisome thing vnto vs, that are burthened with corrupt and dull flesh, to continue in praising God, especially because we haue small delight in it: yet it is farre otherwise with that blessed company of heauen: they are not burdened, it is their whole ioy and felicitie to glorifie God, and they are so rauished with the loue thereof, that they can neuer waxe weary. In that they proclaime *holy, holy, holy*, it is to testifie that all his waies, yea euen all his most seuere iudgements are iust & vpright, & holy, howsoeuer they may seeme vnto men. There is many sore plagues, and horrible iudgements set forth in this booke, to be executed vpon the wicked world, which vnto the corrupt sense of flesh and bloud may seeme to be from rigour and cruelty in God, and the wicked do blaspheme him indeede as a cruell iudge, when he executeth vengeance vpon them: but these heauenly and glorious, and blessed Angels, which are about the throne of his glory, and the ministers to execute his will and his decrees, do pronounce that all that commeth from him, is most holy and iust. Let vs learne hereby when any thing doth fall out which seemeth hard and cruell, to submit our selues, and to rest vntill we be made like to the Angels, for then shall we see, as they see, and know as they know, and proclaime as they proclaime. Next vnto his holinesse they set forth his omnipotent power, for they say, *Lord God Almighty*. And then his eternitie, in which he is vnchangeable, hauing his being of himselfe, and giuing the being vnto all creatures: for they adde, *Which was, and which is, and which is to come.* Thus we see the nature and properties of these heauenly instruments, in which God doth set forth and magnifie his glorious maiesty. And now we are come to the seuenth and last thing, by which the high glory of God Almighty is in this Chapter described, and that is, that he is praised and magnified both of Angels and men. For this praise which the Angels giue being set forth he addeth, that when the foure beasts gaue glory, and honour, and thanks to him that sate vpon the throne, which liueth for euer and euer: *The foure and twenty Elders fell downe before him that sate on the throne, and worshipped him that liueth for euermore, and cast their crownes before the throne, saying, Thou art worthy ô Lord to receiue glory, and honour, and power: for thou hast created all things, and for thy willes sake they are, and haue bene created.* These foure and twenty Elders do represent all the Saints, both of the auncient Church, as also vnder the Gospell. And first that they fall downe before the throne, it is by a signe to testifie their reuerence in praising of him, as also to worship him: for the true Church doth worship him alone: the true beleeuers fall downe to neither Saint nor Angell, nor to any image or reliques, but onely vnto the most high God. In that they cast their crownes before the throne, they emptie themselues before him of all worthines to haue any glory, acknowledging that their crownes of glory are his free gift, without any desert or merite of theirs. For why else should they cast them downe before the throne, but to confesse that God alone is worthy of all honour and glory?

The Papists thinke themselues great friends to the Saints in heauen, and take it they must needs accept of their friendship, when they be deuout worshippers of them, as their *Legenda aurea* and their festiuals are stuffed full for most impudent lies and fables, what such and such a Saint did for such and such that were their deuout worshippers: but this place doth fully confute the vanity of all such wicked and blasphemous forgeries. For what likelihood is there that the Saints in heauen, throwing downe their crownes, confessing their owne vnworthinesse, & ascribing all worthinesse of glory and honor to God alone, can like well that the Lords peculiar glory should be taken from him, and giuen vnto them? For the Church of Rome in praying to Saints, in worshipping them with diuine honour, in making them mediators, authors and patrons of saluation, rob God, and spoyle our Lord Iesus Christ of his ornaments to decke them. But let them go, and let vs learne here that the Angels and Saints in heauen delight that God only should be glorified, and therefore do most highly abhorre and detest, that his glory should be taken from him and giuen to them, yea euen the very least part of it. They will be no patrons, nor they do not thanke those that commit such abominable sacriledge. They loue those which after their example ascribe all glory, and honour, and praise to God alone through his Sonne Iesus Christ. Lastly, they do by words ascribe vnto God the Father all worthinesse to receiue glory, honor, and power, because that of his owne holy will he hath created all things, and doth support them.

Now then to conclude, let vs couet and long with all our hart for that time when we shall be vnburdened, and deliuered from all corruption, and receiued into the societie and fellowship of this heauenly company, euen of the blessed Saints & Angels, and together with them, laud and magnifie our Lord God for euer and euer, euen world without end.

Thus we see the description of the diuine maiesty, euen of the great God, from whom this Reuelation commeth. Whatsoeuer things do follow in the booke, that come to passe in the world, let vs remember from whose prouidence they come, and how the world is like a sea of Christall before him.

THE

THE XII. SERMON.
CHAP. 5.

1. And I saw in the right hand of him that sate vpon the throne, a booke written within, and on the backside, sealed with seuen seales.
2. And I saw a strong Angell which preached with a loud voice, who is worthie to open the booke, and to loose the seales thereof?
3. And no man in heauen, or in earth, neither vnder the earth, was able to open the booke, neither to looke thereon.
4. Then I wept much, because no man was found worthy to open, and to reade the booke, neither to looke thereon.
5. And one of the Elders said vnto me, weepe not, behold that Lion which is of the tribe of Iuda, that roote of Dauid, hath obtained to open the booke, and to loose the seuen seales thereof.
6. Then I beheld, and lo in the middest of the throne, and of the foure beasts, and in the middest of the Elders, stood a Lambe as though he had bene killed, which had seuen hornes and seuen eyes, which are the seuen spirits of God, sent into all the vvorld.
7. And he came and tooke the booke out of the right hand of him that sate vpon the throne.
8. And when he had taken the booke, the foure beastes, and the foure and twentie Elders fell downe before the Lambe, hauing euery one harpes, and golden vials full of odours, which are the prayers of the Saints.
9. And they sang a new song, saying, thou art worthy to take the booke and to open the seales thereof; because thou wast killed, and hast redeemed vs to God by thy bloud, out of euery kindred, and tongue, and people, and nation:
10. And hast made vs vnto our God Kings and Priests, and vve shall raigne vpon the earth.
11. Then I beheld, and I heard the voice of many Angels round about the throne, and about the beasts and the Elders, and there vvere ten thousand times ten thousand, and thousand thousands,
12. Saying with a loud voice, worthy is the Lambe that vvas killed, to receiue power, and riches, and wisedome, and strength, and honor, and glory, and praise.
13. And all the creatures which are in heauen, and on the earth, and vnder the earth, and in the sea, and all that are in them, heard I saying, praise, and honor, and glory, and power be vnto him that sitteth vpon the throne, and vnto the Lambe for euermore.
14. And the foure beasts said, Amen: and the foure and twenty Elders fell downe and vvorshipped him that liueth for euermore.

IN the former Chapter, we haue had the description of the high maiesty of God the Father Almighty, who gaue this Reuelation to his Sonne Iesus Christ. In this

Chapter is set forth vnto vs, first a descriptiõ of this Reuelatiõ: then next a description of the Lord Iesus Christ, who receiueth it at the hand of his Father: and lastly here is set forth the most glorious praise, which by the chiefe Angels, by the Saints, by the multitude of Angels, and by all creatures in heauen, in earth, and vnder the earth, and in the sea, is giuen to Christ. Of these three parts consisteth the whole chapter. Le vs come to the words as they be set downe: *I saw* (saith he) *in the right hand of him that sate vpon the throne, a booke written within, and on the backeside, sealed with seuen seales.* The booke as appeareth afterward by the opening of the seales, is this Reuelation. All the secrets reuealed in it come from the will, the counsell and decree of the most high God, and are ordered by his prouidence, and therefore are by vision shewed to *Iohn*, to be in his right hand. This right hand of the Lord doth all, this right hand of the Lord bringeth mighty things to passe, this right hand of the Lord hath the preheminence: this is one point of the description.

Then further, that they be written in a booke, it is to shew, that they be decreed, and determined so firmely and so constantly in the counsell of God, that none of them shall faile, but come foorth, and be fulfilled in their season. That the booke is written within, and on the backside, we are giuen to vnderstand, that there be many things to be reuealed: for it is not only a whole booke, wherein they be contained, but also written as full as might be, both within, and on the backeside: they be many great things which should fall out in the world, from the time that *Iohn* receiued this prophecy, to the day of iudgemẽt. That it is sealed with seuen seales: we are taught, that they be the counsels and secrets knowne onely to the most high God, vntill it pleased him to reueale them by his Sonne: for the number of the seales doth shew, that they be perfectly sealed vp. No mights, no thrones, no principalities, or dominations in heauen, did or could know any of those things which are written in this booke, before the seales be opened.

Now that we may know, that Iesus Christ, the onely begotten Sonne of God, which is from the bosome of the father, the mediator betweene God and man, is the only reuealer and opener of his Fathers will: here is proclamation made vnto all creatures in heauen and earth, which is a part of the description of this booke, that only the Lord Iesus is found worthy to open the seales thereof. For he sayth, *I saw a strong Angell that preached with a loude voyce, who is worthy to open the booke, and to loose the seales thereof: And no man in heauen, nor in earth, neither vnder the earth, was able to open the booke, neither to looke thereon*. Let vs then know for certaine, that our blessed Lord Iesus hath alwayes had this glory peculiar to himselfe alone, that he is the opener of the counsels of God. He is the eternall word, Iohn.1.vers.1. He is the wisdome of the Father from euerlasting, and before all creatures, as *Salomon* setteth him forth, Prouerb.8.ver.22. *No man hath seene God at any time, the onely begotten Sonne which is in the bosome of the Father, he hath declared him*, Iohn.1.vers.18. He sent his spirit vpon the Apostles, as hee had also of olde time giuen him to his Prophets, and so the holy Scriptures were written.

Here do the Papists lay in for their Purgatory, and for their *Limbus patrum*: indeede

THE REVELATION.

deed the learned Papists do rather defend both *Limbus* and Purgatorie by tradition then by Scripture, but yet where there may the least shew be made of Scripture, they take hold: as the Rhemists vpon these words, that none in heauen, nor in earth, nor vnder the earth was found worthie to open the booke, inferre thus, *He speaketh not of the damned in hell, of whom there could be no question, but of the faithfull in Abrahams bosome, and in Purgatory.* The force of their reason is in this, that touching the damned in hell, there could be no question, whether any among them could be found worthy to open the booke: and so there needed no proclamation to be made to find any there. Therefore vnder the earth, is to be vnderstood (say they) of some other companie, as of the Saints in *Abrahams* bosome, which they call *Limbus Patrum*, or of the tormented soules in Purgatorie.

O foolish ridiculous Papists, which seeke in the cleare light to blind the world with such fooleries: first why do ye here mention the faithfull in *Abrahams* bosome, when ye teach that Christ did fetch them forth, and carie them with him to heauen before this time? Did he leaue some behind him in *Limbo*, or is heauen vnder the earth? And then when ye say, there could no questiō be made of the damned in hell, whether anie there were worthie, I pray ye then what question could be made of those in Purgatorie? could it be doubted that among those, which (ye say) lye in those horrible torments of Purgatorie, peraduenture some one might be found worthy to open the booke? If there could no one be found among the Angels and Saints in heauen, could there thē be question about them in Purgatorie? Why do ye not see, that this Proclamation is made, not for anie question, whether there were some Angell or Saint worthie (for it was knowne and out of doubt there was none) but to teach vs, that indeed among all creatures in heauen or earth, or wheresoeuer, there is no one worthie, but that this honour and worthinesse is peculiar to the Mediator Iesus Christ. Thus much I thought good to note of their peruerse folly.

It followeth now in the text, that *Iohn wept much, because no man was found worthie to open the booke, to reade it, or to looke thereon.* Saint *Iohn* did not doubt but that in this booke were written such things as were verie good and profitable for the Church to know: and when he saw there was none found worthie to opē it, he sorrowed and lamented much, for feare that the Church should be depriued of such a benefite. He loued Iesus Christ dearely, and therefore he loued the sheep and lambes of Christ, which he hath redeemed with his bloud, most feruently coueting that they might be instructed, and fed with all knowledge that might bring them vnto saluation. This was a good shepherd, those are nothing like him, which care not though the people ouer whom they haue the charge, be ignorant in the word of God. Saint *Iohn* did weepe for feare that the things in the booke should not be knowne: they weepe that the people come to anie knowledge, and so espy their wickednesse: here is great ods.

Then next is shewed, how *Iohn* is cōforted touching this matter: *For one of the Elders said vnto him, weepe not, behold, that Lyon which is of the tribe of Iuda, that roote of Dauid, hath obtained to open the booke, and to loose the seuen seales thereof.*

The

The ſtrong Angell then did not preach with a loud voyce, to find if there was any other worthie to open the booke, as a matter that might be, but to make it knowne, that none indeed was worthie but Chriſt Ieſus alone. The Elder calleth him that Lyon of the tribe of *Iuda*, reſpecting that prophecie of *Iaakob* in bleſſing his ſonne *Iuda*: for he ſetteth him forth as a young Lyon that ſhould take the pray, and as a moſt ſtately Lyon, which lying downe to ſleepe, none dare raiſe him vp, Gen. 49. verſ. 9. Now it is moſt certaine, that whatſoeuer dignitie and glorie is aſcribed to that tribe, it is in reſpect of Chriſt, who came of the ſame. He calleth him alſo that root of *Dauid*, for according to the fleſh he was the ſonne of *Dauid*. But the phraſe of ſpeech is from the Prophet *Eſay*, for the Lord did threate ſuch calamitie vnto the Iewes, Eſa 10. that he compareth their cutting downe, to the cutting downe of the trees in a wood, and then miniſtring comfort, chap. 11. leaſt all might ſeeme to faile, he ſaith, that out of the ſtocke of *Iſhai*, who was the father of *Dauid*, and out of his rootes ſhould a branch ſpring vp, vpon which the ſpirit of the Lord ſhould reſt, the ſpirit of wiſdome & vnderſtanding, the ſpirit of counſell and power, the ſpirit of knowledge, and of the feare of the Lord. This mightie Lord in battell, this ſtrong Redeemer hath gotten the victorie, and obtained to open the booke, and to looſe the ſeuen ſeales thereof. Now *Iohn* hath his eyes opened, and ſeeth him that is worthie to open the booke: and that which appertaineth to the deſcription of the booke being finiſhed, now he deſcribeth the opener. For he ſaith, *Then I beheld, and lo in the middeſt of the throne, and of the foure beaſts, and in the middeſt of the Elders ſtood a Lambe as though he had bene killed, which had ſeuen hornes, and ſeuen eyes, which are the ſeuen ſpirits of God, ſent forth into all the world*. Firſt, in this deſcription it may ſeeme ſomewhat ſtrange, that hearing of a Lyon which had ouercome, now he ſeeth a Lambe: what difference there is betweene theſe two, that is to ſay, a Lyon and a Lambe, euerie man knoweth. But we muſt conſider that our Lord Ieſus, in reſpect of the enemies, namely the diuell, death and ſinne, hath ſhewed himſelf as a mightie conquering Lyon, euen that Lord mightie in battell: for he vanquiſhed and ſpoyled them, and tooke from out of their iawes the pray, euen the captiues whom he redeemed frō vnder their power: but in reſpect of his redeemed, he is that Lambe of God which taketh away the ſinnes of the world. Moreouer, we muſt note, that he neuer ſhewed that mightie power of the Lyon more, then when as the vnſpotted Lambe he was ſacrificed vpon the croſſe. The Lambe ſlaine, ouercōmeth all by his bloud: then do not maruell that the Lyon of the tribe of *Iuda* appeareth in the likeneſſe of a Lambe. This Lambe which was ſlaine, ſtandeth in the middeſt of the throne, not as the foure beaſts are ſaid to be in the middeſt of the throne, and round about the throne, which are miniſters, but he as being of equall maieſtie with God the Father, as Saint *Paule* teacheth, Phi. 2. He hath all fulneſſe of power, and of wiſdom, of ſight and knowledge, which is reſembled by his ſeuen hornes, and ſeuen eyes: which alſo are here expounded to be his mighty ſpirit, euen the holy Ghoſt, who he ſent downe into the world, whoſe manifold gifts are powred forth and beſtowed vpon the Church.

Now

THE REVELATION. 123

Now followeth how this Lambe taketh the booke: for he saith, *And he came and tooke the booke out of the right hand of him that sate vpon the throne.* And now followeth the worshipping, the reioycing and praising, wherewith both Angels and men, and all creatures do worship and magnifie the Lambe. He beginneth first with those chiefe Angels and with the foure and twenty Elders: *And when he had taken the booke* (saith he) *the foure beasts, and the foure and twentie Elders fell downe before the Lambe.* Then this Lambe of God, is God, yea God ouer all to be blessed for euer, otherwise how should both men and Angels fall downe and worship him? Is it not said, thou shalt worship the Lord thy God, and him only shalt thou serue? Matth.4. Consider then how great he is, of whome it is said, let all the Angels of God worship him, Psal.97.ver.7. Hebrew.1. Great is the glorie of the Angels in heauen, and yet their greatnesse and glorie is so farre vnder his, that they worship him, euen with the highest worship. And let not vs then giue away any part of his worship vnto any creature; for that is a most horrible wickednesse of the Papists. It is said they *had euery one harpes, and that they sang a new song.* This is to set forth the ioy and reioycing, euen that spirituall ioy, which all the faithfull haue through Christ. Indeed it is great ioy which is wrought by him, which these musicall instruments, and new song do dignifie. This ioy remaineth still as fresh as at the first, and therefore he saith, they sung a new song; for a song is euer the more delightsome while it is new. What the matter of this new song is, we shall see afterward: he saith, *They had also golden vials, full of sweet odours, which are the prayers of the Saints.* The meaning of this is opened by the holy Ghost himselfe, by expounding that those odors are the praiers of the Saints, whereby we see how precious vessels the harts of true beleeuers are before God, and how sweete the praiers are, which are offered vp vnto him out of them: for ye see the vials are of pure gold, and that is the most precious mettall: the praiers offered in them are sweet odours. They did burne incense in the time of the law, which was sweet, not that God was delighted with the smell of any corporall thing, but spirituall things were represented thereby; euen the precious sweetnesse of true praiers offered vp by his people. And therefore the Prophet *Dauid* desired that his praier might be directed before the Lord as incense, Psal.141. We are soone cast downe, & faint in our praiers, as if God had no delight in them: because he often seemeth to turne away his face, and not to regard them, while we aske and obtaine not at the first, or second time.

Let vs therefore for our encouragement remember, they be sweet odors, when they be of faith offered vp in Christ. Thinke vpon this place, when we think prayer is litle worth. But we teach that praiers are to be offered to God through the mediation of Iesus Christ onely; and that the Saintes and Angls are not to haue any part of this honour, as that we should pray vnto them to be mediators and aduocates for vs. And here the Papists draw forth (as they thinke) a strong argument, to confute vs, & to proue that the Saints in heauen do offer vp the prayers of men in earth which seeke vnto them. It is much that our Rhemistes will confesse that the faithfull be Saints while they liue vpon the earth: for the ignorant Popish sort

do

do for the most part scorne it. And now touching their argument from this place: It is not said that the Saints in heauen offer vp the prayers of the Saints in earth, or that these 24. elders had their golden vials full of sweete odours which were not their owne: for these odours were their owne praiers. This may seeme straunge, for do the Saints in heauen pray? I answere, that whether the Saints in heauen do pray, or how they pray, I will not curiously enquire: but I doubt nothing at all, but that these twenty foure Elders do represent the whole Church, euen all the Saints both in heauen and in earth. For if they did represent onely the Apostles and Prophets, how should they say, *Thou hast redeemed vs vnto God by thy bloud, out of euerie kinred, and tongue, and people, and nation?* And now for the matter of their new song, these be the words: *Thou art worthie to take the booke, & to open the seales thereof, because thou wast killed, and hast redeemed vs vnto God by thy bloud, out of euery kinred, and tongue, & people, & nation, & hast made vs vnto our God, kings & priests, & we shall raigne vpon the earth.* This excellent & most noble song, first proclaimeth the praise & worthines of the blessed lambe of God Iesus Christ, to be alone the opener of Gods secrets to the Church. *Thou art worthie to take the booke, & to open the seales thereof.* There could none in heauē, nor in the earth, nor vnder the earth be found, that was worthie to open the booke or to looke thereon, besides him alone: great is the worthinesse then of the Lambe, aboue and beyond all creatures.

Then followeth the confirmation of this worthines, by his humble obedience to his father, his loue and benefits to the Church. For as Saint *Paul* saith: *He humbled himselfe and became obedient to death, euen to the death of the crosse.* And here they say: *because thou wast killed.* How great loue this was towards miserable sinners, to giue himselfe vp for them to the torments of death, no tongue can expresse. And what fruite and benefite came by his bloudie passion to the Church, is set forth in the words that follow. It standeth of two parts, the first is the deliuerance from our bondage and miserie: for being vanquished by death, subiect to the tyrannie of the diuell, and vnder the curse of God; he hath fully deliuered vs: and that the 24. elders declare, in saying, *Thou hast redeemed vs vnto God by thy bloud, out of euery kinred, and tongue, &c.* Then the Gentiles also, euen the people that sate in darkenes, and in the shadow of death, haue seene this great light: Let vs alwaies sing this new song: let vs with glad hearts set forth the worthines of the Lambe, which hath redeemed and bought vs with his most precious bloud. And not onely this, but also (which is the other part of the benefit the Church receiueth by his death,) that he hath exalted vs vnto very high dignitie and glorie. For they say, *Thou hast made vs kings, and priests vnto our God, and we shall raigne on the earth.* It were a wonderfull great benefit to be drawne out of sinne, from the torments of hell, from the power of the diuell, and of death; and to be left in a state without either ioy or paine: but he hath not only deliuered from those former, but also hath so sanctified and clensed vs from our vncleannes, as that we are made holy priests to God, yea sons of the most high, and so great kings; and shall raigne in heauenly glorie for euer. For although it be said, we shall raigne vpon the earth,

yet

yet this kingdome is heauenly: for the Saints shall with Christ receiue the inheritance, and be Lords and kings both of heauen and earth. There shall be new heauens, and a new earth, in which righteousnesse shall dwell, as the holy Ghost saith, 2.Pet.3.13. The Lord giue vs to be of that number which the 24 Elders do represent, that sing this new song vnto the Lambe. It is euen the most ioyfull and the most blessed thing vnder heauen to behold the worthinesse of Christ, to feele his benefites, and to set forth his praise in the same, with spirituall mirth and gladnesse, together with his Saints that do loue his name. And in very deed if our eyes were opened to see a litle into the bottom of that gulf of miseries, out of which he hath redeemed vs by his bloud, and also in some sort to behold the toppe of that glorie vnto which he hath exalted vs, we could not be stayed from singing this new song. The Papists by this place, because it is said, *Thou art worthy, &c. because thou wast killed,* affirme that Christ by his death did merit the high glorie in which he is exalted. Most foolish they are in this, for Christ God and man is but one person, and although for a time he humbled himselfe, and tooke vpon him the shape of a seruant, yet the highest glorie was his owne euen then, and no robberie euen then to be equall with God, as *Paule* teacheth, Philip. 2. Therfore vnlesse they will with one sort of hereticks denie the personal vnion of the two natures in Christ, or with another sort denie his equality in glory with the Father, how shall they stad in this, that Christ by his death did merite his glorie? In the next place the infinite multitude of heauenly Angels about the throne, the foure beasts and the Elders, euen a thousand times ten thousand, and thousand thousands, do with a loud voice set forth the worthinesse of the Lambe. *Worthy is the Lambe* (say they) *that was killed, to receiue power, and riches, and wisdome, and strength, and honour, and glory, and praise.* O most sacrilegious Papists, which rob him of that which all the Angels in heauen do ascribe vnto him! Let vs ioyne with the heauenly companie, & not with the Papists.

Lastly, Saint *Iohn* heareth all the creatures in heauen, and earth, vnder the earth, and in the sea, yeelding praise and glory to God Almightie, and to the Lambe for euermore. This is to be vnderstood of the verie heauens and the earth themselues, & the seas, with all their furniture: as the Sun, the Moone, the stars, & all dumbe creatures below. For as they be all subiect to the bondage of corruption, and in their kind do grone and trauell in paine, waiting when the sonnes of God shall be reuealed, for then they shall also be restored vnto libertie, Rom. 8. so in their kind they laud and praise the Lord God, and the Lambe for their restitution, vnto which praise of theirs the chiefe Angels subscribe, in saying, *Amen,* and the 24 Elders, euen the whole Church fall downe & worship him that liueth for euermore. Then seeing the chiefe Angels, the whole Church, the common multitude of Angels, and all creatures worship, magnifie, & praise the Lambe of God with so great ioy and reioycing, let vs couet to be of this number, and euen set our delight to honour and praise him both by our words and deeds. This shall be our happinesse and glorie for euermore.

THE

SERMONS VPON

THE XIII. SERMON.
CHAP. 6.

1. *After I beheld vvhen the Lambe had opened one of the seales, and I heard one of the foure beasts, as it were the noise of thunder, say, come and see.*
2. *Therfore I beheld, and lo there vvas a vvhite horse, and he that sate on him had a bow, and a crowne vvas giuen vnto him, and he vvent forth conquering that he might ouercome.*
3. *And vvhen he had opened the second seale, I heard the second beast say, come and see.*
4. *And there vvent out another horse that vvas red, and power vvas giuen to him that sate thereon, to take peace from the earth, and that they should kill one another, and there vvas giuen vnto him a great sword.*
5. *And vvhen he had opened the third seale, I heard the third beast say, come and see: then I beheld, and lo a blacke horse, and he that sate thereon had balances in his hand.*
6. *And I heard a voice in the middest of the foure beasts say, a measure of vvheat for a penie, and three measures of barley for a penie, and oyle and vvine hurt thou not.*
7. *And vvhen he had opened the fourth seale, I heard the voyce of the fourth beast say, come and see.*
8. *And I looked, and behold a pale horse, and his name that sate on him was death, and hell followed after him, and power was giuen vnto them ouer the fourth part of the earth, to kill vvith sword, and vvith hunger, and vvith death, and vvith the beasts of the earth.*

THe booke sealed with seuen seales, did the Lambe take out of the right hand of the most high God his Father, none in heauē, or in earth, or vnder the earth besides him alone, being worthie to looke thereon: and now he openeth the seals thereof, and so discloseth vnto his seruant *Iohn* the mysteries contained therein, that he might deliuer them to the Church for the instruction and vse of all Gods seruants. When he had therefore opened the first seale, *Iohn* saith he beheld it, and one of the foure beasts, with a mightie and glorious voyce, euen as it had bene of thunder, willeth him to come and see. And when he looked, *there vvas a vvhite horse, and he that sate thereon had a*
bow,

THE REVELATION.   127

bow, and a crowne was giuen vnto him, and he went forth conquering, that he might ouercome.

What euery part of this vision doth represent & signifie, we are to consider: as namely the horse, his colour, he that sate on him, the bow, the crowne, and his going forth conquering, that he might ouercome. Some do take it, that vnder the figure of these is set forth, how God for the wicked rebellion of the world, wil most mightily and speedily strike them with the arrowes of pestilence, and so triumph ouer them by a conquest. But they doubtlesse are deceiued, which so expound this vision, as the text it selfe will make euident. It is a white horse, marke that, for the white color in the holy Scriptures doth neuer figure out that which is doleful, as the pestilence is a thing verie doleful: but it representeth light, innocencie, puritie, ioy and gladnesse. Againe, as we shall see, here follow shadowed out vnder the other three horses and their riders horrible iudgements, which are executed vpon the world in the displeasure of God, for despising his maruellous mercie and kindnesse offered by Christ. Among which iudgements the pestilence is not the least. Therefore in the opening of the first seale, by the white horse and his rider, by the bow and crowne, and by the going forth to conquer, is represented a farre other matter, and that is, the glad tidings of the Gospell which the Lord Iesus brought, and which he sent abroad by his Apostles and ministers, and conquered and subdued nations vnder him, and which he will still send forth to the end of the world. In this exposition, taking this figure to represent the going forth of the Gospel, euerie part doth most fitly agree, euen by the phrases of the Scriptures: yea, the whole matter of this vision is framed, as it may seeme, by the agreemēt of the speeches out of the 45 Psal. where the marriage of Christ to his Church is figured out by the mariage of king *Salomō* with the daughter of *Pharaoh*. Thus are the words set downe, *Gird thy sword vpon thy thigh, ô thou mighty one, the sword of thy glory and comely beautie. And with thy comely beautie ride on prosperously for the businesse of truth and of meeke righteousnesse, that thy right hand may teach thee terrible things. By thy sharpe arrowes in the heart of the kings enemies, the people shall fall vnder thee.* In these words of the Prophet is set forth the goodly & glorious conquest and victorie of Christ ouer the nations of the world, subduing them vnder him by the Gospell, where he rideth forth; shooteth his arrowes, and getteth the victorie. But let vs compare the words in both places together more particularly. In this place the Prophet speaking of Christ, saith, *With thy comely beauty ride on prosperously, &c.* and Saint *Iohn* at the opening of the first seale, seeth a white horse and one sitting vpon him, which goeth forth conquering. If we respect the colour of this horse which is white, doth it not represent the comely beautie & glorie of Christ & his Gospell? If any will obiect that the Psalme doth not speake of the colour of his horse: I answer, that in the 19 chapter of this booke, Christ is described riding vpon a white horse, and all the armies of heauen following him vpon white horses, which is agreeable to this. The horse and the riding forth, do set out vnto vs indeed, and represent most fitly, that with maruellous swiftnesse the light of the glorious Gospell should be caried & spread ouer the kingdomes of the world. For

it

it is a great wonder to confider, how farre ouer mightie kingdomes and nations of the heathen people, within a few yeares after his afcenfion, the Lord Iefus was preached, and his doctrine was of multitudes embraced. He rode forth indeed profperoufly, and fwiftly vpon this white horfe, euen the minifterie of his Gofpell, for the bufineffe of truth, and of meeke righteoufneffe, & his right hand ful of power, wrought fearefull things. In the Pfalme the Prophet mentioneth no bow, but fharpe arrowes: and contrariwife here Saint *Iohn* feeth him haue a bow, but mentioneth no arrowes. Let not this feeme to make any difference, the bow and the arrowes go together, & fo the matter is all one, for the bow is not to any purpofe without arrowes, which S. *Iohn* fpeaketh of here, & the arrowes fixed in the hart of the kings enemies, which the Prophet fpeaketh of there, are fhot out of a bow. Here S. *Iohn* feeth him haue a crowne giuen him, which betokeneth the victorie which he getteth ouer the inhabitans of the world with his bow & arrowes. The Prophet fetteth it forth in thefe words, that *by his fharpe arrowes being fixed in the heart of the kings enemies, the people fall downe vnder him*. Then here is the crowne of victorie, here is the conqueft and the fubduing of the people by the bow and arrowes. Thefe arrowes, euen thefe moft fharpe and deepe piercing arrowes of the Gofpell, by which the world hath bene fubdued vnto Chrift, Saint *Iohn* hath not fhewed vnto him in vifion, into what part of man they are fhot: but the words of the Pfalme do fhew, for in it the Prophet faith, *thefe fharpe arrowes flicke in the heart of the kings enemies*. And in verie deed all the arrowes of the Gofpell which Chrift fhooteth out of this bow, which is euen the tongues of his minifters, do ftrike the verie harts of men, and do fticke in them, yea they pierce into all the fecret places of the heart. Thefe be noble arrowes, this is a worthie bowe, and here is a glorious victorie. But the queftion may be moued here, why the Prophet fpeaketh as if thefe arrowes were fhot, and did fticke onely in the heart of the kings enemies, that is, in the heart of the enemies of Chrift the king of kings. And moreouer, it may be demaunded what victorie or conqueft the Gofpell obtaineth ouer fuch as remaine obftinate enemies vnto Chrift, which reiect, blafpheme, and perfecute the fame. Firft, we are to confider, that before fuch time as we be in our hearts ftricken with the arrowes of the Gofpell, and conuerted therby to God, we be all of vs by nature the kings enemies, as we may fee, Rom. 5.10. Secondly, we muft obferue, that this victorie of Chrift is of two forts, in refpect of two wayes that the people do fall vnder him. For they whofe hearts thefe fharpe arrowes do ftrike and pierce vnto their conuerfion, as the fweete fauour of life vnto life, and the power of God vnto faluation, they fall downe vnder him with willing & glad hearts, to worfhip, to honour, to obey, and magnifie him as their moft gracious and bleffed king: a moft happie victorie. Thefe fharpe arrowes do not hurt them, but the fafter and the deeper they fticke in their hearts, the better it is for them: yea they couet, & it is moft comfortable vnto them, when they feele them pierce deepeft to kil the old mã. In thefe the arrows may be faid to be in the hart of the kings enemies, not that they remaine ftill enemies, but were before. There is another fort, into whofe hearts alfo thefe arrowes are fhot, & do wound them moft deeply,

THE REVELATION.

ly,but yet do not conuert them,but are the fauour of death vnto death. These do feele the strokes, they rage and are wonderfully moued, they resist, and will not yeeld vnto him that hath shot them,they will none of his yoke, they will not stoupe to obey him, they will breake his bands asunder,they reiect his lawes,they wil not haue him to rule ouer them,they wrastle and struggle with all their might, and yet the arrowes sticke fast in their harts, and by no meanes they can plucke them out, nor heale those deepe and deadly wounds which they make. These do seeme not to be subdued, nor to fall vnder Christ, but the truth is, his arrowes do woūd them deadly, and he doth triumph ouer them. Of this Saint *Paule* glorieth in the Lord with thanſgiuing, 2. Cor. 2. verſ. 14. 15. 16. For he saith, God made them alwayes triumph, both in those that are saued, and in those that perish, &c. Consider then I pray ye, that seeing the rider vpon this white horse with his bow will conquer all, to saue the one part as his subiects which turne vnto him, and to subdue the other as wicked rebels to their destruction, how good it is that we imbrace the Gospell with all loue and gladnesse of hart, and so be of those that come willingly and frankly, as he speaketh, Psalm. 110. Let the other fret as much as they will at the true preachers of the Gospell, yet the arrowes which they shoote sting them so sore, & sticke so fast in their hart, that they biting at them cannot plucke them forth, nor heale the wounds wherewith they haue wounded them vnto eternall death. But why is it sayd that he goeth forth conquering, that he might ouercome? is it meant that the worke is still in hand? yea doubtlesse. For albeit the holy Apostles of Christ had at that time when *Iohn* receiued this prophecy, conuerted great multitudes in many kingdomes, yet the diuell made still all the force he could to suppresse the truth. The Emperors, the kings, the Princes, the Iudges, the Ppilosophers, and all idolatrous people which stood vpon the ancient religion of their forefathers, made fierce war against them, and yet this white horse and his rider proceed and breake through them, yea the Lord with his sharpe arrowes from the mouth of his twelue Apostles, most mightily bringeth them vnder. There be many enemies at this day and shall be euen to the worlds end (for the diuell will neuer giue ouer vntill he receiue his finall iudgement) and therefore this white horse & his rider still go forth: and many by him are dayly conuerted and fall downe to Christ, and the enemies are wounded with deadly wounds which they shall neuer recouer, yea euen the whole kingdome of Antichrist. Beloued consider this vision, the world is bent against the Gospell, great power is made, great cruelty is exercised, and terror euery where to oppresse it, but this rider will conquer all, let vs therefore boldly cleaue vnto it. Thus much for the opening of the first seale.

At the opening of the second seale, he heard the voyce of the second beast say, *Come and see*. We haue seene that there was figured out, vnder the white horse & his rider in opening the former seale, the most ioyfull thing that euer God sent into the world, euen the Lord Iesus with his glorious Gospell, running through the nations of the world. Now in the next three seales being opened, there come forth three other horses and their riders, of other colours, to represent other kind of matters, euen the horrible punishments, and fearefull iudgements of God, which in

K   his

his wrath and displeasure he poureth forth vpon the wicked world for despising his great kindnesse offered, for hating, and blaspheming, and railing vpon his Gospell, and for persecuting his Church. For the greater the kindnesse of God hath bene in giuing his only Sonne vnto vs, with the fulnesse of all heauenly treasures, to enrich, and to make vs truly blessed for euer; the greater and the more execrable is the ingratitude, and wicked contempt of the blind world, in hating and reiecting the same. And from hence it ensueth, that more sore and grieuous plagues haue ouerspread the inhabitants of the earth since the comming of Christ, then in former ages.

In the first of these then, here commeth forth a red horse, he that rideth vpon him hath power giuen him to take peace from the earth, that they might kill one an other, and there was giuen him a great sword. This representeth the bloudy wars, tumults and cruell slaughters among the people of the earth. This plague should swiftly spread it selfe, and therefore commeth also on horsebacke. The colour of this horse declareth what he doth bring, for he is red, that is, all bloud, and very slaughter it selfe. The rider vpon this red horse, is the diuell himselfe: for he is the most fit for such a turne: He is a cruell murtherer from the beginning, hee delighteth in bloud, in hatred and malice, and the same he worketh among men. The righteous God of vengeance giueth him power to take peace from the earth, that men may one kill another, and to this ende a great sword is giuen him for to murther and kill withall. He stirreth vp hatred among kings, and inflameth the wrath of Princes & great men, he raiseth vp tumults and seditions among the rude people, he taketh away all sence of humanity out of the harts of men, and filleth them with such cruelty, that they can without any mercy or compassion shed the bloud one of another. A man is not able almost in his whole life (if he vnderstood all languages and should do nothing else) to reade all the warres and horrible slaughters that haue bene made vpon infinite multitudes, in all countries, since the time of the Gospell. And yet the quantity of the bloud that hath bin shed in killing one another, euen that the riuers sometimes haue bene coloured therewith, is not so strange, as to consider with what sauage cruelty it hath bin done. Many Captaines and souldiers haue bene so cruell and hard hearted, that they haue had no compassion vpon old men, nor vpon women, nor children: but haue thrust their swords and daggers into them, as litle moued, as if they had thrust thē into a stacke of hay. This fellow vpon the red horse hath played his part throughly in the world, and doth still euen at this day. This bloudy cruell tyrant is fit for the world: for God hath giuen a king of peace, vnder whom we should liue, which rideth vpon the white horse; the world will none of him, & therefore this bloudy tyrant the diuell doth receiue power ouer them.

But it may here be sayd, that these bloudy warres in time of the Gospell, doe seeme to be disagreeing, yea quite contrary to that which the Prophets of old did ytter touching the state of the world vnder the kingdome of Christ. For they describe, as I may speake, a golden world. The Prophet *Esay*, Chap. 11. speaking of the branch that should spring out of the roote of *Iesse*, and how the spirit of the

Lord

THE REVELATION.

Lord should rest vpon him, addeth such a description of the cruell beasts & venimous serpents putting off their crueltie and venime, as if there should no noysome thing remaine among men. Looke what hee saith of the wolfe dwelling with the Lambe, the Leopard with the kid, the Lyon with the calfe, and a child to guide them, the beare with the cow, and their young ones together, the yong child putting his hand vpon the hole of the Aspe and Cockatrice. And in the second Chapter he saith, that the law shall go out of Syon, and the word of the Lord out of Ierusalem: and shall iudge among the Gentiles, and they shall cut their swords into spades, and their speares into sithes: nation shall not lift vp a sword against nation, neither shall they learne to warre any more. How can these agree? We are to consider for the reconciling of these things, that our Lord Iesus is the king of peace, he is the reconciler, and the restorer of all things. Before the sinne of man, the beasts did not one dissent from another, nor had any deuouring nature in them any way to hurt. Chrifts kingdome is now but begun, and when it shall be perfected, all hurting shall be taken away. Moreouer, men by nature are cruell and rauening, euen like wolues and beares: when they are regenerate by the Gospell: looke how farre the power of Christ beareth sway in them, so far they cease from those cruell affections, and become tame and meeke. When Chrift shall fully raigne in men, then they shall be perfect. Behold then how the Prophets do set foorth what Chrift bringeth, and what meekenesse and peace he worketh in the chosen, what minds they beare, and what affection they be of, which are regenerate. And were it not the fault of men, all strife and warres should cease indeede, and none should hurt at all. The diuell & his are in such a rage against Chrift, that all is on a broyle. The faithfulll also are so vnperfect, that sometimes they are at sharpe contention. And least any should imagine that the words of the Prophets were so to be taken, as that at the comming of the Messias all should become so peaceable, the Lord himselfe, euen the Messias, foretelleth of this horse and his rider, with his great sword: Thinke not (sayth he) that I am come to send peace vpon the earth, I am not come to send peace but a sword, Matth. 10. ver. 34. These horses go both forth still in the world, and the rider vpon the white horse doth still conquer, euen in the middest of the bloudy swords, and tumults. Let this suffice for the second seale.

When the Lambe opened the third seale, he heard the third beast say, come and see: and lo a blacke horse, and he that sate on him had ballances in his hand. Vnder this figure is set forth dearth and famine. The horse is blacke, which is a sad and dolefull colour: for famine is full of sorrow. The ballances are to shew, that men shall measure and stint themselues in their eating, to make that little which they haue, reach farre and last long. In time of plenty we see how wastfull men are, not regarding measure: but when famine doth oppresse, then euery man hath a little apppointed him by measure, least they should consume in few dayes that which should last many dayes, and so vtterly want and perish before any plenty could come. Therefore when the Lord threatned grieuous famine to the Israelites, he sayth that ten women shall bake together in one ouen, and shall deliuer foorth

K 2   bread

bread by waight, Leuit.16. When a city is ſtraightly beſieged, and the victuals very ſcarſe, euery man hath a litle meaſure, or a little waight for his daily allowance, that ſo they may for a time hold out. To repreſent this plague of famine vpon the world, here is one vpon a blacke horſe with ballances in his hand. Yea further to declare the grieuouſneſſe of the famine, a voice commeth from the throne of God, ſhewing what is decreed, and that is, a meaſure of wheate for a peny, and three meaſures of barley for a peny, and wine and oyle hurt thou not. The meaſure here ſpoken of is a *Chenix*. Writers do ſay it was ſo much as would ſerue a man breadcorne for one day. And the Romaine peny vnder *Domitian* was almoſt ſeuen pence of our mony: and at that time the labouring men did worke for a peny a day. Then ſee what ſtraight here is, when a man had wife and children to ſuſtaine by his trauaile, and the wages or hire for his dayes worke would little more then buy him bread-corne for himſelfe alone, if he did eate wheate bread, and three mens bread-corne, if he would eate barley bread: for how ſhould his labours ſuſtaine with meate and apparell, his wife and children? And for the next clauſe touching wine and oyle, I take it fitter to ſay, thou ſhalt not doe vniuſtly, then to ſay, thou ſhalt not hurt. For this horſeman goeth foorth not to hurt the fruits of the earth, but to repreſent a famine. And then the ſenſe is this, in plenty he that will ſell a litte wine or oyle for a great price, doth deale vniuſtly: but in famine & extreame penury, he that ſelleth a little wine or a little oyle for a great deale of money, doth not deale vniuſtly, when through the ſcarſitie the price can be no lower, the ſcarſitie compelleth him. Let vs conſider what a grieuous plague an extreame famine is. The Prophet *Ieremiah* in his Lamentations, ſayth, They be better that are killed with the ſword, then they that die of famine. Alſo he there, and the Scripture in other places ſheweth, that in ſore famine, the women haue eaten their owne children. Alas what griefe do they ſuſtaine before it come to this, that mothers can be brought to kill and eate their owne children? What are the bowels of a mother to her owne children, yea as Ieremy ſaith, to the children of their ſpan (not of a ſpan long) but to thoſe which the mother whē they be litle ones doth ſpā with her hands, dancing them, & nurcing thē vp? A man wold thinke no extremity could be ſo ſore, as that it ſhold driue her to kill & eate them: and yet we reade of diuerſe that did. And remember how when we haue fealt but ſome ſcarſity of corne (other things being plentifull) how ſore it hath pinched many? Now, if I ſhould ſtand to ſhew at large when, and how the Lord fulfilled this viſion, by plaguing the world with ſore and grieuous famines, I ſhould weary ye: only I will recite ſome few examples. As firſt, about the yere of our Lord 316. the world was miſerably afflicted with famine, peſtilēce, & with ſundry ſorts of calamities, after they had cruelly murthered heapes of Chriſtians. In the yere of our Lord 537. there was a very great famine ouer the world. In 604. there was alſo a grieuous famine, but chiefly in Italy, where Rome ſtandeth. Alſo there was a famine very great and ſore ouer the world in the yeare 946. Likewiſe in the yeare of our Lord 1066. there was a ſtrong famine in all countries. In Fraunce, which hath bene a great vpholder of the ſea of Rome, this blacke horſe came often, and his rider with ballances. For in 660. the

land

THE REVELATION. 133

land was so sore afflicted with famine, that the king sold the vessels of gold and silver, and other precious things in the Churches to relieue the poore. In 898. so grieuous that men were ready to eate one another. Also 931.945.1233. Also in 1235. the famine was so grieuous in France, that men were constrained to eate grasse. And likewise in 1351. What should I mention the famines that haue bene in Germany, in Spaine, in Italy, in Polonia, in Denmarke, in Phrygia, at Venice, at Rome, in England, and in many countries? Surely God hath often sent forth his blacke horse, and besides he hath sent that famine of the word which *Amos* speaketh of, & the yong men and the beautifull virgins haue perished with thirst.

And now followeth the opening of the fourth seale, at which there commeth forth a pale horse, & he that sate on him is called death, & hell followeth. This figureth out the pestilence, & pestilent diseases which God in wrath sendeth vpon the world, and killeth. Men that die of the pestilence looke pale, and therefore here is a pale horse, and death vpon him. A dolefull thing is the pestilence, and this pale horse hath and doth run often through the world. I will mention but some few. In 173. there was a great pestilence ouer the world. Also 254. 1092. 1157. Also in 1305. 1347.1428. these were pestilences general ouer the world. About theye are of our Lord 1315. wehre as such a pestilence that writers report, the third part of men were consumed of it. I will not stand to shew the horrible pestilences that haue bin in seuerall countries and cities, and how often: for it would be a matter infinite. Behold then the grieuous calamities that haue bin in former times, both when the heathen Emperors persecuted and murthered the Christians, and also in the time that Antichrist had set vp idolatry: here is hell following, both the graue, & the infernall torments. The red horse then with blody wars, the blacke horse with famine, the pale horse with the pestilence, haue power giuen them ouer the fourth part of men. For so it is said, that power was giuen them (as I take it rather then to say power was giuē him) ouer the fourth part of mē, to kil with sword, with hunger, with death, and with the beasts of the earth. Thus we see the grieuous plagues that haue bin: and these being sent of God, there is no way to withstand them, but onely with true and vnfained repentance, not despising the blessed Gospell of peace, but obeying it from the hart. For the despising and hating of it, draweth all these horrible plagues vpon the world. When ye see them or heare them, remember the sinnes daily committed, and tremble.

The Lord of heauen giue vs grace
to be warned.

K 3 THE

THE XIIII. SERMON.

9. *And when he had opened the fift seale, I saw vnder the altar, the soules of them that were killed for the word of God, and for the testimony which they maintained.*
10. *And they cried with a lowde voyce, saying, how long Lord, which art holy and true, doest not thou iudge and auenge our bloud on them that dwell on the earth?*
11. *And long white robes were giuen to euery one, and it was said vnto them, that they should rest a litle seafon, vntil their fellow seruants and their brethren, that should be killed euen as they were, were fulfilled.*
12. *And I beheld when he had opened the sixt seale, and lo, there was a great earth-quake, and the Sunne was as blacke as a sackecloth of haire, and the Moone was like bloud.*
13. *And the starres of heauen fell vnto the earth, as a figge tree casteth her greene figges, when it is shaken of a mighty wind.*
14. *And heauen departed away as a scrole when it is rolled, and euery mountaine and Ile vvere moued out of their places.*
15. *And the kings of the earth, and the great men, and the rich men, and the chiefe captaines, and the mighty men, and euery bondman, and euery freeman, hid themselues in dens, and among the rockes of the mountaines.*
16. *And sayd to the mountaines and rockes, fall on vs, and hide vs from the presence of him that sitteth on the throne, and from the wrath of the Lambe.*
17. *For the great day of his wrath is come, and who can stand?*

IN the opening of the former seales, we haue seene figured out, first the going foorth of the Gospell, and then the horrible plagues sent vpon the wicked world for despising the same. In the opening of the fift seale is set forth the state of the soules of those which had beene killed for the Gospell. It was very needefull that this should bee, because they seemed to the world of all other to be the most wretched and miserable. While they liued in the world, they were subiect to the common calamities with other men, and besides this they were put to death most cruelly: yea moreouer, they were put to death as men not worthie to liue vpon the earth. For looke whatſoeuer calamities came, as of the peſtilence, of the famine, and of ſuch like, the cauſe was laid vpon them. The Gods (for ſo the heathen did ſpeake) they ſaid were angry, and did puniſh becauſe of that new learning. If any thing fell out beſide ordinarie courſe, by and by, they cryed to the Lyon with the Chriſtian (as ancient writers which liued in thoſe times do teſtifie). Hereat they ranne vpon them, and murthered thim on heapes, both men and women, with all the moſt grieuous tortures they could deuiſe. How many thouſands did they after this maner ſlay in the firſt ten perſecutions? and they, euen theſe Chriſtians, were reproched, and accurſed among men, as the moſt vile & deteſtable things that euer were vpon the earth: and the Lord God ſeemed to haue no care of them. This might trouble weake mindes, to thinke what is become of them. They haue bene murthered on heapes in all places, their bodies haue bene euen trode downe as the mire. This, as I ſaid, might much trouble the minds of the weake : and therefore here is ſhewed vnto *Iohn* in viſion, that howſoeuer the world did accurſe and cōdemne them, and tread them downe as mire in the ſtreet, yet God had them in price and eſtimation, and had placed them in ioy and bliſſe with their redeemer.

But let vs come to the words as they lie in the text: *When he had opened the fift ſeale, I ſavv vnder the altar, the ſoules of them vvhich vvere killed for the vvord of God, & for the teſtimony vvhich they maintained*. At ſuch time as *Iohn* receiued this reuelation, there had bene many ſlaine for the Chriſtian profeſſiō: but things to come are alſo ſhewed vnto him in viſion, and ſo no doubt the ſoules not onely of thoſe which were then alreadie ſlaine, are in viſion reſembled, but alſo of many other which were afterward put to death vnder the perſecuting Romane Emperors. That they be vnder the altar, it repreſenteth indeed that they be with Chriſt in heauen, and that they be in ioyfull reſt vnder his cuſtodie & protection: for Chriſt is both the prieſt, the altar, and the ſacrifice. It is the ſame thing in effect with that which is in Luk. 16. touching the ſoules of the righteous in Abrahams boſome. And with that which our Sauiour ſaid to the theefe, Luk. 23: *This day ſhalt thou be vvith me in paradiſe*. The thing I ſay is all one, but that here is another phraſe of ſpeech, which is applied fitly to the martyrs. For they were offered vp to God after a ſort as ſlaine ſacrifices, euen vpon that heauenly altar, when they were cruelly murthered for the Goſpell, and therefore he ſaw their ſoules now vnder the altar. They were vnder that altar vpon which they were ſacrificed to God. The papiſts of Rhemes do gather a great matter from hence to maintaine their idolatrous laying vp the the reliques and bodies of martyrs vnder or neare their altars. Chriſt (ſay they) as mā no doubt is this altar, vnder which the ſoules of all martyrs liue in heauen, expecting their bodies, as Chriſt their head hath his bodie alreadie. And for correſpondence to their place or ſtate in heauen, the Church layeth commonly their bodies alſo, or reliques neare, or vnder the altars, where our Sauiours bodies is offered in the holy Maſſe: and hath a ſpeciall proviſo that no altars be erected or conſecrated without ſome part of a Saints bodie or reliques. Thus write our Ieſuites. But we reade of no ſuch thing either commanded or done by the Apoſtles, or by any in the Primitiue Church. We reade that *Stephen* was a martyr, and that religious

religious men tooke him vp and caried him, no doubt to be buried: but we reade not that they buried him vnder an altar. We reade not in all the new Testament of any altar but this one in heauen, nor of any sacrificing the body of Christ but once, when he offered himselfe vpon the crosse. So that in very deede their altars & their sacrifices of the Masse, are euen so many sacrilegious blasphemies, against the only spirituall altar Christ, and the sacrifice which he offered. For Christ offered himselfe to God by his eternall spirit, that is, by his Godhead, and from thence hath his bloud the power to purge sinne, Hebr. 9. Let the Papists proue that any man, yea any Angell is worthy, to offer Christ in sacrifice to his father, Iesus Christ yesterday, and to day, and the same for euer, Hebr. 13. Were not then the fathers vnder the law incorporate into him as we are? How else could the whole Church be his body, and he the head? Could they be incorporate, and not eate his flesh & drinke his bloud, and so mystically and by a spirituall vnion be made flesh of his flesh, and bones of his bones? *S. Paule* sayth (speaking of those fathers) that they did all eate the same spirituall meate, and drinke the same spirituall drinke, 1. Cor. 10. Did they eate Christ but in a figure, & we in truth, as our Papists would beare vs in hand? If they did eate him but in a figure, they were either graffed into him but in a figure, and saued but in a figure : or else Christs mysticall body being but one, yet not all saued after one manner. We cannot be saued vnlesse we eate his flesh, and drinke his bloud, Iohn. 6. No more could *Abraham, Moses, Dauid*, nor all the Prophets. Christ is the bread of life to the whole world: if we eate this bread one way, and *Abraham* and the Prophets another, or they but in figure, that is, in truth not at all, then our faith and their faith is not all one, they are saued one way and we another. What wicked absurdities will follow hereof we may easily see: and therefore it is most euident, that albeit we haue Christ more fully reuealed vnto vs, being come and hauing finished all things which were promised to them, and which were vnder figures shadowed forth vnto them, yet as we eate his flesh & drinke his bloud, so did they . They did eate his very flesh, and drinke his very bloud spiritually, and so do we, they eate it not with their teeth, no more do we. His body once slaine vpon the crosse was auailable to saue them, so is it to saue vs . What correspondence can there be then betweene the soules of the Martyrs vnder the heauenly altar, and the laying of dead bones and reliques neere to these blasphemous Popish altars? Christs body doth not come vpon those altars, and therefore if they haue in the popery any bodies bones, or reliques of such as were true martyrs indeede, the laying of them vp so, is not as their soules are neerest to him in heauen, so their bodies are neerest to his body in earth: but they are vniustly and wickedly abused vnto most vile idolatry, and filthy luker: euen as the Israelites would haue worshipped the body of *Moses*, if they could haue come by it, and therefore the Lord buried him they knew not where, about which the diuell stroue, as S. Iude sheweth. While he was aliue they often rebelled against him, and were ready to stone him, but being dead, they would haue worshipped him. They which murdered Christ, built the sepulchers of the Prophets in their honour, Matth. 23. Euen so the idolatrous Papists, murther the faithfull that come into their hands, and worship

THE REVELATION.   137

ship the martyrs which were slaine by their fathers in old time. Then next he saith that these soules of the martyrs, *cryed vvith a loud voice, saying, How long ô Lord, vvhich art holy and true, doest thou not auenge our bloud on them that dwell on the earth?* This is a vehement crying for vengeance vpon those that had shed their bloud, yea euen for full vengeance. And moreouer, they crie for it speedily, and seeme to be impatient of the delay. Here be two things that may seeme very hard: the one, that the holy martyrs before they died (as we see in *Steuen*, Act. 7.) prayed for their persecutors, that God would not lay that sinne to their charge: and after their death cleane contrarie, they crie onely for speedie vengeance. The other, that they be in such discontentment and disturbance, which agreeth not with ioy and peace, or such happie estate, as they are said to rest in that be in heauen. I will answer to these. For the first, it is most vndoubted, that the blessed martyrs in heauen are not led with any hatred or priuate desire of reuenge, in respect of any wrong or crueltie shewed to them, but with a loue & burning zeale of the kingdome and glorie of Christ: and whatsoeuer desire they haue, it is wholly to that end. Wherefore they are here vnder a figure brought in crying for vengeance, rather to expresse what iudgement of God tarieth for the cruell persecutors, then to shew what mind they beare towards them. For it is indeed their cause that cryeth for vengeance, and as *Abels* bloud, so their bloud crieth aloud in the eares of the Lord of hosts for reuenge. And here their crying is to shew that God hath not forgotten them: but that indeed their cruell persecutors shall come to their account. For these things shewed in vision and figure, are applyed to our capacitie. As the Iudge can neuer forget where the crie is still in his eares, so the Lord hath not forgotten (though he delay for a time) the bloud of his seruants that hath bene shed. Thus we may consider, and not take it that they are caried with desire of reuenge. Touching the other point then, the martyrs haue no disturbance, no impatience, nor vnquietnesse to hinder their peace and ioy in which they rest, the loud crie is not to shew any discontentment or disquietnesse in them. The Saints in heauen (as it must needs be granted) haue not that full glorie which they shall haue when the sonnes of God shall be reuealed, and therfore desire the last iudgement, when they shall receiue their bodies: and no doubt their desire is earnest. Saint *Peter* speaketh of the Angels how they couet to behold the things which shall be accomplished at that day, 2. Pet. 1. And yet the Angels are not hindred in their present ioy by that vehement desire: for they rest in the will of God, and so do the holy martyrs which are here spoken of.

The next words do shew that they be in honour, in glorie, and in peace, when he saith, *Long white robes were giuen to euery one of them*: for these robes are robes of dignitie and blisse. I need not to stay in the exposition of them. And lastly, it is shewed that the full redemption is for a litle season deferred, and they must rest contented, because there are moe of their brethren to be slaine as they were. Surely the beast which maketh warre against the Saints, hath murthered many in sundrie kingdomes, yea exceeding heapes now of late yeares in *Fraunce*, so that the number is filled vp apace: wherby we are admonished to lift vp our heades and

to

strength we shall fall: but if we feele our weakenesse, & trust in God, he will make vs able to stand.

The opening of the sixt seale followeth next, in which there be figured out most fearfull and horrible tokens of Gods displeasure vpon the wicked world, and the horror of conscience wherewith all sorts of worldly men are stricken and terrified at the beholding of them. There were grieuous things at the opening of the second, third, and fourth seales: but now after the crie of the martyrs for vengeance, though the full vengeance be not executed, yet the Lord doth declare his wrath further, euen in a wonderfull maner, and as it were with the astonishment of all creatures. So horrible a thing before God is the sauage cruelty in shedding the bloud of true Christians, and so much is he moued at the cry of their bloud: for the terrible things which now follow are vpon their crie for vengeance. Let vs see the things. First, there was a great earthquake. Then, the Sunne is darkened, & becommeth as blacke as an haire-cloath. The Moone is turned into bloud. The stars fall, euen as a figge-tree casteth her greene figges when it is shaken of a mightie wind. Heauen departeth away as a scrole that is rolled, and euerie mountaine & Ile are remoued out of their places. This is it which Saint *Peter*, Act. 2. did alleage out of the Prophet *Ioel*: *It shall be in the last dayes, saith God, I will powre out of my spirit vpon all flesh, and your sons and your daughters shall prophecie, your young men shall see visions, your old men shall dreame dreames, &c. And I will giue signes in heauen aboue, and tokens in earth beneath, bloud, and fire, and the vapour of smoke: the Sun shall be turned into darknesse, and the Moone into bloud, before that great and notable day of the Lord come.* These signes in heauen aboue, and tokens in earth beneath, are signes and tokens of Gods heauy displeasure: for as his kindnesse exceedeth in the Gospell, in powring forth the greatest gifts and graces of his spirit: so is his indignation the more increased, that such mercies are not only despised and hated, but that also all crueltie is shewed vnto those that embrace them. We reade of mightie shakings and earthquakes in old time, by which many cities were ouerthrowne: we reade of such tumults, commotions, and seditions among the nations, as if all were on fire, & turned into bloud. Moreouer, we reade of such confusion, such sects and heresies, that worldly men haue as sensibly perceiued the wrath and displeasure of God, as if the Sunne it self were darkened, the Moone turned into bloud, and the starres should fall: yea, as if there were such an horrible concussion, as that the heauens should depart, and the mountaines & Iles be remoued out of their places. We do not reade that the Sunne, the Moone, or the starres indeed, or the heauens, the mountains or Iles were thus: but he that shal reade the histories and records of ancient writers, and see the state of the world

for

THE REVELATION.   139

for twelue, or thirteene, or fourteene hundred yeares past, in the times, and immediatly after the times of those cruell bloudie slaughters of Chrifts martyrs, muft needs confesse that God did wonderfully, yea fo wonderfully declare his wrath from heauen, as if thefe things fpoken of the Sunne, the Moone & the ftarres, had bene vifibly reprefented to the eye. Thofe ancient times were wonderfull grieuous and lamentable to behold. And if we come downeward vnto later times, in which the Poperie began to grow & was fet vp (howfoeuer the Papifts fpeake of a golden world) we fhall reade of fuch terrible fignes and tokens of Gods anger, as the like haue neuer bene heard of. For as herefies, fuperftition, idolatrie, and mens inuentions increafed and bare fway, to the defacing of the Gofpel, & of the pure worfhip of God: and as hatred and enmitie increafed againft Gods true feruants, to the perfecuting and rooting of them out: fo God increafed his plagues and heauie iudgements vpon the world. Great commotions, great bloudfheds, great peftilences, great famines, yea great miferies of all forts did euer anon ouerfpread. I do not miflike, in thefe tokens and fignes of Gods wrath in the earthquakes, darkening of the Sunne, turning the Moone into bloud, and the ftarres falling from heauen, the heauens departing away, the mountaines and Iles remouing, that we alfo take a myfticall expofition. As by the earthquakes (as our Sauiour, Math. 24. forefhewed, there fhould be famines, peftilences, and earthquakes in all places) we may take it, were fhewed the fhakings of the people, the changes and alterations of kingdomes, ftates and religions. For the alterations were maruellous in manie kingdomes. There were tumults and commotions, and hideous broyles in all countries. There haue bene flaughters, and turning all into bloud, when tyrants haue perfecuted. The minifters of the Gofpell haue fallen and dropped downe from heauen, euen from their heauenly light, and other fuch grieuous things.

Now followeth the effect of thefe fignes in the hearts of the prophane worldly men of all degrees. All are terrified, and that grieuoufly at the beholding of thefe things. For he faith, *The kings of the earth, the great men, and the rich men, euerie bond man, and euery free man hid themfelues in dennes, and among the rockes in the mountaines.* If a company of wicked fubiects were committing fome wicked facts to the difhonour and dammage of the king, and the king commeth forth to looke vpon them, and teftifieth his anger, they fcatter and runne to hide themfelues: fo the Lord fhewing himfelfe from heauen, with fearefull fignes of his difpleafure at the crie of his martyrs, and for the difhonour offered to his name, the wicked enemies are not able to abide his looke, but fcatter euerie way, and hide themfelues: they defpifed him before, when he feemed to be abfent and to keepe filence. They made a mocke of his Gofpell, and of his fonne: they trode downe his poore feruants. Now when he fheweth by terrible fignes that he beholdeth them and is angrie, they know not which way to turne them. Death is a fearefull thing, but not fo fearfull as his prefence: and therefore they feeke fome comfort if it might be that way, wifhing that the mountaines and rockes might fall vpon

them

them, and hide them from his presence. For they confesse by those signes, that the day of his wrath is come, and that none can abide it. It may be said, when was this fulfilled? when do we reade that there was such a scare among men? We must vnderstand that these things shewed in vision, were not so fulfilled to the bodily eye, but the holy Ghost vnder these figures, doth shew into what terrour of conscience all the wicked enemies haue bene cast into, at the beholding the signes and tokens of Gods displeasure, and being priuie & remembring all the iniuries and contempt shewed against the Lord Iesus and his Church. They do not repent: for an vngodly man comming to faith and repentance, shunneth not the presence of God, though he haue griuously sinned: but these desire they may not come into the sight of God and of the Lambe. They delighted themselues in their vngodly wayes, and now they perceiue that God is offended, for they gather it by his grieuous plagues and fearefull signes, they see they must come to iudgement, and that doth torment and trouble them. How great thinke ye were the troubles and tokens of wrath, when the verie tyrants are made to feele and confesse, and that with such inward trouble and feare, that Christ is displeased for the iniuries which they haue done vnto him? They that reade ancient histories shall find, that when the hand of God hath bene vpon them, some of the most cruell haue bene euen forced to vtter, that it was for tormenting the poore Christians. And looke vpon men at this day, and marke the most wicked and desperate despisers and blasphemers of the truth, and if there fall out any fearefull signe, that God seemeth to come neare in displeasure, ye shall see them quake and perplexed for the time, in such sort that they cannot tell where to become. Their minds do as it were seeke darke dennes to hide themselues in. Why is a Lambe then so terrible? He is a Lambe indeed euerie way to his chosen, but most terrible to all those which oppresse his chosen. They be deare vnto him, yea so deare, that his wrath is kindled against all that hate them. We may see by this place, that wicked and prophane mockers and despisers of the Gospell, though they carie smooth faces, are made oftentimes to feele that which they would willingly be rid of. And let vs learne to kisse the sonne (as the Prophet willeth, Psal.2.) least he be angrie. Let vs embrace with all gladnesse his truth: let vs obey him, and loue his people: and then what troubles and commotions, and fearefull tokens soeuer fall out, we shall haue inward peace and comfort. Yea, when death commeth we shall haue ioy, and be nothing terrified at the iudgement seat nor feare the Iudge: but we shall willingly endure to come into his presence. O what a treasure is this, and now in our life time to be sought for. Lord giue vs wisdome for to do it. Amen.

THE

THE REVELATION. 141

THE XV. SERMON.

CHAP. 7.

1. And after that I saw foure Angels stand on the foure corners of the earth, holding the foure vvinds of the earth, that the vvinds should not blow on the earth, neither on the sea, neither on anie tree.
2. And I saw another Angell come vp from the East, vvhich had the seale of the liuing God, and he cried vvith a loud voyce to the foure Angels, to vvhom power was giuen to hurt the earth and the sea, saying:
3. Hurt ye not the earth, neither the sea, neither the trees, till we haue sealed the seruants of God in their foreheads.
4. And I heard the number of them that vvere sealed, and there vvere sealed an hundreth and foure and forty thousand of all the tribes of Israell.
5. Of the tribe of Iuda were sealed twelue thousand. Of the tribe of Reuben vvere sealed twelue thousand. Of the tribe of Gad vvere sealed twelue thousand.
6. Of the tribe of Aser were sealed twelue thousand. Of the tribe of Nephthali were sealed twelue thousand. Of the tribe of Manasses vvere sealed twelue thousand.
7. Of the tribe of Simeon vvere sealed twelue thousand. Of the tribe of Leui vvere sealed twelue thousand. Of the tribe of Issachar vvere sealed twelue thousand. Of the tribe of Zabulon vvere sealed twelue thousand.
8. Of the tribe of Ioseph vvere sealed twelue thousand. Of the tribe of Beniamin vvere sealed twelue thousand.
9. After these things I beheld, and lo, a great multitude, vvhich no man could number, of all nations, and kindreds, and people, and tongues, stood before the throne, and before the Lambe, cloathed vvith long vvhite robes, and palmes in their hands.

IN the times of the opening the former seales, vnder the persecuting Emperours, there were thousands, yea thousand thousands cruelly murthered for the Gospell, as it was noted before in the sixt chapter. They were iudged of the heathē people, to be so vile and so wicked, that looke whatsoeuer strange plagues fell out in the world, they were said to be the cause of the same, and so they were put to death with execration, as things most detestable. Moreouer, God seemed to haue small care of them, when he suffered them to be tormented and killed: wherfore least this might trouble the minds of the godly, or least they shold
want

want any encouragement or hartning to stand boldly in the truth, in the opening of the fift seale, the soules of those so murthered, are shewed to *Iohn* in vision to be in blessed estate: & moreouer, there is reuealed, that horrible vengeance doth remaine for those which had so cruelly shed their bloud. And further, as we haue seene, after the crie of those martyrs for reuenge of their bloud, in the opening of the sixt seale, the Lord God is so highly displeased, and his anger so iustly kindled for this vile contumely shewed against his Sonne, and against his faithfull members, that he manifestly sheweth the signes and tokens of his wrath in the heauens and in the earth, with such shakings, such darknesse, such horror and confusions, that all the prophane aduersaries are marueilously terrified. Most horrible was the state of the world at that time. Now it might be said, these soules of the martyrs are safe, which are the Church triumphant, they be arriued vpon the hauen of securitie, the waues and tempests cannot come nigh them: but now what shall become of the Church militant, the Church in earth, being in the confused gulfe, and tossed in the darknesse, in the time of the commotions and fearfull signes here spoken of? Yea, when heauen and earth seeme to be mingled together with such confused darknesse, and when all things come to passe which are shewed at the opening of the sixt seale, and many more at the opening of the seuenth, which lasteth to the end of the world; it may be said, what shall become of them? This doubt is answered, that the Lord Iesus doth so prouide for, and so preserue his chosen in the middest of all these horrible things, that not so much as one of them doth miscarrie. To declare so much to the singular consolation of all the faithfull, here is set downe in this chapter, which is placed betweene the opening of the sixt seale and the seuenth, how *Iohn* in vision saw these faithfull in earth sealed, and set in safetie, euen a great & an infinit number, he heard the praise which they giue to God, & had shewed vnto him their happie estate with Christ. So then the Church in earth, though in great assaults, euē in the time of Antichrist, is as safe as the martyrs in heauen. And this same did the Prophet *Ioel* also in a word expresse, as Saint *Peter* doth also alleage it, Act. 2. for hauing told, that there should be signes in heauen aboue, and tokens in earth beneath, bloud, and fire, and the vapour of smoke, and that the Sunne should be turned into darknesse, and the Moone into bloud, &c. he addeth, *It shall come to passe, that whosoeuer shal call on the name of the Lord shall be saued.* Let the heauens and the earth be mingled, let darknesse, horrour and confusion be neuer so great, blessed be the high prouidence, there shall not one of Gods seruants perish.

But let vs come to the words as they lie: that he seeth *foure Angels standing vpon the foure corners of the earth, &c.* It may be demaunded, whether they were good or euill Angels: for there be good Angels, and there be euill Angels: and we may find in the holy scriptures, that God hath executed his iudgemēts or plagues vpon wicked men, as well by his heauenly ministers and holy Angels, as by infernall spirits the malignant wicked diuels. I take it out of doubt that these were vncleane spirits, euen diuels of hell, these foure Angels here spoken of: because the plagues wherewith they are to hurt, are chiefly spiritual, as we shall see, and such as

the

the diuels do execute. That they stand vpon the foure corners of the earth, it sheweth that they haue power giuen thē to plague vniuersally ouer the whole world, and not in some one countrey, or in some few places. For vnder East, West, North, and South, the foure corners, or the foure quarters, the whole world is included. That they hold the foure winds, the question is whether they hold them backe frō doing harme, vntill their power be giuen to loose thē, or whether they haue power to hurt by holding them back. Certaine it is, that the winds sometime when they blow ouer loud, do much hurt both by sea and by land. For they drowne shippes, and ouerthrow houses and trees: but yet the windes cannot be spared, they be so wholesome, and good for all things that liue and grow. Wherefore I take it out of doubt, that these foure Angels holding the foure winds that they should not blow vpon the earth, vpon the sea, nor vpon any tree, do it to hurt, according to the power which was giuen vnto them. God is angrie and giueth them power, and they are readie. Then let vs see what is represented by holding the windes from blowing. No doubt here is a spirituall plague represented, because here is such a speciall prouiso and care shewed for the Church, for her safe keeping from spirituall dangers. The seruants of God haue their part in outward calamities, but that sealing of them which is here spoken of, setteth them safe from spirituall infection, so farre as to be ouerthrowne thereby. The blowing of the winds, do fitly represent the preaching of the Gospell, and that heauenly inspiration and breathing of the holy Ghost which goeth with it. Then on the contrarie the holding of the winds, is the stopping of the course of the Gospell, and so the keeping backe of that heauenly grace. And least any shold take this to be but mans coniecture, vnderstand that the Scripture it selfe vseth this similitude, as we may reade in the 4 chapter of the song of *Salomon*, where the Church speaketh thus: Arise ô North wind, and come ô South wind, blow vpon my garden, and the spices thereof shall flow, &c. What can be meant by these winds which she wisheth to blow vpon her garden, but the heauenly breathings of Gods holy spirit and word? Will any deny this? Then the holding of the foure windes represenreth the great and generall plague of all plagues, euen the stopping of this wholesome breath through the world. That which God said: *I will powre out of my spirit vpon all flesh*, is the highest blessing vnder heauen: for the spirit giueth life. But the world is euer so vnthankfull, & doth set so light by heauenly blessings, doth so hate the truth, & persecute those which loue it, that God is highly offended, & giueth power to the diuels to stay the Gospell, & so to bring in darknesse, and famine, and destruction vpon all nations. Lay all the things then together which I haue noted, that the power giuen to these Angels to hurt the earth is spirituall, because here is such speciall prouision to set the Church and all her children in safetie, sealed with the seale of God: and because the breathing of the windes in the Scripture doth resemble that heauenly inspiration of Gods spirit, which with the preaching of the liuely word bloweth vpon the Church: and moreouer that it is held backe from all the foure corners of the earth: and ye see that there should come a time when the Gospel should as it were cease, and not be published freely and openly in any countrey of the world. Surely this without the heauenly breathing of the holy Ghost, and of the glorious Gospell? Can there be any faith without these? Indeed the vision shewed in this chapter is to answer & to satisfie that doubt. And therefore that we may know that Christ would, and did prouide for his chosen some breath, euen when it was generally stayed, and did not blow: yea that after a miraculous sort euen in the middest of all darknesse, when the whole ayre was corrupted, when mē did suck in no breath, but of filthie poisoned superstition, idolatrie, and stinking rotten dregges of mens inuentions, he did minister light, & quickening breath, and wholesome foode vnto them, and kept them from the generall infection. The next words do shew how this was performed. *And I saw (*saith S. *Iohn) another Angell come vp from the East, hauing the seale of the liuing God, and he cried with a lowd voice to the foure Angels, to whom power was giuen to hurt the earth, and the sea, saying: Hurt ye not the earth, neither the sea, neither the trees, vntill vve haue sealed the seruants of God in their foreheads.* This Angell comming vp from the East, is the blessed Lord Iesus himselfe, as ye shall see it plaine by this, that he hath the seale of the liuing God to set vpon all the elect: for none haue that seale to set the print of it vpon men but Christ, as it will better appeare when we come to see what this seale of the liuing God is. He commeth vp from the East, for he is the Son of righteousnesse that ariseth & shineth vpon his Church, and expelleth all spirituall darknesse from her, euen when all the whole rout of infernall spirits are let loose in the world to couer the earth with the darknesse of hell. *He hath the seale of the liuing God.* What is this seale then? S. *Paul* doth shew what it is, who is a sufficient witnesse, when he saith: After ye beleeued, ye were sealed with the holy spirit of promise, Ephes.1. Then the spirit of God, euen the spirit of adoption, is the seale of God, wherewithall the elect are sealed, and set in safetie in the middest of Antichristes tyrannie. For whosoeuer hath the print of this seale vpon him, he is out of danger. To this agreeth S. *Iohn* in his first Epistle chap. 2. speaking of the comming of Antichrist, for he setteth the beleeuers in safetie by this, as he saith: Ye haue receiued an annoynting from that holy one, and know all things. Ye shall not neede to feare Antichrist, he shall not be able to seduce ye, because ye are taught by the holy Ghost. The Papists would make vs beleeue, that seeing there shall be false Prophets, & deceiuers, & strong delusiō of error, & heresies in the world, the only safetie of the people is to cleaue to Chrifts vicar (for so they call the Pope) he can neuer erre: for so also they speake of the Pope. But this is the diuels subtiltie, to leade men to seeke their safetie vnder his wings, which is the destruction of all. This is according to the old prouerbe, to make the Foxe the gooseheard. Christ neuer speaketh of such a safetie, he neuer saith, cleaue to him that shall be Bishop

of

Papists of Rheimes, is an allusion to the signe of the crosse, which the faithfull beare in their foreheads, to shew they be not ashamed of Christ. I answer, that this is but friuolous, as any man may see, yea a child may see, if he consider that the seale here spoken of is the proper signe of Gods elect, by which they are seuered and discerned from all the reprobate, and by which they stand safe from all spirituall perils. No reprobate is signed with this seale, but many a reprobate is signed with the signe of the crosse. And then seeing the signe of the crosse is common to hypocrites, how can that be an allusion to it which seuereth the true seruants of God from all other? But these Papists would blind the simple people with any shew. Surely they care not what grossenesse other men do espy in them, so the superstitious and idolatrous sort may be kept blind, and haue them still in admiration.

  This mighty Angell crieth with a loude voyce to the foure Angels, to whom power was giuen to hurt the earth, and the sea, saying: hurt not the earth, nor the sea, nor the trees, vntill we haue sealed the seruants of God in their foreheads. The Lord Iesus hath all power in heauen and in earth giuen vnto him. He hath the keyes of death and of hell. He commandeth with authority the very diuels. And when power is giuen them for to hurt (as they haue no power, but as it is giuen them) it is restrained and limited, and so farre, that they cannot plucke out of Christs hand, nor hurt so much as one of his chosen. He sealeth them vp, and setteth them safe. If it were possible (as he saith, Matth. 24.) the elect should be deceiued: but blessed be his holy name, which hath made it impossible. And further we are here to note, that these Angels cannot hurt the earth, & the sea, that is, not euen the worldlings, & reprobate, vntill Gods seruants be set free out of danger. Great is the kindnesse of our Lord towards his redeemed. *Lot* made petition and sute to the Angels that he might haue a city to flie vnto, and the same being graunted, they will him to make haste thither, saying, that they could do nothing vntill he came thither. We reade also, that when the Lord would destroy Ierusalem for all the wicked abominations therein committed, he shewed to the Prophet in a vision, the destroyers comming foorth with their weapons to destroy: also a man girded in a linnen garment which went through as he was willed, and marked all those in their forehead which mourned and cried out for the abominations there committed: and the destroyers were to follow him, & not to touch any that was marked. Ezech. 9. They could not destroy the wicked, vntill the godly were marked and set free. Let vs then be well assured, that in the middest of all Sathans deceits, and in the very prime of Antichrists tyranny, and of all mischiefes and confusions, those shall all stand safe which call vpon the name of the Lord: euen all that call vpon him, as

L   the

the Prophet fayth, in truth: for they be all fealed in their foreheads with the feale of the liuing God. Here is then the wifedome, the power, and prouidence of God highly fet foorth and glorified, that draweth out euery one of his feruants out of this fwelling and raging gulfe, fo full of darkeneffe and ftormes, fo that no one of them doth mifcarrie. The diuels and the tyrants do euen as it were throw wild fire, feeking to confume, to ouerwhelme and to drowne them, but all in vaine, through the goodneffe of God. But why is it fayd that the feruants of God are fealed in their foreheads? If the holy fpirit of promife, euen the fpirit of adoption, be the feale, wherewith they be fealed, he is fet to in the hart, and not vpon the forehead. To anfwer this, we muft here confider that in fpirituall things the holy Scriptures do fpeake as of corporall, applying all to our capacity. The fpirit, the foule, or the heart of man, hath no forehead, as we fee in the head of the body, but yet is fayd to receiue the marke or print of this feale in the forehead, becaufe it doth openly appeare. And further we muft note, that it appeareth not onely to God and his Angels, but alfo vnto men. If ye will demaund, how doth this feale appeare to men? I anfwer, that a man cannot carry fire in his bofome, and no heate appeare. In like manner, à man cannot be fealed with the holy Ghoft, and carry it fo clofe in his heart, but that it will appeare in the outward conuerfation and behauiour and profeffion. The good workes, euen the fruites of the fpirit will fhew themfelues, with the witneffing of the trueth. Such as walke in euill workes, or make no profeffion of the holy Gofpell, fay what they will, there can be no print of this feale feene in their foreheads. If we be fealed, let vs declare our loue and zeale to the Gofpell, and our good deedes, and workes of mercy to our brethren that be in diftreffe.

Now followeth the number of the feruants of God which are fealed: *I heard the number of them that were fealed, and there were fealed an hundred, and foure and fortie thoufand of all the tribes of Ifrael.* The Church confifteth of Iewes and Gentiles: the Iewes had the prerogatiue to be before the Gentiles, and therefore he beginneth firft with them. The Gofpell is the power of God to faluation, to euery one that beleeueth, to the Iew firft, and then to the Grecian, Rom. 1. verfe. 16. They are called the naturall branches, Rom. 11. And in the fame Chapter *S. Paule* difputeth, and fheweth that God hath his remnant ftill among them. Some of them be now and then in one country or other conuerted to Chrift: but this great number vnder the opening of the fixt and feauenth feale, do import a more generall calling of the nation of the Iewes (if they may rightly be called a nation, being fo fcattered among the nations) which thing alfo *Saint Paule* feemeth to prophecie of, Rom. 11. The number of Gods elect among them now in thefe latter dayes, is fet downe to be an hundreth and foure and fortie thoufand. Not that we are to take it fo as that there are iuft fo many, neither more nor leffe: but this number doth arife of twelue times twelue: in that he fayth of euery tribe twelue thoufand. Which we are not alfo fo to vnderftand, as that there fhold be of euery tribe an equal nũber, not moe, nor leffe of one then of another: but this number of twelue is vfed as the perfect and full number, in as much as the Church of the Iewes was founded

vpon

vpon twelue Patriarks, the twelue sonnes of *Iacob*. Vnto which our Sauiour had respect, when for to gather the disperfed and loft sheepe of the house of Israel, he chose twelue Apostles. *Iohn* heard the tribes seuerally reckoned vp, and of euery one sealed twelue thousand. Then God hath not (as S. *Paul* faith) cast off his people which he had chosen : he hath a remnant among them through the election of grace, which he respecteth, and sheweth by this particular rehearsall. But how is it, that here are twelue tribes, and yet some left out? In *Moses* we reade that *Iacob* had but twelue sonnes, and yet there are twelue tribes to whome the land of Canaan is deuided, besides the tribe of *Leui*, which had no seuerall inheritance of a tribe alotted. Thus it came to passe, the eldest was to haue the prerogatiue of the first borne, both touching the principalitie for Christ the king to come of him, & also to haue a double portion of the land. *Reuben* was the eldest, but he committed incest with one of his fathers wiues, and so was cast downe from this dignitie, Gen. 49. verf. 3. 4. *Simeon* was the next, and then *Leui*, they are both depriued of it for their cruell fact in killing the Sichemites, because their fister *Dina* was defloured. *Iehuda* he was the fourth, he preuailed and obtained the principalitie, and so *Iacob* setteth him forth in the same chapter. Thy brethren shall praise thee, thy hand shall be in the necke of thine enemies, thy fathers sonnes shall bow to thee. It is manifest, as it is said in the Epistle to the Hebrues, that our Lord sprong of *Iuda*. But *Iuda* did not obtaine the whole birthright, but part of it befell vnto *Ioseph*, as namely a double portion in the diuision of the land, and his two sonnes *Manasse* and *Ephraim* become two tribes. This is set foorth 1. Chron. 5. verf. 1. 2. Also ye may reade how *Iacob* himselfe doth appoint it so, Gen. 48. verf. 5. Thy two sons (faith he to *Ioseph*) which were borne vnto thee in the land of Egypt, before I came to thee into Egypt, are mine: *Ephraim* and *Manasse*, are mine, as *Reuben* & *Simeon*. So then *Ioseph* being two tribes, there are 12. besides the tribe of *Leui*, which did not inherit as the rest, but was scattered in Israel. Here now in sealing twelue thousand of euery tribe, the one sonne of *Ioseph* is named, and *Ioseph* himselfe for the other. And againe, because the priesthood of *Leui* ceaseth, and all are made priests, & the Leuites inherit as the rest do, in the heauenly land of promise, the tribe of *Leui* is here brought in, and the number of twelue being precisely to be kept, the tribe of *Dan* is omitted. This tribe fell to idolatrie, as ye may reade, Iudg. 18. and continued therein vntill the capiuitie, and are not numbred among the tribes, 1. Chron. chap. 2. 3. 4. 5. 6. 7. 8. where all the other tribes are rehearsed. Some of the Papists do gather a mysterie out of this, that the tribe of *Dan* is here omitted, and haue heretofore stood much vpon it: because some of the ancient fathers did take it that Antichrist should come of the tribe of *Dan*; hereby sundrie fables haue sprong touching Antichrist. This hath bene the cunning of the diuell, to the end that the great Antichrist might not be knowne, to draw mens minds to waite for one that shall come of the Iewes. They may waite long enough: for when the Iewes shall receiue the Messias which they dreame of to come, then shall the papists also see that Antichrist which they imagine. But the truth is, the learnedest Papists, and euen the Papistes of Rhemes, do see the vanitie of this collection,

L 2

tion, that Antichrist should come of the tribe of *Dan*, and do omit it: and then what should we stand to confute it?

Hauing done with the number of those which were sealed of the Iewes, hee commeth then to the Gentiles. Indeed the Church of the Iewes had the priuiledge to be before them: but herein the Church of the Gentiles goeth beyond her, that the multitude of her children is innumerable. God indeede can number them, but no man is able to number them. For thus *S. Iohn* sayth, *After these things I beheld, and lo a great multitude vvhich no man could number, of all nations, and kindreds, and people, and tongues, stood before the throne, and before the Lambe, clothed with long vvhite robes, and palmes in their hands*. Here we may learne first, that we are not to measure Gods Church after our owne senses, when idolatry, superstition, open wickednesse, bloudy persecutions, and slaughters, & darknesse, do ouerspread all. *Elias* the Prophet saw such things ouerspread in Israell, and complained that he was left alone. But he was deceiued, for the Lord made him aunswere, I haue reserued to my selfe 7000 in Israel, which haue not bowed the knee to Baal. If so great a Prophet were so much deceiued in so small a corner: how shall not other which are farre inferior to him, be deceiued among the multitude of the nations? beholding the manifold corruptions in manners which euery where ouerspread in the Churches: but chiefly looking backe into the idolatrous, darke & bloudy kingdome of Antichrist, a Donatist will iudge few or none to remaine. But to correct this boldnesse, here is shewed that euen in the most miserable times, the Lord did preserue his Church; had his elect in the confused heape, and that in a maruellous great number. Then also here is comfort to support weake minds in such times of distresse, and hauocke. But when our Sauiour sayth the gate is streight and the way narrow which leadeth vnto life, and few that find it, how doth it agree with this? Are they few which no man is able to number? Here yee must note that our Sauiour speaketh not simply, but in comparison. The multitude of those that shall be saued is very great, if they be considered by themselues, yea they be so many as no man is able to comprehend the number: but if ye compare them with those that shall be damned, they be but few: their number, I meane the number of the damned, doth in many degrees surmount. When Princes do muster souldiers, if the Captaines should take but ten out of a parish through this land, when they come together they make a great army: but compared with the multitude of men, women and children which are left behind, they scarse are missed. And what is this land to the whole world? and then consider the time, that this innumerable multitude is gathered in so many hundreth yeares. Then further this innumerable multitude doth stand before the throne, and before the Lambe: which is a great dignity and happinesse vnspeakeable, euen to be so neere to God, and to be partakers of his glory. While they bee in the world, they be iudged for the most part to bee so base and vile, and are had in so great contempt, as if they were not worthy in any respect, to come neere the presence of earthly Princes, nay not euen to dwell among men: but here they stand all before the high throne. They be in long white robes, which betokeneth their dignitie,

their

THE REVELATION. 149

their innocency, and glory: but of these robes we shall speake more afterward. It is sayd further, that they haue palmes in their hands. It was in old time the manner of conquerers to beare in their hands palmes of victory. Then it is to shew, that all these are warriers, come out of the battaile as mighty and victorious conquerers. I need not here enter into the discourse of those things which ye haue bene so often taught in, out of diuerse places of the Scripture, but especially out of Eph. 6. touching the spirituall warfare. Ye see there what fierce, and mighty, and subtill enemies we are continually enuironed withall. The greater or stronger the enemies be, the more glorious is the victory. Indeede it is not by their owne strength that they haue preuailed, and carry palmes in their hands: but through the might of the Lord. Christ Iesus is the king of glory, he is their head and Captaine, he hath in his owne person fought the combate, he is the Lord that hath shewed himselfe mighty in battaile: for he hath trode downe Sathan, and all the infernall powers: and all his chosen are through faith armed with his power, and so through him do become mighty conquerers, as it is here shewed vnto *Saint Iohn* in vision. The Lord blesse vs, and make vs to be of this heauenly company.

THE XVI. SERMON.
CHAP. 7.

10. *And they cried with a loud voyce, saying, Saluation commeth of our God, that sitteth vpon the throne, and of the Lambe.*
11. *And all the Angels stood round about the throne, and about the Elders, and the foure beasts, and they fell before the throne on their faces, and worshipped God,*
12. *Saying, Amen. Praise, and glory, and wisedome, and thankes, and honor, and power, and might, be vnto our God for euermore, Amen.*
13. *And one of the Elders spake, saying vnto me, What are these which are arayed in long white robes? and whence came they?*
14. *And I said vnto him, Lord thou knowest. And he sayd to me, These are they which came out of great tribulation, and haue washed their long robes, and haue made their long robes white in the bloud of the Lambe.*
15. *Therefore are they in the presence of the throne of God, and serue him day and night in his Temple, and hee that sitteth vpon the throne will dwell among them.*
16. *They shall hunger no more, neither thirst any more, neither shall the sunne light on them, neither any heate:*

17. *For*

17. *For the Lambe which is in the middeſt of the throne, ſhall gouerne them, and ſhall leade them vnto the liuely fountaines of waters, and God ſhal wipe away all teares from their eyes.*

We haue noted before, that in this Chapter there is ſet forth vnto vs how the Lord Ieſus doth preſerue his Church militant here vpon earth; and euery one of her children in ſafetie from ſpirituall infection, euen in the middeſt of all daungers whatſoeuer, here in the world. He ſetteth the ſeale of the liuing God vpon them, and thereby they are preſerued. This we haue already handled, and ſpoken alſo touching the great number of them, in the former part of this Chapter. Now followeth the praiſe and thankeſgiuing which they offer vp vnto God for their preſeruation & deliuerance: and how not onely they, but alſo all the Angels in heauen do glorifie him for the ſame. And then followeth an expoſition of the viſion, in which their good eſtate is ſet forth both in this world, and in the world to come. *They cried* (faith S. *Iohn*) *with a loud voyce, ſaying, Saluation is of our God, that ſitteth vpon the throne, and of the Lambe.* Their loud crying and lifting vp their voyce, in aſcribing ſaluation to God, and to the Lambe, doth ſhew how earneſtly, how vehemently, and with how deepe affection of heart they do render praiſe to God their Sauiour. For the vehement motions of the mind are vſually expreſſed by the voyce, which vſually is not vehement, vnleſſe the minde be vehemently moued. They be ſo full of it within, that they cannot vtter it ſoftly. They be like the veſſels of new wine that muſt haue a vent: for ſo is it with all that feele the goodneſſe of God. Indeed this is a worthy thing, and doth diſtinguiſh the true, hearty, and cheerfull praiſing of God, from that which is but for faſhion ſake, and hypocriticall, as alſo from that which is but cold, and negligently done, although with ſome ſinceritie. We ſee men in their anger how ſtrongly they thruſt foorth their ſpeech, and likewiſe in their carnall mirth: but when it toucheth the praiſes of God, they can ſcarſe be heard, they do but as it were liſpe. What doth this betoken, but that the heart within hath ſmall feeling of Gods kindneſſe, and ſo hath as ſmall delight to praiſe him? But let vs ſee what might be the cauſe that they be thus vehemently affected to offer vp ſuch ſtrong praiſe to God, and to the Lambe. Indeede here lyeth the cauſe, that they ſee God hath miraculouſly, and after a wonderfull manner ſaued them out of extreame daungers, by the bloud of the Lambe. If we could ſee the depth of our miſery and bondage: if we could diſcerne throughly the tyrannous power of ſinne, of the diuell, and of death: if we did well know our owne corruption, and frailty, and all the ſtrong and ſubtill aſſaults of the diuell, and all the daungers that we are compaſſed about withall, by meanes of Antichriſt, and ſee indeede that God doth ſaue vs out of them: it would make vs crie aloud in praiſing of him, euen with wonderment at his glorious power, wiſedome, and mercifull prouidence. It commeth to paſſe ſometimes, that a man paſſeth through very

great

THE REVELATION. 151

great perill, and doth not espie it while he is in it; but when he is past, he doth wonder, and wonder againe, how he could escape. Euen so it is with vs, for doubtlesse we see but little now in comparison; but when we shall be fully deliuered, & haue our eyes opened, and looke backe into the huge gulfe of daungers, out of which we are drawne by the power of God: we shall then crie aloude, that saluation is of God that sitteth vpon the throne, and of the Lambe. This is not like the cry of the Popish Church, which doth ascribe saluation to mans merits. The holy Angels in heauen do see the glory of this saluation, euen the greatnes of the worke, and that it is wholly of God through Christ, and therefore they do worship, and they do subscribe to the praise of the Church. For he sayth, *All the Angels stood round about the throne, and about the Elders, and the foure beasts, and they fell before the throne on their faces, and worshipped God, saying, Amen*. And then to shew the infinitenesse of his praise, & that they cannot satisfie themselues in praising of him, and that no speech is sufficient fully to expresse his due praises, they heape vp many words, saying: *Praise, and glory, and wisedome, and thankes, and honour, and power, and might, be vnto our God for euermore, Amen*. This manner of praising God is to be obserued that we may learne it, for it is the right manner. I may truly say, and no man can be so impudent as to deny it, that here is the Catholike praising of God, and of our Lord Iesus Christ, through whose bloud hee doth saue vs. That is Catholike, which the whole true Church doth, and all the blessed Angels in heauen: and when we ioyne with the Church and with the Angels, then are we in the Catholike faith. And what is that? We see it set downe in these words, *Saluation is of God, that sitteth vpon the throne, and of the Lambe*. The Papists in defending mans free will, by extolling mens merits, by seeking iustification by workes, by boasting of their workes of supererogation, and by a thousand such like trumperies of their owne deuising, wherein they seeke remission of sins, and to purchase eternall glory, do take away almost the whole praise from God, and from the Lambe of God Iesus Christ, and giue it to creatures. They would leade vs to doe the like with them, and what is their argument which they vrge so much? They say they be Catholike: because so many Popes, so many Cardinals, so many Bishops, so many Doctors, so many Abbots, so many Monkes, so many Friers, so many Nunnes, so many Nations, so many Kings, so many wise Counsellers, haue consented and agreed, and haue held as they hold. They say we haue but a few that consent. Let it be so. What if a man could find but ten in a countrey that agree in this doctrine and in this praise, with the Church, and with all the holy Angels in heauen: are they not (I speake of that heauenly company) sufficient to be opposed against the whole rabblements of Friers, of Monkes, of Cardinals, of Popes, yea & to fill vp the number, of all the diuels in hell? Which company will ye chuse to be Catholike? If a man can find no one in earth to ioyne with him in this faith, that saluatiō is only of God through the bloud of the Lābe, & that God alone is to haue the whole praise of it: let him not be afraid, he is not without company, & that good company, for all the Saints & all the Angels in heauen do ioyne with him. He shall be called an hereticke, but then the holy Angels be heretikes.

L 4   God

God is our whole Sauiour, let vs put our trust onely in him, and giue him all the praise. This is the right faith, this is the Catholike confession. Let Friers & Monks, Cardinals and Popes go, and ioyne with the Saints and blessed Angels.

Now followeth the exposition of the vision. First, one of the Elders doth aske of *Iohn* what these are which are arayed in long white robes, and whence they came. We see the Elder doth not demaund this question for to learne, but for to teach. If any will say then, why doth he which did know, aske him which did not know? We see it is vsuall, it is to moue attention, and therefore the fittest way to make vs learne. A father when he will teach his child some matter which the child indeed seeth, but yet doth not vnderstand, asketh him what is that which thou seest there, or what meaneth that? And so the child is not onely made to see his want of skill, but also is made desirous, and attentiue to learne what the matter is, about which the question is demaunded. So Saint *Iohn* saith: *Lord thou knowest*, therby confessing his ignorance in that matter, and how readie he is to learne. And then he telleth him first, these are they which came out of great tribulation. It is then shewed aforehand, that such as will enter into life with Christ, must passe through great troubles and sorrowes here in the world. The diuell doth enuie them, the world doth deadly hate them, and many griefes take hold of them. What then, if this blessed company enter into ioy and glorie through great affliction, would we be of them, and yet refuse to suffer afflictions? There be many (as we see daily) which take some good liking of the Gospell, but yet they will not suffer any rebuke for it. They would willingly raigne with Christ, but they refuse to suffer with him. Let them take heed, if they will keepe the friendship, & seeke the ease of the world, they can be none of the companie here spoken of: for these come out of great affliction. Againe, let vs learne here to iudge wisely of the Church of Christ and her children: we see them oftentimes in great distresse, racked and tormented here vpon the earth, which worship the Lord in truth, euen after the rules which he hath prescribed in his holy word. We heare how they haue bene murthered vpon heapes, and are in such contempt, so despised and hated, as if they were the of-scouring of men: and looke what mischiefe can be deuised and wrought against them, they shall be sure to haue it. And thus it seemeth, God doth not regard, nor careth not for them. That is false, their bloud is precious in his sight. This warfare is alotted vnto them for their triall, and to their great good. If the Lord himselfe then do chastise vs with his owne handes; if the world do hate and persecute vs for righteousnesse sake; and if the diuell stirre vp all maner of troubles against vs, let vs reioyce and be glad, we be of the multitude here spoken of. Shall anie terrour of affliction for a few daies, driue vs from the possession of so great glorie, which shall last world without end? Nay, let vs be of good comfort, let vs be glad, and reioyce that the Lord hath made vs worthy to be of the fellowship here described. For see and consider well what followeth: *They haue washed their long robes, and haue made their long robes white in the bloud of the Lambe.* What is meant by these long white robes? The innocencie, the holinesse, the puritie and glorie, in which they stand cloathed before the most high God. They may

not

THE REVELATION. 153

not be naked, neither must they come in filthie garments, that shall dwell in his presence. But whence haue they this pureneffe? how come they to be thus royally clothed? how come they to shine thus in glorie, and to be of this shining & pure brightneffe? It is told here, that they haue washed their robes, and made them white in the bloud of the Lambe. All *Adams* children are vncleane and most filthie to behold: but these are come to a fountaine and haue washed themselues, and made them cleane, otherwise they should haue bene cast forth with the rest. This fountaine is the bloud of the Lambe, for that doth cleanse from all sinne. Here is the worke of faith, here is our iustification, here is the treasure of the Church. But how can the washing in bloud make a thing white? Indeed bloud doth make red, but the bloud of the Lambe, becauſe it cleanseth and maketh righteous and innocent, is said to make white. The Papists vaunt much of the indulgences and pardons giuen by the Pope to take away sinne: they say he hath the disposing of the Church treasures, the merites of the bloud of Martyrs: they glory of a righteousneſſe inherent in mens owne workes, and they haue deuised a number of things to purge away sinne, yea some they send vnto the fire of Purgatorie. None of all this heauenly company haue light into their hands: for here is no mention of anie thing wherewith they haue bene washed, but only in the bloud of the Lambe. Againe, if their righteousneſſe and innocency were inherẽt, sticking in them as their owne, euen by the merite of their owne workes, how should it be compared to a robe that is put vpon one? That which we haue not of our owne but by imputation, as the righteousneſſe of Christ through faith, that is fitly reſembled by a garment, yea by a large and goodly garment put vpon vs. Beloued, the bloud of the Lambe, his merits, his righteousneſſe, his innocencie, are sufficient to cloath vs in the preſence of God: let vs ſtedfastly beleeue and truſt to the same, let vs ſeeke to be waſhed and ſanctified in him: and let the Popish ſort alone with their pardons, their Purgatorie fire, and all their other wares which they ſell for money. Such as will haue ſaluation among them, muſt buy it with their ſiluer. Let them keepe their markets by themſelues, and let vs waſh vs only in the bloud of the Lambe. Renounce thoſe ſtinking inuentions of Antichriſt, which derogate from the glorie of Chriſts paſſion. If any thing can purge but his bloud, ſurely the the purging by his bloud is of no exceeding glorie: for that is but meane which hath ſuch companions. Moreouer, by this purity through the bloud of Chriſt, the faithfull are reconciled and brought into fauor with God, he receiueth them into his preſence, euen into the preſence of his glorie, to dwell with him, to ſerue him, and to be partakers of his glorie, to be vnder his protection from all harmes, & to liue bleſſedly in ioyes for euer. For it followeth, *Therefore they are in the preſence of the throne of God, and ſerue him day and night in his temple, and he that ſitteth vpon the throne will dwell among them.* O how great a dignitie is this, vnto which our bleſſed Sauiour hath aduaunced vs? Let vs thankfully receiue it, let vs long to come to it, let vs lift vp our hearts from this miserable world. We shall dwell with the great king of glorie: in what honour and bliſſe shall we be then? what shall be able to hurt vs anie more? Indeed while the children of God liue vpon the

earth,

earth, they be tossed and turmoyled with many miseries. They be persecuted, they be driuen out of their countrey, they be imprisoned, they be poore, they be destitute, they be hungry, they be thirstie, they suffer heate, & cold, & wearinesse; they be sicke, they be subiect to a thousand mischiefes and dangers: but now they shall be rid from all miseries and encombrances. For he saith: *They shall hunger no more, neither thirst any more, neither shall the Sun light on them, neither any heate.* By these are vnderstood all calamities and oppressions, and miseries, which we endure while we be here: not onely in bodie, but also in soule. Men seeke euery way to hurt vs, in our bodies, in our goods, in our names, and in our liues. The diuell he assaulteth, he tempteth, he terrifieth, he raiseth all that he can against vs. The Lord correcteth, scourgeth and chasteneth, as a father doth nurture his children, that they may reuerence him, and stand in awe. What sorrowes, what sighes, what grones, what mournings, and what teares do arise from hence, who is able to expresse? How often do these things come one in the necke of another, euen as the waues of the sea when it is tossed with mightie windes? How terrible vnto flesh and bloud is death it selfe, which we are all sure we must come vnto? And where is the comfort, but onely in this, that after a litle time, euen of triall of our faith and patience, our gracious God will rid vs of them all? that he will bring vs out of this troublesome sea, vnto the hauen of rest? Seeing it is thus, let vs not faint, but take courage and be strong to beare all aduersities. All the elect of God come out of great affliction. Why should we not remember this, and not be cast downe in our temptations, as if it were our case alone, or as if God had forsaken vs? If we endure and suffer affliction as good souldiers of Christ, we shall stand before the throne of God ere it belong, with palmes in our hands, and clothed in long white robes of dignitie and glorie. For our time of triall, our time of pilgrimage is but for a few daies: if we be pinched with pouertie, if we suffer hunger and thirst, or be any way in distresse, God will put an end speedily. We shall be with the Lambe, euen with that blessed Lambe of God which taketh away the sinnes of the world. The Lambe shall be our shepheard, and shall guide, and feed vs with all good things: for he sayth: *The Lambe which is in the middest of the throne shall gouerne them, and shall leade them vnto the liuely fountaines of waters.* Can a Lambe then be a shepheard? Yea, such a Lambe as this, for he is in the middest of the throne. He is a Lambe to the flocke, but yet so full of all might and power, that he is a most victorious Lion vnto all the Wolues and deuouring beasts. The Prophet *Dauid*, Psal. 23. proclaimeth the Lord to be his shepheard, and therefore he shall lacke nothing. He lodgeth him safe in the folds or cotes, where there is plentie of greene pasture. He leadeth him vnto the pleasant streames of still waters, both to coole heate, and to quench thirst, and other duties he setteth forth of a shepheard. They be all included in this, that the Lambe shall gouerne them, and leade them to the fountaines of liuing waters. The Lambe then bringeth vs vnto God, & the Lambe feedeth vs when we be there with all heauenly and spirituall dainties. He is rich, for it hath pleased the Father, that in him all fulnesse should dwell, Col.1. How shold they hunger, how shold they thirst any more, or how should any euill come nigh them, whom he doth guide, and whom he leadeth to the waters of life? Wel, and blessed, and a thousand, and ten thousand times blessed is he that is a sheepe in this flocke: he shall drinke his fill of the waters of life. But what are these waters of life, or liuing waters, whereof the streames do run continually? Our Sauiour saith, *He that beleeueth in me, as saith the Scripture, out of his belly shall flow riuers of water of life.* This (saith the Euangelist) spake he of the spirit, which they that beleeued in him should receiue: for the spirit was not yet giuen, because Iesus was not yet glorified, Ion. 7. ver. 38. 39. We shall then liue by the spirit, the life of God shall be in vs: we shall be filled with ioy and comfort vnspeakeable: we shall be in honour and glorie for euermore. All our miseries, trauels, and sorowes which we endure in this world, shall be quite forgotten and vanish away: for he saith, *God shall wipe away all teares frō their eyes.* If there were no teares in their eyes while they be here, yea if there were not many and plentifull (as the Prophet saith, *Thou giuest thy people plentie of teares to drinke*, and as the Prophet *Dauid* saith, he watered his bed, and made his couch to swimme with teares) it should not be said, *God shall wipe away all teares from their eyes.* They be great sorrowes and griefes that do cause men to weep and lament: yea such valiant men as *Dauid* was. Think not then while ye be here to liue in delicacie and pleasures of the flesh, and yet to come to the heauenly ioyes. No, remember what Christ saith, *Blessed are ye that weep now, for ye shal laugh*, Luke 6.21. *And wo be vnto ye which laugh now, for ye shall lament and weepe*, Luke 6.25. It is much better to weepe here in afflictions for a litle time, and to reioyce for euermore in the world to come, with ioy vnspeakeable and glorious, then to haue delight in the pleasures of sinnes for a season, and afterward to mourne for euer in the torments of hell. Thus haue we seene, that not onlie the Martyrs which be of the Church triumphant are in safety, but also the Church militant in earth. They are gone before, kept by the power of God in the time that they continued in the battell: the same power of the Lord shall keepe vs, and we shall follow and be ioyned with them. They trusted in the Lord, and he did not faile them: let vs trust constantly, and continue faithfull euen vnto the death, and we shall find him the same vnto vs that he was vnto them. For hath he not made the same promise, and doth he not loue his people as well now as he did then? For shall we thinke that he is changeable? or that he will not regard those that trust in him? he is the shepherd ouer the whole flocke, which shall be euen to the worlds end. And seeing we be now in exceeding great dangers in these euill dayes (as the last times are perillous) assure your selues he hath a speciall care ouer vs. O how miserable and wretched are they which despise such a shepheard, and will not be fed by him! Let vs dayly vpon our knees instantly beg of God, that we neuer come to be of that number of such despisers. And thus much for this time.

THE

SERMONS VPON

THE XVII. SERMON.

CHAP. 8.

1. And when he had opened the seuenth seale, there vvas silence in heauen about halfe an houre.
2. And I saw the seuen Angels vvhich stood before God, and to them vvere giuen seuen trumpets.
3. Then another Angell came and stood before the altar, hauing a golden censer, and much odours vvas giuen vnto him, that he should offer vvith the prayers of all Saints vpon the golden altar which is before the throne.
4. And the smoke of the odours, vvith the prayers of the Saints, vvent vp before God out of the Angels hand.
5. And the Angell tooke the censer, and filled it vvith fire of the altar, and cast it into the earth, and there vvere voyces, and thunderings, and lightenings, and earth-quakes.
6. Then the seuen Angels which had the seuen trumpets, prepared themselues to blow the trumpets.
7. So the first Angell blew the trumpet, and there vvas haile and bloud mingled vvith fire, and they vvere cast into the earth, and the thirdpart of trees was burnt, and all greene grasse was burnt.
8. And the second Angell blew the trumpet, and as it vvere a great mountaine burning vvith fire vvas cast into the sea, and the third part of the sea became Bloud.
9. And the third part of the creatures which vvere in the sea and had life, died, & the third part of the ships were destroyed.
10. Then the third Angell blew the trumpet, and there fell a great starre from heauen, burning like a torch, and it fell into the third part of the riuers, and into the fountaines of vvaters.
11. And the name of the starre is called Wormewood, therfore the third part of the vvaters became vvormewood, and manie men dyed of the waters, because they were made bitter.
12. And the fourth Angell blew the trumpet, and the third part of the Sunne was smitten, and the third part of the Moone, and the third part of the starres, so that the third part of them was darkened: & the day was smitten, that the third part of it could not shine, and likewise the night.

13 And

THE REVELATION. 157

13. *And I beheld, and heard one Angell flying in the middest of heauen, saying with a loud voyce, Woe, woe, woe to the inhabitants of the earth, becauſe of the ſounds to come, of the three Angels, vvhich vvere yet to blow the trumpets.*

Eare now come to the opening of the laſt ſeale. For the booke, which was in the right hand of him that ſate vpon the throne, was ſealed with ſeuen ſeales: ſixe are alreadie paſt, and now the Lambe openeth the ſeuenth. This reacheth vnto the laſt iudgement, which is at the ſecond cōming of Chriſt, & therefore vnder this all things are finiſhed. The opening of things vnder this ſeale are diuided into ſeuen parts, at the ſounding of ſeuen trumpets, & vnder the laſt of thoſe trumpets (as we may ſee in the latter end of the 11. chapter) is the day of iudgement deſcribed. And in the tenth chapter, the Angell ſweareth, that *there ſhall be no more time, but in the dayes of the voyce of the ſeuenth Angell, when he ſhal begin to blow the trumpet.* The viſions then which follow from the beginning of the 12 chapter to the end of this prophecie, do ſet forth more largely and more clearely, ſome ſpeciall things, which are deſcribed more darkly in the opening of the ſeales. For the booke ſealed with the ſeuen ſeales, containeth all the whole matters which were to be reuealed. Now to the words as they lye. S. *Iohn* ſaith, that *vvhen he had opened the ſeuenth ſeale, there vvas ſilence in heauen for the ſpace of halfe an houre*. What ſhould this ſilence meane? Some ſay it ſignifieth cōſultation, that as kings and mightie Princes, when they enterpriſe great & waighty matters, conſult with mature deliberation: ſo, though God need not anie conſultation, knowing all, and hauing in his infinite wiſdom decreed all things: yet to repreſent to vs that verie great things are in hand, and that both *Iohn* and all other might be prepared with due attention to receiue them, this ſilence is continued for halfe an houre. Others do take it to ſet forth aſtoniſhment: as namely, that at the opening of this ſeale, there appeare ſuch dreadfull iudgements of God to be executed vpon the world; that all the heauenly companie are aſtoniſhed and abaſhed to behold. Which of theſe is meant, I wil not ſtand to diſcuſſe, becauſe they come both to the ſame effect, for to declare the greatneſſe of the matters now in hand. Great and grieuous things were reuealed vnder the opening of ſome of the former ſeales: but now follow greater and more grieuous: for here commeth the kingdome of the great Antichriſt, and all the horrible plagues which go with it: as alſo the full powring forth of Gods wrath at the laſt day. So that it is no maruell though Saint *Iohn* ſaw the elect ſealed vp, and ſet in ſafetie, when ſuch things ſhould fall out. Then next, S. *Iohn* ſaw ſeuen Angels, to whom were giuen ſeuen trumpets. The Angels are Gods ſeruants & miniſters, which are in a readineſſe to do his will. But what do the ſeuen trumpets repreſent? for we muſt take it that they ſignifie ſomewhat. They do repreſent that God commeth againſt the world as an enemie vnto battell, euen proclaiming open warre with the ſound of trumpets. For as kings when they go to battell, and their armies meet to set each vpon other, do it by sounding of trumpets, proclaiming thereby their enmitie and purpose of warre: so the Lord God seeing how cruelly his seruants haue bene dealt withall, how his holy Gospell hath bene despised, hated and persecuted, and his name dishonoured and blasphemed, commeth vpon the world as an enemie, with the sound of trumpets vnto battell. For before the powring forth of euerie iudgement, an Angell soundeth a trumpet. Wo be to the wicked world when God is thus displeased, and commeth againſt them vnto battell. It may make vs tremble and quake for feare, if we be not fencelesse as stones or blockes, to behold the publication of Gods wrath: for if we be partakers with the world in these sinnes, we shall also be partakers of the plagues. But if the most high be thus displeased for the cruell misusing of his seruants, for the abusing of his Gospell, and for all the wicked abhominable vices committed, that he commeth with the sound of the trumpet one after another to proclaime open enmitie and battell: what shall become of the Church in earth, or how shall it go with her, in the middest of his hot displeasure? The Church hath a Mediatour, and when the displeasure and wrath of God doth most of all shew it selfe, yet she is remembred, and is in safetie with all her children, her prayers comming vp before God, and being accepted through the same Mediatour, she also receiueth heauenly gifts and spirituall graces. This is shewed manifestly in the next words, when Saint *Iohn* saith, *Another Angell came and stood before the altar, hauing a golden censer, &c.* The Rhemish Papists hauing no warrant in the holy word of God to maintaine their deuises, yet to blind the ignorant, lay hold where there seemeth to be any shew: as here they say, the Prieſt ſtanding at the altar praying and offering for the people in the time of the high mysteries, Chriſt himselfe being present vpon the altar, is a figure of this thing, which the Angell doth here at the altar, and thereto he alludeth. Wo be to those which are so blind, as to be carried away with such geere as this, to beleeue the Popish sacrificing Prieſthood, and the abhominable Maſſe. There is no Scripture either for their altar, their prieſthood, or sacrifice: how shall we then thinke that there is an allusion in the Scripture to things which by the holy Scripture are not warranted? This is manifeſt, that in the old law there was a golden altar, and a golden censer, in which the Prieſt did burne sweete incense before the Lord, which did figure the mediation of Chriſt, in which the prayers of the Saints are acceptable: to this figure we are sure he alludeth in this vision: for hauing the Scripture to warrant that, the verie speeches do also accord. There is a golden altar, a golden censer, and sweete odours described in *Moses*, and so are here. As the Prieſthood and mediation of Chriſt was figured by these in time of the Law, so how can we say that the same figure now in visiō, doth signifie any other thing? The holy Sacrament of the Lords supper is the same that Chriſt did firſt adminiſter with his owne hands, sitting at the table with his twelue Apoſtles: and if that their Maſſe were not a filthie prophanation, but a figure of this heauenly vision, then was Chriſt in that action a figure of it also. How wicked and absurd a thing is this? Again, what resemblance can there be, or what figure in a Prieſt offering a

slaine

slaine sacrifice propitiatorie, (for in the Masse they glorie that they offer vp the verie bodie of Christ crucified and his bloud that was shed) and a Priest offering incense vpon an altar that is not an altar of slaine sacrifice, but onely to offer sweete odours? Alas, shall poore blind people be still seduced by such impudent cauils? But they are yet more shamelesse in abusing this place of Scripture. For as they would beare men in hand, that their Popish Masse is so glorious a thing, as that this heauenly vision doth allude vnto it: so they would proue that the Angels in heauen, do offer vp to God the prayers of the Saints in earth, because this Angell offreth with the praiers of all Saints. Thus they find a way to breake in & to spoile the Lord Iesus of his glorie, who is the onely high Priest, and the onely Mediatour betweene God and man, and indeed the beloued sonne, in whom alone the Father is well pleased, Matth. 3. But yet they are here grauelled diuerse wayes, the matter doth not fall out to fit their turne. For first, they dare not affirme that this Angell is not Christ himselfe, but say thus: If this be S. *Michael*, or anie Angell, and not Christ himselfe, as some take it, then Angels offer vp the prayers of the faithfull. Where do ye find that *Aaron* with his golden censer with sweet odors at the golden altar, was a figure of anie but of the Lord Iesus? Did *Aaron* & his sonnes represent anie Angell? Then how will they perswade that this is any *Michael*, or any Angell besides Christ? For doth he not perfourme that which was figured by those things vnder the Law? Indeed the things are finished, but yet for our capacitie the same are set forth againe vnto vs in the vision, by the ceremoniall figure. For how should that heauenly & inuisible thing, the mediation of Christ, be more fitly shewed to vs by vision, then vnder that figure by which it was shadowed out in time of the Law? Who is the Priest figured, but the Lord Iesus? Who is the golden altar, but the Lord Iesus? What are the sweet odours with which the prayers of all Saints come vp before God, but the most sweet mediation of the Lord Iesus? For it is said, *There was much odours giuen vnto him that he might offer with the prayers of all Saints, vpon the golden altar which is before the throne. And the smoke of the incense, with the prayers of the Saints went vp before God, out of the Angels hand.* This may seeme to be somewhat to proue it was not Christ himselfe, because the odours are giuen him: but the Scripture saith, yea Christ saith, *All things are giuen vnto me of my Father*: & this is called the reuelation of Iesus Christ, which God gaue him. It is the most sweete incense of Christs mediation, with which all the most holy place in heauen is perfumed. It is that sweet incense of his mediation, in which God is well pleased and delighted, with which our prayers ascend as it were mixed with it, and so become also sweet and delightsome vnto God. Indeed without these odours our prayers could not be sweete and pleasant to God. For how can anie sweet thing proceed out of so corrupt and stinking vessels as we be? but they are sanctified in him, and made sweet with his sweet odours. The Lord is delighted with the sweetnesse of his sonne, and the prayers of the whole Church come vp before him, mixed and seasoned with his sweetnesse, therefore he cannot but be also delighted with them. Then secondly, vpon these words that the Angell doth offer with the prayers of

all

all Saints, our Rhemists do confesse that by Saints here, as also in other places of Scripture, are meant holy persons in earth. Indeed it is a thing euident by the word of God, that all true beleeuers haue this honourable and glorious title giuen them, and of right belonging vnto them, to be called Saints, euen while they liue vpon the earth. Why then hath it bene the vse in Poperie, and is still among all the ignorant blind Papists, to account none Saints but such as are dead, and the same canonized by the Pope? Though (say they, euen the Rhemish Papists) it be not, against the Scriptures, that the inferiour Saint or Angell in heauen should offer their prayers to God by their superiour there. Behold into what vaine speculations men are carried, when they are bold to set themselues against the truth. What an infinite heape of Martyrs may the carnall reason of man imagine, and say they be not against the Scriptures? But let vs see how this ouerthroweth their owne diuinity, and what absurdities it carieth with it. If the inferiour Angell do offer vp his prayer to God by his superiour, then this Angell is aboue all, for he offereth the prayers of all Saints: And the Papists say, the blessed Virgin is Lady and Queene of heauen, and so superiour to all Angels. How commeth it then that she looseth her place? why doth not she as the most worthie Mediatrix next Christ, offer vp the prayers of all Saints? And if the inferiour Saint or Angell offer his prayer by his superiour, then this Angell offereth her prayer among the rest: for he offereth with the prayers of all Saints, & she is one among the Saints. How shall she offer vp prayers, and be a Mediatrix for others, when her owne prayers are offered to God by another? For as I say, this Angell offereth with the prayers of all Saints: and this Angell offereth alwayes, and none but he: seeing this vision doth set forth not what was done at one time, but what was and is done so long as the Church doth and shall continue vpon the earth. If this Angell then offer vp the prayers of all Saints, and at all times (as it is manifest) where is the mediation of the Virgin *Marie*, and of other Saints and Angels? whose prayers do they offer vp, if one offer with the prayers of all? Againe, if an inferiour Saint or Angell be to offer their prayers to God by their superiour Saints or Angels: then is it not lawfull for anie inferiour Saint to make a petition to God, but by the mediation of a superior. What diuinitie is this? Let it passe, let them alone. It followeth, that *the Angell* (which ye see is the Lord Iesus Christ) *tooke the censer, and filled it with fire of the altar, and cast it into the earth, and there were voyces, and thunderings, and lightenings, and earthquakes.* This sentence is diuersly expounded by diuerse: because fire in the holy Scriptures representeth diuerse things. It is terrible to behold flaming fire, it consumeth and burneth vp with sharpe and bitter paine: and for that cause, the wrath of God is compared to fire. Also it pierceth, it purgeth in burning out drosse, and giueth heat: and for that the holy Ghost is called fire, and represented by fire; as *Iohn* the Baptist speaketh of Christ, saying, *He shall baptize ye with the holy Ghost and with fire*, Matth. 3. And there appeared vnto them clouen tongues, as it were of fire, Act. 2. which were the gifts of the holie Ghost. For he pierceth deepe, he burneth out drosse, and purgeth the hearts of the faithfull, he setteth them also on fire with burning loue and zeale of Gods glorie.

Let

Let vs see then which of these is represented by the censer filled with the fire of the altar, & cast down into the earth. They that take it here to be the wrath of God cast downe by Christ vpon the world, say that the voices, the lightnings, thundrings, and earthquake, are the terrible signes and tokens of his wrath. But seeing all the plagues which God sendeth downe in the opening of the seuenth seale, are at the sounding of the seuen trumpets, there is no reason to take this fire of the altar for to signifie Gods wrath, but indeed for the holy Ghost, euen for those heauenly gifts which Christ bestoweth. Through the mediation of Christ, the prayers of the Church come vp before the throne and are heard, and the heauenly fire, euen the gifts of the holy Ghost are thereupon sent downe: who can deny this to be true? Then follow voices, for the glorious Gospell is sounded foorth, by the operation of the holy Ghost, Christ is constantly professed, the world is reproued of sinne, of righteousnesse, & of iudgement, Ioh. 16. The diuell is disturbed in his kingdome: he rageth full of wrath. The tyrants and wordlings are also molested: herevpon are raised vp all maner of broyles, tumults, vprores, and commotions, with cruell persecutions, and horrible slaughters, which are represented by thundrings, lightnings, and earthquake. We must euer looke for such stirres at the preaching of the Gospell: it cannot be otherwise, while there be diuels. Hauing thus set forth the mediation of Christ for his Church, and how he sendeth downe his spirit vpon her, by which she is comforted and guided, he returneth to set foorth the plagues to be powred forth vnder this seuenth seale. And first as he sayth, the seuen Angels which had the seuen trumpets, prepared themselues to blow the trumpets. These heauenly messengers are most readie to execute the will and the commandement of God, without any doubting or reasoning: for they know he is most holy and iust in all his iudgementes, and no crueltie proceedeth from him. They sound the trumpets then of defiance, & proclaime open warre from God, against the wicked world. It is hard to declare euery particular, but I will wade no deeper then the cleare light and doctrine of the Scriptures may shew the bottome, and as it were the safe places where to tread. First therefore it is manifest, that here are dreadfull plagues powred forth from God Almightie, being highly offended. Secondly, it cannot be restrained to corporall punishments, but indeed the plagues are chiefly spirituall. Thirdly, we are not to take it that a seuerall plague is powred forth at the founding of euery trumpet, but the same, vnder diuerse figures in sundrie of them. This withall, that there is an vniuersalitie, and a progression from lesse to greater in the plagues. For that an vniuersall plague might be shewed as it were vpon all parts of the world, in the sounding of the first foure trumpets, the world is deuided into the earth, the sea, the riuers, and the heauens, through all which the plagues are spread: so that ye can looke no where, but all is ouerspread with the wrath of God, and with terrible iudgements. The first Angell blew the trumpet, and there was haile and bloud mingled with fire, & they were cast into the earth, and the third part of trees were burnt, and all greene grasse was burnt. We may not take these things literally, of haile and bloud, and fire indeed mingled together, nor of the very trees and greene grasse burnt vp: for such a thing hath not bin heard

heard of since Christ. But vnder these there are spirituall plagues figured: as we may consider in particular: for haile, is a thing that doth beate downe corne, & destroy the fruits of the earth, and so hurteth many wayes. Bloud doth cause to corrupt & putrifie. Fire doth consume and wast. As these three should be mingled together in some horrible tempest, and cast vpon the earth: so vpon men, yea euen in the visible Church, a tempest of spiritual haile, bloud and fire, that is, of errors, lyes, and strong delusions, is cast downe, ouerspreadeth and wasteth grieuously. Thus much may suffice for the sounding of the first trumpet.

The second Angell soundeth the trumpet, and this apostasie by Antichristes kingdome first figured by such a terrible tempest, is represented by a great mountaine burning with fire, and cast into the sea. A thing most horrible to looke vpon: but such as the world hath iustly deserued, by refusing to receiue the loue of the truth. This burning mountaine doth corrupt and destroy: for the third part of the sea is turned into bloud: the third part of the creatures which had life in the sea dyed, and the third part of shippes were destroyed. The people indeede are as an huge sea of many waters: and this mountaine is very great which falleth vpon them. The third Angell doth blow the trumpet, and there fell a great starre from heauen burning like a torch, and it fell into the third part of the riuers, and fountaines of waters. And the name of the starre is called Wormewood, therefore the third part of the waters became wormewood, and many men dyed of the waters, becaufe they were made bitter. This doth most fitly set forth the fall and declining of the pastors of the Church. It is euident that the starres in this booke be the pastors, Chap. 1. This is a great starre, representing very many pastors and teachers. For many did decline and corrupt the pure doctrine: or at the least it did represent some speciall great one which drew many downe with him. As when some pastor of great account and authority declineth, may drop downe with him. This great starre doth fall from heauen, when those Bishops which succeeded the former did degenerate, were lifted vp in pride, and in steede of shining with the light of pure doctrine of the heauenly word, did set vp and maintaine their owne inuentions, and liued vitious liues. This starre falleth into the riuers and fountaines of waters, which men do drinke of. The doctrine of Gods word is the waters, euen the most pure waters which are giuen to the Church continually to drinke of. These waters are most sweete, comfortable, and wholesome of themselues. This starre falleth into them, and infecteth them: for by little and little the teachers mixed their owne deuises with the word: they infected with false expositions, mingled and poysoned the waters, making them bitter: and hereupon it followeth that many did die and perish. But seeing the corrupt doctrine, which is agreeable to the sinfull nature of man, is so sweete and delightsome vnto the blind superstitious people, that they greedily sucke it in, and are neuer filled; how can it be sayd that the waters become bitter? I answere to this: that the pure doctrine of Gods word is sweete and comfortable, because it worketh peace in the cōscience, and ioy in the holy Ghost. The false doctrine though at the first taste it seeme sweete, yea becaufe it destroyeth the iustification, and reconciliation through faith, in the bloud of Chriſt, taking away all peace of conſcience, & ſpirituall ioy, filling the heart with doubts, and tortures, it is moſt bitter. For what can be more bitter, then in ſteede of a liuely feeling through faith, that we are reconciled to God through the bloud of his Sonne, and in ſteed of the ſpirit of adoption by which we are ſanctified, which beareth witneſſe to our ſpirits that we are the childrē of God, to haue the doubts and tortures of conſcience, which I ſay do follow of ſuperſtitious and corrupt doctrine? The aſſurance of faith, or full perſwaſion of the remiſſion of ſins, is condemned of the Papiſts as high preſumption: and to be in doubt is deemed great humility.

 In the next place followeth the ſounding of the fourth trumpet, at which S. *Iohn* ſayth, *The third part of the Sunne was ſmitten, and the third part of the Moone, and the third part of the ſtarres, ſo that the third part of them was darkened: and the day was ſmitten, that the third part of it could not ſhine, and likewiſe the night.* This darkening the third part of the Sunne, the Moone and the ſtarres, figureth the darkneſſe brought vpon the Church by ſuch teachers as did daily more and more degenerate. The light of the holy Scriptures, the light of heauenly doctrine was quenched and darkened. This tempeſt of haile, bloud, and fire, the great mountaine burning, the ſtarre falling into the riuers, and the darkening of the Sunne, the Moone and the ſtarres, are moſt horrible plagues: but yet not to the vtter deſolation of the Church, nor yet the full ſetting vp of Antichriſt: for in euery one there is mentioned but a third part deſtroyed, and more grieuous things do follow. This curſed kingdome began and proceeded by degrees, and the fulneſſe of it is ſet forth in the ſounding of the fift trumpet. And that we might know the greateſt plagues are yet behind at the ſounding of the three trumpets which remaine, an Angell doth flie in the middeſt of heauen, and with a loude voyce proclaimeth woe, woe, woe, to the inhabitants of the earth, for the ſounds of the three trumpets which remaine. The woes indeede are denounced but vpon the inhabitants of the earth, that is, vpon the children of this world: for no one of the elect ſhall be hurt by them with ſpirituall hurt, ſo far as to deſtroy them. As in the former, ſo in theſe the Lord preſerueth his Church, they were all ſealed with the ſeale of God. But we muſt note, that albeit great and terrible plagues haue bene already reuealed, yet the three that remaine exceede them all.

THE XVIII. SERMON.
CHAP. 9.

1. *And the fift Angell blew the trumpet, and I saw a starre which fell from heauen vnto the earth, and to him was giuen the key of the bottomlesse pit.*
2. *And he opened the bottomlesse pit, and there arose the smoke of the pit, as the smoke of a great fornace, and the Sunne and the ayre were darkened by the smoke of the pit.*
3. *And there came out of the smoke Locusts vpon the earth, and to them was giuen power, as the Scorpions of the earth haue power.*
4. *And it was commanded them, that they should not hurt the grasse of the earth, neither any greene thing, neither any tree, but only those men which haue not the seale of God in their foreheads.*
5. *And to them was commanded that they should not kill them, but that they should be vexed fiue moneths, and their paine should be as the paine that commeth of a Scorpion, when he hath stong a man.*
6. *Therefore in those dayes shall men seeke death, and shall not find it, and shall desire to die, but death shall flie from them.*
7. *And the forme of the Locusts, was like vnto horses prepared vnto battaile, & their heads were as it were crownes of gold, and their faces were like the face of men.*
8. *And they had haire as the haire of women, and their teeth were as the teeth of Lions.*
9. *And they had habbergions like to habbergions of yron, and the sound of their wings was like the sound of chariots, when many horses runne vnto the battaile.*
10. *And they had tailes like vnto Scorpions, and there were stings in their tailes, and their power was to hurt men fiue moneths.*
11. *And they haue a king ouer them which is the Angell of the bottomlesse pit, whose name in hebrue is* Abaddon, *and in greeke he is called* Apollyon, *that is, destroying.*

I Noted vnto ye the last time, that the three woes to come are the three last woes, and the three greatest woes reueiled in this booke, and therefore proclaimed by an Angell flying in the middest of heauen with this voyce, woe, woe, woe, &c. And now we come at the sounding of the fift trumpet vnto the first of them. It is a woe of darknesse, yea of most horrible spirituall darknesse, & of dead-

ly

THE REVELATION.   165

ly poyſonſome ſtinging vermine, which come with the darkneſſe. We will looke vpon it, as it lyeth in order. When the fift Angell blew the trumpet, *Iohn* ſaw a ſtarre fall from heauen vnto the earth. Here is a ſtarre falling from heauen, the bringer in of this great woe. Some do take it that this is the ſtarre which fell at the ſounding of the third trumpet: becauſe the participle is of the time perfectly paſt. I cannot thinke ſo, vnleſſe *S. Iohn* had vſed the Greeke participle, ſo that it might be ſayd, I ſaw that ſtarre which fell. I take this ſufficient to proue it to be another ſtarre. Some take this ſtarre for an Angell comming downe ſpeedily from heauen, ſent of God to open the bottomleſſe pit. But how ſhall that be ſo, when ſtarres in this booke do ſignifie no other Angels, but the Angels of the Churches, as Chapter. 1. that is, the miniſters of the Goſpell? This ſtarre therefore that here falleth, is ſome great Miniſter, & of high eſtimation in the Church, as his power giuen vnto him may teach vs to ſee. And if ye demand who it was, I anſwer, the Church of Rome was a right worthy and famous Church. The Biſhops of Rome were excellent men many of them ſucceeding each other, and ſuffered martyrdome for the Goſpell: they declined and grew worſe and worſe, ſo farre as to become the great Antichriſt. This ſtarre being of maruellous account, falling from the heauenly brightneſſe of the doctrine contained in Gods word, and from the true godlineſſe, vnto humane inuentions, and wicked life, retaineth ſtill an exceeding great power to do hurt. He hath giuen vnto him the key of the bottomleſſe pit: Sathan by him broacheth in all his helliſh doctrine. The Papiſts boaſt that the power which their Pope hath exerciſed ſo long, is the keyes of heauen, and that at his pleaſure he can ſend and let men in there: and ſo the Pope doth promiſe eternall life at his pleaſure. But the truth is, that his power is the key of hell, that key is giuen vnto him, to bring in dueliſh doctrine, ignorance of the truth, darkneſſe, idolatry, ſuperſtition, and all wicked errors: for he openeth the bottomleſſe pit, and the ſmoke thereof, yea ſo darke a ſmoke commeth vp, that the light of the Sunne and of the ayre are darkened. We did ſee how at the ſounding of the fourth trumpet the third part of the Sunne, and the third part of the Moone, and the third part of the ſtarres was ſtriken, ſo that the third part did not ſhine: this was a great diminiſhing of the light, but nothing comparable to the darkeneſſe here ſet foorth. The courſe of the Goſpel was ſtayed(as we ſee the foure Angels held the foure winds) mans deuiſes and ſuperſtition greatly increaſed, the cleere light of the moſt pure doctrine was much dimmed, and ſo by little and little Antichriſt was exalted: and when he was come to his full ſtrength, the pit of hell being opened, that Sathan might ſend forth what ſtrong deluſion he would, the caſe is farre more miſerable then before. Marke what ſimilitude here is vſed. For like as the Sunne with his bright beames doth peirce through and lighten the ayre, and ſo we haue light vnto theſe our bodily eyes here vpon the earth; and if a thicke darke ſmoke ariſe, it darkeneth the ayre, and keepeth the light of the Sunne backe from vs: ſo Chriſt Ieſus with his glorious Goſpell, ſhining vpon the Church, the ſmoke of the pit of hell, euen the illuſions of the diuell, the inuentions of men, idolatry, errors, and ſuperſtition doe darken, or keepe backe the bright beames thereof from men. We may plainly

M 3   ſee

see by this place, that in the kingdom of Antichrist, grosse and palpable darknesse doth ouerspread all: and that men are ignorant of the truth, and couered in blindnesse, by reason of the thicke smoke arising out of the bottomles pit. The doctrine & worship of diuels is now set vp: this being one proper and infallible note of that horrible kingdome, it is requisite that I should stay a litle vpon it. And if any man will obiect that it is not certaine, that this is a description of the kingdom of Antichrist; I say it is most vndoubtedly certaine, and without all controuersie, a description of Antichrists full exaltation: and if men be not wilfully blind, they cannot but see and confesse so much. For is it not certaine, yea so certaine that the most impudent aduersaries cannot deny, that among other plagues the great plague vpon the world by Antichrist, is reuealed in this booke? Is it not also manifest that in the opening of the seuen seales al things are reuealed which should happen, euen to the end of the world? and therefore at the sounding of the seuenth trumpet is the day of iudgement, as we see in the latter end of the eleuenth Chapter: & as the Angell in the next Chapter doth sweare that there shall be no more time when the seuenth Angell shal begin to sound the trumpet, and that the mystery of God shall be finished. For all that followeth from the beginning of the twelfth Chapter is but larger descriptiōs & plainer, of some things gone before in the opening of the seales. Moreouer, is it not out of doubt, that the kingdome of Antichrist is one of the greatest plagues? And will ye call into question whether the three woes denounced by the Angell, be the three greatest? The last of the three is the dreadful day of iudgement: the last sauing one, is the horrible kingdome (as we shall see) of the Turke: and the first of the three (which is this that we are now in hand withall, is the wicked kingdome of Antichrist. A starre fallen, a great minister of the Gospell still in title, to whom the key of the bottomlesse pit is giuen, is the head of this kingdome next vnder the diuell. This one point ye see, is most euident by the wordes of the text, whereby we come to a second point: namely, that the Popery is this kingdome, which indeed is more fully declared in the Chapters following: but yet to be proued by this. For what kingdome of such power, as to agree with the description here following can be found, that hath a starre fallen to be the head thereof, but the papacie? let it be shewed if they can through the vniuersall world. And now to come further, and to proue it by the darknesse which ariseth by the smoke of the pit: is any so senselesse as not to take it of spiritual darknesse? Is it meant that a smoke shall arise out of the pit of hell, and darken the ayre which we draw in, and the Sun in the firmament, which shineth to our bodily eyes? No, let the most obstinate and rankest Papist in the world deny if he can, that this darkening is not the darkening of the Gospell, in which Christ shineth to the Church, as the Sunne to the world. Let such an one also if he can denie, that this smoke is not the darkenesse of Sathans kingdome, ignorance of the mysteries of Christs Gospell, through mens inuentions and blind errors. And doth not this fitlie agree to the Popery? was not the Gospell buried among them? were not all maner of humane traditions, errors, lies, superstition, and idolatry, set vs in stead thereof? were not the people kept in such exceeding darknesse, as that they receiued and were fed with al maner of lies,

yea

the Churches the whole doctrine of the Gospell, and taught them all the counsels of God in the tongue which they vnderstood, exhorting all pastours to be diligent in teaching, and all people to let the word dwell plenteously among them: which is cleane contrary to that doctrine and practise of the Papists. For they keepe the Scriptures from the people, they will haue them kept blind without any light, least they should espie their treacheries and falshood, and so refuse to sup vp those filthy stinking poysoned dregges which they do giue them. And who hath brought in all this darknesse or smoke of hell, but that starre fallen from heauen, which hath the key of the bottomlesse pit? Beloued, if the word of God be true (which I trust no man here is so wicked to doubt of) the Popery is this darke kingdome, and the Pope that starre which hath opened the Pit of hell, and brought in such horrible darknesse and confusion. If they can shew likelihood in any other, let them, that it may be discussed. Then next he sayth, *There came out of the smoke Locusts vpon the earth, and vnto them was giuen power, as the Scorpions of the earth haue power.* Here is a further misery, for beside the plague of darknesse, there commeth from the smoke another plague of the Locusts: For as the smoke of the bottomlesse pit doth darken the Sunne, so of the same smoke the Locusts are bred. Let vs see what this representeth. Locusts are but a vile vermine, but yet great swarmes of them do eate vp and destroy the greene things and fruites of the earth, and make a fruitfull land wast: as yee may reade the description of them, Ioel. 2. These which are here spoken of be not common Locustes, but haue also the deadly poyson and power of Scorpions, to sting and torment men to death. This is a most pestilent vermine: who are represented by them? By these are represented all the Popish Cleargy, their Priests, their swarmes of Monkes, Friers, and Nunnes. For first, all this vermine is not bred from the light, hauing no ground in Gods word, but indeed from the smoke of the pit. They are bred of ignorance, of error, and blind superstition, they come from hell. Let any Iesuite shew, where vnder a starre fallen, there is any resemblance of the swarmes of locustes bred of error, of ignorance and darknesse but only vnder the Popes, in their heapes and rabblements, yea euen swarmes of Friers, Monkes, & such like. Haue not they ouerspread the earth, euen to eate vp and to lay wast al greene things in the Church? And haue not they euen as it were with the poyson of Scorpions, stong thousand thousands with their damnable errors and diuellish deuises? who can declare the spirituall miseries of those dayes, when together with the hellish darkenesse, through the want of Gods word which lay buried and hid, the venimous locusts did ouerspread, which stong euen as scorpions? Here is againe a doubt to be answered, which is this, When all was thus ouerwhelmed in the darknesse of that smoke, and the earth euery where

crawling

crawling full of these locustes, what became of the Church? this doubt I say might arise. And ye know it is the question which euery Papist propoundeth; where was your Church an hundreth yeres past? This question is answered in the next words. For as we haue seene in euery danger prophecied before in this booke, speciall prouision made to set the chosen in safety: so here these locustes are restrained from hurting of them which are sealed. Their power is limited only vpon the reprobate: for we heard before how al the seruáts of God were sealed in their foreheads, they are sealed with the holy spirit of promise, which is the spirit of adoption. And here is commandement giuen to the locustes that they shall not hurt the grasse, neither any greene thing, neither any tree, but onely those men which haue not the seale of God in their foreheads. We see thē they could not touch the elect of God. Here is the glorious power, the prouidence and wisdome of our Lord Iesus Christ, that in the middest of this darknesse, horrible to thinke vpon, euen when Antichrist raigneth in his full pride, his elect among these scorpion locusts flying about their eares like swarmes of hornets, yet not one of them is stong to death: his flocke is defended. Then there is another commandement giuen to these locustes, which is that they should not kill men, no not euen the reprobate: but that they should be vexed fiue moneths, and their paine should be as the paine that commeth of a scorpion when he hath stong a man. This may seeme hard at the first, that they should not kill them: for doth not the darknesse, and the venime of these locustes bring vtter destruction vnto mens soules? shall not the kingdome or power of Antichrist slay men with the spirituall death? how then is it sayd they should not kill them? It is to be answered, that they should not kil them out right at once, but torment them with a lingring death: and therefore they are compared to scorpions For it is sayd, that he which is stong of a scorpion is tormented two or thtee daies grieuously before he die of it: he hath a lingring paine. And vnto that paine of such as lie in torment stong with scorpions, is likened the paine of those which are stong by these locustes. O miserable state of poore blind superstitious Papists, which drinke in the poyson of Antichrists doctrine: what a sting doth it leaue behind? how is their conscience vnquiet? how is it vexed and tormented? no tongue is able to expresse it to the full: they feele and know that they be foule sinners, they are sure also that they must come to iudgement. They are told of the torments of hell by the Scriptures, and of the fire of Purgatory by the Popish sort: the doctrine of free iustification in the bloud of Christ is hid from them, yea condemned as heresie: all assurance of Gods fauour, all peace of conscience, all ioy in the holy Ghost are quite destroyed: they are sent to seeke ease in the merite of their owne workes, in Popes pardons and indulgences, by running on pilgrimage to this Idoll, and to that Idoll, by punishing their bodies with whippings, fastings, and a thousand inuentions: and when all is done, they are not satisfied, they are not eased, but the horror of iudgement, and tortures of conscience still remaine: these scorpion locustes haue stong them. For if any man will doubt of the torments which they suffered in the blind Popery that were drowned in superstition, being stong with the false doctrine and idolatry of these locustes, doe but marke their ende: for when

they

THE REVELATION.

they haue run, run, run, euery way to seek ease, when they haue spent their goods, and tormented their bodies with all the sharpe penances they can: yet at the last what do they? They giue great gifts, they build Abbeyes to haue trentals of masses, and to be prayed for. Then sing, sing, sing, ring, ring, ring, powre the pardons into the graue: call for the Friers: call for the poore: let plentifull almes be giuen to helpe the poore soule to some ease from the torments it was in: ô filthy cursed locustes, that thrust in such tormenting poison into the consciences of miserable men! ô blessed doctrine of reconciliation through the bloud of the Lambe, which bringeth sweete peace and ioy vnto the wounded soule! It is sayd, they should haue this power to torment men fiue moneths. This is a comfort, yea a great comfort, that albeit the displeasure of God was great, for the contempt and abuse of his holy Gospell, and therefore as Saint *Paul* teacheth, 2. Thess. 2 he would send strong delusion, euen the darknesse and these vile locusts; yet it shall be but for a time, yea lesse then halfe a yeare. I will not stand curiously about the number of yeares, but yet I take it that by these fiue moneths, after the maner of the speeches of the Prophets, some fiue hundred yeares are to be vnderstood. For the poperie hath beene in the power and sway to bring in this hellish darkenesse, about the space of fiue hundred yeares, as we shall haue occasion to note elsewhere. But how is it to be taken that he saith, in those daies men shall seek death and shall not find it, & shall desire to die, but death shall flie from them? This doth shew how fully their torment is like to those which are stong with Scorpions: for they lye in grieuous paine certaine daies, & would faine be rid of it by death, & death lingereth. Surely the superstitious papists void of all true peace of conscience, tormēted with the feeling of their sinnes, and feare of comming to iudgement, in all their seeking for ease do but increase torment. For that which they drinke in as a medicine to ease them, is poison which doth more and more encrease paine. No doubt such as be in that case wish to be dead, so that they might neuer come before the Iudge, and so may be said to seeke death. And thus hauing described the torment wherewith these locusts should vexe the inhabitants of the earth, in the time of the great Antichrist, he returneth to describe the forme of them. He saith the forme of the locusts was like vnto horses prepared vnto battaile, &c. here we haue a maruellous description. What is a pield locust to an horse? and yet these locustes are like strong horses prepared to battaile. The popish cleargie, though the inferiour sort of them were base in shew like paltrie locusts, yet were strong and linked together with readie and prepared minds, as horses to battell against all such as shold anie way but so much as mutter against the vsurped power and tyrannie of their king the Romish Antichrist. Who knoweth not this which either liueth among them now, or that readeth the histories of the times past? they rush strongly like horses to the battaile. There haue bene great troupes and armies of them, and so bold as to bid battaile against the mightiest Emperors & kings in all Europe. Then next he saith, they had on their heads as it were crownes of gold: they be but vile locustes, a deuouring vermine, good for nothing, and yet decked with honour as it were with crownes of gold vpon their heads. To vnderstand this, looke what deuises they had to be in dignitie and estimation: looke what priuiledges & immunities they had, as not to be vnder the power of kings: finally, looke what titles of honour and preheminence euerie Locust did chalenge, and ye must needs confesse that they had crownes vpon their heads like crownes of gold. Indeed it is not said that their crownes were of gold, but like gold. For the honour which God hath ordained, and the maiestie which he giueth vnto Princes, is set forth with crownes of pure gold. But those deuised titles and honours of the Romish Clergie, though they glister, and shew like gold, yet they be no crownes of gold, they be no honours to them which know the truth. Their great Lord himselfe with his triple crowne, whose glorie and magnificence was published and esteemed to excell the maiesty of Emperours, as farre as the Sun doth excell the Moone in brightnesse, is now couered with shame and ignominie, it is no crowne of gold. For who doth not know, that it is no true magnificēce ordained by God, but giuen by the Dragon? What is then the crowne of their Monkes & Friers? do not all men now see it is no gold? In the darke they seemed to be gold, so long as the smoke of the bottomlesse pit darkened the Sunne: but now the Sunne shineth, and we see the crownes were but like gold.

He saith further, that *they had faces like faces of men*. They be not terrible to looke vpon, in as much as they pretend all good, making men beleeue that they can bring them vnto true blessednesse. For they will teach them true religion, true deuotion, and giue them pardon of all their sinnes. Manie things they promise, and make a faire face, that none may be affraid of them. They had haire like women: they are delicious and wanton, and full of whorish entisements: their attire and gestures wholly tending to allure vnto spirituall whordome and superstition: but their teeth are as the teeth of Lyons: they haue strong and sharpe teeth. These are strange Locusts, in forme like horses to battell, that looke like men in their faces, haue haire like women, and teeth like Lyons. They be great deuourers, they eate vp all. Looke how they were planted and seated, & see whether they had not gotten the fattest things in the earth which they fed vpon. Looke vpon the Abbeyes, the Priories, the Nunries, and all religious houses, and iudge what teeth they had. When there was not enough to satisfie them of temporall mens lands, then they prayed vpon Church liuings, and made impropriations. If they had continued, and bred still, and their time of fiue moneths not limited, which is now expired, what almost should haue escaped their teeth? The next words do shew how strongly they were armed: for he saith, *They had habbergions, like to habbergions of yron*. How can this agree, may some man say, to the poore Popish Priests, Monks or Friers, if they be the Locusts? were they armed in any such sort? Yea, they were strongly armed all of them. Their grand Captaine the Pope had so terrified and brought vnder all Kings and Emperors, that none durst meddle with the basest of these Locusts: they were exempted from the secular power, and not to be iudged or corrected by the same. If any King should take vpon him to punish one, though neuer so meane of their Clergie, for murther, for theft, for whoredome, or anie notorious vice, the Pope as a dreadfull God vpon the earth, would by and by they were coniurers, riotous, whoremongers, and most filthy in all wicked and leud life, as the Monks, and Friers, & Priests were for the most part, yet was there no punishment to be laid vpon them by Princes. ¶ Also their wings make a great noise: for he saith, *the sound of their wings was as the sound of chariots, when manie horses runne vnto the battell.* This is not the least matter that they make so horrible a noise: for it striketh a great terrour into mens hearts. True it is, that the noise is confused, as what is all the noyse they haue made or do make, to defend and vphold their bloudie kingdome, but a terrible confused and threatning noise without all reason? The few Locusts which remaine at this day being disturbed, make a great noise; how great was it then thinke ye, when all Europe almost was full of the swarmes and troupes of them? Blessed be God which with a mightie East wind hath cast these clamorous Locusts, which made such a noise with their wings out of our coasts, and drowned them in the sea. He saith, *They had tayles like vnto Scorpions, and they had stings in their tayles.* This is to shew their craftie sleight, by which they wind in for to do hurt, and sting men priuily: their flatteries and faire promises, and goodly smooth words, do shew no such matter that men need to feare them: but in the end, euen as it were with the taile, they leaue a sting behind them, euen the poison of their diuellish doctrine and false worship, into which they seduce men. At this day, now when the light hath bawrayed them, with what wonderfull cunning do they wind in themselues, and sting manie in all pllaces? They make a shew of great zeale for the Catholike Church, for the ancient faith, and for the Fathers, and the end of all is but to leaue the sting of their taile behind them, that is, their owne corrupt and damnable doctrine: for they are gone quite astray from the ancient Catholike faith of the godlie Fathers Doubtlesse I may speake this, that it was no great maruell, that poore ignorant men in the time when the Sun and the aire were darkened, were stong and stong againe: but now in the time of light they are worthie a thousand times to perish which will let them touch them with their taile, to receiue the sting. Touching the time in which power is giuen them to hurt, I haue spoken before. And the last thing is, that they haue a king ouer them, which is the Angell of the bottomlesse pit, which is called *Abaddon* in hebrue, and in greeke *Apollyon*: both the words are of one signification, and that is destroying. Then this great army is not without a Generall, vnder whom as vnder their Emperour they serue, whose honour, dignity and power they maintaine. It is the Angell of the bottomlesse pit: but who is that? whether is it the diuell or the Pope? No doubt properly the diuell is the Angell of the bottomlesse pit. But the starres are Angels of the Churches: and this starre being fallen hath the key of the bottomlesse pit committed to him:

where-

wherefore I do see no reason why he may not be called the Angell of the bottō-lesse pit for this respect, that he opened the bottomlesse pit. These Locusts do all acknowledge him to be their king indeed, vnder him & for him they do warre. It is also very certaine that the diuell is their king, for he is the king of their king. The Pope destroyeth by the power of Sathan, who is indeed the great destroyer. It is a maruellous shame for vs that we are not as earnest to warre vnder our Captaine Iesus Christ, as they be for their king, the Angell of hell, the Pope and the diuell.

THE XIX. SERMON.

CHAP. 9.

12. *One vvoe is past, and behold yet two vvoes come after this.*
13. *Then the sixt Angell blew the trumpet, & I heard a voyce from the foure hornes of the golden altar which is before God,*
14. *Saying to the sixt Angell, which had the trumpet, loose the foure Angels, which are bound in the great riuer Euphrates.*
15. *And the foure Angels vvere loosed, vvhich vvere prepared at an houre, at a day, at a moneth, and at a yeare, to slay the third part of men.*
16. *And the number of horsemen of vvarre were twenty thousand times ten thousand: for I heard the number of them.*
17. *And thus I saw the horses in a vision, and them that sate on them, hauing fiery habbergions, and of Iacinth, and of brimstone, and the heads of the horses vvere as the heads of Lyons: & out of their mouthes went forth fire, & smoke, and brimstone.*
18. *Of these three vvas the third part of men killed, that is, of the fire, and of the smoke, and of the brimstone, which came out of their mouthes.*
19. *For their power is in their mouthes, and in their tailes: for their tayles were like vnto serpents, and had heads vvherewith they hurt.*
20. *And the remnant of the men vvhich vvere not killed by these plagues, repented not of the vvorkes of their hands, that they should not vvorship diuels, and idols of gold, and of siluer, and of brasse, and of stone, and of wood, which neither can see, neither heare, nor go.*
21. *Also they repented not of their murther, and of their sorcerie, neither of their fornication, nor of their theft.*

Of the three last woes which the Angell proclaimed, we haue had one in the former part of this chapter, and that is, the darke kingdome of Antichrist which we passe briefly ouer, because it is afterward set forth largely.
And

THE REVELATION.

And now we come to the second wo, being the first of the two which yet remaine. It is (as we shall see) a great armie which in horrible manner slayeth the third part of men. This wo is also vsually expounded of the kingdome of Antichrist, as namely in a further increase. But I do take it to be otherwise, being led by these reasons following. First, the Angell denouncing *Woe, vvoe, woe*, denounceth three seuerall woes: and therfore it is said, *One vvoe is past, and behold yet two vvoes come after this*. If the kingdome of the Pope should be painted out both by the Locusts, and by these horsmen, I see not how they should be properly called two seuerall woes. The same woe might be augmented, and yet still the same, but this is another, or a seuerall woe from it, and so called the second woe of the three. He that will then expound this second woe to be the tyrannie of the Pope, must not take the former to be a description of the Poperie, because, as I said, they be two seuerall woes. Secondly, the slaughter of the third part of men is both a slaughter of the wicked, and not of the Saints, and also a bodily slaughter, as may euidently appeare by the latter end of this chapter. For Idolaters that worship diuels are spiritually slaine already, this slaughter is vpon such vngodly ones, and they that escape the same, repent not of their idolatrie. It is a plague, if we consider it well, vpon the idolatrous kingdome of Antichrist: it is a great slaughter made vpon those that worship idols. The Pope indeed with his armies of scorpion Locusts, besides the stinging to death of the soules of the reprobate, slayeth the bodies of the Saints: but that is far another thing from this slaughter. Thirdly, no man of any iudgement, as I suppose, can doubt, that this reuelation reuealing & describing all the greatest calamities and plagues that should come vpon men in the world, should not set forth the kingdome of the Turkes. There are indeed some things which at the first may seeme to make against it: but I take this cleare, to be the description of the great plague of Turcisme. For as I said, I am out of doubt, that the kingdome of the Turkes is described in this booke: and if this be not it, let any man shew where we shall find it. Let vs then come to the words as they lye. When the sixt Angell blew the trumpet, Saint *Iohn* heard a voice from the foure hornes of the golden altar which is before God. This Prophecie vseth the phrases of the Prophets vnder the Law, where things were figured by ceremonies. And because the mediation of Christ remaineth fresh and alwayes effectuall, there is said to be a golden altar before God in heauen, which is the altar of sweet incense. And indeed our altar is in heauen: for whatsoeuer spirituall sacrifice of praise and thankfgiuing we offer, it is vpon the mediation of Christ. From this altar the voice commeth to the Angell which blew the sixt trumpet, that we might know it is the voyce and commaundement of our Lord Iesus Christ, it is the voyce of the mightie God. The voyce commandeth the Angel to loose the foure Angels which are bound in the great riuer *Euphrates*. These Angels thus bound at *Euphrates* are diuels: their binding is no more but a restraint, by which they were held backe from doing that mischiefe which they desired to do; and were readie. Their loosing giueth them power to performe that which they wished. We may not take it that they were iust foure in number: but because they should raise an horrible

plague

Plague that shold spread East and West, North and South, ouer a great part of the world, they are said to be foure. The sense is, that the diuels haue yet further and greater scope giuen them then before, to plague and destroy the inhabitants of the earth. They had exceeding great power in the kingdome of Antichrist, I meane the diuels, but they are insatiable, and so after a sort lye still bound vntill they haue their desire. The place where they lye bound is Euphrates: wherein is a mysterie. It is the name of a great riuer which ranne so nigh the citie Babylon in Chaldea, that it was a mightie defence to the citie, so that the citie could not be easily taken, vntill they that laid the siege cut out trenches and deriued the waters another way. This is the letter, Now for the mysterie. Rome in this booke is called Babylon mystically, and after the same maner the great riuer Euphrates (as we shall see after in chap. 16.) signifieth the power and force, which that citie Rome, euen this great Babell hath to defend it selfe. Then in this power of Rome lye the diuels bound. This causeth Interpreters to take this plague also to be the popish armie. But this one circumstance of the place doth not carrie so great force in it, as to enforce that sense, as we may consider. It is out of doubt that Sathan waited through the power of the citie of Rome to worke all mischiefe: and therefore may well be sayd to lye bound there so long as he was restrained. Also from Rome the greatest cause of Turcisme came, seeing it was not onely raised vp to be the plague of Idolaters: but also the darknesse which made way for that error, euen the religion of the Turke, came also from Rome, whē the starre euen the Angel of that Church had opened the bottomlesse pit. I thinke it therefore no hard matter to say, the diuels were let loose at Rome which brought the Turcisme: for I thinke they all waited there for their helpe from that citie. He saith these Angels were prepared at an houre, at a day, at a moneth, and at a yeare, to slay the third part of men. This ascending by degrees from a short time vnto longer and longer, I know not what it meaneth, vnlesse that they be presently and in short time readie to worke their mischiefe, and as readie also to continue on the same still without wearinesse: and withall that God doth limit their times. For certaine all these be most true, they be readie with speed, they be neuer wearie, and God doth limit them. First that the diuels are in a wonderfull readinesse to worke the destruction of men, if they may be let loose, can any doubt? What a bloudie tyrant is Sathan? Secondly, they be neuer satisfied with any time, but would continue: for they be wrath that their kingdome draweth toward an end. And thirdly, (which is our comfort) the Lord God doth set their bounds how farre they shall go, in plaguing and destroying, and how long. Well they are loosed now, and here followeth presently the description of a terrible plague which they raise. It is a murthering armie, and he beginneth in the description with the number of them. The number is twentie thousand times tenne thousandes. Or as some expresse it, which is all one, two thousand times an hundred thousands: or two hundred thousand thousands. One thousand thousands is a great armie, and such as hath bene but seldome in the world in comparison: How great is an armie then of two hundreth such armies of a thousand thousands put together? I say how huge is an armie which is of two

hundreth

hundreth armies, and euerie of them a thousand thousands? But it may be said, where shall we find that the Turkes murthering armies haue bene so great? I answer that it is not meant, that this armie was all at a time: here is the full plague of manie yeares set forth. Then it may be obiected, that this number commeth short of the number of warriours which haue bene in the armies of the Saracens and Turkes, if we take the space of sixe or seuen hundred yeares: for in this space of time their whole armies would rise to a greater number then two hundreth armies of a thousand thousands in euerie armie. I do not doubt of that: for it is not the purpose of the holy Ghost to set downe the iust and full number, but by this great and maruellous multitude to leade vs vnto an innumerable companie which should kill and destroy men. How could Saint *Iohn* number such an armie? or did he stand to number them, may some say? He answereth this doubt, and saith, he heard the number of them. He did not number them, but the number was told him.

Then next followeth a description of these warriors, & their horses, a descriptiō indeed full of terrour. For thus they appeared in vision: first, the riders had fierie habbergions, and of Hyacynth, and of brimstone. Fire is a bitter thing, especially when it is ioyned with brimstone and with smoke, which doth choke and strangle: for smoke is resembled by the colour of Hyacynth: and the horses and their riders therein are alike. For after he hath reported that the heads of the horses were as the heads of Lyons: which sheweth their stomacke, strength and fiercenesse: he addeth, that out of their mouthes went forth fire, and smoke, and brimstone. They come with a terrible crueltie & fiercenesse. Then followeth the great slaughter; which is, that *the third part of mē were slaine by the fire, the smoke, & the brimstone, which came out of their mouths.* They are slaine with maruellous barbarous cruelty, either killed with bodily death as multitudes were, or drawn to that wicked religion of *Mahomet.* For partly by externall violence, and partly by a suttle shew of religion and deuotion, they destroy: and therefore it is said, *their power is in their mouthes, and in their tailes:* and that *their tayles are like serpents, and haue heads vvherewith they hurt.* These horses may be diuels themselues for ought that I can see, for the diuels haue set the Turks a worke and do.

And now that these things may the better appeare, I will briefly note vnto ye the beginning, the proceedings, and the order of the Turcisme. About the yeare of our Lord 591 was *Mahomet* borne, of base parentage, in a certaine village of Arabia called Itrarix, (for so histories do report.) This *Mahomet* by fraud and cousinage grew into great credite and fame among the sedicious Arabians, and Egyptians. In the yeare of our Lord 623, he was made Captaine and Prophet of the Saracens and Arabians. It fell out to be so vpon this occasion. There was an armie of Saracens, which with *Heraclius* the Emperor did warre against the Persians. Their wages were denied them, and not onely that, but also reprochfull words were giuen; for the Treasurers of *Heraclius* said, they could hardly giue wages to the Romane and Grecian souldiers, and that they had no money remaining to cast to this rout of dogs (for so they tearmed the Saracens.) They hearing this reproch, in a great rage spoyle all the townes neare about *Damascus.* They renounce their subiection and obedience to the Romane Emperor, & created *Mahomet* their Captaine: for he hauing maried a verie rich wife, had won the hearts of many with gifts. This filthie man fained himselfe to be a Prophet, and said that he had visions and reuelations, and talke with Angels. And so by the helpe of *Sergius* a Monke, an Arrian (who denied the eternal Godhead of our blessed Sauior) he framed a new worship and religion, patched together out of the old testament, and out of the new which he depraued. He raigned in the parts neare *Damascus* nine yeares, and so died in the yeare of our Lord 631.

 Then succeeded this *Mahomet* in the kingdome of the Saracens, *Ebubezer*, he raigned two yeares, and tooke *Damascus*, and made it the head of the kingdome: he wasted Gaza and Ierusalem. After him succeeded *Haumar*, who raigned 12 yeares, and greatly enlarged the kingdome: for subduing a great part of Syria, he possessed Egypt. In his dayes the Persians craued aid of the Turkes against the Saracens, but the Persians went by the worse, and then the Turkes entred into league with the Saracens; and receiued their religion, ioyning their forces also together vnto the warres, and from that time the Saracens and the Turkes were counted almost for one people. Then was the kingdome farre larger whē the Persians were ouercome: for then had they all these regions, Syria, Cilicia, Cappadocia, Mesopotamia, the Iland Cyprus, Egypt and Ierusalem In all these parts the religion of *Mahomet* was set vp: at Babylon was then the seat of the kingdome. They ruled the prouinces by Presidents, who they called Souldans: the Souldan of Egypt was the mightiest: he tooke Cæsaria of Palestine, in the yeare of our Lord 642. And in the yeare 654. he possessed the most noble Iland of Rhodes, frō whence he caried verie great riches. The fourth king of the Saracens was *Hoam*, vnder whom they inuaded *Africa*. *Muhauias* succeeded him, and raigned 24 yeares, vnder whom they inuaded Africa the second time, & caried away captiues fourescore thousand. In this kingdome of the Saracens, which held now the Empire of Asia and Persia, there succeeded one another to the number of 26 kings, & continued 200 yeares without ciuill discord among themselues. In this space of time the borders of their kingdome were yet somewhat further enlarged, manie sore battels were fought, great slaughters of Christians, and manie carried captiues: for they tooke the Iland Creta, they entred into Italy, spoyled some townes, and would haue set vpon Rome it selfe; but the citizens of Rome put thē to flight. But about the yeare of our Lord 832. the Souldans through emulation and ambition, began to warre and contend among themselues, so that their power diminished; and the power of the Turkes by degrees increased so farre, that in litle more then two hundreth yeares, besides the regions of Armenia the greater, & the lesse, Cappadocia, Galatia, and Bythinia, which they had gotten, they cast the Emperour of the Saracens forth of his kingdome, and set vp in his place a king of the Turkes. Their first king was *Zadoke*, in the yeare of our Lord 1051. In two yeares space he subdued a great part of Asia. Three of his successours Emperours of the Turkes preuailed, and did great things against the Christians: but afterward there

was

THE REVELATION. 177

was much ado to winne from the Turke the holy land. The Pope, and the kings and Princes of diuerſe countries ioyned together, and ſent an army vnder *Godfrey* of Bullaine, of three hundreth thouſand footmen, and one hundreth thouſand horſ-men.

In the yeare 1099. *Godfrey* wan Ieruſalem, and was crowned king: there ſuc-ceeded him fiue or ſix kings in Ieruſalem, which with the loſſe of much bloud kept the holy land (as they call it) which to maintaine the warres againſt the Turkes, did ordaine certaine orders, as of Templars, and knights of the Rhodes. Ieruſalem was loſt againe, with great ſlaughters of Chriſtians in all parts thereabout, in the yeare 1187. And within ſhort time after that, the *Tartari* a barbarous people, be-gan to be of power. Their firſt Emperor was *Changius Can*. Diuerſe ſucceeded, which greatly diminiſhed the dominion of the Turkes, vntil about the yeare of our Lord 1300. for then the Empire of the *Tartari* was ouerthrowne, & the Empire of the Turkes did flouriſh more then euer before. Now come the greateſt mon-ſters, and moſt ſauage and cruelleſt tyrants of all. *Ottoman* was the firſt of them: he and his ſucceſſours with moſt cruell ſlaughters ouercame the Chriſtians in ma-ny countries, and ſpred the Turkes dominion very farre: but yet in the middeſt of their glory, there is a great gap made. Thus it was, *Baiazethes* the fourth Emperor of the Turkes wonderfully preuailing with great ſlaughters of Chriſtians, and lea-ding innumerable multitudes captiue out of Hungary which he inuaded: and ſet-ting vpon the Emperour of the Grecians, waſting and deſtroying with ſuch ter-rour, that the Emperor craued aid, and *Charles* the ſixt king of France, ſent a po-wer, and *Sigiſmund* king of Hungary went himſelfe with an army, which were o-uerthrowne miſerably, and *Sigiſmund* hardly eſcaped. This was in the yeare of our Lord 1395. *Baiazethes* in this his glory, being for his terror and quickneſſe in war called *Hildrin*, that is lightning, proceeded yet forward, and waſted Thracia, Myſia, Dardania, and Macedonia, and to the great terror of all Chriſtendome, be-ſieged Conſtantinople. It was ſuppoſed the city would be taken and vtterly de-ſtroyed: but in the meane time (as it is reported) by the requeſt of the Emperour, came *Tamerlan* the Scythian, with an exceeding great army againſt the Turke out of Scythia. *Baiazethes* was conſtrained to raiſe his ſiege againſt Conſtantino-ple, and to go and fight with this *Tamerlan*. It is ſayd that the army of *Tamer-lan* was an hundreth myriades, that is, an hundreth times ten thouſand, or a thou-ſand thouſands. *Baiazethes* army was fiue hundreth thouſand, that is halfe ſo much. They fought this battaile in the yeare of our Lord 1397. neere to the great riuer Euphrates, which is by Babel in Chaldea. There were ſlaine aboue an hun-dreth and forty thouſand of the Turkes. Euphrates ſeemed rather to runne with bloud then with water. The victory fell to *Tamerlan*, who tooke *Baiazethes* the great Turke and put him into an iron cage, and caried him about in ſhew through Aſia, he trode vpon his backe, as vpon a ſtoole when he went to horſebacke: he made him alſo gather vp ſcrappes vnder the table like a dogge. He cauſed the Em-preſſe the wife of *Baiazethes*, to be clothed in a ſhort garment which did ſcarce couer her ſhame, and ſo to waite and fill the cups to the Nobles of Scythia, in the

N ſight

SERMONS VPON

fight of her husband. The Turke tooke this so heauily, that he beate his head against the iron grate of his cage, and so killed himselfe. Thus was Constantinople for that time, & all Grecia, freed from the most sauage tyranny of the Turke. And then that horrible kingdome might seeme euen as good as pulled downe: but God had in his iustice determined the plague for the wickednesse of those which professed his Son in word, and liued in so foule idolatry. *Tamerlan* thus preuailed, who though he shewed this fauour and compassion to the Emperor of Grecia, yet was he one of the most cruell tyrants that euer liued. He was a poore mans sonne, and became a Captaine among robbers, and grew so strong that hee found the meanes vpon occasion to become the king of the Persians. If he besieged a city, the first day he set vp white tents: to shew that if they would yeeld they should haue mercy. The second day he set vp red tents, by which he threatned death. The third day he set vp blacke tents, in token of extreame calamity: and after these were vp, no yeelding could be accepted, but they must all die, both great and small. And therefore besieging a city which yeelded not at the first, nor the second day, but stood the setting vp his blacke tents, the Citizens fearing his cruelty, sent forth all their litle children, their sonnes and their daughters clothed in white, and palmes in their hands, thinking by the innocency of these poore infants to mitigate the cruelty of the tyrant: but he sent his horsemen vpon them, and trode them downe most cruelly. One demanded of him why he was so cruell towards all? And it is said, that he with a frowning sterne countenance looking awry, made this answer: Thinkest thou that I am a man, and not rather the wrath of God dwelling vpon the earth to the destruction of me? The king of Hungary thought it a fit time after this great victory of *Tamerlan*, to set vpon the son of *Baiazethes*, and vtterly to roote out the name of *Ottoman*, not only out of Europe, but also out of Asia. But he tooke the foile, and *Calepine* the Turke preuailed: and after the death of *Tamerlan*, *Mahomet* recouered againe all that his Grandfather *Baiazethes* had lost, and dyed in the yeare 1419. And from that time the kingdome grew more larger, and more terrible then euer before, for the wrath of God was kindled against the wickednesse of the Christiās. For *Amurathes*, who came next to be Emperor of the Turks, subdued many places to the great destructiō of the Christiās. He was indeed strongly resisted in Hungary, and by *Ladislaus* king of Polonia. This *Ladislaus* and the Turke concluded a peace for fourteene yeares with a solemne oath. But Pope *Innocent*, & *Iulian* the Cardinall with wicked counsell perswaded *Ladislaus* to breake his oath, affirming that he might lawfully do it to an enemy of Christ. *Ladislaus* gathered his power, and there ioyned with him the power of the Pope, and of the Duke of Burgundy, and of Venice. He thought to intercept the Turke suspecting no such matter, because of the peace concluded betweene them by oath, But the Turke smelt the matter, & with wonderfull speed came to Verna where *Ladislaus* was, not looking for him. There was a most famous battell fought: it continued three dayes and three nights without any apparance which side should preuaile. The fields seemed to stand with pooles of bloud: At length the Turke preuailed, to the great slaughter of the Christians. *Ladislaus* the king was slaine, and so was the wicked Cardinall *Iulian*,

which

THE REVELATION.

which perswaded him to breake and violate his league and solemne oath. This battell was fought in the yeare of our Lord 1444. After this the Turke did maruellously rage against Hungary, thē against Grecia, & other places. At this time *Scanderbeg* the son of a Christian Prince which was ouercome by the Turke, and so his foure sons caried away, among whom this *Scanderbeg* was one, being a man of wonderfull valour (for therefore the Turke called him not by his owne name which was *George*, but *Scanderbeg*, that is, *Alexander* the great) reuolted from the Turke, recouered his fathers possession, and was a great plague to that sauage kingdome. But yet the Lord God which was wrath for the wickednesse of men, would haue it further preuaile.

For now followeth another *Mahomet* a most cruell tyrant, which meant to subdue the whole world, and indeed exceeded all his predecessors in power. For he besieged and wan Constantinople, and so did ouerthrow and put an end to the Empire of the East. He wan it in the yeare 1453. and there hath euer since bene the Royall Pallace of the Turke. The winning of this city, and the ouerthrow of that Empire of the Grecians, was a manifest token of Gods heauy wrath, and did strike such a terrour into all Christiandome, that many yeelded themselues to the Turke, and many regions and cities he ouercame by violent warres. If I should stand now to recite the horrible slaughters of Christians, and the innumerable multitudes which the Turkes haue led into captiuity, I should be more then tedious. I suppose that by the Saracenes, the Turkes, the Tartarians, and Scythians, the third part of men haue bene horribly slaine: as it is sayd by *Saint Iohn*, that the third part of men were slaine. Many, did confesse that these plagues came vpon them for sinne, euen that the word of God was despised, and that all foule vices did abound among the prelates: but yet there was no amendment of life, no repentance, but all grew worse and worse. For marke what *Saint Iohn* sayth: *And the remnant of the men which were not killed by these plagues, repented not of the workes of their hands, that they should not worship diuels, and idols of gold, and of siluer, and of brasse, and of stone, and of wood, which nsither heare nor go. Also they repented not of their murther, and of their sorcery, neither of their fornication, nor of their theft.* If we looke through all Europe, so farre as the Pope bare sway, ye shall find that euen to the very time that the light of the Gospell brake foorth againe, the more the Turke with sauage cruelty and tyrannie, did leade into captiuitie infinite multitudes, so that there was a terrour striken into all mens hearts, that as he had subdued all the East Churches, so hee would also ouerrunne all the West Churches, yet horrible idolatrie increased, and other wickednesse dayly more and more. How were the people besotted? how did they runne from Idoll to Idoll, which were but of gold, or siluer, or brasse, or stone, or wood, and had no sense to heare, to see, or to go? The truth is, they worship deuels which worship not the Lord as *Saint Iohn* here speaketh. And none worship the Lord which worship Idols. Likewise what cruell murthers did they commit, especially vpon the true seruants of Christ? The Monkes, the Friers, the Priests, the Nunnes, how full of charmes, sorseries, witchcrafts, and coniurations were they,

N 2   with

with innumerable whoredoms, murthers and thefts? The common people, yea all sorts did follow them. What should I here stand to enter into particular demonstrations, when all that be of yeares can testifie, vnlesse it be such as be wilfully blinded, how all agreed to that which Saint *Iohn* here setteth downe? And now let the most slie and subtill of all the Iesuits which warre for Antichrist, shew vs where they be in the world that haue bene plagued with this terrible armie, sent in Gods wrath for worshipping of Idols, and the other vices here named, but onely in the Poperie? If they will leade vs vnto more ancient times, they may not: for this is in the opening of the seuenth seale of the booke, & in the blowing of the sixt trumpet, and therefore in the latter end of the world, seeing the day of iudgemēt commeth when the seuenth Angell bloweth the trumpet. If they would turne vs ouer to the heathen nations, the West or East Indians: indeede the West Indians haue bene slaine in such multitudes, as it is almost incredible: but then the Popish Spaniards haue bene this murthering army, for they haue killed them. But alas who cannot see that this prophecy is chiefly fulfilled vpon those nations which professe Christ? Poore and miserable is the shift of our Rhemists vpon this place, which say here are meant the portraitures of the heathen Gods: seeing they be gone long since, & this is spoken of the latter end of the world, in which none worship Idols of gold, siluer, &c. but the Papists. Blessed be the Lord who by the light of the Gospell hath deliuered from worshipping dumbe Idols, and so from the feare of this horrible army. For where men haue imbraced the Gospell, and repented of their abominable idolatry, they haue no feare of him any longer.

THE XX. SERMON.
CHAP. 10.

1. *And I saw another mighty Angell come downe from heauen clothed with a cloud, and the rainebow vpon his head, and his face was as the Sunne, and his feete as pillars of fire.*
2. *And he had in his hand a little booke open, and he put his right foote vpon the sea, and his left foote vpon the earth.*
3. *And cried with a loud voyce, as vvhen a Lyon roreth: and when he had cried, seuen thunders vttered their voyces.*
4. *And when the seuen thunders had vttered their voices, I was about to write: but I heard a voyce from heauen saying vnto me, Seale vp those things which the seuen thunders haue spoken, and write them not.*
5. *And the Angell which I saw stand vpon the sea, and vpon the earth, lift vp his hand to heauen:*

6. *And*

6. *And sware by him which liueth for euermore, which created heauen, and the things that therein be, and the earth, and the things that therein be, and the sea, and the things that therein be, that time should be no more,*

7. *But in the dayes of the voyce of the seuenth Angell, when he shall begin to blow the trumpet, euen the mystery of God shall be finished, as he hath declared to his seruants the Prophets.*

8. *And the voyce which I heard from heauen, spake vnto me againe, and sayd, Go take the little booke which is open in the hand of the Angell, which standeth vpon the sea, and vpon the earth.*

9. *So I went to the Angell, and sayd vnto him, Giue me the little booke. And he sayd vnto me, Take it, and eate it vp, & it shall make thy belly bitter, but it shall be in thy mouth as sweete as honey.*

10. *Then I tooke the little booke out of the Angels hand, and eat it vp, and it was in my mouth sweete as honey: but when I had eaten it, my belly was bitter.*

11. *And he sayd vnto me, Thou must prophecy againe among the people, and nations, and tongues, and to many kings.*

His vision is ioyfull: for after the darke kingdome of Antichrist, and that horrible murthering army of the Turkes, a mighty Angell commeth downe from heauen to relieue the poore Church, and to be auenged of those cruell enemies. The Lord preserued a remnant in the middest of those plagues, euen when the smoke of the bottomlesse pit did darken the Sunne and the ayre, when those scorpion locustes did sting and torment men, and when that horrible army whose horses had heads like Lions, and fire, smoke and brimstone comming out of their mouthes, and destroying the third part of men: but now he sendeth forth the Gospell againe, dispelling the darknesse and errors which came by the smoke of the pit, scattering and destroying the stinging locustes, reforming his Church, and gathering great multitudes of his Saints together. This vision is fulfilled, or at the least begun to bee fulfilled in our dayes: for we liue vnder the opening of the seuenth seale, and vnder the sounding of the sixt trumpet, as it doth euidently appeare by this Chapter. I will come to the text as it lieth. The mighty Angell which commeth downe from heauen is the Lord Iesus Christ himselfe: for the things which are here attributed vnto him, and by which he is described, bee such as belong to none other but to the diuine maiestie. For that he is clothed with a cloud, it is a note of Christs peculiar glory. The rainebow about his head (which of olde time was the sacrament betweene the Lord and all flesh, that he would not any more drowne the whole earth) is no lesse. This rainebow, also doth testifie, that albeit he be come downe with great wrath and terror against his enemies, euen as the God of vengeance, yet full of mercy to his faithfull seruants. That his face doth shine as the Sunne, it is to the

comfort

comfort and deliuerance of his Church, euen to difpell all that fmoke of the bottomleffe pit, as we fee the Sun fcattereth and driueth away the thicke miftes. And as the ftinging locufts were bred of the fmoke, fo now the brightneffe of his countenance doth fcatter and deftroy them, as vermine which cannot endure the light. The fwarmes of them were exceeding great, and like to moft terrible Locufts they did craule in abundance, & fpread themfelues ouer the face of the earth: but now their nefts be deftroyed, and they are become very few in comparifon of that they were, and withall they be greatly diftreffed which remaine yet behind. The bright fhining countenance of this Angell caufeth them to appeare moft vile and bafe, not onely to thofe which imbrace the truth, but alfo to the very fubiectes of Antichrift. Their glorie is defaced, their fhame is layd open, and their ftrength decayed. *His feete are as pillars of fire*: This is fet downe for the terrour of his enemies, whom he will tread downe vnder his feet, & confume them with the fire of his wrath. Before he commeth, the locufts are of wonderfull power, Antichrift held all the Kings in Europe in awe, and excercifed tyrannie at his pleafure, the Turke was terrible: but what are they vnto this mightie and glorious Angell? what is their power to withftand him? Then further it is faid, that he had in his hand a litle booke open. This booke is the booke of the holy Scriptures: for as we fee, the Bible is a large booke, if we confider it by it felfe, but yet in comparifon of the huge volumes of the ordinances and decrees in the popifh Church, it is but a litle booke. The booke in the hand of him that fate vpon the throne was fhut, and fealed with feuen feales, that no man could looke vpon it: but this booke is open, to fignifie that it is to be looked vpon of all men, and openly taught vnto all the feruants of God. It was fhut vp in the poperie, and lay buried in a ftrange tongue: no man taught it, which embraced the Romifh religion, but in fteed thereof mens decrees and inuentions, and all lyes and fables were preached by the popifh cleargie, and beleeued of the people. The Laitie (as they call them) were in no wife to meddle with it. Fourefcore yeares paft, ye fhould not fee it in the hands of any: now it is open in the hands of thoufand thoufands, and ten thoufand thoufands of Gods people, which out of it do learne to know God, and to worfhip him aright in fpirit and in truth. It hath brought fuch light euery where, that the fcorpion locufts cannot deuoure vp the greene things of the earth, nor fting men any longer in fuch multitudes as they did. It was faid before, when the third part of men were flaine by the fire, by the fmoke, and by the brimftone that came out of the horfes mouthes, that the remnant of the men which were not killed of thofe plagues, repented not of the workes of their hands, that they fhould not worfhip diuels, and idols of gold, &c. and the fame kingdome and tyrannie of the Turke being fent of God in his wrath to plague Idolaters, as Idolatrie encreafed, fo it alfo encreafed: for the more the Lord plagued the world by the Turke, the more Idolatrie encreafed, and they were further and further from repentance: fo that euen vpon the time that the Gofpel began to peepe forth, darkneffe was growne euen to the full, Idolatrie was exceeding groffe, and the Turkes power did fo encreafe, that he was a terror vnto all Chriftendome, & it was feared that as he had throwne

downe

THE REVELATION. 183

downe the Empire of the East, and ouerrun all those Churches, so he would throw downe the Romane Empire and spread himselfe ouer all the Churches in Europe. For as a terrible fire doth hang in the ayre, and men looke with feare when it should fall vpon them: so did he seeme to hang ouer all. But when this mighty Angell had brought this little booke open from heauen, and that men did looke vpon it, and repent of their idolatry, and turne to the liuing God, the plague hath departed euer since, and the Turke hath not bene feared in these parts where the Gospell is preached: but God hath drawne his power another way, and set him a worke elsewhere. So that if men cannot be brought to beleeue, that God raised him vp as a scourge and plague for idolatry, and other foule sinnes in the Church, according to the wordes of the former Chapter, when he sayth *They repented not of the workes of their hands, &c.* yet when they see that at the opening of the booke of God, and forsaking idolatry, the feare of him is remoued, let them beleeue it. What can we haue more plaine, then that this open booke in the hand of the Angell, hath deliuered vs both from the Pope and from the Turke? a most happy opening of this blessed booke.

Then it is sayd further, that he put his right foote vpon the sea, and his left foote vpon the earth. This sheweth that he is Lord and ruler both ouer sea and land: for he treadeth vpon both, and standeth as stedfast and as firme vpon the sea, as vpon the fast earth. He cried also with a loud voyce, as when a lion roreth. This is to manifest and to declare his wrath against his enemies, euen against the Locustes, and the horsemen of warre, and their horses. He let them range for a time at their pleasure, but now they shall feele his hand, and the power of his mighty and terrible voyce. If the Lion rore, the beasts of the forrest tremble. The Lord hath vttered his voyce againe in earth, and hath scattered his foes, he will in the ende make them tremble. And when he had cried (sayth *S. Iohn*) seuen thunders vttered their voyces. It is not expressed what he vttered in his strong and mighty voyce, with which he cried as when a Lion roreth: but it appeareth euidently that it was concerning the terrible vengeance and seuere iudgements to be executed vpon the destroyers and oppressors of his Church. For that which seuen Angels do vtter, at his call, is vttered as if seuen thunders should vtter their voyces. Thunder is a most terrible thing, and for that cause the most fearefull iudgements of God against the aduersaries are vttered by the voyces of thunders. He will thunder vpon them in his wrath, and horror shall oppresse them. The number of seuen, is a perfect number in the Scripture: for the Lord made all things in sixe dayes, and rested the seuenth day: and therefore to denounce the fulnesse of all his iudgements, here are seuen thunders vtter their voices. These thunders did speake so as they might be vnderstood: for *S. Iohn* was about to write the things which they spake: he tooke it they were vttered for that end and purpose, that he shold deliuer them in writing to the Churches: but he recciueth a commandement to the contrary. He is willed not to write, but to seale vp the things which the thunders had spoken. Why then were they vttered? or was it not in vaine, seeing they be concealed? It was not in vaine: for first, though the particulars be not expressed what the thunders spake, yet here we are taught, that there remaine most fearefull iudgements for Gods enemies, which he hath thundred out with terrour against them. And then moreouer, when the time commeth they shall be seene and vnderstood, for they be sealed vp vntill that time: as we see the Angell spake to *Daniell*. These things are sealed vp vntill the time determined, chap. 12. vers. 9. Let vs then fully assure our selues that there is great wrath and vengeance of the Lord to be powred forth vpon the papists, and vpon the Turkes, & vpon all such enemies of the truth, for all their crueltie shewed towardes his poore seruants. Their wickednesse hath bene and is exceeding great many waies, both against Gods truth, and against his people: and no maruell though the Lord denounceth his wrath and vengeance against them for the same by seuen terrible thunders. Who shall be able to stand whē this commeth, euen when the great God shal thunder against them from heauen? Let the Pope make merrie, with all his stinging Locustes which yet remaine, yea with all such as fauour and take his part: this is their lot, and ye see what cheare is prepared for them: most horrible vengeance shall light vpon them.

The next part of this chapter setteth forth, how the Angel with a solemne oath, euen by the liuing God which created all things, affirmeth that the great day of God, the day of the generall iudgment is at hand. This is for our instruction chiefly, which liue in this last age of the world: that we may be warned that the last day is at hand. The booke in the right hand of him that sate vpon the throne, was sealed with seuen seales, which the Lambe hath opened: vnder the seuenth seale commeth this great day. This seuenth seale is opened and as it were deuided into seuen parts, at the sounding of seuen trumpets: sixe of these trumpets are sounded alreadie. Yea it is euident that the sixt trumpet was sounded long since: because it draweth well towards fourescore yeares since this Angell came downe from heauen with the litle booke open in his hand, and that the light of the Gospell began to peepe out, and to disclose the foulnesse of poperie. For in the yeare of our Lord 1516. or in the yeare 1517. *Martin Luther* began to call some matters into question touching the poperie.

There remained but the last trumpet to be founded when the Angell made this solemne protestation, and a good part of the time since is expired. It is therefore as I sayd, euen to warne vs that liue now in these daies, and haue seene all these things fulfilled, to be prepared, and to wait for the second comming of Christ. But let vs looke vpon euery part and circumstance in this oath, as the words of the text do leade vs. *The Angell* (saith *Iohn*) *which I saw stand vpon the sea, and vpon the earth, lift vp his hand to heauen*. It is a cleare case, that in old time, they that sware, did lift vp their hand to heauē, thereby testifying as by an outward ceremonie or gesture, that they called the God of heauen to witnesse. And therefore *Abraham* when he would haue the king of *Sodome* vnderstand that he had sworne by the most high God, that he would not take any thing that was his, whē he had brought backe the captiues, vseth but this speech: I haue lift vp mine hand to Iehoua the God most high, possessor of heauen and earth, Gen. 14. 22. Then it is expressed, that this Angel sware by him that liueth for euermore, &c. The liuing God

alone

THE REVELATION. 185

alone is to haue this honour, that we sweare by his name in truth: and so the Angell sweareth by him and by none other. I wil not stand here to confute the Anabaptists, which because of these words of our Sauiour, *Sweare not all*: do hold it vnlawfull now vnder the new Testament to take an oath: we see here the Angell sweareth. But if anie shal thinke, how it can be, if this Angell be Christ, & so the liuing God, that he should sweare by the liuing God? the matter is easily answered. Christ in the person of the Mediatour is both God and man. And againe the scripture saith, *When there was no greater to sweare by, the Lord swore by himselfe*. He saith not, the creator of all things, or the Creator of heauen and earth: which is as much in effect as he speaketh, and doth teach vs, that he hath the ordering of all things, & hath in his owne counsell decreed the time when the world shal haue an end: but which created the heauen, & the things which be therein, & the earth, and the things which therein be, and the sea, and the things which therein be, &c. Here we see the whole world is diuided into three parts: the heauens, the earth, and the sea with their furniture. Euerie one of these is verie great, & furnished with maruellous creatures: and when we looke vpon them seuerally, it may leade vs into a greater wonderment at his glorie. And that is one cause no doubt, why he doth speake of them euerie one, as it were apart. We are negligent in considering the creatures to see how they set forth the magnificēce of their creator. The Lord no doubt could haue created all things at one instant, but he made them in sixe dayes, and so we haue them distinguished, to the end we might be moued and led vnto deeper consideration.

And now followeth what he sware, and that is, *Time shall be no more, but in the dayes of the voyce of the seuenth Angell, when he shall begin to blow the trumpet, euen the mysterie of God shal be fulfilled, as he hath declared to his seruants the Prophets*. The time that shall be no more, is the time as it is now, for the state of things as they be: and that there shall be no more delay or deferring of matters, but all shall be brought to iudgement. For now we see commonly good matters troden downe, and euill causes maintained, and no redresse to be had: but then there shall be no more delay, but euerie thing righted that is amisse. And this the Angell sweareth shall be euen when the seuenth Angell beginneth to blow the trumpet. But why doth the Angell take such a solemne oath that the day of iudgement shall shortly come? The cause is euident: we see how men in these last dayes are drowned in worldly cares and pleasures, euen with as much greedinesse, as if the world were new begunne, and should last for euer. Our Sauiour telleth how they shall eate and drinke, marrie wiues, plant, build, &c. and how the day shall come vpon thē vnawares euen as a snare. The things be lawful in themselues, & that causeth the more danger: for many thinke so long as they be about lawfull & honest things, though they be euen drowned and ouerwhelmed in them, and expell all care and delight in heauenly matters, that they cannot be blamed. Yea euen the faithfull need to be stirred vp: for the wise virgins do slumber and sleepe. We haue warning giuen vs in many places of the Scripture: but this warning, if we be not vtterly as dead flesh, may touch and moue vs, euen to prepare our selues with our loynes girded, and our Lampes burning, to waite for the comming of our maister.

But what is this that he faith, *Euen the myfterie of God shall be finished?* It is the rewarding of the iuft, and the punifhing of the wicked. The word of God, not onely the writings of the Apoftles, but alfo of the Prophets, doth plainely fet forth & teftifie both: that is to fay, what glorie God will beftow vpon all fuch as be faithfull and true vnto him, which loue, obey and ferue him: and on the other fide, what terible wrath fhall be powred forth in full meafure vpon all vngodly finners, and yet they be ftill a myfterie: for the greater part thinke litle of any fuch matter, and the faithfull which beleeue it, come farre fhort of comprehending it as it fhall be. For the high glorie of God fhall be exceedingly magnified both in the faluation of the iuft, & in the deftruction of the wicked, which we cannot now fully comprehend. Let vs thinke of it, and long for it, and be affured we fhall then fee the greateft and the moft wonderfull fights that euer haue bene feene. And aboue all, let vs labour that the myfterie of God may be finifhed vnto our ioy and comfort. Now is the time, beware ye be not of thofe that fhall be made veffels of wrath.

Now all that remaineth to the end of this chapter, is concerning the litle booke which the Angel brought downe open from heauen in his hand. Firft, *Iohn* is commaunded by the voice which fpake to him from heauen to go take the litle booke which is in the hand of the Angell ftanding vpon the fea, and vpon the land. Saint *Iohn* obeyeth that commādement of the heauenly voice, and goeth to the Angel, requiring of him that he would giue him the booke. The Angel doth not only deliuer it to him, but withall commaundeth him to eate it vp: and he telleth him he fhould find the tafte thereof fweete in his mouth as honey, and bitter in his bellie. Which he found fo indeed: for he tooke the booke and did eate it, and it was fweete in his mouth, but when he had eaten it, his bellie was bitter. What this doth fignifie, the Angell doth tell him in thefe words, that *he muft prophecie againe among the people, and nations, and tongues, and to many kings*. It is for great purpofe that this booke is brought, and for that refpect here is much faid of it. It is as I haue noted before, to declare that after the darkeneffe of the Poperie, in which the holy Scriptures lay buried, and mens inuentions & lies were taught, now towards the latter end of the world the Gofpell fhould be preached againe. For ye fee there remaine no trumpets now to be founded but the laft: there is but the laft woe to come. *Iohn* then in taking the booke, eating it vp and prophecying vnto kindreds, tongues, people, and manie kings, reprefenteth not the Minifters of old in the ages paft, but the Minifters of our time, which fhall preach the truth for the throwing downe of Antichrift. Then let vs examine euerie parcell. There is firft a voyce from heauen, willing them to take the booke at the hand of Chrift. The Minifters are called of God, and by him they are fet on worke: otherwife there could be no power, no authoritie, nor no good fucceffe in their minifterie. Againe, fee how the voyce from heauen fendeth them vnto that litle booke: for therein lyeth all the power and authoritie. And do we not fee this fulfilled? Did

not

THE REVELATION.   187

not *Luther*, and all the rest of those noble instruments that God raised vp to recouer his Church from vnder the tyrannie of Antichrist, euen by the direction of the holy Ghost, as by a voyce from heauen, leaue all humane deuises, and flie to the holy Scriptures for triall of all matters? And haue we not found, that so soone as euer the Lord sendeth his Ministers to take this booke, then beginneth the worke against Antichrist? Doth it not wound them so deeply? doth it not so discouer all their treacheries and abhominations, that they will not abide to be tried by it? They say there is no certaintie in the Scriptures to decide controuersies. They say the Scriptures be not sufficient for all matters. Yea which is most wicked, they set themselues aboue the Scriptures, affirming that the Scriptures haue no authoritie in respect of men, but that which dependeth vpon their Church. Thus Antichrist and his ministers set themselues aloft aboue all, and will be tried by nothing but by their owne decrees, that is, by themselues: for this is their bulwarke, that their Church cannot erre: the Pope in his chaire iudicially cannot erre. But they come downe, and let vs in no wise be driuen from this litle booke which is deliuered vnto vs by the Angell.

Then next, the Ministers of Christ are to eate vp the booke: that is, they must be so painefull in the studie of it, so learne it, and know all points of doctrine and instructions in it, and haue the power thereof in their heart, euen as if they had eat vp the whole booke. All their studies in other bookes must be but helpes to bring them to the knowledge of this booke. How sweet is it in the mouth, what ioy and delight, the finding out and knowledge of the true doctrines bringeth to a man while he is in the studie thereof, all godly students do know. How bitter it is in the belly, what indignation and griefe it worketh when it is knowne and digested, to see it despised, to see errour, falshood and abhominable wickednesse exalted and magnified, all godly zealous men do feele. Who is a right student in the holy Scriptures, which feeleth not that booke as sweete as honey in his mouth, & bitter in his bellie? If this bitternesse in the belly were not, men wold keepe it still within them: but they as the Angell sayth, must prophecy: againe, they must out with it among the nations and people. They must instruct in doctrine, they must couince, reproue, and exhort. The sweetnesse that a man feeleth in the doctrine, doth not carry him sufficiently to do all this: but the bitternesse which he feeleth, the indignation that falshood shold beare sway, the griefe to see the desolations of the Church, and the burning zeale of Christs glory, do thrust him forward. What is a minister of the Gospel, if he seeme to haue eat vp the whole booke of God, & it make not his belly bitter? Looke vpon those worthy men which receiued the booke at the hāds of the Angell, at the first disclosing and bewraying of Popery: some in Germany, some in France, some in England, some in other countries. But specially looke vpon *Luther, Caluine, Peter Martir, Bucer, Bullinger*, and *Beza*: and ye shall see that as they euen eate vp the booke of God, and became very mighty in the holy Scriptures, feeling such wonderfull sweetnesse therin: so also they were caried with a wonderfull zeale and indignation against the wicked doctrine of Antichrist, their bellies were made so bitter, that they prochecied, and through their prophecying,

cying, the light of the truth hath spread it selfe among nations, tongues, & people, and kings haue embraced & maintained it. Praised be the Lord, blessed be his holy name for this great woik which he hath wrought in our dayes. When ye see all things fal so fully out according to this vision, let vs be bold in the truth, & magnifie this litle booke, which will vtterly destroy Poperie, & bring downe the proud Antichrist, do all which fight for him what they can.

THE XXI. SERMON.

CHAP. 11.

1. *And there was giuen me a reed like vnto a rod, and the Angell stood by, saying, Arise and measure the Temple of God, & the Altar, and them that worship therein.*

2. *But the court which is without the Temple, cast forth and measure it not: for it is giuen vnto the Gentiles, and the holy city shall they tread vnder foote fortie and two moneths.*

3. *But I will giue power vnto my two witnesses, and they shall prophecie a thousand, two hundreth and three score dayes cloathed in sackcloth.*

IN the latter end of the former chapter, Saint *Iohn* representing the Ministers of the Gospell, whom the Lord would raise vp in the latter end of the world, to recouer his Church from vnder the tyrannie of Antichrist, taketh the litle booke of God which was open in the hand of the Angell, and eateth it vp, and it was sweete in the eating, but bitter in his belly, because he must prophecie againe among people, and nations and tongues, and to manie Kings. The Gospell of the kingdome (as our Sauiour saith, Matth. 24. verse 14.) shall be preached in the whole world, (which is begun to be accomplished in our dayes) and then shall the end be. In this chapter here is first set forth the effect of this prophecying againe in the latter dayes: as namely, the restoring, reforming and building vp of the Church, which was so oppressed and wasted by the great Antichrist: and then by occasion therof in the second place, here is the historie of the builders, that is, of the faithfull ministers of the Gospell, not onely of those which in these last times should take and eate vp the litle booke, and restore the Churches, but also of those which were raised vp, and withstood Antichrist all the time of his raigne, euen when his power was at the greatest, and when he did chieflie flourish. This historie containeth

diuerse

diuerse worthie things, and profitable to be knowne. The first point, that is, the restoring, the repairing, and building vp of the Church, is resembled by the measuring of the Temple of God. For he saith, there was giuen him a reed like vnto a rod, and he was willed to arise, and to measure the Temple of God, and the Altar, and them that worship therein: for ye may see in *Ezechiel*, chap. 40. that by measuring is signified the restoring of the Church. The Church of Israell was afflicted, and led into captiuitie by the King of Babell, and seemed to be ouerthrowne: but the Lord doth comfort the faithfull with the promise of restauration by Christ, & figureth out the same by measuring. For there Christ hath a reed to measure with, of sixe cubits, and measureth all parts about the Temple, and in the Temple. And from thence is this figure taken, that *Iohn* in the person of all the Ministers hath a measuring reed giuen him, and is willed to measure. We all do know that men do not measure to throw downe and to destroy anie building, but to repaire, and to build vp. Thus much touching the measuring.

Now for the things which he is commaunded to measure: that is, *the Temple, the Altar, and thē that worship therein*. This prophecie setteth forth spirituall things by the same figures vnder which they were represented in the time of the law: and therefore by the Temple and the Altar, & they that worship, are signified the pure and spirituall worship of God, and all the true worshippers. These were oppressed, troden downe and defaced by Antichrist, and now are measured to be repaired & built vp.

Then followeth another commandement giuen vnto *Iohn*, which is in these words: *But the court which is vvithout the Temple, cast out and measure it not, for it is giuen to the Gentiles: and the holy citie shall they tread vnder foot two and forty moneths*. What is the meaning of this? I will shew ye. The visible Church, & such as will beare the name of the Church hath great heapes in it of false Christians. There be sundrie sorts of heretikes, there be hypocrites, there be Idolaters, and corrupters of the true worship, as all the swarmes of Papists. These shall be all cut off from the true Temple of God, euen from the fellowship of the liuely members of Christ, being but as hangers on, resembled by the court without the Temple, and shall not be measured. The Lord God will build vp and saue his true Church, and yet cast them forth. Then let vs marke further, that the court without the temple, is not only allotted vnto those which were hangers on, & in words professe Christ, but yet for their prophanenesse are called Gentiles, but also that these same which possesse the same court are they which tread vnder foot the holy citie two and fortie moneths. The false hearted hypocrites, the wicked heretiks, & idolatrous sects of Antichrist, are they which tread downe the truth and the true seruants of God. The Church, called the holy citie, was indeed grieuously persecuted almost for the space of three hundreth yeares at times, by the heathen Emperors: they are here after a sort included, but properly and peculiarly these Gentiles that possesse the court without the Tēple, are the false Christians, the heretiks, and those which are vnder Antichrist: these do defile, lay waste, and tread vnder foot most grieuously the pure worship, and the true worshippers. The Gentiles
which

which vtterly renounced Christ, cannot in so full a maner be said to be the vtter court of the temple of God, for they be further remoued. Then note how it was in the Temple: first, there was the most holy place into which the high Priest alone entred once a yeare. Then was there the holy place, into which the Priests did enter at all times. Thirdly, there was the court, into which all the people might, and did come to worship. This last, that is, the court where all the people were, was the largest roome, and had farre the greatest multitude in it, Let vs see then how it is to be taken.

Through Iesus Christ all the elect are made holy Priests to God, & do not remaine in the vtter court of the Temple, as the figure was vnder the law, but haue an entrance into the most holy place, as we are taught, Heb. 4. ver. 16. and 10. ver. 19. 20. And then on the other side, so many as professe Christ and yet are not sanctified, they are called Gētiles, for they be still prophane: the court without is giuē to them: they worship, but haue no accesse into the most holy place, and so shall be cast forth, and shall not be measured with the true worshippers. These are they which indeed proudly chalenge the name of the Catholike Church, because they are by manie degrees the greatest multitude. These take vpon them authoritie to frame a worship of God: these do tread downe the holy word of God as much as as in them lyeth, and murther the true worshippers. Let all the heretikes and Idolatrous Papists then boast and glory of their multitudes, that they be Catholike, and despise the true worshippers, because they be so few. Let them proudly lift vp and aduaunce themselues, because they professe Christ in word, and chalenge authoritie to do eue what they list. We see the holy Scripture is plaine against thē, their multitude shall not excuse, they shall be cut off, and not measured and built vp with the true temple, which are the holy worshippers of God. Then next here is shewed how long the great Antichrist and his rout of prophane Gentiles, possessing the vtter court of the Temple, shall tread downe the holy citie. The time is set to be two and forty moneths: and that is three yeares and a halfe: for twelue moneths to a yeare, three times twelue is thirtie and sixe, and then sixe moneths for the halfe yeare, do make vp two and fortie. From this place the Papists do draw one argument, by which they would proue that the Pope is not Antichrist. After this maner they reason: The Pope hath gouerned the Church many yeares: the great Antichrist shall raigne but two and fortie moneths, which is three yeares and a halfe: (for they do rightly confesse that the Gentiles which possesse the vtter court of the temple, are the rout of Antichrist) therfore say they, it is impossible that the Pope should be Antichrist. For answer vnto this: let it first be demanded, doth not Saint *Iohn* in this prophecie speake mystically, euen as the Prophets did in old time? they cannot denie this. And then demand further, is not euery day put for a yeare in the seuenty weeks which *Daniel* the Prophet speaketh of? & so euery weeke is seuen yeares. And why may not euerie moneth here then be put for thirtie yeares? which then do amount vnto 1260 yeares. Which indeed is a long time in comparison of three yeares & an halfe: but cōpared with the eternity of Christs kingdome, it is as nothing. And that is one cause why the Lord numbreth it by

dayes

THE REVELATION.

dayes & moneths which quickly run out. But then here will arise another scruple: If the kingdome of Antichrist shall continue twelue hundreth and sixtie years, we must either say that the Bishop of Rome was Antichrist more then a thousand yeares past, yea aboue thirteene hundreth, if we take his raigne to be no longer thē vntill he was disclosed by the Gospell: or else we must say he hath yet long to continue. Let not this trouble vs, seeing it is most cleare and out of all controuersie, that in this booke, a number certaine is put for an vncertaine. As in the seuenth chapter of this booke it is said, that of euerie tribe there was sealed twelue thousand. And because twelue times twelue amount vnto one hundreth fortie & foure, it is sayd chap. 14. that so manie thousands stand with the Lambe vpon mount Sion. Is any man so vnwise, as to take it, that of euerie tribe there should be saued iust twelue thousand neither more nor lesse, and so in all of the Iewes in these latter dayes iust an hūdreth fortie & foure thousands to be saued? & not rather that the Lord by a nūber certaine doth declare that euē when his Church doth seeme vtterly to faile, he saueth a great number, of which he expresseth not the iust sum. So in this place when God will comfort his people, he sheweth that Antichrist shall tread downe the holy citie but for a short time, that is, two and fortie moneths, which is but three yeares and an halfe, he meaneth not to note the iust number of yeares that he shall continue.

Thus much for the time of Antichrists treading down the holie citie: Now we come to the builders, the true ministers of the Gospell, which should be in all the time of this treading downe. *But I will giue power to my two witnesses, and they shall prophecie a thousand two hundreth and sixtie dayes, cloathed in sackcloth.* Antichrist and his companie being those Gentiles which possesse the vtter court, do treade downe the holy citie, that is, the true Church of God, but shall they quite destroy it? or doth God in this time of Antichrists raigne forsake it? or shall there be none to resist the tyrannous proceedings of Antichrist? This might be demanded, and here is a full answer, God doth not forsake his Church, it shall not be so troden downe as to be quite destroyed he doth not leaue it without true teachers, which resist that wicked companie, by maintaining the Gospel, so that they cannot vtterlie abolish the truth. The multitude indeed to whom the court without the temple is giuen, is exceeding great, and the true worshippers are few in comparison of them: that huge multitude conspire against the pure truth of Gods word, and set vp lyes: but God will haue some witnesses at all times to witnesse his truth, and to condemne their falshood and lies. And because the law did require that to establish euerie matter two witnesses should be at the least, and his faithfull seruants in the prime of Antichrists raigne were verie few, he speaketh of the least number, which is sufficient by the law to be admitted for witnesses. These are not to be taken then for two and no more, but for all those worthie seruants of Christ, which frō time to time, both in the time of the persecuting Emperours, and also when the Poperie bare sway, were raised vp and did teach the true wholsome doctrine, and impugne the great Antichrist, and his wicked Clergie. These two witnesses of the Lord do prophecie, that is, they expound the

liuely

liuely word, and feed Gods elect with wholesome doctrine, condemning by the holy Scriptures all errors, idolatrie, and false worship. And how long shall they prophecie? euen all the time of Antichristes raigne: for that is clearely expressed. For take thirtie daies to the moneth, and the thousand two hundreth and sixtie daies, is all one with two and fortie moneths. Antichrist shall with his companie tread downe the holy citie two and fortie moneths, and the Lord will yet giue it, euen that holy citie (for so I take it rather then to say he will giue power) vnto his two witnesses, to instruct, to comfort, and to build vp in the truth 1260. dayes, that is, all that whole time of 42. monethes. If Antichrist tread downe the holy citie seuen hundreth yeares, yea if it be a thousand or more, all that same time the Lord would raise vp some or other, still to succeed in the true ministerie, to preserue the remnants of his people. There was no time then in all poperie, but some haue preached the Gospell, and shewed boldly and plainely that the popish kingdome, is that bloudy kingdome of Antichrist, and their worship, euen the worship of diuels.

It may be some will demand, how shall this appeare, that there were euer some raised vp, which preached against the Pope and his cleargy? I answer, that all things are not written which were done in all places, but yet histories of all times do testifie sufficiently of these two witnesses, that is, of a competent number of true teachers. It shall not be needfull to mention those which were in the times of the heathen Emperours, or before the kingdome of poperie was growne strong against the truth, but those onely which in the middest of the darkenesse, which (I say) in the midst of the darknesse, when the smoke of the bottomlesse pit did ouerspread all, did preach the truth, and were persecuted. In the yeare of our Lord 1158. which is now more then foure hundreth yeares past, *Gerhardus* and *Dulcinus Nauarensis*, did earnestly preach against the Church of Rome, and taught that the Pope is Antichrist: that the cleargie and prelates of Rome were reiect, & were become the very whore of Babylon, prefigured in the Reuelation. These (as histories do testifie) came into *England*, and brought certaine others with them, who were by the king and the prelates burned in the forehead, and sent out of the Realme: & after were put to death by the Pope. In the yeare 1160. *Waldus*, one of the chiefe men of the citie of *Lions* in *France*, was terrified at the sight of one that fell downe dead suddenly: he shewed great fruits of repentance, both by excercising the workes of mercie in relieuing the poore, and also by instructing himselfe and his family in the word of God, and exhorting all that resorted vnto him to the same, and by translating certaine parts of the holy Scriptures into the French tongue, which he deliuered vnto many. He and a great number that receiued instruction by him, maintained the same doctrine drawne out of the holy Scriptures which we do now, condemning the Masse to be wicked, the Pope Antichrist, and Rome Babylon, &c. They were threatned, and by violence of persecution scattered into many places, and some of them remained long in *Bohemia*. In the yeare 1212. the Pope caused an hundred persons in the countery of *Alsatia*, whereof diuerse were noble men, to be burned in one day, for maintaining doctrine against the doctrine of the Romish Church. About the yeare 1230 almost all the Churches of the Grecians renounced the Church of Rome, becauſe of their execrable ſimonie, and ſuch abominable wickednesse. In the time of the Emperour *Fredericke* the ſecond, about the yeare 1240 there were in the countrey of Sueuia many preachers, which preached freely againſt the Pope and his prelates, affirming boldly that the Pope and his ſayd prelates were heretickes, & ſimoniakes, and ſuch like. In the yeare 1250 or thereabout, roſe vp *Arnoldus de noua villa*, a Spaniard, a man famously learned and a great writer: he impugned the errours of the Popiſh Church, and taught that the Pope led the people to hell. This *Arnoldus* was condemned as an heretike. About the ſame time *Guilielmus de ſanƈto Amore*, a maiſter of Paris, and a chiefe ruler of that Vniuerſitie, applied all the teſtimonies of Scripture which are touching Antichriſt, againſt the Popiſh Cleargy. The Pope & his prelates condemned him for an heretike, he was baniſhed, and his bookes burned. About the yeare 1290 *Laurence* an Engliſhman, a maiſter of Paris, mightily proued the Pope to be Antichriſt, and the Synagoue of Rome to be Babylon: the Pope after his death cauſed his bones to be taken vp and burned. At the ſame time *Robertus Gallus*, a man of noble parentage, impugned the Pope and his cleargy, calling the Pope an Idoll, and threatning the iudgements of God againſt their abominable ſinnes. Alſo about the ſame time *Robert Greſted* Biſhop of Lincolne, a man famouſly learned in three tongues, wrote diuerſe inuectiues againſt the Pope. And when he was ſicke, and lay vpon his death-bed, which was at Bugden, he called one *Iohn Giles* a preaching Frier, complaining of the diſorders of the Friers and Romane cleargy, prouing the Pope to be an hereticke. And ſpeaking of the manifold abuſes of the Church of Rome, and particularly about their couetouſneſſe and lechery, he ſayd they ſhould not be deliuered from the ſeruitude of Egypt but by force. And being ſcarſe able to vtter his words, with ſobbing and weeping his breath went away, and ſo he departed in the yeare 1253. which is now more then three hundreth yeares paſt. After his death the Pope would haue had his bones digged vp, but was terrified by a viſion. About the yeare 1350 the Lord raiſed vp diuerſe learned men, which openly and boldly impugned the Church of Rome: as *Gregory Arminenſis*, who layd open the abuſes of the Romiſh Synagogue, and confuted the popiſh doctrine of free will. *Taulerus* in Germany a preacher taught likewiſe. *Franciſcus Petrarcha* at the ſame time, who calleth Rome the whore of Babylon, the mother of error, the temple of hereſie. And a little before that, *Iohannes de rupe Sciſſa*, was caſt into priſon for rebuking the popiſh prelates for their great enormities, and for that he calleth the Church of Rome, the whore of Babylon, the Pope the miniſter of Antichriſt, and the Cardinals falſe Prophets. And being in priſon he wrote a booke, prophecying of the affliction which hung ouer the heads of the Spirituality for their vngodly life: he called his booke, *Vade mecum in tribulatione*. Then was there Maiſter *Conradus Hager*, who taught more then twenty yeares againſt the Maſſe: he was afterward ſhut vp in priſon. *Gerhardus Rhidor* wrote a booke againſt the Monkes and Friers, which hee intituled *Lachrima eccleſiæ*. About the ſame time were

were *Michaell Cesenas*, and *Petrus de Corbona*, and *Iohannes de Poliaco*: these were condemned by the Pope and his adherents. The sayd *Michael* wrote a booke against the pride, the tyrannie, and primacy of the Pope, accusing him to be Antichrist, and the Church of Rome the whore of Babylon, drunke with the bloud of the Saints, &c. he left behind him many followers, of whom a great part were slaine by the Pope, some of them were burned. About the same time two Friers were put to death at Auinion for matters which they held against the Pope: one of them was called *Iohannes Rochetaillada*, who did preach that the Church of Rome was Babylon, and the Pope and his Cardinals Antichrist. About the yeare 1360. was set forth a writing against the Pope and the popish Cleargy, called a complaint of the plowman. About the same time, *Armachanus* an Archbishop in Ireland, was raised vp against Antichrist, he was a man of great learning and godlinesse, his troubles were many, and the deliuerances great which God gaue him. In the yeare 1364 one *Nicholas Orem* preached a sermon before the Pope and his Cardinals, in which he rebuked the popish prelates, and denounced their destruction not to be farre off for their most wicked abhominations. About the yeare 1370 liued *Mathias Parisiensis*, a Bohemian, who wrote a large booke of Antichrist, and noteth the Pope to be the same. About the yeare 1384 *Nilus* Archbishop of Thessalonica, wrote a large booke against the Romane Church. About the yeare 1390 many were put to death for the Gospell, refusing the doctrine and worship of the Romish Church. As at Bringa there were burned 36 Citizens of Maguntia. In the prouince of Narbone there were to the number of one hundreth and fortie which chose rather to suffer all torments then to receiue the Romish religion, and to deny the truth of the most glorious Gospell. A good while before this time, there were 24 put to death at Paris. There were foure hundreth noted to be heretikes, foure score beheaded, Prince *Armericus* was hanged, & the Laſie of the Castle was stoned to death. In the dayes of king *Edward* the third, about the yeare 1371 began *Iohn Wickliffe* of Oxenford openly to deale against the Pope and popish doctrine. The times were then very grieuous, the popish kingdome of Antichrist being risen vp vnto very great strength and cruelty. King *Edward* the third himselfe being well learned and a valiant Prince greatly withstood popery: he much fauoured and defended *Wickliffe*, so did diuerse Noble men, in so much that Maister *Wickliffe* and others openly preaching against the Church of Rome, the Pope & his prelates doing what they could, were not able to hurt him. After the death of King *Edward*, he was greatly supported by the Londoners: and so escaped the hands of his aduersaries, still proclaiming the holy and heauenly doctrine of the Gospell against the Romish Antichrist. It pleased God by his preaching, and by his bookes to giue light vnto many in the land. Sundrie were put to death, of whom the Lord *Cobham* was one, and diuerse fled out of the land, because they would not deny the truth which they had learned from him. That popish Councell of Constance 41 yeares after his death, condemning his doctrine, caused his bones to be digged vp and burned. And as *Wickliffes* doctrine tooke place here in England and spread farre, so were some of his

workes

THE REVELATION.   195

works caried into Bohemia, where they did more preuaile, for about the yere 1410 *Iohn Huffe*, who taught in Buhemia, with diuerfe others the holy Gofpell of Ielus Chrift, which a multitude zealoufly imbraced, & thereupon renounced the Church of Rome, was cited to appeare before the Pope, which he auoided. And about the yeare 1414 he was charged againe to appeare at Rome, then was he excommunicated, and much moleftation followed, but he continued a conftant witneffe of Chrift, and openly impugned the Romifh Synagogue, vntill the Councell of Cóftance, where he was condemned as an heretike and burned.

In the fame Councell alfo *Ierome* of Prage, a worthy feruāt of Chrift in refifting the Romifh harlot, was condēned and then burned. Thefe men were put to death, but Antichrift and all his power could not roote out the Gofpell in Bohemia. God raifed them vp a valiant Captaine *Iohn Zifca*, and they put to flight great armies of the Papifts that came againft them . I will not ftand to fhew what perfecutions followed about this time in England, and what a number were vexed, and many put to death: they called them at that time Lollards. Come downe lower: Whē the Romifh prelates had now long perfecuted, and feemed to haue rooted out with fire and fword almoft all the profeffors and preachers of the Gofpell, the Lord raifed vp new witneffes, men famoufly learned and godly. Among thefe *Vifelus Groningenfis*, who died in the yeare 1490 which is now an hundreth and three yeares paft : he was fo worthy a man, that he was called *Lux mundi*, that is, the light of the world . He difputed mightily and boldly againft Poperie, and proued their doctrine falfe and wicked, and that the Popes keyes do not open but fhut heauen gates.

In the yeare 1500 *Hieronimus Sauonarola* a Monke in Italy, with two other Friers named *Dominike*, and *Siluefter*, were condemned to death at Florence. They taught and maintained againft the Pope and the popifh doctrine, the things which we do now. Thefe faithfull witneffes were not fruitleffe, as may appeare by the perfecutions and murtherings which followed after them in diuerfe places. In the raigne of King *Henry* the feuenth, liued *Iohannes Picus* the Earle of Mirandula: he was but 32 yeares old when he dyed, and yet of great learning. He made open chalenge at Rome to difpute with any , againft fundry points of popery : The popifh prelates wold not difpute, but did article againft him touching fufpition of herefie. We are now come downe euē within a very few yeres of the time that God raifed vp his worthy feruant *Martin Luther*, and then together with him fundry others to pull downe Antichrift, and to deliuer his poore Church from grieuous thraldome and miferable bondage, fo that I need not to proceed any further. We may fee by this that I haue noted, that the Lord euer had fome faithfull witneffes which withftood the Romifh Antichrift, and taught the truth to his people. Thus much then touching that one thing that the Lord had alwayes fome faithfull minifters of his Gofpell , euen in the depth of popery.

That he fpeaketh of fo fmall a number of witneffes : we are taught thereby not to depend vpon the greater multitude in the miniferie , but vpon thofe which purely teach the trueth, and leade a godly life agreeable to the fame, following the

O 2   fteppes

steppes of Chrift and his Apoftles. The Papifts brag much of their multitudes, and would thereby oppreffe the faithfull minifters of Chrift as being few in number. Some are much troubled at the fame: but what if the diuell and Antichrift haue two thoufand feruants, for euery two true feruants of the Lord? are they the leffe to be regarded? was not one *Elias*, being one true Prophet of God, better then foure hundreth falfe Prophets of *Baal*? Be not troubled, be not difmayed whē it fhall be obiected, thefe be but few againft many, but looke to the way of truth and found godlineffe, looke which haue the right on their fide. The malignant Church oftentimes haue exceeding many goodly prelates, when the true Church feemeth to be almoft vtterly banifhed out of the earth. The truth of God dependeth not vpon the multitude of the voyces of men which confpire together. It is fayd further that thefe two witneffes fhall prochecy a thoufand two hundreth and fixtie dayes clothed in fackcloth. This fetteth forth the apparell of Chrifts minifters. In olde time when men did faft and mourne dolefully, they did vfe to put on fackcloth.

This prophecy fpeaking myftically, and vnder figures is not to be taken here according to the letter, that the true witneffes of Chrift, euen his faithfull preachers fhall all the time of Antichrift be clothed in facke: but that indeed they fhall haue a forrowfull life here vpon the earth, yea fo full of griefe and lamentation, as if they did alwayes faft and mourne. A very good place to ftand a little vpon, to note the difference betweene the true minifters of Chrift, and the wicked pompous Antichriftian prelates. Begin with the Prophets in the time of the law. They were fent of the Lord to rebuke al eftates, & to reclaime thē from their wicked waies. Whē they faw how ftifnecked the people were, and how rebellioufly they defpifed the counfels of the Lord: When they were hated and perfecuted, what was their life but a continuall forrow ? what could they do but mourne from day to day ? And how meane were they then in the eyes of the world ? were they in pompe and iolity? No verily, for with them it was as if they had alwayes bene clothed in facke. When other men did folace and fport themfelues, they did lament and forrow. What fhould I fpeake of the glorious Apoftles of our Sauiour Iefus Chrift ? what was the whole life of that chofen veffell *Paul*, after he was called to preach the Gofpell? The hiftory of the Acts of the Apoftles fheweth his life. Shall we thinke that *Peter* found any better entertainment then he did? Was *Iames*, or *Iohn*, or any of the reft in outward iolity? we are fure they were not. Then leaue them, and come downe to thofe that fucceeded, and efpecially in the time of Antichrift, and what fhall we find but men clothed in facke ? God did manifeft his trueth vnto them, and raifed them vp, and appointed them to be his witneffes. They did lay open the way of life, and reproue the whorifh Babylon, and all abominable vices. Their word, & their teftimony which they bare was defpifed, & condemned almoft of all men, euen as herefie. All that gaue credit to the fame, were deemed ranke heretikes. They were cruelly perfecuted, accurfed, and murthered. They faw the wicked florifh. They faw idolatry, fuperftition, and errours moft abominable, fet vp and maintained, and the worfhip and glory of God troden downe. They faw the people feduced by the great Antichrift, fitting in the temple of God, & led by lea-

pers

pers into hell. Alas what could they find but sorrow & griefe of hart? how could they now but be clothed in sacke? how could they but mourne and lament ? Then looke vpon the contrary side, the Pope & his Cardinals, his great prelates & Cleargy maisters, were they clothed in sacke, were they in bitter griefe and sorrow? Nay they haue bene with pompe, and pride, and outward glory arrayed in all precious costly things, like to the Princes of the earth : as with gold, siluer, pearles, precious stones, silkes, scarlet, purple, and with all fine clothing. They liued in all pleasures & delicacie, feeding vpon all the fattest things, and sweetest that might be gotten for mony. Here we see then a very great difference betweene these, and the true and faithfull witnesses of Christ clothed in sacke. The histories of those times do shew, what great complaints there were of the pride and excesse of the Popish Cleargy.

And now what shall we say for our time ? Doubtlesse the true ministers of the Lord haue no cause to giue themselues to the mirth, the iolity, and brauery of the world. But there is cause still, yea euen in these daies to be clothed in sacke: that is, to lament and mourne. For how do we see the voice of God despised ? how is his glory defaced, the proud magnified, & vanity extolled? Alas there is cause of great mourning to all that loue the Lord, & we are not to thinke that it will be better.

If we therefore will approue our selues to be the Lords faithfull witnesses, we must not seeke the pompe, the riches, the pleasures, the ease, and the delicacie of this world : let those things alone for the ministers of Antichrist, whose bellie is their God, which mind earthly things : but we must painefully labour to aduance the truth, to pull downe errours and wicked vices : we must lament and mourne to see the truth so much despised, the Lord our God so highly dishonored, and men running headlong to destruction. Then shall we please God, and our ministery shall be blessed. Thus much for this time.

THE XXII. SERMON.
CHAP. 11.

4. *These are two Oliue trees, and two candlestickes, standing before the God of the earth.*

5. *And if any will hurt them, fire proceedeth out of their mouth, and shal deuour their enemies: for if any will hurt them, so must he be killed.*

6. *These haue power to shut heauen, that it raine not in the dayes of their prophecying, and haue power ouer waters to turne them into bloud, and to smite the earth with all manner of plagues, as oft as they will.*

7. *And when they haue finished their testimony, the beast that commeth out of the bottomlesse pit shall make war against them, and shall ouercome them, and shall kill them.*

8. *And their corpses shal lie in the streetes of the great city, which is called spiritually Sodome and Egypt, where our Lord also was crucified.*

9. *And they of the people, and kindreds, and tongues, and Gentiles, shall see their corpses three dayes and an halfe, and shall not suffer their corpses to be put in graues.*

10. *And they that dwell vpon the earth shall reioyce ouer them, and they shall be glad, and they shall send gifts one to another, for these two Prophets tormented the inhabitants of the earth.*

11. *But after three dayes and an halfe, the spirit of life which came from God, shall enter into them, and they shall stand vpon their feet, and great feare shall fall vpon them which see them.*

12. *And they heard a great voyce from heauen, saying vnto them, come vp hither. And they went vp into heauen in a cloude: and their enemies saw them.*

13. *And in that houre there was a great earthquake, and the tenth part of the city fell, and in the earthquake were slaine names of men, seuen thousand, and the rest were terrified and gaue glory to the God of heauen.*

Aint *Iohn* proceedeth forward in the description of these two witnesses, of whom we spake the last time in the former verses. And because to the eye of the world, or in externall shew, the true ministers of the Gospell seeme very base, very weake, and contemptible, and to haue nothing excellent or precious in them: and moreouer it seemeth that they be ouercome, troden downe, and vtterly vanquished by their enemies:

least

THE REVELATION.

least we should be caried awry with that opinion, they are here set forth to be honourable in the sight of God, and full of spirituall treasures wherewith they enrich the Church; and heauenly power also is in them, wherewith they be armed, euen vnto a maruellous victory and triumph ouer those which seeme to ouercome thē. This place is then, as we shall see, for to teach vs, that we must not esteeme of Christs ministers according to outward appearance in externall glory and worldly pompe, which indeed they haue not: but according to the heauenly and spirituall graces and power with which they are furnished, for the weapons of their warfarre are spirituall.

Let vs looke vpon the words as they lie. He sayth they be two oliue trees, and two candlestickes, &c. We reade in *Moses*, that the oyle of oliues is very sweete and precious. And it is vsuall in the holy Scriptures (as all do know) by sweete precious oyles wherewith they did vse to annoynt them, to represent the graces of the holy Ghost. This heauenly precious oyle, euen these sweete graces of the holy Ghost, the Lord powreth vpon his Church by his faithfull ministers: and therefore they are sayd to be two oliue trees, they haue the sweete oyle of the spirit, not to themselues alone, but for others. They be also two Candlestickes: ye know what the vse of candlestickes is. They beare vp the pure light of Gods word, which from them shineth vpon men, as the candlestickes do beare the candles set vpon them. Then that they are sayd to stand before the God of the earth, it is to shew, that they be his instruments which ruleth not only in the heauens, but also in the earth, yea euen then when all things seeme to be ordered at the will of Sathan & wicked men: for we will acknowledge that God ruleth in the heauens, but in such times we can hardly beleeue that he ruleth in the earth. We may note from hence what a precious vse there is of the ministerie of the Gospell: and what blessings God doth giue by it. For what can be more necessary? what can be more for our spirituall comfort and eternall blessednesse, then to haue the Lord powre into our hearts the heauenly and spirituall graces of the holy Ghost, which is figured by the oliue trees, and to shine vnto vs with the true light, which he doth by his ministers, as they are sayd to be candlestickes? Here also the ministers of the Gospell may learne, if they will be true ministers of Christ, what manner of persons they ought to be, euen fresh oliue trees, and candlestickes, that is, full of heauenly graces dropping from them, and full of cleere light, both in pure doctrine, and godly conuersation. Blessed be such instruments, that stand before the God of the earth, yea a thousand times blessed of God, their worke is so precious. And wo be to them which hold the place, & through their darknesse and fleshly mind, are nothing lesse, then oliue trees and candlestickes. Thus we see what precious instruments they are vnto the children of God: now let vs see with what might and power they be armed against the wicked enemies and prophane worldlings. *And if* (sayth he) *any will hurt them, fire proceedeth out of their mouth, and deuoureth their enemies: for if any will hurt them so must he be killed. These haue power to shut heauen that it raine not in the dayes of their prophecying, &c.* It may seeme strange, that we ascribe this which is here written vnto the ordinary ministers and preachers

G 4

preachers of the Gospell: for where haue those preachers bene seene or heard of, that haue had fire proceeding out of their mouthes to deuoure their enemies? Where haue we known of such as could shut the heauens that it should not raine? or that haue turned waters into bloud, and stroke the earth with all maner of plagues when they would? are there any such ministers now? or haue we read of such in time of poperie? For answer vnto this, ye must know that this booke vttereth almost all things mystically. For indeed the doctrine of Gods word, which proceedeth out of the mouth of his faithfull witnesses, is a fire that shall deuoure and slay all the wicked enemies. It shall not slay them with bodily death, for that way the beast preuaileth against the seruants of Christ, but as a fire it shall deuoure them for euer with a spirituall death. O mightie is the glorious word of the Lord, and it triumpheth ouer all: for those whom it doth not purge as pure gold, it burneth them vp like drosse. Let vs take heed how we despise and resist it, and let vs beware how we become enemies vnto the true ministers of it. For they be starke mad, and know not what they do, which oppose themselues against the ministers of Christ. They must be killed and deuoured with this terrible fire, and yet they know it not. This is plaine enough touching the fire which proceedeth out of their mouth: but how shall we vnderstand that which followeth, that they haue power to shut heauen that it raine not, that also they can turne waters into bloud, and strike the earth with all maner of plagues, which of all the preachers hath done these things? Thus it is, *Elias* did shut the heauens, that it rained not in three yeares and sixe moneths. *Moses* turned the waters into bloud, and stroke the land of Egypt with sundrie plagues. And now the faithfull witnesses of Christ, the true ministers of his Gospell are compared to these two great Prophets *Moses* and *Elias*, not that they shall worke those myracles which they did in such outward things, but that they shall be furnished with a power in spirituall things, which is no lesse. The great power of God is in the ministery of the Gospel, as ye may reade 2. Corinth.10. euen to cast downe euery thing which exaulteth it selfe against God, &c. This power is not visible, and therefore it pleased God to furnish his prophets and his Apostles with the power to worke wonders vnto the bodily sight of men, that thereby they might be led to consider of that inuisible power of God with which they were armed. Now although the faithfull ministers haue not the power to worke these externall signes and wonders: yet because they haue that glorious inuisible power which is the greater, they are sayd to haue also that power to do outward signes & wonders, which was but as a witnesse of that other. I know that this is farre from the common opinion of men, because they can see if a wonder be wrought before their bodily eyes, but they haue no eyes of the soule to behold the most wonderfull and glorious power of the Gospell, in throwing downe the power of darknesse, euen the kingdome and power of the diuell, in sauing the faithfull, and destroying the rebellious. The Lord our God by these speeches of shutting of heauen, that it raine not in the dayes of their prophecying, of turning waters into bloud, and striking the earth with all maner of plagues, doth lead vs to the consideration of that inuisible power which is in the true ministerie

of

of his word. Saint *Paul* faith, the Gofpell is the power of God vnto faluation, to euery one that beleeueth, Rom. 1. It is the arme of the Lord, Efay. 53. Therefore let not vs be blinded to thinke meanly of it according to the outward fhew of the minifters. I would ftand no longer vpon thefe words, but it is needfull here a litle to anfwer the papifts. For from hence they draw one of their chiefe arguments, by which they would proue that the Pope is not Antichrift. Thus they reafon (if I may call it reafoning, which yet indeed is plaine doting.) If *Enoch* and *Elias* haue not yet come and refifted the Bifhop of Rome, then is not (fay they) the Bifhop of Rome Antichrift. But thefe two men *Enoch* and *Elias*, haue not come and refifted the Pope, therefore he cannot be Antichrift. For they take it that the two witneffes here fpoken of are indeed *Enoch* and *Elias*, and that they fhall come downe from heauen in perfon, and preach againft Antichrift three yeares and an halfe, & then be killed by him. They haue for this, the opinion of fome ancient writers, but in deed with varietie, & nothing as they vaunt and would make fhew of. They ftand alfo to proue the fame by the holy Scriptures, but faile vtterly therein. For although the holy Scriptures do teftifie, that *Enoch* was tranflated and faw not death, and that *Elias* was taken vp in a fierie chariot: yet to fay that their bodies were receiued into heauen we cannot: much leffe can it be proued that they fhall come downe from heauen, and liue among men, and preach againft Antichrift, and then be killed. Yes (fay the papifts) touching *Elias* it is cleare, that he fhall come againe in perfon, euen by the words of the Prophet *Malachy*: Behold I fend you *Elias* the Prophet, &c. How importunate would thefe papifts be, if our Sauiour himfelfe had not expounded that faying of the Prophet touching the comming of *Elias*? So they might haue fome colour of matter to proue that Antichrift. is not yet come, they will ftrengthen the Iewes in their opinion, that the Meffias is not yet come. For when the Lord Iefus Chrift the redeemer was come, the Scribes faid he was not the Chrift, and why ? becaufe (faid they) *Elias* muft firft come and reftore all things, as the Lord promifed by the Prophet *Malachy*. This you may fee in Matth. 17. verf. 10. They erred becaufe they looked that *Elias* fhould come in perfon: whereas the meaning of the Lord by the Prophet was, that he would fend one to prepare the way before the face of his Sonne, which fhould come with the fpirit and power of *Elias*, as the Angell doth expound it vnto *Zacharias* the father of *Iohn* Baptift, Luk. 1. verf. 17. Our Sauiour made anfwer vnto his Difciples, that indeed *Elias* muft come, and then addeth further that he was alreadie come, and they did not know him, Matth. 17. And when he had fpoken much in the commendation of the greatneffe of *Iohn* the Baptift, in the end he addeth, and if ye will receiue it, this is that *Elias* which was for to come, Matth. 11. verf. 14. Can the papifts with any face ftand now to maintaine that this place of *Malachy* was and is to be taken, that *Elias* fhould come in fpirit firft before Chrift to prepare his way, and then in perfon to refift Antichrift: If *Iohn* Baptift be that *Elias* which fhould by promife come, what can moue vs to looke for another *Elias*? What, fhall we with the Iewes looke for *Elias* to come in perfon, and fo call into queftion whether the true Meffias be yet come? The prophet *Malachy* fpeaketh from the Lord vnto his owne nation, saying, Behold I will send vnto ye *Elias* the prophet, he shall turne the harts of the fathers to the children, and the harts of the children to the fathers, &c. Whereby it is euident, that if *Elias* must come in person, it must be vnto them, that is I say, to the Iewes, and to restore all things among them. But the Angell, and our Sauiour himselfe haue shewed that this prophecie is alreadie fulfilled, and all things therein haue bene performed by *Iohn* the Baptist. And so for ought that the Iesuites can cauill vpon this place touching the two witnesses, it remaineth still as cleare as the Sunne, for ought that is here against it, that the Pope is the great Antichrist.

Thus much touching the spirituall and heauenly power wherewith the true ministers of the Gospell are armed, and for which they be likened and compared to the two great prophets *Elias* and *Moses*. Let vs now proceed to the rest. Here is set foorth in the next place the sauage crueltie that Antichrist, and his seduced multitude of idolatrous subiects, should exercise vpon these true and faithfull witnesses of our Lord Iesus Christ. One way, that is touching the bodily death, they preuaile against them, and ouercome them: but another way (as we shall see) these worthie seruants of the Lord do triumph in victorie ouer them most gloriously. These are the words: *And when they haue finished their testimonie, the beast which commeth out of the bottomlesse pit shall make warre against them, and shall kill them.* As the fire which commeth out of their mouthes deuoureth their enemies, and slayeth them with a spirituall death: so the power of the Antichristian kingdome shall be bent against them, ouermatch them, and slay them with the corporall death: so farre shall the Romish tyrannie preuaile ouer them. The beast is sayd here to come out of the bottomlesse pit, that is, out of hell. And some do hold that the great Antichrist shall be a very diuell indeed, and it may be that they which thinke so, are moued by this place so to thinke: for no men, but diuels do come from hell. But indeed their opinion is vaine, and this speech maketh nothing at all for it. Seeing (as we shall obserue when we come to the 13. chapter) the beast is not put so much for the men, as for the sauage and beastly power which those men doe exercise. And also the power is of the diuell, which the beast should exercise: for the Dragon giueth to this beast his power, his throne, and great authoritie, as we reade chap. 13. vers. 2. Then it commeth out of the bottomlesse pit of hell. This cruell power which the diuell giueth to Antichrist and his ministers, is wholly bent against the faithfull preachers & ministers of the Gospell: for it is sayd, that he shall make warre against them. As indeed there is great cause: for their doctrine, euen the pure and most wholesome doctrine of God, doth discouer their blasphemous filthie abhominations. And so if that take place, downe goeth their credit and estimation, which in no wise they can abide, and therefore make warre. Then further, we see it is the holy will of the Lord, that the beast in warring against the Prophets, shall preuaile against them, ouercome them, and kill them.

This must not seeme strange, seeing all sorts of enemies haue bene permitted so farre at one time or other; when the Lord would giue this high honour vnto

his

his seruants, that they shold be his witnesses, euē with the shedding of their bloud. Then let all men take heed, when they see or heare of the cruell murthering of the Preachers & professors of the Gospell, that these thoughts, or this maner of reasoning enter not into their mind, as to thinke or say thus: The Pope and his do preuaile againſt the Preachers and professors, & cut them downe, therfore God doth blesse and fauour the Church of Rome: he alloweth their worship and religion. Or thus: the Preachers and professors are with all dishonour, contempt, and reproch cut off and trode downe euen as the mire in the streets, therefore God careth not for them: for if they were deare and precious vnto him, he would not suffer them to be so vsed. This reasoning is farre awrie, for ye see it here plainly expressed, that God giueth power to the beast, cruelly to murther his faithfull witnesses, which yet notwithſtanding are verie deare and precious in his sight. Nothing is or can be more euident then this: and yet many are aſtoniſhed, and many are seduced at the beholding of the same. Their sight can pierce no deeper then to the externall apparance and view of matters, & according to that they do iudge. Here is yet one thing worthie speciall obseruation, and that is, that the beaſt shall not preuaile againſt them to kill them, vntill such time as they haue finished their teſtimonie. They muſt firſt performe their seruice to the Church, for which they are appointed. The Lord doth protect them from the power & rage of Antichriſt, vntill such time as they haue done their whole message. The moſt high gouernour ouer all will haue his truth vttered, & his worke finished: he will haue his seruants accompliſh (as I said) their whole seruice, before they be cut off. We reade in the Gospell, that the enemies would haue laid hold of Chriſt, but his houre was not yet come: euen so vntill their houre be come they cannot touch these. It is added, that *their corpses ſhall lie in the ſtreets of the great citie, which ſpiritually is called Sodom and Egypt, where our Lord was crucified.* These words do declare a moſt bitter hatred, and a moſt sauage crultie in the men of Antichriſts Synagogue, againſt the Saints of God. For they are not satisfied nor contented with the killing of thē, no not with all the torments, tortures and reproches, which they cause them to endure while they be aliue: but after they be dead, they do them all the dishonor which they can, by caſting forth their dead bodies into the open places, denying them the honor of buriall.

Their whole drift and purpose in this, is to haue those precious bodies of the holy Martyrs, eſteemed to be no better then dead carrion, euen the dead bodies of dogges or swine: and so they would terrifie others. Whereby we may see how low here in the world, the Lord doth suffer his glorious witnesses to be caſt into al outward ignominie. If they could put them vnto a thousand deaths, this place sheweth that they ſhould be sure of it. And because they wold make it (as I said) a ſpectacle and a terrour vnto others to driue them from their doctrine, they caſt their slaine bodies into the open ſtreetes of their bloudy citie. Why, will some say, will they suffer the dead carcaſſes of men to lie in the ſtreetes? will it not annoy thē, & be so vnwholsome that they ſhal not be able to abide it? And if it be cleere that Rome is this great citie, the seat of Antichriſt, what Preachers of the Gospell haue

haue bene slaine there, and cast forth into the streets thereto lie? I answer, that we may not take this to be spoken of the streetes within the walles of the citie of Rome, but looke how farre the power and dominion of Rome hath spread it self, looke how farre Antichrist the Pope hath exercised tyrannie ouer the Churches in manie great and large kingdomes, so farre go the streets of the great citie. Those which haue bene cruelly murthered in Fraunce, and cast forth into open place in the fields, haue lyen in the streets of the great citie. Likewise in England, in Scotland, in Spaine, in Germanie, and in all the rest: for hitherto reached the streetes of the great citie. In those countries there haue bene many faithfull Ministers of Christ cruelly put to death, and all the dishonour that might be was then shewed to their dead bodies. This same great citie, this Church or Synagogue of Antichrist, boasteth her selfe to be the holy, the pure, and the chast Spouse of Christ, euen the mother of all the faithfull children of God: when as indeed for her vncleannesse and filthinesse of life most detestable, the Lord calleth her Sodome: and for her idolatrie, and sore bondage in which she hath held and oppressed Gods people, he calleth her Egypt. Sodome was filthie in her wickednes not to be spoken, but not more filthy then Rome, & the Romish Synagogue, and rabblement of Popes, Cardinals, Monkes, Friers and Nunnes. Egypt was full of superstition, and of most foule and grosse idolatrie, when she held the children of Israel in cruell bondage, but Rome hath exceeded her in both. And marke how the Lord saith that this great citie is spiritually called Sodom & Egypt: for this teacheth vs that the literall name is another: as we shall see it plaine in the 17. chapter, that the seat of the beast is literally to be called Rome. Then Rome in letter, but spiritually Sodom and Egypt. Then he addeth, *Where our Lord was crucified.* Full glad are the Papists of this clause, for hereby they say it is euident, that Rome is not the great citie which spiritually is called Sodom and Egypt; seeing all do know that Christ was not crucified at Rome, but at Ierusalem. Ierusalem, Ierusalem, say they is the great citie where Antichrist shall raigne, and therefore the Pope cannot be Antichrist, because he hath his seate at Rome, and not in the Temple at Ierusalem where Christ was crucified. Let this trouble no man, for doubtlesse Christ was crucified at Rome. If any shall replie, that the foure Euangelists do testifie that he was crucified at Ierusalem: I answer, that is most true: but yet he was also crucified at Rome. Was he then twise crucified? No, but thus: if we respect the place, he was crucified at Ierusalem: if we respect the power and authoritie that put him to death, he was crucified at Rome: Rome ruled at that time in Ierusalem. Reade the Euangelists, and ye shall find that Ierusalem at that time was in subiection vnto the Empire and dominion of Rome. *Pontius Pilate* was Deputy for the Emperor of Rome in Ierusalem. The Iewes (as they confesse) had no authoritie to put any man to death, Iohn 18. vers. 31. & therfore they accuse him before *Pilate. Pilate* saw that they did it of enuie, and would haue deliuered him. Then they cried out, that if he did deliuer him, he was not *Cesars* friend, because he maketh himselfe a King. In which words they did accuse our Sauiour of treason against the Emperour, because he made himselfe a King. Hereupon *Pilate* did condemne him to

death,

death, and set this title vpon his crosse, as the cause of his death: *Iesus of Nazareth, king of the Iewes.* Then lay all these things together, Christ is crucified by the power of the Emperour of Rome in his deputie *Pilate*: he was accused and put to death for treason against the Emperour, which they wickedly laid to his charge. And therefore the holie Ghost saith plainly he was crucified at Rome. Rome then crucified the head: Rome hath since cruelly murthered the members. Rome is that purple whore, which is drunken with the bloud of the Saints.

Hitherto the crueltie of the beast against the Lords witnesses, and now followeth the rage of the blind multitude which are seduced by the beast. He saith, that *they of the people, and kindreds, and tongues, and Gentiles shall see their corpses three dayes and a halfe, and shall not suffer their corpses to be put in graues.* O sauage crueltie! they dishonour them all that they can, allowing the crueltie of Antichrist in shedding their bloud: what beastly crueltie is this? The time is also noted in which they shall see their corpses lie vnburied to be three dayes and an half. Before he spake of 42 moneths, which is three yeares and an halfe, and of a thousand, two hundreth and three score dayes, which is the same: but here because he speaketh of the lying of dead bodies vnburied, he mystically calleth it three dayes and a halfe, which is the same time with the former. Then next is noted the ioy, the gladnesse & mirth which the inhabitants of the earth shall make that these Prophets are ouercome by the beast & so cruelly slaine. For he saith, that *the inhabitants of the earth shall reioyce ouer them, and be glad, & shall send gifts one to another.* This doth shew what an extreme hatred the blind world doth beare against the true Preachers of the Gospell. We may learne by it, how farre they be from all excuse, which in the darkest times of Poperie were led awrie into idolatrie & false religion, that they loued and liked so well of the proceedings of the beast, and hated so bitterly the pure heauenly doctrine of the Gospel. It is euen the same which S. *Paule* speaketh, 2 Thes. 2. that because they receiued not the loue of the truth, that they might be saued, God shall send them strong delusion to beleeue lyes: that all they might be damned, which beleeued not the truth, but had pleasure in vnrighteousnesse. For in the raigne of Antichrist, such as gaue eare to the Lords witnesses, and imbraced their holy doctrine were saued, but the other had pleasure in vnrighteousnesse, & were so exceeding glad at the murthering of the Prophets, that they send gifts one to another, as the maner is at ioyfull times when mens hearts are merrie. But this is more euident by the clause that followeth, whē he saith, *these two Prophets tormented the inhabitants of the earth.* Men are glad and reioyce exceedingly when such are destroyed and taken away as did torment them, and these prophets did torment them. If the preachers of the Gospell be the tormenters of the world, why should the world be blamed for hating of them? Yes, for that they torment, it ariseth from the fault of the inhabitants of the earth, and not from the fault of the preachers. For what is it which doth torment, but the fire which commeth out of their mouth? and that is the pure doctrine of God. Now this doctrine to such as loue God, is most sweete & wholesome, as the Prophet *Dauid* wittnesseth, Psalm. 19. but to those which loue darknesse, and that take

pleasure

pleasure in vnrighteousnesse, it is a tormenting fire, yea euen a flame that shall burne them vp, and deuoure them for euer. Marke the contrarie effect in the ministrie of the true Prophets of the Lord, or the diuerse working. To the faithfull that loue the Lord, there is nothing more sweet and comfortable, then the heauenly doctrine of Christ vttered by his faithfull seruants, it doth euen feed their soules, and fill them with ioy and gladnesse, so that they tenderly loue the messengers which bring it, euen as the instruments of their eternall blessednesse. But on the contrary part, to the inhabitants of the earth, euen to the men which haue their portion in this life, which delight in the wayes of their flesh, and follow such a religion as agreeth to their owne wisedome, this pure doctrine of God bringeth grieuous torment, and therefore they hate most deadly the men which do vtter it. This place doth teach vs what a tormēt it is to the reprobate, whē they heare they holy word of God nakedly and purely preached. This place doth open vnto vs what is the cause that the holy Prophets in old time, and the Apostles and faithful ministers of the word since Christ, haue bene hated persecuted, & cruelly murthered: euen this, that their doctrine did torment the wicked world so sore, that they could not abide it. Maruell not (brethren) that the godly Preachers at this day haue manie bitter enemies, for there be innumerable whose consciences are so euill, and that take such delight and pleasure in their owne sinfull lusts, that the holy word of God, when it is rightly preached, doth torment and vexe them wonderfully. Some do account it a great fault in the Preachers, when any of the people do storme and rage at their doctrine, and they would haue them so to vtter the word, as to grieue or displease none: but look vpon that which is here said, the true seruants of Christ so faithfully deliuer their message, that it stingeth and tormenteth the inhabitants of the earth, and maketh them euen as mad men to rage in wrath and furie. Gods truth must be vttered, let the inhabitants of the earth, whom it tormēteth, broyle and take on neuer so much : yea let them with mad furie run vpon the Ministers of the Lord and murther them, yet they must not keep silence, they may not keep backe that fire which proceedeth out of their mouth, which doth torment and deuoure the enemies. Againe, let all people here be warned how they oppose thēselues against the holy word, for it will torment them exceedingly. Seek to purge the heart, and then it shall not be a tormenting fire, but a sweet and precious food vnto the soule. Blessed are they which find it so: and most wretched is euerie one whom it tormenteth.

Hauing thus farre set forth the victorie of the beast in killing the Lords witnesses: as also his crueltie, and the sauage furie of his seduced multitude in dishonouring them after they be dead : he commeth now to declare the spirituall victorie and heauenly honour which these holy seruants of the Lord obtaine euen in the sight and view of the world. They were alwayes in triumph & honor with God : but in the world all the time in which Poperie preuailed, they lay as men couered with ignominie and reproch, condemned and accursed as heretikes. And then were canonized for Saints such as shewed themselues valiant champions for the defence of the tyrannie of Antichrist. After three dayes and a halfe, euen when
the

the time was come that Poperie must be disclosed by the light of the Gospell breaking forth, there followeth a great alteration. These Prophets are raised vp againe, for he faith, that *the spirit of life which came from God, shall enter into them, and they shall stand vpon their feete*. This is somewhat strange: but we may not take this so, as that the witnesses of the Lord, the Prophets which the beast slue, shall be raised vp in their owne persons (which yet they shall be at the generall resurrection) but God doth here raise vp other witnesses endued with the same Spirit which they were, vttering and maintaining the same truth, & the same cause against Antichrist, and pulling downe his vsurped power. This was first fulfilled when God raised vp his noble instruments and most worthy seruants, maister *Luther*, Maister *Caluin*, *Peter Martyr*, *Bucer*, and manie other. This is fulfilled dayly in all the faithfull Ministers of Christ, raised vp in all countries. Let no man thinke that this expofition is beside the holy Scriptures, when ye see that the Lord said that he wold send *Elias* the Prophet, & yet *Elias* came not in person, but *Iohn* the Baptist in the spirit and power of *Elias*. And looke well vpon the cause, the seruants of the Lord which were murthered in time of Poperie, or which were condemned as heretikes, and so lay vnder all ignominie and reproch among men: as *Wickliffe*, *Husse*, *Hierome of Prage*, and many other, are they not after a sort also euen raised vp to life, yea euen in their owne persons, when their doctrine and their cause is most mightily defended by the liuely word which is come frō God? Do they not euen as it were stand vpon their feet againe? Is there not a great feare fallen vpon manie that see it? They neuer looked for such an alteration, which worshipped the beast.

And touching the words which follow, is there not a great voyce from heauen to bid them come thither? and are they not ascended vp euen in the sight of their enemies? doth not the mightie voyce of God in his word which is from heauen, cleare them from being heretikes, and manifest that they were true Prophets of the Lord, and now partakers of the heauenly glorie? This word (I say) carrieth them vp into heauen, as it were in a cloud. This word sheweth that those Popish Saints whom Antichrist did canonize, as *Thomas Becket*, and such like, were wicked Idolaters. The Papists, and especially the Iesuits do bite and gnaw at this, but cannot tell how to remedie it. They labour with all their might, still to dishonour those worthie witnesses of the Lord, whom their king Antichrist slue, and to honor those Popish champions, but all in vaine: for this great voyce frō heauen, euen the cleare word is too strong for them, and doth beate them downe. It layeth open the filthinesse of those whom they extoll, and it aduanceth euen to the heauens the true ministers of the Gospell whom they condemne.

Here is yet another thing remaining, an earthquake and the effect thereof. He faith, *In that houre there was a great earthquake*. Euen at the time in which God raiseth vp his seruants to spread the light of his Gospell, to discouer all the wicked abominations of Antichrist and to giue honour to his former Prophets, falleth out this great earthquake. But will some say, when heard we of such an earthquake? I answer, that by this earthquake are meant the commotions, the seditions, the tumults

SERMONS VPON

mults and warres among the kingdomes and nations of the world, which haue bin verie great euer since the Gospell brake forth. All that be of yeares do know what great shakings there haue bene, and yet are. And now touching the effect of this earthquake, the tenth part of the great citie doth fall. The Romish Sinagogue cōmeth downe, yea it commeth downe dayly, there is such a mightie shaking. Manie are departed from them, their glorie is impaired, yea they are constrained to forsake some of their owne superstitious inuentions, & to confesse that they were errors. And further, there is this effect of the earthquake, that in it there are slaine seuen thousand. Seuen is vsed in the Scriptures for a full and perfect number, and so by seuen thousand are meant many thousands, euen all those vpon whom the grieuous iudgements of God do fall, and roote them out. And it is said, *the rest were terrified and gaue glorie to the God of heauen*. Blessed be God, many repent in these dayes, euen in the midst of these commotions & fearfull iudgements of God. Yea they turne from the worshipping of idols, and giue glorie to the God of heauen. In the time of the murthering armie, chap. 9. when the third part of men were slaine, it is said, that the rest repented not of their idolatrie: blessed be the times into which we are fallen, although they be otherwise troublesome, for in them God giueth repentance to manie.

THE XXIII. SERMON.

CHAP. 11.

14. *The second wo is past, behold the third woe will come anon.*

15. *And the seuenth Angell blew the trumpet, and there were great voyces in heauen, saying, the kingdomes of this world are our Lords and his Christs, and he shall raigne for euermore.*

16. *Then the 24. Elders vvhich sate before God on their seats, fell vpon their faces, and vvorshipped God,*

17. *Saying, vve giue thee thanks, ô Lord God Almightie, vvhich art, which wast, and vvhich art to come: for thou hast receiued thy great might, and hast obtained thy kingdome.*

18. *And the the Gentiles vvere angrie, and thy wrath is come, and the time of the dead that they should be iudged, and that thou shouldest giue reward vnto thy seruants the Prophets and Saints, and to them that feare thy name small and great, and shouldest destroy them which destroy the earth.*

19 And

19 *And the Temple of* GOD *was opened in heauen, and there was seene in his Temple, the arke of his Testament, and there followed lightnings, and voices, and thundrings, and earthquake, and much haile.*

THe opening of the seuenth seale of this booke, is as yee know diuided into the sounding of seuen trumpets: whē foure of them were sounded, an Angel flyeth in the middest of heauen, saying with a loud voice, woe, woe, woe, to the inhabitants of the earth, that is three woes, becauseof the three trumpets which were yet to be sounded. At the first of these three greatest woes, wee had briefly described the darke kingdome of antichrist. At the second trumpet sounded, there was painted out the horrible destroying armie of the Turkes. These two being fulfilled, there remaineth but one which is the third. And therefore as it is sayd at the first of the three, one woe is past, and beholde two woes will come after this: so at the next it is here saide, the second woe is past, and behold the third woe commeth anon. This third woe is the greatest woe of all woes, euen the last woe, that is to say, the wo of eternall iudgement and vengeance. This is here described at the sounding of the last trumpet. Here is then the day of iudgement, and some description of the things which follow that day both vpon the good, and vpon the bad. For this description, as wee shall see, deuideth it selfe into these two partes, that is to say, the ioyes of the good, and the torments, of the wicked. The former two woes, that is, the kingdome of the Pope, and the kingdome of the Turke being much spent, we are now to waite for the great day: for as the holy Ghost sayth, *The third woe will come anon.* It is no time for men to liue now in securitie.

Then he sayth, *The seuenth Angell blew the trumpet, and there were great voyces in heauen, &c.* The Angell did denounce a woe, and it is sayde, the third woe will come: and now at the sounding of the trumpet, here are voyces heard of triumphing ioy and gladnes. How doth this agree to a woe? Ye must note that the three great woes are denounced only against the inhabitants of the earth, the children of this world, euen the reprobate. Now the ioy which is here set forth is of another companie, euen of the blessed Angels, and of all the elect and redeemed of the Lord. For when the greatest woe of all beginneth vpon the deuils, vpon Antichrist, and vpon all the wicked, then beginneth also the greatest ioy of the church, and of all the heauenly companie. How do the holy Angels and the Saints expresse the cause of their ioy? or what cause of ioy vtter they? Saint Iohn saith, there were loud voices heard, saying, *The kingdomes of this worlde are our Lordes, and his Christs, and he shall raigne for euermore.* Here is the cause of ioy expressed. Then all their ioy is in this, and for this, that the kingdome of God, and of his sonne Iesus Christ is set vp, and shall stand for euermore, euen world without end. Here is indeede full cause of triumphing and reioycing, for in this kingdom of our Lord consisteth the glory of God, the glory and the ioy of all the heauenly companies: and

P there-

SERMONS VPON

therefore no maruell though there bee loud voyces of ioye and triumph, at the full setting vp of the same. But it may be said, doth not the Lord God raigne as king ouer all the world euen now?. or did hee not euen then rule when Antichrist bare sway? Yea hath he not alwaies raigned? and is not the Lord Iesus lifted vp in glory at the right hand of God, & hath all power giuen vnto him in heauen and earth, and doth raigne as Lorde and king ouer all? How then is this applyed to the day of iudgement, as though the kingdome of God, and of his Christ, should then, and not before then, be set vp? To answer this, wee must note, that although the most high God of glory is king ouer all, and hath exalted his sonne vnto the highest maiestie, yet by his permission, Satan the prince of darkenes, with his Angels exercise a kingdome and a dominion in darknes, in vnrighteousnes, and sin, and beareth great sway in the world by his ministers and seruants the wicked and reprobate, and shall doe euen to the day of the generall iudgement. But at that day, the whole kingdome of Satan, of Antichrist, and of all the wicked enemies, shall bee quite and vtterly beaten down, no reliques, nor remnants of the same remayning. The deuils and the wicked shall all be cast into the prison of hell, and there be shut vp in darknes, & in euerlasting torments. They shall range no more abroad to molest the seruants of God, nor to worke wickednes vpon the earth. For we looke (as Saint Peter sayth) for new heauens, and a new earth, in which dwelleth righteousnes, 2. Pet. 3. This is it which we are taught to pray for dayly, when we say, Let thy kingdome come. And to all that hate the power of the deuill, with the workes of darknes, and that loue the glory of God, and of his Christ, it is a most ioyful time to thinke vpon. The Lord Iesus Christ shal raigne (as the heauenly spirits do here pronounce) not for a thousand yeares vpon the earth, which is the errour of the Chiliastes, but for euermore: Euen so shall the blessednes of the saints be with their head and king world without ende. For so long as God and his Christ shall raigne, so long shall the Church inioy true blessednes: and that is so long as neuer shall haue an ende.

Men are carefull about the things of this life, and an hundreth yeares seemeth a long time, but if our eyes could be opened to behold the time, euen the eternitie and euerlasting continuance of the kingdome of Christ, it would make vs despise and set light by the time present, and the transitorie things which are in it, and so set our whole hart vpon this glorious kingdome which shall neuer decay or draw towards any end. Thinke often I pray ye, vpon these reioycing words of the holy Angels, the kingdomes of the world are our Lords, and his Christes, and hee shall raigne for euermore. Thus much for the triumphant ioye of the Angels. Now followeth the reioycing of the Church.

The 24. Elders doe represent all the chosen which are saued, both in the time of the law and of the Gospell. The number of twelue doubled, respecteth the twelue tribes, for the one: and the Church gathered by the Lambes twelue Apostles, for the other. These first doe fall downe vpon their faces and worship God. They doe not worship one an other, they worship no Angell, but they all worship God. And yee shall neuer finde in the holy scriptures, that the true Church or any member thereof,

thereof, doth worship any but God. For the diuine worship is peculiar to the most high God alone, who will not (as he sayth by the prophet) giue his honour to any other. It is heinous sacriledge and robbery to giue away any part of it vnto creatures. The popish Synagogue the Church of Rome, doe worship Angels, and pray vnto them. The popish Synagogue do worship Saintes, and call vpon them, making them mediators of intercession. They do worship and call vpon the blessed Virgin, vpon the Apostles, and Martyrs. The popish Synagogue doe worship dead bones, and rotten reliques, yea euen the bones somtimes of wicked men, such as Thomas Becket. Finally, the popish Synogogue doe worship Idols of siluer and gold, of brasse, of wood, and of stone, which can neither goe nor see, and therefore indeed they worship deuils, as the holy Scriptures doe flatly charge all Idolaters: therefore the popish Synagogue are nothing like to the heauenly company, which worship none but God. Learne therefore out of the holy Scriptures, and take heed to what companie of worshippers yee ioyne your selues. If yee ioyne with them which worship God alone, there is plaine warrant enough in the liuely worde: If yee will ioyne with them that make others Gods, (for what a man offereth diuine worship vnto, that hee maketh God) yee follow the wicked inuention of the flesh, and the diuilish suggestion of Satan, and the Lord in his word doth terribly threaten against the same. Keepe your selues chast, bee pure worshippers of God, commit not spirituall whoredome with deuils.

It followeth, that they giue thanks and praise to God: *We giue thee thanks Lord God Almightie,* (sayt they) *which art, which wast, and which art to come,* &c. The Saintes receiue very great benefites at the day of iudgement, for it is the day of redemption vnto them: it is the day in which they beginne to enter into the possession of their full glory; the they receiue their bodies. They cannot therefore but with vehement affection breake foorth into thanksgiuing for the same. Such of Gods children, as now being clogged with the burthen of the flesh, are dul to giue thanks for their redemption, shall then with most quicke affection sound forth thanksgiuing and praise to God alone. Indeed we haue the promises of God, which cannot lye, nor deceiue vs, that we shall be plucked out of miserie, and made partakers of his glory in eternall blessednes: but our nature is such, as that wee are most moued with the things present, which our sences doe apprehend. Let a man haue the promise and gift of some rich inheritance here in the worlde, which is to come a long time after, and it will moue him, but not so much, as when he taketh the possession. The faithfull doe worship God, and giue him thankes while they be here, but nothing as it shall be at the latter day. Then see with what tearmes they set forth God: *Lord God* (say they) *Almightie, which art, which wast, and which art to come.* They see now most cleerely, that God by his almightie power treadeth downe all the enemies, yea euen the strongest of them, and plucketh forth his redeemed out of their hands. They see in more perfect sort then while they liued here, that hee is God eternal, and vnchangeable, and shall continue the same for euer. That he hath giuen the being vnto all creatures, and supporteth them by his mightie worde. These things they now see perfectly.

In the next words they render a reason of their thanks, saying, *For thou hast receiued thy great might, and hast obteined thy kingdome.* Is this the cause of their thanks? And had not the Lord alwaies his great might? and doth hee not alwaies raigne as King? The Lord hath alwaies retained the fulnes of his might, and shall haue no greater power at the latter day then he hath now. Also he raigneth as king ouer all: but as it was said before, he doth permit a kingdome & a power to the deuill, which when he throweth down, he is sayd then to receiue his great might, & to obtaine his kingdome. The receiuing then of his great might, is the exercising and putting forth of the same, for the vtter ouerthrow of all the enemies, and full deliuerance of the Church. While Satan and wicked men doe beare such sway here in the worlde: while the godly are oppressed and iniuried many waies: while death hath stil dominion ouer their bodies, and they lie in the dust, subiect vnto basenes, vnto vile rottennes and corruption, where is the mightie power, and where is the kingdome of God? Doe they not seeme to be laid aside for the time? But when he sheweth his power, and beateth quite downe the power of Satan, and plucketh his chosen out of the iawes of death, then is he sayd to receiue his great might and kingdome.

And now marke well what cause the Church hath to giue him thankes for receiuing his mightie power & kingdom: for by this meanes she is brought to her perfect saluation and glory. Our ful deliuerance, I say, doth stand in the mighty power of the Lord. And when he doth beate downe all his enemies and raigne, then blessed shall we be. When our Lord God shall raigne, let all reioyce and be glad, that bee of vpright heart, for we shall raigne with him. Hitherto appertaine all the exhortations in the Scriptures, which will vs to reioyce in his holy name. Then to conclude this point of this triumphant song of the Church: see how all saluation is ascribed to the mightie power of God: and how the Saints doe thanke him alone for it. It is written, as you know, saluation is of the Lord. And who giueth thanks for that which is his owne? If our works, or merites, or righteousnes did saue vs, these thanks to God for his power and kingdome could not stand. Wee might in some sort thanke our selues: yea, wee might glory in our selues, and in our owne, strength. But the true Church giueth thankes onely to God, and glorieth onely in his power and kingdome. Therefore the popish Synagogue which glorieth in her owne righteousnes, is nothing like to the chast spouse of Christ. O beloued, trust in the Lord, and in his glorious power, for he alone is our Sauiour, and our redeemer.

Then it followeth: *And the Gentils were angrie, and thy wrath is come, and the time of the dead that they should be iudged, and that thou shouldest giue reward to thy seruants the Prophets, and to the Saints, and to them that feare thy name, both small and great.* This is the latter parte of the ioyfull and triumphant song of the Church. In the former, as we haue seene, they gaue thanks to God, that he had receiued his great might and kingdome: because by it, and in it, consisteth the felicitie of the chosen. And now comming to mention the wrath and vengeance which is to be poured forth vpon the wicked: they first doe say, the Gentiles

were

were angrie. As if they should speake thus, the Gentiles, euen all the prophane enemies of thy Church, both forraine and domestical, haue had their time, in which they were angrie with thy people, and in their wrath did afflict and vexe them very sore: And nowe the case is altered, and the time of thy wrath is come to punish them for the same their wicked crueltie. The speech is very fitte, seeing there hath been no time, but the Church of Christ here in earth hath had very angrie enemies, and in their anger and furie, they flie vpon her, reuile and persecute her, and most cruelly murder her children. This wrath of the Gentiles, and bitter rage against the Church, which is most deare & pretious to the Lord, is most highly displeasing his heauenly Maiestie: and therefore though hee suffer them, and seeme to wincke at them, yet there is a time to declare his wrath vpon them, and that, as the elders say, is now come.

It is a strange thing to see how blind the world is: The Ministers of Antichrist, how angrie they be, and how they fret and rage at al those which loue and imbrace the pure doctrine of the most glorious Gospell of Iesus Christ? And how madde they bee, that men wil not reuerence the lawes and cursed decrees of Antichrist, and so together with them worship the beast? And in their anger, how cruelly they runne vpon yong and old, both men, women and children, sparing none, and murder them vpon heapes? Againe, the prophane worldlings, which take pleasure in the lusts of sin, & would gladly walk without rebuke in all vncleannes, how exceeding angry be they, when the liuely cleere word is vttered, which doth disclose and bewray them? And if they see any of the people imbrace the holy doctrine of God, and eschew vncleane waies, how their wrath is then inflamed, they could euen find in their hearts to beate out their braines: because the Lord letteth them alone, (I meane he doth not powre forth vpon them the full measure of his wrath) they imagine that they shall neuer come to any account for the same. But let men remember that which is here written, *The Gentiles were angrie*, that is, they had their time to shew their wrath: *and the time of thy wrath is come*. Men haue a number of excuses, to colour their wrath and furie against those which publish and professe the doctrine of Christ, they will say it is for their lewd and naughtie behauiour and euill manners: (as though they which can and doe make much of the most filthy vncleane persons bare any misliking to sinne) but they can not cloke matters before God, let them therefore take heed, that their anger bee not against the light, euen of a loue which they beare vnto darknes. And for vs, beloued, let vs the more patiently beare the anger of the Gentiles, seeing they haue but their time: and there is a time when the wrath of the Lord shall come vpon them for it. We were better to endure their anger, which is but for a time, then to vndergoe the wrath of Almightie God, which shall torment as a consuming fire, for euer and euer. Manie doe not consider well of this, but feare the wrath of men, more then the wrath of God. They see so many angrie at the gospel, and some of them of power, that they will professe it no further, then that they may kindle the wrath of none against them. Such and such will bee offended with vs, say they, they may worke vs great harme and displeasure, and why should wee displease and anger any? Nay, why wilt

wilt thou displease and anger the Lord God, that thou fearest the wrath of man, and fearest not his wrath? Let vs learne here to be armed stronghly, and euen to stand fast, euen fully perswaded, that if we will eschew the dreadfull wrath and heauie displeasure of almightie God, we must make full account to endure the anger of the Gentiles. For this is the portion and lot of the Church, and of all her children, to beare the anger of the Gentiles.

The next words are: And the time of the dead that they should be iudged. The Angell in the tenth chapter did sweare, that time shuld be no more but in the dayes of the voice of the seuenth Angell, when he shal beginne to blow the trumpet. We see here how this agreeth with the same, that now the dead shall be iudged. Then they are deceiued, which expound these thinges to bee such as goe a little before the last iudgement. For when this trumpe shall sound, the dead shall bee raised vp incorruptible: Christ with this commeth to iudge the quicke and the dead. As to this also those former things, the receiuing his great might and kingdome, and the time of his wrath doe agree. And what shall be done at this iudgement? The next words doe shew, that when they say, that thou maiest giue reward to thy seruaunts the Prophets, and to the Saints, and to all that feare thy name, both smal and great: and that thou maiest destroy them, that destroy the earth. This yee see reacheth to both parts, to the reward of the godly, which shal receiue the crowne of glory, and to the rendring vengeance and destruction to the wicked, for all their wicked waies. The blessed ones which now shal raigne with the Lord in glory, are diuided into these three sorts, the prophets, the Saints and all that feare God, both small and great. No doubt men shall in their seuerall degrees, not of merite (because there is none in the works of man) but of the fruites of faith receiue the reward of glory. If a man sowe sparingly, he shall reape sparingly and if he sowe plenteously, he shall reape plenteously, as Saint Paul telleth the Corinthians, 2. Cor. 9, vers. 9. We are called vpon to be rich in good workes, 1. Tim. 6. We are willed to make vs friends with the vnrighteous Mammon, Luk. 16. Our Sauiour saith, *Whosoeuer shall giue vnto one of these little ones to drinke, a cup of colde water onely, in the name of a disciple, verily I say vnto ye, he shall not lose his reward.* Math. 10. By Prophets are meant in a large signification, all that haue faithfully taught and instructed the Church in the holy doctrine of Christ, whether priests or prophets of old in time of the law, or apostles, prophets, Euangelists, pastors, and teachers in time of the Gospell. All these, euen according to their faithfull seruice, and labours, shall receiue their reward. It is said in the Prophet Daniel, that they which haue taught other, shall shine as the firmament, Dan. 12. Great shall be the reward of glory vpon the faithfull, and true Prophets.

Then next it is said, He will giue reward to the Saints, and then to all that feare his name, both small and great. It is euident by the Epistles of Saint Paul, as also by diuers other Scriptures, that the true beleeuers are all of them called Saints: how is here then a distinction of Saints, from those that feare his name? for they say to the Saints, and to them that feare thy name. We must either take it thus, to the Saints, euen to all that feare thy name, seeing all that feare the Lord be Saints: or els these

former

THE REVELATION.

former are called Saints by an excellencie. For while they liued in the world, some haue farre excelled others in holines. But all that feare the Lord shall bee rewarded, both the small and the great. This is a great spurre to pricke vs forward vnto al good workes, wherein we may serue the Lord, and glorifie his holy name. And as on the one side, here is ioyfull reward proclaimed to the good, so on the other side, here is destruction denounced to the euill: and shouldest (say they) destroy them, that destroy the earth.

The godly receiue their reward from the free mercie, and bountifull goodnesse of the Lord, not for any merit or desert of their owne: for how can any worke done by man, merit or deserue eternall glorie? But the wicked and vngodly, the reprobate are punished and destroyed in eternall perdition, euen according as they haue deserued. And therefore it is sayd here, the Lord shall destroy them, that destroy: for they that destroy, deserue, and are worthie to be destroyed. But why are vngodly men sayd to destroy the earth? I answer, wickednes doth corrupt, and destroy. And as godly men by holesome doctrine, sound aduise, and good example in life, as meanes, are sayd to saue others; which is a blessed thing: So euill men with their vngodly opinions, euill perswasions, and wicked deedes, do corrupt and defile, and euen vtterly destroy many. If ye marke it, this is a most cursed thing, which yet many wicked men doe glorie in, that they can hinder all goodnesse, and draw many after them into euill. Woe bee to such, for as they doe destroy, so ye heare that they shall be destroyed. The Lord sendeth his holy word to be preached, which is the arme and power of God to saluation, drawing men out of the power of sinne, of death, and of the diuell. Thou opposest thy selfe against it because thou canst not indure the light, thy workes being euill, thou railest vpon those that preach it, thou hatest such as professe it, and so warring for the diuell, thou destroyest the earth, and therefore thou shalt be destroyed. The Lord hath redeemed vs that we should serue him in holines and righteousnes all the dayes of our life: thou doest not onely despise this, and walke in sinne thy selfe: but art a maister, and a ringleader vnto all vices, yea euen a perswader and a setter on of others. For thou art not onely a foule swearer thy selfe, but doest euen deride him that will not sweare. Thou doest not content thy selfe with thine owne drunkennes, but hast a delight, and a sport, to make others drunken. Thou entisest to whordome, to theft, and to a thousand vanities, thou destroiest the earth, and therefore most iustly thou shalt be destroyed.

Thus farre we haue seene the reward of the good, and the destruction of the bad expressed by words: now in the next verse they be both of them figured vnder figures. And the Temple of God was open in heauen (sayth S. Iohn) and there was seene in his Temple the arke of his couenant: and there followed lightnings, and voyces, and thundrings, and earthquake, and much haile. The faithfull are reconciled vnto God by Christ, and shall dwell with him in the heauenly kingdome of glorie for euermore: which is figured by this, that the Temple of God is open in heauen, and in the same Temple was seene the arke of his couenant. For by this

P 4   arke

arke wee must note that our Lord Iesus is represented, euen the mediatour betweene God and man, in whom the couenant of reconciliation and peace is made and ratified. There shall be no such carnall things (as the holy Ghost speaketh in the Epistle to the Hebrues) in heauen: but the arke did figure Christ in the time of the law: and this booke setteth foorth heauenly and spirituall things, by those same externall figures which were then vsed. Then he sayth, there followed lightnings, and voices, and thundrings, and earthquake, and much haile. The faithfull being receiued into blisse, here is expressed the terrible wrath and vengeance of God sent downe vpon the reprobate. And all is here painted out vnder a most grieuous tempest. For as the Prophet Dauid, Psal. 11. describeth the iudgement of God, that he will make it raine vpon the wicked snares, fier, and brimstone, and tempest, which shall be the portion of their cuppe: so here shall be such a tempest as neuer was seene, with lightnings and voyces of terrour, and thundrings, with earthquake, and much haile. Indeed there is nothing here in this world so terrible, as that it can fully represent the horror of Gods wrath, which shall at the day of iudgement be powred foorth vpon the damned: but some shadow thereof is resembled by these terrible thinges. Let vs feare the Lorde, and glorifie his holie name, that wee bee not found among those vpon whom this tempest shall light.

THE XXIIII. SERMON.
CHAP. XII.

1 *And there appeared a great wonder in heauen, a woman clothed with the Sunne, and the Moone vnder her feete, and vpon her head a crowne of twelue starres.*

2 *And she was with child, and cried trauelling in birth, and pained, readie to be deliuered.*

3 *And there appeared another wonder in heauen, behold a great red dragon, hauing seuen heads, and tenne hornes, and vpon his heads seuen crownes.*

4 *And his taile drew the third part of the starres of heauen, and cast them to the earth: and the dragon stood before the woman, which was readie to be deliuered, to deuoure her child when she had brought it foorth.*

5 *And she brought foorth a manchild, which should rule all nations with a rod of yron, and her sonne was taken vp to God and to his throne.*

6. And

6 *And the woman fled into the wildernesse, where shee ha|th a place prepared of God, that they should feede her there a thousand, two hundreth, and threescore dayes.*

HE second vision of this prophecie, which beginneth at the fourth chapter, and continueth to the end of the eleuenth, being finished, we are come now to the third vision; which reacheth to the ende of this booke, in which there bee sundrie particular visions. There be in this no new matters (for all things were contained in the booke sealed with seuen seales, all which seales are opened, and the secrets disclosed, in briefe and darke manner) but here wee shall haue some of the same things, euen the chiefe and principall which haue beene so briefly, and so darkly vttered in the opening of the seales, more largely and more cleerely for our better instruction, painted out. For we shall now see in goodly manner described by a vision, first the Church militant vpon earth, vnder the figure of a woman clothed with the Sunne, &c. Then is there a description of her chief enemie the deuill, who as a most vgly monster doth seeke to destroy the blessed seede, and so to deuoure her also, by dispossessing her of that eternall blessednes, of which she hath the promise. Then next follow the descriptions of the chiefe and principall instruments, which this monster the dragon, euen the deuill vseth against her, which are described vnder the figures of a monstrous beast with seuen heads and tenne hornes, and of a beast with two hornes like a lambe, whose dominion & tyrannie against the Saints are set foorth. Then doe follow the ruines and vtter ouerthrow of the power of these beasts, and the plagues vpon the malignant Church which doth worship them, with the condemnation of them all, that is to say, of both the beasts, and of them that take their part; and of the deuill. And lastly a most sweete and comfortable description doth follow of the victorie, of the glorie, and of the eternall felicitie of the true Church, after the finall destruction of all her enemies. These things are reueiled in sundrie particular visions, but may bee called all one. But before she come vnto this victorie and glorious triumph, she must encounter with those huge and vgly forenamed monsters, as wee shall see by their description.

Come now to the words: there appeared (sayth he) a great wonder in heauen, a woman clothed with the Sunne, &c. Here beginneth the description of the holie Catholike Church, which is called the Spouse of Christ, the Lambes wife. And that wee may haue our mindes prepared vnto a due regard and reuerend estimation of the whole matter, which is here handled: S. Iohn sayth, there appeared a great wonder in heauen. We are moued at great wonders, and he telleth that here is a great wonder shewed. Looke not then here for common matters, and for such as are but of small moment and little to be regarded: but for such indeede as are to be wondred at for their greatnes, and which for our profit and saluation, it
standeth.

standeth vs greatly vpon for to know. First this being (as none can denye) a description of the Church militant vpon earth, here ariseth a question: How is it that shee appeareth in heauen, for this woman appeareth in heauen, and the Church militant is vpon the earth? The answer is plaine and easie enough to this. For we must vnderstand, that her birth is from heauen, shee is borne of God, her inheritance is in heauen, where she shall raigne with Christ in glorie, she is but a stranger and a pilgrime, and that for a time vpon the earth. This is the cause that shee appeareth in vision, not vpon the earth, but in heauen. This is a great and a wonderfull thing to consider, if wee could throughly way it. But the wonder is farre greater in the next words, namely, that the Church appeareth in the person, and vnder the figure of a woman, and hath such monstrous enemies. How shall a woman stand to fight against such horrible enemies, and preuaile? What is a woman to the cruell monster the dragon here painted out? What is a woman to those great monstrous beasts which follow in the next chapter, whom the world wondreth at and worshippeth? How shall she fight against these? how shall she be in safetie, or how shall she stand? Is it not a wonder of wonders, that she is not vtterly swallowed vp, and quite destroyed? She hath indeede one which is on her side to vphold her, who is most mightie & inuincible, in power farre aboue all her enemies, otherwise she should be swallowed vp & vtterly deuoured, a thousand thousand times. The most glorious power of God, and of our Lord Iesus Christ, sheweth it selfe in preseruing this feeble woman, and in giuing her victorie ouer so mightie enemies. All that haue eyes to see, must needes confesse that this is a very great wonder indeede. And let vs for our instruction learne, that wee being but as a weake woman in our selues, all our strength wherewith we be armed and made able to stand against the deuill and against Antichrist in the spirituall battaile, is from our Lord God. Wee are kept by faith, 1. Pet. 1. vers. 5. Our victorie is our fayth, 1. Ioh. 5. vers. 4. Let vs also, as S. Paul willeth in his Epistle to the Ephesians, put on the whole armour of God, otherwise wee are but as a weake woman before these huge enemies. Then it is sayd, that this woman is clothed with the Sunne, the Moone is vnder her feete, and on her head a crowne of twelue starres. Here is goodly attire: this is pretious and heauenly decking, farre aboue the rich and costly robes, and princely ornaments of the greatest Queenes that euer liued vpon the earth. Here is a glorious woman, and full of light; the brightnes of God is vpon her, she shineth pure and cleere, she is clothed with the righteousnes, and with the innocencie and puritie of Iesus Christ, who is the sonne of righteousnes, and therefore he sayth, she is clothed with the Sunne. O blessed woman: She treadeth vnder her feete things mutable and transitorie, euen the things of this world, which are fitly resembled by the Moone that doth alter & change, which he saith is vnder her feet. Her affectiō is vpon heauenly things, euen vpon the glorie promised and prepared for her, in the world to come, and in respect of the same, shee treadeth vnder her feete, that is, shee despiseth and setteth light by all the transitorie riches, glorie, pompe, and carnall pleasures of this world. She is crowned, for verely shee is a great Queene, euen the spouse of the king of kings: and her crowne is not of golde, or pretious stones, or pearles, or of any corruptible thing, such as Kings and Queenes do vse, but of an heauenly matter, euen of twelue bright stars. For she shall bee crowned with heauenly glory, and light which shall neuer faile. She is brought to the fruition of this heauenly glory, by the pure shining doctrine of the holy Apostles, and therefore it seemeth the number of twelue is vpon her crowne. This is a thing also of great wonder, that out of so base and miserable estate, yea euen from the bondage of corruption and thraldome of eternall damnation, into which we were cast downe, the Lord doth lift vp his Church into so exceeding high glory. And here I pray ye all to consider, and to take it as a cleere doctrine deliuered in this place, that so many as will be the true children of the church, they must put on Christ, they must despise this world, and all the vaine pompe and the glory thereof, with all riches and carnall pleasures, and as citizens of the heauenly citie, euen long after their countrie: And the word of God, euen the doctrine of the Apostles must be their crowne. In the next verse it is sayde, that the woman was with child, and so neere her time to bring forth, as that shee was in the paines of her trauaile to be deliuered. Here is a great matter to be noted.

It appeareth plainly by the fift verse following, that the child which the woman trauelleth in paine withall to bring forth, is Christ Iesus the blessed seed of the woman, who was promised as the Sauiour that should breake the serpents head. For there it is sayd of him, that he should rule all nations with a rod of Iron. And who is that but Christ the Sauiour? Hee was promised vnto Adam, and Eue at the first in paradise, immediatly after their fall. This promise was renued vnto the Patriarches, and vnto all the faithfull in the time of the law. The whole people of Israell waited for the comming of this Messias, which should vanquish the deuill and death. And albeit hee was borne but of one member of the Church, that is, of the blessed Virgin Marie, in whose wombe onely he tooke his flesh, yet may it be said that the whole Church, euen all the elect of God: which were before his comming, did euen trauaile with paine to bring him forth, they had such a longing, they had through faith in the promise so vehement and feruent a desire and expectation of his birth. And therefore he faith, that the woman, that is the whole Church, cryed trauailing in birth, and was pained, they brought him forth by faith. Thus far Saint Iohn hath proceeded in the description of the woman, which is euen now readie to bring forth her Sauiour: now who painteth out that vgly foule monster her enemy the deuill, as he was resembled and shewed in the vision vnto him. And thereappeared (saith he) an other wonder in heauen, behold a great red dragon, &c. Wee saw good cause why the woman appeared in heauen, although she be warring vpon the earth: but this may seeme a strange wonder, that the deuill appeareth in heauen. Hath this dragon any thing to doe there? hath he the power to enter into the heauens? Is not hell his place? what shall we say to this? I noted vnto yee before, that the woman hath her birth from heauen, she is borne of God and heauen is her countrie, there lieth her inheritance. I need not stand to proue these things, for who is it that will doubt of them, or call them into question? Now because the dragon seeketh to cast her quite downe from this her high dignitie and glorious life, and

vtterly

vtterly to depriue and to dispossesse her of that heauenly inheritance, he appeareth by vision also in heauen. It is to teach vs, that hee pursueth her euen thither, when he laboureth to cast her downe from that dignitie. For the whole practise of Satan is, to bring downe into condemnation in hell with himselfe, euen all the elect and chosen children of God if it were possible. Hee enuieth the felicitie of the Church, and would draw her downe into perdition: and so we see then why in vision he appeareth in heauen. It is not then that he hath any right, any interest or place in heauen: but that he pursueth the woman in some sort thither. Hee is a most enuious, a most hatefull and cruell enemie of ours.

And now let vs see what manner of one he is, what his disposition, qualities, and properties be. He is resembled by a dragon, which is a beast so fierce and cruell, that he cannot be appeased. We doe all abhorre it, and euen as it were tremble at the name of a dragon: and therefore vnder this figure is painted out the most sauage monster of all, full of all dragonly selnes. He is said to bee a great one, and so the more terrible: for looke how much the greater, so much the more terrible is a dragon, huge in greatnes, very mightie and strong, and a dragon that is fell. Besides his greatnes, his colour doth also bewraye what is in him: for hee is all fierie red. He doth burne, yea hee is on a flame as it were with hatred and malice, both against God and man. Hee delighteth in nothing so much as in murther and crueltie, he is all bloudie. He is a murderer from the beginning (as our Sauiour sayth) and abode not in the truth, Iohn 8. His bloudie and fiery nature seeketh nothing continually, but to destroy and murder both the soules and the bodies of men. And he doth destroy and swallow vp so many as God doth not blesse and keepe from him.

We see here plainely what the woman is to looke for at the hands of such an enemie: and we are continually to craue the blessing and protection of God. Is hee any way to be appeased or qualified? Is it good to obey his will? May there be any reconciliation, or any truce so much as for one hower had with him? But when as the holy scriptures doe teach, that there be great multitudes and armies of deuils which doe compasse vs about and seeke our endlesse destruction: How is it that he speaketh here but of one dragon, whom he afterward calleth the deuill and Satan? The answere vnto this is euident: namely, that this one dragon doth represent the whole kingdome of the deuils, euen the whole infernall power. If there be an head or a master deuill, yet all the rest doe ioyne in one. Yea they all of them so ioyne together in malice and mischiefe, as if they were but one, and not manie deuils. Their malice, their power, their craftines, and their indeuours, doe all concurre. Our Sauiour teacheth, that Satans kingdome is not deuided, Matth. 12. Then further, this dragon hath seuen heads, and ten hornes, and vpon his heads seuen crownes. Here is a wonderfull, and I may say, a most dreadfull description of his subtiltie, of his strength, and of his victories, which by his force and subtilties he hath obtained. He hath seuen heads, and marke well what that representeth, for as we vse to say commonly of a craftie man, hee hath a subtle head: so the perfect number of seuen heads here do represent the fulnes of his subtilties and craftes. The

number

ber of seuen is vsed in the scripture for a perfect number to signifie many, and so by these seuen heads, are signified the manifould and sundry deepe sleights and subtilties of this horrible enemie, and as I sayd, euen the fulnes of them. He is most vglie and most foule in al things, and yet through sleight he can colour the matters that he dealeth in, so farre and with so great cunning as to transforme himselfe into the likenesse (as Saint Paul saith) of an angell of light, and make the things seeme good which he perswadeth. Without the speciall wisedome of God therefore to guide vs, he should out of doubt deceiue all; none, not euen the wisest should be able to espie out, and to auoyde his subtilties. He hath ten hornes: and by hornes ye knowe right well that the Scripture euery where setteth foorth, and resembleth, strength, and power, and might. Then it is euident, that besides the manifold subtilties of this cruell dragon, he is of wonderful force and might: for ten is also a perfect number. They be mightie spirits the deuils and full of terrible power: For these ten hornes doe pretend so much. Wee all of vs doe vnderstand this, that strength can do much by it selfe, and subtiltie alone doth often preuaile to effect very great matters: what shall wee thinke then, where such exceeding great strength resembled by ten hornes, and so manifold subtilties as his seuen heads containe, meete and are ioyned together? These do indeed concurre in this fierie dragon, the fierce and cruell enemie of mankind. And what effectes they haue wrought, is declared in the next words, when he saith. And vpon his heads seuen crownes. Who do vse to weare crownes I pray you but conquerours, which in deed get the victorie and doe raigne?

Now because the dragon by his subtilties especially hath gotten many victories, and hath seduced the nations of the worlde, euen to worship him in stead of God, and so hath brought them vnto eternall perdition, hee is crowned and hath raigned ouer them as a king, and as a most mightie conquerour. And because his subtilties haue so often preuailed, all his heads are crowned. There is not one head that wanteth a crowne. This is that mightie tyrant, whome Saint Paule calleth the God of this world, who blindeth the eyes of the infidels, 2. Cor. 4. And whom the same Apostle calleth principalities, and powers, euen the rulers of the darkenes of this world, and spirituall craftines in the high places. And Saint Peter calleth him a roring Lion, Ephes. 6. 1. Pet. 1. 5. Indeed all his dominion is in falshood, in lyes, in error, in darkenes, in superstition, in Idolatrie, and in all filthines of other wicked sinnes. As his subtiltie is very great for to seduce, so is hee mightie and strong in the corrupt heart of man to leade vnto all these. The light, the truth, the pure worde of God in deed do vanquish him: and the spouse of Christ is armed therewith, as with the spirituall sword, Ephes. 6. It is a very good thing for vs, that the holy ghost doth thus paint him out, euen in this terrible manner, euen to raise vs vp from securitie, that we may seeke continually to God, to bee preserued by his gratious and mightie protection from this dragon. He destroyeth many thousands, and yet maketh them beleeue he neuer commeth nigh them: he holdeth them in such blindnes and contempt of Gods word. He woundeth their soules to death with all abominable sinne. He worketh mightily in their hearts so farre that they obey his will

and

and so honour him as their God, and yet they doe not perceiue it. If ye will be wise, be instant with the Lord God night and day, and let it be your continuall prayer to be deliuered from him.

It is sayd further, that his taile drew the third part of the starres of heauen, and threw them downe to the earth. This is a maruailous thing, and which we may indeed greatly wonder at, that this monster the dragon is so huge and so great, that his taile reacheth vnto, and doth cast downe the third part of the starres of heauen? what is the bignesse of the whole bodie, and what is his strength that hath such a taile? Hereby I take it euident, that dragon representeth the whole bodie of all the deuils. How easily were he able to swallow vp the woman, if the mightie power of God did not keepe her? What is she in her selfe compared vnto him? Glory, honour, thanks, and praise, be to the most high God, which is greater and mightier then he, and doth so arme euen the least and the weakest of all his chosen, and maketh them so strong, that they vanquish and ouercome this monster. And it is a glorious victorie, that weake flesh through the power of God is so mightie as to ouercome him. But it may bee demaunded, what is meant by this, that his tayle doth draw the third part of the starres of heauen, and cast them downe to the earth? How is it to be vnderstood? We know it is not to be taken literally, that the deuil with a very tayle euer drew downe the starres themselues of the firmament, which doe shine vnto our bodily eyes: Wee must then take it mystically, and not as the letter soundeth. And ye see before by Christs owne words, when hee sayth, the seuen stars, are the seuen Angels of the seuen churches, that by stars are signified preachers of the Gospell, because they must shine to the world with pure doctrine, like starres. A great part of them are by the deuils taile cast downe. They seemed which are thus cast downe, for a time to shine like starres of heauen, both by the light of heauenly doctrine, and also of vpright conuersation: but the deuill casting in his taile, that is euen tempting them with ambition, with vaine glory, with couetousnes, and with other fleshly lusts and earthly desires, pulleth them downe from their brightnes. They become euen like the rest of the worldlings, which are called the inhabitants of the earth, which he sheweth when he sayth, the dragon doth cast them to the earth. This place doth instruct vs al, for this is declared to the end that we may not be astonished, nor stumble at it as at a strange matter, when wee see many learned men, that haue zealously preached the gospel, and were famous that in continuance of time doe become euen meere worldlings, scarce retaining so much as any little shew either of zeale for to set forth the trueth, or yet of godly conuersation: all graces doe wither in them. This prophecie must needs be true in all ages and times. The dragon fighteth against the woman very fiercely, and although he can not cast downe the least of Gods elect, for Christ sayth, the father that gaue them me is stronger then all, and none can take them out of his hands, Ioh. 10. yet hee preuaileth against multitudes which are in the visible Church, and which did seeme for a time to be very good Christiãs, zealous of good works. And no maruaile, for if he draw down with his taile so many learned teachers, and make such hauocke among them, what hrpes of others which are but common professorts thinke ye, he doth ouercome? Here is then a very good lesson for al the preachers and ministers of the Gospell, yea euen a warning for them (if men will bee warned) to take heed, that they be not of those starres which the dragons taile shall cast downe. He striketh in his taile continually among vs, and tempteth with couetousnes and ambition. It standeth vs vpon to feare and to tremble, and to depend vpon the Lord with humble supplication and prayer. For this place ought to moue vs to crie continually, Lord Iesus preserue thy ministers: because doubtles, as he preuaileth against many of the teachers, so his taile is walking, and he doth most furiously assault vs all: yea we shall all be cast to the earth, if the Lord Iesus doe not preserue and keepe vs.

Then it is sayd further, that the dragon stoode before the woman, which was readie to be deliuered, to deuoure her child, when she had brought it foorth. This is a most wicked practise, this is a most daungerous attempt, that he watcheth so narrowly to deuoure the blessed seede, euen the Sauiour of the world, so soone as euer he should be borne. This was the readie way to ouerthrow the woman also: for all the health and felicitie and saluation of the Church, dependeth wholy and altogether vpon the Messias. If he should faile, all were lost. The time of his birth foretold by Daniel the Prophet was now come. And marke the subtill practise of Satan, who watcheth when, and where he should be borne, and stirreth vp Herod the king subtilly to seeke him out by the wife men, Matt. 2. that he might kill him. And whē he did not preuaile by one means (that is, the wife men being warned of God, returned home another way) he attempted another: for he sent and slew all the young children in Bethelem, and round about in the borders thereof, from two yeares old and vnder, thinking by that meanes to kill Christ among them. O monstrous cruell dragon, which hath the tyrants of the world at his becke to commaund! For indeed he wrought by such wicked rulers against Christ, and by such he worketh continually against the whole Church of God. Well, shee bringeth foorth, and she bringeth foorth a manchild, and such an one, as should haue all the nations of the earth for his possession, and ouer whom as a most mightie king, he should raigne and rule with an yron scepter. This may in some sort be applied to all the faithfull, in as much as they shall raigne with the Lord Iesus their head, but most fitly it is here to be vnderstood of Christ himselfe, euen as the second Psalme doth shew. This infant is the king of all kings. This babe is he which of old was promised by the Prophets, that with his kingly power was to tread downe Satan and his kingdome, and to deliuer the prisoners and captiues out of his hands. No maruell therefore, though the dragon seeke to deuour him so soone as he should be borne. But we shall see how he misseth of his purpose, for the child is taken vp to God, and to his throne, he is set farre aboue the reach of the dragon, he cannot deuoure him. After a sort indeede the babe so soone as he was borne, was taken vp to God, and to his throne, though he remained still vpon the earth, when the Lord gaue warning to the wisemen, not to returne backe againe to Herod, and when he willed Ioseph to flye into Egypt, and when, by his most mightie arme he kept him continually from all perill, Satan seeking all wayes and meanes for to deſtroy him. For the preſeruation of Chriſt while hee was an infant, and likewiſe while he entred into his office, was as miraculous, as if he had been taken vp into heauen, euen to the throne of God and kept there. Thus the infant is ſet in ſafetie from the iawes of this foule greedie dragon, and after his paſſion he aſcended in deede vp to the throne of God in heauen: but what becommeth of the woman, how ſhall ſhee doe, how is ſhee prouided for, or how ſhall ſhee eſcape him? Wee ſhall ſee, that ſhe is alſo well prouided for. It is ſayd, that ſhe fled into the wildernes. Behold here how Satans rage was ſuch, that when he could not deuoure the child, then he attempted ſome other way vtterly to roote out, and to deſtroy the woman. But ſhee eſcapeth him alſo: for ſhee hath power giuen her to flye away from him into the wildernes. This plainly ſheweth what he purpoſed: for if hee ſought not vtterly to ſwallow her vp, why fled ſhee away from his preſence? But what way is this to bee vnderſtood? what reaſon is here for vs to thinke that ſhee could thus eſcape? Are not the deuils as ſwift to flye after, as ſhe was to haſte and to remoue her ſelfe out of their ſight? Can fleſh and bloud make quicker ſpeede then thoſe nimble ſpirits? I will tell ye, we muſt vnderſtand this flight of the woman from the preſence of the dragon, to haue bin then when the Lord did ſpread his Church into waſt, wide, and wild barren places, as it were into the wildernes. I will ſhew ye more plainly, how this flight is to be vnderſtood. When the Church began to increaſe, after our Sauiour had taught while he liued vpon earth, and then his Apoſtles after his aſcenſion, (and had gathered a right excellent and famous Church) Satan was in a marueilous rage: and that Church being then in a narrow compaſſe, euen the moſt of them that profeſſed Chriſt in that one citie Ieruſalem, he attempted as it were to ſpread his net ouer them, and to roote them out all at once, and ſo to deuoure the woman. And therefore as wee reade, Act. 8. after the ſtoning of Steuen, he raiſed vp a great perſecution: and then hee had Saul in his campe, as a moſt cruell perſecutor, who thought hee ſhould doe high ſeruice to God, if he could roote them out all. The high prieſts, the princes of the Iewes, the Phariſees, & doctors of the law, were all ſo inflamed in wrath againſt the Church, that they meant to deſtroy all that ſhould confeſſe Chriſt Ieſus. And this the dragon led them into by his ſubtiltie, though they did not perceiue ſo much, but ſeemed to doe it in zeale of the law. But how ſhall we vnderſtand this that he ſayth, the woman fled into the wildernes? What is this wildernes whither ſhee fled from the preſence of the dragon? Doubtles, the heathen countries might very well be called, and ſo they are called in the Prophets, the wildernes. When God ſeparated the Iewes to be his onely people, and ſuffered the Gentiles to walke in their owne vanities, what could they bee but a wildernes? He gaue his word to the Iſraelites by Moſes and the Prophets, and ſo they were planted, and dreſſed as his vineyard, as the Lord calleth them, Eſay, 5. They were, as S. Paul alſo ſpeaketh, the Lords husbandrie, 1. Cor. 3. There was plowing, and ſowing, planting and watring among them, by the Lords labourers, the prieſts and prophets: there were ſome fruites brought foorth. The Gentiles in the meane time, euen all other the great and mightie nations and kingdomes of the world, lay deſolate and barren,

euē

THE REVELATION. 225

euen as a wildernesse: no dressing there, no tilling, no fruite, but all couered with thornes. Into this wildernesse then the woman flyeth from the furie of the dragon. For at the persecution raised, when Steuen was stoned, as we reade Act. chap. the 8. the Disciples were scattered, as ye may there see, into diuers nations, and countries of the Gentiles. They were before as it were penned vp in a narrow corner in Iudea, but now they are scattered and dispersed farre and neere among the heathen. Thus doth she escape from the dragon. But how durst the woman attempt to flye into the wildernesse? how did she know she should be safe there? I answer, that she had the speciall direction of God: for it is sayd, where she hath a place prepared of God. The woman then dooth nothing by her owne strength, nor by her owne wit: but by the hand and power of the Lord, and by the speciall wisedome of his spirit, she flyeth to her place assigned. Those worthie seruants of the Lord which fled from Ierusalem, being persecuted there, & preached the Gospell in farre countries, did it not rashly, nor of their owne head. For(as ye see) God hath prepared her place whither she should flye. But now it might be sayd, how shall she liue in the wildernesse? how shall she doe for sustenance? If one haue neuer so safe a place for defence in a wildernesse, and haue nothing to feede vpon, what is he the better? There is no tilling nor sowing, nor planting, there groweth no corne, there is nothing to bee had either for foode or raiment: how then shall the Church doe in the wildernesse? Marke what followeth, and ye shall vnderstand, that God doth not onely prepare a place for her in the wildernesse, but it is added, where they should feed her, a thousand two hundreth, and threescore daies. Then the Lord God doth also send vnto her, and see that she shall lacke no food while she is in the desert.

When the great famine was in Israel, in the dayes of Elias, wee reade, that the Lord sent the rauens with bread and flesh morning and euening vnto Elias, whē he lay hid where Ahab should not finde him. When the children of Israel came foorth of the land of Egypt, they were led in the wildernesse fourtie yeares, as Moses reporteth. They had neither feede time nor haruest, and yet they were fed. He fed them from heauen with Manna. And as the Psalme sayth, man did eate the bread of Angels. It was not the bread of ẏ bakers, but the bread of Angels, that is, such as God gaue to them by the ministrie of Angels. So now the Church flyeth into the wildernesse, but God sendeth vnto her those which shall feede her, and nourish her plenteously. Now the Lorde sendeth foorth into all places of the wildernesse, euen among the rude sauage people of the Gentiles, his faithfull ministers, well furnished. Such as our Sauiour compareth to housholders that bring foorth of their treasures with all store of heauenly, and spirituall foode, things new and old, Mattit. 13. vers. 52. Yea euen from among those which fought for the dragon, to destroy the woman, and which caused her to flye into the wildernesse, the Lord plucked out one speciall chosen instrument, euen Paul, whom he sent after her, with exceeding abundance and plentie of foode to nourish her. Happie are they whom God doth feede, we may safely depend vpon him. His store neuer faileth, and if they be in the wildernesse, he will send vnto them, he neuer wanteth meanes. Hebr. 13. And wee haue his promise, that hee will neuer leaue vs nor forsake vs.

Thus wee see how by the prouidence of almightie God, the woman escapeth the daunger of the dragon, and the perill also of famine. The dragon thought vtterly to roote her out, that she might neuer after bring forth any children to God: but the Lord dooth protect her, and multiplieth her children abundantly in the wildernesse. Great multitudes of sonnes and daughters she bringeth foorth, and nourisheth vp, among the Gentiles. The dragon and all the cruell tyrants are thus by the wisedome of God disappoynted. God doth often turne the furie of his enemies to the enlargement of his Church. Let vs not then faint, nor despaire when wee see all on an vprore against the faithfull Christians, and such strength and terror bent, as if all should downe, this woman shall neuer bee ouercome by the dragon, nor by all that he is able to make. Blessed is she, blessed are all her children. Wee haue now in the last place the time set foorth, that is, how long they shall feede her in the wildernesse, euen a thousand two hundreth, and threescore dayes. This is the same number of dayes, that he sayd in the former chapter, his two witnesses should prophecie. Reckoning thirtie dayes to the moneth, it ariseth vnto two and fourtie moneths, in which he sayd, the Gentiles should tread vnder foote the holy citie: and two and fourtie moneths make three yeares and a halfe. And therefore hee sayth afterward in this chapter, that the woman fled into the wildernes, vnto her place where she is fed; a time, times, and halfe a time. All these times of dayes, and moneths, and yeares meeting in one, the Papists, as wee noted before, will needes vnderstand not mystically, but literally for the space of three yeares and an halfe, as wee in common vse doe take yeares. And thereupon they inferre, that Antichrist shal raigne but three yeares and an halfe: but the Pope hath raigned diuers hundred yeares (say they) and then cannot he be Antichrist. If they will needes take it literally, then let them shew how the Church in all countries of the world, shall for those three yeares and an halfe bee fed by two men. The Church shall be fed in the wildernes, and the two witnesses shall feed her all that time of three yeares and an halfe, for so long they prophecie, and so long the woman is fed in the wildernes. Can two men be in all countries at once? If they will say there shall bee more then two, then according to the letter the things are vnperfectly set downe. For those that prophecie so long, are they which all the while doe feede the Church. The two witnesses shall feede her in the wildernes, that is, in all nations of the world, and must needes therefore be more then two. Euen so the certaine number of dayes, is put for a number indefinite, euen for the whole time that the Church shall be persecuted by the dragon, and not for three yeares and an halfe. Let no man thinke this strange: for can any bee so foolish as to imagine, that of euery one of the twelue tribes of Israel there should bee saued iust twelue thousand? But of this no further.

T.H.

THE XXV. SERMON.
CHAP. XII.

7 *And there was a battell in heauen, Michael and his Angels fought against the Dragon, and the Dragon and his angels fought:*
8 *But they preuailed not, neither was their place found any more in heauen.*
9 *And the great Dragon was cast forth, that ould serpent called the deuill, and Satan, which seduceth the whole world: hee was cast into the earth, and his Angels were cast out with him.*
10 *And I heard a great voice in heauen, saying, Now is saluation wrought, and the strength, and the kingdome of our God, and the power of his Christ: because the accuser of our brethren is cast downe, which accused them before our God, day and night.*
11 *And they ouercame him by the bloud of the Lambe, and by the word of their testimonie, and they loued not their liues, euen vnto the death.*
12 *Therefore reioyce ye heauens, and ye that dwell in them. Woe be to the inhabitants of the earth, and of the sea, for the deuill is come downe to you, which hath great wrath, knowing that he hath but a short time.*

N the former part of this chapter, wee had first the description of the true Church: and then next we had figured out her great enemie the deuill, and how he endeuoured and waited to destroy the blessed seed euen Iesus Christ so soone as hee should be borne, and so to take away the saluation of the Church: and missing thereof, hee sought to roote out of the earth all that should bee found to confesse his holy name. Christ is taken vp to the throne of God, out of the reach of the dragon, hee cannot destroy him being from his birth miraculously protected, and after hee had finished all things, ascending vp into heauen. The Church also is so prouided for by flight into the wildernes, that hee can not vtterly destroy her from the earth. These things we had in the former verses. In this part which I haue now read, here is an other thing set forth, which is the chiefe and principall matter of all, wherein our whole ioy and comfort doth rest: and that is, how Christ ouercommeth. Here therefore the dragon, as it was promised, the seed of the woman shall breake the serpents head. Here therefore wee shall see a great battell fought betweene him and Christ, in which the dragon is ouercome, yea all the faithfull ouercome him by the bloud of Chriſt. Theſe be high and excellent things, yea euen the higheſt, which we are with great ioy, and with great attention to giue eare vnto. Let vs now come vnto it.

And there was (ſaith hee) *a battell in heauen.* The place is named firſt where this battell was fought to be heauen. Did not Ieſus Chriſt fight this battell vpon the earth? Did the deuill leade his armie vp into heauen and fight there? Did he not ſpoyle (I meane the Lord Ieſus) principalities, and powers, and triumph ouer them in his croſſe? Surely he ouercame the deuill by his death vpon the croſſe. If then this battel were fought vpon earth, how is it ſaid here, that the battell was in heauen? could it be in heauen, and yet fought in earth? For anſwere vnto this, wee muſt conſider that which I noted vnto ye before, namely, why the dragon appeared in heauen, not that he had any place, or right, or power, or entrance there, but becauſe the woman is from heauen, her inheritance is in the heauens, and the dragon would caſt her downe from it. Then yee may ſee that the reaſon why hee appeareth in viſion in heauen, and why he is ſaid to fight in heauen, is all one, euen this the battell is about heauenly things, he would plucke downe the woman from thence, from euerlaſting glory into eternall miſerie. Thus much concerning the place.

Then next here are named the captaines on both parts in this battell, together with their armies. Michael and his Angels on the one ſide for the Church, and the dragon and his Angels on the other ſide againſt the Church. Here is then the ioyning of the battell, they both fight, yea they all fight on both ſides, both the captaines and their armies. Michael is the captaine on the beſt part, and he is Ieſus Chriſt. This name is giuen him in the tenth chapter of Daniel, where hee is called the firſt of the chiefe princes: becauſe he is the head of Angels, who are the chiefe princes, being as the bleſſed apoſtle Saint Paul calleth them, principalities, mights, thrones, and dominations. In the twelfth chapter of Daniel, hee is called Michael the great, or the greateſt prince. The word is an hebrue name, compoũded of three words, which conſiſt euery one but of one ſillable, which are theſe, Mi, cha, and el. Mi, ſignifieth who or which, cha, equall or like, el, the ſtrong God: Michael then ſignifieth who which is equall with God. And we are taught that Ieſus Chriſt touching his Godhead is equal with the father. For Saint Paul (as ye know the place in his epiſtle to the Philippians) ſaith, that Chriſt being in the ſhape of God, thought it no robbery to be equall with God. Then this Michael is Ieſus, for hee is equall with God. Here may now a queſtion be moued, as thus: Did not this Michael only ouercome the dragon? Is there any other power beſides the power of our Lord Ieſus, which he vanquiſhed Satan? If not, how is it ſaide, that Michael and his Angels fought againſt the dragon? This is eaſily anſwered, that how ſoeuer Michael hath his Angels that doe fight, yet he alone hath the power which ouercommeth the deuill: for they all fight, in his name, and in his power. Yea to ſpeake more properly, they bee but the miniſters and inſtruments of his power. They bee then ioyned with him in this battell, not that they fight in their owne ſtrength, but becauſe they be his miniſters.

Now

THE REVELATION.

Now besides the heauenly spirites which are not to be excluded, the blessed Apostles, and other ministers of the Gospell whom the Lord raised vp, were the Angels of Michael. These fought and doe fight against the dragon, when they deliuer forth the light of the heauenly truth: when they teach the true worship of God, and beate downe all false worship which is in Idolatrie and error. Yea when they lay open the power of Iesus Christ, and his sauing health: Downe goeth Satan and his kingdome euen by these. So then, when Peter, and Paul, and all other holy seruants of God, euen as the Angels of this most mighty prince Michael, doe fight against the dragon and against his Angels, and ouercome them: they fight not in any power of their owne, neither doe they ouercome by any might of their owne, but they fight and ouercome only in the strength and power of their captaine. This may teach vs, that it is not because Christ needed any helpe, that his Angels doe fight with him: neither is it to shewe that Satans power is subdued by any other might then by his alone. All that fight against the deuill and his Angels, and ouercome, fight with the power of Christ. Thus much may suffice for the answering of that question.

Come now to the other part, The dragon and his Angels fought. This great tyrant hauing obtained a kingdome, is very loth to haue it pulled downe or diminished, yea he fighteth and endeuoureth not onely to vphold that he had, but also to enlarge his dominion, yea euen so farre if it were possible, as vtterly to pull downe the kingdome of God. Here is fighting then for two kingdomes, euen betweene two great princes, the prince of darknes, and the king of glory. The Lord of hoasts, euen the Lord strong and mightie in battell, which is the king of glory, Psalm. 24. will breake downe the tyranous power and kingdome of the dragon, and set vp the kingdome of grace, and saluation, and from hence ariseth the battell. But who are the dragons Angels which doe fight for him? Shall wee take the dragon to be but one deuill, euen the chiefe, whome the Pharisees called Beelzebub, and all the rest of the deuils to be his Angels? Or as the papistes say, this great dragon is Lucifer, for so they call the prince of the deuils, because in the 14. chapter of Esay, ver. 12. it is said, how art thou fallen from heauen Lucifer? which is spoken of the kingdome of Babell, and they ignorantly apply it to the deuill. For the king of Babell is compared for the brightnes of his glory, to the morning starre, which is called Lucifer. It may bee there is one deuill chiefe as king ouer all the rest, but I doe not yet see how it is cleerely proued by the holy scriptures. I know the vanitie of some is such, that they doe not onely beleeue that there is (as I sayd) one deuill as king ouer all the rest, which I will not affirme nor denie, but also beleeue the coniurers, which set forth that according to the gouernments here among men, there be also among the deuils, vnder the chiefe deuill, Princes, Dukes, Earles, and great captaines which haue their armies vnder them. If the holy word of God hath taught no such thing, then who hath taught it but the father of lies? But if any man shall reply, and say it is cleere by this place, that there is one prince of the deuils, and all the rest be called his Angels. And likewise, Math. 25. Goe ye cursed into euerlasting fire, which is prepared for the deuill and his Angels. I say as I did before, I doe not denie,

nie, as I doe not affirme, but that one deuill may bee the chiefe, and as the prince, but yet I doe not see, but that rather by this dragon the kingdome of deuils is represented, and that if there be seuerall orders or degrees, because Saint Paul calleth them principalities, and powers, and the rulers of the darknesse of this world, Ephe. 6. yet they may be all included in this dragon. Who then will some say, be the angels of the dragon which here doe fight? It is no absurditie to call particular deuils the Angels of the dragon, howsoeuer they bee all figured by him, seeing they all fight to maintaine and hold vp one kingdome. And moreouer by the Angels of the dragon, are not onely deuils vnderstood, but also tyrants, false teachers, corrupters of the truth, and heretikes: for all these do fight for to vphold the power and kingdome of the dragon. As Christ and his angels fight on the one part, so these with the dragon fight against him, on the other part.

It followeth, that the dragon and his Angels preuailed not, neither was their place found any more in heauen. This may seeme to bee but halfe a comfort, that he saith, they preuailed not: for a power sometime doth nor preuaile, and yet is not ouercome, nor diminished. Doth Satan goe away, and his Angels from this battell onely not peuailing? Are they not subdued and vanquished? Yes, that is out of question, that our mighty prince hath broken or crushed the head of the serpent. He triumphed in his crosse ouer principalities, and powers. Satan commeth down from heauen speedily: As ye know how our Sauiour speaketh in the Gospel, I saw Satan fall downe from heauen like lightning. They preuailed not, not onely in oppugning the whole Church, but also in not retaining that power which they had. For hauing seduced the large and mightie kingdoms of the world, insomuch that the deuils by the Gentiles were worshipped as Gods; now Christ finishing the blessed worke of redemption so long before promised to the fathers; and now the pure light of the glorious gospell shining into the hearts of Gods chosen in all places, great multitudes were translated out of darkenesse into the kingdom of light. Now is not the dragon able to plucke out of the handes of Christ, so much as one soule of his elect: and therefore the conquest ouer him is great. But that which followeth seemeth somewhat darke; namely, that he sayth, their place was found no more in heauen. Had the deuils any place in heauen after they were become deuils? had they place in heauen till Christ suffered? Nay we are taught that they were cast downe from heauen when they sinned, 2. Pet. 2. By this is meant that they could no longer impugne or assault the Church touching her blessed estate in the heauens, with any hope to dispossesse her. Satan and his Angels had place in heauen only to fight against the chosen; and now the same is quite taken away from them at the comming and death of the Lord Iesus. If any will say, he tempteth all the elect stil as he did before; he seeketh to cast them downe from heauen into the gulfe of hell as he did before: And moreouer, it may be sayd truely, that hee could neuer from the beginning of the world pluck down one of Gods elect. What difference is there then? why is it more sayd, that his place is found no more there? True it is that he could neuer disinherite the Church, nor plucke downe into eternall destruction so much as one of her true children, and so in that respect there can appeare

no.

no difference at all: But yet wee muſt conſider, that becauſe the battaile is now fought, and all things before promiſed are now finiſhed by the death and reſurrection of Chriſt, the victorie of Chriſt and his Church is aſcribed to this time, that now Satan is caſt down. Againe, whereas this huge monſter, partly by his ſtrength, and partly by his craftines, had long time preuailed, and thereby was made ſo bold that euery way hee aſſailed Chriſt Ieſus himſelfe: now hee feeleth that he is ouercome, and that there remaineth no hope for him euer to aſſaile againe in battaile, either the Sauiour himſelfe, or the ſaluation of the Church. Their place in that reſpect is found no more in heauen. Where is their place then found? for they be not quite put downe as yet from fighting, they haue a place, they be not yet quite diſpoſſeſſed of their kingdome?

It is expreſſed in the next verſe, that they be caſt forth into the earth, out of heauen then into the earth. Not vtterly put downe then (as I ſaide) from their kingdome, nor from fighting, but caſt out from fighting any more in heauen, to fight in the earth. Of this we ſhall ſpeake more anon, but firſt touching the ſpeeches which are to ſet out the dragon. The great dragon (ſaith Saint Iohn) was caſt forth, called the deuill and Satan, which ſeduceth the whole world, &c. looke vpon the words, he is a dragon fierce and fell: He is a very great one, and of wonderfull power: He is that old ſerpent, and therefore not only ſubtill, but through long experience wonderfull deepe in manifold crafts and ſleights. He is called the deuill, that is, a falſe accuſer by his calumniations. He is called Satan, which is an aduerſarie, burning with hatred againſt God and man. He hath with his craft and ſubtiltie preuailed and ſeduced the whole world, (only thoſe fewe excepted which the Lord hath choſen out of the world) and yet in this battell he is ouercome and caſt forth. For what is he for all his fiercenes, ſtrength, and ſubtilties, when he encountreth with Chriſt? for he is Michael, equall or like to the ſtrong God. Indeed yee may well perceiue that al we are nothing to this vgly monſter, he could eaſily ſwallow vs vp: but there is one on our ſide, euen our redeemer who is too hard for him, and hath caſt him forth, he hath caſt him into the earth, and his Angels with him. Well then come, he is not yet caſt downe into hell and ſhut vp there. Hee is caſt but into the earth, he is not ſpoyled of all power, but vpon earth he renueth the battell, and fighteth. And the Church is and hath beene vpon the earth. Very true, & he fighteth againſt her vpon the earth, he tempteth her children, he perſecuteth them with ſlaunders, and with all kinde of cruell torments: but her ſaluation is ratified and ſealed vp, and ſo hee cannot fight againſt her in heauen. Hee hath then ſome power left to fight with all againſt the Church in earth, to vexe and afflict her in this worlde, but hurt her eſtate in heauen, nor diſpoſſeſſe her hee cannot, being ſpoyled of all that power, neither remaineth in him any hope thereof. Againe hee hath his power, his kingdome, and dominion remaining whole ſtill in the earth, that is, ouer the reprobate and wicked worldlings. He is caſt forth and his Angels out of heauen, but not from amongſt them. They be his ſubiects, they be his vaſſals, they honor him by doing his will.

Thus farre then we ſee his kingdome doth yet continue after this great battaile: and

and shall continue to the great day, that is, the day of iudgement. But hath not the Lord Iesus fully ouercome him? hath he not fully trode downe his aduersaries? or did he want might for to doe it? He wanted no might euen at once vtterly to tread them downe all, and to leaue them no power. The worke which he wrought was not in it selfe vnperfect, either for the full deliuerance of his chosen, or for the vtter ouerthrow of all his enemies: but it pleaseth God in his heauenly wisedome, that this power should not shew forth it selfe at once, but by degrees, and in some measure for the time, and then perfectly to take effect when all the dead shall bee raised vp. Then let vs not be discouraged, that the dragon after this battaile fought, retaineth still a kingdome, and great power, and doth still muster his bands, and armies, and doth fight. He cannot fight any more (as wee haue seene) in heauen, and that which he retaineth of his power in earth, is but by permission for a time: for Christ at the latter day (as Paul sheweth, 1. Cor. 15.) will put downe all rule and authoritie, and shall haue all his enemies made his footestoole. Thus farre touching the battaile.

Now as it hath been the manner of old, when any great battaile was fought, that the side which preuailed would sing a song of victorie, and set forth the praise of the conquerors: As ye may see how in such a song Moses, and the children of Israel, magnifie the Lord God as the most strong and mightie warrior, when he had ouerthrowne Pharaoh and his hoast in the red sea, Exod. 15. Also wee reade how Debora in the booke of Iudges, after the greate victorie gotten ouer Sisera, made a song, in which she setteth foorth the praise of the conquerors, Iudg. 5. The Lord is magnified, and the instruments, euen her selfe, and Baruck, and Iael the woman which draue the naile into the head of Sisera, and likewise such of the children of Israel in their tribes, as behaued themselues valiantly. And we reade also, that when Dauid had slaine Goliah, and the victorie was gotten ouer the armie of the Philistims, the women came foorth and did sing, that Saul had slaine his thousand, and Dauid his tenne thousand, 1. Sam. 18. These were songs of victory: this was the manner to extoll the conquerors. So here, when the dragon and his Angels are ouercome, there is a ioyful song of victorie, which S. Iohn heareth vttered with a loude voyce from heauen. This is indeede a most excellent song, in which first the kingdome and power of God, and of his Christ, are magnified for ouercomming the dragon, then the glorious victorie which the Church hath ouer him through Christ. Thirdly, there is a calling vpon the heauens and vpon all that dwel in them, to reioyce for this glorious victorie. And lastly, woe is proclamed to the reprobate, which receiue no good by the same victorie, but through their owne corruption, turne it to their further destruction.

Touching the first of these, wee see it is sayd, now is saluation wrought, and the strength, and the kingdome of our God, and the power of his Christ. There is nothing darke or difficult in these words: but as ye see the praise of God. and of his Christ are founded foorth, in that the most high power of God, and his kingdome, hath shewed it selfe in Christ, by vanquishing the dragon, and thereby working and ratifying the saluation of the Church, that it can neuer be shaken. Mark well

(I

THE REVELATION. 233.

(I pray you) how it is fayd, that faluation is wrought in heauen, and then the kingdome of God, and the power of his Chrift are annexed. For hereby we are taught, that the faluation of the Church is wrought onely by the power of God in Chrift, and wholy dependeth vpon the fame. Here is no part afcribed to the Angels, nor to any other creature, but all wholly vnto God and his Chrift. It is the kingdome and power of God in his fonne, and not the kingdome of any creature, in which the faluation of the elect confifteth. We muft afcribe vnto God and his Chrift, all the glorie and praife thereof. It pleafeth God indeede, to vfe both the minifterie of men and Angels in working this faluation, yet they doe nothing but in and by his ftrength: Then let vs note here that which wee fpake of before, namely, how the dragon is caft foorth from heauen, that is, wherein his power to fight did confift, and how it is taken away. For the words of this fong doe expreffe it, when they fay, becaufe the accufer of our brethren is caft foorth, which accufed them before God day and night. This dragon did ouercome our firft parents Adam and Eue and brought them into the guiltines of finne: yea all their pofteritie are of neceffitie borne from them vncleane finners. Then is the iuftice of God, fuch that where there is the guiltines of finne, there is damnation. All then being guiltie, the dragon doth ftand before God night and day, and requireth and iudgeth euen by the iuftice of God to haue all damned in hell for euer. Herein then ftood his power againft all: and as vnder a certaine right herein he fighteth: and the Lord God cannot deny iuftice and right, becaufe he cannot deny himfelfe. How is the dragon then caft foorth from this? Thus he is caft foorth, the Lord Iefus is borne, euen Michael the moft mightie prince. He taketh all the finnes and guiltines of his people vpon him, euen to beare them in his bodie vpon the tree. He fuffereth all the wrath and torments due for the fame, fo that with his owne bloud he wafheth the whole Church, and maketh her cleane from all fpot. Then fhe being thus iuftified and clothed in Chrift with perfect holines and puritie; the deuill can accufe her no longer, nor lay any thing iuftly to her charge. All his right and power agaynft the elect is taken away: and fo his place is found no more in heauen. This is it which S. Paul glorieth of, Rom. 8. Who fhal lay any thing to the charge of Gods chofen? It is God that iuftifieth (fayth he) who is he that condemneth? it is Chrift which dyed, yea rather which is raifed againe, which is alfo at the right hand of God, and maketh interceffion for vs. Who then fhall feparate vs, from the loue of Chrift? Behold then, beloued, the dragon caft foorth, becaufe he can no more lay any guiltines of finne to our charge. Behold our faluation ratified in the death and refurrection of chrift. Behold the kingdome and might of God, and of his Chrift herein, and let vs afcribe all glorie, and praife, and honour, onely to him which indeed hath wafhed vs from the guiltines of our finnes, and made vs fo perfectly pure, that the deuill can lay nothing to our charge. This is the firft part of the triumphant fong, proclaming the glorie and praife of the chiefe conquerors. Now to the fecond.

I noted before that in fongs of victorie, not onely the chiefe doers had their praife, but alfo all that dealt valiantly: as in the fong of Debora next after God, her selfe, Baruck, Iael, and others: So here after the praise to God and his Christ for ouercomming the dragon, the Church also, euen all the faithfull, haue their praise and commendation, for their valiantnes in conquering the deuill and his armie. These be the words, And they ouercame him by the bloud of the Lambe, and by the word of their testimonie, and they loued not their liues euen to the death. Then here is a praise of the elect, that they vanquish the dragon, here is their valiant strength which they tread him downe withall in battaile celebrated: but not to take any thing from the praise and glorie of Christ. For they doe not ouercome by any might of their owne, but by the bloud of the Lambe, and by the word of their testimonie, &c. Christ then is hee that hath ouercome, and euery one that hath the true faith, in him and by him dooth get the victorie. Saint Paul, when he setteth foorth the spirituall battaile, willeth vs to be strong in the Lord, and in the power of his might, and to put on the whole armour of God, Ephe.6. Euen so may we learne in this place, how euery true Christian soule is armed to fight, and to get the victorie ouer the deuill. It is euen thus, to haue the true and and liuely faith in the death of Christ, and so by his bloud to be purged from all sinne: and to imbrace the most pure and holy word of Christ, and openly to professe it, and not onely in the time of peace, but euen when they be so persecuted for it, that it cost them their liues. For then are they sayd not to loue their liues euen vnto the death, when they chuse rather to suffer all the cruell tortures and torments, which the deuill and the tyrants can deuise, then to deny the trueth and name of Iesus Christ. It is called the word of their testimonie, not that it is the word of man, but because they doe witnes the same: For it pleaseth our God to giue this honour to his people, as to bee witnesses to his most sacred trueth. And our Sauiour saith, that he which doth not forsake father and mother, wife, children, and his life, for his sake, he is not worthie of him. And one thing is here to be obserued, that euen in death and martyrdome, euen in all reproaches and torments which tyrants and persecutors lay vpon the holy seruants of God, they ouercome the dragon. Will he then gladly escape from the iawes of this dragon, that he swallow you not vp with him into hell? Set all your trust in the bloud of the Lambe of God, Iesus Christ, for the remission and free pardon of all your sinnes. For being through a liuely faith iustified in him, the dragon hath nothing to lay to your charge wherein hee may iustly accuse ye before God. Take the sharpe sword of the spirit, euen the pure word of God, and fight against him with the same, for it shall cut and wound him deeply. Stand in the profession of this trueth, and be not ashamed to beare witnesse vnto it before men: and if it shall cost thee thy life, and that thy bloud shall be shead for it, faint not: thou art one of those which get the victory in the great battaile, euen ouer the dragon, and ouer his Angels. For let not this depart out of thy minde, they ouercame him by the bloud of the Lambe, and by the word of their testimonie, and they loued not their liues, euen to the death.

The next part of this heauenly song of victorie, sayth, Therefore reioyce ye heauens, and ye that dwell therein. That God and his sonne Iesus Christ doe raigne, that the deuill and his Angels are cast foorth, that the chosen haue the victorie ouer

THE REVELATION.

uer him through the bloud of the Lambe, and that the saluation of the Church can neuer be shaken, are so happy things, that it behoueth the very heauens to reioyce, and all the Angels of God, yea and all the redeemed which haue their inheritance in the heauens. The heauenly spirits doe ioy wholly in the glorie of God, euen that his sonne doth raigne. The heauens and the earth in their kinde are glad also and reioyce: and how much greater cause haue we to reioyce then? which are not onely deliuered out of the hands of our enemies, euen out of the power of the deuill and of death, and set free from eternall damnation: but also lifted vp into heauenly dignitie, euen into the fellowship of Angels, made heires of glorie, and the sons and daughters of the blessed God. They which haue faith cannot but bee filled with ioy, euen with spirituall ioy, and despise all the vaine and transitorie pleasures of the flesh. They sell all that they haue to buy this pearle, and this treasure, which is like treasure that is hid in the field, Matth. 13. If wee doe not reioyce, it is an argument that wee haue not felt the power of the deuill conquered in our hearts. And hauing thus moued the heauens, and them that dwell therein to reioyce for this great victory, then he commeth to the last part, in which there is woe denounced to the reprobate, whom he calleth the inhabitants of the earth and of the sea, they haue no part nor inheritance in the heauens. And the cause is rendred of their woe, which is vttered thus, for the deuill is come downe to you, &c. The Church (as I noted before) with all her true children be citizens of the heauenly citie, and but strangers and pilgrimes vpon the earth. The wicked which haue none other portion but in this life, euen the worldlings, they be called the inhabitants of the earth and of the sea. Well, the deuill is cast out of heauen, that is, he cannot impugne the saluation of the elect for to hazard the same: but all his power that way is bent and lighteth vpon the Infidels, I meane he conquereth and subdueth them, raigneth ouer them as king, and draweth them into hell. But the speech may seeme strange, that here is woe denounced to these inhabitants of the earth and of the sea, as it were from the victorie which Christ hath gotten ouer the deuill. Was not the deuill downe here below among them before? Were they not also vnder the woe and curse of God vnto eternall damnation, though Christ had neuer ouercome the deuill? For answer to this, we must confesse that all men are by nature, as the holy Apostle speaketh, the children of wrath. And so if Christ had not conquered Satan, all, not onely the reprobate, but also those which shall bee saued, should haue been vnder the woe. Also Satan before Christ fought this battaile, was among the inhabitants of the earth: but now being by our prince ouercome, hee commeth downe more heauie and in more tyrannous sort vpon them, and so their woe is as it were doubled. The victorie of Christ is turned to their deeper condemnation. How is that will some man say? Thus, Sathan being out of all hope euer to pull downe the saluation of the Church, that is, being cast out of heauen, hee will now wrecke his ire vpon the inhabitants of the earth: his power ouer them is not destroyed, and hee will now exercise it to the full, and leade them deeper into all horrible sinne and condemnation. The holie Ghost sayth hee hath great wrath, knowing hee hath but a short time. The

Church

Church he may a litle afflict and vexe in this world, but hee cannot hurt: and therefore he will, as we vse to say, haue his penniworth vpon those which be still in his hand: he maketh them his vassals to fight for his kingdome against Christ, and against his Church: he hardeneth their hearts and blindeth their eyes, leadeth them into the loue of darknes, and hatred of the light. Thus, I say, is their woe, through the wrath and tyrannous rage of the dragon, which is more heauilie come downe vpon them, greatly increased. And so wee see, that the faithfull haue all ioy by this victorie, and the reprobate through their owne corruption haue their woe increased. Satan doth now ride vpon them. And though the time from the passion of Christ to the day of iudgement may seeme vnto men to bee long, yet the deuill knoweth it is but a short time. Thus much touching this song of victorie.

THE XXVI. SERMON.
CHAP. XII.

13 *And when the dragon saw that hee was cast vnto the earth, hee persecuted the woman which had brought foorth the manchild.*

14 *But to the woman were giuen two wings of a great Eagle, that shee might flie into the wildernes, into her place where she is nourished for a time, times, and halfe a time, from the presence of the serpent.*

15 *And the serpent cast out of his mouth water as it were a flood, after the woman, that he might cause her to be carried away of the flood.*

16 *But the earth holpe the woman, and the earth opened her mouth, and swallowed vp the flood which the dragon cast foorth of his mouth.*

17 *Then the dragon was wroth with the woman: and went and made warre with the remnant of her seede, which keepe the commaundements of God, and haue the testimonie of Iesus Christ.*

18 *And I stood vpon the sea sand.*

E had the last time (in that which goeth next before in this chapter) the battaile betwixt our great prince Michael, and the dragon. The dragon (as we saw) tooke the foyle, was ouercome, and cast downe from heauen to the earth. Also we heard the heauenly and most ioyfull song of victorie. And now S. Iohn sheweth that the dragon for all this doeth not giue ouer, but still pursueth the woman, and her seede: wee must still looke for trouble at his hands. When the dragon saw (sayth S. Iohn) that

he

he was caſt into the earth, hee perſecuted the woman, which had brought forth the manchilde: hee being then ouercome of the head, ſetteth vpon the bodie. Yea, knowing further that the ſaluation of the bodie is moſt finally ratified, ſo that the bleſſed eſtate of the woman cannot bee ſhaken in the heauens, he now endeuoureth to roote her out of the earth. For his perſecuting of the woman, ſheweth that his purpoſe is if he can vtterly and wholly to deſtroy with cruell death all and euery one which ſhould be found to profeſſe the name of Chriſt. He ſought by ſtirring vp the high prieſts, the Phariſees, and other cruell tyrants, to roote out the name and memorie of chriſtianitie. And conſidering how few they were in compariſon, which imbraced the doctrine of the Goſpell at that time, while all the Apoſtles remained in Ieruſalem: and wayiṅg on the other ſide the great multitude, the mightie power and cruell rage of the aduerſaries, which were ſtirred vp and inflamed by the dragon, it is a very great miracle that the whole companie, being almoſt all in one citie, were not of a ſudden ſet vppon and cruelly murdered. The dragon purpoſeth euen to ſpread his net ouer thē al at once, and not to let any one eſcape. He hath for to effect this his purpoſe ſeruants & miniſters euen in great nūber, armed with power, and burning with furious rage, and which indeede, beginning with Steuen, ſet vpon the reſt. Why are not all deſtroyed? why doe they not with the like furie runne vpon all, that they did vpon Steuen? The Lord doth euen miraculouſly preſerue and protect his Apoſtles and other which abode in Ieruſalem: and many eſcape by flight into other places, as ye may ſee if ye reade. Act. 8. This flight and this diſpertion, is ſo ſpeedie and ſo without let and danger, that he ſayth here, that to the woman were giuen two wings of a great Eagle, that ſhee might flye into the wildernes. Theſe be the wings of Gods prouidence and mightie protection, opening and preparing the paſſage, and the place where his Church ſhould now reſt and be harboured and fedde in the wilderneſſe, euen among the Gentiles. The time of her abode in the wilderneſſe was before numbred by daies, as a thouſand, two hundred and threeſcore daies, and here he ſayth, a time, times, and halfe a time. Touching this time we haue ſpoken before how myſtically it is to be taken, and not as the Papiſts, which apply it vnto three yeares and an halfe, as yeares are taken in common vſe, and ſo would proue that Antichriſt ſhall raigne but ſo long. Our Sauiour did in his owne perſon preach three yeres and an halfe, and therefore ſome doe interprete that that time is vſed here to ſignifie the whole time that the Church ſhall be fedde in the wilderneſſe of this world. And indeede we ſaw in the former chapter that the two Prophets doe propheſie euen ſo long. So long alſo he ſayth there, the holy citie ſhall be troden vnder foote of the Gentiles. Then all the time that the Church ſhall be perſecuted & vexed in this world, ſo long yet ſhe ſhail be ſedde. But how is it ſayd that ſhe might flye into the wilderneſſe from the preſence of the ſerpent? It is not the deuill in all places of the world? where ſhould any one get from his preſence? The Gentiles did worſhip deuils (as S. Paul teſtifieth, ſaying, The gods of Gentiles are deuils, 1. Cor. 10.) and the diuels had their kingdome ouer the nations of the world. Alas then, ſhe flyeth from the preſence of the deuill: but is it not ſtill into the preſence of the deuill?

uell? There be diuels plentie before she come, aed wheresoeuer she come, or any other children, they be euen compassed about with armies of deuils: and if they had not been there before, is the dragon such a lumpe that hee cannot make haste and speede to ouertake her? Can the Church here in earth flye swifter then the diuels? For answere to these things, we must note, that the flight of the Church from the presence of the serpent, is not meant that shee did or could flye from the presence of the diuels, for they alwayes compasse the faithfull, if we take his presence absolutely: but after a sort she flyeth his presence, when the power of the tyrants and persecutors which hee raiseth vp cannot reach vnto the Church or ouertake her, to murther and kill her. Thus it is then, the deuils touching themselues could be with the Church wheresoeuer she became in the world, and how swiftly soeuer she fled: but they could not carrie the power of the murthering persecutors, and that is here called the presence of the serpent. Then marke those which fledde from Ierusalem, could not flye from Satans temptations, wheresoeuer they became: but he could not reach them with the power of the high Priests and princes of the Iewes, that presence of his she fled from. Indeede he attempted to pursue her that way, if he could haue brought it about, and Saul had letters and authoritie from the high priests vnto Damascus, Act.9. but he could doe little. For now Samaria receiued the Gospell, shortly after Antioch a great citie of the Gentiles had a most famous Church planted in it, and they were the first that were called Christians, as we reade, Act.11.vers.26. Then Paul and Barnabas were sent forth among the Gentiles, and the other Apostles also went foorth, and great Churches were planted in all kingdomes almost in the world. Now what hope could the dragon haue to roote out the woman from the earth? which way can hee now turne him? Is he yet in hope to roote out from the earth the whole Church? will he yet endeuour such a thing? That he doth: he is so monstrous great, he hath so often preuailed, and hath so many wayes, he is so bold that he yet attempteth vtterly to rid the earth of her.

And marke what S. Iohn sayth: And the serpent cast out of his mouth water, as it were a flood, after the woman, that he might cause her to be carried away of the flood. This is a strange thing, and wonderfull to bee considered, that the dragon, when the woman was fled from his presence, into the large and wide wildernes, cast out of his mouth such abundance of water, as to make a swift and mightie flood that should drowne the woman, and vtterly sweepe her off from the face of the earth. It was sayd before, that his taile drew the third part of the starres of heauen, and cast them to the earth, which sheweth the huge greatnes of the monster: and this casting foorth a flood out of his mouth sheweth no lesse: a flood to ouerflowe and runne through the great wildernesse, and so to ouerwhelme and drowne her wheresoeuer she were. This greatnes of the power of Satans kingdome causeth him to be so bold, as still to maintaine warre agaynst the kingdome and power of almightie God. Do not thinke (beloued) that the deuils are weake in power or in practise agaynst the Church: but when ye reade such things as this, consider what a most glorious power of God it is which doth vanquish him, and

plucke

plucke the poore woman out of his iawes. For indeede, though the power of the deuill in the kingdomes of this world which be exceeding great, he is a mighty terrible prince, and can commaund great things, yet compared to our great prince Michael, the Lord Iesus, hee is nothing. For our Lorde, vnder whose banner wee fight, is the king of kings, and the Lord of hoastes, whose power is infinite, and lasteth for euer and euer. But what should this same floud be which commeth out of the deuils mouth? Do ye not suppose, that the waters which come forth of his bellie, bee as sweete and holesome as the fountaine it selfe out of which they flowe? Sweete things no doubt these waters are, euen as sweete as the deuill himselfe. But what are they that he would drowne the woman withall? Euen a floud of all foule heresies, of lyes, of reproches, and slaunders, and such like. For hee raised vp heretikes, euen monsters, which drew many counterfeite Christians into perdition, and although (as Satan did know) hee could not destroy the faith and the saluation of the elect; yet by this meanes he could bring them all into extreme danger of their liues, for the heresies were such as the very Pagans might loath to heare of. And then those heresies comming out of his mouth as a part of those waters, yet he perswaded that the Gospell bred them. Men cryed out that there were no such things before that doctrine came, & that they did by and by spring vp with it. The gospell being thus charged and made odious as a most foule doctrine, and such as bred monstrous opinions, all that did professe it were extremely hated, euen as men not worthy to be suffered to liue vpon the earth. Thus were the mindes of bloudie tyrants stirred vp, and persecutions grew hot and bitter. Then were the poore christians euen compelled to meete in the nights in caues, and in secret places, & there to haue the holy excercises of religion. Vpon this Satan tooke occasion to accuse them of most horrible filthines: as if they should eate their children, and that men and women meeting together, out were the lights put, & filthines committed, euen adulteries and incests, fathers with their daughters, the brethren with their sisters, and such like.

Then further the heate of persecution being terrible, and sundry reuolting, the persecutors hired and procured some of them, to say indeed, that when they were at those meetings of the Christians, there were such filthie thinges committed, and that they themselues had there committed such thinges. This gaue strength and credit to the slanders, and what think ye was the rage and furie of the heathen? who would not think he did euen a good worke to destroy such? There is now nothing but killing and murdering vpon heapes. And yet the danger is further increased: for the wrath of the Lord being kindled for such wickednes committed against his sonne against his pure word and Church, hee powred forth horrible plagues vpon mightie swift streame: So that without the wonderfull power of God, prouiding for the woman euen miraculously, how can shee but bee caried away of the floud? how can she but be rooted out of the earth? Well, the blessed Lord doth indeede prouide for her: and deliuereth her from being swallowed vp of this great floud, of all these stinking waters which issued out of the dragons bellie. For as the Lord hath ratified the saluation of this woman in heauen, and set it so fast that the dragon cannot shake it, so also he preserueth her in the wildernes of this world, vntill such time as she hath brought forth all her children. The dragon doth cause thousands of her children indeed to be cruelly slaine in all places, but he cannot roote her out, nor make her barren, but she shall still continue in the world, bring foorth and nurse vp blessed children to God, euen to the day of the generall iudgement. Then the deuill doth tempt, the deuill doth persecute, but he cannot plucke downe the Church from heauen, from her saluation, nor yet destroy her with bodily death out of this world. These things are fixed and established by God, and it is impossible that they should be altered. But let vs see how the woman escaped drowning, for the floud pursueth her into the wildernes. The earth (sayth Saint Iohn) holpe the woman, and the earth opened her mouth, and swallowed vp the floud which the dragon cast out of his mouth. Here is a wonderfull deliuerance, beholde and consider.

Our Lord is the Lord of hoastes, and hath all creatures both the liuing and the dead at his commandement to helpe his Church. For as al things, when he willeth, stande vp and fight against the wicked, so also they fight for the defence of the Church when he commaundeth them. The earth is the Lords, and all that is therein: The earth acknowledgeth her Lord, and obeyeth his commaundement: the earth doth helpe the woman. Wonderfull is God in his prouidence: doth the earth helpe the woman? yea, which of his creatures shall not helpe his chosen, euen willingly when he wil haue it so? for though it be said that the earth holpe the woman, yet wee must looke vp higher, and knowe that it is the Lord which doth it. For the earth doth it but as the Lordes handmaid, and being thereunto by him appointed. Then the holy Ghost doth not vse this speech to draw our eyes from God, to seeke succour elsewhere: but indeed setteth forth his wonderful power and prouidence, which commaundeth and directeth all creatures to the seruice of his Church. But now it may be demaunded whether this be to be vnderstood of the very earth indeed, euen the ground that we tread vpon? Nay, ye know that in this booke things are to be taken mystically: and as hee compareth the heresies, the lies, reproches, and slaunders to a floud of waters cast foorth of the dragons mouth to carry away the woman: So he compareth the drinking & drying vp of the same, as if the earth should cleaue and swallow vp a floud of waters: for there is no way to restraine a great floud, but if the earth open and drinke it. This it is then, all the heresies, all the slaunders and lyes cast forth as a mightie floud to drowne the Church, haue by the good prouidence of God euen as it were suncke in the earth, and haue been swallowed vp. The Church remaineth in the world at this day after all those ancient crimes and slaunders cast forth against her, they being as it were suncke into

THE REVELATION. 241

the earth, and vanished. She is long since iustified and cleered from those foule faults which the subtill serpent caused her to be charged withall, and brought into hatred. Great multitudes, euen of the wicked haue been compelled to confesse her innocencie, and to praise her. The heresies of al the auncient heretikes are euen as it were drunke vp by the earth. Some indeed Satan raiseth vp in all places, as fit instruments to renue those former heresies, but cannot preuaile to rend & teare all in peeces, and to vexe and make hauock as of old. Indeed the errors of poperie did ouerspread almost all in time past, euen like a flood; but now, euen as if the earth had opened her mouth a great part are suncke, and euen the papists themselues confesse that they were abuses: and the rest of their matters can hardly retaine credit, no not among a few. For not only the true beleeuers, which in these last times are many, but also multitudes of meere worldlings doe see the vanitie of poperie, and doe despise it. And in this high prouidence of God, euen the earth, that is, the state of wordly things, and worldly men, haue ministred some helpe. For when any mightie cruell tyrant, beleeuing the filthie lyes and slaunders raised against the faithfull, purposeth to roote them al out, and ioyneth with other of the same mind: one thing or other riseth vp euen of and about the earthly state, and holdeth them occupied and busied, so that they cannot performe their desire against the church. Great kings and princes in these latter daies haue sworne each to other in a cursed league, which yet they call the holy league, that they wil ioyne all together, & euen destroy from the earth all that professe the holy Gospell, whom they indeed iudge to be wicked heretikes. Why haue they not preuailed? the earth hath opened her mouth, the worldlie state hath been such that they neuer could: but one way or other haue had their hands full. The floods of lyes, of reproches, and slaunders cast forth by those that worship the beast, against the faithfull and holy seruants of the Lord, and with which the eares of princes haue been filled, and their mindes enflamed to wrath and crueltie, and euen by this meanes suncke. Indeede there haue been horrible slaughters committed, and many slaine in France and other countries, but the dragon is farre from drowning the woman with his stinking flood. If ye consider what a few the true professors of the Gospell be, and what wonderfull power there is in the world in the hands of them that hate them deadly, and wish them rooted out: ye shall be constrained to confesse that it is euen a great miracle, as if the earth did open her mouth, and drink vp the floods of the dragons lies, that the state of kingdomes and earthly things is such, that they cannot according to their desire ioyne together to destroy the woman. And euen as the Gospell was through the subtilty of the serpent, charged in old time to breed al those monstrous heresies which sprung vp: so also at this day the enemies cry out, that our doctrine doth bring forth all the heresies that arise. The Anabaptists, the Libertines, those of the familie of loue, yea all such execrable monsters, are by the seruants of Antichrist, termed as it were the children of those which preach the Gospell. But the falshood of this appeareth, and euen the earth openeth her mouth and drinketh in the flood of their false accusations. Furthermore, it hath pleased God in all ages to vse the men of this world sundry waies to helpe his Church: who are euen as the

R earth,

earth, in respect of any heauenly thing. Thus we see how the woman doth escape the flood which the dragon casteth out of his mouth. The Church then cannot be rooted out from the face of the earth. Let this comfort and stay vs when the rage is greatest against the seruants of Christ. Ye shall at sometime see such tempests raised by Satan, as if heauen and earth should bee mingled together: Yee shall see such power bent against the Gospel, and so great terror, as if al should down. Nothing but slaughters, and terrible threatnings: yea so terrible as if fire came out of their mouthes euen to deuoure all. Be not then dismaid, nor do not faint: the Gospell cannot be beate downe, the cause of God cannot be ouerthrowne, neither can Satan euer bring to passe by all his sleights and cruell practises, but that there shal euer some stand vp boldly to professe, to teach, and to maintaine the same.

Now it followeth: *Then the dragon was wrath with the woman, and went and made war with the renant of her seed, &c.* What, was he not wrath with her before? Yes, but this is to teach vs, that the heat & fury of his wrath still increased. But what is the reason that his wrath thus increaseth? Because his interprises faile, and that he can by no meanes haue his purpose to destroy the woman, therefore he is more & more enflamed in wrath against her. In this is set before vs a right diuelish wrath: for he hath no cause to bee so moued against the woman, but that he cannot hurt nor destroy her. What hath she done to him? hee sought to cast her downe from eternall blessednes, and tooke the foyle, and himselfe was cast to the earth and all his. He laboured then to roote her out from the face of the earth, and all the waies which he deuiseth faile of bringing his desire to passe: and now he is more & more wrath, that he can no way destroy her. Is not this a mad kind of wrath? as this is in the diuell, so shall ye see it euident in many men whom he doth worke in. If they be once inflamed with burning malice against any man, it carrieth them with a desire to do them all the mischiefe which they can. It is euen meate and drinke to them when they can hurt.

Now if they practise and deuise many wayes and meanes, and see nothing will preuaile, they cannot hurt those whom they so bitterly hate; that is a wonderfull sting, it grieueth them and tormenteth them sore, and euen kindleth in them a greater fire of wrath and displeasure, and the heate of their furie burneth hotter within them. For as it is some kind of quenching or slaking the heate and fire of their malice, when they can execute their desire vpon those whom they so deadlie hate, so the missing of their purpose, kindleth the same. Let men take heede, for it is a most cursed thing to be like, & to resemble the wicked diuels. Such as abound in malice are like the diuell, and resemble him exceedingly: If Satans wrath bee kindled, then he will not yet giue ouer. Giue ouer? No, hee will neuer giue ouer vntill he be quite cast down. For he could not preuaile against Christ but was cast down, yet he set vpon the church. When he saw one way succeeded not, he sought another: when he could not destroy her out of the heauens, he attempted to roote her wholly out of the earth. When he findeth that he cannot doe that, his wrath is still kindled more and more, and he will doe what he can to afflict her. Here is the thing, he cannot doe what he will: therefore hee will doe what hee can. His fierie

cruell

THE REVELATION.

cruell hatred and malice will not suffer him to rest. He will still be deuising what harmes and mischiefes he can: and therefore it is sayd, *he was wrath with the woman, and went and made warre with the remnant of her seede, &c.* He is then come downe thus low that he can proceed no further, but to make warre with the true children of the Church, and that remaineth to all the faithfull, and shall remaine euen to the end of the world. There is no pacifying of this enemie, there is no truce to be made or had with him for so much as one minute of an houre: but it behooueth vs to be alwaies armed, and alwaies to stand readie to repell his assaults. Behold here also euen as it were the image of the diuel in many men (for as the regenerate doe beare the image of God their father who hath begotten the in the new and spirituall birth, so the wicked doe beare the image of their father the diuell) which being ouercome with malice that raigneth in them, can neuer cease nor giue ouer, seeking and deuising how to hurt those whom they hate, although they take neuer so many foyles. If they cannot wrecke their anger to the full, they will also assay to doe what they can. If they bee foyled and foyled againe, yea euen shamed, and can see no hope to doe halfe so much harme, nor the hundreth part which they wish: yet they will not giue ouer, but if they can hurt but in a small trifle it shall come. Here is the very image of the diuell, where ye see this. Ye will say, it is a great thing which Satan is here sayd to doe, that hee warreth against the faithfull. He doth wonderfully vexe and torment the true Christians here in the world. It is very true, this is a great thing considered in it selfe: but compared with the other two, the one, that he sought to ouerthrow the saluation of the church: the other, that he sought to destroy her at once out of the earth, that she might neuer bring forth any moe children to God, it is but a small thing. And so I say, note it in men which burne in malice and wrath, & they can neuer giue ouer, their diuelish mind can neuer rest, though it bee but in small trifles, yet will it shew it selfe. The reason is euident, Satan the fierie red dragon cannot rest, and hee possesseth their mind, therefore they cannot rest, for he thrusteth them forward, and wil in no wise let them rest.

If they haue lied, if they haue slandered, if they haue done iniuries other wayes, and be conuinced, rebuked, & for the time euen suffer shame, yet they must on againe, he euen thrusteth them vpon their noses. O wofull and lamentable estate of slauerie and bondage, which the seruants of Satan are held in, when the fierce dragon filleth them full of his fierie malice, & will haue them as restles as himselfe, euen till he bring them together with himself vnto endles miserie. Resist him therefore, beloued, giue not place vnto him by anger, and wicked enuie: for if he once get hold in them, that is, to fill the heart with malice, he can hardly be cast foorth. But let vs returne now againe vnto that former point of Satans making warre. He maketh warre with the remnant of her seed. Here is that which we are to look for, euen continuall warre with the dragon, and with all the power which he can make: we haue him our cruell & fierce enemie. Al the true children of the church must make full account of this so long as they liue, and stand prepared. For although

though he finde it (as I said) beyond his reach to roote out the mother, yet he will not ceafe to torment as many of her children as he can, that he may terrifie others from imbracing the holy faith. We are put in mind of this by Saint Paul, and willed to put on the whole armour of God, that wee may bee able to refift, Ephef. 6. Here is alfo to bee noted, that Saint Iohn maketh a fhort defcription of the right feede, or true children of the woman: for he faith, which keepe the commaundements of God, and haue the teftimonie of Iefus Chrift. It is but fhort, but it is a pithie defcription of the right feede, he noteth two things which both goe together in the found Chriftians.

They hold the doctrine and faith of Iefus Chrift in an open and bold profeffion, that is one: and walke in obedience to the law of God, that is the other. They profeffe the Gofpell, and will not denie it though it fhould coft them their liues. And they profeffe it not with a dead faith, but that liuely faith which worketh by loue: for he faith, they haue the teftimonie of Iefus, and they keepe the commandements of God. And this is one chiefe caufe why the dragon doth rage in wrath fo fore againft them, that they will not with the reft of the world obey and worfhip him: but cleaue to the Lord God in faith and obey his lawes. The children of this world alfo, the minifters of Satan cannot abide them, becaufe their workes bee good; and they loue the light, and they themfelues loue darkneffe more then light, becaufe their deedes bee euill, Iohn 3. verfe 19. Hereupon it followeth, that the dragon fhall alwaies haue them for to take his part, and moft readie to perfecute the true children of God, becaufe they cannot but hate, euen as hee hateth. Thus much touching the dragons making war with the remnant of the womans feede.

It followeth in the text, *And I ftood vpon the fea fand.* This fhort claufe maketh a paffage vnto that which followeth in the next chapter, touching the vifion and defcription of the beaft that rifeth out of the fea. But whether Saint Iohn faith of himfelfe, I ftood vpon the fea fand, or whether he faith that the dragon ftood vpon the fea fand, is the doubt: becaufe the Greeke may bee interpreted, either I ftood, or hee ftood. Some expound it, that Saint Iohn in a vifion ftood vpon the fea fand, that he might behold the rifing vp of the beaft. But I take it the more probable, that the dragon ftood vpon the fea fand, as it were working and framing out of the fea his chiefe inftrument the huge and terrible beaft, by whom he warreth againft the feruants of God. It is not much materiall whether way wee take it, and therefore I will not ftay vpon it, but will here make an end.

THE XXVII. SERMON.
CHAP. XIII.

1 *And I saw a beast rising out of the sea, hauing seuen heads, and ten hornes: and vpon his hornes ten crownes, and vpon his heads a name of blasphemie.*

2 *And the beast which I saw was like vnto a Leopard, and his feete were as the feete of a Beare, and his mouth as the mouth of a Lion, and the dragon gaue him his power, and his seate, and great authoritie.*

3 *And I saw one of his heads as it were wounded to death, and his deadly wound was healed, and all the world wondred after the beast.*

4 *And they worshipped the dragon which gaue power to the beast, and they worshipped the beast, saying, Who is like vnto the beast? who is able to warre with him?*

5 *And there was giuen vnto him a mouth speaking great things and blasphemies, and power was giuen vnto him to doe two and fortie moneths.*

6 *And he opened his mouth vnto blasphemie against God, to blaspheme his name, and his tabernacle, and those that dwell in heauen.*

7 *And it was giuen vnto him to make warre with the Saints, and to ouercome them: and power was giuen him ouer euery tribe, and tongue, and nation.*

8 *And all the inhabitants of the earth shall worship him, whose names are not written in the booke of life of the Lambe, which was killed from the beginning of the world.*

9 *If any man haue an eare, let him heare.*

10 *He that leadeth into captiuitie, shall goe into captiuitie: he that killeth with the sword, shall be killed with the sword. Here is the patience, and the faith of Saints.*

And I saw a beast, &c. In the former chapter, wee haue had the description of the womans greatest enemie, namely, the great red dragon. In this chapter are painted out the next greatest enemies which she hath, euen the chiefe instruments which the diuell vseth to warre against her and her children here in this world. For the dragon, as it is sayd in the latter end of the former chapter, doth make warre agaynst those which keepe the commandements of God, and which haue the testimonie of Iesus Christ: and he doth worke and make this warre by instruments, and now S. Iohn hath them shewed vnto him in vision, and doth accordingly describe them. First he sayth, *I saw a beast rising out of the sea.* Her enemies are beasts, we shall see nothing but beastly qualities. Wee finde in the holie Scriptures, that by beasts are figured certaine great kingdomes or Monarchies. As for your better instruction, reade the seuenth chapter of Daniel, and yee shall see that the Angell doth so expound it, touching the foure beasts which Daniel sawe in vision. Then we are out of doubt that this beast representeth a great Monarchie, power or dominion, which the diuell vseth as his instruments to warre against the Saints. In deede we must note by the way, that the holy Ghost doth not represent the ciuill power of the kings by sauage beasts, for the ciuill power is of God: but he figureth out the pride, the ambition, the crueltie, the rauening, and the sauage qualities of those mightie kings, which erected and vpheld those great Monarchies. We see then what is meant by the beast: but how is he sayd to rise out of the sea? doth a Monarchie arise out of the sea? As the beast is not to be taken literally, no more is the sea to bee vnderstoode of the very sea indeede, where the fishes doe swimme, and where the shippes doe saile: but it must bee interpreted in a mysticall sence. And that is thus, the tempestuous and troublesome estate of the nations of the world, is called a sea. And from the boyling and broyling estate of the nations, did this beast arise. For the Romane Empire (which is figured by this monstrous beast) did spring and grow vp from the contentions and discords, and diuisions among the kingdoms, which are as a raging sea. For while they through ambition and vaine glorie vexe and weaken one another, commeth a stronger and subdueth them all. Thus the beast ariseth out of the sea: this yee see is verie plaine.

Then he sayth, that he had seuen heads, and tenne hornes, and vpon his hornes tenne crownes. The dragon in the former chapter had seuen heads and tenne hornes: and this beast his child is very like him, yea as like as a child may be to the father. Here is a difference, that the dragon hath his crownes vpon his heads, and not vpon his hornes, and this beast his child, hath his crownes vpon his hornes, and not vpon his heads. What is the reason of this? I will tell ye how I take it. The dragon hath great power, which is signified by his hornes: but he hath preuailed most by his craft and subtilties, which are signified by his heads, and by them hath gotten greatest victories, and therefore they are crowned. This beast hauing very much of the subtiltie of his father, hath yet preuailed most by force and power, euen by the power of kings, which his hornes besides strength doe represent, and therefore these hornes are crowned. That there is the name of blasphemie vpon his heads, it fitly expresseth the qualitie of the father, who is euen the fountaine of all blasphemies against the most high God, and against all goodnesse. Wee may also perceiue by this what the seruants of God are to looke for at the hands of this beast. That which is blasphemous against the God of glorie, how will it spare me? all crueltie is here to be looked for.

Then next this beast is described as a compound of diuers beasts: and so indeed a very monster of monsters. For his body is like to a Leopard, which some call the

cat

THE REVELATION.

cat of the mountaine, a beaft (as they fay) very fierce, fwift and fubtill. His feete are like to the feete of a Beare: and we know a Beare, and how vgly, and rauening he is. His mouth is like the mouth of a Lion. The Lion is the moft ftately proud beaft that liueth. Well then we fee that this beaft, this Romane Empire (as wee fhall fee it plainly proued to be the dominion of Rome, when we come to the 17. chapter, by the expofition of the Angell) hath the properties of thofe three beafts. There is craft, there is rauening, there is pride, and many other fauage and beaftly lufts. What fhall the Church looke for at the hands of this beaft, but that which commeth from Leopards, Beares, and Lions? And now leaft wee might thinke that this monfter fhould not bee able to doe much harme, it is added, that the dragon gaue him his power, his throne, and great authoritie. The dragon is the great mightie prince of darknes, the god of this world, he is worfhipped and obeyed, he is of great power and might in all maner of vngodlines, it is therefore a very high throne, it is great dignitie and power among the inhabitants of the world, which he giueth vnto him. This mightie prince then the dragon fetteth him that is the beaft aloft in might and glorie and dominion, that he may execute his will in oppugning the trueth, and murdering the Saints. But it may be demaunded: Doth the dragon refigne ouer all vnto him? doth he goe out of his throne, and let him haue all his doings, and all the glorie and the worfhip? Nay, it is not meant fo: for Satan holdeth his throne, he is ftill the god of the world, the prince of darknes, and worketh mightily in the children of difobedience, and is worfhipped ftill together with the beaft: For Saint Iohn fayth in that which followeth, they worfhipped the beaft, and they worfhipped the dragon which gaue power to the beaft. Then the dragon doth not forgoe any honour in giuing his throne and power to the beaft, but vfeth the beaft as his chiefe inftrument, by whom hee worketh, to get glorie to himfelfe: for the throne of the beaft and his throne doe become all one, fo that by the beaft hee fetteth vp all his abominations: they worke together, and are worfhipped together, in as much as the beaft maintaineth idolatrie, and worfhip of diuels. But here will arife another doubt: for S. Paul fpeaking of the powers, fayth, that they bee of God, and willed that men fhould obey the Romane Emperors, when they were heathen: how then is it fayd, that the diuell fet vp this beaft, euen the Romane Empire? This is eafie to bee anfwered. The Lord God difpofeth the kingdomes of this world to whom it pleafeth him. The ciuill power alfo is ordained of God, and is good, and to bee obeyed euen for confcience fake. But now as the men come vp to it by craft, by fraud, by oppreffion, by crueltie and rauening, and as they rule with tyrannie and all wicked lufts, whereby they impugne the trueth, they are fayd to bee fet vp by the diuell, and to worke by the diuell: for all thofe things are of the diuell, and the Empire is called a beaft, not in refpect of the ciuill power, but for thofe beaftly qualities, which are of the diuell.

Then it followeth, that S. Iohn fayth, he faw one of his heads, as it were wounded to death. Here is fome difficultie to finde the perfect fence of this: becaufe it is not faid which of the feuen heads was wounded, nor yet when it was wounded.

The Angell in chapter 17. sayth, that the seuen heads are seuen hils, & seuen kings. He saith that fiue of those kings were fallen, one of them was standing at that time when this reuelation was giuen, and one was to come. Wee must take this according as the like is to be taken in Daniel, chapt. 7. where the Angell sayth, the foure beasts are foure kings. Hee meaneth not by foure kings no more but foure men which were kings: but by euery one a succession of kings. As by the Lion was signified the king of the Chaldeans, that is, all the kings which succeeded each other in that Empire. So must we take it for these heads, when he sayth seuen kings, not for seuen men which were kings, whereof fiue were fallen, one was, and one was to come: but indeede, for seuen seuerall gouernments which had kingly power, in euery one of which many succeeded each other. And of these seuen, the Empire stood at that time, for Rome was gouerned then by Emperors, which was the sixt head, and the Papacie the seuenth head, which was not then come. Now it is most probable that this wound was made either in the sixt head, that is, in the Empire, or els in the seuenth, which is the Papacie. For such a deadly wound is not read of in any of the former fiue that were past. Wee reade of some wound giuen to the Papacie before it was risen vp to the full, as in the dayes of *Wickliffe* and *Husse*: but the wound was not so deadly. I take it therefore cleere that the wound was in the Empire, that is in the sixt head. Now when this deadly wound was, is to be inquired. Here some say at one time, and some at another. To let all other passe, no doubt the most deadly wound was made by an Emperour, euen by Constantine the great, somewhat more then three hundreth yeeres after the birth of Christ. It may bee sayd, that the Empire did flourish in his dayes, how then can it be taken that the deadly wound was made by him in the sixt head of the beast, which was the Empire? To answere this, we must remember that which I said before, namely, that the ciuill power which is of God, is not figured by beasts, nor by the heads of the beast; but the beastly qualities of those which rule. So then Constantine was Emperor, but, whereas all the Emperors of Rome before him were heathen, and maintained the worship of diuels, and oppressed the Church, murdering many thousand of Christians, (such an instrument was the sixt head of the beast for the dragon) he the same Constantine became a Christian, and greatly aduaunced the Church: was not here euen a deadly wound giuen to this head of the beast? The whole power of the Empire was by the wicked Emperours turned against the Church, euen to roote her out and to destroy her children, and now quite contrarie the same power is by this Christian Emperor applied altogether for her honor and defence. Where is now the dragons beast which he set vp to warre against the woman? hee lyeth now for a time wounded euen as it were vnto death. This in deede was but for a time, because this deadly wound was healed vp againe by wicked Emperours that succeeded, and by the Popes, for it came to passe that the whole power of the Empire, and of the Papacie ioyned together against the Church, and became as beastly in setting vp Idolatrie, and murdering the Saints, as euer were the heathen Emperours. The wound is healed. Hereupon it followeth, that the world wondred after the beast. The dominion and the power of this

beast

beast spreadeth it selfe againe farre, and is wondred at for the greatnes. Doubtles there be great kingdomes and nations of the world (as we know) which were neuer subiect to the Empire & Papacie of Rome: but the Scripture vseth this speech and sayth, all the world wondred, and worshipped the beast, when the greatest part or very many nations became subiect to this tyrannie. This is indeede to giue vs a note what a mightie enemie the woman (that is the Church) hath, besides the dragon. The world doth not onely wonder after the beast, but doe also ioyne themselues, as it is the manner of all ineere worldlings, where they see the greatest power, there to ioyne themselues, howsoeuer the power be wickedly and blasphemously abused against God and his trueth. And therefore it is said, that they worshipped the dragon that gaue power to the beast, and they worshipped the beast. They fall downe and worship Idols, and so indeede they worship diuels. They reiect the holy doctrine of God, and imbrace the decrees and doctrines of men, vpheld and maintained by the power of wicked Emperours and vngodly Popes. We must needes confesse that men worship them, whose decrees and whose religion they imbrace: therefore let it not seeme straunge, that he faith, they worshipped the beast. If we imbrace sincerely the lawes and ordinances of God, then we worship him. If wee receiue the doctrines of diuels, and the worship inuented by them, then wee worship diuels: who can deny this with any shew of reason? If we follow the decrees of Popes and Emperours, setting vp Idolatrie and superstition, then as we worship diuels, so we worship the beast, howsoeuer in our blind intents wee imagine that wee worship God. The dragon then and the beast are worshipped together, that is, the diuell and the Romane tyrannie. And S. Iohn addeth, that the world wondring, sayth, who is like to the beast? who is able to warre with the beast? The riches, the dignitie, the glorie, and the power of the beast are such, and so great, that there is none comparable in the whole world. For since the Papacie sprung vp, and the power of the Romane Empire ioyned with it, there hath beene none such, in the opinion of men, vnder heauen. For who knoweth not that the eyes of the world were so dazeled with the glorie of the Papacie, that they thought the power of the Popes was not onely aboue all the high things in this world, but also did reach euen into the highest heauens, and vnto the lowest hell? They tooke it that the Pope might carrie to heauen whom hee would, and whom he would he might cast downe to hell: then who could warre with the beast? Doe yee not see the reason of their wonderment, and of their speech?

It followeth, that *there was giuen vnto him a mouth speaking great things and blasphemies.* O most horrible wicked beast that must blaspheme the liuing God, his trueth and sanctuarie! But it may here first bee demaunded, who giueth him this wicked mouth to vtter great things and blasphemies? You will say, who but the diuell? as it is sayd before, that the dragon gaue vnto him his power, and his seate, and great authoritie. No doubt such horrible blasphemies come from the diuell: hee is euen as the welspring and fountaine of them all. But doubtles Saint Iohn telleth vs here, that GOD gaue to the beast this mouth

to

to speake great things, and blasphemies. It wilbe said, how can the most holy God bee sayd to giue such a mouth to speake blasphemies? I will shew you. Saint Paul speaking of the comming of Antichrist, sayth, that becaufe men receiued not the loue of the trueth that they might be saued, God would send them strong delusion to beleeue lyes, &c. 2. Thess. 2. How doth God send them strong delusion? Euen thus: when in his iust iudgement for the wicked contempt of the trueth, he giueth scope to Satan to set vp the great Antichrist, and by him to spread forth al his poyson. So in this place we are to look thus high as vnto God, who iustly for the wickednes of the world, letteth the diuell loose to set vp such a blasphemous mouth: and so after a sort the Lord God giueth him this mouth. But this beast hath seuen heads, and euery head doubtles hath his mouth: it may therefore be demaunded, of which of the heads is this mouth? I answere, that euery one of the seuen heads had a blasphemous mouth: for those fiue seuerall states of gouernment by which Rome had beene gouerned, which were fallen when Iohn receiued this prophecie, were bent against God and his truth, and did speake blasphemies. The sixt head, that is the persecuting Emperours, had an exceeding blasphemous mouth against God, and against his truth. But the seuenth head exceedeth them all, and therefore no doubt Saint Iohn speaketh chiefly of that seuenth head here. For who is able to set forth the greatnes of the things which the papacy hath boasted of, and the monstrous foulnes of their blasphemies, euen beyond all blasphemies of heathen tyrants? What power was it almost that belongeth vnto Christ which the pope did not challenge? and what is there in the office of Christ, which he hath not vttered his blasphemies against? Looke vpon the authoritie which he vsurpeth ouer the word of God: See what power he challengeth to remit sinnes: Consider how many mediatours hee setteth vp, and what he ascribeth to the merits of man: yea goe through all their worship, and ye shall finde almost nothing but horrible prophanations of Gods trueth, and foule blasphemies. A man might write large volumes of this thing.

It is added, That power was giuen him to doe, two and fortie moneths. This is also to be referred to the God of heauen, who ruleth ouer al, that in his righteous iudgement he giueth power vnto this huge beast to work his tyranny in the world to the destruction of infinite thousands, which wickedly despise the holy doctrine of God. They would not deny their corrupt and filthie lusts, euen the pleasures of sinne, they would not submit themselues to the glorious Scepter of grace, that the king of glorie might raigne in them vnto their eternal blessednes: and therfore this beastly tyrant hath power giuen him to raigne ouer them, and to exercise his spirituall tyrannie, euen to plunge them deepe into the bottomlesse gulfe of eternall miseries. For all the power which is giuen to this beast to doe, is in these two points, the one in afflicting and murthering the seruants of God, which turneth to their good: and the other in seducing the children of this world vnto damnation. The time that this beast shall raigne is expressed to bee two and fortie moneths. This is the same time which wee had in the eleuenth chapter, in a thousand two hundreth and threescore daies. It is three yeeres and an halfe: but we must not be

so.

so grosse as to take it literally, as the papists do for three yeeres and an halfe, as we reckon our common yeeres, but according to the tenor of this prophecie, we must take it mystically, seeing one head of this beast, that is, the heathen persecuting Emperours made hauocke of the Church with many cruel slaughters, about three hundred yeeres. Wee may not imagine that the time which this head raigned, is excluded, or not contained in these two and fortie moneths. The time that this beast shall haue power to doe in the world seemeth very long vnto vs, which take a thousand yeeres to be a long time: but with the eternall God, a thousand yeeres are but as yesterday, they bee almost as nothing: and to bring vs to see into the shortnes of the time that this beast shall raigne, compared with eternitie, he setteth it foorth by a few moneths. Because it ministreth great comfort to consider that the Church is in her pilgrimage and sorrowfull conflicts but for a time, and shall remaine in glorie for euer and euer. Let vs waite patiently, and the end of this tyrannie will come.

The next verse sayth, that hee opened his mouth vnto blasphemie against God, to blaspheme his name, his tabernacle, and them that dwell in heauen. This beast, this Romane dominion, exerciseth to the full all that power to doe euill which is permitted vnto him. For he openeth that wicked mouth which is giuen him vnto blasphemie, euen against the most high God, against his name, euen his holie and pure worship, against his tabernacle, that is his church, and against the Angels and spirits of iust men which are in the heauens. All these doth the beast blaspheme. Well, no man can denie, but that the heathē persecuting Emperors did blaspheme all these: for they denied God the father of our Lord Iesus Christ. But if we affirme that the papacie is one head of this beast, how can it be shewed that the said papacie blasphemeth the true God, his worship, his Church, his Angels and Saints in heauen? I answere, that they blaspheme God many waies, and for example, what horrible blasphemie is it, that they take vpon them to picture the Godhead, which is inuisible and incomprehensible, yea that they picture the glorious trinitie, & wil resemble it by a man with three faces in one, which is a monster? And doth not the papacie horribly blaspheme the name & worship of God, when they condēne the holy & pure religion of God to be heresie? when they establish their owne decrees aboue the holy Scriptures of the Prophets and Apostles. They doe also blaspheme his tabernacle, when they accurse and condemne for heretikes all the true worshippers of God, euen al those which will worship him according to the prescript rules of his holy word. They blaspheme the Angels & Saints in heauen, whē sacriligiously ascribing vnto them diuine honor, as by praying vnto them and making them mediatours, they say that the Angels and Saints doe allow of the same. Also many other waies they blaspheme them, when they make thē to be patrones of their abominations. For like as he may bee said to blaspheme God, which sayth that God alloweth periuries, whoredomes, and cruell murthers: so may they bee sayd to blaspheme the Saints and Angels in heauen, which say that they allow of the highest sacriledge, of Idolatrie, of superstition and of many abominations.

Then next it is said, That it was giuen vnto him to make warre with the Saints, and

and to ouercome them: and that power was giuen him ouer euery tribe, & tongue, and nation. Here be two things set forth, the one is the terrible might and power which is granted vnto him to make warre withall against the true worshippers of God, and to ouercome them: the other expresseth the largenes of his dominion. Touching the former of these, it is certaine that he doth ouercome them but by an outward force and victorie in tormenting & killing their bodies, he cannot cause them to forsake the truth, that way they get the full victorie ouer him. A good meditation is here to be had, that the Saints of God are cruelly troden down, oppressed and murdered here in the world. For if we were not thus taught aforehand by the holy Ghost, we should think that God regarded not these, but fauoured those that haue such power to tread them downe. O it is the lot of the Saints, to be cruelly murdered by the beast, that is, by the Romane tyrãnie. How many thousands did the Emperors slay in the ten great persecutions? And what slaughters haue the popes and their adherents caused to be made? It is wonderfull to consider the victories which they euen as rauening wolues, haue had ouer the poore lambes of Christ: and not in some one countrie or nation, but in many great kingdomes, for power is giuen him ouer euery tribe, and tongue, and nation, (which is the other thing set forth in this verse) and looke how farre his dominion reacheth, so far his fierce and sauage crueltie against all that will not worship him, spreadeth it selfe. Hereby it hath come to passe that great heapes haue been slaine here in England, in Scotland, in France, in Germanie, in the low countries, and in other kingdomes farre distant from Rome, yet by the power and lawes of the Romane beast. What other Monarchie hath there been ouer the kingdomes of the world since Christ, but the Empire and papacie of Rome? There be indeed that haue large dominions, but nothing to that which is here spoken of. And if any will reply that Rome neuer had dominion ouer all the kinreds, and nations, and tongues of the earth; I answere, that the holy Ghost here as in other places, and names, Act. 2. nameth all nations, to signifie very many.

Now let the papists brag of their multitude, of their vniuersalitie, and consent, and that therefore they be catholike: Ye see here that the beast with seuen heads (one of which heads is the kingdome of Antichrist) hath power giuen him ouer euery tribe, and tongue, & nation. Doth the largenes of his dominiõ make it good? Hath he the truth on his side, becausehe can slay in all nations, those that will not worship him? How foolish are the papists in glorying of their multitudes, and that they haue alwaies preuailed ouer those which haue withstood them? seeing the kingdome of the beast is here described to be so large, and so mightie, and killing in all nations those that will not worship the beast.

Now as it hath been declared, that hee shall make warre against the Saints, and ouercome them, that is, by an outward victorie killing their bodies: so in the next words hee sheweth the victorie which he shall haue ouer the children of this world, by seducing them vnto eternall damnation. For it followeth, *And all the inhabitants of the earth shall worship him, whose names are not written in the booke of life of the Lambe which was killed from the beginning of the world.* Antichrist
then

THE REVELATION. 253

then preuaileth ouer the bodies of the faithful, & ouer the soules of the vnfaithful. In the one he murthereth the bodie, but cannot hurt the soule: in the other, he casteth both soule and bodie into hell. For what shal become of all those which worship the beast? do they not forsake God? And marke here, how when Saint Iohn hath set forth that the beast shall haue power ouer all nations, and shall make war with the Saints, and ouercome them; he addeth by and by, that all the inhabitants of the earth shall worship him: which is to note vnto vs, that looke vpon which side the outward power goeth, thither do all the worldlings turne themselues. And because the beast condemneth the true worshippers of God to bee heretikes, and cruelly putteth them to death: they can see no further, but gather by and by that God is with the beast, and so fall downe and worship him, receiuing all his ordinances, his lawes, his decrees, and his doctrines as oracles from God, not calling any thing that he doth into question. Such force there is, I say, in the outward power to perswade the blind world, which see but according to the flesh. We are to note further in this verse, when he saith, that al the inhabitants of the earth do worship the beast, that by & by he restraineth it to the reprobate, saying, whose names are not written in the booke of life of the Lambe, &c. Although the multitude be exceeding great that receiue the religion of the beast, yea so great that the holie Ghost termeth them all the inhabitants of the earth: yet some are excepted, some doe renounce him, and that is all the elect, whose names are written in the booke of life, he cannot seduce any one of them vnto damnation. This is a goodly comfort, that all his glorying of power, of multitude, of learning, or whatsoeuer, yea all his tyrannie against those which will not ascribe vnto him that which belongeth only to God, cannot deceiue nor terrifie any one, no not euen the least of the elect, but onely the vngodly which proudly despise the holy doctrine of the Lord. Speaking of the holy election in Christ, (which he calleth the book of life of the lambe), he addeth, that this lambe was killed from the beginning of the world. Christ was offered in sacrifice as the vnspotted lambe of God which taketh away the sinnes of the world: And although he was manifested in the flesh in the later end of the world, and not slaine before, yet because the holy Patriarches, euen from Adam were saued by his blood: it is said, he was killed from the beginning of the world. His death is also as effectuall now, and shalbe vnto the worlds end, as it was when he did hang vpon the crosse. The redeemer by the Lambe shal be safe in the middest of all dangers:

It followeth now, *If any man haue an eare, let him heare.* This is to giue a note, that the things which are here vttered be mysticall: they are not to be vnderstood by the fleshly eare, but spiritually. If any man haue his eare opened by the holie Ghost, he may heare and vnderstand them: otherwise he cannot. For they whose eare God openeth, vnderstand the mysteries of the prophecie, and they are cleere vnto them: but to the rest, that is, to the worldlings they be sealed vp, the cannot heare nor vnderstand the, they shall worship the beast, ascribing vnto him diuine power and honor. After the descriptio of the beast, and calling vpon such to heare, as haue an eare, he commeth to denounce iudgement and vengeance against this

terrible

terrible monster. For shall his power defend and support him alwaies against the mightie reuenging hand of God? shall he neuer bee called to iudgement for his horrible blasphemies, and tyrannie? Yes verely, for here it is sayd, hee that leadeth into captiuitie, shall goe into captiuitie: he that killeth with the sword, shall bee killed with the sword. Here is the patience and the faith of the Saints. The Iudge of the whole world is iust, and wil recompence euery one according to his deeds. This bloodie Romane Empire both former and latter, which hath so tyrannouslie oppressed the Church with bondage, and drawne infinite thousands into euerlasting captiuitie, shall also it selfe bee cast downe, and the vpholders thereof shall become the bondslaues of hell world without end. They put to death with the sword the holy seruants of Christ: and the sword of Gods wrath shall kill them for euer. The Saints are with faith to beholde it, they are with patience to waite for it. For by faith wee are to behold cleerely, that the most righteous God will rescue and saue his afflicted seruants, and destroy their oppressors: and because in his holy wisedome he appoynteth the times and seasons, we must patiently waite for the same.

THE XXVIII. SERMON.
CHAP. XIII.

11 *And I beheld another beast ascending out of the earth, hauing two hornes like a Lambe, but he spake like the dragon.*

12 *And he did all that the first beast could do in his presence, and he causeth the earth and them that dwell therein, to worship the first beast, whose deadlie wound was healed.*

13 *And he doth great wonders, so that he maketh fire come downe from heauen on the earth in the sight of men.*

14 *And he seduceth the inhabitants of the earth by the signes which he had giuen him to doe in the sight of the beast, saying to the inhabitants of the earth, that they should make the image of the beast which had the wound of a sword and did liue.*

15 *And it was giuen vnto him to giue a spirit to the image of the beast, so that the image of the beast should speake, and should cause that as many as would not worship the beast should be killed.*

16 *And he made all both small and great, rich and poore, free and bond, to receiue a marke in their right hand, or in their foreheads.*

17 *And that no man might buy or sell, saue he that had the marke, or the name of the beast, or the number of his name.*

18 Here

18 *Here is wisedome, let him that hath vnderstanding count the number of the beast: for it is the number of a man, and his number is sixe hundreth, threescore and sixe.*

E had the description of the beast with seuen heads in the former part of this chapter: and now hee painteth out the beast with the two hornes like a Lambe, which also doth warre against the Saints. A beast, as wee haue seene, is a kingdome, a dominion, or a power exercised with tyrannous and beastly qualities. And by this beast with the two hornes, is the kingdome of the great Antichrist, euen the kingdome of the Papacie described: This beast is called the false prophet, chapter 19. But here ariseth a great doubt at the first: for if the seuen heads of the former beast, bee seuen seuerall states or gouernments, by which Rome hath ruled ouer the world: and that the Empire (which then stood when Iohn receiued this prophecie) was the sixt of those heads, and the monarchie of Popes the seuenth, which the Angell sayth was then to come, chapter 17. why, or how shall the Papacie be described againe vnder another beast? Can that Empire of the Popes be both the seuenth head of that former beast, and also a beast by himselfe? Yea verely that he is in respect of the double power which this second beast did challenge. For they, that is to say the Pope, challenge the highest power ciuill, ouer all Emperors and Kings, and the highest power spirituall ouer the faith, ouer the consciences and soules of all men: which power is peculiar to Christ, one is your doctor euen Christ, Matthew 23. So that this second Empire of Rome is set foorth not onely as an head of the former beast, but also as a seuerall beast by it selfe. And this may as well be, as that the Angell, chapter 17. saith, that the head which was not then come, should bee both one of the seuen and the eight. If he bee one of the seuen, and also the eight, then is he somewhat besides an head of the beast, yea euen a seuerall beast by himselfe. But more of this when wee come to that chapter.

Now let vs proceede to the description of this monster, which is not onely the seuenth head of the beast, but also for his differing power from all the rest, is also a seuerall beast by himselfe. Saint Iohn saith, that he saw him ascending out of the earth. Here is noted in this first clause, his originall, of what progenie or stocke he commeth, that the seruants of God may know what his dignitie is, howsoeuer he glorieth thereof. For the Papacie doth boast with full mouth, that their dignitie and power is from heauen. They glorie and bragge that Christ gaue it to Peter, and that they haue it by succession from him. Thus I say they make their boast. But the holy Ghost telleth vs, that it ariseth out of the earth: for as that is right excellent and glorious which commeth from heauen, so that which springeth from the earth is vile, base, and contemptible. Moreouer, in the phrase of the holy Ghost, to say he ascendeth out of the earth, is as much to say, as that this beast is bred and springeth from the sensualtie of man, and from the very diuel of hell. For S. Iames

ioyneth

ioyneth these three together as agreeing in one, earthly, sensuall, and diuellish. Iam.3.vers.15. Let them then bragge while they can, that their power is from heauen, we haue the cleere word of God that it is from the earth, it is of man, it is of the diuell.

In the next clause he sayth, *This beast hath two hornes like a Lambe, but spake like the Dragon.* Here is a great difference in this beast in deede and trueth, from that which he pretendeth in shew. For he pretendeth and maketh shew as if hee were an innocent Lambe, and sayth that both his hornes (that is, the two powers which he challengeth, euen the ciuil and the ecclesiasticall) are the hornes of the Lambe of God Christ Iesus: when as he hath receiued the sayd powers from the diuel, and in working is as the dragon, which is noted in these words, *but he spake like the dragon.* I might here stand to shew at large how the Popes of Rome since the time that they vsurped to be vniuersal Bishops, call themselues Christs Vicars, and affirme most stoutly that he hath committed into their hands both the temporall sword ouer all Emperours and Kings in the earth, to place and to displace at their will, and also the spirituall sword and power ouer all mens soules, to carrie to heauen, and to throw downe to hell at their pleasure. I might likewise stand to shew, that the Lambe indeede is king of kings, and Lord of Lords, and that he is our great high priest, and hath the lordship ouer the faith and conscience of men, and that he hath not resigned either of these powers to any, but sitting at the right hand of the highest maiestie, doth exercise them himselfe, to the great ioy of al the faithfull. I might (I say) stand to handle these things at large: but it is sufficient only to note them, seeing there haue neuer been any so blasphemous as to challenge these high powers which are peculiar to Christ, but the Popes which are the head and standerd bearers in the kingdome of the Papacie. And marke this well, how the Lord doth not say, that he hath indeed the two hornes of the Lambe, but two hornes like to the Lambe. For howsoeuer they bragge in the Papacie, that their kingly and priestly power doe bring sauing health vnto all that obediently submit themselues to the same (as being the hornes or powers of the Lambe of God committed vnto them) yet the holy Ghost to the end that the godly may not bee deceiued, saith, they are but like the hornes of the Lambe, and that they be indeed the very hornes and powers of the diuell, for he doth speake like the dragon. Here againe is a large field, if we should runne through all particulars to shew how the Romish beast boasting of Christs power, is no more but the mouth and instrument of the great red dragon the diuell, to blaspheme God and his trueth, to persecute his Church, to tread downe the holy worship, and to set vp the worship of Idols, yea to teach and establish heresies, errors, and doctrines of diuels. O the Papacie make shew of hornes like a Lambe, but speake like the dragon. Wee must not then bee troubled with their vaine bragges, but looke what the pure word of God doth teach vs, and rest in that. Whosoeuer teacheth against that holy word, speaketh like the dragon.

It followeth, *That he did all that the first beast could doe in his presence.* Here is the great power of the Papacie and the efficacie thereof set forth, that it is as mightie

THE REVELATION. 257

mightie and performeth as much in the seruice of the dragon against God and his Church, as euer the Empire of the heathen and wicked Emperours could doe. This is much, if we consider both the maiestie, and power of the Empire before it receiued the deadly wound, and also what horrible things it did against God and his Church, throwing downe the trueth, and setting vp Idolatrie, and murdering the holy seruants of Christ: and yet this second beast goeth as farre. Yea doubtles (as we shall see) he doth more, but the holy Ghost noteth first that he doth all that the former could doe. And he causeth the earth (sayth S. Iohn) and them that dwell therein, to worship the first beast, whose deadly wound was healed. These words doe minister a great doubt vnto some, how this second beast may represent the Papacie, seeing the Popes doe cause the inhabitants of the earth to worship them selues, and not to worship the heathen Emperours which were before them. This doubt is easily remoued, if wee consider but two poynts. The one, that the beasts are not y men that ruled either in the Empire or in the Papacie, but the tyrannous power exercised by the men with cruell and beastly qualities. The other is, that albeit the power in the Papacie commeth vnder the name of Christ, and with other termes, as it were vnder another cloake, yet is it the very same in effect, or a liuely image of that which the Emperours did exercise. The heathen Emperours condemned the true worship of God, persecuted all those with cruell death which did imbrace it, and set vp the worship of false gods, and doctrines of deuils. When that head had receiued a deadly wound, and was somewhat reuiued againe, the Papacie raiseth and reneweth all that former beastly tyrannie, impugneth the trueth of God, maintaineth the worship of Idols and doctrines of diuels. Now when the inhabitants of the earth are compelled to worship this beast, that is, to submit themselues to this vsurped tyranny, to imbrace the lawes, the decrees, the religion and worship which it setteth vp, they doe indeede worship the olde Romane tyrannie, which is brought in againe by the Papacie. Indeede the popes, and the papisme doe not allow of the old Romane tyrannie, but doe condemne it to be of the deuill, because it denied Christianitie, set vp the worship of false gods, and murdered the Saints; and yet they compell all men to worship that beast. If this shall seeme strange vnto any, let them consider that the holy Ghost doth not heere teach what the second beast thinketh or intendeth, but what he doth: for Satan can so farre delude the blind hearts of men, that when their intents are to worship God, they worship deuils. If a man in the darke intendeth to set vpon his enemie to kill him, and vnawares in stead of his enemie killeth his owne father, shall wee say that he hath not killed his father, but his enemie, because his intent was onely to kill his enemie and not his father? If wee confesse that to be absurd in the darknes of the bodily eyes: why shall wee not confesse it to be as absurd in the darknes of the minde, to say a man worshippeth God, when he worshippeth deuils, because his intent is to worship God, and not deuils? Then seeing it is so, whatsoeuer the papists intend, because they bring in againe the old Romane tyrannie, they cause men to worship the former beast. They themselues are deceiued in their intents: for the holy Apostle S. Paul prophecying of them, sayth vnto

S Timothie,

Timothie, that the euill men and deceiuers shall waxe worse and worse deceiuing, and being deceiued, 2. Timoth. 3. ver. 13. Let it be, they thinke they do right when they pray to Saints and Angels, and make them mediatours, and when they worship Images: yea let it be, they take it they doe God high seruice when they put to death all that will not obey their lawes: yet in truth they bring in Paganisme, and murther the Saints. The popes are worshipped, not as men, but for their power which they haue vsurped, which power of the deuill, and so the former beast is worshipped in them, which the deuill set vp.

Then next it followeth, that this beast did great wonders, so that he maketh fire come downe from heauen in the sight of men, and deceiueth them that dwell on the earth by meanes of those signes which he hath power to doe in the sight of the beast. In these words, there be set forth vnto vs two things, the one is the signes and wonders which antichrist shall worke: the other is the efficacie of those signes in seducing the blind worlde. Our Sauiour saith, that the false prophets should arise and worke such signes and wonders, that if it were possible the very elect should be deceiued, Matth. 24. And Saint Paul shewing the comming of the great Antichrist saith, his comming shal be by the efficacie of Satan, with al power, & signes, and lying wonders, 2. Thess. 2. Here is then the proper marke of the kingdome of Antichrist, lying signes and wonders.

Now that we may see how fitly this agreeth to the papisme, let vs call to minde how they that are for ye bloudy kingdome doe boast of their miracles, their signes, and wonders. Their *Legenda aurea*, their festiuals, and other their writings doe set foorth infinite miracles and wonders, which they say were wrought to confirme their religion. As some for purgatorie and prayer of the dead, some for the reall presence of Christ in the sacrament, to shew that the bread and wine are turned into his very fleshe and bloud: but most plentifull are their miracles which were wrought for those that were very deuout in worshipping of Saints, and their Images. All is miracles, miracles, among the papists, and all but lying signes. S. Iohn nameth one wonder here which is this, namely, that the beast causeth fire to come downe from heauen in the sight of men. The great Prophet of God Elias, as wee reade, caused fire to come downe and to consume the captaines and their fifties which were sent from the king of Israell to fetch him. Likewise at his prayer the fire came downe and consumed the sacrifice, when the priests of Baal could not doe the like. But where doe we find that any such thing hath been done in the poperie: I answere, that it is not the meaning of the holy Ghost, that this beast, the kingdome of Antichrist, shal in very deed haue power to cause fire to come downe from heauen: but in the opinion of the blind world he hath as great power as had Elias. For as the fire came downe from heauen at the prayer of Elias in the sight of the people, to confirme that to be the true worship of God which he maintained, and to proue the worship of Baal to be false and wicked: so partly by counterfeit miracles, and partly by some strange things done by the power of Satan, the world hath verily beleeued that this beast, the papacie, or those popish prelates had as great power to worke miracles as euer had Elias, both to confirme their religion to be true, and also to condemne the worship of those which withstand the same. Then we see the reason, why the efficacie of Satan to worke wonders in the poperie, is compared to fire comming downe from heauen in the sight of men, euen because the whole controuersie betweene Elias and the Prophets of Baal was decided by that fire which came downe to shewe whether part had the true religion. We may note then what a great aduantage the Romish beast taketh to seduce the blind world: As thus, when religion was in question in the dayes of Elias, the controuersie was decided by the fire that came downe from heauen, in so much that al the people fell vpon their faces and cride, Iehouah hee is God, Iehouah hee is God. Reade the historie, 1. king. chap. 18.

Now this beast the papacie came in, in times past euen as if he had bin an other Elias, saying vnto all that withstood him, let it be tried by miracles, whether part hath the true religion. The holy and true worshippers of God make answere, our religion is expresly deliuered in the word of God, it is fully confirmed by the miracles of Christ and his Apostles, wee worke no miracles to confirme that which is alreadie confirmed. This I say, is the answere of Gods true seruants. Then cried out the popish rout, we haue miracles wrought in our Church to confirme all that we do: Behold all people, and yee shall see. Then came the effectuall power of Satan to doe some strange things which seeme wonderfull vnto the ignorant. Then downe fell the inhabitants of the earth wondring at these lying signes and wonders, nothing doubting but that the beast can cause fire to come downe from heauen, not onely this materiall fire, but the fire of Gods wrath to consume all his aduersaries, both the captaines and their fifties. Thus hath Antichrist seduced the world with the power of his signes and wonders, and caused them to murther the true seruants of God as no better then the priests of Baal, that could worke no miracle to confirme their worship.

Now the world commeth to be at the commandement of Antichrist, whome they take to haue so great power to confirme all that he doth with miracles from heauen. And now he hath gotten them vnder, he layeth his commaundement vpon them, saying to them that dwell on the earth, that they should make the image of the beast which had the wound of a sword and did liue, for so it followeth in the text. Here is a matter of some difficulty to be well vnderstood. Wee are sure that the holy Ghost doth hereby declare that Antichrist enlargeth and spreadeth his power by causing this image to be made. But what is this image of the beast, there lyeth the difficultie.

The sixt head of the beast, that is the Empire, so farre as it was tyranous and beastly, had receiued a deadly wound when Constantine imbraced and defended the faith of Christ. After also the Empire was rent in peeces, so that there was the Emperor of the East, and the Emperor of the West. The Empire of the West fell quite downe, so that for the space of three hundreth yeares and more, there was no Emperour of the West, vntill the Bishop of Rome Leo the third, made Charles the great the king of France, Emperour. Now here was an Empire of the West againe erected, but not of such maiestie and power as the old Romane Empire had been.

What shall wee take this to bee the image of the beast, whose deadly wound was healed? I see not how that can be, because the Empire is the beast, for the beast still remaineth though not in like power ỹ it was before, for this second beast doth all that he doth in the presence of the former beast, which cannot be both the beast and the image of the beast. Therefore the setting vp of the Empire, cannot be the making the image. What then, where shal we find this image of the former beast, euen in the presence of the beast, and that in the papacie. For substance of matter, as I haue noted before, the papacie hath set vp the olde Romane tyrannie which was in the heathen Emperours against the true worship of God, and against his Church, and hath brought in the doctrine & worship of deuils. And now Saint Iohn sheweth, that as they set vp the same matter in effect; so likewise they erect an externall forme of their ecclesiasticall gouernment, after the very patterne and forme of the gouernment of the old Empire, yea so like, that it is called an image of the same. It shall suffice to shew this in a few things.

As first, behold the policie or forme of gouernment of the ancient Roman Empire, which seemed to be an Aristocratie, because there was a Senate: there were graue Senators, which seemed to haue high authoritie, but yet in very deed it was a monarchie, yea and cruell tyranie, in as much as they were all vnder the rule of one man, the Emperour who bare the sway. In like manner ye may behold in the papacie the like forme, yea the perfect image of that policie; for there is at Rome the high Senate, the colledge of Cardinals, which take the vpper hand of kings, which also seeme to holde the power of an Aristocratie, but they also are all of them subject to one monarch, to one head, which is the pope that ruleth ouer them, and ordereth all things at his pleasure as a God vpon earth, for they all as his vassals extoll his power, and affirme that he cannot erre, neither as they say, is he to be iudged of any.

Then further in the ancient Romane Empire, the heathen Emperours tooke vpon them not onely the highest kingly power and Empire ouer all men, but also the priesthood & power ouer religion: and moreouer to be the Tribunes of the people, which had the power of forbidding and disanulling all decrees made by other magistrates. We haue the very true image of this in the papacie, while the popes haue vsurped the highest ciuill power ouer all kings and Emperors, the fulnes of authoritie of the priesthood to rule ouer religion, and as the high Tribunes of the people to be exempted from all iurisdiction, and to disanull the decrees of all other Bishops, yea of generall councels if they be not ratified by them. Doe wee not here see the very image of the old Romane Empire, although I should goe no further in this matter? But now as the head ouer all, that is, the Emperour, was at Rome, and the Senate which next vnto him were the highest, so were there in all lands (so farre as the Empire did reach) presidents and great rulers ouer prouinces, which had all their authoritie from the Emperour, and were as his sworne men, at his becke and commandement. At Rome also hath been and is the head ouer all in the papacie, euen the wonder of the worlde, the pope whome they extoll as a God vpon earth, and there also is the high Senate the colledge of Cardinals, and according to the old patterne this Monarch had in all kingdomes (so farre the papacie did reach) his great presidents ouer prouinces, which were all of them his sworne men, and had their whole power from him, euen the mightie prelates, which were able to iustle with kings. I might here also stand to shewe, how the poperie hath set vp againe that externall forme of worship which the idolatrous Romanes of olde vse about their Idols with candles, with holy water, with processions, and with a great number of other thinges, which they vse in their chiefe solemnities: but this little may suffice.

Wherefore to conclude this point, as the second beast hath in substance of matter set vp the former beast to be worshipped, whilest he bringeth in againe that old tyrannie against the Church, that oppressing and condemning the true worship of God, and that erecting of idolatrie and worship of deuils, euen the same, though not vnder the same termes: so likewise hath he in his spirituall tyrannie, framed his hierarchie, after the very forme of the auncient Romane policie, and so hath set vp the liuely image of the former beast. Thus may ye see what the image of the former beast is, here erect. Yet there remaineth one doubt, for it is sayd that this beast with two hornes like a lambe, willeth the inhabitants of the earth to make the Image of the former beast. Whenas the popes themselues, did vsurpe to haue that highest power in all things as the heathen Emperours had, and to haue all gouerned according to that forme of gouernment which was in the Empire, how can it be said that the inhabitants of the earth make the image? Doth not the beast himselfe make it? yea, but this is to be answered that the kings of the earth, and the people their subiects giue their consent, or else it could not haue been. For if the malignant Church, the Synagogue of Antichrist, that Romish clergie, had not seduced the kings and the people with the power of their lying wonders, and made them beleeue that they could bring downe fire from heauen vpon their enemies, they might haue required this image to be made, but not haue obtained it. But now it might arise in a mans mind thus, an Image is but a dead shew of a thing, and can doe nothing. The holy Ghost doth preuent this obiection, and sheweth that it becommeth more then a dead or an idle Image: for he saith, the beast had power giuen him to put a spirite into the image of the beast, so that the image of the beast should speake, and should cause, that as many as would not worship the beast shouldbe killed. Here is a wonderfull Image, that hath life put into it, and power to doe so great matters. The popish hierarchie is not a bare resemblance of the old Romane policie to stand as a picture in a wall, but hath a spirite put into it by the false prophet (which is the whole bodie of all the false teachers in that Romish apostasie) and spreadeth it selfe and speaketh with such power in all kingdomes, that it causeth all such to be put to death, as will not worship the beast. Who knoweth not this? that as many as would not in all countries imbrace the whole popery (and so in such worship that old tyranie which maintained idolatrie) the popish hierarchie whereof the pope is the top, then his Cardinals, then his great prelates, inquisitors, and other officers did speake and condemne them as heretikes, deliuering them ouer being condemned to the secular power, to bee put to death. And wee know

SERMONS VPON

know that the kings then durst not but put them to death, least it should light vpon themselues. Thus were the poore sheepe of Christ killed by the mightie power of this image, and looke into those kingdomes where the parts of it yet remaine, and ye shall see how it oppresseth the Church. This is very much, but the beast is not yet satisfied, but will haue all sorts of people brought into bondage vnto him as his marked seruants. Yea, as men vse to set a brand vpon their sheepe and other cattell, and to eare-marke them, that it may openly and manifestly appeare to whome they appertaine: so doth Antichrist this Romish beast, cause all men in all kingdomes to carry in open view his marke or brand, whereby all may see that they doe apperteine vnto him. For thus it followeth in the text, And hee made all both small and great, rich and poore, free and bond, to receiue a marke in their right hand, or in their foreheads: and that no man might buy or sell, saue he that had the marke of the name of the beast, or the number of his name.

Then we see that among the people there is none so smal, or so base, either man or woman, whom Antichrist doth neglect, but will haue them marked and branded. Among the Kings, the Princes, the Dukes and nobles, there is not one so great, or so high, but he must stoope to receiue this brand: seeing hee causeth all both small and great to receiue it. There is no man which by the abundance of his riches and worldly wealth, can buy out this matter. There is not the poorest begger that shall be let go. All free men must be bond to him: and bond men besides their masters according to the flesh, must haue a spirituall Lord. None of all these shall be permitted to trafique in the world, or to be conuersant among men, vnles the marke appeare vpon them, either in their foreheads or in their right hands. Their hand is put for their actions, and the forehead for their open profession, and in one of them at the least, euery man must openly declare that he acknowledgeth the Pope of Rome to bee the Lord ouer his faith. Is there any man which doth doubt of the trueth of this, I meane that this was in euery respect fully performed in the Papacie? Doe not all that be of any yeares know, that so many of all sortes whatsoeuer, as did not openly professe the Pope to bee their Lord, yea euen in Christs stead, Lord and head ouer the whole Church, were cruelly put to death? Could any, I pray you, which would not doe this, bee suffered to buy and sell, or to be conuersant among men? Goe now into Spayne, and see how you can liue there: where a part of the image of the beast yet standeth. I call it but a part of the image, not because it is not as an whole image, but because the image of the beast is called but one in all kingdomes, so farre as it was spread, and in sundrie kingdomes it is broken downe.

It may here be demaunded, whether all these three bee put for one, the marke of the beast, his name, and the number of his name? I take it they are not all one, but that the marke is a more speciall thing then his name or the number of his name. For who knoweth not, that some were more neerely marked vnto the Pope, or with a more speciall brand then others? All the Laitie (as they called them) bare his name, or the number of his name, and did professe their humble submission vnto all his decrees, did worship him as their spirituall Lord that had

the

the power ouer the spirituall life, and death. But his clergie of all sorts, as his Cardinals, his Bishops, his Abbots, his Monkes, Friers, Nunnes, and Votaries, had speciall markes, and were most neerely bound vnto him. Then wee see it is not in vaine that the holy Ghost maketh a difference of the marke, seeing all are branded, but not all alike: but some besides the common marke, haue also their seuerall, and speciall marke. Thus we see that all sorts of people become as the marked or branded cattell of the beast, and must be subiect to his will.

The papists thinke they put a great question vnto vs, when they say, where was your Church an hundreth yeares past? To answere this, aske them where the true Church of Christ was, when the second beast, the beast with two hornes like a Lambe, did cause all both small and great, rich and poore, free and bond, to receiue the marke of the beast, and that none might buy or sell but such? were they not persecuted, condemned as heretikes, and murdered in all lands, which would not become his marked seruants? What can be more cleere then this? What true Church of Christ should wee looke for, all the time that this beast raigneth, but a persecuted, scattered remnant? And what doth the vniuersalitie, the multitude and consent of so many kingdomes submitting themselues to the Papacie, and worshipping the Pope and his decrees, but plainly declare that they bee the very malignant Church, the synagogue of antichrist here painted out? Reade all auncient histories of things that were done in the times of poperie, and see what one thing can bee found which doth not in all respects most fitly agree with the description of this second beast? Reade how they haue been vsed in all countries within the popish dominion, which haue denied to imbrace the popish idolatrous religion, and see whether they doe not likewise in all respects agree with the estate of the true Church here described in this booke. Then if it be so, that the Romish synagogue the papisme, euen that idolatrous kingdome, doe so fitly and fully agree with the description of this second beast, and that the true Church oppressed by them, should al that while be but as a scattered remnant persecuted and slaine, why should they aske where our Church was? It was persecuted, oppressed, and scattered by the Romish beast: they condemned and cruelly murdered all the true worshippers of God that they could lay holde of: for they cause all to bee put to death that will not worship the image of the beast.

Now last of all S. Iohn commeth to shew what the number of the name of this beast is: for if wee come to know his name, what would we desire more? But the holy Ghost will not tell his name plainly; but mystically, as other things in this booke, that the worldlings which shall fulfill them may not see them, and yet the faithfull seruants of God doe attaine to the knowledge of them. Therefore he saith, here is wisedome, let him that hath vnderstanding count the number of the beast, for it is the number of a man, that is, such as a man may be able to finde out. And then he sayth it is sixe hundreth, sixtie, and sixe. The sillables of his name shall not bee set downe, but the letters of his name being numbred, are in number as they signifie, put all together, sixe hundreth, sixtie, and sixe. Here the papists doe laugh, saying, that there be many names to bee found both proper and common, whose letters

letters being numbred doe amount to this number 666. and therefore no certaintie can be had that way. Also they say no one Pope can bee named, the letters of whose name make that number. These papists herein are most grosse and absurd: for we are not here to enquire about the name of any man, but about the name of a kingdome, for the beast is a kingdome. And what is the name of the Romane Empire, and the name of the popish hierarchie? Are they not the Latines? The Popes of Rome are all for Latine, and will haue no exercise of religion but in Latine. They condemne the Greeke Church, because it will not bee subiect to their Latine lawes. They compell all men to pray in Latine. And touching the Bible, whereas the olde Testament was written in the Hebrue tongue by the Prophets, and the new Testament in Greeke by the Apostles and Euangelists, they condemne the same, being the originall, as corrupted, and will haue the Bible to bee authentike in no tongue but the Latine. I might proceede in moe particulars: but who knoweth not that the papacie is the kingdome of the Latines? What then will some say? what is this for the number of his name? Thus it is, S. Iohn wrote this Reuelation in Greeke, and the Greeke word *Lateinos*, which signifieth Latine, containeth the number sixe hundreth sixtie and sixe. The beast is a kingdome, and the Papacie is the kingdome of the Latines: what other Monarchie can bee shewed since the Reuelation was giuen, the letters of whose name containe this foresayd number? *Irenæus* an ancient father of the Church, yea so ancient, that he reporteth, that hee sawe and heard *Polycarpus*, who was one that was a disciple of S. Iohn, that receiued this prophecie, mentioneth this word *Lateinos* as the name of the beast. Also wee may note, that is the letters of the Greeke word *Lateinos*, being numbred doe amount to 666. so doe the letters of the Latine *Ecclesia Italica*, that is, the Church of Italie, and the letters of the Hebrue word *Remiyth*, which signifieth Romane. This is much that it fitteth in all the three principall tongues, the Hebrue, the Greeke and the Latine. Some doe like better that the number of his name should be deferred to the time of his comming, as that hee should come about the yeare sixe hundreth sixtie and sixe: but that cannot agree with the words of the text, that all should receiue the marke of the beast, or his name, or the number of his name. Men professing poperie carrie not the number of the yeare in which Antichrist did come, but they professe themselues to be of the Latine kingdome, to be of the Italian Church, to bee of the Romish religion: and so carrie his name and the number of his name. Thus much for this time.

THE

THE XXIX. SERMON.
CHAP. XIIII.

1 *And I looked, and behold a Lambe stood vpon mount Sion, and with him an hundred and foure and fourtie thousand, hauing his fathers name written in their foreheads.*

2 *And I heard a voyce from heauen as the sound of many waters, and as the sound of a great thunder, & I heard the voyce of the harpers, harping with their harpes.*

3 *And they did sing as it were a new song, before the throne, and before the foure beasts and the Elders: and no man could learne that song but the hundreth, fourtie and foure thousand, which were brought from the earth.*

4 *These are they which are not defiled with women, for they are virgins, these follow the Lambe whither soeuer he goeth, these are brought from men, being the first fruites to God and to the Lambe.*

5 *And in their mouthes was found no guile, for they are without spot before the throne of God.*

N the two former chapters the 12. and 13. wee haue had the description of the enemies to the true spouse of Christ, the holy Church: as in the 12. chapter there is painted out the great red dragon the deuill himselfe with all his Angels: and in the 13. chapter the beast with seuen heads, and the beast with two hornes like a Lambe. Now in this chapter here is first set forth her protector and defender against those huge monsters, and then afterward their decay and ruine. And I looked (sayth S. Iohn) and behold a Lambe stood vpon Mount Sion. In the dayes of the great Antichrist they were killed that would not worship the beast, and no man might buy or sell saue he that had the marke, or the name of the beast, or the number of his name: and this was ouer many nations, kindreds and tongues. Where then was the true Church? did she vtterly faile in the earth? as the papists say vnto vs, where was your Church an hundreth yeares past? The spouse of Christ did not faile vpon the earth euen in the middest of those grieuous times; for here is still a mount Sion, that is, a true Church in the world, here is a Lambe standing vpon the same as her protector, and here be many thousands of pure worshippers her true children, which are not defiled with the idolatrous worship of Antichrist.

The

They condemne them as heretikes, persecute and ki ll them, but they can neuer cause them to forsake the truth. Thus much is here plainely set before vs.

But this is strange that a lambe is here set forth to be the defender of the church against those mightie enemies. What a mighty huge monster is the great red dragon? Of what maruerlous power is the beast with seuen heads, and likewise the beast with two hornes? what is a lambe vnto all these? Yes this lambe is too strong for them all: for hee is the lambe of God that taketh away the sinnes of the world. He is throughly able though he be a lambe to defend his church against those monsters, though they were ten thousand times stronger then they be. But seeing this lambe in the fift chapter of this booke, is called the lyon of the tribe of Iuda: it may be demaunded whether he might not in this place more fitly appeare in the shape of a lion to encounter with those mightie enemies. It is out of doubt, that our Lord Iesus is called a lion in respect of his terrible power wherewith he doth teare downe his enemies. But we must note withall, that the greatnes of his power against the deuill and all his instruments hath shewed it selfe as hee is a lambe, yea the lambe slaine in sacrifice: for it is the power of his death that vanquisheth, and the church hath her victorie through his bloud. So that it is indeed a lambe that ouercommeth these terrible enemies, and protecteth his chosen. They ouercame him by the bloud of the lambe, chap. 12. vers. 11. And marke well how it is said, that this lambe standeth vpon Mount Sion: for albeit he be in bodie ascended vp into heauen, yet he said, behold I am with you, euen to the ende of the world. Why then doth the pope bragge that all power ouer the whole Church in earth is committed into his hand, and that he is in Christs stead? Ye see Christ is not absent, that hee needeth a vicar to supply his roome and office. The Church hath the lambe that was slaine present with her, by whom she doth ouercome. Thus much for the protector, now for the protected. And with him (saith the text) an hundreth and foure and fortie thousand. This is that number which are sealed before in the seuenth chapter. It is a number certaine, for an vncertaine: for it is not the purpose of the holy Ghost to teach vs that the Lord Iesus did preserue iust so many thousands in the dayes of Antichrist, but that when there seemed to be few or none, yet the Lord preserued many thousands. As Elias sayd to God, Lord they haue digged downe thine Aulters, and killed thy prophets, and I am left alone. But the Lord made him this answere, I haue reserued to my selfe seuen thousand in Israel, which haue not bowed the knee to Baal. Elias (as it appeareth) sawe fewe or none, and yet there were a great number. So in the dayes of poperie when they killed all those which would not worship the beast, few appeared, but yet the Lord preserued many thousands scattered in the kingdomes and great nations, ouer which the Romish Antichrist had gotten the dominion. An hundreth foure and fortie thousand are a great number, and these are sayd to be of the tribes of Israel: and it seemeth that this number is put for a farre greater. It may then bee obiected, that so great a multitude could not but appeare and make some shewe, yea a faire greater shewe then euer was made in the dayes of poperie, by those that withstood it. To this I answer, that looke but into our owne land, which is but a smal countrie in comparison of some

other,

other, and see when there is mustring of souldiers, a man or two out of a parish which are not missed, & may seeme to be little, yet when they come together they make a great armie of many thousands: So the true worshippers of the Lord scattered thinne in many great kingdomes, set all together make a goodly companie.

Moreouer, besides the largenes of the kingdomes in which they be scattered, we must also note the length of the time: For the poperie was in the strength and did flourish foure or fiue hundreth yeares: in this time a few at once amount to a great number, being gathered out of so many nations. Howsoeuer the marked seruants of Antichrist despise this scattered remnant, bragging of their infinite millions of millions, yea of so many thousand thousands, almost as here bee persons, yet this small number (small I call it in comparison of their innumerable heapes of people) shal be found to be the true Catholike Church, and their multitude the Synagogue of Satan whom they doe worship. This booke doth plainely shewe that the true Church is farre lesse in number then the false Church, and that the false Church shall preuaile in the world against the true seruants of God, and murther them: what do they then boast of their strength and multitude? Doth it not make against them? yes verily. It is also here to bee noted, that howsoeuer the true worshippers be dispersed and scattered one from another here in the world, yet they meet all together in the vnitie of faith, & are ioyned to the lambe their head. Our papists contend for a visible bodie in the world, or els it canot be the church of Christ: As now at this day since the disclosing of Antichrist there be many visible assemblies that doe professe the gospel. But how could there be such assemblies in the dayes when the kings and their subiects did worship the beast, and those which refused to worship him were put to death? True it is that in some places, there were some companies of those which professed the Gospell, and which condemned the doctrine of the church of Rome to be Antichristian: whome the Romish beast with all his power could not subdue, as the histories doe shew of the Bohemians, and of those whome they call the Waldenses. The Lord had many scattered people in this our countrie of England also, which imbraced the true doctrine, and refused to worship the beast, but especially in the dayes of Wickliffe, and certaine yeares after.

Then it followeth, Hauing his fathers name written in their foreheads. As the children of the malignant Church, which are called the inhabitants of the earth, haue the marke of the beast in their foreheads, or in their right hands, euen the name or the number of his name: so the pure and holy worshippers on the contrary part haue written in their foreheads, the name of the Lord God, who is the father of the lambe. What is this, but that as the seruants of Antichrist are not ashamed openly to beare his marke and to professe his religion: so these are not ashamed of the holy religion and worship of God, but doe openly professe it before men. It is great reason that this shuld be so: nay it is a very absurd thing, that the popish sort shuld glory in the name of the pope, and openly reioyce in the profession of his wicked inuentions, euen in the worship of deuils, & that on the contrary part, the true worshippers should be ashamed of the name of God, that is, of his gospell, of his religion

SERMONS VPON.

on and true worſhip: and therfore it is ſayd here, his fathers name is written in their foreheads. Ye haue many which are time ſeruers, that wil ſay, they keepe their conſcience to God, whereas outwardly they do ioyne with falſe worſhip. They beare openly and outwardly to the view of the worlde the marke of the beaſt, and are aſhamed to beare openly the name of God, that is, the profeſſion of his holy trueth, which condemneth all falſe worſhip; but ſay they carrie that ſecretly in their conſcience, which they ſay is enough, ſeeing God lookes vpon the heart. Let ſuch mē learne out of this ſcripture, that notwithſtanding all the tyrannie of Antichriſt, the true worſhippers doe carry the profeſſion of his religion, as openly to the view of the world, as the other doe carry the marke and name of the beaſt. Yea moreouer aske ſuch men whether it be tolerable, that the ſeruants of God ſhould bee more aſhamed of his name, then the ſeruants of Antichriſt are aſhamed of hel? Shal God haue leſſe honour then the deuill? Let them alſo remember that our Sauiour doth not ſay he will deny them, and bee aſhamed of them that ſhall denie him, and bee aſhamed of him before his father in their heart and conſcience: but he ſaith, he wil denie them, and be aſhamed of them, which are aſhamed of him, and denie him before men, Math. 10. verſ. 32.33. Whoſoeuer will be of this companie which are with the Lambe vpon Mount Sion, they muſt not be aſhamed to haue it written in their forehead, that they profeſſe the doctrine of God deliuered vnto vs in the ſcriptures of the Apoſtles and prophets, and that they vtterly renounce all idolatrie and falſe religion, brought in by the Romiſh Antichriſt. Now as I ſaid, there be many which in the times of perſecution, will lend their bodily preſence to the Idol ſeruice and worſhip of deuils, flattering themſelues in this, that they keepe their conſcience free to God, profeſſing the faith of Chriſt ſecretly to themſelues, but dare not beare his fathers name written in their foreheads: ſo are they not a few euen in the daies that the goſpel is maintained by Chriſtian princes, which carry themſelues ſo cloſe and ſo warily, that a man ſhall not diſcerne what religion they be of, or which part they fauour. There is ſtrife and contention, one part for the holy doctrine of God, and an other for the Romiſh inuentions, and theſe men are loath to diſpleaſe either part, and ſo ſwim betweene two ſtreames. How will ſuch bee bolde to carrie the fathers name written in their foreheads in the heate of perſecution, which dare not in the daies of peace, when the power of their prince maintaineth the goſpel openly and boldly profeſſe the ſame?

Well, to conclude this point, let vs remember, that theſe hundreth, fourtie and foure thouſand, which are with the Lambe vpon Mount Sion, haue his fathers name written in their foreheads. If we make account to bee of this companie, that is, if we will be true worſhippers, and cleaue vnto Chriſt in his Church, euen vpon Sion his holy hill, then muſt wee not bee aſhamed openly to profeſſe the holy doctrine and pure worſhip of God, both in time of peace, and in time of perſecution. Wee muſt diſdaine to ſee the marked ſeruants of the beaſt cairie his name, and wee our ſelues aſhamed of the truth of Chriſt. Let vs honor the Lord our God, as much as they honour the beaſt, and the dragon, which hath giuen his power and throne to the beaſt.

Let

THE REVELATION. 269

Let vs now goe forwarde with that which followeth in the text: And I heard a voice from heauen, as the sound of many waters, and as the sound of a great thunder, and I heard the voice of harpers harping with their harps. Here is set forth how this companie of true worshippers doe magnifie and praise God for his great benefites and graces bestowed vpon them. This is out of all doubt to declare, that do the dragō what he can, and when the beast ẏ dragons vicar that Romish pope hath spent all his power and policie to roote out all true worshippers, yet God wil haue a companie in earth that shall praise and glorifie his name: he will be worshipped in earth amoūg the sonnes of men. For we must remember that the chiefe end of our creation and redemption is, that we should glorifie, and extoll the praise of the creator and redeemer. The deuil laboureth to haue all worship him, and that there shuld none remaine to praise the true and liuing God vpon the earth: but the Lord withstandeth his practise herein, and reserueth at all times a remnant, at sometimes more, and at sometimes lesse, which call vpon his name in truth, and glorifie him with praise and thanksgiuing. And this is it which Saint Iohn vttereth here, when he sayth, hee heard a voyce from heauen, as the sound of many waters, and as the sound of a great thunder, and the voyce of harpers, harping with their harpes. But it may here be said, if this companie with the Lambe vpon Mount Sion, doe represent the faithfull here in the world, whom the lambe doth preserue in the times that the great Antichrist doth raigne and lay wast the Church: how then is this voyce heard from heauen? Is not this song of praise vttred vpon earth? I answere, that howsoeuer the Church bee vpon the earth as a pilgrime for a time, yet her birth is from heauen, her conuersation is in heauen, her inheritance is in heauen, shee is taught from heauen to praise and glorifie her God. In these respects the voice and sound of her praising God may be said to be from heauen, although it bee vttered vpon the earth. Ierusalem (sayth S. Paul) which is from aboue, is free, which is the mother of vs all.

Then further, here be three comparisons to expresse the sound of this praise, the first, that it is like the confused roring noyse of many waters: the second, that it is as the terrible noise of a mightie thunder: the third, that there is the sweete melodie of harpers, harping or playing vpon their harpes. What these things do meane is somwhat difficill to find: for they are expounded by diuers, after a diuerse manner. If we take it that the sound is all one in it selfe, & the difference to be as the person that heareth it, differeth or altereth his estate, thē it is thus: A meere natural man heareth nothing whē the praises of God are sounded forth but as the confused noise of many waters. When the same partie hath his eares opened by the gracious worke of the spirit, and seeth his owne vnthankfulnes and misery, then the sound of the word, and the praises vttered by the Church, are as a terrible thunder: but after a more through and sound conuersion all is sweete and pleasant, as most delectable musicke. Doubtlesse these things are most true in many: and it may be, this scripture is to signifie so much. But if we will rather apply it both to the parties that vtter the voyce, and to the seuerall exercises of the Church, then it is to be taken thus: waters doe signifie (as the Angell sheweth chap. 17.) multitudes, tongues, and kinreds of
people.

people. So the noyse of many waters, may very well be here taken, that the voyce of this prayse is the voyce of a multitude gathered out of many kindreds, nations, tongues and people.: For the Lord gathereth his elect out of many kingdomes and nations. And albeit they bee seuered by seas and distance of places, yet they meete together in the vnitie of faith in their head Christ. Yea, howsoeuer their languages doe differ, yet like as many waters meeting together they make but one sound, and in this respect that the substance and summe of their seuerall voyces is all one, euen the magnifying the praise of God, and the vttering his trueth, it is sayd, that their voyce is as the sound of many waters.

Then for the second, that it is as the voyce of a great thunder, it may very well represent the terrible iudgements & threatnings which the seruants of God do denounce against the wicked corrupters of his holy worship. Although the ministers of Antichrist, and the vngodly worldlings doe heare it with deaffe eares, yet is it in deede as a most terrible thunder. In the last place, the sweete melodie of the harpers, doth shew, with what spirituall ioy and gladnes the true beleeuers doe praise God, To praise God is nothing, vnlesa man take great ioy, delight, and pleasure therein. In the time of the law God appoynted that his people should praise him in the publike assemblies with all manner of sweete instruments of musicke: what shall wee imagine that God is delighted with the sweete noyse and harmonie of Instruments? That were most foolish, if wee should thinke so, seeing his ioyes are in himselfe, and infinit: but it was to shewe indeede that the heart and minde of man must ioy and reioyce in praising the Lord: As Saint Paul requireth of the Christians, that they make melodie in their hearts to the Lord. It is a place worthie great and deepe consideration: for it may teach vs that when men do vtter the praises of God, if it be onely with a pleasure in the voyce, and for custome and fashion, it is a dead thing, not pleasing to God at all. But if we delight and ioy in glorifying and praising God, so that it is euen like sweete and pleasant musicke to our hearts: then doe we praise him indeede with his Saints, and that is pleasing vnto him. O how men delight to heare the praise of those whom they loue : if yee loue the Lord, let your heart and tongue agree to magnifie his praise, and reioyce in his honour. The deuill applieth all his might and force to destroy the praise of God, and therefore seeketh by all meanes to draw aside the hearts of men from reioycing in the Lord. Wee see the perturbations, and distempered affections that many are in, whereby, vpon euery light occasion, euen as at the wagging of a straw, they are tormented, and disquiet others, so that they cannot reioyce in the Lord, and with glad hearts sing forth his praise: but rather doe murmure. We must take heede of that, and seeke to haue our harpes well tuned, that is our harts, that euen with sweete and pleasant harmonie, they may sound foorth the praises of God. The same deuill also who corrupteth whatsoeuer he can, draweth the melodie from the heart into the mouth onely: for some looke onely to the outward tune, and are delighted with the skill of that: they chaunt and make a pleasant noyse to the outward eare, but the strings of the heart are not tuned, there is no spirituall delight in praising God, and what doe such but euen bellow?

It

It followeth, And they did sing as it were a new song before the throne, and before the foure beasts and the Elders. As S. Iohn told vs of the melodie of harpers, so now hee addeth, that they did also sing as it were a new song, which also is to declare with what gladnes and mirth of heart, the faithfull doe sound forth the praise of Gods glory. Men doe vse for to sing when they be merrie and glad, as the Apostle saith, *Is any merrie, let him sing Psalmes*, And it is to bee considered that, he saith, their song was as a new song. Wee knowe that a song doth delight most when it is new, and lesse as it waxeth common, and, as we say, stale. The praising of God by the faithfull is most auncient and continuall; and yet they continue it with such delight; as if it were still new. For if men vpon a custome or common fashion vtter the praises of God, without feeling of ioy and gladnes in the same, it is euen as a stale song. Therefore the godly receiuing daily new benefits, doe still renew their song, that it remaineth as fresh and pleasant as at the first, it neuer waxeth olde in the motions and affections of their minde. This is it that the holy Prophet Dauid so often calleth for, saying, Sing to the Lorde a new song, cheerefully praise the Lord. Here is then no more expressed in this place to bee done by the Church, then that which the holy Ghost alwaies called vpon the seruants of God for to performe. We must then make account, that it is our part and duty to ioyne with them; and to take more delight in setting forth the praise of God, then in all earthly ioyes: we ought to make it euen as the top and crowne of our pleasures: wee must goe cheerefully vnto it, both in priuate by our selues, and also in the publike assemblies. Behold then his benefits and louing kindnes towards vs, that we may alwaies reioyce and triumph in his most holy name.

It is said that they sing this new song before the throne, before the foure beasts, and before the Elders. Although the praise be vttered by the Church vpon earth, yet the sweete harmonie of their harpes and song, commeth vp into the heauens, before the throne of God, and before his holy Angels, in as much as the Lord heareth their praise, and it is pleasing vnto him, and also all the holy Angels and Saints do reioyce in the glorifying of God. It is the whole delight of the blessed heauenly spirits to praise the Lord, and to heare his praises vttered by men. It is euen the sweetest melodie and song that can be vnto them. We doe not reade of any praise offered vp by the faithfull in all this booke vnto any Angell or Saint, but onely to him that sitteth vpon the throne, and to the Lambe: for none is to be with him partaker of his worship and glorie: none is worthie to bee ioyned with him: hee, is God alone. The ministers of Antichrist crie out vpon vs as aduersaries to the holy Angels, to the blessed Virgin, and to the Apostles and Martyrs, that we refuse to call vpon them, or any way to ascribe vnto them that which is peculiar to God and to his Christ. They imagine that they haue them on their sides, and that they be set against vs because of this: As their popish bookes are full of tales, what such or such a Saint did for those that were their deuout worshippers. If it were so, doubtles wee should bee in a heauie case, to haue all the heauenly companie againfl vs. But it is farre otherwise: for the Angels and the Saints in heauen haue their whole ioy in this, that God is glorified, they delight not in horrible sacrilege,

that

that is, that the glorie which belongeth onely to God, should be giuen vnto them. Nay, they are against all those which doe not together with them, worship onely the great God.

It is added further, That no man could learne that song but the hundreth, fourtie and foure thousand which were bought from the earth. What language then might this song bee vttered in, that none can learne it, but the redeemed? Is there any tongue peculiar to them in which they sing praises to God? Wee must note that he speaketh not here of the outward voyce, or sound of words: for what forme of praise is there, or in what laguage, but some or other euen of the enemies of God, as it falleth to be in their tongue, can learne it? But this song is to bee vnderstood of the ioyfull praising of God in the heart, it is the spirituall ioy, or the ioy of the holy Ghost, which neuer any can attaine vnto, but only the elect. No man can rightly praise God, vintill hee feele in his heart that God hath chosen him vnto life and glorie: no man can attaine vnto that but hee that receiueth the spirit of adoption. Whereupon it followeth, that none but the elect can learne this song. Outwardly then hypocrites and wicked persons may learne to vtter this song in outward voice and speech (for what words that tend to glorifie God cannot the most wicked tongue pronounce, if we respect the sillables?) but that which is in the heart, they cannot learne. Let vs then bee afrayd least we deceiue our selues in this, that we can speake as good wordes to the praise of God as any; and come to the same prayers and praises that the best doe, and thinke that is all, or sufficient. For if we doe it but in word, not reioycing in heart, we neuer learned this new song, we can haue no testimonie vnto our conscience, that we be of the number of the faithfull, and pure worshippers of God. If wee labour not to learne this new song, wee faile in the whole: we are none of this companie, for they all sing as it were a new song. Lay hold of the promises then, apprehend the loue of God, and yee shall loue him againe, and then shall your greatest ioy and delight bee in praising his blessed name.

Here followeth next, that this companie which are with the Lambe vpon mount Sion, are all virgins, and not defiled with women. Here is a companie, yea a great companie of chast and pure ones. It is meete indeede that all they which accompanie the vnspotted Lambe should be such: All virgines, all chast and pure virgins, here is a goodly assemblie. Here the papists steppe in and lay hold for the commendation of single life, and say it appeareth hereby, that virgins alwayes accompanie Christ in heauen, and so haue greater dignitie then others haue. This maketh (as they take it) for the single life of all their Priests, Abbots, Monkes, Friers, Nunnes, and such like: for they be all vnmarried persons. If S. Iohn had said here these bee vnmarried, it had been well for their purpose: but he sayth not so, but that they are virgins, not defiled with women. For all vnmarried persons are not virgines, all that liue in single life keepe not themselues vndefiled with women. We graunt that the popish swarmes of such vermine liue a single life, but we will not graunt them to be virgines, or not defiled with women: for the earth hath been filled with the stinke of the whoredomes, incests, and abominable filthie lustes of their Popes, their Cardinals, their Bishops, Monkes, Friers and Nunnes. These hundreth, fortie and foure thousand virgins which are with the Lambe, come not out of their cloysters, they must seeke for them some where else. But to answere them more fully, I say they are very much ouerseen to expound this place of single life, or as I may speake, of bodily virginitie. They speake indeed reprochfully of marriage, but dare they say that the marriage bed is defiled? The holy Ghost saith, Hebr. 13. that it is vndefiled. Then when S. Iohn sayth, these are not defiled with women, if wee will vnderstand it of this corporall virginitie in single life, must it not needes secretly charge all married persons to bee polluted by their marriage? When the holy Scripture plainly affirmeth, that the marriage bed is not defiled, we may not expound this place to contrarie that plaine doctrine: which we must needes doe if wee will expound it of single life: because in this place, virgins, and such as are not defiled with women, are put for the same thing, and as I sayd, if we take it so, then secretly it imputeth a defilement vnto all married persons. Then seeing wee may not charge the holy ordinance of God with pollution, wee must heere flye vnto another kinde of virginitie, and that is a spirituall virginitie: as S. Paul sayth he did labour to present the Corinths as a chast virgin to Christ. The Lord sheweth that hee dooth take his Church as his spouse, and she is called the Lambes wife. There is then a spiritual whoredome when men commit idolatrie, and follow the worshippe of Idols, and the superstitious inuentions of men, and doctrines of diuels. And there is a spirituall virginitie where men are not defiled with such whorish women as the Idols and false worship. How often doth the Lord vse such speeches by the Prophets, (as all that reade them can tell) that his people went a whoring when they worshipped Idols? Then thus it is: these hundreth, fortie and foure thousand are such as kept themselues from worshipping Idols of gold, of siluer, of brasse, of stone, and of wood, which should be, and were worshipped in the kingdome of Antichrist, as it is euident by the latter ende of the ninth chapter of this prophetie. A great part of this companie also consisting of married men, and married women, were also chast and pure as well as the rest, from the bodily fornication. Therefore beloued, if wee will bee with the Lambe, imbrace and hold fast that holy and pure worship which is prescribed in the word of God, and vtterly renounce all Idolatrie and all mens deuises: for such chast and pure virgins are meete to accompanie Christ. Such as bee polluted with fornication either carnall or spirituall, bee not as chast virgins to bee coupled vnto Christ.

He describeth this companie yet further, and sayth, they followe the Lambe whither soeuer he goeth. The Lambe is their shepheard, they know his voyce, and goe to whatsoeuer he calleth them, and they will not heare the voyce of strangers, but doe flye from them, Iohn 10. Antichrist, euen all the false prophets in the poperie, haue sought to make the whole Church in all kingdomes obey their voyce, and they drew infinite multitudes to imbrace their doctrine, and to take their wicked decrees to be euen as the oracles of God: but these they cannot neither by

T deceit,

deceit, nor yet by violence draw from following the Lambe. These doe acknowledge no doctrine nor no worship; but that which he hath deliuered by his holie Apostles and Prophets. Where shall we find Christ but in the scriptures, & where shall we find the true Church but with Christ? In the next words he sheweth, how it commeth that these are so nigh vnto Christ, & that indeed as he declareth is not through their own indeuour or worthines, but that they are bought, as he saith, frō men. The Lambe bought them, and he bought them with a great price, not with corruptible things, (as S. Peter saith) as gold, or siluer, but with the precious blood of Christ, as of a Lambe vndefiled and without spot, 1.Pet.1.19. He sheweth also to what end they be redeemed, in these words, being the first fruits to God and to the Lambe. By this wee must vnderstand that they be consecrated and set apart to God, and to his Christ. They are not to liue vnto themselues, they are not to serue sinne: but they are in all puritie to walke with the Lord their God. That he saith, there was no guile found in their mouthes, and that they are without spot before the throne of God, it is not to be referred to their own holines, but to that perfect righteousnes which they haue by faith in Christ.

THE XXX. SERMON.
CHAP. XIIII.

6 Then I saw another Angell flie in the middest of heauen, hauing an euerlasting Gospell to preach vnto them that dwell on the earth, and to euery nation, and kinred, tongue, and people,

7 Saying with a loud voyce: Feare God and giue glorie to him, for the houre of his iudgement is come: and worship him that made heauen and earth, the sea, and all the fountaines of waters.

8 And there followed another Angell, saying, it is fallen, it is fallen, Babylon that great citie, for she gaue to all nations to drinke the wine of the wrath of her fornication.

9 And the third Angell followed them, saying with a loud voyce, if any man worship the beast and his Image, and receiue his marke on his forehead, or on his hand,

10 The same shall drinke of the wine of the wrath of God, yea the pure wine which is powred into the cup of his wrath, and he shall be punished in fire and brimston, before the holy Angels, and before the Lambe.

11 And the smoke of their torments shall ascend vp euermore, and they shall haue

no rest day and night which worship the beast and his Image, and whosoever receiueth the print of his name.

WE had the description in the former chapter, of the beast with seuen heads that should afflict the Church, and more particularly of the seuenth head, which was not then risen when Iohn receiued this prophecie, which is also set forth by himselfe as a beast with two hornes like a Lambe, being indeede the kingdome of the great Antichrist. In this chapter wee haue had the vision which was shewed to Iohn touching the protector of the Church, and the remnant by him preserued in the dayes of that horrible darknes and confusion; least wee might thinke that the Church vtterlie failed in earth when that beast was worshipped in all lands, and when those were cruelly murdered that refused to worship him: And now after this he commeth to set forth the ruine and decay of this foresayd Idolatrous kingdome of great Babell. This may we hearken vnto with so much the more cheerefulnes of minde, because it is not onely very comfortable in it selfe, but also that it falleth out in our daies, and we see and behold with our eyes the fulfilling of it, being begun not yet full fourescore yeeres past.

The words of this text which I haue read vnto ye that doe concerne this matter, do deuide themselues into 3. parts, being the voices of three angels one following after another. The first Angel publisheth the Gospell of Christ vnto the nations of the earth. The second followeth, and proclaimeth, that great Babell (euen the bloodie kingdome of the beast) is fallen. The third Angell crieth out with a loud voice, and denounceth the dreadfull vengeance of Almighty God against al those that doe not turne to his true worship, from that idolatrous worship of Antichrist. Here is the summne of that which I haue read vnto ye. These three Angels doe represent the ministers of Christ raised vp in these last daies, to throw downe the wicked poperie with the pure light of the Gospel of Christ, which I need not stand to proue, because the ministers of the Gospell are called the Angels of the Churches, chap. 1. It is therfore said, that the first Angel hath an euerlasting gospel to preach. The true gospell is called euerlasting. The popes of Rome vsurping the power of the Lord to make lawes to the conscience of men, set vp the dunghill of their own most filthic abominations, supposing that they had established them so sure, that the holy doctrine of God deliuered by his Apostles and prophets, should neuer rise vp againe, they condemning it to be heresie, & al those to be heretikes which imbrace it. But it is an euerlasting Gospell, they cannot roote it out, nor so keepe it down, but that it wil rise vp and flie abroad: & therefore it is said here, that the Angell that flieth in the middest of heauen, hath an euerlasting Gospell to preach. Let no man thinke that euer any power of man shall bee able to abolish it, seeing the whole power of y Romane beast, which al the world wondred at, could not keepe it vnder. And let the Romane prelates reuile it as new doctrine, because it discloseth their wickednes, yet it is an euerlasting Gospel, not inuented by man, but deliuered

T 2

SERMONS VPON

uered by God himselfe from the beginning, and shall continue to the end, Al doctrine of men shall fall, for it is not euerlasting.

And now mark how he saith, that the Angell which preacheth this euerlasting Gospell, flieth in the middest of heauen: This may seeme very strange. What doth this figure out vnto vs? It figureth out these two things: the first, that when the time was come, that God would cast downe the poperie, the Gospell should bee most swiftly carried and spread ouer many kingdomes and nations: and then the second, that no power vnder heauen should bee able to stay the course thereof. These be two great things, and here plainly figured: and now marke well how it standeth. The Romane beast had great kingdoms subiect vnto him that did worship him: this Angell must preach the Gospell vnto them, therefore it is sayd hee must preach it to euery nation, kinred, tongue, and people. The kingdomes are very large, and therefore here is neede of expedition to carrie and spread it ouer them. Wherefore it is not sayd, that the Angell standeth to preach, but that hee flieth in the middest of heauen, that is, he carrieth it away very swiftly vnto the kingdomes and nations of the earth. Was not this fulfilled perfectly, when God raised vp first Martin Luther, and then many other worthie instruments which carried the Gospell into many kingdomes, and spread it farre and wide? How swiftly hath it runne ouer large kingdomes since that time? I neede not stand to name the countries vnto ye into which it is spread.

Then to the second poynt, This Angell flieth with it in the middest of heauen: which figureth out vnto vs, that it is beyond the power and reach of the beast, and beyond the reach of the Kings that stand for the kingdome of the beast, to stop the course of it. Kings and Emperours haue had great power, and the Popes haue had greater then they all: but let all the Emperours, Kings, and Popes, ioyne their whole forces together, and see if they can stop a cloud when it flieth aboue in the ayre. If they cannot, then how will they stop this Angell that flieth in the middest of heauen with the Gospell, and publisheth it to the nations? The ministers of the Gospell whom the Lord raised vp, as Luther, Melancthon, Bucer, Peter Martyr, Caluine, Virete, and many others, walked vpon the earth, and published and spread the truth through the nations: and yet they were so far aboue the reach of the beast, from laying hold of their persons to kill them, or to stop the course of their preaching, that they are figured out here to flie with it in the middest of heauen. Such as haue not obserued this are very senceless and dull. Thus we see how speedily the Gospell should bee carried ouer the kingdomes of the world, when great Babel should downe, and how no power vpon earth should be able to stop it, the Angel flying with it in the middest of heauen. Now let vs heare the doctrine it selfe which he preacheth, for the summe of it is here reported, which is this, saying with a loud voyce, Feare God, & giue glory to him, for the houre of his iudgement is come: and worship him that made heauen and earth, the sea, and all the fountaines of water. What a wonderfull comfort and confirmation vnto vs here is giuen, to stand in the doctrine now published against ỹ Romish Antichrist, seeing the Gospel which this Angel flieth withall, containeth the whole summe of

all

THE REVELATION. 277

all the doctrine which M. Luther, M. Caluin, and the rest haue taught out of Gods word, no difference at all to be found? For reade ouer all their bookes which they haue written and published, and see if this be not the summe of all their doctrine which they preached, namely, that men should turne from fearing, glorifying and worshipping creatures, to feare, to glorifie, and to worship God alone, which hath made all things. The papistrie worshippeth and glorifieth euen with diuine honour, men and Angels, yea idols of gold, of siluer, of brasse, of stone, and wood, with the reliques and rotten bones of dead men. This Angell (euen those holy ministers whom God raised vp in these last dayes to deliuer his Church from the tyrannie of Antichrist) publish with a loude voyce, that the true and liuing God which made the heauens, the earth, the sea, and all the riuers and fountaines of waters, is alone to be feared, glorified, and worshipped with diuine honour. This Angell cryeth out with so mightie a crie, that all the nations doe heare the same, and are brought to see that it is wicked and blasphemous sacriledge against the glorious Sonne of God, to seeke remission of sinnes in the merites of men, and in the blood of Martyrs, and to pray to Saints or Angels, seeing there is one mediatour betweene God and man, the man Iesus Christ, who alone hath made the reconciliation by his crosse. This Angell hath now almost these fourescore yeares sounded forth ouer many great kingdomes, that it is horrible idolatrie, and euen the worship of deuils, to bow and pray to Images, which are nothing but vanitie and lies. Finally, this Angell hath proclaymed, and proclaymeth still at this day, prouing by the holy written word, that all the inuentions of poperie are nothing else but horrible prophanations of the worship of God, and therefore that men are to turne from them, and to feare, to glorifie and to worship the true God alone, with that pure worship which he hath prescribed in his written word. Let men examine euery syllable of that which S. Iohn reporteth here to be the voyce of the Angell that flyeth in the middest of heauen, with an euerlasting gospell to preach to all nations, and see if it be not in euery respect the same that hath been, and is now preached by the Ministers of the gospel. And then considering that the poperie is flat contrarie, ascribing to creatures the things which are peculiar to God, and to his Sonne Iesus Christ, why should not we take courage to stand against them, reioycing in that holy doctrine which the Lord hath here vttered in vision so long since? And now let vs see what effect the voyce of this Angell hath. Is this euerlasting gospell which chalengeth all honour, glory, and worship to God alone, published in vaine to the nations of the world, against the kingdome of the beast? No verily: It throweth it downe. For marke what he sayth: And there followed another Angell, saying, it is fallen, it is fallen, Babylon that great Citie, for she gaue to all nations to drinke the wine of the wrath of her fornication. So soone as euer the gospell brake forth and was published among the nations, calling vpon men to turne from the worship of creatures, to worship the true God, downe falleth the kingdome of Antichrist, the kingdome of confusion great Babel, which oppressed the Church, that Romish tyrannie of popes, which consisteth altogether of Idolatrie, superstition, and worship of deuils. The

T 3   light

light hath disclosed them, and men haue turned from those abominations. The Pope suppressing the holy word of God, and so bringing in thicke darknes vpon the nations in which hee had couered them, set vp himselfe euen in the place of God, and did what he lust in the darke, all his decrees being holden as the oracles of God, and he was worshipped as one that could both saue and destroy. Now at the voyce of this Angell, there is such light, that great kings and princes and rulers, with great multitudes of their subiects, had their eyes opened to behold that the Romish religion is idolatrous, that the Papacie is the very kingdome of the great Antichrist: and so whereas before, they worshipped the beast, now they holde vp their hands onely to the God of heauen, and glorifie him in his sonne Iesus Christ. Now were lawes made in kingdomes and prouinces, to abolish that vsurped power of the Bishop of Rome. Now were lawes and iniunctions set forth, to destroy, roote out and deface all monuments of his idolatrous and superstitious worship, which he had erected in all kingdomes. Now the Popes which were honoured, euen as Gods vpon the earth, while men sought remission of sinnes at their hands, and the blessing of eternall life, as if they could bestow it at their pleasure, are so farre from this honour and glory, that they be iudged the most vile and abominable that liue. Is not Babell then fallen? where is their glorie, where is their dignitie and estimation, yea, where is all their terrible power which they exercised in times past? If any will obiect that the dominion of Rome is not quite downe. That is nothing: for it is not meant that the fall of Babell, and her vtter abolishing should bee all at once, but her ruine shall be by degrees. It is a thing determined with God, and pronounced, that she shall downe: and therefore the Angell for to declare the certaintie thereof, doubleth the speech, saying, it is fallen, it is fallen, Babylon that great citie. Who is there in the worlde, which is not almost a blocke, which seeth not that the Romish power and tyrannie is cast downe by the voyce of the Angell, that is, by the doctrine of the Gospell now preached?

Behold here the power of Gods trueth in throwing downe Babell. Who could haue thought, liuing an hundreth yeares past, and beholding the power and glory of that Romane tyrannie, that such a Monarchie should so suddenly be cast down, neuer to be recouered againe? But as the Angell sayth, the time of his iudgement is come, and in very deede strong is he that iudgeth her. Nay, this is more then wonderfull, that whereas all the power of kings could not pull it downe (the kings fearing the Popes curse) the voyce of doctrine vttered by a few men of no worldly power hath done it. Yea I may say further, that there is no power of kings now able to hold it vp. For as it was beyond the power of kings to pull it downe, so is it farre from them now to be able to hold it vp. The beast hath bestirred him, and sent into all lands for to stirre vp the Princes to put to death all that will not worship him. And diuers mightie kings and princes haue so farre giuen their power to the beast, that they entred into a league (which they call the holy League) and vowed to ioyne together to roote out from the earth al that imbrace that gospell here vttered by the Angell, and will not imbrace the Romish religion, & worship the beast. But what haue they preuailed, seeing the Gospell hath spread fur-

ther

ther and further? Many make doubt whether the poperie bee that kingdome of the great Antichrist which should come. They cannot see it to be a matter of full certaintie, wherein we may rest out of all doubt and controuersie. Let them consider well of this place, what the euerlasting Gospell is which the Angell preacheth to all nations, kindreds, tongues and people. Let them also consider that the second Angel after the publishing of that doctrine, proclaimeth the fall of Babylon that great citie. Then further let them see whether it be not the same doctrine now of late preached among nations, which the Angell here vttereth. And finally, marke whether the poperie bee not cast downe by it. Finding these things thus to concurre, why should wee doubt, but that the papisme is the very beast with two hornes like a Lambe, euen the great Antichrist? And now brethren, how happie are we, and how great thankes and praise are wee with glad mindes to offer vp to God almightie, that we are borne and liue in the daies, in which the Angell flieth with this heauenly Gospel, and see the ruines of that idolatrous kingdomes, which hath murdered so many true worshippers of God, and seduced so many thousand thousands, vnto the worship of diuels? Yea howsoeuer they raile vpon them, happie and thrice happie are those great seruants of God, Luther, Caluin, Bucer, Martir, Bullinger, Cranmer, Ridley, and others, which haue succeeded and followed since their dayes, and are indeede the Angell that flyeth in the middest of heauen, to call men with the pure doctrine of the Gospel, from worshipping the beast and dumbe Idols, to worship the true and liuing God. Let vs also for our part step in, and with all our might so farre as the Lord doth inable vs, and call vs, strike at the head of this monster, and increase the ruines of wicked Babell. We all see how the seruants of Antichrist bestirre them, and especially those wicked traytors the Iesuites, to heale the wounds that are giuen to their Idoll, and to recouer the breaches, which are made in the walles of their great citie: and shall not we be as forward in the seruice of the Lord? Is there any thing here wherein we may so much reioyce, as in the ruine and downfall of Babylon, being so horribly wicked? For see what the Angell addeth as the cause why the Lord God will execute sharpe vengeance vpon her: for she gaue (sayth he) to all nations to drinke of the wine of the wrath of her fornication. Here bee but few words, but yet they expresse a sea, or gulfe of most wicked abominations committed by Babel, the Romish synagogue. For marke well euery part of the sentence: Her filthines is not compassed in with narrow bounds, as committed in some one kingdome: but spreadeth it selfe ouer all nations: for she sayth, she gaue to all nations to drinke of the wine, &c. It is a foule thing before God to corrupt one man: it is more to corrupt a familie, and so goe vp by degrees to a whole citie and to a kingdome, which is very much: and if it stayed there, yet how horrible must it needes bee in the sight of God? But Rome hath not stayed there, but hath corrupted and seduced all nations vnto Idolatrie, superstition, heresies, and worship of false Gods: who is able then to declare the largenes of the sea or gulfe of all her abominations? What madnes is it in the papists to boast of their multitudes? seeing it is plainly expressed, that the great Antichrist, the whore of Babylon shall giue to all nations to drinke

drinke of her cup. And this is the cause why the holy Ghost calleth Antichrist the man of sinne. Ieroboam made Israel to sinne when he set vp the golden calues to be worshipped and so might be called a man of sinne: but what was his fact, being in a little corner among the tenne tribes, if it bee compared to that which the Popes of Rome haue done in all nations? There is the man of sinne indeede. Neuer was there any kingdome vnder heauen, that corrupted and seduced so many nations vnto wicked idolatries, as the kingdome, or beast with two hornes. Thus much touching the large spreading of Babels abominations: now marke with what speech he expresseth her sinne. He calleth it the wine of wrath of her fornication. Because the Lord vseth this metaphor, that Babell offereth the nations a cup to drinke of, he also continuing the metaphor, calleth all her abominations wine, which she putteth into the same for them to drinke. And then further that we may vnderstand what wine it is that she hath caused them to drinke out of her cup, he calleth it the wine of her fornication. Although the Popes haue set vp or allowed stewes, and filled the earth with such kind of whoredomes yet this is not so much to bee taken for that, as for that spirituall whoredome, that idolatrie, superstition, and all filthie inuentions, by which they corrupted the holy ordinances of God, and set vp a false religion. This is their chiefe whoredome, wherein they haue drawne infinite thousands of thousands from God, to commit fornication with stockes and stones. And then last of all, it is not onely the wine of her sofnication, but the wine of the wrath of her fornication. This sheweth that the Lord is prouoked to wrath and displeasure, and so to execute vengeance for her abominations. This wine of wrath, may be taken both these waies: first, that the Lord being moued to wrath with the world, for despising his trueth, gaue scope to Satan to erect the kingdome of Antichrist, and so to bring in all abominable idolatrie. For that Saint Paul teacheth, 2. Thess. 2. Then secondly, that it prouoketh the Lord God to wrath, who is a iealous God, and will not suffer his glorie to be giuen to creatures, yea Idols, and to diuels, but he will be reuenged. Then wee see that the spirituall whoredome of the Church of Rome, is the wine of wrath. So lay al these together, Babylon that great citie hath spread her filthines so farre and wide, that she hath corrupted all nations, making them to drinke of her cup, so that there is a deepe gulfe of her abominations. She hath filled her cup with all filthie fornication, vnto which she hath led both the kings and their subiects, who haue greedily supped vp the same, euen to the dregs. It is the wine of wrath, for the iust God is prouoked thereby: therefore Babylon is fallen, it is fallen. It is not possible that this proude kingdome should stand, the most high God comming to iudgement against her, euen to powre forth his wrath and vengeance. Here is a generall doctrine for vs all to meditate often vpon. And that is, if the mightie kingdome of the world come downe for wickednesse, who can escape that prouoketh him? For if he iudge the nations, how shall any one man escape? And when yee see wicked men flourish, and be so mightie in the world that yee thinke they must needes stand, remember how great Babell which made all kings to tremble at her power, is fallen for her wickednes. So will the Lord God of heauen cast downe all the workes of iniquitie.

quitie. Now wee come to the voyce of the third Angell, who denounceth iudgement and vengeance vnto all those which will not turne from worshipping the beast, to worship the true God. And first it is to bee noted, that this Angell is also sayd to vtter his message with a loude voyce, which is to shew the vehementie thereof, which the slow, the deaffe, and dull eares of many causeth. For albeit the light of the Gospell hath turned so great multitudes from poperie, that Babell hath caught a very great fall, yet experience doth teach vs, that many hauing bin nuzled vp in poperie, stand vpon the aintiqultie of it, and condemne the holy Gospell of Christ as new learning: Therefore least such should flatter themselues, and least the weake should bee seduced by the, it is very necessary that the wrath & vengeance of God should bee strongly denounced against them. Thinke not therefore that it is an intemperate heate (or as some smooth Atheists terme it rayling) when the true seruants of Christ that publish the Gospell, doe with great vehemencie denounce vengeance against the popish idolaters: seeing the Lord hath here figured it long before by an Angell. Nay rather know that this Angell figureth the true ministers of the Gospell, and therefore they execute not their office faithfully, which do it not. There be many also which account so little which religion be set forth, that they think they worship God in both. They cannot see, but that the papists also bee good Christians, and worship God: the voyce of this Angell is very needfull for them, that they may see what dreadfull vengeance the Lord denounceth against the popish worshippers. Well, let vs come to the words which this Angell proclaimeth with so loude a voyce: They may all bee deuided into two partes, whereof the one, noteth out with supposition the worshippers of the beast: the other describeth the wofull torments which they shall endure for the same. The former is thus, If any man worship the beast and his image, and receiue his marke on his forehead or on his hand: that is to say, if any man professe and take the Church of Rome, euen that idolatrous strumpet, which vsurpeth power ouer Gods worde, to bee the true Church, euen the chast and beloued spouse of Christ: If any man acknowledge the Pope to bee the Vicar of Christ, the head of the Church, and that hee hath power and authoritie to make lawes to binde the faith and conscience, which men are to obey vnder paine of damnation, and so receiueth all his decrees as the oracles of God: If any hold, that there is no remission of sinnes but in that societie and vnder that head, and so will haue his pardon from him, or from some that haue that power from him, beleeuing that the Pope hath that power committed to him, to pardon whose sinnes he will, and that the same power is deriued from him as from the head and fountaine vnto all his chanelings: If any man hold these foresayd things, or carrie an open profession or marke to shew that he holdeth them, & ioyneth in the Idol seruice with that synagogue, or wisheth to ioye being restrained, the same worshippeth the beast and his image, and carrieth indeede his marke. That same is hee to whom, or against whom the Angell denounceth this sharpe vengeance.

One part of the words which denounce the horrible damnation vnto the popish worshippers, set forth the vengeance of God by two comparisons, namely of

wine

wine powred into a cuppe and giuen them to drinke, and of fire and brimstone in which they shal burne: the other declareth that their torment shal neuer haue any end, nor any intermission. When God by his Prophets of old, did threaten destruction to the wicked nations, hee sometime vsed this figuratiue speech, that they should take the cup and drink: So here, like as the Idolaters haue willingly receiued the cup at the hands of the whore of Babylon, to drink vp her filthy abominations, the Angell threatneth that they shall be made to drinke of another cup, that is, of the cup of Gods wrath. And he calleth it the wine of Gods wrath which is powred into this cup. Wine is a piercing thing when it is receiued into a mans bodie: and so by this similitude is meant, that the worshippers of Antichrist shall as it were euen drink and be filled both in soule and body, euen as vessels, with the piercing wine of the wrath of God. There shall bee no part of them free from it. And the Angell doth amplifie the matter, that he saith, it shall be vnmixed wine, which is not delayed, and therefore so much the more piercing and searching. O wofull creatures that drinke this wine, it will leaue no corner free in them, in all parts both of bodie and soule.

The other comparison, which is of fire and brimstone, declareth in most fearefull manner the bitter torments of the wrath of God. What torment is like vnto fire and brimstone? who is able to abide it euen for one day? If a man should lie a whole yeere in such torment, were it not a wonderfull horrour? And the Angell saith here, that they shall be tormented in fire and brimstone before the holy Angels, and before the Lambe. They shall be a gazing stocke in their torments vnto the Angels and Saints, who shal not pitie them, but reioyce to see their confusion. And moreouer, they shall not lie in these torments for a yeere, or for yeeres, but for euer, as the Angell sheweth. The smoake (saith he) of their torments ascendeth vp for euermore. We know that if smoake ascend vp, the fire is not quenched: therefore it declareth that this fire shall neuer bee quenched. Yea further, it is shewed, that it shall not be with them, as it is with men that suffer grieuous torments here in their bodies which come by fittes, with some intermission, and sometimes they haue things that refresh and comfort, and sometimes they sleepe and forget, or feele not their paine: but the euerlasting torment of these, as it were in fire and brimstone, shall neuer bee eased one minute of an houre, neither by day nor by night. This is the portion of those that worship the beast and his image, & receiue the print of his name. Here is the good which the Pope doth bring vpon all that loue and honour him. O consider it I beseech ye: and imbrace the pure and holie worship of God which he hath prescribed in his word. Cleaue fast vnto it, and bee not drawne by any torments to drinke of that whores cup: least yee drinke of the cup of Gods wrath. It is much better to giue your bodies to bee burned for the Lords trueth, then to be tormented world without end in fire and brimstone.

THE

THE XXXI. SERMON.
CHAP. XIIII.

12 *Here is the patience of the Saints, here are they which keepe the commandements of God, and the faith of Iesus.*
13 *And I heard a voice from heauen, saying vnto me, write, blessed are the dead which die in the Lord from henceforth, yea saith the spirit, because they rest from their labours, and their workes follow them.*

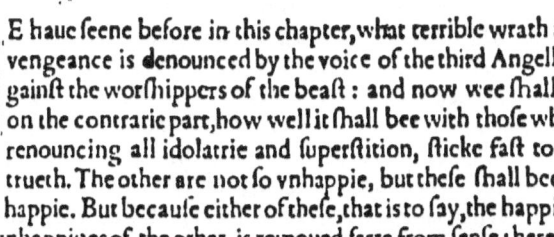E haue seene before in this chapter, what terrible wrath and vengeance is denounced by the voice of the third Angell, against the worshippers of the beast: and now wee shall see on the contrarie part, how well it shall bee with those which renouncing all idolatrie and superstition, sticke fast to the trueth. The other are not so vnhappie, but these shall bee as happie. But because either of these, that is to say, the happines of the one, and the vnhappines of the other, is remoued farre from sense: here is a sentence interlaced, to stirre vp and to prepare the minds of the godly vnto a deep consideration. For he saith, here is the patience of the Saints, here are they which keepe the commandements of God, and haue the faith of Iesus. It is sayd that all the popish worshippers of Idols shall be cast into hell, and tormented with eternall flames, because they forsake the true God, and follow the lawes of the beast: in the meane time they glory that the heauens are theirs, that their Pope can bring them thither: they insult ouer the godly, they reuile them as heretikes, they persecute and tread them downe. Here then is need of patience, here the holy seruants of God are tried.

Then on the other part, what precious promises are made vnto all those that shall faithfully and constantly imbrace the pure worship of the Lord? But what appearance is there now of any such thing? They be afflicted and tormented here in the world, so that of all men they seeme to bee the most miserable. Here therefore their obedience to the lawes of God, and their faith is tried: here may wee learne a good lesson, when we see the wicked enemies of Gods truth florish in the world, and oppresse the poore seruants of Christ. If we can looke vp vnto the high prouidence of God, who gouerneth and disposeth all by his heauenly wisedome: if we can with patience wait his time, we shal euen in the greatest assaults that can come, rest assured of this, that God will pull down al proud tyrants which oppresse his seruants, and which corrupt at their pleasure his holy worship. And that he will

powre

powre forth his vengeance vpon them. And further, we shal nothing doubt howsoeuer the faithfull be afflicted in this world, but that they shall bee raised vp vnto glory: their state shall be exceeding good. While men iudge by outward appearance, and by their owne wisedome, and carnall sence in these things, they be caried cleane awry, and chuse to cleaue to the stronger part. O let vs learne indeede, that we must haue our patience tried, our obedience also and faith, to see how we will stick to the truth. Many do stumble when they see the proud corrupters, euen like giants as it were raigne ouer the godly, and presse them downe at their pleasure, boasting of their wisedome, of their knowledge, of their faith and hope, as if they were the very maine pillers of all trueth vpon the earth, reuiling as base dung or drosse, such as vnfainedly studie in all singlenes of heart to pleaseGod, and that cleaue wholly to his word: but if they could behold what is threatned to the one, and what is promised to the other, it would stay and vphold them very much. We ought to fasten our eyes vpon it, that it may stay vs in patience.

As wee haue therefore seene the torments of Idolaters laid open, so let vs come now to the sentence vttered, which declareth the state of the godlie after this life: For we haue heard the vengeance denounced against the worshippers of the beast, and the preparing of the minds of the faithfull. I heard (saith he) a voice from heauen, saying vnto me, write, the dead are blessed from henceforth that die in the Lord, euen so saith the spirit, because they rest from their labours, and their works doe follow them. This is a most noble sentence, and worthy not onely to be grauen in letters of gold, but also, euen in the tables of the hart, and I beseech ye write it vp there. And we are to note first for expofition, that the chiefe or whole pith of matter of this sentence is set downe in few words in the middest thereof, and the matters of circumstance to commend the same, goe partly before, and partly follow it. For the whole matter is in these words, The dead are blessed that die in the Lord from henceforth. The matters of circumstance which goe before it to set forth the worthines and authority therof, are in these words; I heard a voice from heauen, saying vnto me, write. And that which followeth sheweth reasons why those dead are blessed in these words, The spirit sayth so, because they rest from their labours, and their workes follow them. I will deale with the words in that order in which they lie. Saint Iohn heard a voice from heauen, which sheweth the truth and excellencie of it, because it commeth from God. That which is from the earth, or from man, is of no dignitie, of no authoritie or credit, because there is nothing in man by nature but spirituall darknes, error, falshood, and vntruth. There is nothing but that which is polluted, vncleane, and abominable, which Satan the prince of darknes, hath brought in. Contrariwise, in heauen all is pure, and cleere, and free from errour, all is excellent and full of dignitie, and this voice commeth from heauen: This voice commeth from the throne of God, that we may giue credit vnto it, as vnto an infallible oracle. It is most requisite that this saying, the dead are blessed which die in the Lord, from henceforth, should bee confirmed in this maner, it is so farre remoued from all sence and reason of man. For the faithfull haue from time to time been reproched, reuiled, dishonoured among men, and

THE REVELATION. 285

many of them cruelly murdered, and haue left no shew behind them in the world why they should be in better case then others. The world reioyceth and triumpheth against them, as if their end were meere follie and madnes. Well, a voyce from heauen is to be opposed against all voyces of men whatsoeuer, and wee may safely rest in it. Although wee doe not see how blessed the dead are which die in the Lord, yet we may stedfastly beleeue it, because this voyce commeth from heauen which affirmeth it.

Then it followeth, *Saying vnto me, write*. Saint Iohn sheweth, that he did not only heare the voice pronouncing such a matter, but also before it is pronounced, he is willed to write it. Write (saith the voice) the dead are blessed which die in the Lord from henceforth. He had a commandement in the first chapter to write in a booke the things which he had seene, & being now againe commanded to write this saying, that it might stand in record vnto all posterities, it is to teach vs that it is a saying right excellent & necessary for al the seruants of God, euen to confirme them against all troubles, daungers, reproches, infamies, and against the terror of death it selfe. The most high God himselfe from heauen, hath willed his seruant Iohn to write, that the dead are blessed which dye in the Lord. But see how the speech is framed, it is not sayd indefinitely, generally, or absolutely without restraint, that the dead are blessed, but those that dye in the Lord: For there is a difference of the dead. Such as dye in their sins, death doth not dispatch or rid them from their miseries, but is as the gate through which they passe into the gulfe of endlesse woe. They passe from the lesse miseries (which they haue endured in this life) vnto the greater. Such as die in the Lord, that is, all such as are found in Christ, death is as the gate through which they passe from all the calamities which light vpon them in this vale of miseries, vnto endlesse ioy and blisse. For Christ hath ouercome sin, the diuel, and death it selfe: He hath led them captiue and triumphed ouer the in his crosse. All such as are found in him, haue all their sins abolished, his innocencie is put vpon the, they are reconciled vnto God, how shall any euill then come nigh vnto them? Behold what a goodly thing it is to die in the Lord: It is the fulnes of blisse. And they that liue in ỹ Lord, as ye must obserue, are they that shall die in the Lord. I doe not denie, but that some which spent their life wickedly haue dyed in the Lord, as the theefe for one, which did hang at the right hand of Christ. But this is a rare gift of God, they be more then mad fooles which presume vpõ it. He that will be wise, let him bend all his studie and care, euen in the whole course of his life to apprehẽd the faith and liuely power of Christ, euen to liue in him, that he may die in him. Yea let all the whole life bee no more but to learne to die well and blessedly. For if a man lay hold of the holy faith, and study to please God with a pure conscience, if hee seeke the mortification of the old man with all his corrupt lusts, and fulfill not the desires of the flesh: If hee put on the new man, and walke in the vertues of the spirit, the vertue and power of the death and resurrection of Christ is in him, he doth liue in ỹ Lord, when death approcheth he shal haue peace of conscience, he shall reioyce that he shall also die in the Lord. There is no goodlier matter for vs to endeuour then this same. And marke well how he saith from

henceforth

SERMONS VPON

hence-forth, which is as much to say, presently, or forth-with. They that dy in the Lord are blessed by entring into ioy presently, there is no delay. Their soules wander not vp and downe, that it need to be said, God rest their soules, God rest their soules, as the superstitious papists vse to say. They are not boyling in purgatorie, and so neede praiers, almes, Dirges, masses, and the Popes pardons to helpe them out, nor any other popish filthy trash. Ye see that the voyce of God from heauen pronounceth, and willeth Iohn to write it, that the dead which die in the Lord are not onely blessed, but also from hence-forth, that is to say, euen so soone as euer they bee departed out of this life, because they enter presently into rest, and are freed from all their calamities, labours, and afflictions, which they endured while they walked vpon the earth. What then, shall we beleeue this voyce of God, which S. Iohn is willed to set downe in writing, or shall wee beleeue the popish Church which affirme, teach, and stifly maintaine the flat contrary? Which (think you) deserueth to be credited, the voyce of God from heauen, which telleth vs that they are presently in blisse and rest from their labours which dye in the Lord? or shall we beleeue the pope and his shauelings, which for their gaine, do teach that many which dye in the true faith, and so in the Lord, goe into the greiuous paines of purgatorie, and must haue their helpe by Masses and pardons to come out? There bee three places (say they) vnto which the soules of men doe goe when they depart this life, heauen, hell, and purgatorie. They which dye in a perfect good estate, goe immediatly to heauen: they that on the contrarie are found in a state so wicked that they bee not at all in the state of grace, goe directly to hell: and such as bee in a middle estate betweene these, not perfect, but hauing some drosse of their sinnes, and yet not out of the state of grace, these before they can goe to heauen, are cast into that purging fire, and tarrie there longer or shorter time as the matter of their sinne is, or as they receiue helpe from the liuing. This is the popish doctrine. And when wee say it is wicked, and that it dooth derogate from the bloud of Christ, which onely doth purge the soule of man from sinne: when we say it is blasphemous that the Pope dooth challenge such power, as to fetch out soules out of purgatorie by his pardons, which he selleth for money: and when we truely affirme that there is no such purgatorie taught in Gods word, but that it is mans inuention, alleadging this place against it, that the dead are forth-with blessed which dye in the Lord, because they be at rest: the Iesuites reply, that this place maketh nothing against purgatorie, and certaine vaine shifts they haue deuised to auoyd it. As first they would haue these words in the Lord, to be taken for the Lord, or for the Lords cause, and so they say it is to be vnderstood onely of the Martyrs which were slaine for witnessing the Gospel, whom their Church denyeth to goe to purgatorie, but directly to heauen without delay. So they wil haue it thus, the dead are blessed that dye in the Lord, that is the Martirs, they goe forth-with to heauen, as this text teacheth; but yet others (say they) goe to purgatorie. Let it be that in the Lord may be taken to be, for the Lord: yet what reason can be shewed why such restraint should bee made in this place? Are not al that dye in Christ, true members of his mysticall bodie? Are not his members coupled vnto

him

him as to their head by a spirituall vnion? Then doth not S. Paul say, that hee was made sinne for vs, which knew no sinne, that we in him might be made the righteousnes of God? 2.Cor. 5. What is this, but that the things which are in the body are imputed to the head: and that contrariwise the things which are in the head are imputed to the bodie? seeing the head, and the body stand as one ioyned together. All the redeemed are the body, and Christ the head, they be in him, and he in them. That which is theirs, is imputed vnto their head Christ: as namely their sinne, their curse, their penaltie, their death, all which he bare vpon the crosse, that he might abolish them. That which is his, is imputed vnto his body, euen his obedience, his puritie; and all good things that be in him. He hath abolished their vnrighteousnes, their curse, and their death: and hath put vpon them his righteousnes, his blessing, and his life. If these things be thus, (as those words of S. Paul doe plainly shew) how should any that dyeth a true member of Christ, whether he die as a martyr, or otherwise bee sent any where else to bee purged, but onely in the blood of Christ? Haue not all true beleeuers their pardon through Christ, and die in him, as well as the martyrs? If Christ were made sinne for all the members of his mysticall bodie which is the Church, and if euery true member of the Church, bee made the righteousnes of God in him: then how shall not all that dye in him forth-with be blessed? Hath not the death of Christ sufficiency in it selfe fully to abolish sinne, but his very true members which be in him and he in them, must be cast into a fire to purge them? Nay, they are from henceforth blessed that die in him. Our Iesuites reply yet further, that although these words, the dead are from henceforth blessed that die in the Lord, be taken generally for all that die in the state of grace, yet it proueth nothing against purgatorie. How so? Forsooth they shew reasons to proue, that such as bee in purgatorie, bee in a more blessed estate then the godly which liue vpon the earth, which yet are called blessed euen while they liue. First, because the words of the text here be plaine, that such as die in the Lord doe rest from their labours, they affirme that the soules in purgatorie may bee sayd to rest in peace. Is it not strange that purgatorie must become a place of such happie rest? But let vs heare what reasons they bring. The soules in purgatorie (say they) are set free from the labours, afflictions, and persecutions of this life. See how contrary the popish seducers are vnto themselues. For when they would make their greatest gaine of purgatorie, they terrifie the rich men by describing the horrible and vnspeakeable torments thereof, that they may bee readie to buie their pardons and their Masses with any exceeding great price, rather then to lye there one day. The fire of purgatorie (say they) differeth not in sharpnes, or bitternes of torment, from the fire of hell, but onely that it lasteth not but for a time, the soule commeth out of it, but they that bee in hell neuer come out. And then further they say, that the fire of hell exceedeth in heate our common fire which wee haue here, as much as our fire exceedeth painted fire. Painted fire doth burne but a little, and we al know that our fire doth burne with great smart, and if the smart of the fire of purgatorie bee as farre beyond that, as that is beyond the smart of painted fire, I thinke they haue small rest which be in purgatorie. When the Pope would

would fill his coffers, then purgatorie fire burneth with vnspeakeable torments: but when the holy Ghost pronounceth, that the dead which dye in the Lord are forth-with blessed, becaule they rest from their labours, then rather then there shall be no purgatorie, purgatorie shall be a place of happie rest in comparison of the afflictions of this life. Sure if this doctrine of the Iesuites stand, the Pope were euen almost as good to haue no purgatorie at all. They say, there goe no Martyrs into purgatorie, such then as goe thither, goe but out of the ordinary afflictions of this life, and the state there (they say) is better then the state here: then the rich men, if it be so, will not giue their money and their lands very fast to get out so speedily from thence, but euen arme themselues to beare it: for they bee very loath to goe from hence, and if their estate here bee lesse blessed then there, what should they make such haste to get out from thence? Yea, say the Papists, for there they are out of the danger of sinning. What then? if they lye boyling in torments vnspeakable for their former offences, doe they rest from their labours? Can it be sayd that they be blessed because they be at rest? Yea (say they) although the torments be great, yet because none goe into that purging fire but such as goe to heauen, they are sure of their saluation, they know they shall goe to heauen after a time, which they could not for certaintie know while they liued here, and so they rest and are blessed. Then it seemeth, that the soule may at the same time feele, both vnspeakable torment, and vnspeakable ioy: which is absurd. The whole man consisting of bodie and soule, the bodie being in paine, the minde may reioyce: but how both those should be in the minde at once let them shew. Well yet further, because they perceiue that these their friuolous cauils cannot auoyd the force of this place, they proceede and say, the word from hence-foorth, doth not signifie from this present time forward, as if the Apostle had sayd, that after their death and so forward they are happie: but noteth the time past of the Fathers vnder the law, with the time of the Gospell, in this sence, that in the time of the law, the Fathers that dyed in the state of grace went into *Limbus Patrum*: but now, except the impediment be in themselues, such as dye in the state of grace goe straight to heauen, and so are blessed in comparison of them that went into that *Limbus*. It is a straunge thing to heare men reason vpon their owne inuentions: for this *Limbus Patrum* is euen as hard to proue, as the purgatorie, I meane as the papists doe teach of it: for they make it to be as it were the brimme of hell, and therefore they say Christ descended into hell, to fetch out the Fathers. Christ sayth, that the soule of Lazarus was carried by the Angels into Abrahams bosome where it was comforted: by which it is euident that the soules of the godlie were in blessed rest before the comming of our Sauiour Christ. To say therefore that the dead that now dye in the Lorde are blessed because they goe straight to heauen, and not to *Limbus*, is a rotten cauill, and not worthie any answere. Well, thus this place which pronounceth that the dead which dye in the Lorde, doe rest from their labours and are blessed, quite ouerthroweth the popish purgatorie: God hath pronounced it from heauen, the Iesuites haue beat their braines to inuent cauils and shifts to defend their inuented purgatorie from the dint of it, but cannot.

Therefore

Therefore beloued, lay hold of Christ to liue and die in him, and bee assured that so soone as euer yee depart this life, your soules shall bee carried into rest and ioy. Beleeue not that fearefull purgatorie which is blasphemous against the blood of Christ, and is maintained by the Popes of Rome to get plentie of money for their Masses and pardons.

It followeth, The spirit sayth so. This is added for confirmation, because wee are so hard of beleefe. The holy Ghost is the spirit of truth, and he affirmeth from heauen, that the dead which die in the Lord, are blessed from henceforth: shall we not beleeue him? Shall we doubt of his word? Although they seeme to make an end of their life here without all honour, yea euen to perish, the world doth so insult ouer them, yet doubt not but that they are blessed, because the spirit sayth so. He sayth so, then ground vpon it. His credit is more then the credit and all his shauelings: beleeue them not, for they speake by the spirit of Antichrist. And although wee ought to giue credit to the voice of God vttered barely without reasons to confirme the same, yet he staieth not there, that is, in bare affirming, but yeelding to our weaknes, addeth confirmations. For he sayth, they rest from their labours, and their workes doe follow them. Their happines is here set foorth in two parts, to shew indeede that it is a true blessednesse. The one is, that they rest from their labours: the other is, that their workes doe follow them. As touching the former, it is a great part of happines to be deliuered and set free from calamities, from sorowes, from labours, and from the troubles of this life, especially in the godly, who as Saint Paul sayth, are of all other the most miserable in this life, 1. Cor. 15. for they are subiect to the common calamities, as of sicknes, pouertie, losses, and painfull labours, and besides those, the world doth hate them, reuile and persecute them, and that so bitterly, that many of them haue been imprisoned, racked, tormented, and cruelly put to death by the Romish beast. It is, as I sayd, a great part of happines to rest from all these labours: but it is not a perfect happines, vnlesse we will say that the horse which hath been sore trauelled, is happie, when he is dead, because he resteth from his labours. The dumbe beast being dead feeleth neither good nor euill, but in that respect is it well that he resteth from his miseries which his cruell master put him vnto: And least any might imagine that the dead in Christ had none other blessednes but that, euen to rest from their labours, here is added the other part, namely, that their works follow them. This maketh vp the true blessednes, this sheweth that they do not rest from their labors as feeling neither good nor euill, but that they bee in ioy. For God hath promised, that he will honour them that honour him. He hath promised that he will reward with glorie euery good worke of his seruants: and here it is said, that their workes do follow them: their good deeds which they did in loue of God, and of his truth, are not forgotten, but doe accompanie them. Death seemeth to cut off all from them, and quite to strip them, as indeed he cutteth off honours, riches, wiues, children, and friends: but he cannot cut off, nor separate them from their good works. Indeed it is most certaine that a man goeth naked and bereft of all things that he inioyeth in this life, sauing his works, for they doe still accompanie him, as we are

V   here

here taught. It is a thing worthie great confideration. Men glue their mindes to feeke for fuch things as they think fhall do them good: as for humane wifedome, for riches, for honours, for dignities, for delights, and for friends. And fome vfe there is indeede of thefe things here in the world: but they doe not well confider that death fhall cut them off from all thefe things, and leaue them vtterly naked. They do not wifely weigh what it is to haue great troupes and trains attend vpon them for a time. Of fuch as death will fhut the doore vpon, and thruft backe from following of their mafters, They doe not wifely prouide fuch a traine as death can not keepe backe, but that they fhall accompanie and follow them: For there is fuch a traine, and who are they? euen their workes. For fo it is here faid, and their workes fhall follow them. O that we could well confider what a bleffing this is: how would we then while wee liue here, prouide to haue fuch a traine to accompanie that our death as cannot be kept backe, when all other things fhall leaue vs alone & vtterly forfake vs? We fee the great men of this world what great troupes they haue follow them of houfhold feruants, and retainers: what wealth, what honors, what ioyes and pleafures they poffeffe. O how happy are they, if at the houre of death when all thofe fhall forfake the, they haue as goodly a traine alfo of good workes to attend vpon them! For they that imbrace the true faith of Chrift Iefus, and bring forth plentifull fruits thereof, (as Saint Paul willeth Timothie to charge them that be rich in this world to be rich in good workes) fhall finde the comfort and ioy thereof at the houre of their death. It may be demaunded, fhall men then come to bleffedneffe or bee faued by their owne workes? The holy fcripture faith plainly, that he which is not a forgetfull hearer; but a doer of the worke, fhall bee bleffed in his deed, looke Iam. 1. verf. 25. And bleffed are the mercifull, and bleffed are the peacemakers, Matth. 5. &c. but yet wee may not bee fo groffe as with the papifts to hold that mens good deedes doe iuftifie them, or merit eternall life. Chrift is our iuftification whom we apprehend by faith: good works are the fruits of faith, and do declare that the life and power of Chrift is in vs. For before we be in him, we can doe nothing, Iohn 15. verf. 5. Moreouer, albeit they bee not of that value to merit eternall glorie, our workes we doe of faith: yet God hath promifed to reward them with glorie, which commeth of his free grace. We are therfore, if we be wife, to endeuour not onely to fhunne wicked workes, but alfo to abound and to be rich in all good workes. A great ioy it fhall bee vnto vs at the houre of our death, when all other comforts fhall faile vs; for what is it that can then doe vs any good? But if we haue imbraced the truth, and ftudied to pleafe God night and day, performing with a good confcience thofe duties which hee requireth at the hands of his children, both towards his holy maieftie, and towards men: It fhall refrefh vs with fweete ioy to looke backe into the race that we haue runne, it fhal eafe and comfort vs in the middeft of all griefes which we endure in the body: and when the eyes be clofed vp, a goodly troupe fhall attend vpon the foule, euen of holy deedes, whofe reward fhall be great. We all know we fhall die: wee doe all of vs confeffe that our life here vpon earth, is but as a fhadow and as a vapour. Wee can difcourfe vpon the vanitie of riches, and honours, and pleafures: what a great
follie

THE REVELATION.

follie and madnes is it then for a man to haue abundance of riches, whereby hee might be able to ouerflow in good works, in aduancing the glory of God, and relieuing the needie, and doth remaine as a barren withered tree which is planted where it hath no moisture? Whatsoeuer gift God hath bestowed vpon vs whereby we may be able to doe good deedes, let vs not neglect the time, but take all occasions to be doing, that when wee die our workes may follow vs, and that we may receiue the blessed reward that is promised. Some neede instruction for the soule, some reliefe for the bodie, doe what thou canst to helpe them; thou shalt heape vp treasure, and lay a good foundation against the time to come, 1.Tim.6. But shall not the wicked men haue their workes follow them also? Yea, euen to their great shame: for all shall be accompanied. And as the good workes of the righteous doe follow them vnto their praise and glorie: so the euill deedes of the wicked shall accompanie them vnto iudgement, and euen into hell; that there they may receiue the reward that those their workes haue deserued. It were well for the vngodly if they might any way wind themselues from the traine of their euill deeds: but they cannot, for they shall follow them with a loud cry for vengeance. Let all such therefore as be wise, prepare themselues for death, in doing such good works as they may reioyce in.

THE XXXII. SERMON.
CHAP. XIIII.

14 And I looked, and behold a white cloude, and vpon the cloude one sitting like vnto the sonne of man, hauing on his head a golden crowne; and in his hand a sharpe sickle.

15 And another Angell came out of the Temple, crying with a loude voice to him that sate on the cloud, thrust in thy sickle and reape, for the time is come for thee to reape, for the haruest of the earth is come.

16 And he that sate on the cloud thrust in his sickle on the earth, and the earth was reaped.

17 Then another Angell came out of the Temple which is in heauen, hauing a sharpe sickle.

18 And another Angell came out from the Altar which had power ouer fire, and cryed with a loud voice to him that had the sharpe sickle, and said, thrust in thy sharpe sickle, and gather the clusters of the vineyard of the earth, for her grapes are ripe.

19 And the Angell thrust in his sharpe sickle on the earth, and cut downe the

grapes of the vineyard of the earth, and cast them into the great winefat of the wrath of God.

20 *And the winefat was troden without the citie, and blood came out of the winefat euen vnto the horse bridles, by the space of a thousand and sixe hundreth furlongs.*

Here hath been set foorth vnto vs before in this chapter, the ruine of great Babell, which is the kingdome of the beast, and the same ruine wrought by the preaching of the Gospell. The light of the trueth bringeth them down. There was also vengeance denounced against the worshippers of the beast, and that in most grieuous maner. Now in this which I haue read vnto you, here is described their vtter ouerthrow, and the vtter ouerthrow of all the wicked, which shall be at the day of the generall iudgement. For here is a description of the last iudgement, and of the wrath of God that shall be powred forth vpon all wicked sinners. The whole matter is painted out vnder two similitudes: the one of the haruest, the other of the vintage. In the former of these similitudes, there is first a representation, or a description of our Lord Iesus the high iudge, comming in his glory to iudge the world. When he walked vpon the earth, and spake of the iudgement day, Matth. 25. he said he would come in the cloudes of heauen, and sit vpon the throne of his glorie: and here Saint Iohn saith, I looked, and behold a white cloud, & vpon the cloud one sitting like to the Sonne of man. Here then is such a throne, and such a glorie, as all the kings and Iudges of the earth come farre short of. They verily sit vpon high thrones, and in great maiestie vpon the earth, but the throne and the maiestie here described is far greater, for it is heauenly. There is no iudge but he that can lift vp himselfe so high as to sit in the cloudes of heauen. This is a peculiar glorie to that iudge, and it is not to bee passed by, that hee saith, It is a white cloude vpon which he sitteth, for thereby is represented the vprightnes and integritie of the iudge. The Iudges vpon earth doe faile often in iudgement, being carried awry sometime with ignorance, sometime with affections either of loue or of hatred, & sometimes through feare, yea and some no doubt at sometime are corrupted with bribes: but here is no such thing, this seate is white, euen cleere, innocent, and pure from all spot or staine. This is a right worthie commendation of the Iudge, that no man shall receiue wrong iudgement from his mouth. The sentence shall bee vpright, iust, and perfect, both to the one part, and to the other.

It followeth, That this iudge sitting vpon the cloud, hath on his head a golden crowne. This sheweth his authoritie and power, for Christ is as it were crowned king of kings, and Lord of Lords. He hath receiued all maiestie, and power, in so much that euery knee shall bowe, and all tongues shall confesse that Iesus is the Lord, to the glory of God: as here he that representeth him sitting vpon the cloud, is crowned with a golden crowne. Then it is said, that hee hath a sharpe sickle in his hand. Our Sauiour himselfe in certaine parables, Matth. 13 likened the end of the world vnto haruest, and so accordingly in this place the last iudgement being

ing represented by harueft, the Iudge hath a sharpe sickle in his hand, with which he commeth for to reape. For a sickle is for that vse, a sickle is for harueft. But what is resembled by this sharpe sickle, may some man say? I answer that by this sharpe sickle is signified the sharpe seueritie of iustice and vengeance, with which, all the wicked shall at the dreadfull day of iudgement be cut downe. The sentence of iustice pronounced against them by the iudge, shall they feele to be a right sharpe sickle indeed: it shall cut (as we say) euen to the bone. It shall reape them euen as corne is reaped, and they shal be bound into sheaues, and cast into the lake of fire. They shall feele the sharpnes of this sickle world without end. It may be said that the iudgement shall bee both of the iust, and of the vniust. Yea but this figure is shewed to set foorth the terrible wrath against the vniust onely: for the iust shal feele no such seueritie of iudgement. It shall be a most happie and ioyfull day vnto them, euen the day of redemption.

Then it followeth: *And another Angell came out of the Temple, crying with a loud voyce to him that sate vpon the cloude, thruft in thy sickle and reape, because the time is come for thee to reape, for the harueft of the earth is ripe.* The Lord Iesus shall come to iudgement at the time which his father hath decreed, and therefore here commeth a commandement from the throne of God, to him that sitteth vpon the cloud to thruft in his sickle, and it is said, that the time for him to reape is come. Wee must also marke how he rendreth the reason, namely, that the harueft of the earth is ripe. For as men doe know when to reape their corne, namely when it is ripe and well withered: so the Lorde knoweth the time of iudgement, euen when the wickednes of the world is fully ripe. We see great and horrible abominations daily ouerflow in the world; wee may wonder at the long suffering and patience of God, yet we must not thinke that he regardeth not, because men are let alone, but remember what is here said, that the harueft must be ripe, and then the Lord will come and cut it downe. God promised to giue the land of Canaan to Abraham, and to his seede, and for the wickednes of those nations which dwelt therein, he would deftroy them: to plant in his people: yet he telleth Abraham, that his seede should bee foiournor foure hundreth yeeres. Adding moreouer that they should in the fourth generation returne thither, beeaufe (faith the Lord) the sinne of the Amorite is not yet full, Gen. 15. ver. 16. As the Lord deferred to caft out and to deftroy those nations vntill such time as their wickednesse was growne to the full: so we learne here that he deferreth the great day of iudgement vntill the iniquities and sinnes of the earth be fully ripe: then is the Lords harueft, then will he cut downe his corne. Doubtles if then haue this wisedome not to thruft in sickle vntill the corne bee readie: the moft high God the fountaine of all wisedome, knoweth much more the time when the sinnes of the world are come to their full ripenes. Doubtles so farre as we can discerne, the regions are already white vnto the harueft, we may euen looke daily for the sharpe sickle to cut them all downe: but yet wee know not but that there may bee some good diftance of time yet remaining to their full ripenes, onely let vs be sure the time will come of this iudgement: and therefore I befeech ye, let it bee your greateft care to ftand faft in the

true

true feare of God, that wee bee not found among those that shall feele the sharpe sickle. Then it is said, that he which sate vpon the cloud thrust in his sickle on the earth, and the earth was reaped. It is a great haruest, and yet this reaper can reape it all. Behold the mightie power and strength of the iudge, which none shall be able to withstand. For euen as the corne is easily cut downe with the sickle, and hath no power to resist the reaper, so shall all the wicked, be they neuer so many, and neuer so mightie, bee cut downe with the sickle of Gods iudgement; and no way be able to resist. They shall be all as ripe corne vnto the sharpe sickle of the iudge. Men doe now encourage themselues in wickednes, because they be many that ioyne therein together, and because they be mightie: but let them thinke vpon this sharpe sickle which shall be thrust into the thickest of them; and shall cut them downe by handfuls. The mightie warriours, the great princes, and the kings of the earth, with all their nobles and traine, shall be but as weake straw to the sickle. This iudge, when his haruest is once come, will thrust in his sharpe sickle, and cut downe euery high thing which exalteth it selfe against God. He will cut downe the kingdome of the great Antichrist, that Romish beast. He will cut down the whole kingdome of darknes: he will cut downe the diuels themselues, there shall nothing remaine now, the whole haruest shall be reaped. O that men would consider this before hand, and be wise, and not bolden themselues for to doe euill, by their strength and multitude. Now they stand for thick, euen as whole regions of corne, and thinke there is none but they: who shall be able to hurt them? Well, let them be so, here commeth the reaper, and they shall finde that there is one too hard for them, which will destroy them all, who indeed hath a scattered remnant which he will saue. Thus wee haue seene one figure by which the iudgement day is represented: but the Lord doth represent it by two, and therefore now followeth the other, which is of the vintage.

In our countrie we make no wine, and therfore this comparison is not so cleere to euery one, as that other of the haruest is, how the corne is reaped downe when it is ripe, that euery man knoweth. In the hot countries where the vines grow, when the time of the vintage commeth, the husbandman commeth with a sharp instrument, which is here also called a sickle, & cutteth off the clusters of grapes. Then is there a winepresse, and into that he casteth those clusters; and then after that the presse is troden, to the end that the iuyce may be pressed out. Now to this the Lord compareth the destruction of the vngodly at the last day: The wicked shall be cut downe as grapes, cast into the presse and troden. If any shall demaund, why this vengeance which the Lord will execute vpon the wicked at the day of iudgement, is described by two similitudes, the one of the haruest, the other of the vintage: I answere, that it is not onely to declare the full certaintie of the thing, as the holie scripture vseth to double a thing for certaintie, but also to raise men vp from their securitie and drowsines. For wee see how men delight and sport themselues in all maner of abominable sins, and how little they think of such vengeance to come, as if their doings shuld neuer be called to any reckonings, yea when they do think of it, it is but euen as it were in a dreame, or a matter so farre off, as if it should not

be

THE REVELATION.

be, and therefore that the godly may be strengthened, and shake off securitie, (for the wicked will take no warning) the thing is doubled. Let vs therefore beloued, howsoeuer the Lord let wickednesse here escape vnpunished for a time, and the wicked which prouoke God doe flourish) assure our selues that there is a day comming when vengeance shall be powred foorth in full measure vpon all those which haue corrupted their waies vpon the earth.

But let vs come to the words of this text: *Then another Angell came (sayth he) out of the Temple which is in heauen, hauing a sharpe sickle.* This Angell also representeth the Lord Iesus, who shall iudge both the quicke and the dead. He is ascended into heauen, he is exalted in glorie aboue all, sitting at the right hand of God, and exercising the fulnes of all power, and from thence he shall come with great glorie to iudge the world, as it is sayd here, that the Angell commeth out of the temple which is in heauen. Hee hath also a sharpe sickle, because the iudgement is likened to the vintage: for with his hooke or sickle he will cut and gather the grapes of the earth. What it signifieth I tolde you before: for this sickle representeth the same thing that the sickle of him that sate vpon the white clowde, which reapeth the haruest. The sentence of iudgement shall cut downe very seuerely and sharply. Well, the Iudge hath this sharpe sentence readie, and expecteth the fulnes of time, which the high wisedom of God hath appointed, when the clusters of grapes shall be fully ripe for the vintage. For so soone as that time is come, hee shall presently cut them downe, and therefore see what followeth. *Another Angell came out from the Altar which had power ouer fire, and cryed with a loud voyce to him that had the sharpe sickle, and said, Thrust in thy sharpe sickle, and gather the clusters of the vineyard of the earth, for her grapes are ripe.* Now then the time is come, because wickednes is growne to the full: the clusters are ripe, and euen readie for the winepresse. O most wise God, which hast appoynted the times and the seasons, thy patience and long suffering is great, it is meet that we should wait thy good pleasure and will, which disposest all things to thy glorious praise, and to the good of thy chosen people.

But let vs come more particularly to the matter. He saith, an Angell came out from the Altar which had power ouer fire. There is some difficultie in these words, but we must bee wise with sobrietie. The Lord is said to dwell in his holy temple in heauen. In that temple and most holy place wee haue a great high priest, our Lord Iesus, who is our Mediatour, and intercessor. There is sayd to bee an Altar, which Altar indeede he is: for hee is both priest, sacrifice and Altar. It is sayd before in this prophecie, that the soules of them that were slaine for the testimonie of Iesus, were vnder the Altar. Then wee may take it, that the time of the last iudgement is decreed in the secret counsell of God, and commeth from the innermost place in the temple to represent so much. For in the time of the law there was a golden Altar in the most holie place, euen in the presence of God. But why is this Angell said to haue power ouer fire, or what is meant by that, there is the difficultie? Some doe take it, that by fire here is meant the vengeance of God, which vsually in the holie Scriptures is called fire. And so they take the sence to bee this, that

V 4   the

the Angell is the executor of Gods wrath vpon the bloodie kingdome of Antichrift, and that hee is fayd therefore to come out from the Altar, becaufe it is fayd before, that vnder the Altar lye the foules of thofe which were killed for the teftimonie of Iefus, crying for vengeance. This is a godly fence, & I could yeeld vnto it, but that there is in the 16. chapter an Angell called the Angell of the waters. For thereby I take it plaine, that this is fpoken of the materiall fire, becaufe that other in chap. 16. is to bee taken of the materiall waters. Then thus wee reade, that S. Paul fpeaking of the exaltation of Chrift, faith, God hath placed him at his right hand in heauen, farre aboue all principalitie, and power, and might, and domination, Ephef. 1. verf. 21. By which tearmes he noteth the Angels: And they are alfo called thrones, principalities, mights, &c. Coloff. 1. verf. 16. Thefe titles are giuen vnto them, becaufe the Lord God doth vfe their miniftrie in ruling and preferuing the world. Then although we are not curioufly to difpute, yet we may take it that God hath giuen power to fome Angels ouer the fire, and to fome ouer the waters, and to fome ouer other creatures; for the ordering and preferuation of them. Then further wee are plainly taught, that at the day of iudgement, the Lord will come in fire. For thus fpeaketh S. Paul, *When the Lord Iefus fhall be made manifeft from heauen with his mightie Angels, with flaming fire, to render vengeance to all that know not God, nor obey the Gofpell of our Lord Iefu Chrift.* 2. Theff. 1. verf. 7. Alfo Saint Peter in his fecond epiftle and fecond chapter doth teach, that the heauens and the earth are kept for fire: and that the elements fhall melt with heate, and that the earth and the things which are therein fhall bee burnt vp, 2. Pet. 3. Then feeing it is fo, that the Lord will come to iudgemēt with flaming fire, wherwith the creatures fhall be burnt, we may fee, that the Angell which had power ouer fire is here fitly brought in, when the iudgement fhall bee. When this Angell had cryed with a lowd voyce to the other, that hee fhould thruft in his fickle and gather the clufters of the earth, becaufe her grapes are ripe: it followeth that by and by the Angell thruft in his fickle and cut them downe, and caft them into the great wine fatte of the wrath of God. I tolde ye before, that where the wines are made, they haue a preffe or fatte into which they caft the clufters, that their iuyce may bee preffed out. And according to that, it is here fayd, how the Angell cut downe the clufters of grapes of the earth, and caft them into the fatte or preffe where they fhall be preffed. Then what are thefe clufters of grapes? They bee the wicked men of the world. And why are they compared to clufters? Becaufe they grow fo thicke, euen on heapes like grapes. Yee haue great partes of the worlde which renounce the name of Chrift: as the Heathen, the Iewes and the Turkes. There bee very large kingdomes of fome of thefe. Againe, come to thofe which acknowledge the name of our Lord Iefus Chrift, what heapes and multitudes are there of Idolaters? Come neerer euen to thofe kingdomes in which the Gofpell is preached, bee there no clufters among them of thefe ftinking grapes? Verely the whole vines doe feeme to bee ouerfpread almoft with nothing els. It is hard to finde any great clufters of godly men any where: they bee fcattered and growe thinne. When the Sonne of man fhall come (faith our Sauiour) fhall he find faith

vpon

THE REVELATION. 297

vpon the earth? Wee see how it is alreadie, and the worlde shall not amend, but waxe worse and worse euen to the ende, so that when the iudgement day commeth, there shall be almost nothing vpon the whole earth, but heapes of vngodlie men, which are compared euen to clusters of grapes, which the Iudge commeth to cut downe with a sharpe sickle. And no more power shall there bee in all the inhabitants of the earth to resist the cutting of this sickle, then is in the clusters of the vines, to withstand the force of his sharpe hooke, which cutteth them for the vintage. Most fit then we see is this figure to expresse the cutting downe and destruction of all the wicked which shall bee at the great day of the Lord. Then what is that great wine fatte of the wrath of God into which they shall be cast? It is the place of execution, and of torment, it is hell: for all the vngodly shalbe cast into hell, as into a great large winepresse: for it is the great wine fat of the wrath of God. The Prophet Esay calleth it Tophet, and describeth it thus: Tophet is prepared of old: it is euen prepared for the king: he hath made it deepe and large: the burning thereof is fire and much wood, the breath of the Lord like a riuer of brimstone, doth kindle it, Esay 30. vers. 33. This is the great winepresse into which all the clusters of stinking grapes shall be cast, and pressed.

Now to set foorth the horror of Gods vengeance vpon the wicked in hell, the allegorie is continued: for as it was said, that the clusters were cut downe and cast into the great fatte or winepresse, so he saith now that the fatte is troden. For when the grapes were in the presse, they had a way to tread it, to the end that the licour might issue out: and so he saith heere, that this fat is troden without the citie. This is out of all doubt, that hell is without the citie, that is, without the heauenly habitation of the iust: for all that worke wickednes shall be put apart into a place by themselues, where they shall be tormented together. For the heauenly Ierusalem is described in the ende of this prophecie, the citie of the Saints: and it is said that they that do keep the comandements, may enter in through the gates into the citie; and without shall be dogges, and enchanters, and whoremongers, and murtherers, and idolaters, and what soeuer loueth or maketh lyes, chapter 22. vers. 15. Then it is said, that blood came out of the wine fatte euen vnto the horse bridles. It seemeth that to tread the great winepresses they did vse not onely men, but also horses: and so according to that the figure is here expressed, when he speaketh of horses. We know also that when the presse is troden, the iuyce of the grapes issueth out: and for that it is said here, that blood came out of the wine fatte euen to the horse bridles. And it is said, by the space of a thousand and sixe hundreth furlongs. Eight furlongs are a mile, then eight hundreth furlongs are one hundreth miles, and so the thousand and sixe hundreth furlongs amount vnto two hundreth miles. This is a large winepresse, as need requireth for to containe the whole multitude of the vngodly. It is not spoken to declare the iust or full bredth of hell: but by this large space, and by the blood comming forth to the horse bridles, to giue vnto vs some resemblance of the wonderfull slaughter which the Lord will make of all his enemies. Men may consider by this how fearfull the vengeance is that shall be powred foorth vpon all the wicked. They cluster together now like clusters

sters of grapes, and each doth encourage and embolden other vnto all sinne, yea many comfort themselues thus; if I goe to hell, I shall haue good store of companie. Yea but the companie shall not comfort thee at all, but make the iudgement more horrible: for they shall be cast on heapes like grapes into a great lake, where they shall bee pressed together, vntill they doe euen as it were swimme in their owne blood. Let vs be warned, let vs studie to keepe a good conscience, that wee may escape from this horrible vengeance of the great God. For all woes, all sorrowes, all euils and miseries shall be vpon those which shall be cast into this great wine fatte of Gods wrath. What a follie is it, not onely to lose eternall glorie, but also to fall into this wofull destruction, euen for a few vncleane lusts and pleasures of sinne, which last but for a season?

THE XXXIII. SERMON.
CHAP. XV.

1 *And I saw another signe in heauen great and maruelious, seuen Angels hauing the seuen last plagues: for by them is fulfilled the wrath of God.*

2 *And I saw as it were a glassie sea mingled with fire, and them that had gotten victorie of the beast, and of his image, and of the number of his name, stand at the glassie sea, hauing the harpes of God.*

3 *And they sung the song of Moses the seruant of God, and the song of the Lambe, saying, Great and maruelious are thy workes Lord God almightie, iust and true are thy waies king of Saints.*

4 *Who shall not feare thee O Lord, and glorifie thy name, for thou art holy, and all nations shal come & worship before thee, for thy iudgements are made manifest.*

5 *And after that I looked, and behold the temple of the tabernacle of witnes was open in heauen.*

6 *And the seuen Angels came out of the temple which had the seuen plagues, clothed in pure and bright linnen, and hauing their breasts girded with golden girdles.*

7 *And one of the foure beasts gaue vnto the seuen Angels seuen golden vials full of the wrath of God which liueth for euermore.*

8 *And the temple was full of the smoke of the glorie of God and of his power, and no man was able to enter into the temple, till the seuen plagues of the seuen Angels were fulfilled.*

WE had the fall of Babylon set forth in the former chapter, and how it should come to passe by the preaching of the Gospell. Wee had also a description
of

THE REVELATION. 299

of the wrath of God which shall come vpon them at the day of iudgement. And now, least we might imagine, that the worshippers of Antichrist should be let alone, and flourish at their pleasure here in this world, and escape free from punishments vntill the latter day: here is a vision in two chapters, euen of purpose to set forth the plagues of God vpon the kingdome of the beast, not onely that endlesse torment before spoken of, but all the grieuous punishments which shall come vpon them in this life also. That idolatrous and bloodie kingdome ruled long, and with mightie tyranny oppressed the people of God, but marke now how the righteous God doth recompence them here in this world: For these two chapters doe declare and set it forth at large.

But before we come to the view of them, here are other matters to be considered: as first, the entrance which Saint Iohn maketh vnto this vision, which is to moue and prepare the mindes of the godly vnto attention. For when matters are not common, nor such as are light or trifling, but great and wonderfull, men ought to giue diligent heede, to the end therefore that we may be attentiue. He beginneth in this wise, And I saw another signe in heauen great and marueilous. If the signe be as hee sayth here, great and marueilous, then let vs looke for great things, and such as we are to wonder at. Then he telleth what hee saw, euen seuen Angels, hauing the seuen last plagues: This is the signe which he calleth great and marueilous. God doth execute his wrath and vengeance vpon the wicked by his ministers the holy Angels, which are here therefore said to haue the plagues in a readines, euen the seuen last plagues. Seuen is the number of perfection, and therefore it is here vsed to signifie the fulnes of all the iudgements of God against wicked sinners. They are called the seuen last plagues, because (as hee saith) the wrath of God is fulfilled in them. There is the full accomplishment and finishing of all plagues in them. They reach from the time that they begin, vnto the ende of the world, and the last of them beginneth that plague that shall last for euer and euer. Then in these seuen the whole wrath of God is powred forth. There remaineth no one plague after these. Hauing thus briefly made his entrance to the matter, then before he come to declare the execution of these plagues by particular, he expresseth also a vision which he had together with the same, touching the true seruants of God. For euer, when there is any grieuous thing shewed and denounced against the wicked, there is also some vision to teach, that the Lord God, euen in the middest of the execution of his vengeance, setteth his seruants in safety, so that the wrath toucheth not them. When a showre of raine commeth down, or a storme of haile, it lighteth vpon al both good and bad, which are abroad in the fields. But it is not so in the tempests of Gods vengeance: for when he raineth downe the same from heauen, although the good bee mingled in the world with the bad, yet hee preserueth them. This whole matter of the preseruation of the good, is declared by a figure. For it is likened to the safe passage of the children of Israel through the red sea, in which their enemies which pursued them were all ouerwhelmed and drowned. For when the children of Israel came out of Egypt, Pharaoh pursuing them with his hoast, the Lord parted the waters of the red sea, so that the tribes passed

through

through on drie land, the waters standing as a wall on both sides, as Moses reporteth, Exod. 14. King Pharaoh and his whole armie doe follow them, and the waters ouerwhelme them, so that not one of them escapeth. Saint Iohn therfore, saith, that he saw as it were a glassie sea mingled with fire. This glassie sea representeth the world, which is euen a gulfe full of tempests, and stormes of afflictions, troubles, temptations, and daungers of all sortes. In this sea the deuill that great Pharaoh, with all his armies pursueth the seruants of God. But it is a glassie sea, it is so hard to the faithful, that they go vpon it as vpon firme ground. They passe through the sharp afflictions in it, for he saith it is mingled with fire. This fire doth not consume them, but it doth purge them: for they be in it as gold is in the furnace, which consumeth not by the fire, but the drosse is burnt out, and so it becommeth more pure. Saint Iohn saith therefore, that he saw them standing at the glassie sea, euen all those that had gotten the victorie of the beast, and of his image, and of the number of his name. He saw them as hauing passed through, and now standing vpon the shore. For he alludeth to the armie of Israel, which being passed through the red sea, stood vpon the shoare, and beheld how their enemies were drowned. For al they which stedfastly cleaue to the holy word of God, and worship him in truth, euen with that holy and pure worship, which he himselfe hath prescribed, keeping themselues free from idolatrie, and superstition, and from all the abominations of the Romish beast, all they (I say) are here said to haue passed through this sea, and to stand at the shoare. For albeit they be but in passing many of them, yet in vision they appeare as set in a serie vpon the shoare, because their victorie and saluation, is as certaine, and out of doubt, as if it were alreadie finished. But as for their enemies, it is not a glassie sea to them, so hard as to be safelie troad vpon, but a deuouring gulfe which doth swallow them vp vnto perdition. The fire which is mingled in it doth not purge them, but is as the beginning of those flames of wrath that shal burne and torment them for euer. For all the plagues of God which follow in this vision, and all other afflictions which come vpon the wicked idolaters here in this life, doe not bring them to repentance, and so draw them neerer vnto God, but are, as I said, euen the beginning of the flames of Gods wrath, yea euen a certaine entrance into hell. These are ouerwhelmed, and drowned in the sea of this worlde, euen as Pharaoh and all his armie were in the red sea.

But to returne againe to the godly, S. Iohn saith, he saw them hauing the harps of God. What are these harps of God but instruments of melodie? They are the spirituall ioy, the gladnes, and the comfort which God hath giuen them, with which they prepare themselues to sing praises to the Lord for the victorie and deliuerance which they haue obtained through his blessing and free grace. For looke how it is said, that the Israelites being come to the shoare, and there beheld the Egyptians dying, Moses and they did sing a song of praise to God, both for their deliuerance, and for the ouerthrow of their enemies, Exod. 15. so is it said here, that they which get the victorie of the beast, passing safe through the gulfe of this world, standing at the shoare, and beholding the greatnes of their owne deliuerance through the grace of God, and the iudgements and wrath of the Lorde vpon their enemies,

haue

THE REVELATION. 301

haue harps wherwith they prepare themselues to sing praises to God for the same. And he saith, they did sing the song of Moses the seruant of God: not that these holy worshippers doe sing the same words of that song of Moses, Exod. 15. but he continueth the figure, and the meaning is that they laud and magnifie the Lord for their deliuerance, and for his iudgements which he executeth vpon their enemies, as Moses and the children of Israel did for theirs out of the red sea. It is then the song of Moses, in that they extoll the name of the Lord as Moses did, that saueth them from drowning in this great tempestuous sea of the world, & that with his plagues ouerwhelmeth their wicked enemies in the same: as Moses and the Israelites praised God, so doe these: this is the song of Moses. He saith also, that they did sing the song of the Lambe. This must needes be: it is meete they should sing the song of the Lambe, for it is through the blood of the Lambe, that they get the victorie: the Lambe is their great captaine by whose conduct they passe through this great sea. The lambe doth teach them how to offer vp their praises, and thankes, and honour, and glorie to God his father through his name. It is therefore the song of the Lambe. And it is a right ioyfull and sweete melodie which they make with their harpes, being the harpes of God. They sing with exceeding great ioy and gladnes of minde.

In the time of the law, God appoynted that there should bee musicall instruments and melodie in the publike assembly where they did praise him. What shal we thinke that the Lord God taketh pleasure in sweete tunes? No, but when men praise him with ioy and gladnes of heart, that is acceptable vnto him. And what a dull and dead praising of God is it, if men vtter with the mouth, and take not delight and pleasure in their hart in his praise? If to magnifie & praise the high name of God bee as pleasant and delightsome to the heart, as the sweetest musicke is to the eare, then doe men praise him indeede: then doe they loue his glorie. And to shew this were those instruments of musick in the publike worship vnder the law. And to that which was the manner then, doth this vision allude, saying, that these had the harpes of God, that is, they extoll and praise God with great ioy and gladnes of heart. It is the sweetest and the most comfortable melodie vnto them that can bee, to glorifie the Lorde. Heere must wee looke to our selues, whether wee haue these harpes of God: for wee come together and make shew that wee praise our God. If we doe it of custome or fashion, and not with delight and gladnes of heart, taking more pleasure therein, then in all the sweetest melodie in the world, we haue not the harpes of God, our praise is not acceprable vnto him. Well now let vs see what their song is. It is in these wordes, Great and maruelous are thy works Lord God Almightie, iust and true are thy waies, king of Saints. Who shall not feare thee O Lord, and glorifie thy name, for thou art holy, and all nations shall come and worship before thee, for thy iudgements are made manifest?

Before I lay open the particular poynts of this worthie song, it shall not bee amisse to consider well to whom it is sung, I meane whose praise it setteth forth, or to whom it ascribeth al glorie. Reade it ouer, and marke it well, and you shal finde that it magnifieth the praise of God alone, and not of any creature. Yea reade in

all

SERMONS VPON

all places of this booke, where either the Angels in heauen, or the Church in earth doe praise and magnifie the great God, and ye shall finde that there is no creature worshipped, and glorified with him. Nay, I may say further, reade and search all the whole Bible, both the old Testament and the new, euen all the writings of the Prophets and Apostles, which haue deliuered to the world, the doctrine of the Lambe, and ye shall not finde any where, that any Angell or Saint is worshipped, and praised with diuine worship. The word of God, which is the doctrine of the Lambe, out of which this song is drawne, and therefore called the song of the Lambe, teacheth men to ascribe all glorie, and praise, and worship, and honour, and maiestie to God alone. And that there is no creature in heauen or earth worthie to be ioyned with him, to be partaker with him in his glory, or to be worshipped with any part of his worship. For looke what the creatures haue, they haue receiued it from him, and are all of them, though some be more glorious then other, to worship and praise his name together. There is no one to be set vp so high, as to haue any part of his glorie. It is wicked sacriledge, and blasphemous impietie, to take any part of the diuine worship and praise, and to giue it to any creature. The Church therefore being taught by the Lambe, and altogether guided by his spirit doth sing this ioyfull song of the Lambe. They worshippe, they praise, they magnifie, and extoll the name of the Lord God almightie, ioyning none other with him. It is not therefore the song of the Lambe which is sung in the popish Church, because they worship and praise and magnifie creatures, they giue thanks vnto them, as vnto patrones and mediators vpon whom they call, and vnto whom they ascribe their deliuerance and preseruation. The Dragon, and that beast with two hornes haue taught their songs, of which their Masse booke is full. For they that reade them, if they haue their eyes opened, shall see them stuffed full of blasphemous sacrilegies, while they worship the creatures, and ascribe vnto them the glorie and praise which is due onely to God, and to his sonne Iesus Christ. Which part then is it best and safest for vs to follow? Shall we ioyne with these that stand at the glassie sea, which haue gotten the victorie of the beast, in praising God alone? Or shall we ioyne with the Church of Rome, which honoureth euen with diuine honour, the creatures, in stead of the Creator? Shall we worship God or ly, (as the Lambe teacheth, Matth.4.)or shall we ioyne with the papists that worship and glorifie the creatures, with the glorie and worship that is peculiar to God? In their Masse booke they haue songs of praise to the Virgin Mary, in which they call her their Mediatrix and say she is placed in the throne with God the Father, and that she raigneth with God: this is in the Masse of her Assumption. They call her the starre of the sea, the Mother of grace, the fountaine of mercie, in the Masse of her Visitation. They call her the cause of saluation, and the gate of life, in the Masse of her Purification. They craue by her grace to be set in the hauen of saluation, in the Masse of her Conception. They pray that they may bee deliuered from the flames of hell, by the merites and prayers of Saint Nicholas. What should I stand in making particular rehearsall, they worship the Saints, and ascribe vnto them the office of Mediators, which belongeth only to Christ. Shall wee, I say,

ioyne

THE REVELATION. 303

ioyne with them in this their wicked facriledge? No, let vs ioyne with the true Catholike Church, and worſhip God onely, for ſo doe the Angels and Saints in heauen. For there is no creature worthie to be ioyned with God, to haue any part of diuine worſhip: he is God ouer all to be praiſed for euer.

And now let vs come to the matter of this ſong. I will not diuide it into any parts, but ſhew euery branch as it lieth. They firſt proclayme that the workes of God are great and maruellous. We may vnderſtand this generally of al the works of God, which the faithfull doe beholde and wonder at: and wee may reſtraine it to the particulars here in hand. The generall doth reach to the wonderfull creation, and ſetting vp the frame of the whole world, with all other things which haue fallen out in the gouernment and preſeruation thereof. The particulars here in land, are the great and miraculous preſeruation of the true beleeuers in this gulfe of the world, that the Dragon and the beaſt doe not drowne them: and the execution of Gods iudgements vpon them that worſhip the beaſt. All circumſtances conſidered, they be both to be greatly wondred at. And in them both, the Lorde doth euidently declare that he is almightie, as they doe here praiſe him. What are the faithfull in themſelues in compariſon of the Dragon and of the beaſt, which purſue them in the ſea of this world? It is the mightie hand of God that bringeth them ſafe to the ſhore. It is the miraculous power of God from heauen that preſerueth them, for which they doe celebrate his praiſe. Againe, that the Lord plagueth ſuch mightie enemies, and pulleth them downe, yea bringeth to ruine that mighty monarchie of Antichriſt, the wonder of the world, it euidently manifeſteth his almightie power and prouidence, which none can withſtand. All things are great, all things are maruelious in theſe his workes, if our eyes were open and cleere to behold them.

Then it followeth, iuſt and true are thy waies, king of Saints. As in the former clauſe, they celebrate the praiſe and glorie of God, in that his almightie power hath manifeſted it ſelfe by workes great and wonderfull: ſo in this they magnifie him, that as a iuſt king, ruling and iudging with vprightnes, all his waies are iuſt and true. When he executeth vengeance in moſt ſharpe and ſeuere maner vpon the wicked, it ſeemeth vnto the ſenſe and wiſedome of the fleſh, to bee cruell rigour, and the vngodly doe murmure and fret at it: but all the faithfull, which haue their mindes lightened with the grace of the holy Ghoſt, doe ſee cleerely, that all his waies are iuſt, and ſo they glorifie and praiſe him for his righteous iudgements, and plagues, executed vpon the wicked. And looke whatſoeuer he hath vttered in his holy word, either in promiſes to thoſe that obey him, or in threatnings againſt the rebellious, he performeth the ſame, and ſo all his waies are true. The vnfaithfull ſee the godly paſſe through great afflictions in this life, and they imagine that the promiſes which are made to ſuch as feare the Lord are but words. Againe, they behold that wicked men for a time doe flouriſh and proſper, euen in the middeſt of their wickednes, and they promiſe to themſelues ſafetie from all euill, as if all the threatnings of God againſt the euill doers ſhould come to nothing. This maketh them ſo bold in diſhonoring God: but the godly doe ſee that nothing

ſhall

shall fall to the ground of all that hath proceeded out of the mouth of God, and therefore they proclaime that his waies are true. In that they giue the Lord this title, that he is king of Saints, we must not so vnderstand it, as if he were king only ouer them, and not also ouer the vnholy, but that the Saints doe receiue good by his kingdome. He is their king to defend them, to comfort them, and to set them vp in life and glorie, his kingdome is their ioy. Hee hath also dominion and doth raigne ouer the wicked, but so as it is to their griefe and endles woe. For as in a kingdome the faithfull subiects receiue much good, and doe reioyce in their iust, victorious and mightie king, and contrariwise the rebels doe feele his power to their griefe: so is it in the Lords kingdome. The iust receiue all good, but the rebels are troden downe, and shall feele his iustice, his hand and power, to their eternall woe.

It is then added, Who shall not feare thee O Lord, and glorifie thy name, for thou art holie? The Lord is so great a king, that he is to bee feared and glorified of all. The good doe feare him with a reuerend feare that is ioyned with loue: and they doe delight in setting foorth his praise and glorie, euen the glorie of his great name. And the wicked which doe despise him, shall be made to tremble & quake at his presence with seruile feare: and albeit they loue him not nor his glorie, yet shall he be glorified by them, yea he is glorified in their destruction. For howsoeuer they shall curse and blaspheme in their horrible torments, yet the iust shall proclaime that therein he is holie, and that he sheweth no rigour nor crueltie, but layeth that which is iust vpon them. It is said further, All nations shall come and worship before thee, for thy iudgements are made manifest. By this it is shewed, that howsoeuer the multitudes in the world doe conspire together in casting off the yoke of the Lord, and rebelling against him, yet they shall in the ende at the full manifestation of his iudgements bow before him, and acknowledge him to be Lord and king ouer all. We see daily what desperate boldnes there is in many, as if they were lawles and vnder no king. We may see also (if we be not wonderfull blinde) that some of the most wicked, which seemed to bee armed against all terror, at some strange hand of God vpon them, do tremble & bow for the time: how much more then shall all the stoutest be made to bow before him, and to acknowledge his supreme power and gouernment, at the terrible day of vengeance? when all nations shall come and worship before him, when (as the Apostle Paul sayth) all knees shall bow vnto him, and euery tongue shall confesse that Iesus is the Lord, to the praise of God. It is good therefore that we acknowledge the Lord to be king, and that withall dutifulnes we submit our selues to the obediéce of his holesome lawes, and so worship and glorifie him with holy worship. The rebels shall euery one of them euen to the stoutest, be made to stoope before him, and to confesse his soueraigne power, when it shall be to their griefe and sorrow: but the Saints shall reioyce in their king, whom they haue carefully obeyed and worshipped. And thus haue we seene the ioyfull triumphant song of those which stood at the glassie sea, which had gotten the victorie of the beast, of his image, and of the number of his name. The battell yet continueth betweene the beast

and

THE REVELATION.

and the faithfull, and if we be not of this companie, which with the harpes of God doe sing this song of victorie to our Lord God, we are but in euill case: for if we get not the victorie wee drowne in this horrible sea. The true worshippers being thus set in safetie vpon the shore, hee returneth to the description of the plagues which are powred foorth vpon the kingdome of the beast. *After that* (saith he) *I looked, and behold the temple of the tabernacle of witnes was open in heauen.* This booke setteth forth the matters vnder figures, and it alludeth to the figures which were vnder the law. There was the teple, which was as a signe that God did dwell among them: for it was the royall palace of their king. In this temple, there was the most holie place, where was the arke of couenant, and the mercie seate: euen the signe of Gods presence. To shew therefore that these seuen last plagues doe come from the counsell and decree of the most high God vpon the kingdome of the beast, the tabernacle is open in heauen, and the seuen Angels, which haue the seuen last plagues come out from thence. The destruction of the kingdome of Antichrist, and all plagues vpon the popish worshippers come from the throne of God in heauen. He sendeth forth the ministers of his wrath, which doe execute his will in plaguing the wicked. These holie ministers the blessed Angels, are readie with all integritie to doe his will: and therefore he saith, they were clothed in pure bright linnen, and girded at their breasts, with golden girdles. Then it is sayd, that one of the foure beasts gaue vnto the seuen Angels, seuen golden vials full of the wrath of GOD which liueth for euermore. I will not take vpon mee to speake further touching the ministrie of Angels then thus, that the Lord God doth vse them as his ministers, both for the preseruation of the good, and for the execution of his iudgements vpon the wicked, as we see in this place. He sayth, the vials are of gold; because the workes of God are pure and precious euen in the destruction of the wicked. It is sayd, that they are full of the wrath of God, that we may know that the Lord will be throughly reuenged vpon his enemies. And that he sayth, it is the wrath of God that liueth for euermore, it amplifieth the grieuousnes of it. For the wrath of princes is heauie, but it hath an ende, because they die: but the wrath of God neuer endeth, because he liueth for euer. Then last of all he saith, *that the temple was full of the smoke of the glorie of God, and of his power, and no man was able to enter into the temple, till the seuen plagues of the seuen Angels were fulfilled.* This doth allude to that which is written, 1.King.8. where it is sayd, that the clowd filled the house of the Lord so, that the priests could not stand to minister. This smoke signifieth the presence of the Lord, and his glorie. And we must note that the same are represented vnto vs by a thick, and darke clowd of smoke, because his iudgements are vnsearchable, and none can behold his glorie: but when all the plagues are fulfilled, which shall be at the last day, then shall we haue a more full sight of his maiestie so farre as creatures may, and see into vprightnes of all his waies. And thus much for this time.

X THE

THE XXXIIII. SERMON.
CHAP. XVI.

1 *And I heard a great voice out of the Temple, saying to the seuen Angels, Goe your waies, powre out the seuen vials of the wrath of God, vpon the earth.*

2 *And the first Angell went and powred foorth his viall vpon the earth: and there fell a noisome grieuous sore vpon the men which had the marke of the beast, and vpon them which worshipped his image.*

3 *And the second Angell powred forth his viall vpon the sea, and it became as the blood of a dead man, and euery liuing thing dyed in the sea.*

4 *And the third Angell powred forth his viall vpon the riuers and fountaines of waters, and they turned to blood.*

5 *And I heard the Angell of the waters say, Lord thou art iust, which art, and which wast holy, because thou hast iudged these things.*

6 *For they shed the blood of the Saints and Prophets, and therefore thou hast giuen them blood to drinke: for they are worthie.*

7 *And I heard another Angell out of the Altar saying, Euen so Lord God almightie, true and righteous are thy iudgements.*

8 *And the fourth Angell powred forth his viall vpon the Sunne, and it was giuen vnto him to torment men with heate of fire.*

9 *And men boyled in great heate, and blasphemed the name of God which hath power ouer these plagues, and they repented not to giue him glorie.*

WE had in the former chapter, as it were the preparation of the seuen last plagues which were to bee powred forth vpon the kingdome of the beast, and now in this chapter followeth the execution of the same. The Angels had the vials full of the wrath of God deliuered vnto them, and were in a readines, but did not powre them forth vntill they had commandement from their Lord God. And therfore he saith, he heard a great voyce out of the Temple, which willed them to powre them forth. The Lord vseth the ministerie of Angels, and as we see they depend wholly vpon his will. They stay till he commaund, they presently fulfill his commaundement, and leaue nothing vndone which he willeth. There is a perfect obedience in them: so that our Sauiour teacheth vs to pray, *Thy will bee done in earth, as it is in heauen.* We may note yet further in this first verse, that they are willed not to distill as it were by drops, or by little and little, but to powre forth the vials of the wrath of God vpon

the

the earth. The vials are full, and must as it is sayd bee powred forth, which sheweth that God is so highly displeased, that he will execute vengeance vpon the enemies of his trueth in great measure. We may not wonder that the Lord is so wroth against the popish worship, and worshippers: for there is in it the corrupting of all his holy ordinances, and the very worship of diuels, in maintenance whereof, they murther the seruants of God. Such as haue any true sight in thẽ, must needes confesse that these are most horrible things. Well, the Angels receiuing charge, the first then powreth foorth his viall vpon the earth, and there fell a noysome and grieuous sore vpon the men which had the marke of the beast, and vpon them that worship his image.

For the better vnderstanding of these plagues, we must vnderstand, that as the great citie of Antichrist is called spiritually Sodom and Egypt, chapter 11. so the plagues which the Lord plagueth them withall, are set forth sundrie of the vnder the same names that those are, with which Pharaoh and his people of Egypt were striken. We reade in Exodus, chap. 9 that God commanded Moses and Aaron to take their handfuls of the ashes of a furnace, and to cast them into the ayre before Pharaoh, which they did, and there followed a sore all ouer Egypt vpon men, yea euen vpon the inchaunters themselues, so that they could not stand before Pharaoh for the grieuousnes of the sore. This was the sixt plague of Egypt: and of the seuen last plagues which are powred foorth vpon the kingdome of the great Antichrist, which hath held the Church in thrall & bondage as Egypt did, it is the first. But now it may be demaunded what this sore should be? The plague sore is very grieuous, and that hath raged mightily among the Papists: but it will be said that the Churches of the Protestants haue not been free from the same, but are diuers times sharply chastised therewith: and here he speaketh of a sore which is more peculiar to the popish sort, first to their votaries which haue the mark of the beast, and then to the common multitude which worship his image. There is a new sore which is called the French pock, which is a most grieuous, and a most loathsome disease. It is called also, *Morbus Neapolitanus*, the disease of Naples, because it began first there. For about the yeere of our Lord 1494. the French-men and the Spaniards warring at Naples, this most filthie disease grew among them from the whores which were there in great number with them, being a sore that was neuer heard of before that time. This sore (as it cannot bee denied) is sometimes taken by the infection of others, and so by that meanes lighteth vpon some honest persons: but vsually lighteth vpon filthie whoremongers, being a most loathsome plague cast vpon them for their vncleane life. Now we may reade in the first chapter of the epistle of Saint Paul to the Romanes, that when the Gentiles tooke vpon them to represent the inuisible God by images and likenesses, and so turned the glorie of the incorruptible God, into the similitude of a corruptible man, and of birds and creeping things; God gaue them ouer into a reprobate sence, and into vile lusts to defile themselues. Euen so in the poperie, when they became so wicked, as to make the similitudes of the inuisible and most glorious Godhead, not onely in likenes of a corruptible man as the heathen, but also (which is horr ble rible and blasphemous) like a man hauing three faces in one : and likewise when they did worship those images, and others also of Saints, the Lord gaue them ouer into all vncleannes. For where the spirituall whoredome is committed, the bodily whoredome followeth. Hereupon it came to passe in the poperie, that whoredome & al filthines not to be named, did ouerflow especially among those which had the speciall marke of the beast, as among the great prelates, the Monkes, the Friers, and the Nunnes. The earth was filled with the stinke of their horrible filthines and whoredoms. And vpon these the Lord hath also sent this noisome sore, so that it hath been among them for the space of this hundreth yeeres. It hath light vpon the popish French-men, Spaniards, and Italians, which are they that most deuoutly worship the image of the beast, but especially vpon their Bishops, Abbots, Priests, Monkes, Friers, and Nunnes, as writers doe report. Thus much for this plague, which is the first of the seuen.

It followeth: *And the second Angell powred out his viall vpon the sea, and it became as the blood of a dead man, and euery liuing thing died in the sea.* This is a sore plague to the kingdome of the beast, that the sea is turned into blood, as the waters in Egypt were. But what is meant here by the sea, and how is this turning into blood to be expounded? It is said in the 13.chapter, that the beast, that is, the Romane empire, rose out of the sea: where by the sea is meant the wauering, tempestuous, and troublesome state of the nations, full of tumults, vprores, and seditions. For the state of the nations for these respects may wel be compared to a tempestuous sea. This broyling sea then of the kingdomes, among which and out of which the beast ariseth, is turned into blood, yea like to the blood of a dead man which is loathsome and putrifying, which words are vsed to continue the allegorie. Then when ye see what is meant by the sea in this booke, ye may easily perceiue what way it is turned into blood. The sword turneth this sea of the people into blood: The warres, the cruell warres, are here represented, which God would send vpon the popish kingdomes. There hath been much bloodshed in all ages, and among all nations, but most horrible in the kingdomes of the poperie, and especially of latter times. The Popes themselues (as histories do report) haue been the chiefe raisers vp of warres in setting the kings at variance: for the vial of Gods wrath which the Angell powreth forth, giueth scope to the diuell to worke mischiefe. The diuell he practiseth by his vicar Antichrist, and filleth all the kingdomes full of blood, and so destroyeth infinite thousands of liuing things. The Psalmist saith of the Egyptians, hee turned their waters into blood, and slew their fish. To that same he alludeth here, saying, that euery liuing thing died in this sea, the waters thereof being turned into blood. This may also be extended to the famines, to the dearths, and to the pestilences which haue followed the warres, and through which innumerable multitudes haue been deuoured. Wee had the description of a most horrible destroying armie, killing and destroying great multitudes of idolatrous wicked people, which very fitly representeth the cruell wasting armies of the Turkes, and although that hath been described before, yet is it not here vtterly excluded. For the great Turke hath been a chiefe doer in turning this se-

THE REVELATION.

into blood, and that in dreadful wise in sundrie places vnder the Popes dominion, and especially within little more then one hundreth yeeres past. I will not enter into the declaration of particulars to declare these things, but such as will bee further satisfied in them, let them reade the histories which describe the warres, the bloodsheds, the commotions, the seditions, the tumults, and the slaughters which haue been in Italie, France, Germanie, Hungarie, and other countries of Europe, and see whence they sprung. It will bee sayd, that warres come vpon all lands, as well where the Gospell is preached, as where the poperie is maintained. It is true, for the wrath of God is prouoked by many in all lands, not onely where his word is denied, but also where it is openly professed. For where it is plentifully preached, many despise it vtterly and haue it in derision, euen like to swine which tread precious pearles vnder their feete. Also some like dogges rend and teare them that bring it. Others, and that not a few of them which professe it, doe not frame their liues so well as they ought, but cause the weake to stumble, and open the mouthes of the enemies to blaspheme and to raile vpon the holy way of God. For these things the Lord sendeth chastisements, as sicknes, famine, and bloodie warres, to correct his people for their amendment. Although we may say God is displeased, yet it is his mercie and fatherly chastisement to his true worshippers. It is farre otherwise in the gulfe of the papacie, where the shedding of the blood hath been farre greater, and not to their amendment, but euen in wrath. For there, as I sayd before, are the most horrible blasphemies and abominations committed, which pull downe bitter plagues vpon them. Thus much touching the second plague: now to the third.

And the third Angell powred foorth his viall vpon the riuers and fountaines of waters, and they were turned to blood. As in the former it was sayd, that the sea was turned into blood, so now he sayth, all the fresh waters of which men vse to drinke, doe also become blood. This setteth forth the same plague in some sort, but yet another, because it toucheth more neerely and in an higher degree. When the waters of the sea are blood it is a plague, but when it lighteth vpon the fresh waters it is a sorer plague, because of the speciall vse which men haue of them. The plague of warres then and bloodsheds among the papists, are here compared with the plague of Egypt, by which their riuers and fountaines were turned into blood, and they were constrained to digge into the ground to get waters to drinke. O how dolefull, and how heauie a case is it, when men are made to drinke blood in stead of pure refreshing waters! This turning the waters into blood is spoken hyperbolically, to declare the horriblens of the slaughters that should bee made among the worshippers of the beast. All ouerfloweth & aboundeth so with blood, that they haue giuen vnto them their owne blood to drinke. For so it is meant, as we may see by the next words, which the Angell of the waters is said to vtter.

And I heard (sayth Saint Iohn) *the Angell of the waters say, Lord thou art iust, whichart, and which wast holie, because thou hast iudged these things.* The Lord God in the gouernment and preseruation of the world vseth the ministrie of Angels (as I said before) and before in chap. 14. we had the Angell brought in, which had

had power ouer fire, and now the Angell of the waters: becauſe there he ſpeaketh of vengeance that ſhall be executed at the laſt day by fire, and here of the plague vpon the waters. This Angell proclaimeth, that the eternall God which is, which was, and which ſhall be (for ſo we may tranſlate it) is iuſt, becauſe he hath iudged theſe things. This latter clauſe ſheweth, that it is to be taken that the vnchangeable God declareth himſelfe to bee iuſt by taking vengeance. When hee ſuffereth the wicked to range vpon the earth at their pleaſure, to corrupt and defile all things, to blaſpheme his name, to tread down his holy worſhip, and to murther his faithfull ſeruants; all holy Angels doe know, and ſo doe the faithfull among men, that although there be no execution of iuſtice and iudgement for a time, but the ſame is deferred and delayed, yet hee is a moſt righteous iudge, and will in due time, which is knowne to his holy wiſedome, ſtand vp to doe his office. It is vnpoſſible that he ſhould let goe the execution of iuſtice: for hee is the iudge of the whole world, he is iuſtice and iudgement it ſelfe. And therefore vnles he can be changeable and denie himſelfe, he cannot leaue iuſtice vnexecuted. When hee doth declare himſelfe by execution, then doe the creatures ſee it, and acknowledge that he is iuſt, as the Angell here ſaith, becauſe thou haſt iudged theſe things.

If we conſider well of the matter, as it is in the Lord himſelfe, it is very certaine that he doth not become iuſt, becauſe he iudgeth theſe things: but indeed he iudgeth theſe things becauſe hee is iuſt. For the execution of this iuſtice, is the effect of a cauſe which is precedent. But as I ſayd, the Angell ſpeaketh ſo, becauſe by iudging he manifeſteth to the creatures, that he is a iuſt & a moſt righteous iudge: for the creatures cannot ſee the things which are in God, but as he reuealeth them. We poore men, beholding moſt horrible enormities & abominations ouerſpreading the earth, and perceiuing no vengeance of God to follow, but all to paſſe away ſmoothly, as if he regarded not the matter, are often halfe amazed: but when the time commeth, and iuſtice is executed, then we crye out, Lord thou art iuſt, becauſe thou haſt iudged theſe things, that is, wee ſee by this execution, that thou art a iuſt God, and wilt not ſuffer wickedoes to eſcape vnpuniſhed. This is a very neceſſary doctrine for vs to bee well perſwaded in, that God is a righteous iudge. For if we be not, we ſhall with the wicked bee boldened vnto the committing of all ſinne. For they ſeeing, as Salomon ſayth, that ſentence is not executed ſpeedilie againſt a matter, and their hearts are full in them to doe wickedly: they imagine that they ſhall euer eſcape, becauſe they doe eſcape for the preſent time. And this is it that the Pſalmiſt ſaith, The foole hath ſayd in his heart there is no God: they are corrupt and become abominable. For he that ſaith in his heart that iuſt vengeance ſhall not bee executed vpon all wickednes, denyeth that there is any righteous iudge. And if there be no righteous iudge, then is there any God? Surely God is a moſt righteous iudge. Indeede it is ſo that hee doth not puniſh all offences here in this life, but reſerueth them vnto the great day, but yet hee letteth not the wicked altogether eſcape vntill that time, but meeteth with them now and then, and that in ſuch ſort that the faithfull doe ſee plainly it is Gods hand, and do proclaime when they ſee the vengeance, as the Prophet ſayth in the Pſalme, Surely

there

there is a God that iudgeth in the earth, doubtles there is a reward for the righteous, Psal. 58. Whereby we may see it is a great bridle to the seruants of God, euen for to restraine them from wicked sinnes, that they behold how God executeth some vengeance vpon the vngodly in this world, as also it is an encouragement to set them forward in the way of righteousnes without fainting. For beholding that he is so seuere a iudge against the euill doers, they must needes collect that he will plentifully reward such as doe obey his holy will.

Then the Angell addeth further, For they shed the blood of the Saints and Prophets, and therefore thou hast giuen them blood to drinke: for they are worthie, least it might seeme ouermuch rigour and seueritie that God dooth plague these wicked ones withall in giuing them blood to drink: and that they doe as it were swimme in blood, the Angell expresseth their sinne, by which they haue deserued such horrible punishment, and for which he saith they are worthie to bee so handled. They haue many grieuous sinnes those Idolaters, both against the first table of the law, and against the second: but here is but one named, which is both for the greatnes, and also that the plague is fitted vnto it. Touching the greatnes of the sinne that it might appeare, he calleth them the Prophets and Saints, whom they slew. The Prophets are the teachers of the Gospell, and the Saints are all the true beleeuers. These be all the children of the most high God, they be very deare and precious vnto him. All men ought to loue and regard them highly for their fathers sake. Then how horrible a sinne is it not onely to despise, to hate, and to reproach them, but also most cruelly to murther and kill them? What plague can bee sufficient for such despite offered to God? If one should take the children of a king and intreate them in such cruell and despitefull maner, hauing not deserued euill, who would not say that the sharpest death were too little for such villaines? And what are the greatest kings of the earth, in comparison of the high God? The dignitie of the children is according to the dignitie of their father. Then may we see that they which cruelly murther the Prophets and Saints, are worthie of all torments. As the Angell sayth here, for they are worthie. This may stop the mouth of man, when he shall repine at the seuere plagues which God sendeth vpon the world. Their sinne is so great that they be worthie. Who then can charge God with ouer much rigor or seueritie? Shall the wicked world worship the diuell, and performe his will in murthering the holy seruants of God, and shall not God plague them for so doing? This for the greatnes of their offence, now for the fitnes of the plague. They shed blood, so cruell and sauage they bee, and the Lorde giueth them blood to drinke. They shed blood among themselues, euen vntill they doe as it were drinke their owne blood. They that reade the histories, shall finde how the papists haue murthered the true worshippers, and how euen among them againe there haue followed cruell slaughters: and the cruell persecutors especially haue been as it were bathed in their owne blood. The Lord doth thus fit his plagues to their sins. The Egyptians were so cruell and bloody, that they tooke the male children of the Hebrewes when they were borne and cast them into the riuers, at the time when

Moses

Moses was borne, and when Moses was sent, the same riuers were turned into blood: so the plague it fitted to their sinne. At this plague there is another Angell whom S. Iohn heard from the Altar, saying, Euen so Lord God almightie, true and righteous are thy iudgements. That this Angell also is sayd to proclaime that God plagueth iustly, and is heard from the Altar, it hath this sense, that God reuengeth the blood of his martyrs. For at the opening of the fift seale, Saint Iohn sayth, hee saw the soules of them that were killed for the testimonie of Iesus, vnder the Altar. This voyce then commeth as it were from them, and in their behalfe. Their blood cryeth aloud for vengeance, and the Lord beginneth to execute some part of the same vpon the seruants of Antichrist while they bee vpon the earth: and reserueth their full reward vntill the great day, when he will powre out all his wrath. Thus much as concerning the third plague.

And the fourth Angell powred forth his viall vpon the Sunne, and it was giuen vnto him to torment men with heate of fire. This fourth Angell, as we see, powreth forth his vial vpon the Sun in the heaues, to this end & purpose, that we may know that no part of the world may be free from bringing plagues to these wicked Idolaters. For the first was vpon the earth, the second vpon the sea, the third vpon the fountaines and riuers, and this fourth vpon the Sunne. For as they dishonour the creator, who is God ouer all to be blessed for euer; so all the parts of the world which are his creatures, which shew foorth his glorie, and were made to serue man, are armed to execute his wrath vpon such wicked rebels. The earth, the sea, and the riuers with all fountaines of waters, doe affoord what plagues they are appoynted from below, and the Sunne from the heauens on high doth his part. For by this, men boyle in heate, and are tormented. We doe all know by experience, that the Sunne is of wonderfull great and necessarie vse to the inhabitants of the earth, not onely for his light; but also for his cherishing heate, by which things grow and waxe ripe. Now the plague commeth when the heate thereof becommeth immoderate, whereby not only the fruits of the earth and all greene things are scorched and dryed vp, but also the bodies of men are distempered. Hereupon follow dearths, and sundrie grieuous diseases, as pestilences, and hot agues, with many noysome and grieuous paines. This plague hath been sore in the hot countries which are popish, as in Spayne, Portugall, France, and Italy. And he sayth, that men boyled in heate, and blasphemed the name of God, which hath power ouer these plagues: and they repented not to giue him glorie. Here is set foorth what effect these plagues worke among the wicked. Yea verely we are here taught that there is not that effect which ought to be, but the cleane contrarie. When the Lord sendeth plagues, men ought by and by to enter into this consideration, that hee is a iust iudge, and that they haue by their sinnes prouoked him to wrath. Then ought they to bee sorrowfull, to bee humbled, and to repent that they haue dealt so vngratiously, against so louing and so gracious a God. They ought to glorifie and praise him by all the wayes and meanes which they can, whom they haue so wickedly dishonoured. And doubtles the children of God

doe

THE REVELATION.

doe this, but the wicked reprobates when he chastiseth them, doe quite contrarie. They dishonour him, and when hee doth strike them, although their conscience doth accuse them of wickednesse, and they doe in some sorte acknowledge that God sendeth the plagues, and can either increase or diminish them, yet such is their proude stiffenes, that they are nothing humbled, but the sharper his rods be, the more they doe blaspheme him.

Many waies haue the wicked idolatrous papists blasphemed the holy name of God: and first this is common to them all, to raile vpon the holy Gospell, and to charge it to bee the cause of all euils. Then further, it is an vsuall thing among the Italians and Spanyards in their furie and rage, to vtter blasphemous speeches directly against God. The whole Papisme aboundeth with such monsters. And doubtles the more heauilie the hand of God doth presse such, the more aboundantly they vomit out their poyson. But now it will bee sayd, that these plagues before named, as warres, dearths and pestilences, come and light vpon those also which professe the Gospell, and that bee aduersaries to the Bishop of Rome: for they dwell together vpon the face of the earth. I answere, that God doth chastice his seruants for their offences, not in wrath and displeasure to their destruction, but in fatherly loue and mercie, for their good: as yee may see how Saint Paule teacheth, 1.Corinth. 11. toward the latter ende of the chapter. The Lorde doth correct and chastice his children, that they may not bee condemned with the world. And as hee sayth, all things worke together for good to them that loue God. Rom. 8. Let vs therefore in time of these calamities humble our selues vnder the mightie hand of God, to giue glorie to his name, and not rage and blaspheme with the wicked.

THE XXXV. SERMON.
CHAP. XVI.

10 *And the fift Angell poured out his viall vpon the throne of the beast, and his kingdome waxed darke, and they did gnaw their tongues for sorrow.*

11 *And blasphemed the God of heauen for their paines, and for their sores, and repented not of their workes.*

12 *And the sixt Angell poured forth his viall vpon the great riuer Euphrates, and the waters thereof dried vp, that the way of the kings of the East might be prepared.*

13 *And I saw three vncleane spirits like frogs, come out of the mouth of the dragon, and out of the mouth of the beast, and out of the mouth of the false Prophet.*

14 *For they are the spirits of deuils working miracles, to goe out to the kings of the earth, and the whole worlde, to gather them to the battaile of that great day of God almightie.*

15 *Behold I come as a theefe, blessed is he that watcheth, and keepeth his garments, least he walke naked, and men see his filthines.*

16 *And he gathered them into a place called in the hebrew tongue,* Armageddon.

17 *And the seuenth Angell poured forth his viall into the ayre, and there came a great voice out of the temple of heauen, saying, it is done.*

18 *And there followed voices, thundrings, and lightnings, and there was a great earthquake, such as was not since men were vpon the earth, so mightie an earthquake I meane.*

19 *And the great citie was deuided into three parts, and the cities of the Gentiles fell, and great Babylon came in remembrance before God, to giue vnto her the cup of wine of the fiercenes of his wrath.*

20 *Euery Isle fled, and the mountaines were not found.*

21 *And there fell a great haile as it had been talents out of heauen vpon the men, and men blasphemed God because of the plague of the haile, for the plague thereof was exceeding great.*

WE haue had foure of the seuen last plagues in the former part of this chapter, at the pouring forth of the vials of the foure Angels, and now in the rest of the chapter we haue the other three, the former whereof is the fift plague. And to come to that, he saith, that the fift Angell poured forth his viall vpon the throne of the beast. The former plagues were very grieuous, but not like vnto this, for this commeth neerer, euen to the top, or to the head, and so spreadeth ouer the whole bodie. For in that wicked apostasie, the throne is euen the very top, and that being touched, all the whole societie which is subiect to the same, is also touched. Wee must therefore note that here commeth a plague that toucheth to the quicke, the effect whereof is expressed in these words, And his kingdome waxed darke. We haue seene before how high the throne of the beast was exalted, where hee sayth, the dragon gaue him his power, his throne, and great authoritie: and all the worlde wondred and followed the beast, and worshipped the beast, chapter 13. And now at the pouring foorth of the fift viall, here is shewed, not the quite ouerthrow or vtter pulling downe at once, but the decay and diminishing of the same. For he sayth not that the kingdome of the beast is cast downe, when the fift Angell poured forth his viall vpon his throne, but that it is darkened. The maiestie, the power, the dignitie, the pompe, and the estimation of Antichrists kingdome commeth now into decay, waxeth obscure, and is diminished. It may here bee demaunded, Is not the kingdome of the beast, a kingdome of darkenesse? Yes verily, it is a kingdome of all darknes and confusion. How then can it be said to be darkened? Can darcknes

be

be darkened? or is the power of darkenes diminished by darkenes? To make this cleere, we must distinguish: for in respect of heauenly and spirituall light, the poperie is darkenes, and blinde ignorance, euen a gulfe of confusion. But in respect of this world, the throne & kingdome of that Romish beast did shine in wonderfull brightnes, in pompe, and glorie. Now the darkening is in respect of these latter, for their worldly power and glory is obscured and waxeth darke. That throne was taken to be the chaire of Peter, and the Pope was esteemed to bee his successor, and to haue Christs power here vpon earth, euen as a God to doe what he lust. All men were glad to haue his blessing, trembling at his curse, and seeking remission and pardon of their sinnes at his hands. They did all magnifie and extoll him as the most holy father: Emperours and Kings did worship him. But when the Angell had poured forth the viall vpon that throne, when the time was come that the light of Gods word should breake forth againe: his throne commeth in question, his authoritie commeth in question, and is found by the euident testimonies of the trueth to be vsurped. Whereupon it followeth, that all his lawes and decrees are not of God, but wicked and abominable. Whereupon further it is found, that it is the kingdome of the great Antichrist, the man of sinne, the whore of Babel. So that great Kings, Princes, and multitudes of people, which honoured him before as God, hauing their eyes lightened with the cleere brightnes of Gods word, haue now loathed and despised him, as the most horrible and filthie Monster in the world. This is the darkening of that kingdome, this is it that hee saith, their kingdome waxed darke. And how sore a plague this is vnto them, and how neerely it doth touch them, the words following doe shew, when he sayth, that they did gnaw their tongues for sorrow. At the first when the Gospell began to peepe forth, they did despise it, as a thing which they could easilie suppresse, but within a short time they found, that neither by their excommunications, wherewith in former times they had euen as it were with lightning and thunder, caused kings and nations to tremble, neither by force of warres, nor by bloodie slaughters, neither by any skill in learning, nor by treacheries, they could any thing preuaile, but that it did more and more, lay open their filthines and shame. Then did they become, and so doe they continue at this day, euen as mad men in sorrow and rage, which the holy Ghost expresseth, in saying that they gnaw their tongues for sorrow. They be full of fierie hatred, and cannot tell which way to be reuenged: for the more they striue, the more they loose dailie. Faine would they haue the Poperie restored to the ancient glorie, and they deuise what they can to bring it about: but it will not bee, for their kingdome waxeth darker and darker. This is the griefe of all griefes vnto them.

He addeth, and they blasphemed the God of heauen, for their paines, and for their sores, and repented not of their workes. Here againe the holy Ghost sheweth what effect the plagues which God sendeth, doe worke in the reprobate. The more neerely men are touched and pressed with the hand of God, the more they should be humbled and become penitent, as wee noted before. But these are so farre from that, as that indeede they breake forth into open blasphemies against the Lord God of heauen: and turne not from their wicked workes. It is not possible for a man to recken vp all the blasphemies which the Bishops of Rome with their Cardinals, their Bishops, Abbots, Monks, and Friers, haue vttered against the holy doctrine and worship of God, and especially since it hath made their kingdome to waxe darke, and their pompous glorie to come downe. And it is a thing to be wondred at, to behold their impudencie in colouring and defending all the wicked abominations which haue been, and which are committed among them. They defend the superstition, the idolatries, the heresies, and foule errors which in former times their Church hath set vp. Also the wicked maners of their Votaries, and other most filthie deedes, they seeke to cloake: yea they adde treasons, periuries, and murders. This is the repentance of the papists, now when the gospell hath bewrayed them. But let vs goe forward to the pouring forth of the sixt viall.

It is said, that the sixt Angell poured forth his viall vpon the great riuer Euphrates, and the waters thereof dried vp, &c. The kingdome of the beast waxed darke at the pouring forth of the fift viall, but the sixt payeth them home neerer. For it drieth vp the waters of Euphrates, so that the way is laid open for those that shal spoile and destroy their citie, to enter into it, and to take it. Let vs giue eare vnto this, for it is ioyfull vnto all Gods people, and it is euen now in working. The waters of Euphrates are dried vp by little and little, and do waxe euery day more shallow, to become such as men may wade ouer into Rome, euen to rouse Antichrist out of his pallace. But things are here spoken mystically, and must bee interpreted. Rome the citie of Antichrist, or the kingdome of the beast is called in this prophecie Babell. We all know the reason, euen because it hath held the people of God in bondage, for so did Babel in old time. Then looke what the scripture teacheth concerning the destruction of that Babel, and ye shal find that the holy Ghost vseth those speeches here to set forth the destruction of Rome, and of the kingdome of Antichrist. In Daniel, chap. 5. is set forth how Babel was taken by Darius, and Cyrus Kings of the East. For they were the Kings of the Medes and Persians, which besieged Babel. This citie Babel was so strong that they could not preuaile. On the one side of it, and iust by it, did run the riuer Euphrates, a riuer very broad and deepe, which was such a defence, that on that side there was no passing into the citie. Cyrus had this deuise, he caused the army to cut out great trenches and ditches, and so to let out the riuer aboue before it came to the citie, and so drawing out the waters, and deriuing them another way, he made the riuer so shallow before the citie, that the souldiers waded ouer, and entred. To this the holy Ghost here alludeth. Then is it easie to see what is here meant, when he saith, the waters of the great riuer Euphrates were dryed vp. For by this riuer is signified the fortification of Rome this great Babel. It was of late a great deepe riuer, and not to be waded ouer. For when the world wondred after the beast, and said, who is able to warre with the beast, how strongly was that kingdome, or that great citie fortified? The riches, the glorie, the honour, and the strength thereof were exceeding great, these are Euphrates, and the waters of these are dried vp. The waters of this riuer are a great deale shallower then they were some fiftie yeares past, and doubtlesse

lesse they drie vp by little and little daily. The Popes coffers waxe emptie, his credite is impaired very much, his friends haue forsaken him, his old reuenewes out of sundrie kingdomes doe faile: and so the passage beginneth to lie open to the kings of the East. Rome beginneth to lie open to her enemies, the waters of her Euphrates are become so shallow, that men may almost wade ouer them, and in processe of time they will bee dried vp, that men may easily passe ouer. They were so deepe that no kings could leade their armies ouer them: but the way shall be made easie. But here it will be demaunded, who are these kings of the East, and how shall the citie of Antichrist be taken? The things being yet to come, it is hard to tell how they shall be, or by whom. Rome shall downe, that is most certaine: and whether by Christian princes, or by the Turke's, or other Easterne princes, we cannot tell. If any shall say, that the text is plaine, that the way shall bee prepared for the kings of the East: I answere, that is but an allusion, because Darius, and Cyrus that tooke Babell, drying vp the waters of Euphrates, and leading ouer their armies, were kings of the East.

? Well let vs goe forward, the waters drie vp and they perceiue it, and bestirre them exceedingly. For when men let out the waters of a great pond that is full of fishes, when the water waxeth low, ye shall see the fishes take on wonderfully: so is it with the Romish Antichristian rabblement; they feele the waters of their riuer drying vp, and they tumble and tosse euery way. For behold what S. Iohn addeth, *I saw three vncleane spirits like frogs come out of the mouth of the dragon, out of the mouth of the beast, and out of the mouth of the false prophet.* Now the matter waxeth hot. And marke here who ioyne together, the dragon, the beast, & the false prophet. The dragon is the diuell, the beast is the Romane Empire, the false prophet is the papacie, who is also in one respect a chiefe head of the beast, and as he is the false prophet, a beast by himselfe. These three are no meane ones, & they consent, and conspire together against the Gospell, to maintaine poperie, which is here represented by three spirits which come out of their mouthes, which are all alike, for they be all like frogs, they be al of one nature and qualitie, for he saith, They be the spirits of diuels working miracles, and they goe foorth all vpon one busines: for he saith, they goe forth to the kings of the earth, to gather them to the battell of the great day of God almightie. Doe ye not see how they all three agree together in one? The diuell is the chiefe, the beast and the false prophet are led by his spirit: for the spirits that come out of their mouthes are the same with that which commeth out of his. They haue all three one minde, one purpose, one desire, and practise one thing. What are these spirits then that are the spirits of deuils, like frogs, which goe forth to the kings of the earth? Surely the Iesuites and Seminarie priests, which are sent foorth into all lands vnto kings and princes to moue them against the Gospell, are most fitly resembled by these vncleane spirits. For first they come with the minde of the Pope, and of the Romane Empire, and so with the very mind and spirit of the dragon. They come with the very spirits of diuels, and with great efficacie of error do worke strange things, euen wonders to deceiue the blind. They be like frogs, not onely that their delight is in the

stinking

stinking puddles of filthie superstition, as frogs delight in marish places, but also that they keepe a croaking and make a tedious noyse. They seeke by treacheries, and all maner of lewd practises to moue seditions, and rebellions, and treasons, and all for the maintenance of the poperie. I will not here enter into any discourse of their particular doings, which haue been so famous here within our land, that euen children cannot be ignorant thereof. How many of them haue conspired the death of our prince, and haue their heads standing ouer London bridge? Let them croake and take on while they will in all lands, and gather as great armies as they can, yet the waters of Euphrates shall dailie diminish and drie vp, and they doe but assemble and prepare themselues to the slaughter in the great day of God almightie. It is God that bringeth them downe, and no power of man can withstand him.

Then in the next place, because here was mention made of the great day, there is a warning added, for to stirre vs vp vnto watchfulnes, to waite our Lords comming. Behold (saith he) I come as a theefe. The Lord will come suddenly, and when he is not looked for, as he teacheth by this comparison, Matth. 24. and Luke 12. That if the good man of the house did know at what houre the theefe would come, he would not sleepe but watch, and not suffer his house to be broken vp. A theefe commeth at vnwares vnto them that be asleepe. For which cause our Sauiour saith here, Beholde I come as a theefe, I will come when men shall thinke least, and they shall bee caught as in a net. Wherefore they are blessed that doe watch, and keepe their garments, least they walke naked, and men see their filthines. This watching is to be vnderstood of the minde, that it fall not asleepe in carnall pleasures, in cares of this world, or securely wallow in sinne, and so be spoyled of the precious garments of the soule, which are giuen vs in Christ Iesus. This admonition is giuen more then once in the scriptures, and reasons added to moue and to perswade, because the neerer the end of the world is, the more worldly mē will grow, and lesse watchfull in minde vnto good things. I doe therefore beseech ye to consider of it, and be warned. Doe not follow the multitude of the worlde herein, which as men asleepe in sin walke naked, and their filthines is seene both to God and men. They will not be warned: but (beloued) be ye warned at the voice of the Lord himselfe: who is to be beleeued, and telleth what is for our good.

And now where it was said, that the vncleane spirits, which came out of the mouth of the dragon, out of the mouth of the beast, and out of the mouth of the false prophet, went forth vnto the kings of the earth to gather them together vnto battaile: it is shewed that they preuaile therein, I meane thus farre as to gather them to the battaile. These wicked ministers of Antichrist, guided and led with the spirit of Satan, although they cannot preuaile with all kings and princes, yet they stirre vp some, whom they perswade to bend their force against the cause of God, and against his faithfull seruants. For such Kings and Nobles as God doth not by his speciall grace lighten to beholde his trueth, lye open to bee seduced by their sleights. They are so impudent in their false slaunders, with which they burthen the professors of the Gospell: they are so importunate in boasting of the authoritie

THE REVELATION.

thoritie of their Romish synagogue: they are so cunning to depraue and to peruert the holy Scriptures, that they much preuaile with some. It is said therefore that they gather the kings with their forces together into a place called in hebrue *Armageddon*. Here is darke speech, but the meaning is this, that the Lord will destroy these enemies of his Church with so horrible slaughter, that the place shall take a name thereof. For so we may reade, that among the Hebrewes it was an vsuall thing where any famous thing fell out, to call the place where it fell out, by a name that did report the same vnto posteritie. This is so vsuall a thing, as I sayd, that whosoeuer readeth the olde Testament shall finde it very often, so that in so cleere a matter, I will not alleage any particulars. This is hard to bee expounded what the word *Armageddon* doth signifie: because Saint Iohn wrote it not in hebrew letters, but in the greeke, and somewhat also in forme of a greeke name. For there bee hebrew letters, which when a word is turned into another language, I meane expressed with the characters of another tongue, cannot fitly be expressed, and therefore are sundrie times left out. And this name *Armageddon* is compounded of two hebrew words, but with what letters in the hebrew it is hard to tell, or with what change also of vowels. Some say it commeth of *Har*, which signifieth a mountaine, and *Megiddo*, which is the name of the place where the godly king Iosias was slaine: and so this place should be called *Armageddon*, the mountaine of Megiddo, for the slaughter of kings that shall bee there. Others doe expound it to come of *Cherem*, which signifieth a killing, a destruction, and *Gedud*, which signifieth an armie, and so together it should signifie the destruction of an armie. Some other doe take it to be expounded of *Arma* with the letter *Ain*, as to say, *gnarma*, which is subtile, and *gada* with the letter *Ain* also, which signifieth to cut downe, as to say, *gidnon*, and so the sense should be the subtiltie of cutting downe, because the kings and their armies are seduced by the subtiltie of Antichrist and of his ministers, to their vtter subuersion and cutting downe. All these come to one thing in effect, which is, that the armie of these wicked ones which assemble themselues in battaile against the Lord, shall be destroyed: and therefore it is not much materiall to dispute which is the more likely signification of the word. This is our speciall comfort, that albeit the beast and the false prophet led by the spirit of the Dragon, doe make great sturres, and gather great armies and powers to fight against the Gospell, and against all that doe professe it, and that onely for the maintenance and support it on of their owne pompe and glorie, yet they shall not preuaile, but shall be vtterly cut downe and destroyed: as we shall see, it more at large set forth in the 19. chapter.

Now to the last plague: The seuenth Angell powred forth his viall into the ayre, and there came a great voyce out of the temple of heauen from the throne, saying, it is done. This plague containeth the most generall and the most grieuous wrath and vengeance of almightie God, vpon the whole bodie of the kingdome of Antichrist. It containeth indeede sore iudgements vpon them immediatly before the last day, with the wrath that shall then come vpon them: and therefore it is sayd to bee powred forth into the ayre: for that doth compasse them all in on-

every

euery side. And moreouer, that wee may note the grieuousnes of this vengeance, here is the voice of almightie God from his throne in heauen. Moreouer, this voice is to teach vs, that God in his vnchangeable decree hath determined to beate the downe, and that now the time is come, and hee will endure them no longer. Hee hath touched them with former plagues, and that neerer and neerer, but no repentance hath followed, no amendment: but contrariwise they haue waxed worse and worse, and haue more wickedly blasphemed him and his holy truth, to maintaine their owne inuentions, and therefore now he beginneth to come vpon them with more horrible vengeance, euen to their vtter ouerthrow.

He sayth, *It is done*. Now they must come to their reward. There is no way for them now to escape: for can men escape from the hands of God? Although their plagues haue been great, yet they are so stone hard, that they seemed little to feele them. Nay, the Lord seemed to winke at them in some sort, and but to dallie with them: but now he will lay on downe blowes, euen to breake the stonie rockes in peeces. O beloued, let vs take heede that we haue nothing to doe with the popish sort, let vs flie and eschew their religion and their manners, least we come also to be partakers with them in the plagues which here doe follow. For first hee sayth, that there followed voyces, thundrings and lightnings, and that there was a great earthquake, such as was not since men dwelt vpon the earth, so mightie an earthquake. These speeches are not to be taken according to the letter, but mystically: and they doe set foorth that all shall bee full of horrour and shakings. If there were so great a tempest in the ayre, with terrible thunderclaps, and flashes of lightning, and roring noyses, and withall the earth trembling and shaking vnder mens feete, would it not bee a most terrible thing to behold? Could any man endure and not quake for feare at the sight and hearing thereof? Would it not bee thought then, as we vse to say, that it seemeth heauen and earth would be mingled together? There shall come then (as is heere figured by such a tempest) horrible things vpon the kingdomes which are subiect vnto Antichrist. Terrible iudgements of God shall light vpon them. They shall bee as it were beat downe with lightnings and thunders, and the earth shaking vnder them. Where shall they haue any comfort, or succour? There shall bee not onely terrible and dreadfull plagues vpon them, but also such shakings of their estate, such commotions and tumults, as the like were neuer since the beginning of the world. There haue been great shakings, great commotions, great broyles, great alterations and chaunges, but neuer any like vnto those which shall fall out when this tempest is begunne. Thus may wee see the chiefe cause why the Angell is sayd to powre foorth his viall into the ayre, because these horrible iudgements are represented by a terrible tempest, and earthquake. Now ye shall see what effect this tempest and earthquake doe cause, or what matters come to passe by the same. It is first sayd, that the great citie was deuided into three parts. The great citie in this prophecie is Rome, and the dominion of Rome, euen so farre as it extendeth. For looke how farre her authoritie stretcheth, so farre may it be called the great citie: and all that worship and serue the beast, may be sayd to bee citizens and to dwell in the great citie.

citie. Then as it falleth out in mightie tempests and great earthquakes that cities are torne and rent, so is it here sayd, that by this tempest and earthquake, the great citie is clouen into three parts. Many doe expound this thus, that the multitude in all nations, which with one consent did professe poperie, and worship the beast, shall be diuided from that vnitie into three parts. As namely, one part at the voyce of the Gospell forsake the Romish religion, euen with zeale and pure affection, to worship the true and liuing God, according to the rules of his holy word. Another part shall stiffely cleaue to the poperie, euen blinded and besotted in their errors. A third part not caring for the one side nor the other, but as men voyd of religion, shall stand as it were indifferent. Doubtles of this latter sort there be wonderfull many, which being men of this world, so they may inioy the world, the riches and delights thereof with peace, they care not much what religion come. They can goe through in poperie, and when they be among papists commend it: and they can make some shew of the Gospell among Gospellers. No man can denie but that this is most true: but yet I thinke wee cannot for certaintie affirme that it is here meant by the cleauing of the great citie into three parts. For mine owne part I thinke the time of the powring foorth of this seuenth viall is not yet come: and therefore we cannot precisely say what it shall be. Sure we are, it shall be a very grieuous calamity, and a grieuous rent, but in what manner, we must not take vpon vs to set foorth, seeing the fulfilling of prophecies is the cleere and perfect interpretation of them. It may be it shall be in Rome it selfe, and not to be vnderstood of the whole societie, which is subiect to that Romane tyrannie: they that liue when it commeth, shall see it.

Then is it said further, And the cities of the Gentiles fell. This is vsually expounded of the kingdome of the Turke, and of other kingdomes of the Heathen which deny Christ: but I see no reason to force thereunto. Indeede vsually in the holie Scriptures the Gentiles are taken for those nations, which in no sorte did professe the religion and worship of the true God: but yet they that marke shall finde that sometimes in the Psalmes and in the Prophets, the prophane multitude in the visible Church are called Heathen. And so in the 11. chapter of this booke the Romish multitude, partly Pagans vnder the cruell Emperours, and partly false Christians vnder the Popes, are called Gentiles or Heathen: and so this may be vnderstood of the cities of those prophane and wicked Idolaters which cleaue to the poperie, that they shall fall, I leaue it also as a thing as yet darke.

Then next he sayth, that great Babylon came in remembrance before God, to giue vnto her the cup of the wine of the fiercenes of his wrath. This whore of Babell did imagine while the Lorde let her alone, that God did not regard her doings. And such is the weakenes of man, that euen the faithfull are readie to feare when the wicked are suffered to raigne, that God doth not remember them: and therefore when this time commeth, the Romish synagogue shall see and feele, that God remembreth her. And when she shall bee made to drinke of the cup of the fierce wrath of the Lord, all men shall acknowledge that she is not forgotten, and that although her abominations do escape for a time, yet shall they not escape

Y   for

for euer. Then is there further added, that euery Isle fled, and the mountaines were not found: which sheweth that there shall be no place of refuge for these wicked men, whereunto they may flie for succour. For in time of great calamities men vse to flie to the mountaines to hide themselues, or into Isles. But in this tempest and earthquake when the terrible God standeth vp to execute vengeance vpon these vngodly enemies of his Gospel, there shall be no place for them wherein they may hide themselues from him, but his hand will finde them out.

Then last of all he sayth, that there fell a great haile as it had been talents out of heauen vpon the men, and me blasphemed God because of the plague of the haile, for the plague thereof was exceeding great. Wee reade how the Lord God cast downe great stones from heauen vpon the wicked, whome hee rooted out of the land of Canaan, when Iosua came and fought to place the tribes of Israell there: and so it is said, that vpon these wicked in Antichristes kingdome, hee will cast downe haile stones of great waight. Hee will fight from heauen against them to beate them downe, vnto eternall destruction. But they will not relent, but still blaspheme him. And thus yee see what a tempest of wrath remaineth for the wicked Papists. Let vs therefore cheerefully and louingly imbrace the holy Gospell of God, that we may reioyce, when the enemies shall houle. For with this haile they shall bee beaten downe into hell, where shall bee weeping and gnashing of teeth world without end.

THE XXXVI. SERMON.
CHAP. XVII.

1 *Then there came one of the seuen Angels, which had the seuen vials and talked with me, saying vnto me: come, I will shew thee the damnation of the great whore that sitteth vpon many waters.*

2 *With whom haue committed fornication the kings of the earth, and the Inhabitants of the earth are drunken with the wine of her fornication.*

3 *So he caryed me away into the wildernes in the spirite, and I sawe a woman sit vpon a scarlet coloured beast, full of names of blasphemie, which had seuen heads and ten hornes.*

4 *And the woman which I saw was arraied in purple and crimson, and girded with gold, pretious stones, and pearles, hauing a golden cup in her hand full of abominations and filthines of her fornication.*

5 *And in her forehead was a name written a mystery, great Babylon the mother of whoredomes, and abominations of the earth.*

6 *And I sawe the woman drunken with the bloud of the Saints, and with the*
bloud

bloud of the Martyrs of Iesus: and when I saw her I wondred with great meruaile.

7 *And the Angell said vnto me, wherefore meruailest thou? I will shew thee the mysterie of the woman, and of the beast that beareth her, that hath seuen heads and ten hornes.*

E haue had the description of the beast with seuen heads, which is the former dominion of Rome, and of the beast with two hornes which is the latter, euen the kingdome of the great Antichrist that should come. The plagues also which GOD would send vpon that idolatrous Synagogue haue beene set forth, and the ruine thereof. And now that the people of God might know for certaine, and not by coniectures who should bee this beast, and where he should raigne: here is not onely a vision shewed vnto Saint Iohn of the beast, but also of the citie where he should raigne, and moreouer the mysterie of them both expounded. The Lord sent his Angell vnto Iohn to open the meaning of these visions, so that wee doe not rest vpon any vncertaine coniectures, but haue the exposition of God himselfe. Why should wee any more complaine, and say the things be so darke that they cannot be vnderstood? or that wee can haue no certaintie of them? what can we require more but the exposition of the Lord God himselfe? Here the Iesuites vse what sleightes they can to defend Rome, and their Pope, but they are so euidently noted, that they cannot couer their shame but with such thinne couerings as euery one may easily see through them. But now beloued, seeing the Lorde doth so graciously by his holy Angell expound vnto vs the mysterie of the whore of Babell, and of the beast which beareth her, let vs thankfully and reuerently apply our minds to learne: and especially because the exposition of the mysterie of this woman, and of the beast that beareth her, is a cleere opening of the greatest part, and euen of all the chiefest matters in this prophecie. This chapter is euen as the key to open the closet of the mysteries of this booke. But let vs come to the words of the text.

Then (saith he) there came vnto me one of the seuen Angels, which had the seuen vials, and talked with me, saying vnto me, come, I will shew thee the damnation of the great whore which sitteth vpon many waters. Here is for this vision (as ye see) first set downe the minister by whom this vision is shewed and expounded vnto Iohn, that is the Angell. And hee was one of those seuen which had the seuen vials of the wrath of God, because here followeth not onely an exposition of the mysterie of the great whore, but also her damnation in the next chapter. For this Angell is one of them which poureth forth vpon her the wrath and iudgement of God.

Secondly, it is noted how he calleth Saint Iohn to the receiuing of this speciall vision. For he saith, come I will shew thee. And then is added what he will shew him, namely, the damnation of the whore. The words after some phrase may bee expounded thus, I will shew thee that damnable great whore which sitteth vpon many waters. For as yet Iohn had not seene her in any vision. And in that he saith, She sitteth vpon many waters: it sheweth that she hath dominion ouer many nations and peoples, as we shall see afterward in this chapter: for the angell doth so interprete them. In the next words there is a reason rendred, not onely why she is called a whore, but also the great whore. She is a whore, because she hath committed fornication: she is the great whore, because she hath committed whoredome with such great ones, and with so many: for he sayth, with whom haue committed fornication the kings of the earth, & the inhabitants of the earth are drunke with the wine of her fornication. The church of Rome boasteth her selfe to be the chast spouse of Christ, but she reiecteth his lawes, she condemneth his pure worship, and setteth vp a worship of her owne, euen all idolatrie and superstition, the worship of deuils, and so like a most abominable filthie whore, hath allured and drawen the kings of the earth, and their subiects euen mightie nations to commit spirituall whoredom with her: for so the scripture speaketh of all those that turne from the pure worship of God vnto mens inuentions. And here we are to note that he saith, the inhabitants of the earth are made drunke with the wine of her fornication, For this in a word expresseth with what greedie desire the blind idolatrous people should receiue the decrees of the Bishop of Rome, euen as drunken men seeke stil to poure in wine. No man is able with words sufficiently to expresse how much and how madly men in the time of popery doted vpō the rotten filthy inuentions of the Pope. How did they drinke vp his pardons and indulgences euen as men drinke vp sweet wine? How ranne they after stockes and stones at his appoyntment? and euen like men that are mad drunke, looked to saue their soules by swilling in the very dregs of his inuentions. It is rare to find any that haue the like true zeale to receiue into their soule the holy and pure oracles of God. Doubtlesse the drunken zeale of papists to commit whoredome with this great whore of Babylon, in vehemencie goeth farre beyonde the zeale generallie of those that professe the holy Gospell. Which thing indeed ought to make vs much ashamed. For shal they be more zealous of mens inuentions, nay of the deuils inuentions which poyson the soule vnto death? then we shall be of the liuely words of God which bring grace and saluation. Let it somewhat stirre vs vp.

It followeth, So he caryed me away into the wildernes in the spirit. The angell being to shew vnto Iohn the great whore of Babell, caryeth him away in the spirite. He is againe rauished in the spirite as sometimes the prophets were when visions were shewed vnto them. And he saith, he is caryed into the wildernesse, and there he hath the sight of her set before him. What meaneth this, that the great whore is in the wildernes? I will shew yee. The Lord in the prophet Esay calleth the gentils the wildernes: for among them there was no fruitfulnes to God, but all lay barren and wast. Therefore it is sayd, chapter 12. of this booke, when the Church was spread among the gentiles, that shee was fled into the wildernes. By the same reason, the visible Church is called a wildernes, when it is once laid wast and desolate. And Saint Iohn Baptist commeth crying in the wildernes. The

great

great whore of Babell, is seated in the Church which is the vineyard of the Lorde, but she so wasteth and destroyeth so farre, that she turneth almost al into a wildernes, and therefore in the wildernes is she shewed vnto Iohn. No fruitfull thing can grow neere her she maketh hauocke, and so right wel she appeareth in the wildernesse.

Now after the place noted where hee saw her, Iohn commeth to paint her out and to describe her. And I saw (saith he) a woman sit vpon a scarlet coloured beast. The true Church in the 12. chapter of this booke, appeared in vision vnder the shape of a woman clothed and decked with heauenly and spirituall ornaments: And here the malignant Church the Romish Synagogue, and the citie of Rome it selfe is figured and represented by a woman also in goodly decking, and in verie pompous and costly attyre, but not heauenly, but such as this world doth affoord: for it is all but whorish, she hath no spirituall ornaments. This woman sitteth vpon a beast. It hath been shewed you before in the 13. chapter, that a beast doth signifie a dominion, a rule, a monarchie. For so much the Angell doth shewe in Daniel. The Romish rout, the Synagogue of Antichrist, and the citie of Rome hath been supported by a mightie Empire and dominion which they haue helde ouer the nations: Therefore the woman sitteth vpon a beast. And this beast is scarlet coloured: for it is a bloudie kingdome. Yea and the Popes and Cardinals in their greatest pomp are clothed in scarlet. This beast is ful of names of blasphemy. For that citie, and that Church hath been held vp by a most blasphemous gouernment, and by most wicked lawes. There is nothing in it but blasphemie vpon blasphemie against the holy doctrine of Christ.

Then further he saith, this beast vpon which the woman sitteth, hath seuen heads and ten hornes. Whereby ye may see it is that same beast, euen that same Empire, which is described, chap. 13. What is meant by the heads, and by the hornes of this beast, the Angell afterward in this chapter doth shewe, which I will not touch vntill we come to that place. And now for the attyre of this woman, he saith, The woman which I saw was arraied in purple and crimson, and girded with golde, pretious stones, and pearles. In few wordes the holy Ghost doth here declare, that the citie of Rome, and the Romish Church should be most richly and pompously decked with all costly things. For by purple, crimson, gold, precious stones, and pearles, are signified not onely the things so named, but also all other pretious things for pompe and ornaments. Whores doe trim vp themselues, and this great whore is decked and trimmed aboue all other. The harlots doe decke themselues for to entice and allure louers, and so to draw them to commit fornication. So this whore of Babell thinck in all outward pompe and glorie in earthly thinges, euen to the intent that she may allure the nations to commit whoredome with her, euen the spirituall whoredome. Looke vpon the citie of Rome in time past, looke vpon the Popes and Cardinals, and other great prelates, yea looke vpon their whole religion, and you shall see nothing but pompe, glorie, & beautie in outward things: and by these they haue dazled the eyes both of high and lowe, and haue drawen them into superstition and idolatrie. Beloued, here is a speciall thing to bee noted, which I will lay open vnto you: and iudge in your selues, whether it bee not most plaine and euident.

The enemies doe graunt first, that the true Church is described with her ornaments, chap. 12. And also they cannot denie, but that here is described the malignant Church. Then let the wise consider the descriptions of them both: the true Church hath her ornaments, and her decking altogether heauenly and spirituall. She is cloathed with the Sunne, the Moone is vnder her feete, and on her head a crowne of twelue starres. Here is all from Christ, here is all spirituall and heauenly bewtie. The false church, shee setteth forth her selfe, shee is very pompous to the outward eye, but all her decking and ornaments bee earthly. She is not cloathed with the sunne, shee is not adorned and bewtified with the righteousnes of Christ: shee hath not a crowne of twelue starres vpon her head, the doctrine of the Apostles is not her crowne, it doth not shine in her, shee hath no spirituall riches: but shee glistereth with golde, precious stones, and pearles, and in all costly ornaments of purple, scarlet, crimsin, and of all manner of silkes. And now iudge whether our Church which doth professe the Gospell, or the popish Church be likest to that woman, chapt. 12. Yea, and iudge whether their Church or ours, be likest vnto this woman here described, sitting vpon the beast. Ye shall finde that the Churches which doe renounce the poperie, and professe the Gospell, make no shew in any outward pompe, but haue all their glory in the sonne of God. Their bewtie is spirituall, inuisible, and hid from the eyes of flesh and blood: the pure doctrine of our Lorde Iesus Christ doth shine among them: it is their crowne, their glorie and bewtie. They seeke not to drawe men to their religion, by the glittering shew of outward things: but by the heauenly treasures and rich graces which are giuen vnto vs in Christ Iesus. On the other side, the Church of Rome, which extolleth her owne righteousnes, glorieth in her own doctrine, and in her owne decrees, hauing no spirituall treasures for to lay open, for to drawe men by, vnto her religion, trimmeth vp her selfe, and all her religion with outward pompe of riches, and precious attyres: all is in outward glorie, and in goodly shewes. There is gold, pearles, precious stones, and costly garments: and take away these, and you take away all: for there will remayne nothing that is worth the looking on. It falleth out sometime, that notorious harlots which trimme and decke themselues with costly apparel, and goodly ornaments, and haue paynted their faces, doe seeme very bewtiful, comely and amiable, which yet, those goodly garments taken off, and they put into meane apparell, and the painting of their faces gone, are as homely and as hard fauoured women, as a man shall lightly see. And this is the very case of the great whore of Babylon, the Romish Church. Shee hath trimmed her selfe with costly ornaments aboue all other whores in the world. Shee hath painted her face, and hath set forth her selfe in such worldly pompe, bewtie, glory and riches, as the like hath not been seene, and thereby hath won great kings and multitudes, to commit whoredome with her, both while shee was heathen, and since shee hath been vnder the Popes: and take away her outwarde

THE REVELATION. 327

pompe, and shee is the most euill fauoured and beggarly whore that may be. She hath no true spirituall bewtie, she hath no true heauenly treasures to bestow vpon her children.

It is added further, that this woman sitting vpon the beast, hath a golden cup in her hand, full of abhominations of her fornication? The Angell sayd before, that this great whore had made the inhabitants of the earth, drunken with the wine of her fornication: and now here in vision, is shewed the cup in which she hath offered the same wine. For he saith, she had in her hand a golden cup. It is not in vaine that the cup is mentioned, because it may be demaunded how men should be so easilie led to drinke vp such abhominable filthie things? Surely the cup doth intice them. It is such a goodly fine cup, for it is a cup of golde: who would suspect, that such horrible and filthie abhominations of spirituall whoredomes should come forth of such a fine precious cup? It is indeede a golden cup, and such as the wisest man may easilie bee deceiued withall, that is led but with humane wisedome. And so yee will confesse when ye know what it is: for what is this cup which this gorgious whore of Babel holdeth in her hand, of which the kings and nations doe drinke? What is it by which shee broacheth all her filthie abominations? It is euen this, the title of the Catholike Church, of Peters chayre, and Christes Vicar: for they boast that they bee the Catholike Church, Peters chayre they say is at Rome, and the Pope hee is the Vicar of Christ. Is not here thinke ye a golden cup, will any man be afraide to drinke of it? Now into this golden cup, hath this whore put all her swill: for looke whatsoeuer filthines in superstition, in idolatries and heresies, the Romish Church hath deuised, they haue put the same into this cup, and so offered it to the kings and nations to drinke, and the cup hath made them drinke, making no question what they did drinke: for be it neuer so contrarie to the holy word of God, if it were once put into this golden cup, that is to saye, the holy Catholike Church hath decreed, Christes Vicar sitting in Peters chayre doth commaund, who almost would refuse to suppe it vp? All lyes, doctrines of deuils, euen filthie abhominations being put into this golden cup, the world was so greedie of them, that well was hee which might get the first draught: and they did swill themselues, euen vntill they were drunken. Here lay the chiefe deceite: for if the filthie whore had not craftily made her such a cup, shee could neuer haue entised the kings and nations to committe such abhominable whoredome with her. Could shee haue made them drinke vp heresies and errors condemned by the expresse written word of God? Could she haue brought them contrarie to his flat commaundement, to worship Idols of golde and siluer, of brasse, of wood and stone? Could she haue brought them not onely to worship the dragon, but also to condemne, to persecute and most cruelly to murther the holy and pure worshippers of the Lord? but that shee had vsurped and chalenged this title of Catholike Church, and of the power of Christ, and the blind world did beleeue her. They tooke it, that nothing could come forth of this cup, but that which was for the saluation of their soules. Wee are here taught a good lesson to bee wise, euen to looke what is put into the cup before we drinke of it: or else out of a goodly cup of gold, we may drinke deadly poyson. So many in times past as by the wisedome of gods holy spirit, and by the light of his pure word did examine and trie the things which were put into this cup refused to drinke thereof, and saued their soules, though to their trouble in this world: thus much touching the cup.

Then it followeth, and in her forehead was a name written, a mysterie: Great Babylon, the mother of whoredomes and abominations of the earth. Shee hath her name and her qualities written in her forehead, to bee openly seene and read of all men. Wee vse to say, if euerie mans faults were written in their foreheads, some would pull downe their hats very low: but this whore hath a name expressing her qualities, and all her abominable whoredoms written in her forehead, and yet is so impudent that shee is not ashamed at all. Shee hath the whores forehead indeed: this is the great goodnes of God, that this whore hath her name written in her forehead, to the end that all his chosen seruants might eschew her, and take heed of her whoredoms. The name which is written in her forehead, is great Babylon, and then her qualities are noted thus, the mother of whoredoms and abominations of the earth. Babel is confusion; Babel held the Church in captiuitie, Babel was full of idolatry. Rome is the great Babel, shee hath mixed and confused all in Gods worship: she hath oppressed the Church: she hath abounded in all abominable Idolatries: Shee hath not onely committed all manner of whoredoms and abominations and filthines, but euen as a mother of all these things, she hath bred them, brought them forth, and spread them ouer the kingdoms and nations of the earth. Shee is the mother indeed of all filthines: for so is great Babylon. But it will be said, if her name be so openly grauen in her forehead, and her filthie whoredoms so manifestlly expressed, how commeth it to passe that so many haue been led away, and seduced by her to commit fornication? Did they reade the name, & yet imbrace her? The holy Ghost answereth this in a word, that though her name and her qualities were written in her forehead, yet the world did not, nor could not reade it, for he sayth it is a mysterie. The whore braggeth, that she is the chast and pure spouse of Christ: her whoredoms and abhominations are so euident that they be euen written in her forehead, and the Lord hath set a brand vpon her forehead with this name, great Babylon the mother of whoredoms, &c. But yet it is a mysterie, it is hidden from the blind world, and none of that Romish sort can reade it: but Gods true and faithful seruants by the pure light of his trueth, as it were putting spectacles, doe behold most clearely the letters of this name in the whores forehead. Oh say some, if Rome be Babylon, if the Church of Rome be the Synagogue of Antichrist, which carrieth her name written in her forehead, why should not so many learned men of that side espie so much? Yee see here that her name is written in a mysterie, which the papists cannot perceiue, being blinded and besotted with the loue of the whore: for this place sheweth euidently what an exceeding blindnes the popish sort are taken and held withall, that a name being written euen in the forehead, and that in cleare letters yet can not they reade it. This it is, when men despise the light of Gods word, and will fol-

lowe

lowe their own inuentions: they blind themselues and are worthily blinded. But let vs imbrace the heauenly light of Gods word, & we shal see the letters as plaine in the whores forehead as may be, that she is great Babylon the mother of whoredoms and abominations of the earth: for it is the light of Gods word which maketh vs able to see and to vnderstand mysteries. And thus shall we escape from the deceits of the cup of this abominable harlot, and stand vpright in the feare and true worship of God. And if any doe not see that the Romish Church is great Babel, it is because they be blind, or vnskilfull in the mysteries of God. Giue a faire printed booke to a man that cannot reade, which knoweth not a letter, and what is it to him? Euen so to such as haue not the light of Gods word, what is it that the name great Babylon is written in the forehead of the Romish Church? they cannot reade it: they cannot perceiue it: they may easily be made beleeue that it is a right holy Church. Well, we may see then that such as bee seduced by the whore of Babylon, it is through their own fault, they despise the true light, and so cannot reade the name that is written in her forehead. Againe we may note here the folly of the papists, for they would beare men in hand because the name is great Babylon, that Antichrist should be one man, who should bee borne at Babylon in Chaldea.

Moreouer, the cauill of the Rhemists is friuolous, when they haue confessed that Rome was called Babylon in the time that the Heathen persecuting Emperours did raigne there: when yet there was a glorious Church there which was not Babylon. And so doe inferre that if Rome bee the seate of Antichrist, yet the Pope and his Church are not Antichrist. As though it were not euident, that the Empire of Rome, that is, the beast which beareth her vp, should haue heads succeeding each other to support her as Babell euen to her ende, and that the seuenth head was onely remaining to come when Iohn receiued this prophecie. Haue not the Popes borne her vp euen as the Emperours did? And let them shew what other head there shall be of the beast. Saint Iohn doth describe this whore yet further, saying, I saw the woman drunken, with the bloud of the Saints, and with the bloud of the Martyrs of Iesus. This part of the description is to shew that this great Babylon is the cruell murtherer of all the Martyrs in the time of the Gospell. It is the bloudie citie, yea so bloudie, that she is euen drunken with the bloud of the Martyrs. This is a cleere marke to shew vnto vs the citie which is called in a mysterie great Babylon, the mother of whoredomes and abominations of the earth. For let the Papist shew vnto vs any other citie besides Rome, which in the time of the Gospell hath shed the bloud of the martyrs. If any will reply and say, their bloud hath been shed in all lands, and in cities very farre distant from Rome. I answere, that that is very true, but yet it was onely Rome that put them to death. For in olde time when the first persecutions were, and many thousands were cruelly murthered in all lands, were they not put to death by the authoritie of Rome? Did not the Emperours of Rome commaund it? and was not the thing executed in their name and authoritie? Who can say that Rome was not then the sheader of the bloud of the Martyrs? And now of later times, all that haue been slaine for the

testimonie

testimonie of the Gospel, in France, in Spayne, in England, and in other countries, who hath put them to death but Rome? At whose decree haue they been slaine, and by whose authoritie, but of the Popes of Rome? Rome, Rome, hath put them to death. Rome is guiltie of their bloud: yea Rome the great whore is euen drunken with the bloud of the martyrs of Iesus. Haue you read or heard of any other besides Rome? Hath there been any other power since the Heathen Emperours, that hath there borne sway and persecuted besides the power of the Popes, or shall we looke for any other to come? If not, why should wee bee in any doubt to say Rome is great Babell that bloudie citie, and the persecuting popish Church of Rome is the wicked synagogue of Antichrist? Well, Saint Iohn was in great admiration, and wonderment when he beheld this woman. He saw her sit vpon such a monster with seuen heads and tenne hornes, he saw her so richly arraied and decked with precious costly ornaments, he saw such a goodly cuppe in her hand, filled with filthie whoredomes and abominations, he saw her name in her forehead, and her qualities painted out, and especially that she was drunken with the bloud of the martyrs, and wondred with great admiration. For is it not a strange and a wonderfull thing, that such a fine and daintie harlot should so drinke vp the bloud of men, that she should become euen drunken with the same? It is a monstrous thing, and most sauage, so to gorge in bloud. And let vs obserue how it falleth out with the murtherers of the true seruants of God: euen as it is with drunkards, the more they drinke, the more they couet still to powre in more. The more they shed bloud, the more greedily they desire still, and as drunken therewith they doe become insatiable. This is the righteous iudgement of God vpon them. Let it admonish vs for to take heede, how wee make any beginning to warre against the people of God, for hauing begun, there is very great danger.

The Angell asketh Iohn why he maruelleth? Not that the sight was not to bee wondred at, or that he simply reprehendeth his wondring: but he would not haue him stay as it were astonished, or amazed with admiration, but rather attend and couet to vnderstand the meaning. For that is mans frailtie to wonder so much as to be hindred, and therefore the Angell calleth him from his wonderment, saying, I will shewe thee the mysterie of the woman, and of the beast that beareth her which hath seuen heads, and tenne hornes. Here is a goodly thing, that wee may not follow vncertaine coniectures, but haue a full and an vndoubted interpretation of the miseries of this booke, the Angell expoundeth them. For the exposition that the Angell here giueth, is euen as a key to open the closet into all the chief things in this booke. For if we vnderstand what is meant by this beast, by his heads and hornes, and likewise what the woman is, wee shall vnderstand the chiefe and almost all the whole argument of this booke. Shall we then set light by this exposition, when the Lord hath sent his Angell to giue it? Nay, let vs with all thankfulnes and reuerence giue eare vnto it, and receiue the fruite thereof, that we may vnderstand this prophecie, and not bee seduced by Antichrist. Thus much for this time.

THE

THE XXXVII. SERMON.
CHAP. XVII.

8 *The beast which thou hast seene, was, and is not, and shall ascende out of the bottomles pit, and shall goe into destruction: and they that dwell on the earth shall wonder, whose names are not written in the booke of life from the foundation of the world, when they behold the beast that was, and is not, and yet is.*

9 *Here is the mind that hath wisedome, the seuen heads are seuen mountaines whereon the woman sitteth.*

10 *They are also seuen kings: fiue are fallen, one is, and another is not yet come, and when he cometh he must tarrie a little space.*

11 *And the beast that was, and is not, is euen the eight, and is one of the seuen, and shall goe into destruction.*

12 *And the tenne hornes which thou hast seene, are tenne Kings, which as yet haue not receiued a kingdome, but shall receiue power, as Kings at one houre with the beast.*

13 *These haue one minde, and shall giue their power and strength to the beast.*

14 *These shall fight with the Lambe, and the Lambe shall ouercome them, because he is Lord of lords, and King of kings, and they that are with him, called, and chosen, and faithfull.*

15 *And he sayd vnto me, The waters which thou sawest, where the whore sitteth, are peoples, and multitudes, and nations, and tongues.*

16 *And the tenne hornes which thou sawest in the beast, these shall hate the whore, and shall make her desolate and naked, and shall eate her flesh, and shall burne her with fire.*

17 *For God hath put into their hearts to doe his will, and to doe with one consent, to giue their kingdome to the beast, vntill the words of God be fulfilled.*

18 *And the woman which thou hast seene, is the great citie, which hath the kingdome: ouer the kings of the earth.*

Now we come to the expostion: where the Angel doth not tel what the beast signifieth: and yet men may thinke, that that should be the first thing in the exposition. And doubtles so it should, but that the Angell doth not expound that which the Scripture before had cleerely expounded. For by beasts, the Angell telleth the Prophet Daniel, are signified kings: but yet not the persons of kings, but the tyranous power exercised by them by succession.

succession. Wherefore wee must here consider that this beast is not to bee taken for certaine persons, but for a dominion exercised by those persons, which haue therein succeeded each other, knowing then what is meant by a beast, which the Angell doth here omitte because it is in Daniel cleerely expounded, wee may the better vnderstand that interpretation which followeth. The beast saith hee, which thou hast seene, was and is not, and shall ascend out of the bottomles pit. This may seeme a very strange and hard speech, to say the beast was and is not, and should ascend againe out of the bottomles pit. Had the beast been in the world before the time that Saint Iohn receiued this reuelation? was he then gone out of the world, and should he afterward returne againe? Yea verily, let not that seeme strange: for the tyranous power of Rome had been very great before Iohns time, it was deminished in this time, and afterward should rise vp againe to the former maiestie. Before that Rome was gouerned by Emperors, and also in the dayes, and vnder the raigne of her first Emperors, Iulius, Augustus, Tiberius, and Claudius, the maiestie and power of that Monarchie was exceeding great. In the dayes of these Emperors Nero, Galba, Otho, Vitellius, and Domitian, that former maiestie and power was greatly diminished: And the same was raysed vp againe by the popes.

But it will be obiected, that although the maiestie and power of the Romane Monarchie was not so great when Iohn receiued this reuelation, as it had been in former times, yet it could not be said, not to be, but the Angell saith, the beast which thou hast seene was and is not. I answere, that the Angell himselfe taketh away this doubt, for that wee might know it is not to be taken absolutely, that he saith the beast is not, but for some respect, and in comparison he addeth that the beast is not, and yet is. How shall wee expound these words, the beast was and is not, and yet is, but that he is, but not such as he had been, nor such as he should be? Then we see there is no difficultie in these words, so we take them altogether. It may also be demaunded, seeing the powers are of God, how this Empire may bee sayd to ascend out of the bottomles pit? The bottomles pit is hell, that which commeth from hell commeth from the deuill? I answere, that a beast doeth not represent simplie the power of gouernment, which in deed is the ordinance of God, but the vsurpation, the crueltie, and the tyrannous abuse of the power, against the trueth and against the Church of God: and so wicked tyrannie of the heathen Emperors and the papall power ascendeth out of hell euen from the very deuill. They bragge and boast in the papacie that they haue it from Peter, and he had it from Christ, and say that they be cast away that will not obey it: and the very trueth is, it is of the deuill, and they fall from God, which submitte themselues vnto it, and verily the Angell saith it shall goe to destruction, for as that which is of God doeth not perish, so all that is of the deuill must needes goe to destruction. When this beast ascendeth againe out of the bottomles pit, hee shall carrie such a maiestie, that the inhabitants of the earth shall wonder. Surely neuer any power in the world was so much wondred at as the vsurped power and maiestie of the Pope. They supposed that hee had

power

power euen as a God vpon the earth, and that hee might send to heauen, and cast downe into hell whome hee would. He might depose kings and Emperors, and set vp also euen at his pleasure. O how did the world wonder and tremble at this power? but yet the Angell restraineth it to the reprobate, for none wonder at the beast but such, whose names are not written in the booke of life. The faithfull in all ages cried out vpon the blasphemous vsurped power of the popes, and did not wonder at it. The Angell addeth, here is the minde that hath wisedome: which is a preface to moue attention, when men shall vnderstand that it is found wisedome, yea it is such wisedome as God himselfe commendeth, for a man to vnderstand the interpretation of the beast, and of the woman: for hee that vnderstandeth will not be seduced by the poperie, but will abide firme in the true worship of God. There hath alwayes beene much subtiltie vsed to drawe men to the Romish religion, but the minde which hath wisedome, that is to say, that minde which God doth instruct, and vnto which hee giueth vnderstanding, doth vnderstand the interpertation which the Angell here maketh, and knoweth that the Romish church is the whore of Babylon, euen a most filthie and idolatrous synagogue. Well the Angell sayth that the seuen heads of the beast are seuen mountaines vpon which the woman sitteth, and they bee also seuen kings. Then it is euident that two things are signified by the heades: for seuen mountaines, are one thing, and seuen kings are an other. The papists here vsing all their cunning to defend Rome, doe cauill and say, that the seuen hilles are seuen kings. If it had beene sette downe thus, the seuen heads are seuen mountaines, that is seuen kings, it had made for them that hilles and kings here were all one. But when hee saith that the seuen heads of the beast are seuen kings, and that they bee also seuen mountaines, who seeth not that here are two seuerall things represented? They doe also cauill that the number seuen is put indefinitly and not for iust so many, as sundry times in this booke. But let them bee asked how many are fiue, and one, and one, are they not iust seuen? Fiue sayth the Angell are fallen, one is, and one is to come, are not these iust seuen? Is not this to tell vs that wee must take it of iust seuen? well then to the matter, the Angell telleth Iohn that the woman which sitteth vpon the beast is the great citie, &c. Then he speaketh of a citie here which for her situation is builded vpon seuen mountaines, and for her power and regiment hath been supported by seuen seuerall kindes of gouernmentes which are called kings. Rome was builded vpon seuen mountaines: all the papists in the world cannot denie it: for not onely the poets of old times spake so of it, but also the seuen mountaines on which the citie is built are thus named, Capitolinus, Palatinus, Auentinus, Celius, Exquilinus, Viminalis, and Quirinalis. Let vs see if any papist in the world can denie but that Rome was builded vpon these seuen hilles, not one more nor lesse. Indeede they heere seeke a little poore shift, and say that Rome in olde time did stande vpon these seuen hilles. How faintly and howe coldely is this vttered? Faine they would say that Rome now standeth not vpon those seuen hilles, because it now standeth in the plaine of Campus Martius, and the pope sitteth on the other side of the riuer: but they dare not for feare it should bee sayd, if your pope sitte not in that Rome where ye say Peter sate and had his chaire, then doeth not your pope sit in Peters chaire. For if Peter were Bishop of Rome, hee had his chaire and was Bishop of that Rome, which was builded vpon seuen mountaines. So that if they will deriue their power from Peters chaire, it must be from that same Rome built vpon seuen mountaines, in which, if S. Peter were Bishop of Rome, he had his chaire, and not from another Rome. Let them looke to it. But what though the citie bee remoued, and the pope remooued also into another part, is it not still a citie builded vpon seuen hilles, when as the buildings vpon those seuen hils doe still partly remaine inhabited, and the popish religion there practised? Doth the building in the plaine, make it not to bee vpon the seuen mountaines? Let the papists deny if they can, that there bee either churches or monasteries or both vpon euery one of those seuen mountaines. Let it bee that for the inhabitants the prime as it were of that citie is remooued from those mountaines, yet let vs see how they can shift it, that those churches and monasteries, be not in Rome and of Rome. Then that he sayeth, the seuen heades are also seuen kings, it sheweth that the citie Rome that gorgious whore, which is drunken with the blood of the Saintes, hath been borne vp not onely by seuen hilles vpon which she was built, but also by seuen kinds of gouernment, which hee calleth seuen kings. Hee saith that fiue of these were fallen, before the time that Iohn receiued this reuelation, one was then present which was the sixt, and one, that is the seuenth, was to come. It will peraduenture be obiected, that the Angell doeth not say, the seuen heads are seuen orders of states of kingly gouernement, but seuen kings. It seemeth to note out seuen men which raigned as Kings in Rome, and not seuen kinges of gouernement, in which there was the kingly power in euery one, I suppose this hath led some to expound it of seuen of the Emperors; fiue past before the time that the Angell spake this to Iohn, the sixt then present, and the seuenth to come. But what reason is there to leaue out the other wicked Emperors? Because they were not Romanes. They were Emperors of the same citie, and as wicked as the other. What then, shall wee not thinke that the Angell speaketh here, as the Angell speaketh in Daniel? The foure great beastes (saith the Angell to Daniel) are foure Kings which shall rise vp in the earth, Daniel. 7. verse. 17. Is it not as cleere as the sunne, that by foure Kings are meant there, not fower men which raigned as Kings, but foure kingdomes or monarchies, in which many men succeeded each other, and raigned as Kings? the whole Empire then or Monarchie of the Babylonians is called a King, which stoode long, and had many Kings by succession. The like is to bee said of the Kingdome of the Medes and Persians, and also of the rest. Why then shall wee not take seuen Kings here to bee seuen kingly gouernements, by which the woman had been borne vp? Rome was not onely builded vpon seuen hils, but also hath been vpholden by seuen seuerall orders of kingly power. For Rome was builded by Romulus and Remus: and Romulus raigned King. After him succeeded other Kings of Rome, of which Tarquinius Superbus was the last. The Angell saith fiue of the heads were fallen, of which fiue, this was the first that fell in the said Tarquinius: for there the Kings ended. Then next were

THE REVELATION.

Confuls chofen, and they gouerned the citie with kingly power: there is the fecond head. Afterward the Decemuiri bare the chiefe fway, and fo haue ye the third head. Then followed the gouernement of Dictators, as the fourth head: and then was there a fift ftate which were the Triumuiri. And thefe fiue heads were fallen before our fauiour was borne. For none of thefe then bare the chiefe rule in Rome: but the fixt head, which was of Emperors, was then vp, when the Angell talked with Iohn, which head begun in Iulius Cefar, for hee was the firft Emperor. This fixt head is it of which the Angell faith, one is: and one is to come, This one to come is the feuenth and the laft, yea euen the laft ftate by which Rome fhall bee fupported in her magnificall pompe and delicacie. And this head is the papacie, this hath fucceeded the Empire, and this is euen tho greateft head of all. For vnder the Popes hath Rome been in her higheft exaltation and glorie. And now as this laft head commeth downe, downe alfo fhe whore commeth. For the ftrength of the beaft that beareth her vp, decaying and fayling, fhee cannot but faile and lye on the duft. The Angell faith, that this feuenth head when hee commeth, muft tarrie a little while. But will fome man fay, doth not this fhew that it is not to bee taken of the dominion of the Popes, for they haue raigned a long time. I anfwere, that if wee confider of time according to man, feuen or eyght hundreth yeares is a great time: but if wee efteeme thereof according to the fcriptures, a thoufand yeares is but a fmall time, for what is it if it bee compared with eternitie? It is now well fpent, and the beaft that beareth vp the whore will taile vnder her, and fhee fhall come downe with her golden cuppe. The Angell addeth yet further, faying, the beaft that was and is not, is euen the eight, and is one of the feuen, and fhall goe into deftruction. Thefe wordes be very myfticall, that hee fayth, the beaft was and is not, applying it to the laft head, that is, to the Antichriftian power which was not yet come. For how can it bee fayd that it was before, when as yet it was not come? For the tyranny of popes had not been in the worlde. Surely confidering all things here together which the Angell fpeaketh, efpecially that hee fayth he is the eight and yet one of the feuen: For hereby it is moft euident, and without all contradiction, that hee fpeaketh of two powers, the ciuil, and fpirituall: for in refpect of the ciuil power hee can be but the feuenth head. And therefore that he is alfo fayd to be both one of the feuen, and the eight, it muft needes followe, that as for ciuill kingly power one of the feuen, fo for the higheft fpirituall inrifdiction which he would vfurp he fhould be the eight.

Then marke what I fay, the greateft power of the beaft fhould be in the fpirituall iurifdiction. He is faid before to haue two hornes like the lambe: and this is that which he hath moft preuailed withall of the two. And in refpect of this horne S. Iohn faith, the beaft that was and is not. For the ciuill tyrannie of Rome was when the Angell fpake thefe things vnto Iohn, but the ecclefiafticall tyrannie was not as yet come, I meane in fuch a kind and maner as the Popes had. O this ecclefiafticall tyrannie ouer the faith and confciences of men is fuch, that Saint Iohn giueth the name of the whole beaft vnto it. For doubtleffe in refpect of the terrene gouernment

uernment, it could not well be fayd, the beast which was and is not, but in respect that at that time when the Angell spake this, there was not (as I fayd) the like spirituall tyrannie which afterward the deuil of hel aduanced the popes vnto, although the Emperours tooke vpon them touching religion. It will be here obiected, how can it be so taken, when he sayth, the beast was and is not, and should afterward ascend. For in that hee sayth he was, it sheweth cleerely that the tyrannie he speaketh of, had been exercised in the world before the time of Iohn: But who will say that the spirituall iurisdiction of the Popes had been before the dayes of Iohn? Is it not out of controuersie that it was raised long after? This then seemeth flatly to ouerthrow that former exposition, seeing that the beast which the Angell faith to Iohn, is not, yet was, that is, had been in the world before that time. I answere, that albeit the spirituall tyrannie of the Popes was not then, nor yet had been exercised by any popes before this time that he receiued this reuelation, yet it had been practised in the worlde in some measure before. For the wicked Priestes in Israell, the Scribes, and the Pharisies, had long time exercised a spirituall tyrannie against the people of God, against the Prophets, and against the sonne of God himselfe. The Church had now escaped from them, and so this beast was downe: but the Popes were to raise it vp againe, and to exercise it more cruelly then the priests and Pharisies had done. Thus wee see why the Angell saith, the beast that was and is not, is euen the eight, and is one of the seuenth, and shalt goe into destruction. Onely it remaineth to know how one and the selfe same, should be both the eight, and one of the seuen.

 This is very easie, if ye consider the two powers which the papacie hath chalenged, and both of them the highest, that is, the kingly terrene power ouer all men both high and lowe, euen ouer Emperours and kings: and the Lordship ouer the faith and conscience of men. Both these in the Pope doe concurre, and doe make but one beast. And in respect of the ciuill kingly power hee is the seuenth head of the beast which beateth vp the woman: for hee is the seuenth order of kings by which Rome hath been gouerned. Now if we respect the spirituall tyrannie, which in old time the wicked priests and Pharisies had exercised, though not in such full power, which tyrannie now was downe, Ierusalem being destroyed before Iohn receiued this Prophecie, and therfore the Angell faith, the beast that was and is not: and if we regard this, how the Popes did againe raise vp the same, and practise it in more execrable manner then the other, yee may easily perceiue why this beast is both the eight, and one of the seuen. This is the reason why in the 13. chapter also, the papacie is described as a beast by it selfe with the two hornes, and yet is one of the seuen heads of that other beast. There are two beasts, hee is one of them himselfe, and by himselfe, and yet he is the seuenth head of the other. Here are seuen heads, hee is one of the seuen, and yet the eight, as the Angell sayth, so wee see how fitly these things concurre.

 Now he commeth to the hornes. And the tenne hornes sayth he, which thou hast seene are tenne kings. Wee know that hornes in the scripture doe represent strength and might: and so here for their might and power, ten kings are figured

by

THE REVELATION.

by the ten hornes of the beast. For kings are mightie. Then behold what a mighty beast is this Romane Monarchy, which hath the power of ten kings & kingdoms, euen as hornes to strike or to push withall? In the seuen heads of the beast, we see that it must needes be taken for iust seuen, because the Angell saith, fiue are fallen, one is, and one is to come. Now for the tenne hornes, whether we shall take them for iust tenne, or for more, there is the question, there remaineth the doubt. For if we number the kings and kingdomes, which were subiect to the Pope, wee finde them more then tenne. But yet some (who I suppose not led thereto by this place but simply considering the matter) haue described the kingdomes of the earth, and make iust ten of those which were subiect to the Pope of Rome. Whether it bee so or not, this is euident, that there were tenne kingdomes which deserued to bee accounted as hornes, for their power and strength which they gaue to the church of Rome. These are the kings of the West, the kings of Europe. But the Angel said to Iohn, that they had not as yet receiued a kingdome, but should receiue power as kings at one houre with the beast. This is somewhat hard to be vnderstood. For had not these kingdomes kings ouer them, at that time when the Angell spake this to Iohn? They were almost all of them vnder the Emperor of Rome at that time. And they were subiect in such sort that they had not a kingdome. Now when the speciall beast grew vp, euen the second beast, that is, the papacie, together with him, they receiued power as kings. For doubtlesse there was a great alteration in the kingdomes vnder the Popes, from that which they had beene vnder the Emperours. They receiue greater power, and they carrie another minde toward the papacie then the nations before did toward the Empire. The Empire held them vnder by force and might, and set rulers as ouer prouinces, and against their liking they in the kingdomes obey: but to the papacie they submit themselues for conscience and of loue, euen as to the holy Church. The false prophet hath seduced them, and with him they receiue power as kings, he aduanceth them, for now their power maketh for him, they be his owne hornes. For marke what the Angel saith: These haue one mind, and shall giue their power and strength to the beast. These kings had all one minde in time of poperie: For being seduced, they all held the Pope to be Chrisls vicar, and that he might carrie to heauen, and throw downe to hell. They tooke it, that looke whatsoeuer the Church of Rome decreed, it must be obeyed vnder paine of damnation. And being all of this minde, they giue their power and strength to the beast. They doe all that they can to vphold him: and so they become his hornes: and he calleth them his sonnes: and whilest they raigne, he saith he raigneth. Looke what he willeth they are readie: and therefore the angell addeth, *these shall fight with the Lambe*. The dragon is against Christ, the Romish beast the papacie is set vp by the dragon, and hee vnder the name of Christ, seduceth the kings to fight against the holy Gospell, and against the Church of Christ, in the defence of idolatrie and popish superstition. Beloued, did not the kings thus fight against the Lambe? But the Lambe ouercommeth them, for he is aboue all, he is king of kings. And those that be on his side, euen his faithfull seruants, his true worshippers, get the victorie also. For albeit the beast condemned

Z   them

them as heretiks, and then the kings put them to death, yet they gate the victory, for they could not cause them to forsake the holy faith, nor to drinke of the whores cup. Here be chosen, here be called, here be faithfull ones. These conquer and triumph when they seeme to the world to be ouercome, because their blood is shed. The Lambe hath ouercome, his truth doth stand and flourish, his Church doth increase, when the Romish monster with his ten hornes hath done all that he can. Beloued, when worldly powers are bent against the trueth, let vs not forsake it, for it shall get the victorie: assure your selues Christ will preuaile ouer them all.

 It followeth, and he said vnto me, the waters which thou sawest where the whore sitteth, are people and multitudes, and nations, and tongues. Saint Iohn in vision saw the whore sit vpon many waters, as he hath set downe. And the Angell expoundeth what these waters doe signifie: euen multitudes of people of diuers nations and tongues. Then it is as much as to say, that the whore shall raigne ouer great nations and peoples: her dominion shall be very large. This is to meete with the proude bragges of the papists, when they vaunt themselues of their multitudes, vniuersalitie and consent. They deride and scorne the true professors of the gospell, because they haue been so fewe, and chalenge to themselues the title of the vniuersall and catholike church, because they haue so great multitudes. You (say they) you can shew but here and there a fewe in all ages for this seuen or eyght hundreth yeares, which haue taught and beleeued as you doe: but we haue had the consent and agreement of whole kingdomes and nations, and tongues, which with one consent haue professed the religion of the church of Rome. Is it like that your few, or our multitude, is the true church? We answere, that if kingdomes, nations, multitudes, tongues, and people, be an argument to proue a true church, because they all agree in one religion, then the whore of Babylon is the true church, for she sitteth vpon many waters, which the Angell saith are people, and nations, and kindreds, and tongues. Shall we acknowledge her to be the true Church, because she hath with her golden cup, seduced so many great nations to drinke the wine of her fornication, and to commit most abominable whoredome and filthines with her? Doth a multitude conspire against the truth, euen to set vp and to maintaine mans deuises against the written word of God, make that they doe well, and that the trueth is to be condemned, because fewe doe follow it? I thinke any man may see the vanitie of this argument of the papists, and how it maketh flatly against them, because the malignant church is described to bee so great: and yet it is one of the principall reasons to drawe the blinde sorte withall; for they vse it thus, is it like that God would suffer so many nations, and that for so long a time to goe awry? Alas poreblinde creatures, doe they not see, that the whore of Babylon should deceiue the nations and people, and multitudes, and kindreds, and tongues? What would they haue spoken more plainely? But wee see if the Lorde doe not open the eyes, men wander in the darkenes, and cannot see the cleere light. Well you see beloued how this agreeth with that which we had before in the 13. chapter: where the beast with two hornes, causeth all sorts of people, and that of all nations, to

receiue

receiue the marke of the beast, or the number of his name: and that those which had not the same, might not buie or sell. Yea they must be killed that would not worship the image of the beast. Here is the holy catholike church of the poperie, here is their multitude, their vniuersalitie and consent: here is great Babel, the mother of whoredomes and abominations of the earth: here is shee that with her golden cuppe, hath entised the kings and the great nations to commit all filthie whoredome with her, yea and to be euen drunken with the wine of her fornication. And shall this whore because of her multitude brag that she is the true catholike church?

Let vs proceed: And the ten hornes which thou sawest in the beast, these shall hate the whore, and shall make her desolate and naked, and shall eate her flesh, and shall burne her with fire. In this the Angell sheweth, that the same kings which did hold vp the whore, shall pull her downe. Wee may not take it of the same men, but of those that succeede in the same kingdomes. For the kings of England, of Scotland, of Denmarke, of France, and of other countries which gaue their power to the beast, are dead and gone, if we respect the persons of the men: and those which succeede them now in these kingdomes, which pull downe that vsurped power of Rome, are other persons: but because they succeede and gouerne in the same kingdomes, they are sayd to be those tenne hornes of the beast. This prophecie, or this interpretation of the Angell doth euidently shew vnto vs, that the kings of the same countries which maintained the poperie, shall pull it downe. You may iudge by our owne countrie. The kings of England, at the least diuers of them, in times past were one horne of the beast, and gaue their power to him, for to defend him. But King Henry the 8. King Edward th 6. and Queene Elizabeth, haue pulled him downe what they can. They haue for their part made the whore desolate and naked: and so haue diuers kings of other lands done. This goeth forward daily, and in the end they shall destroy her. Are they not more then blind which see not the fulfilling of this prophecie? Did not the kings of Europe with one consent giue their power to the beast? were they not euen as hornes for him to push withall? And haue not diuers of their successors now hated the Romish whore, and made her naked? These be also called the ten hornes in the beast, not because they be any strength vnto him, but because they sit vpon the same thrones of their auncestors, which maintained the poperie. In that respect they bee the same hornes, but not for the whore, but against her. And that wee may know the whole worke commeth of God, the Angell addeth, For God hath put into their hearts to doe his will, and to doe with one consent, to giue their kingdome to the beast, vntill the words of God be fulfilled. This may seeme hard that the Angell sayth, God put it into the heart of the kings to maintaine the poperie. Did not the diuell seduce them? Yes verely. But yet after a sort the Lord doth it, when for the wickednes of the world, hee in his righteous iudgement letteth loose Satan to deceiue. For so the Apostle writeth, God shall send them strong delusion to beleeue lyes, 2. Thess. 2. The Lord threatned for the contempt of the Gospell, that he would send the great Antichrist, and that these words of God might be fulfilled, by his iust iudgement the kings were deceiued, & stood for the maintenance of Antichrist. But now the time being come that the man of sin should bee disclosed, and that most filthie whore should be pulled downe, the eyes of the kings are opened, and they banish out of their kingdomes that Romish power and Idolatrous religion, and set vp the true worship of God. Here is an alteration in the hornes: and this as I said commeth of God.

Now the last thing remaineth, and that is, what this woman is which sitteth vpon the beast. The Angell doth not in plaine tearmes say, the woman, the gorgious whore which thou sawest with the golden cuppe in her hand, is Rome: for that had been open to all the wicked, from whom the matter is hid: but he sayth as much in effect to those that haue their eyes opened, as if hee had named Rome: when he sayth, and the woman which thou hast seene is the great citie which hath the kingdome ouer the kings of the earth. What citie held the dominion ouer the kings of the earth at that time when the Angell told this to Saint Iohn, but Rome? Miserable poore are the shifts and cauils of the Iesuites vpon this place. Faine they would defend Rome from being this filthie whore, and they say if it bee Rome, it was while the Heathen Emperours liued. That is true, but doe they not see plainly in this booke that the great Antichrist should raigne in the same citie where the Heathen persecutors were? VVell, let them that will be blind, be blind still: wee see it is most euident, for the Angell telleth vs, that Rome is this filthie whore of Babylon. Let vs hate her, if we loue God.

THE XXXVIII. SERMON.
CHAP. XVIII.

1. *And after these things I saw another Angell come downe from heauen hauing great power, and the earth was lightened with his glorie.*
2. *And he cried out mightily with a lowd voyce, saying, It is fallen, it is fallen, Babylon the great citie, and is become the habitation of diuels, and the hold of all foule spirits, and a cage of every vncleane and hatefull bird.*
3. *For all nations haue drunke of the wine of the wrath of her fornication, and the kings of the earth haue committed fornication with her, and the Marchants of the earth haue waxed rich, of the abundance of her pleasures.*
4. *And I heard another voyce from heauen, saying, Come away from her my people, that yee bee not partaker of her sinnes, and that ye receiue not of her plagues.*
5. *For her sinnes are come vp vnto heauen, and God hath remembred her iniquities.*

6. *Reward*

THE REVELATION. 341

6 *Rewarde her euen as shee hath rewarded you, and giue her double according to her workes: and in the cuppe that she hath filled to you, fill her the double.*

7 *In as much as she glorified her selfe, and liued in pleasure, so much giue yee to her torment and sorrow: for she saith in her heart, I sit being a Queene, and am no widow, and shall see no mourning.*

8 *Therefore shall her plagues come at one day, death and sorrow and famine, and shee shall bee burnt with fire: for strong is the Lorde God that iudgeth her.*

He fall of great Babylon, and her destruction, hath been briefly touched before in this booke: but here it is set foorth more at large. For from the beginning of this chapter, vnto the end of the last chapter, it may well bee sayd, that there is nothing but the generall conclusion of the whole prophecie. For through the booke, there hath beene set foorth and described, the power, the dominion, the pompe, and the crueltie of the enemies of the Church, and what great afflictions they haue cast her into: and now the conclusion painteth foorth their vtter downfall & destruction, and how she is drawne out of all her miseries, vnto a most happie estate of endles glorie. Almost all that followeth may bee reduced to this one poynt. So that the conclusion is thus: These proud tyrannous enemies haue bin aloft, they haue enioyed their riches, honours, pompe and pleasures, they haue condemned, persecuted and afflicted the Church of Christ and her children, and most grieuously pressed them downe. But now the case doth alter, the proud persecutors come vnder, and the afflicted is raised vp into glorie. This being the summe, let vs now come more particularly to the matter.

After these things (saith Saint Iohn) I saw another Angell come downe from heauen, hauing great power. Here is he that beateth down the kingdome of Antichrist, here is he that bringeth the great whore of Babylon to ruine, euen a mightie Angell from heauen. For it is the Lord from heauen that iudgeth that bloodie kingdome. But what Angell is this, or what doth he represent? That is first to bee enquired. In the 14. chapter he saith, that an Angell did flie in the middest of heauen with an euerlasting Gospell to preach, and forthwith downe went great Babylon. Where it is euident, that by the Angell is represented the ministers of the Gospell whom the Lord hath raised vp, and sent in these last times, for to recouer his afflicted Church from vnder the captiuitie of Babylon. This Angell representeth the selfe same thing, euen the ministrie of the Gospell: which seemeth to bee weake and contemptible in the view and iudgement of the world: but yet the efficacie thereof being from heauen is strong and mightie, as it is here said. And we see by experience the mightines thereof, in that it hath cast downe the pompe and the glorie of Babell. It hath ouerthrowne the power & pride of the Romish beast,

which

which the kings of the earth did tremble at. It is not said here in vaine that this Angell hath great power: for he pulleth downe a mightie beast, euen the wonder of the world, the Romane Monarchie.

He saith further, That the earth was lightened with his glorie. The power of this Angell consisteth in light: as the power of the enemie consisteth in darknes. The brightnes of the light, expelleth and vanquisheth the darknes. The kingdome of Babylon is nothing but spirituall darknes and confusion: as wee haue seene before in this booke how the bottomlesse pit was opened, and how the smoke of the pit ascended vp and darkened all. The deuill from hell thrust forth by the ministrie of his vicar the pope, all ignorance, errours, lies, and superstition. This Angell with the brightnes of the pure word of God expelleth all these: and therefore it is said that the earth was lightened with his glorie. O what darknes had couered the earth, and what foolish things did men beleeue in the time of poperie? And what a wonderfull light hath the word of God giuen, so that euen the simple, yea euen children doe laugh at the things as most fond, which great wise men did then beleeue. Yea I may truly say, and whosoeuer doth narrowly obserue the matter hee shall find it so, that the brightnes of this Angell is such in lightning the earth, that the beames of his light do pearce euen into the holes of the night birds, which yet doe what they can to hide and couer themselues from the light, I meane the grosse papists, which labour all that they can to vphold their darknes: for they are euen constrained in many things to seele the power of the light though they cannot abide it, but faine would vphold the whore of Babell. God for his infinite mercies sake blesse and prosper the holy ministrie of his word, that the earth may be more and more lightened, and that these wretched papists these ministers of Antichrist, may haue neuer a darke hole to couer themselues in. We see the boldnes of those impudent men, and their trauailes, I would it might moue all the seruants of God, to become more zealous and vehement to spread the light of the holie Gospell. Publish and spread it, and let the Lord worke his holie will and pleasure, for it is the light and the power of the trueth, which must strike the stroke.

And he cryed out mightily with a loud voice, saying, It is fallen, it is fallen, great Babylon, &c. The faithfull ministers of the Gospell proclaime and that vehemently, that the poperie is fallen, yea that it is most certainly fallen, and shal neuer recouer againe. They publish with mightie zeale that Rome is great Babell, and that her dominion ouer the kingdomes of the earth is come to an end. And albeit the papists labour with tooth and naile, omitting no treacherous practise to recouer her fall, and to restore her againe to her former dignitie, yea and beare the ignorant sort in hand that in time they shall preuaile: yet this Angell mightilie denounceth the contrarie. If ye demaund how the ministers and preachers of the Gospel can for certaintie publish this, seeing they be no prophets to see what shall be in time to come. I answere, that this prophecie hath declared and doth declare euidently, that Rome shall neuer recouer her fall, the pope shall neuer bee esteemed againe, but labour he, and all that be for him, both kings & Iesuite priests, what they can, he shall daily by degrees come downe more and more, euen till the vtter and finall

THE REVELATION. 343

nall deſtruction. And now what is Babylon, what is Rome, what is the Church of Rome now ſhee is fallen? The Angell telleth vs, ſhe is the habitation of deuils, a cage of euery vncleane ſpirite, and a cage of euery vncleane and hatefull bird. Doe ye not ſuppoſe here be a ſweet companie to ioyne withall? Al that haue any goodnes in them, doe forſake Rome with her moſt filthy abominations. The deuils and vncleane ſpirits, and vncleane birds, beare all the ſway there. Wee muſt note that the Angell here in deſcribing the deſtruction of the Romiſh Babel, followeth the deſcription which the old Prophets, Eſay and Ieremy vſe in ſetting forth the deſolation of that other Babell in the Eaſt. For Eſay chap. 13: and Ieremy chapter 51. doe ſet forth what vgly and horrible beaſts ſhould dwell in that Babel, and what hatefull vncleane birds ſhould neaſt there. Now as thoſe vgly beaſts and euill fauoured fowles were of old time the inhabitants of Babell in the Eaſt : ſo the holy ghoſt ſheweth, that Rome the Weſterne Babell, is the habitation of diuels, and the hold of all vncleane ſpirits. See beloued the glorie of the Church of Rome, which boaſteth her ſelfe to be the pure ſpouſe of Chriſt. No man, ſhe ſaith, can be ſaued, vnleſſe he become one of her obedient children: and the Lord ſaith, that ſhe is the habitation of diuels. Their doctrine is the doctrine of diuels, their worſhip is the worſhippe of diuels, their workes is the workes of diuels. For what doctrine doe they teach (a few things excepted) but flat contrary to the written word of God? What worſhip but of Idols, and of rotten bones? And what are their workes but treaſons, ſeditions, periuries, and ſlaughters? If men bee not blinde they may ſee, that Rome is the very habitation of diuels. Is it then good ioyning with them, or is it (as ſome take it) a matter ſo indifferent to bee of their Church? Iudge in your ſelues brethren. Yea but will ſome man ſay, if it were certaine that Rome is Babylon. Alas that men ſhould doubt, there is nothing more cleere. If there were but one man in the world of ſtature, proportion, and viſage ſame differing from all other, and a right cunning painter ſhould draw his picture in all points from top to toe : could any doubt that had ſeene the ſame man, and then ſhould ſee his picture, but that it were his onely picture? The holie Ghoſt in this propheſie hath perfectly drawne the picture of Babell, and they that peruſe the picture and looke vpon Rome, finde them ſo like in all parts as nothing can be more : and they ſhall finde none other in the whole world, whom the picture doth reſemble. The only reaſon or cauſe why men bee not fully reſolued that Rome is Babylon, is that they doe not diligently peruſe this picture. Be diligent in this booke, and thou ſhalt bee out of all doubt that Rome is the whore great Babell, and the power of the papacie, the beaſt. If thou wilt when thou knoweſt this, ioyne thy ſelfe with the habitation of diuels, and with the holde of vncleane ſpirites, thou ſhalt together with them bee ſaued. But now what is the cauſe of this heauie indignation of God againſt Rome? What is it wherewith ſhe hath prouoked the wrath of the almighty, to deſtroy her, and to make her the habitation of diuels? The cauſe is repeated, which hath been before rehearſed, that all nations haue drunke of the wine of the wrath of her fornication, the kings of the earth haue committed fornication with her, and the marchants of the earth haue beene made rich of the abundance of her

Z 4   pleaſures.

pleasures. Behold what an hainous thing it is before God, that Rome hath so corrupted religion, and that she hath made the nations drunke with the raging wine of her fornication, and that she hath drawne both the kings and their subiects to commit spirituall whoredome. For whereas men ought to keep themselues chast and pure to God in his holy worship, that is, to worship him alone in spirite and trueth, euen according as he hath prescribed in his holy word: the Romish whore hath entised them to her inuentions, euen to worship Idols, and so to commit spirituall whoredome with diuels, and with her false wares hath enriched her marchants. Is not this a great matter, especially when wee consider vnto how many she hath spread these her whoredomes? then in a ueile not though it bee sundrie times repeated.

And now Saint Iohn saith, he heard another voyce from heauen saying, Come away from her my people, &c. Here is a calling for separation, and a reason rendered to perswade thereunto. The voyce is from heauen that willeth the seruants of God to come away from her. It is therefore the voyce and the commaundement of the Lord and not of man. This voyce in these latter daies hath been and is founded forth by men vpon the earth : but because it is by the word of God, the voyce is said to be, and that rightly, from heauen : for that which is of God is from heauen. There is much adoe about this point : the papists crie out against the preachers that call for this separation, and against the Christian princes which compell their subiects vnto it, that they be Schismatikes. Ye make separation, say they, from the true Catholike Church, ye forsake the chaire of Peter, ye renounce Christs vicar the pastor of your soules, with other such thundering speeches: but wee see they are Babell that abominable whore, wee regard not their vaine speeches, but follow the voyce and commandement of God which is from heauen, both in separating our selues, and in perswading and drawing as many as we can from their wicked societie. Wee see the daunger which is the reason that is here vsed to perswade, namely, least wee bee partakers of her sinnes, and so consequently of her plagues. For how can a man be of that societie, and not be partaker of their sins? And if he be partaker of their sinnes, must he not needs be partaker with them in their plagues ? In the 14. chapter there is set forth the heauie vengeance of God vpon those that forsake not the worship and societie of the beast. And it is, because many are so loath to bee drawne from the Romish religion, in as much as it hath been so long imbraced by their ancesters. In like manner here is a great terror set before vs, least wee might imagine it to bee as a thing indifferent to be of the popish assemblies. If her sinnes were but few and light, small punishment, in comparison should belong vnto the same : for the punishment followeth according to the greatnes of the sins. As men deserue, so are they plagued. And for the same cause that all men may well vnderstand, that the societie with the whore of Babel, the ioyning with the poperie, the imbracing the lawes of the Romish Antichrist, shall plunge them deepe into the gulfe of most horrible plagues, and dreadfull vengeance of almightie God, the voyce from the Lord saith, that her sinnes are come vp to heauen, and God hath remembred her iniquities. What plagues

thinke

THE REVELATION. 345

thinke ye shall follow those sinnes which reach vp vnto heauen? What an heape of sinnes hath great Babell the mother of whoredomes heaped and piled vp? How hath Rome filled the world with abominations? This voyce doth set them before vs in a lumpe, and if a man would take the suruey of them in particular, hee shall neuer bee able. Who is able fully to declare the corruptions, errors, abominable inuentions, superstitions, and idolatries, which Rome hath spread vpon the face of the earth? Who is able to set out the filthie life of Popes, Cardinals, Abbots, Monkes, Priests, Friers, and Nunnes? The earth doth stinke of their vncleannes. Their owne histories doe testifie very much. Moreouer, what crueltie haue they shewed? what slaughters and murders haue they committed vpon the holie seruants of God, which haue reproued their enormities? What treacheries, and what treasons doe they worke and daily practise, if they could bring them about?

Now consider this I pray you, that who so dooth not separate himselfe from them, but is of their societie and religion, hee is a member of that bodie, hee hath his part in all those sinnes. Let not men thinke thus, I neuer did commit whoredome nor incest: I did neuer persecute nor shed blood: therefore I haue nought to doe with their sinnes, if they haue so heaped them vp, that they reach vnto the heauens. O bee not deceiued: for if thou doest not separate thy selfe from Babell, the voyce from heauen telleth thee, that thou shalt bee partaker of her sinnes, and so consequently of her plagues. Her plagues shall bee exceeding great, because her sinnes doe reach vp vnto heauen, and so thy plagues shall bee great, because thou art guiltie of her sinnes. This is it that he said, whosoeuer dooth worshippe the beast or his image, or hath his marke or the number of his name, he shall be tormented with fire and brimstone in the presence of the holie Angels, and of the Lambe. If ye take them to bee grieuous plagues which God doth inflict, not onely in this life, but especially in the torments of hell, then separate your selues and come out from Babylon, renounce the poperie and all Romish trash, and cleaue fast to the holie Gospell of Iesus Christ, which shall saue your soules. Regarde not the clamors of the wicked papists, but obey this voyce from heauen. They call vs vnto all filthie abominations, and spirituall whoredomes, and this voyce calleth vs vnto the pure worship of God. Be not seduced by those which shall speake thus vnto ye. Doth not the Church of Rome beleeue in Christ? are they not Christians? what though they differ in some things, yet as long as they denie not Christ, why may not men safely ioyne themselues with them? Indeede they doe not denie Christ in word, but they both denie his doctrine and persecute it. They professe some godlinesse in shew, but haue denied the power thereof. And now further where the voyce saith, that God hath remembred her iniquities: It may bee said, did the Lord God euer forget them? or did he not regard them? Doubtlesse they were alwaies before the Lorde, and he could neuer forget them: for there is no ignorance nor forgetfulnes in God. He is not like vnto a mortall man. But when the Lord passeth by, and suffereth the wicked to goe vnpunished, when he doth not execute vengeance, they doe imagine that he doth not regard their doings. They suppose that they shall neuer

bee

be called vnto any reckening. Also the faithfull are weake, and according to flesh and blood thinke it long, and are assaulted with some doubts, as if God had forgotten al those hard dealings of the wicked enemies. When therefore the Lord taketh the matter in hand, and beginneth to execute the office of a iudge, then doth he declare that he remembreth the iniquities which are past, and so is said to remember: for the holy Ghost in the scripture applieth himselfe vnto our capacitie, speaking of God. The godly seruants of Christ which liued in former times, and beheld the blasphemies of the Romish beast, and withall considered how long the same had continued, and saw no appearance of vengeance vpon them, had nothing but faith in the word of God to support them, there was none outward thing to lead them to see that God did regard or remember the iniquities of Babel: but in these dayes we haue besides the word of God, the sight and view of the thing before our eyes. Wee see how God hath begun to execute vengeance, and how that he remembreth, and will not let passe the wicked deedes of the papists. The voyce from heauen addeth yet further, saying, reward her, euen as she hath rewarded you, and giue her double, according to her works: and in the cup that she hath filled to you, fil her the double. The sum of this is, that the seruants of God are not onely to remoue and to separate themselues from great Babylon: but also to execute vengeance vpon her: for the Lord God that iudgeth and casteth her downe, doth it by instruments. And as the 137. Psalme pronounceth them blessed that should execute vengeance vpon Babel, for the crueltie which she had shewed to the church: so doubtles we are to make account, that it is a thing most highly pleasing God, when his seruants seeke reuenge, euen to the full vpon this Romish whore, for all the euill which she hath wrought vnto the Church. And to assure vs of this, the Lord from heauen willeth to rewarde her, and that double, yea euen to the full, for all the euill which she hath done to the holy worshippers of God. But it may be sayd, vengeance is to be executed onely by such as beare the sworde: priuate persons are forbidden to reuenge. How then is this to be taken? Are all the faithfull here willed to be reuenged vpon her, and to recompence her for her euill deedes? Or is this spoken onely vnto such as be publike magistrates? To this I answere, that the recompence of vengeance here spoken of, is of diuers sorts, and some way to bee executed by all the faithfull people. Rome hath murdered the Saints, and shed the blood of the Martyrs of Christ: now to reward this, and to shed her blood, belongeth onely to princes, and ciuill magistrates. They be here called vpon, that way to reward her: and are much to be blamed if herein they be negligent. Downe with her, make no doubt, the Lord from heauen doth will ye. And how, shall the christian princes answere it before God, if they neglect this holy worke? Againe, the Romish synagogue, hath glorified her selfe, and her own decrees, boasting that she hath authoritie ouer all: and reuileth, reprocheth, and condemneth them all as heretikes, which reiect her abominations. Now to be reuenged vpon her in this, the ministers of the word are to disclose and to paint her forth to the world. They are to lay open all her whoredomes and most filthie treacheries. They are to manifest that her doctrine and worship, is the doctrine and

worship

THE REVELATION. 348

worship of diuels: that the Kings, and Princes, and people, may hate and abhor her. Such as be seduced by this whore, crye out that the zealous preachers of the Gospell doe raile and blaspheme when they doe this: but what are they to care for the reproches of sinfull men, when the voyce from heauen willeth them to be reuenged vpon her, and not to spare her? And then touching the priuate persons, thus far they are to be readie to execute vengeance vpon her, euen to be readie and most willing at the commandement of their princes to destroy and pull her down. They are also as far as priuate men may, to lay her open in speech, to help to withdraw such from her societie as be seduced. And thus ye may see, that all the seruants of God, both high and lowe, euen of euery calling, are called vpon from heauen, to set vpon great Babel, the mother of whoredomes and abominations of the earth, and to be reuenged vpon her for all the euill which she hath done to the Church of God. Would to God this voyce, euen this heauenly voyce did sound more shrill in the eares of all men; that they might be earnestly moued vnto this holy worke. It is the worke which the Lord from heauen doth call men vnto. It is that which is highly pleasing vnto the Lord, and in which we shall doe him great seruice. Wherefore we are to remember what is said by the Prophet, stirring men vp to execute the Lords vengeance vpon the other Babell in the East, as namely, Cursed is he that doth the worke of the Lord negligently. Is Rome and the Romish religion so abominable to the Lord, for al their vngodly doings, both against his holy worship and people? Is the time come, that he will haue his iudgements and vengeance executed vpon them? And hath his voice from heauen called vpon all men to reward that bloodie citie and wicked synagogue, and to recompence them double, for all the euill which they haue done to vs? and shall wee then bee excused, if we be negligent? Doth not the curse then belong vnto vs? Are we not of the number of slouthfull seruants? Doe we regard how much God is glorified, and his Church eased, by the decay and ruines of that horrible kingdome of the great Antichrist? Let the Christian princes be readie to doe their office: let the preachers of the Gospell performe their duetie: and let all good people be readie and not wanting for their part, to execute the vengeance of God vpon this filthie harlot. Doth not the Lord himselfe as it were sound the trumpet vnto vs from heauen? Ye see how the seruants of Antichrist doe bestirre them to maintaine their kingdome: They fight and striue for the diuell, and are most vehement: and shall we be slacke in the cause of God? Shall they be more forward and bold for their worship of the dragon and of the beast, then wee for the holy worship of God? When yee heare of the great trauailes and labours of the Iesuite priests, of their zeale for the defence of poperie, and how they aduenture euen vnto the perill of death, let it make vs much ashamed. For is it meet that they in such a cause should goe before vs? Their reward is from the dragon, and from the beast, or rather together with them, euen endles destruction. But we, if we fight valiantly vnder the banner of Christ, in the defence of his trueth against Antichrist, against the whore of Babel, euen to pull her downe, and for to destroy her, shall raigne in glorie with our great Captaine.. What shall we then say vnto these neuters, which haue no

zeale

zeale nor heate in them against the whore great Babell? Doe they any thing at all regarde this heauenly voyce? Or be they worthie to bee numbred among the seruants of God? The heauenly voyce doth yet further declare what vengeance God will haue to be executed vpon the Romish Babell, or in what measure: for here is a proportion noted, that according to the height and loftines of her pride and glorious magnificence, vnto which she hath by trecherous meanes aduanced her selfe, and according to the great abundance of her daintie and delicate pleasures in which she hath taken her solace, the greatnes of her shame and sorrowes should bee answerable. Beloued, this is a very great thing which the voyce vttereth, because it requireth and denounceth her torment and shame in an exceeding measure. For if ye will stand vpon this proportion, what glorie, and pompe, and magnificence vnder heauen hath been comparable to the glorie of Rome, vnder the dominion of Emperors and Popes? If also ye might take the view of her pleasures in the time of the papacie, as namely, in what delights touching worldly things her Popes, Cardinals, and chiefe prelates haue liued, where should they bee matched? Then if her shame, and infamie must exceed as much as her glorie hath exceeded, and her sorrowes and torments must abound according to the abundance of her delights, ye may easily see that all things denounced here against her be exceeding great. All such then as are to execute vengeance vpon the whore great Babel, must not be moued with pitie. They must not doe as King Saul did in sparing Agag and the fattest things: but where the Lord commaundeth all seueritie, they ought not to remit. Shall man spare and shew mercie where God will not?

And now to come somewhat neerer, the voyce leadeth vs to behold the toppe of her pride, glorie and pleasures: for it followeth, She sayth in her heart, I sit being a Queene, and am no widowe, and shall see no mourning. In the daies of her prosperitie, euen when she helde the dominion ouer the kings of the earth, Rome was in this securitie, that she did promise to her selfe (for she said in her heart) that her pompous estate should indure for euer. I sit as a Queene, I haue the superioritie ouer the kings of the earth for temporall matters, and I am the head of the Catholike Church, I am the spouse of Christ, I haue all authoritie and power in causes ecclesiasticall, I am eternall, my power shall neuer faile, I shall neuer be remoued. I am not as a solitarie or desolate widowe, I haue many louers which are strong to defend me, I shall neuer feele any want or sorrowe. Is not this a great height of glorie, wherein she hath glorified her selfe by vsurping such power? And being so horrible a filth, is it not wonderful presumption to promise to her selfe an estate so durable? But wee see how she hath been deceiued, the Lord pronounced it before, and her pompe is decayed, she is come downe, euen the Ladie of the world, and hath alreadie lost the greater part of her louers, and of her wealth. And now looke how much higher in glorie and pleasures she hath been aboue all, so much deeper must she be cast downe into shame and sorrowes. Then Rome and the Romish Church are in the extreames: the highest in glorie here in the world, and the lowest in shame and infamie: the most abounding in al pleasures, the deepest

pest in sorrowes. I pray you obserue, what was higher in this world then the Romish synagogue ruling ouer al as the spouse of Christ? And now what baser, what viler, and what more dishonorable thing is there in the world, then to bee esteemed and called the great whore of Babel, the mother of abominations & whoredomes, euen the synagogue of Satan, the kingdome of the great Antichrist? She was aloft, pull her downe to these, saith the Lord, lay her open and disclose her to the full. She did flow in pleasures and delights, giue her the like measure of torments. These things are well come to passe alreadie, and shall fully bee accomplished, for ye may reade what followeth, therefore shall her plagues come at one day, death, and sorrow, and famine, and she shall bee burnt with fire: for strong is the Lord God that iudgeth her. Shall wee doubt of this, when the Lord hath thus before hand denounced it? Shall we not wish for the time when this shall be fully accomplished, and doe the best wee can to bring it forward? I know it seemed a thing vnpossible when the pope sate with his triple crowne, in his glory & pompe, euen as a God vpon earth, that euer that kingdome should bee cast downe: for what power should ouermatch it? Here is declared what power, euen the power of God from heauen: for he saith, strong is the Lord God that iudgeth her. VVhat is able to stand which hath the Lord God almightie against it? Therefore bee sure Babell shall downe.

THE XXXIX. SERMON.
CHAP. XVIII.

9 *Then shall the kings of the earth bewaile her and lament for her, which haue committed fornication with her, when they shall see the smoke of her burning.*

10 *And shall stand a farre off for feare of her torments, saying, Alas, alas, that great citie Babylon that mightie citie, for in one houre is thy iudgement come.*

11 *And the marchants of the earth shall weepe and waile ouer her, for no man buyeth their ware any more.*

12 *The ware of gold and siluer, and precious stones, and of pearles, and of fine linnen, and of purple, and of silke, and of scarlet, and of all manner of thin wood, and of vessels of Iuorie, and of all vessels of most precious wood, and of brasse, and of iron, and of marble,*

13 *And of Sinamon, and odors, and oyntments, and frankincense, and wine, and oyle, and fine flower, and wheate, and beasts and sheepe, and horses and chariots, and bodies and soules of men.*

14 *And the apples which thy soule lusted after, are departed from thee, and all things*

15 *things which were fat and excellent, are departed from thee, and thou shalt finde them no more.*

15 *The marchants of these things which were made rich, shall stand a farre off from her, for feare of her torment, weeping and wailing:*

16 *Saying, Alas, alas, that great citie which was clothed in fine linnen, and purple, and scarlet, and gilded with gold and precious stones, and pearles: for in one houre so great riches come to desolation.*

17 *And euery shippe gouernour, and all they that occupie ships and shipmen, and as many as worke in the sea, stood a farre off,*

18 *And cried when they saw the smoke of her burning, saying, What citie is like to this great citie?*

19 *And they cast dust on their heads, and cried weeping, and wayling, and saying, Alas, alas, that great citie, wherein were made rich all that had ships in the sea, by reason of her costlines: for at one houre is she made desolate.*

Vch as will diligently reade the old Prophets, shall finde it their vsuall manner, whensoeuer they would in most liuely and effectuall sort describe the destruction of any kingdom or famous citie, to set forth or to call for a song of lamentatio: for by this meanes the matter was more cleere, and did more affect and moue the minds of the people. Now ye are to remember that this prophecie, doth imitate those prophecies of old: and so the more liuely to paint out the ruines, and the vtter subuersion of the Romish Babell, euen of their monarchie, religion and citie it selfe, yea to declare how horrible the destruction of these shall be, heere are brought in her louers of sundrie sortes lamenting and bewayling her case: and these are kings, marchants, and shipmasters. Here bee indeede reasons rendred of the sorrowe, and lamentation which euery sort of these doe make. Some of them loued Babel for the pleasures and delights in which they liued vnder her, and others for their gaine. Her destruction bringing an end to both, they lament grieuously. VVee may heere note by the way vpon the cause of their lamentation, what things haue allured men to bee in loue with the whore great Babell, euen carnall pleasures and riches. He beginneth with the kings of the earth, they sing the first part of this dolefull dittie. They sorrowe, they weepe, and they howle for her. But it is most euident by this prophecie, that the kings of the earth shall pull downe and destroy this monstrous whore. How then is it sayd that they shall bewayle her fall? We must consider that this is but a figure, in which after a sort the kings of the earth which are dead and gone in time of poperie, are brought in lamenting. Wee are not to bee scrupulous more then for the scope of the matter, which is to paint out an horrible destruction.

Moreouer this is manifest, that although the kings of the earth shall pull down the monarchie, the religion and citie of Rome, yet some kings are still for her, and seeke to vpholde her: and if they also should fall from her, yet she hath her kings. For her chiefe prelates as Cardinals and Legates, are euen kings: They take themselues

selues kings fellowes, and were wont to take the vpper hand of kings. How wantonly these Cardinals and great Prelates haue liued, in what pompe, pleasures, and iolitie, vnder the whore, and what whoredomes they haue committed with her, both carnall and spirituall, the world knoweth. The Romish doctrine is delightsome to those great persons: in as much as it openeth the gappe vnto all filthie abominations in carnall delights, by teaching that for money they may obtaine pardon at the Popes handes, or by their riches they may make some satisfaction and merit eternall life, or blot out their offences by some penance. O what a griefe shall it bee vnto them, when they behold the smoke of her burning? The destruction of Rome shall bee such, as that into farre countries the smoke as it were of her burning shall bee seene. Yea her torment shall be so horrible, that these kings shall not dare for all their might to come nigh for to rescue her: but for feare shall stand a farre off. And this dolefull voyce shall they vtter, Alas, alas, that great citie Babylon, that mightie citie, for in one houre is thy iudgement come. How it grieueth them, and how much they sorrow and lament to remember what the riches, the power, the pompe, the glorie, and the magnificence of Rome hath beene, and to see her now quite destroyed in so dreadfull manner. They were perswaded that no power should bee able to destroy so mightie a citie. Who could resist such a monarchie? All the worlde wondered at it, and the kings did tremble and quake for feare to displease the Pope. They could neuer looke for such an alteration: for from whence shoulde they come that shoulde worke it? Wee see that the voyce and sound of the holie Gospell is so mightie, that it hath alreadie shaken the maine pillers and towers of great Babell. Rome hath lost alreadie the greatest part of her preheminence and dignitie. The Pope which was honoured and feared as a petie God, is now despised as the most vile minister of Satan, the head, and standerd bearer of the wicked apostacie, which is the kingdome of the great Antichrist. The riches of that citie are diminished, her friends haue forsaken her, shee waxeth feeble: And yet the Iesuites and other papists doe vaunt and glorie that their kingdome shall neuer bee cast downe. Peters shippe (say they) may be tossed in the surges and waues, but it can neuer bee drowned. Most true it is that the spouse of Christ, euen the true Catholike Church shall neuer miscarie in this huge gulfe of the worlde: for shee is founded vpon the rocke, shee is supported by the trueth which is infallible. If the Church of Rome were indeede the Catholike Church, as they vainly boast, then should it neuer fall. But the light of Gods worde doth not cast downe, but build vp the true Church: It casteth downe Rome and that Romish religion, being nothing but mans inuentions. One thing wee may yet note further in the speech of the kings, when they doe confesse that it is Gods iudgement. It teacheth vs that, which indeede wee finde true by experience, that the wicked men doe beholde indeede the hand and power of the Lord God, and doe acknowledge it is his iudgement for wickednes, but yet doe not repent them of their euill. They beholde how the glorie of Rome decayeth, they shall see her full destruction in time, and shall say it is for sinne, but yet they will loue and pitie her. Let not

this

SERMONS VPON

this seeme strange vnto any man: for when the heauie hand of God is vpon any notorious vngodly man, ye shall heare him acknowledge that it is for his vngodly behauiour, by which he hath prouoked the Lord: And he will wish hee had liued otherwise, feeling that all the delights and pleasures of the sinnes are vanished, and that the sting remaineth, and yet repenteth not; but if he recouer doth follow the same waies againe as greedily as euer before. Some will say perhaps, if a man in that estate doe feele and confesse that God pursueth his wickednes, and wisheth hee had neuer liued in such sort, doeth hee not repent? I answere, in some kinde of repentance, hee repenteth for the time, but not vnto amendment: Hee is grieued not for the fowlnes of the sinne, or hatred thereof, hee doth lament not of any loue of God or of goodnesse, but indeed at the torment which he feeleth sinne doth bring. And therefore when the dread and feeling of the horror of vengeance is ouer, he rusheth againe into the same sinnes, and liueth euen as he did before.

It followeth in the text, that the marchants of the earth shall weepe and waile ouer her, for no man buyeth their ware any more. Kings (wee haue seene) which committed whoredome and liued in pleasure with her, lament for the fall of Babel: and now come the Marchants with their part of the lamentation. They weepe and waile, and the holy Ghost noteth the cause, euen this, that no man any more buyeth their wares. Worldly men delight in gaine, it is a sweete thing vnto them, yea a very sweete thing, nothing sweeter. Looke then how much the sweeter, so much the more bitter and grieuous is the losse thereof. And hereof it commeth, that the hope of gaine failing, men lament and weepe dolefully. Take away the gaine of earthly minded men, and yee euen as it were plucke out their bowels. Beholde then how the Marchants doe lament, becauſe with the destruction of the Romiſh tyrannie, the hope of their gaine faileth, in as much as their wares lie in their hands, and no man will buy them. But let vs know who are these marchants, and what be their wares. The wares are noted in the next verses following, and there we are to enquire what they be. The marchants themselues are not named, but knowne by their wares, euen popish marchants, euen all that made gaine of the trash and trumperies which were solde very deere in the poperie, by which men sought helpe for their soules. To recken vp all sorts of these marchants which solde the popish wares, would bee a tedious matter, and to no great purpose, seeing it is knowne that in the Church of Rome all things, and euen among all sorts, from the highest to the lowest, haue been set to sale, and solde for readie money. The histories of former times doe shew, that in the papisme there was all ouer, nothing but euen a marte of buying and selling, in which the marchants of all sorts were assembled. Who had any office or roome almost among them, but as it were in some riuer or ditch spread his nets, and did fish for golde? These marchants then doe bewaile and lament ouer Babel, becauſe no man any longer buyeth their wares, and they be very many. And now touching their wares which no man buyeth any more, they be rehearsed.

They be some of them of the richest things and most pretious in the world, as of gold,

gold, siluer, precious stones, and pearles. And all of them besides, of great account: As one sort of fine linnen, purple, silke, and scarlet. An other sort of costly wood, as of thinne wood, of Iuorie, & of precious trees. An other of brasse, Iron, and marble. Then come synamon, odours, oyntment, and frankincense, wine, oyle, fine flower, wheate, beasts, sheepe, horses, chariots. And last of all, the bodies and soules of men. Are these the wares of the kingdome of the great Antichrist? and will no man buy them any more? Do men set light by gold or siluer? do they not esteeme pretious stones and pearles? Are silkes and scarlets now begunne to bee dispised? Or were any of these euer more esteemed then they be at this day? Will not men in all landes couet after these things euen so long as the world standeth? And will they not gladly buy them? How then is it sayd here, that no man buyeth their wares any more? I answer, that the things whereof their wares were made are still in price: but they had greatly increased the value, and made their gaine very much, by turning them into their wares, which gaine is decayed. Gold is valued and esteemed at the same price it was, so is siluer, pearle, and pretious stones. But now as they were in their hollowed thinges in the Church of Rome, in their Masses, in Crosses, Chalices, Images, Myters, and such like, or in their adorning of shrines, and temples, they be not regarded since the poperie went downe. They be no longer in request, they be no marchandise for any honest man. Men will buy them as the metal or pearle, or stone is worth, but not at that excessiue price which they sold them at before as their wares. True it is that by stealth they send abroad their *Agnus deies*, their hallowed beades, and other such trash vnto the blind superstitious papists in all landes, and so picke vp as it were pedlers, some siluer, both nothing to the gaine which they made in the times that are past. For them now to buy fine linnen, silks, purple, and scarlet, to sel againe, they can doe little or no good, there be other marchants can doe it better, and now turned into coapes, vestiments, and all manner of popish attire, no man will giue one penie the more, but the lesse, and so their gaine is gone. No man doth seeke vnto them now for their Iuorie and other fine wood, for brasse, and Iron, and marble, to adorne Temples, Idols, or monasteries. Their market for these things is past, they can dazle the eies of men no longer with these pompous shewes. Wonderfull great was their gaine in these thinges when they made the world beleeue that by such toyes they should haue pardon, and merite eternall life: but now the word of God hath shewed their false packing, they haue cold takings. In their ceremonies, and about their Idolatrous worship, they had their wares of sweet odours, of oile and franckincense, of ointments, and wine, and fine flower, of which they made great gaine, which now is also gone. To feed the bellies, and to serue the pompe of the great prelates, there were such as prouided wheate, beasts, sheepe, horses, and chariots. Now their kitchins waxing cold, and thier pompous traine decaying, such officers may beg. Thus haue ye seene sundrie sorts of their wares, which since the poperie decayed, are but little in request, and the marchants haue but small takings, by which the marchandise of the Romish Church is so cleerely noted, that no man which hath had any sight or knowledge how all was for money in the poperie, can doubt but that the downfall of

popery

poperie is here described. But yet here is the last braunch remaining, which doth more perfectly set them forth then any of the rest, in as much as there can none be found in the world, which haue made such gaine of mens soules as they haue. The Pope for money by his pardons could bring what soules he lusted to heauen. The Abbots and priors would send them also thither, and assure them of eternall blessednes both in soule and body, which would giue liberally to the maintenance of their dennes. Euery popish priest for a sum of money could draw out of his budget his wares, euen trentals of masses, and diriges to bring the soules of the dead out of Purgatorie. What should I speake of their common and ordinarie buying and selling benefices, whereby the bodies and soules of men are euen bought and sold, as horses and oxen are in the market? A sweete gaine made the pope and his Cardinals, Bishops, Abbots, Monkes, Friers, and popish priestes, with all the rablement of pardoners and confessors of the bodies and soules of men. Beloued, what cleerer description can bee made of the Romish Church, then this which yee haue here? Was not the whole poperie a marte in which there was byingand selling of wares? And where are the soules of men sold for money, but among them? When ye see so many sorts of wares which haue been esteemed as most pretious, being hallowed by the pope or popish prelates, that men did giue great sums of money for, which now no man will giue ought for, remember this prophecie: and behold the wonderfull kindenes of God, which for the establishing of his seruants in the truth, hath so long before described the downefall of great Babel. For if men might doubt so long as she stood in the loftines of her glory, yet the manner of her fall taketh away all doubt, and manifesteth her to be the great whore. And hauing thus declared that the wares of her marchants are no longer salable, no man will giue money for them, their market is done, they may packe and be gone: the holy Ghost proceedeth to manifest, how the Church of Rome shall lose and forgoe all her pleasant, delicate, daintie, rich, and pompous things. He calleth them the apples which her soule lusted after, and the fat things. These were sweet apples which euery tree doth not heare: but yet euery kingdome and nation vnder the papacie did affoord great plentie of them. They were very great apples: as monasteries, abbeyes, and great dignities which caryed with them much pompe, delight, and pleasures. These were fat things, euen of the fattest vpon the earth. And they are departed from them, they haue lost them: yea which is the more grieuous, they haue lost them, and shall neuer find them any more. Such as neuer had a thing, the want thereof doth not so much grieue them, as it doth those which had it and haue lost it. And he that hath lost a goodly pleasant rich thing, his griefe is so much the greater, if he hath lost it, not for a time, but euen as they say, for al euer. When the popish sort do passe by the great Monasteries, and Abbyes, and see the ruinous heapes, and remember the fat reuenewes and pleasures which they had, and al the glorie and pompe which their great prelates had, it grieueth them, they shake their heads, they wish to haue those goodly apples and fat things restored to them againe: but that shall neuer come to passe, they haue lost them for euer. This glorious harlot, the Romish church, feasted and fed her children daintily with sweete and costly fat things: but now her table is is bare, and her dishes are empty: and her children in many places are glad to gnaw vpon a crust. What abundance of wealth had those popish marchants heaped vppe, and at her destruction they shall stand a farre off, weeping and howling. They loue her for the riches and pleasures which she brought them, and therefore they are sorrowfull at her fall. But although they loue her neuer so much, yet they stand a far off and dare not approach neere for to rescue, or for to ayd her, becausehertormentand vengeance shall be so horrible. Rome then, and the Romish Church and monarchy shall be destroyed with such terrible vengeance, that not one of all her louers and best friends shall dare to come nigh, but shall stand a far off. The most which they can doe is to crie out, alas, alas, that great citie, which was clothed in fine linnen, and purple, and scarlet, and girded with golde, and precious stones, and pearles: for in one houre, some great riches com to desolation. Marke here beloued what it is which greeueth the papists, which cause them to cry out, alas, alas: for it is worth the marking, because they pretend the care of Gods glorie and of mens soules: but it is farre otherwise. They haue gloried in the exceeding greatnes of their citie and Church: and now see it brought to nought, and that is it which causeth them mournfully to say, that great citie. The greatnes sticketh in their minde. Moreouer they haue in Rome, and in the Romaine monarchie been very rich, and richly decked with all precious things which they here recite, and wherein all their glory did consist, the losse of these doth greeue them full sore. For these things being gone, what is there in all the Romish religion worthy to be looked vpon? The true Church of Christ is decked with many heauenly gifts and spirituall graces,which doe make her very glorious euen in the middest of all distresses, afflictions, and pouertie. The Synagogue of Antichrist, that great whore Babell, being destitute of all graces, and spirituall ornaments, and shining in the rich attyre of corruptible things, as of gold, of pearles, of pretious stones, of purple, and of silks, when these are gone, she is a foule, filthie, vgly, and deformed beast. Her friends doe lament, that these so rich and pretious things come so sodainly vnto vtter desolation.

Then here follow a third sort which were made rich by her meanes, and they also doe greeuously lament and bewaile her destruction. These are mariners and shipmaisters. While Rome had dominion ouer the kingdoms, and the Pope ruled ouer all euen as a terrible God vpon the earth, there was nothing but trudging ouer the seas thither out of all landes, and againe from thence there was carying and recarying, in so much: that an infinit multitude of mariners and shipmen were continually set on worke and gained greatly thereby. To Rome, and from Rome, to Rome, and from Rome, out of all countries, and into all countries. Kings and great princes, Cardinals, and chiefe prelates which had the riches of the world, were caried and recarried. No maruaile then though these shipmen and mariners are brought in among other her friends, bewailing her destruction: when they shall see the smoke of her torment, standing also a far oft, and not daring to offer her any helpe, they shall cry out, what citie was like vnto this great citie? It is here sayd further that they shall cast dust on their heads. Among the Isralites (as the holy histories doe testifie) men in great sorrow, did vse to cast dust on their heads. And therefore to expresse the great griefe of such as lose their gaine by the fall of Babylon, the holy Ghost saith, they cast dust on their heads. And they cry weeping and wailing, and say, alas, alas, the great citie wherein were made rich all that had ships on the sea, by her costlines. Wee see the cause here also expressed of their sorrowe, euen the hope of their gaine taken away. Gaine is so sweete a thing vnto worldly men, that the losse thereof doth vexe them sore. The Kings for pleasure, the marchants and shipmasters for their gaine, doe lament and bewaile the fall of Babylon. Her vtter destruction is not yet come, but greatlie decayed shee is, and many doe greatly mourne for the same. Some of her well-willers are in good hope still to holde her vp, and recouer her ruines with the repayre of her breaches: and herein they bee exceeding industrious, and venturous: for as in the wars ye shall haue many hardie men that will rush forwarde and hazard themselues with extreame perill to doe some famous exploit onely on this mind, that if they can worke the feat they are made for euer, they shall bee magnified and honoured, they shall come to riches and dignities. Euen so in the poperie, these Iesuites thrust themselues forwarde into most desperate attempts, hoping that if they can by treacheries and treasons bring their matters about, and so vpholde the Babylonish whore, shee will aduance them with great dignities and preferments. For looke but vpon our owne land, and if the popery should get the dominion in it againe, what great things should the Bishop of Rome haue to bestow vpon those his forward souldiers? All is for gaine, but they shall labour in vaine, and neuer come vnto it, but be diminished euen to the vtter ouerthrow of their citie and kingdome, which shall come in the time that the Lord God almightie in his holy wisdome hath appoynted. Thus we haue seene the lamentation for the fall of Babell: now it shall not be amisse here to answere vnto one shift and cauill of the papists. They see it so cleere that this prophesie describing the great Babylon, euen the kingdome of Antichrist, speaketh of a citie ruling ouer kingdomes, which hath shed the blood of the martyrs of Christ. There is no citie can bee found in the world but Rome, vnto which this description can agree. This plainely condemneth the papacie, and Romish monarchie: and vnles the papists can shift it off from Rome, they bee quite vndone. Let vs see then how they shewe their cunning about this matter. They say the whole companie of the reprobate, is called the great whore, chap. 18. They say, that the great citie which the Angell said had dominion ouer the kings of the earth, is the whole companie of the reprobate, as on the contrarie, the whole societie of the faithfull is called the citie of God. Marke well, I pray you, is it a fit kinde of speech to say that the vniuersall corpes of the reprobate, or the whole companie of the wicked raigneth ouer the kings of the earth? Or shall Kings, Marchants, and Mariners stand a farre off at

the

THE REVELATION. 357

the deſtruction of the whole ſocietie of the wicked, and mourn for their fall? Theſe bee vaine ſhifts, it is a citie, and none other citie in the world, but Rome. Obſerue euery thing well, and ye ſhall ſee it moſt cleare.

THE XL. SERMON.
CHAP. XVIII.

20 *O heauens reioyce ouer her, and yee holy Apoſtles and Prophets, becauſe God hath giuen your iudgement on her.*

21 *And a mighty Angell tooke vp a ſtone like a great milſtone, and caſt it into the ſea, ſaying, with ſuch violence ſhall that great citie Babylon be caſt, and ſhall be founded no more at all.*

22 *And the voice of harpers and muſitions, and of pipers and trumpetters ſhall be heard no more in thee at all: and no craftſman of whatſoeuer craft he be, ſhalbe found any more in thee: and the ſound of a mill ſhall be heard no more at all in thee.*

23 *And the light of a candle ſhall ſhine no more at all in thee, and the voice of the bridegroome and of the bride ſhall be heard no more at all in thee: for thy merchants were the great men of the earth, and with thine inchantments were deceiued all nations.*

24 *And in her was found the bloud of the Prophets, and of the ſaints, and of all that were ſlain vpon the earth.*

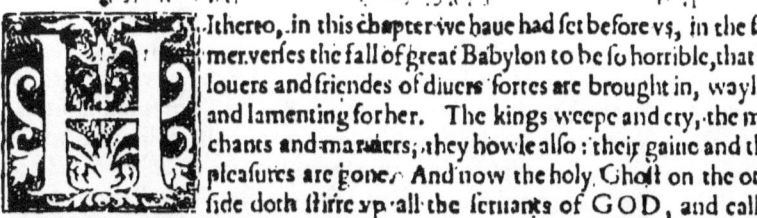Itherto, in this chapter we haue had ſet before vs, in the former verſes the fall of great Babylon to be ſo horrible, that her louers and friendes of diuers ſortes are brought in, wayling and lamenting for her. The kings weepe and cry, the merchants and marriners, they howle alſo: their gaine and their pleaſures are gone. And now the holy Ghoſt on the other ſide doth ſtirre vp all the ſeruants of GOD, and calleth vpon them to reioyce at her deſtruction. For as on the one ſide they lament, ſo on the other ſide there muſt be reioycing. Reioyce ouer her O heauen, ſaith the Lord. Is her fall and deſtruction ſo requiſite for the glorie of God, and the good of his Church, that euen the very heauen, the ſenſeles creature muſt reioyce thereat? Indeede to ſpeake properly, the heauens cannot reioyce, being voyde of vnderſtanding and ſenſe; but to expreſſe the thing with the greater vehemencie, and to declare what abundant matter of reioycing there is in her fall, the heauens (euen as if it ſhould affect them) are called vpon, in ſtead of thoſe that dwel in

Aa 3   the

the heauens, or that shall possesse them: great Babel with her whoredomes defiled all. She condemned the truth, and set vp lies: she persecuted and murdered, and blasphemed the true worshippers of God. Therefore who is there that loueth the glorie of God, that esteemeth the truth, and wisheth well to the Church, but must needes reioyce at her destruction? The holy Angels in heauen, cannot but reioyce at it. The holy Apostles and prophets, the Martyrs, and all the Saintes, must needes bee glad thereof. And so many vpon the earth as haue their conuersation in the heauens: For now shall this monster no longer oppresse them, nor yet blaspheme the truth any more. All that are good then, yea euen all that loue the glorie of GOD, doe greatly reioyce at the horrible destruction of Babell. And this is to bee obserued, as an vndoubted principle, that looke how much the more godly any are, so much the more they reioyce at the destruction of poperie. And looke how much more they reioyce, so far further they be off from pitying great Babell. Most true it is, that the godlier the man is, the more perfect in mercie and pittie, and compassion: for those bee speciall partes of godlines. But this must bee where pittie is to be shewed: and not where God will haue vs to shew none. For our perfection is to agree with the blessed will of God. Now this reioycing ouer her fall, is no small increase of her torments. For where any man is in great calamitie, it somewhat easeth that men are moued with pitie and compassion towards him. And if those that beholde his miserie be so far from pitying his case, that they reioyce and triumph at the same, what an exceeding increase of sorrow doth that bring? Then when the hand of God is vpon the whore of Babell, euen vpon Rome and the Romish Church, to execute the seueritie of his wrath and vengeance, we are for our parts to take heede that wee bee not moued with any compassion, but are in deede to adde as much torment as wee can, euen by reioycing and triumphing at her destruction. Let no man here crie out, that this is crueltie: The Lord God himselfe calleth for it at our hands, but hee calleth not for crueltie. And there is a cause rendered why we should be glad and reioyce: it is in these words, for GOD hath giuen your iudgement on her. That is, the Lorde God hath reuenged your cause: Rome condemned the doctrine of the holy Apostles and Prophets, as wicked and hereticall: And shee hath most cruellie shed the blood of the Saintes and Martyrs, because they would not be driuen from the same pure truth, to imbrace her inuentions, and wicked decrees. And now whereas shee so sore afflicted and oppressed the Church, the Lord for the same afflicteth her, and will powre forth his vengeance on her. Thus hee executeth the iudgement of his Apostles and Prophets vpon her, euen the iudgement which they before denounced in the name of the Lorde; and the vengeance which is due vnto her, for all the euils which she hath committed against them, and against all that feare God, both small and great. Is not this a matter of ioye and gladnes vnto vs all? I know there be some which will say, O ye be malicious, ye be cruell, ye be full of spite and rayling. If the Church of Rome haue faulted, yet are wee not to loue our brethren? Are wee not to pitie those that bee in calamitie? You seeke to pull

downe,

downe, to defame, and to disgrace, what loue doth appeare in you? I answer it is no malice, it is not any want of pitie, neither is it any vncharitable rayling, to lay open their filthie abominations, euen to the full: neither is it crueltie to reioyce in their destruction: seeing God calleth for all these things at our hands: and so worthie a cause is rendred. But on the contrarie part, this we may boldly affirme, that whosoeuer hee bee which doth not reioyce at the fall and destruction of this Romish monster, euen at the destruction of Rome, and of that bloodie Antichristian kingdome, hee neuer loued God, nor his truth, nor his Church, he commeth not within the compasse of these. O heauen reioyce ouer her, and ye holy Apostles and Prophets. Is it not a most euident thing by the cleere words of this text, that such as reioyce not at the grieuous iudgements of God, and at the execution of his seuere vengeance vpon Rome, and the Romish Idolaters, haue no part in the heauens, nor with the holy Apostles and Prophets? Ye haue many men which care not at all, whether the dominion of the Pope stand or fall, these bee indifferent, these bee meere worldlings, not regarding the worship of God, nor the saluation of mens soules, being children of this world, which haue their portion in this life. These are not here called vpon to reioyce: when he saith, Reioyce ouer her O heauen. But if it had been sayd, reioyce ouer her ye inhabitants of the earth and of the sea, it might concerne them. But they haue receiued no such harme by Antichristies kingdome. Againe, there bee many, with either for gaine, or else made drunken and besotted with the wine of her whoredome, doe entirely loue the whore: these are none of the companie here called vpon to reioyce at her fall: for they mourne for her in their heartes. They long to see her set vp againe in her former pompe and iolitie, they wish to see the day that shee might preuaile against all those which doe inueigh against her which the word of God, and that doe bring her vnto shame and contempt. They wish to see them all rooted out, and that all againe with one consent would receiue the golden cup, and drinke whatsoeuer the harlot doth put into it They wish that she might sit as a queene againe, and as the Ladie of the world abounding in all riches, delicacie and pleasures. Then this, O heauen reioyce, is spoken of another companie, whose cause is iudged and reuenged. And beloued if we be not of this societie, woe be vnto vs, wee haue no part in the heauens, we haue no fellowship with the holy Apostles and Prophets. Therefore brethren let vs consider what an horrible monster Rome hath been against the truth, and reioyce in the free passage of the Gospell, which shall throw her downe: yea, let vs doe what wee can to set this holy worke forward. Hauing thus called vpon all the seruants of God, to triumph with gladnes for her destruction, euen because God executeth his vengeance vpon her, for all the euill shee hath done to his people: Now the spirite of the Lorde declareth that shee shell neuer recouer her selfe, nor bee restored againe from this destruction. The Papists doe worke apace in all lands, and aduenture themselues in most desperate manner, to recouer againe the credit of poperie, and to set vp againe the dignitie and the power of their Pope, and the glorie of their Church and Citie; and their bolde enterprises

terprises doe make many, euen to doubt that they will againe one day preuaile. But surely we are to make full reckening, that although here and there they may support for a time some ruinous parts of their rotten frame, yet doe what they can, it shall downe vpon their heads, and come to vtter desolation. For marke what followeth here in the text: and yee shall see that all things to the end of this chapter, are onely for this purpose, euen to shew her vtter desolation? It is first sayde, that a mightie Angell tooke vp a stone, like a great milstone, and cast it into the sea, saying, with such violence shall the great citie Babylon bee cast, and shall be found no more. Here the Lord declareth by a forcible signe, that the citie and kingdome of Antichrist shall be cast deepe into perdition, and shall lie ouerwhelmed and drowned in the same for euer and euer. The signe is so cleere of it selfe, hauing the wordes of the Angell to expound it, that there needeth little to be said for to open the meaning: but yet somewhat shall not bee amisse. And first yee may call to minde, that as Babell in olde time did oppresse the Church, being a most wicked idolatrous citie: so Rome in this Prophecie for the like qualities is named Babylon. Secondly, In as much as Rome surmounteth in all abominations, that auncient Babell, she is called not onely Babylon, but great Babylon. Thirdly, the phrases of speech, and the signes which the Prophets vsed, to declare the destruction and desolation of that olde Babell, are here alluded vnto in the destruction of Rome. The men of Iuda were carried away captiue to Babell: the Lorde by the Prophet Ieremie doth promise, that he will deliuer them, and bring them backe againe from that bondage and captiuitie, threatning destruction vnto that proude Babell. And Ieremie hauing written in a booke all the euill that should come vpon Babell: euen all these things that are written against Babell: hee said to Seraiah, when thou commest vnto Babell, and shalt see and reade all these wordes, then shalt thou say, O Lord thou hast spoken against this place, to destroy it, that none should remaine in it, neither man nor beast, but that it should be desolate for euer. And when thou hast made an end of reading this booke, thou shalt binde a stone to it, and cast it in the middest of Euphrates, and shalt say, thus shall Babell be drowned, and shall not rise from the euill that I will bring vpon her, although they wearie themselues, Ierem. 51.

This is the type, and these are the words vsed against olde Babel: and now consider how that agreeth with the same which is here set downe: and yee shall see that the differences are onely in this, that all things are here with greater force of iudgement, to expresse as it were a deeper vengeance, and a more heauie and vnrecouerable destruction. First there is a man, here is a mightie Angell. The man taketh a stone which indeed will sincke in the waters: here the Angell taketh vp a great stone like a milstone: there the stone is cast into the riuer: here into the deepe sea. All these doe amplifie the matter, if yee looke vpon them. To represent that Babel in Chaldea should sincke downe into miserie and destruction and not rise vp againe, but lie ouerwhelmed, a stone is cast into the riuer which doth sincke downe to the bottome and lieth there. To figure out a

more

more horrible destruction of Rome and of the Romish synagogue, which for their most horrible abominations farre passing that other, is in a mysterie called great Babylon, here is an Angell with great might, who taketh vp a very heauie stone, and with violence casteth it into the deepe sea, where it sincketh downe to the bottome, and lieth couered, past all meanes and helpe of man to fetch it vp againe. So shall the Romish Babel, euen with violence bee cast into the deepe gulfe of perdition and desolation, and shall neuer rise vp againe. It is in the Prophet Ieremie, that Babel should so be drowned or sincke as that stone, and neuer rise againe, although they should wearie themselues. If a little stone cast into the riuer did figure so much, being cast in by a man: shall wee thinke that Rome shall lift vp her head againe, whose drowning, ouerwhelming, and sincking deepe into perdition, is resembled by a great stone like vnto a milstone cast with violence by a mightie Angell into the deepe sea? Let the papists wearie themselues, as indeede their labours are exceeding great, and their interprises desperate; yet they shall neuer set her vp againe. Shee is cast downe deepe with violence, like a very heauie stone into the bottome of the sea of Gods vengeance. Indeede Rome standeth yet, and the poperie is not quite downe, but they are disclosed, and their credit is cracked, their power decayeth, and so this thing is begun, and the time draweth on, when it shall bee fully accomplished. Hee that had beheld the power, the maiestie, the pompe, the riches, and the estimation of that church, about some foure-score yeares past, and looke vpon it now, should see a wonderfull alteration. It seemed then to bee without all danger of being shaken, the Emperor and the Kings, with all their might stoode vp to maintaine it. If any man did vtter but a word against the vsurped power of the Pope, there was a solemne calling vpon Peter, and Paul for helpe against him, and it was thought hee must downe to hell without speedie repentance. Who could abide the tertor of their curse? Did not the Kings tremble and quake for feare at it? And now hee may cast forth his lightnings and thunder (I meane the Pope,) like a terrible god, Who doth regard the same? Doe we not see that all is but an illusion, and an emptie shadow or visor? If then that terrible bloodie kingdome be so farre come downe, beyond all thought and expectation of man: why should we doubt, but that in the time which God hath appoynted, it shall be vtterly cast downe, and for euer?

Now followeth the description of her eternall desolation, which is by deniall of those things which are in the cities inhabited: Wee knowe that rich and mightie cities are full of mirth and iolitie: There be harpers, and other musitians, there bee pipers and trumpetters. These are denyed vnto great Babell, it is sayd, that there shall neuer bee the voyce or sound of these heard any more in her at all. The mirth then of Rome is come to an ende. Shee hath been full of these, euen as the Lady of the world, wanting no pleasant delights. There hath been mirth vpon mirth, and all sweete melodie: but now farewell all this for euer and euer. Shee hath raigned ouer the world, shee hath mustred her armies, and the stately sound of trumpets hath been heard in her: but now all shall bee husht. Here is

one

one note then of vtter desolation. Then to another: And no craftsman of whatsoeuer craft he be, shall be found and more in thee. A citie may stand without melodie or pleasant musicke: but it hath not been seene. Put case it might, yet this cutteth downe Rome vtterly, and sheweth her extreame desolation, that there shall neuer be found in her any artificer of what trade soeuer. Can any citie stand without artificers? Who shall build and repayre their houses? who shall furnish them with houshould stuffe? what shal they do for their apparell and other necessaries? In Babell there shall be none of all these, therefore she shall not be inhabited, but lye desolate for euer. Vnlesse we will imagine that a citie may stand, and the people liue in the same, without the vse of those things which the artificers of all trades doe make and vtter. It may bee some kind of trade being wanting, people might make shift to liue: and therefore it is sayd here, that in great Babylon there shall not bee any one artificer of what trade soeuer, which sheweth her vtter desolation.

Then further it is added, *And the sound of a mill shall bee heard no more at all in thee.* This is yet a further note of an vtter destructiō. Of all necessaries the people must haue bread, or els how shall they liue? If they haue bread, it must come this way, that they haue mils to grinde their corne of which their bread is to be made. And he sayth that in Rome, which is great Babell, there shall neuer bee heard any more at all the sound of a mill. There shall be no more grinding, there shall be no more baking: who then shall dwell there? The Popes, the proud Cardinals and other great prelates, as the Emperours before them, haue long time been pampered and fed in her with the finest flower of wheate. Many others of great estate haue liued daintily within her palaces. The millers and the bakers haue gayned much, and liued euen like gentelmen, through the abundance of her delicacie: all this shall be quite cut off, the sound of a mill shall no more bee heard in her at all. Desolate then, destroyed, wasted, and not inhabited of any, shall shee lye for euer.

Here is yet further added, *And the light of a candle shall shine no more in thee at all.* God giueth vs the cleere and comfortable light of the Sunne by day, by which men see to walke, to busie themselues, and to performe all their works and necessarie affaires of this life. When the night commeth, and darknes ouer spreadeth the face of the earth, then are they faine to vse the artificiall light of fire and candle. Without these they can see to doe nothing, they cannot well stirre about, all is dolefull and dumpish, and therefore wee see that the vse of the candle is very necessarie and great, in all cities, townes and villages. Hereupon it doth followe, that seeing the light of a candle shall neuer shine any more in Rome, that Rome shall lye desolate and forsaken for euer. There shall bee nothing but horrour and darknes, none shall dwell there to shut vp his windowe by night for to light a candle.

There is yet one thing more, and that is, *And the voyce of the bridegrome and of the bride, shall be heard no more in thee at all.* If cities be neuer so populous, yet if there be no generation, they must needes in short time come to be desolate and emptie.

THE REVELATION.

emptie. For men doe weare away, and continuance is by a new supplie that ariseth: As Salomon saith, One generation passeth away, and another commeth, but the earth abideth for euer, Ecclesiast. 1. Well, to shew that Babylon shall not be inhabited, it is here sayd, the voyce of the bridegrome and of the bride, shall be no more heard in thee at all. There shall be no more marriage in Rome, there shall be no more procreation of children, which may succeede and inherite the houses and lands and roomes of their fathers. In all these things then Rome shall be cast downe and layd desolate. There shall be none to inhabite, there shall be no buildings, there shall be nothing but vtter and horrible desolation. These bee very heauie things denounced against so great, so mightie, and so glorious a citie. And least any might thinke that here is ouermuch rigour and seueritie, the holy Ghost againe repeateth briefly the causes of this destruction, that all men may see that shee hath deserued no lesse. There bee three causes set downe, the first is in these words, For thy marchants were the great men of the earth. What fault is there in this, that her marchants were growne so great? Is the greatnes of the marchants so foule and so detestable a thing? Verely the greatnes of marchants is not simply in it selfe, if we consider the matter generally, to be condemned, but here in the Church of Rome it dooth argue a most hainous offence: And that is, that they in the poperie set all things to sale, euen Christ himselfe and all holy things, and the soules of men. They had a number of false wares wherewith they deceiued the people: they turned all into a very matte. The holy Ghost noteth their abominable filthie lucre in a word, when he sayth, thy marchants were the great men of the earth. All that professe the feare of God in simplicitie, do abhorre, and crye out vpon that buying and selling of all things in the poperie. What infinite treasures did the Popes themselues heape vp by many things that they sold? And it is wonderfull to consider the prices which they set vpon their wares. They would and did for money dispense, and giue pardon for all offences. It is most horrible to be spoken. The Cardinals, the Bishops, the Abbots, the Monkes, the Friers & the priests, with sundrie other sorts, had their packes full of wares which they made money of, and in such plentie; that many of them did grow exceeding rich. Marueile not therefore that here is noted as one cause of the vengeance of God vpon the Romish Church, that her marchants were growne to be the great men of the earth: seeing her sale and marchandize of all things hath been such, that we may wonder that the Lord hath spared them so long.

Then followeth the second cause of this vengeance vpon her, in these wordes, And with thine inchauntment were deceiued all nations. This is a wonderfull abomination, which hath drawne the heauie indignation of almightie God vpon her, that this Rome, and this Romish synagogue hath played the witch, and by her witchcraft hath bewitched all nations, and seduced them to commit whoredome with her. The Popes of Rome and their clergie haue set vp and maintained their vsurped power, with lyes, with sleights, and with the illusions of the deuill: and that the nations and kingdoms of the earth did beleeue them, the holy Ghost calleth

leth it a witcherie. And verely if Satan had not euen bewitched the minds of men, how could they haue doted in such sort vpon so foule a strumpet? Looke whatsoeuer she offred in her golden cuppe, of errors, of heresies, of superstition, and of idolatrie, or of any spirituall whoredomes, wherewith she did corrupt and pollute the holy worship of God, the seduced and bewitched nations did receiue and drinke vp the same greedily. O the filthie whoredomes and most foule abominations, into which she drew the people, hauing so bewitched their mindes. And now shall she for the same, receiue her iudgement, and beare the burthen of the vengeance of God, which shall destroy and lay her desolate for euer. Then we see two causes of her extreame miserie: the first, that they set all things to sale: the second, that they bewitched with the illusions of Satan, the mindes of the people in all kingdomes, and seduced them to the worshippe of deuils: and now the third cause remayneth which is not the least, which concerneth their crueltie against the holy seruants of God, whose bloud they haue shed. It is expressed in these words, And in her was found the bloud of the Prophets, and of the Saints, and of all that were slaine vpon the earth. Is not here a sufficient cause of destruction? Is not here a bloudie citie? For when he sayth, that the bloud of the Prophets and of the Saints was found in her, it is not to be taken as the papists doe glorie, that they haue the treasure of the Church, they haue the bloud and the merits of the martyrs, which for money they bestowe; but that indeede Rome hath shed the bloud of Gods seruants, and is guiltie thereof. In that sense he saith, the bloud is found in her, it is vpon her, shee is defiled with it, the Lord God hath sought and found it out. And now since the comming of Christ, what citie can the papists shew vnto vs that hath shed the bloud of the Prophets and Saints, but Rome? In olde time, who shed the bloud of so many thousand Christians in all lands, but the Emperours of Rome? Was not all done by their authoritie? The papists themselues, do confesse this, for it is so cleere that it cannot be denyed. In these latter dayes, the slaughters and persecutions that haue been for the Gospell in all lands, by whose power and authoritie haue they been, but of the popes of Rome? Rome shed the bloud of old, Rome doth shed the bloud in these dayes. Rome therefore is great Babel here spoken of, that shall bee destroyed for murthering the Saints of God. Other Babell so guiltie of bloud, they can shew none. And thus wee see the causes of her destruction, the Lord Iesus for his chosen sake, bring it speedily to passe. Amen.

THE

THE REVELATION.

THE XLI. SERMON.
CHAP. XIX.

1 *And after these things, I heard a great voyce of a great multitude in heauen, saying, Halleluiah, saluation, and glory, and honour, and power, be to the Lord our God:*

2 *Because his iudgements are true and righteous, for he hath condemned the great whore, which did corrupt the earth with her fornication, and hath auenged the bloud of his seruants shed by her hand.*

3 *And againe they said Halleluiah, and the smoake of her torments rose vp for euermore.*

4 *And the foure and twentie Elders and the foure beasts fell downe, and worshipped God that sate on the throne, saying, Amen, Halleluiah.*

5 *Then a voice came out from the throne, saying: Praise our God all his seruants, and ye that feare him, both small and great.*

6 *And I hearde like the voice of a great multitude, and as the voice of many waters, and as the voice of strong thundringes, saying Halleluiah: for our Lord God almighty hath raigned.*

7 *Let vs be glad and reioice, and giue glory to him: for the mariage of the Lambe is come; and his wife hath made her selfe readie.*

8 *And to her was granted, that she should be arayed with pure fine linnen and shining: for the fine linnen is the righteousnes of the Saints.*

9 *Then he saide vnto mee, Write, Blessed are they which are called vnto the Lambes supper. And he said vnto me, These wordes of God are true.*

10 *And I fell before his feete to worship him: but he saide vnto me, See thou doe it not: I am thy fellow seruant, and of thy brethren which haue the testimonie of Iesus. Worship God: for the testimonie of Iesus is the spirite of prophecie.*

Ehaue seene in the former chapter the destruction of greate Babel painted out, and the lamentation, howling and mourning that her louers and friends do make for her. Now in this chapter in that which I haue read vnto you, here is set forth on the contrarie parte the ioy, the reioycing, the triumph, the praysing, and the magnifying of the name of God by all the heauenly companies of Angels and of blessed soules, and by all the faithfull vpon earth, for her fall and destruction, in that God hath

iudged

iudged her. Her deſtruction is taken heauily of them that loue her: but moſt ioy-full it is vnto all that loue God, and his glory. And that we may know how the holy companies in heauen are affected with the downfall of this filthie harlot, all is by viſion opened and reuealed vnto Iohn, and hee teſtifieth it in writing vnto vs, all things in order. This is no ſmall fauour, theſe be not trifles, that the Lord doth reueale vnto vs, what the heauenly companies doe. Let vs be attentiue that we may ioyne with them.

There be thouſand thouſands of holy Angels, as the holy ſcripture doth teach, there be many ſoules of the Patriarks and other holy men, and for this cauſe Saint Iohn heareth a great voyce of a great multitude, for all ioyne together in praiſing the high God. And although they bee manie, yet it is not a confuſed voice that they vtter, but a moſt ſweete and pleaſant harmonie, in which hee vnderſtandeth euery word, as well as if the voice were vttered onely by one. This is miraculous, euen to teach, that the praiſes of God are ſet forth in moſt excellent and pure maner, without all confuſion, among the heauenly companies. The firſt word which they vtter is *Halleluiah*. It is an hebrue worde, which is compounded of *Hallelu*, which is, praiſe ye; and *iah*, which is God. Whereby ye may ſee that they doe firſt incite and ſtirr vp each other to praiſe and magnifie the Lord. For this is the effect of true zeale, where the creature loueth God indeed with ſome integritie, not onely to glorifie him, but alſo to call vpon all others to doe the ſame. They all crie out, *Halleluiah*, that is praiſe ye the Lord. And then they vtter his praiſe thus, Saluation, and glorie, and honour, and power, bee to the Lorde our GOD. Heere be foure words in which they ſet forth his praiſe. In the firſt, they aſcribe vnto him ſaluation. For he is the onely Sauiour, all health and ſaluation commeth from him alone. Both men and Angels haue their ſaluation from him. There is no creature which doth ſaue it ſelfe. And here the ſpeciall occaſion is, that hee doth ſaue his choſen ſeruants, euen his whole Church, from the tyrannie of Antichriſt, and from the cruell dragon.

Then next they aſcribe vnto him glory and honour. For who is worthie of glory and honour but he alone? There be many glorious and honorable things in his Angels, and in his Saints, but they haue them not of themſelues, he is the fountaine they haue receiued them from him, and vnto him is the praiſe, the glory & the honor to be giuen for the ſame. The papiſts are all in worſhipping, honouring, and glorifying the creatures: and vainglorious men ſtand vpon their owne worthines, and couet to be magnified: but the heauenly company is whole in glorifying God. Let vs (beloued) eſchew ſuch vaine glorie, let vs flie from ſuch abominable popiſh ſacriledge, and ioyne with this heauenly companie in glorifying and praiſing our God.

Laſtly, they aſcribe the power to the Lord God in this heauenly praiſe. There be creatures which are ſtrong and mighty in power: but in God we liue, we moue, and haue our being, as Saint Paul teacheth, Act. 17. ſo that all power is from him. Looke whatſoeuer great thing is done by any might, (as here the caſting downe of great Babel) whatſoeuer the inſtruments be that he vſeth, either men or Angels,

the

THE REVELATION. 367

the whole glory redoundeth to God, in as much as they haue all their mightinesse from him. This praise being thus sounded forth to God, there is ioyned therewith, and rendred a cause, in these wordes: For true and righteous are his iudgements: for he hath condemned the great whore, which did corrupt the earth with her fornication, and hath auenged the bloud of his seruants shed by her hand. Is not here great cause why his glorious praise should bee sounded forth? Hee is the iudge of the whole world, he hath threatned seuere vengeance against all impietie, and in time he doth execute the same, thereby manifesting that his iudgements are true, and shall not faile. Hee doth oftentimes deferre them, but in the ende they come. Moreouer, when his wrath is poured forth, it seemeth to flesh and bloud, to be with ouermuch rigour and seueritie: but all the holy Angels and Saints doe plainely behold, and so they proclaime, that his iudgements vpon the wicked are righteous and iust. The torments indeed which they suffer and endure are most grieuous, but no more then they haue deserued, & that doth all this heauenly companie acknowledge. True and righteous (say they) are his iudgements. If any thing do trouble vs when either wee behold the heauie wrath of God almightie vpon the wicked, or remember what he doth threaten against all the workers of iniquitie: call to minde how the whole heauenly companies do subscribe to his iudgements as true & righteous: and hold this as a most firme and vndoubted principle, that if any thing do seeme otherwise vnto vs, it is because we are corrupt and blind, and that when we are fully set free from all burthen of corruption, we shal iudge euen as the holy Angels doe. Wee cannot now see into the righteous waies of our Lord God, as wee shall then: and therefore wee must now for the time rest in this, that wee are sure there is no vnrighteousnes with God. Here wee must note then further, that the whole heauenly companies doe laud and magnifie the Lord God, for his iudgements: For he doth shew forth his glory, not in the riches of his mercy alone which he extendeth vnto many of his creatures, but also in the seueritie of his iudgements. His vnspeakable glory doth vtter it selfe on both sides: and all his holy ones do proclaime it.

And then they come to the particular, saying, For he hath condemned the great whore. All this magnifying then of God is for condemning and destroying Rome and the Romish Synagogue: for that is great Babell the mother of whoredomes and abominations of the earth. And here they recite two generall heads of her impieties, for which the Lord God in iustice doth execute this vengeance vpon her. The one is, that shee corrupted the earth with her fornication, which hath been sundrie times mentioned: because it is a thing most detestable before the Lord. His word and the true light thereof was spread by his faithfull seruants farre and neere among the nations: his pure worship was set vp and imbraced of many. Rome vnder the persecuting Emperours a long time did impugne, but could not preuaile. Afterward rose vp the vsurped power of the popes, and by them this whorish citie bewitched and seduced the nations and kingdomes of the earth, and led them into idolatrie and false religion, euen vnto spiritual whoredome: and this is it which they say, that shee had corrupted the earth, with her fornication. Is shee not

worthy

worthie to bee destroyed with horrible destruction? Is there any pitie to bee taken vpon her, which hath corrupted so many great kingdomes with her fornication? Yea are not all the seruants of God to reioyce at the destruction of such an one? It is no malice, it is no want of charitie, to wish the vtter downfall and subuersion of Rome, and of those Romish Antichristian lawes, yea and of so manie wicked popish enemies of the Church and Gospell, as in obstinate malice persecute the truth: vnlesse we will affirme (which is most wicked) that the holy Angels and blessed Saints are in malice and doe want charitie: seeing all these doe glorifie and praise God for the same. What greater perfection in the creature, then to be like them? Are wee not taught to pray, Thy will bee done in earth, as it is in heauen?

And now marke the second generall head which they recite of her impieties? And hath (say they) auenged the bloud of his seruants, shed by her hand. It was matter euen enough to moue all creatures that loue the glory and truth of God, to be glad and to praise him for the destruction of so monstrous a whore, which had corrupted the earth with her fornication: but yet here is further matter as yee see added: and that is her great crueltie in shedding the bloud of Gods seruants. Doth not the innocent bloud of so many thousands of holy Martyrs cruelly murthred by the heathen Emperours of Rome in former times, and of latter times by the Popes, call and crie aloud in the eares of the Lord for vengeance vpon that bloudie citie? Is it not euen the office of God the righteous iudge to bee auenged? Is it not then our part to wish for the time in which it shall bee accomplished, and when it is come, together with all Gods holy seruants in most reioycing manner to glorifie his holy name for it? The Lorde open our eies more and more, that we may see cleerely the filthie whoredomes of Rome, how shee hath corrupted the earth with the same, and how horrible the crueltie is that shee exercised vpon the true worshippers of God, that so we may more earnestly, euē long to see the wrath of God powred foorth vpon her in full measure: and with these heauenly companies, ascribe saluation, glory, honour, and power, to the righteous iudge for the same.

It followeth, and againe they said, *Halleluiah*. At the first entrance of their praise which they offer vp to God, they beganne with *Hallelniah*, declaring their vehement zeale which they haue to set forth his glory, in that they stir vp and prouoke each other to the same. And now when they haue ended, they vtter *Halleluiah* againe. What doth this teach vs? It doth teach vs that the holy Angels and all the blessed companie in heauen do neuer cease praising and glorifying the Lord God. Their loue, their zeale, & their delight neuer diminished, but when they haue vttered his praise, they call for it againe, saying, praise ye the Lord. They haue neuer done, they neuer waxe wearie, they neuer slacke. Our case while we liue here is far differing, for partly through blindnes, wee see not how worthie hee is of all glorie and praise: and partly through the remnants of corruption which remaine, wee haue small delight to magnifie him, and we do soone waxe wearie. But when we shall be made perfect like to the Angels in heauen, then shall it be otherwise with

vs.

THE REVELATION.

vs. For then shall the whole ioy and delight of our heart, be to glorifie God. And that wherein the creature doth take delight, it doth not waxe wearie of. Maruaile not therefore when yee heare in the scripture, that the holy Angels cease not day and night, saying, holy, holy, holy, Lord God almightie: for it is with exceeding delight. There is nothing so sweete and pleasant, there is nothing so full of ioy, as it shall be vnto vs to glorifie God without ceasing and intermission. Wee shall with full affection sound out *Halleluiah*, saluation, and glorie, and honour, and power, be to the Lord our God, for his iudgements are true and righteous, and his mercie endureth for euer, and when we haue done, we shall still retorne and say, *Halleluiah*. This shall bee our whole delight, as we are here taught, when hee saith, and againe they said, *Halleluiah*.

Then there came a voyce (saith hee) out from the throne, saying, praise our God all his seruants, and yee that feare him, both small and great. This voyce commeth out from the throne, but yet not vttered by him that sitteth vpon the throne, but by some of those glorious Angels which are sayd to be in the middest of the throne, and round about the throne, chapter 4. The voyce, as yee see, saith, praise our God, so that the vtterer thereof ioyneth himselfe with those whom hee calleth vpon as a seruant of the same God: which doth not agree to any of the persons in the blessed trinitie. It is a most sweete voyce, mouing and stirring vp all the seruants of God to praise him, euen all that doe feare him, of what estate, or degree, or condition so euer they be: for it is said, both small and great. God almightie is so worthie of all praise and glorie, and it is so much the duety of all creatures to sound it forth, that here is no stay nor intermission. For vpon the vttering of this sweete voyce, it followeth, that Saint Iohn heard like a voyce of a great multitude, and as the voyce of many waters, and as the voyce of strong thunderings, saying, *Halleluiah*, for our Lord God almightie hath raigned. Then this voyce was not vttered in vaine, it was not without effect, for the multitude of Gods seruants sound forth such a strong praise, or so mightilie stirre vp each other to praise him, that Saint Iohn compareth it to the voyce of many waters, and vnto the voyce of strong thunderings. These are mightie voyces: but it may bee said, where are these heard vpon earth? where doth so great a multitude so strongly praise the Lord, and with so mightie courage and delight? If a man looke vpon the multitudes which are vpon the face of the earth, hee shall heare them sweare and curse, and abuse the name of God generally. Hee shall finde few that with vehement affection doe praise him. Yea if we respect the publike assemblies, in which they sing psalmes, and praises to God, the greater part doe sing with the mouth and outward tune, and not with the melodie of the heart. And it is not the outward voyce that ascendeth to God, but the sincere affection of the minde: when men with a true faith, and feruent loue of the glory of God, doe sound forth his praise. If these be thin sowne, where is this multitude which make this thundering noise? I answere, that albeit the true worshippers of God be scattered thin vpon the earth, yet as they meete in the vnitie of faith, so their praises doe meete together, and ascend vp vnto the Lord God. The voyce com-

Bb meth

meth from the throne which willeth vs to praise our God. Let vs looke vpon the worthines and glory of his praise. Let vs delight therein. And although we light vpon few in comparison which doe feare and honor him, yet let it not discourage vs, as though our praises should be weake and slender: but know that they meete together with the praises of all the saints, and ascend vp so strongly as it were with the voyce of mightie thunderings. This doth also teach vs what an acceptable thing it is to God, that his seruants doe praise him. He is to be worshipped, to be honored, to be glorified, and to be praised aboue all: and no greater thing is there for vs to doe. It is the ende for which wee are created and redeemed, that wee should set forth his glorious praise: and it is our glorie and felicitie, as ye may see in the reason which is added in these words, for our Lord God almightie hath raigned: If God by his almightie power getteth the victorie ouer all his enemies and doth raigne, it is that which we are to reioyce and to glorie in, and to praise him for. And why? Because wee are partakers of the same. He breaketh downe and destroyeth the power of the dragon, of Antichrist, of sinne and of death, euen the power of all our enemies. He doth draw vs out of their hands, from vnder their tyrannie, yea euen from endles miserie, and lifteth vs vp into glorie, to raigne with his most blessed sonne. Is not this a kingdome of grace? Is not this a ioyfull kingdome? Are we not to praise and magnifie him for the same, seeing it is to our endles ioy and felicitie? The whole church is taught by our sauiour Christ to pray with ardent desire, Let thy kingdome come. Tread downe O Lord all thine enemies, breake downe the kingdome of the diuell: raigne ouer the mighty tyrants and subdue them. Let them not tyrannize any longer ouer thy chosen, but aduance and lift them vp out of all oppressions into glorie, that thy glorie may bee magnified aboue all. Being taught to pray thus, as for the chiefest matters of all, which we are to long for, when God bringeth them to passe, shall not all honour and praise, and glorie bee founded forth vnto him in heauen and earth, both by men and Angels? Then yee see here is great cause rendred of his praise. So long as Satan hath a kingdome, and so long as his ministers euen Antichrist and others doe raigne, there is much dishonour to the trueth, and great oppression to the church, whereby the seruants of God are cast into heauines and sorrow: When the Lord God destroyeth the power of these tyrants, so that they cannot hurt any more, then is he said to receiue his kingdome, which commeth with such aboundance of blessings vpon all that feare him, that there is exceeding ioy and exultation, and praising of the high name of God. And therefore they say, let vs bee glad and reioyce, and giue glorie to him, for the mariage of the Lambe is come, and his wife hath made her selfe readie. Here is as yee see, more particularly set forth the matter of ioy, and of glorifying God, vnder the mariage of Christ and his Church. He hath betrothed himselfe vnto her of olde; she is his spouse, as Salomon plentifully setteth forth in his song: and now commeth the time to solemnize the mariage. It hath been the maner of olde, both in Israel, and among the Gentiles, that first for a time there was a contract, a promise of matrimonie of each party to other, and then after that, a day was appoynted, in which they

did

did celebrate the mariage: So long as the church is in this world, she is but betrothed to Christ, and then is the mariage when he taketh her vnto him, into the possession of the heauenly glorie, which shall be at the day of iudgement. For so soone as the mariage is celebrated, the wife entreth with her husband, to bee partaker of all that hee possesseth. And therefore it is here said, that the mariage of the Lambe is come. Shee shall now no more, nor any of her children, be vnder affliction, being receiued into the heauenly inheritance. The mariage of the Lambe is come. He redeemed her with his blood, he hath washed her, and sanctified her, and made her a glorious church to himselfe by the same his blood: and therefore Saint Iohn calleth it the mariage of the Lambe: for all this he wrought as the vnspotted Lambe of God sacrificed vpon the crosse, which taketh away the sins of the world. Then further, it hath been euer the maner when a mariage was to be solemnized, that the bride doth prepare and decke her selfe with iewels and ornaments, and costly apparell: and accordingly it is said here, that the Lambes wife hath made herselfe ready. We must needes confesse that this is a thing most necessarie, that this bride should be decked and beautified: for her husband is most glorious and pure. There must be no spot or blemish, there must be no impurity, nor no deformitie, but all pure and glorious as is meete for the wife of such an husband. The decking and the ornaments wherewith shee maketh her selfe ready, are not such as the brides here in this world doe vse, which are the iewels and ornaments of golde, of siluer, of pearles, and of silks and precious garments, and of other like earthly and corruptible things: but they be heauenly, and incorruptible. And least we should be ignorant what her ornaments be, they are set forth in the next words which are these, and to her it was graunted that she should be arraied with pure fine linnen and shining. This is her decking wherewith she maketh her selfe readie. It may be said, is this the most precious and the most glorious attire, or is this incorruptible? Pure linnen and shining which in olde time they had, was very precious, but the brides of this world also had it, and it was corruptible. And there bee other ornaments more costly. I answere, that yee must not take this literally, for this pure shining linnen is but a borrowed speech to represent another thing. And so hee doth expound it, saying, the fine linnen is the righteousnes of the Saints. It is not then such fine linnen as is made and worne in this worlde. It is heauenly, it is incorruptible, it is glorious. But what is this righteousnes, or iustifications of the Saints? We know how the scripture teacheth that we are iustified or made righteous by faith in Christ. Our sinnes are washed away in his blood, his righteousnes is imputed vnto vs. And from this faith there proceede holy works which doe declare the same, and in that sense are sayd to iustifie. This teacheth vs how carefully we ought to prepare our selues againft the comming of our Lord Iesus, that we may be found holy and chast and pure before him, to come to this mariage. Now the Angell willeth Saint Iohn to write, that they are blessed which are called to the Lambes supper. Here are still borrowed speeches, to set forth the matter. It was the vse at a mariage, to make a great feast at night: and therefore all the heauenly ioyes vnto which Christ receiueth

ceiueth his church, are set forth vnder this word, the Lambes supper. Hee maketh them this feast at his mariage. This mariage feast replenished with all heauenly dainties lasteth for euer. There shall be ioyes and delights, world without ende. At the mariage of his sonne a man of dignitie and wealth, will doe all that he can for to entertaine the guests in the best maner. The kings of the earth then shew their glorie and magnificence: and therefore the kingdome of heauen is likened to a king that maried his sonne, Matth. 22. How great is the feast of a king at the mariage of his sonne? What royaltie is there? And what good thing is wanting that can be gotten for money? How great then is the banquet of the most high God, the King of all kings, and in comparison of whom all the mightiest princes are but beggers, at the mariage of his sonne? The liuing God is an infinite treasure of all good things, the abundance whereof, shall now be shewed forth in this great supper: and therefore Saint Iohn is first willed to write, that they be blessed which are called to the Lambes supper. And for confirmation he saith further vnto Iohn, these words of God are true. Here is a wonderfull great thing set before vs. Let vs take heede we depriue not our selues, and be found without the wedding garment. O beloued, labor for the holy faith, to be sanctified and made meete to come to this heauenly supper. Despise all these worldly vanities, and vaine delights, in comparison of it. For here is the honour, here is the life, here is the ioy and eternall felicitie, and the God of trueth hath promised them. Beleeue God, for his words, as the Angell saith here to Iohn, are true. Neuer doubt but that there is such a mariage, and such a supper prepared, and the happie guests shall be called thereunto.

In the next words, Saint Iohn doth record a fault which he himselfe did commit: namely how he fell downe before the feete of the Angell, to worship him. Where we shall see how also the Angell doth forbid him, shewing reason why he may not in any wise doe so. For when S. Iohn hath told what he did, and what he purposed, as that he fell downe before his feete to worship him: he sheweth also what the Angell sayd, as thus, See thou doe it not, I am thy fellow seruant, and of thy brethren which haue the testimonie of Iesus, worship God: for the testimonie of Iesus, is the spirit of prophecie. Vpon this scripture we are first to note, that it is for the speciall instruction and good of the whole Church, that Saint Iohn reporteth his owne fault. For be yee well assured, that where the holy scripture recordeth the errors, the slippes, and the falles of the most excellent seruants of God, it is for singular purpose, and for the necessarie instruction, and great good of the whole Church, euen of all Gods faithfull seruants. We may first consider here how easie the fall is vnto Idolatrie, when so notable a seruant of God as Saint Iohn doth slippe. He meant not to worship the Angell as God, but being rauished with the glory of the Angell which he beholdeth, he forgetteth himselfe, and is ready to offer vnto him some diuine worship: as wee see Act. 10. How when the Angell of God had willed Cornelius to send for Peter, and saide hee should tell him what he should doe, that when Peter came, he fell at his feete to doe that which is not to be done vnto any creature. The heathen people, being

left

left to walke in the vanitie of their owne minde, did worshippe wheresoeuer any diuine gift did appeare in any creature: and this led them to make many gods. And is it not to bee wondred at in blinde men, when this great Apostle at the brightnes and glorie of the Angell forgetteth himselfe? The papists in the church of Rome haue fallen vnto as grosse idolatrie as euer did the heathen, if not grosser: for wheresoeuer any excellent diuine gift hath been in any creature, or imagined to haue been, there vnto that creature they offer diuine worship, which belongeth onely to God. They worship Saints and Angels, they pray vnto them, they dedicate Churches and Temples vnto them: they make them mediatours, patrons, and defendours. They bowe downe also vnto images, and dead blocks, they make supplication vnto them, which, as the prophet saith, haue eares and heare not, eyes and see not, &c. They doe also worship reliques and dead bones, of such as either haue been holy men, or at the least whom they haue so esteemed. Should I stand here to reckon al things which they worship with diuine honour, which is due to God alone, I should be very tedious vnto you: for how many sorts of base creatures thinke ye I might rehearse of wood, and of iron and such like, before I come to the stinking breeches of Frier Francis which they doe worship?

Well, beholde now in the second place (after ye haue obserued how easily men fall into idolatrie, as to worship creatures in which there appeare diuine graces) what a singular goodnes and prouidence of God here sheweth it selfe towards his Church. This prophecie was giuen to instruct and to arme the true seruants of God, against the idolatrous kingdome of Antichrist, that they might not bee drawne away from his pure and holy worship, vnto the worshipping of creatures. Saint Iohn that receiueth it as the holy seruant of God, and as the penman of the holy Ghost, doth slip, and is readie to worship a creature. He recordeth this his error vnto all posteritie, to take notice of it. And not onely that, but he sheweth also how the Angell did forbid him, and shew reason why neither hee nor any other might doe it. Beholde here (as I said) the singular goodnesse and prouidence of God, that the slip of his seruant should be an occasion euen in that booke which painteth out Antichrist, to cut downe all Antichristian worship: for by the words of the Angell vnto Iohn, al the whole poperie is ouerthrowne, which is in adoring creatures. For if it bee not lawfull to bow downe and to worship so glorious an Angell, then is it not lawfull to worship any Saint. If it be not lawfull to worship those holie and excellent creatures, then is it not lawfull for to worship things which are baser, as images of gold and of siluer, of brasse, of wood and of stone: nor all those reliques and rotten bones. For it is a most cleere thing, that if any creature may be worshipped with religious worship, they bee those which are the highest in dignitie and glorie. But the words of this glorious Angell doe shew plainly that he may not in any wise be worshipped. See (saith he) that thou doe it not. And he doth not onely thus forbid him, but sheweth a reason, which is in these words: I am thy fellow seruant, and of thy brethren, which haue the testimonie of Iesus. Worship God.

O worthie speech to set vp the worship of God alone, which the wicked idolaters doe cauill at, but can neuer darken the cleerenes thereof. Thus it standeth, no fellow seruant is to haue that giuen vnto him by his fellow seruants which is due to their Lord: Then there is but one Lord ouer all, which is God. All his creatures yea euen the highest, those glorious Angels in heauen haue receiued from him all the good things which be in them, they be but his seruants, and the fellow seruants of his Saints. The fellow seruants vnder one Lord must not worship each other, and therefore the Angell saith, Worship God. There bee degrees of excellencie, of gifts, and of dignitie in men and angels, but yet they be all vnder one Lord whom they are to worship alone: which is here ratified thus: I am thy fellow seruant, see thou doe it not, worship God. The testimonie of Iesus, saith he, is the spirit of prophecie. The Angell comming with this testimonie of Iesus, as the holy Apostles and Prophets did, saith he is their fellow seruant, hee commendeth to extoll and to magnifie the same Lord Iesus. What exclamation the papists make against vs that wee will not worship Angels and Saints, that wee will not bow nor kneele to their images, nor make our prayers vnto any but to God, al men doe know. O these heretikes, say they, these heretikes are not friends to the Saints and Angels, but doe hold from them their right and doe dishonour them. And these popish idolaters suppose that they doe highly delight and please the holy Angels and blessed Saints, when with sacriledge they ascribe vnto them the honour, the glorie and worshippe which is due to God alone. Whereas it is most certaine, that as it is the whole delight and ioy of the blessed companies in heauen to haue the glorie of the Lord magnified: so nothing doth more displease them; then when his worship and honour is giuen away from him, either to themselues or to any other creature. And all of them will say as this Angell sayth here; See ye doe it not, we are your fellow seruants, worship God.

This place being so cleere, and so strong against all idolaters, that with diuine worship doe adore Angels and Saints, and images of dead creatures, the Iesuites haue bent all the power of their wittes to weaken and to darken it by cauils, that so they may hold sillie ignorant papists still in their poperie. First, they make this distinction, that there is a diuine adoration called *Latria*, and that say they, is peculiar to God, and whosoeuer giueth it to any creature, committeth idolatrie. Then they say there is a religious worship inferiour vnto that, which is called *Dulia*, which they say is lawfully giuen vnto Angels and Saints, and to their images. This is a friuolous cauill: for in the Hebrew tongue, both in the second commandment, and in many other places of the olde Testament, this *Dulia*, which in the Greeke tongue signifieth seruice, is challenged peculiarly to God. And it is to bee proued, that in the ancient vse of the Greeke tongue *Latria*, and *Dulia* did signifie one thing, sauing that *Dulia* was vsed for the deeper subiectiō in seruice. Now say the Iesuites, Saint Iohn mistooke the Angell, for he tooke him to bee Christ, because he appeared vnto him in that sort, which we reade in the first chapter, and so offereth vnto him the highest worship called *Latria*, which the Angell forbiddeth,

deth, shewing that hee is not Christ. I answere, that to their former vaine distinction, here they adde an vntrueth: for that was Christ in the first chapter, and ye may see how S. Iohn saith in the beginning of chapter 17. that this Angell which sheweth him the damnation of the great whore, and before whom hee falleth downe, was one of the seuen Angels which had the seuen vials.

This cauill being answered, let vs come to another. They make an equalitie betweene Saint Iohn and the Angell in honour with God: so that the Angell knowing his great graces and merites before God, would not accept of any worship or submission at his hands: though he in humilitie did offer it, as againe in chapt. 22. which he would not haue done, if he had been precisely aduised by the Angel but a moment before, of error and vndutifulnes in his fact. If this bee so, why would not the Angell haue tolde it, that the Church might know how farre her children might proceede in worshipping of Angels? Nay, why doth hee speake so, as that he refuseth it at the hands not of Iohn alone, but of all that haue the testimonie of Iesus, yea of all the seruants of God: for he saith, chapter 22. that hee is the fellowe seruant of all that keepe the words of this booke. Then no Christian is to worship this Angell, but, as he willeth euery one, worship God. Doth the Angell say, thou shalt not doe it, thou art as good as I.? If he doe, because he saith, I am thy fellow seruant, then he maketh all the faithfull his equals, and so will bee worshipped of none. But say they, Abraham adored the Angels that appeared vnto him, Gen. 18. Iosua fell downe flat, and adored the Angell that appeared vnto him. I answere, Abraham did take them to be men, and bowed to giue them ciuil worship, which was vsuall and lawfull to bee done to men. It was the Lord himselfe which appeared to Iosua, as also to Moses in the bush. Men haue bowed downe before Kings and Prophets to giue them ciuill honour and reuerence, but otherwise not lawfully. But they demaund whether we ought not to carrie a religious reuerence vnto the holie Angels, vnto godly men, and vnto things sanctified? What a fond cauill is this, that because wee are to loue and reuerence the Angels, and so the Saints, that therefore we ought to kneele to them, to worship them with religious worship, and to make prayers vnto them. Are wee not to reuerence the holy Sacrament of Baptisme, and yet wil ye say that we must therfore kneele down to it and worship it? Let vs renounce that abominable idolatrie of poperie, let vs loue and reuerence both holy men and blessed Angels, but as the Angell willeth, let vs worship God.

THE XLII. SERMON.
CHAP. XIX.

11 *And I saw heauen open, and behold a white horse, and he that sate vpon him, was called faithfull and true, and he iudgeth and fighteth righteously.*

12 *And his eyes were as a flame of fire, and on his head were many crownes, and he had a name written, which no man knoweth but himselfe.*

13 *And he was clothed with a garment dipped in blood: and his name is called the word of God.*

14 *And the warriors which are in heauen, followed him vpon white horses, clothed with fine linnen and pure.*

15 *And out of his mouth went a sharpe sword, that with it he should smite the heathen: for he shall rule them with a rod of iron: for he it is that treadeth the winepresse of the fiercenes and wrath of God almightie.*

16 *And he had vpon his garment, and vpon his thigh a name written, the King of Kings, and Lord of Lords.*

17 *And I saw an Angell stand in the Sunne, who cried with a loud voyce, saying to all the fowles that did flie by the middest of heauen, Come and gather your selues together, to the supper of the great God,*

18 *That ye may eate the flesh of kings, and the flesh of the high captaines, and the flesh of the mightie men, and the flesh of horses, and of them that sit vpon the, and the flesh of all free men, and of bondmen, of small and great.*

19 *Then I saw the beast, and the Kings of the earth, and their armies gathered together to make warre against him that sate on the horse, and with his armie.*

20 *And the beast was taken, and with him the false prophet which wrought miracles before him, with which he seduced them that receiued the beasts mark, and them that worshipped his image, both these were cast aliue into a lake that burneth with brimstone.*

21 *And the rest were slaine with the sworde of him that sitteth vpon the horse, which commeth out of his mouth: and all the birdes were filled with their flesh.*

IT was tolde vs in the eleuenth chapter of this booke, that the beast ascending out of the bottomles pit, should make warre against the ministers of Christ, and ouercome them. And againe it is said in chapter 13. that it was giuen to him, to warre with the Saints, and to ouercome them. This hath been fulfilled and is past,

and

and ouercomming them. The conquerors shall now be conquered, the destroyers shall be (as I said) all destroyed. First S. Iohn faith, that he saw heauen open, and from thence commeth forth this mightie captaine and his armie. We haue seene before in this booke, that the beast ariseth out of the bottomles pit, all his power is from hell, euen of the diuell: and now the power that shall cast him downe, and destroy him is of God from heauen: and therefore Iohn seeth heauen open, & this armie comming foorth to the battell. As the bottomlesse pit before was opened chap. 9. so here heauen is opened. And as the great captaines, & mightie warriors, ride vnto battell vpon strong horses: so here our great Lord Iesus comming forth to warre against Antichrist, appeareth in vision vpon a white horse, and all the warriors on his side, and also vpon white horses: which is to shew, that hee commeth with his armies, very swiftly and strongly to the battell. By the white horse vpon which Christ rideth, is figured the ministrie of the Gospell: for by that the light of the trueth of Christ, and the power of his grace are caried and spread swiftly ouer the large dominions of Antichrist, and do disclose all his errors and filthie abominations, and so ouercommeth and destroyeth the beast. This battell is begun already somewhat before our time, and is now in fighting, and shall continue and proceede, casting those enemies downe more and more, euen to the day of judgement. Wee haue seene before how their citie Babell shall fall, euen so their poperie shall down and their power, yea and the papists in all countries shalbe so weakened, that they shall fall and be slaine by the sword, great multitudes of the. The Lord Iesus, I say, is come forth alreadie vnto this battell vpon his white horse. The blessed Lord put his spur to this horse, that he may yet run more swiftly to the casting downe of the Romish tyrants: it shall be the comfort of his Church.

Then next he setteth forth, that he that sitteth vpon this horse is called faithfull and iust. Verily he is most faithfull to performe al his promises, & nothing he doth but with perfect equitie and iustice. Concerning the former of these, he hath promised to his Church, that hee will roote out and vtterly destroy all her cruell enemies: and albeit he seemeth to forget his promise, because he hath let them range at pleasure so long: yet now at the last he maketh it euident and manifest vnto all how true he is of his promise, so that they publish his fame and praise herein: for, as Saint Iohn saith, he is called faithfull. All that haue eyes doe proclaime this his fame. Likewise the vengeance which he executeth vpō these wicked aduersaries, which is the other poynt, although it may seeme vnto some, to be with extreame rigour and crueltie, yet indeede it is with iustice, it is no more then they haue deserued: and therefore in the next words it is added, that hee iudgeth and fighteth righteously. The kings vpon earth oftentimes doe seeke to make warre each vpon

other

other to doe wrong, to winne vnlawfully and to possesse kingdomes which are not their owne: but this king dealeth not in his warres any way iniustly. There is iust cause why hee should come foorth vnto the battell against the beast, and the false prophet, and against the kings of the earth which take their part. They bee most wicked enemies, euen set against his glorie, his trueth, and his Church: and haue done all the harme and mischiefe which they could any way bring to passe. And they are not satisfied with all the euils and abominations which they haue committed, but they studie and bend their whole minde, by all euill practises to worke greater harme. Well, they shall not haue their will, this captaine commeth foorth against them, to execute true iudgement, and to fight righteously.

In the next place he saith, that his eyes are as a flame of fire: which teacheth that he doth see into all corners of that darke confused kingdome of poperie, he seeth through all those pretenses and shewes which those Romish seducers set vpon matters pretending the zeale of his name and glorie, to seduce the ignorant. And moreouer, whereas that Antichristian generation is exceeding subtill, and in deepe secret conspire mischiefe continually against the true Church, the piercing sight of this our great captaine doth beholde the same most cleerely (for nothing can bee hid from his eyes) and doth disappoynt them. How craftily the Iesuites haue practised treasons in this land, who is it that hath not heard? And how our Lord Iesus fighting against them, in defence and preseruation of his Church, hath with these his eyes like a flame of fire, espied out their secrets and brought them to light, wee haue all seene to our comfort. So that we may fully ground our selues vpon this, to our singular consolation, that although the Romish sort be wonderfull subtill, and full of many deepe sleights as the craftines of the olde serpent can affoord, in this battell which they make against the Church, yet wee neede not feare, seeing our great leader hath such eyes as doe pierce into their deepest secrets. Valiant men of warre are sometimes ouer reached by the craft of their enemies: but none can ouer reach this captaine, his sight is so cleere.

It is then further added, that hee hath vpon his head many crownes. Ye knowe that kings and conquerors are crowned. Here then is the great king of all kings, and the conqueror of conquerors, which is figured heere by that he hath vpon his head many crownes. He hath vanquished the diuell, and death and hell: hee hath made the proudest in the world among men for to stoope, and downe shall the beast and his companie goe, as not able any way to stand in his hands. The Popes haue vsurped great power, yea euen the power which is peculiar to the Lord Iesus: and therefore they haue worne triple crownes, as hauing kingly power in heauen, in earth and in purgatorie. For this their wicked and blasphemous sacriledge, the Lord Iesus commeth forth in battell against them to execute iust vengeance. Here commeth that Lord which hath the power in deede, euen hee that conquereth all his enemies, then downe goeth the beast with all his force, euen of necessitie. Let vs be wise then and ioyne with this Lord: for men would gladly be of that side which shall ouercome: and this side shall surely ouercome.

Then it is added, that he had a name written, which no man knew but himselfe.

Wher

THE REVELATION. 379

What is this name, but his infinit and incomprehensible glorie, and maiestie, and power, being eternall God ouer all equall with the father? There be none among men, nor yet among the holy Angels, that can knowe this name. Yet as yee see, S. Iohn saith that the name is written. All doe reade and know that he hath such a name: but know it or comprehend it, they cannot. He knoweth it, being the eternall wisedome of the father. For this ye must hold as an vndoubted principle, that the blessed Angels in heauē, which are said to behold the face of God, cannot behold him in his perfection: for he is infinit, and how can any creature comprehend that which is infinit? In the next part of the description, he sheweth how he is arayed, for in what manner of clothing he commeth: for he saith, he was clothed in a garment dipped in blood. This is the attyre of him that hath made slaughter of his enemies: for a mightie man which in battell slaieth with the sword, hath his garments sprinkled and stained with blood: and such as trode the wine-presse, the red iuyce of the grapes did staine their clothes. This great Lord of ours hath made slaughter of his enemies in all ages, and hath troden them like grapes in the winepresse of Gods wrath: and therefore comming foorth now to battell against the beast, and the kings of the earth which take his part, he is shewed in vision clothed with his warlike garment, all stained with blood, to represent what shall befall these enemies. This declareth that hee will now execute vengeance vpon them and destroy them. Then ye may see what his garment dipped in blood, doth pretend. And wee must note, that all this is according to the ancient figure: for the Prophet Esay, chap. 63. bringeth in Christ, hauing made slaughter of the enemies of his Church, with his garments all stained with their blood. The wicked papists now at pleasure doe blaspheme his trueth, and persecute those which doe professe it: they make small account of any threatning which hee hath vttered: but they shall finde him a'most terrible God of vengeance. His vengeance is here foreshewed in his garment. Woe be to all his enemies, when his garment is once put on: for how shall they escape? Let vs take heede that wee be not found in the campe of his enemies: as all those bee which impugne and hinder the course of his Gospell. Yea to be sure, that wee shall not bee found among the enemies, let vs fight valiantly on his side in maintenance of the holy faith, against all the wicked corrupters of the holy and pure religion, otherwise we doe not our dutie.

Then he addeth, that his name is called, the word of God. He had before, as we haue seene, a name that none did know but himselfe, which is his incomprehensible maiestie: and here hee is set foorth by a name that wee may vnderstand and know, and that is, hee is called the word of God. This is not to bee taken for that word of God which is written in the Bible, or which is pronounced: but as Saint Iohn speaketh in the first chapter of his Gospell, In the beginning was the word, and the word was with God, and the word was God. This word of God is very God himselfe, euen the eternall wisedome of the Father, the second person in the most glorious trinitie. He openeth and manifesteth all the counsels of God: he is the publisher of his will, in him; and by him th' father hath manifested himselfe to the world: whereby we may perceiue why he is called the word of God. For as in man, the counsels and intents, and purposes lye secret and vnknowne, vntill by word he vtter them, and it is his word that manifesteth the same: so the Lord Iesus as the essentiall worde, (which no similitude can expresse fully) openeth the counsels of the father. Antichrist, against whom hee commeth foorth to battell, chal'enged to himselfe this glorie, that what he vttered and decreed, it must be taken as the vndoubted trueth of God, and so robbed this great Lord of his honor, for which he will now be reuenged vpon him.

In the next place is shewed, how the warriors in heauen doe follow him, which be on his part. For although he bee of that power, that hee can alone without the helpe of any, destroy at once al his enemies, yea euen with the breath of his mouth: yet notwithstanding, he vseth the ministrie both of men and Angels, & hath great armies of noble warriors to fight against the beast. They are sayd to bee warriors in heauen, not that they bee onely the Angels: but because the ministers of the Gospell vpon earth, and all the right valiant men of warre which fight with the materiall sword against Antichrist, doe not fight for any earthly cause, nor with earthly power, but for the kingdome of heauen, and with heauenly armour: for those respects they are likewise sayd for to be warriors in heauen. All these follow the great captaine Iesus Christ, they fight vnder his banner, armed with his might, for his cause, and by his direction. These ride all vpon horses, they be swift, strong, and well appoynted also to the battell. Their horses bee white, which signifieth innocencie and puritie: for these fight not as men heere in the world commonly doe, led thereunto with furie and wrath, and with bloodie and cruell affections, or for vaine glorie: but with the loue and pure zeale of Gods glorie. Then may wee note, that as they haue a good cause, so they doe handle it well: they follow their captaine, and stand in the defence of the trueth, and of Gods holy worshjp against the Romish beast, with all integritie and simplicitie. O what a blessed thing it is, beloued, to be of this company, to fight vnder this captaine, with so holy and pure affection! Take courage and stand for the glorious Gospell, that wee may bee of this armie that follow Christ vpon white horses.

It is sayd further, that out of his mouth went a sharpe sworde, that with it hee should smite the heathen. This is the weapon which he dooth fight withall, with which he shall strike the heathen, euen all his prophane enemies. They bee Christians in name which worship the beast, but yet heathen in deede. This sworde commeth not out of any mouth but his, it is his owne mightie worde. It is verie sharpe, yea as it is sayd in the epistle to the Hebrewes, chapter 4. sharper then any two edged sword. With this he striketh and slayeth not onely wicked men, but euen the diuels. This pure word doth not only slay Antichrist with spirituall death, but also manifesteth and discloseth their abominations, and so weakeneth their multitude, and layeth them open to the materiall sword of princes. For in this last battell of Christ against the beast, there shall bee not onely a spirituall slaughter, but also a killing of their bodies here vpon earth with the sword in warres. In the next place here is a saying out of the second Psalme, that he shall rule them with a rod of iron. The Prophet Dauid in that Psalme describing the kingdom of Christ, vseth this speech, that he shall breake them with a scepter of iron, and dash them in peeces like a potters vessell. An iron mace doth easily beate an earthen pitcher all to sheards, and with such power shall Christ beate downe all the wicked, they shall be but euen like pot sheards. The enemies are very many, and they be mightie: for Satan mustereth great armies, but Christ Iesus alone is too strong for them all. They bee arrogant and proude, and lift vp themselues in their multitude and strength, as if they could doe at pleasure what they lust: and yet in very deede are but as earthen pitchers before him, when he shall strike them with his iron rod.

Here is also by another similitude expressed, how hee shall destroy all the wicked. The clusters of grapes are cut downe and cast together into the wine-presse, and then they do tread the presse to crush out the iuyce of them. Hell is the great wine-presse of the wrath of God, all the vngodly shall bee cast into it on heapes euen as clusters of grapes, and the Lorde Iesus shall (as he sayth here) tread this wine-presse of the fiercenes of the wrath of God almightie. There is yet one braunch of the description of this captaine remaining, which is, that he had vpon his garment, and vpon his thigh a name written, the King of kings, and Lorde of lords. This is a name of great dignitie and glorie; that he is King of kings, and the ruler ouer al rulers. The kings of the earth and the great men haue many vnder them which be their subiects: but these kings theinselues bee subiect vnto Christ, and he doth raigne ouer them. We see then what manner of one he is which here commeth foorth vnto battell; doubt not of the victorie; for who is it that shall withstande him? The beast and the false prophet are strong indeede, they haue kings on their side, they haue great armies and powers, they be fierce and cruell: but yet they shall all downe, here is one that is too hard for them all, if they were tenne thousand times as strong as they bee. And that followeth now in the text: as S. Iohn hath set forth the glorious description of this most mightie captaine, so now he commeth to shew the victorie which he obtaineth. And that we might the better consider of it, as of no small conquest, it is here proclaimed, described, and set forth in a right excellent and goodly manner.

I saw (sayth S. Iohn) an Angell stand in the Sunne. Here is the proclaimer of the victorie, and the place in which he stood for to proclaime it. It is an Angell, euen one of the heauenly ministers, which God hath appoynted to this work. And as they that proclaime any matter, seeke some place to stand in where they may bee best heard: so this Angell standeth in the Sunne. The Sunne giueth light to the whole world, it compasseth about, and the eyes of all are turned towards it, and therefore the fittest place to bee chosen for this purpose. But here it may be sayd, the battell is not yet fought, here is then proclamation of victorie, before the battell. Is that a right order? I answere, that in mens matters it is a preposterous order: but not in Gods matters. It hath fallen out oftentimes in the warres, when as princes haue gone to battell with their armies each against other, that the smaller armie and farre the weaker hath gotten the victorie. It is as it pleaseth the Lord God of hoasts to dispose. Wherefore in those battailes to triumph before the victorie, is no wisedom, because the euent of the warre is vncertaine. Ben-

hadad

hadad king of Aram, boasted against the king of Israel comming vnto battell. But the king of Israel sent him this word, Let not him that girdeth on his harneis boast, as hee that putteth it off, 1. King. 20. 11. And indeed Benhadad had sustained two great ouerthrowes, and yet there was such oddes in the armies, that it is said, The Aramites filled the countrie, but the children of Israel pitched before them like two little flocks of kiddes. The Lord God of hoasts, as I said, did often ouerthrow the stronger by the weaker. But now wee must note that the matter resteth not in any doubt at all in the battell of Christ against his enemies. He is most sure to o-uercome them: and therefore no preposterous order here to proclaime the victo-rie before the battell.

Then next let vs see after what manner this victorie is set foorth. It is vnder this figure of calling a great number of guests to a feast. When men are slaine in great number in the wars, their bodies lie as meate to the fowles of the ayre. Now here al the fowles are called, and promised a great supper made them by the great God. Their dainties are reckoned vp, euen the flesh of kings, of high captaines, of migh-tie men, of horses, and of their riders, of free men, of bondmen, of small and great. Here is their cheere. It may be demaunded, shall Christ ouerthrow them with a bodily slaughter? Is it not a spirituall sword with which he shall strike them? How then is here mention made that the fowles shall be filled with their flesh? I answer vnto this, that it is chiefly a spirituall slaughter that our Sauiour Christ will slay the withall, which is here figured out (according to the manner of this booke) by the bodily slaughters of great armies, where the dead bodies do lie and are meate to the fowles of the ayre: but yet the other slaughter is not excluded: for the word of God doth disclose them, and make them appeare so abominable, that the Christi-an princes shall in the defence of the Gospel make warre vpon, & slay thousands of thousands of them, & let them lie as meate for the fowles of the ayre. The Lord will ouerthrow them euery way: for many of them shal haue their blood shed vp-on the earth, and they shall al be slaine eternally. Now after the description of our captaine, and of the victorie which he shall obtaine; here followeth a briefe men-tion of the captaines and armies of the aduersaries, which are shewed vnto Iohn in vision also. For as it is with the kings of the earth when they go forth vnto the wars, that they bring their armies, where they meete together and try it out, so bere these armies doe meete. There is mustring, there is leuying of power, and there is mee-ting, and assembling, and preparing as fast as may bee on the enemies part. I saw (saith Iohn) the beast, and the kings of the earth, and their armies gathered toge-ther, to make warre against him that sate on the horse, and with his armie. Here ye see that which I noted in generall, that here is great preparation, and the meeting of the armies: and now we may obserue sundrie particulars. As first, the captaine of this armie appeareth, for hee sayth, I saw the beast. Christ commeth formost as the leader in the other armie, and here in this armie the beast: for the beast is their Generall. Some may demaund, Is not the diuell the graund captaine ouer all the armies of the wicked enemies of God? Doe they not all fight vnder his banner, and in the defence of his kingdome? How is it then that the beast is seene as the

chiefe

chiefe on this part? For answere vnto this, ye must consider these three things: first, that the diuell, as it is in chapter 13. hath giuen to the beast his power and throne, and great authoritie. Whereby wee are giuen to vnderstand, that Satan worketh by the beast, the beast is but his instrument which he vseth, and therefore Satan is not here excluded, although he appeare not in vision.

Then for the second, we may note, that in this vision here are shewed vnto Iohn, onely those which in open apparance make warre against the Gospell, & against those which professe it. Satan doth indeede worke all this warre which is made against our Lord: but he doth it closely. He stirreth vp the beast and the kings of the earth which take part with the beast and all their armies, but yet so as he seduceth them: for he doth not tell them plainly that they shall fight for him, to maintaine his kingdome, or to be his seruants, for that would take away their courage: Neither doth he let them vnderstand, that hee leadeth them against the Lord Iesus, against the most glorious Gospell of God, and against his Saints: for that were horrible, but he beareth them in hand that they shall fight for the Catholike faith, and for the Catholike Church, against heresies, and heretikes, and against newe learning. Thus I say, he seduceth them, and leadeth them vnto the battell against Christ. Then may ye note, that although he doe not appeare in the vision at this battell, because he worketh closely, yet he is their graund captaine, vnder whose banner they doe all of them fight.

The third thing then, why he is not here set forth, in this vision comming to this battell, is that he hath been so generall a doer In all ages, that here followeth a speciall vision for him in the next chapter. For as the beast and all his power is here ouerthrowne, so in the next chapter wee shall see how this great captaine ouer them all, euen the dragon, is taken, which set them all on worke. Thus may ye see some reasons, why he doth not in this vision appeare.

Now touching the beast heere spoken of, which is the captaine in this armie, with whom some kings doe ioyne, it is he which is set forth and described, chapter 13. it is the Romane Empire, both the former and the latter, that is both of the Emperours which were heathen, and of the Popes, as it is most euident in that 13. chapter. This beast hath beene the murderer of the Saints, euer since the time of our Sauiour Christ. And although the power of this beast, through the preaching of Gods holie worde, is greatly diminished, yet hee ceaseth not to warre still against Christ, and shall doe euen vntill he bee vtterly ouerthrowne: yea and moreouer wee see it euident, that some kings and great potentates shall still take his part, euen to the ende. Also marke how it is shewed Saint Iohn, that the kings and their armies are assembled with the beast, to fight against Christ. They ioyne close and fast together, they haue entered into a league, which they call the Holy League, and bound themselues by othe and vowe, to roote out all those that professe the holie Gospell, which they call heresie. It is greatlie to bee wished that all kings and princes and Churches which haue renounced that idolatrous tyrannie of Antichrist, and imbraced the holie Gospell, would ioyne as firmelie agaynst them. They doe not onely at this day ioyne so together, but also

also are so industrious and so full of their craftie sleights, and subtill deuises, and colourable shewes as it is wonderfull to consider. And shall they bee so diligent, and so forward in so bad a cause, euen to fight against Christ, and that to serue the diuell to their eternall destruction? And shall not we be as readie and forward to stand in the defence of the holie worship and glorie of the Lord our God, seeing it shall be vnto our euerlasting saluation? Shall they doe more for their rewarde with the diuell in hell, whose seruants they bee, and whom they doe obey: then we for the reward which Christ in heauen, whom as our most gracious Lord, wee ought most willing to serue? Let vs be euen ashamed to come behind these wicked souldiers of Antichrist, which here are gathered to the battell. Shall they bee more faithfull to their wicked Lord, then wee to our good Lord? They assemble to the battell, and it followeth presently, the beast was taken, and the false prophet with him. It is done without any difficultie to Christ, though their power be great: for he is of infinite power. Wee may note that here is a warre-like phrase vsed when hee saith the beast is taken, and with him the false prophet: for in the warres they vse to take the great captaines aliue if they can: so be they here taken aliue, not for to spare them, being so monstrous rebels against God, but for their greater torment, as we shall see it here also expressed.

But what shall we say to this, that here is mention of the beast, and of the false prophet also? If the beast comprehend all the Romane Empire, both the former which was of the heathen Emperours, and the latter which was of the Popes, who is this false prophet, that wrought miracles, that seduced them that worshipped the beasts image, and receiued his marke? Is not this false prophet the Pope and his Clergie, which seduced the world with lying wonders? Wee haue answered this before in the visions which haue bin shewed to S. Iohn, as in chapter 13. there were two beasts, the one with seuen heads, the other with two hornes like a lamb. That beast with two hornes is the papacie. He is a seuerall beast by himselfe, in that he exerciseth another power, besides the power of the heathen Emperors of Rome, and he is one head of the same beast, in that he set vp the image of that former beast, and exercised that power also which that former beast had done. And so the Angel, chap. 17. saith, that the seuenth head of the beast is also the eight. In that hee is one of the seuen heads of that former beast, he is included in that beast: and in that hee is the eight, that is, an head by himselfe, besides that other beast, therein he is the false prophet. And therfore as in chap. 13. there appeare two beasts which oppresse the Church: so here againe they be set forth by two, that is, the beast and the false prophet, that wee might know that all the tyrannie of the empire of Rome goeth downe, both in their ciuill, and in their ecclesiasticall power. Their dominion goeth downe, and downe goeth their worship and religion also. These Romanes with all their power and falsehood in religion, are cast aliue into a lake of fire and brimstone. Here is a short description of those torments of hell; and of that most horrible vengeance into which those wicked ones shall bee cast, and euen in most fearefull maner, which is expressed by this, that they are cast in aliue. For there are degrees of torments, and those great masters of mischiefe

shall

THE REVELATION.

shall haue the greatest torment, next vnto the diuels. All that take part with them are damned, for hee saith, they are slaine with the sworde which commeth out of Christs mouth, that is, with the word of God. And that is a spirituall death and euerlasting. Thus ye see the end of all Gods enemies, euen of all that oppose themselues against his trueth, and against his Church. And to expresse the greatnes of the slaughter, it is said, and all the birdes were filled with their flesh. Thus much touching this vision.

THE XLIII. SERMON.
CHAP. XX.

1. *And I saw an Angell comming downe from heauen, which had the key of the bottomles pit, and a great chaine in his hand.*
2. *And he tooke the dragon that olde serpent, which is the diuell and Satan, and and bound him a thousand yeares.*
3. *And he cast him into the bottomles pit, and shut him vp, and sealed ouer him, that hee should not seduce the nations any more vntill the thousand yeeres were expired: for afterward he must be loosed for a little time.*
4. *And I saw seates, and there were that sate vpon them, and iudgement was giuen vnto them. And the soules of them that were beheaded for the testimony of Iesus, and for the word of God, and which had not worshipped the beast, neither his image, neither receiued his marke in their foreheads, or in their hands, and they liued and raigned with Christ a thousand yeeres.*
5. *The rest of the dead liued not, vntill the thousand yeeres were finished, this is the first resurrection.*
6. *Blessed and holy is he that hath part in the first resurrection for on such the second death hath no power, but they shall be the priests of God, and of Christ, and shall raigne with him a thousand yeeres.*

He fall of great Babell, and her finall destruction, is set foorth before in the 18. chapter. That great Babell is the citie of Antichrist, described in the 17. chapter vnder the figure of a woman drunken with the blood of the Saints. Where it is manifest by the words of the Angell, that Rome is that woman, which hath drunke so much blood. Then further wee haue had in the 19. chapter the vtter ouerthrow and condemnation of the beast, and of the false prophet, and of all that take their parte, for the Lord Iesus commeth forth vnto battell against them. The beast is set forth chapter 13. with seuen heads, which are seuen hils, vpon which Rome was built, and seuen kings, that is, seuen kindes of kingly power by which that citie hath beene supported. The dominion of Popes is the seuenth head of that beast, and the Angel calleth it also the eight, because it challenged a double power. And for that cause that monarchie of the Popes is set forth not only as one head of the beast, but also as a seuerall beast by it selfe, which here is called the false prophet. Then wee see, that the Empire goeth downe, the papacie goeth downe, the whole kingdome of Antichrist goeth downe with their whole religion and worship, yea with all that take their part, when Christ commeth forth vnto battell against them. And now after we haue been told how these shall be destroyed, he commeth to set forth the condemnation of the greatest and chiefest of them al, euen of their grand captaine which set them all on worke, and that is the dragon, which is described before chap. 12. He is the beginner, he is the raiser vp of the rest, he is the great worker of all mischiefe, and now commeth his iudgement and condemnation.

It may be demaunded, shall not Satan be ouerthrowne, and damned together with his instruments? Yes no doubt. Why then is he not ouercome in that battel with the beast and the false prophet? I answere, that he is ouerthrowne and taken in that battel, but not there set forth, but in a vision by it selfe. His armies are brought in with him, with whom he is ouerthrowne, but vnder other titles. Now ye may note that there is an euident cause, why the historie of his condenation is brought in by it selfe after all the other, and that is, that his mischiefe hath extended it selfe further then by the Romane power, and he hath other armies besides the beast and the false prophet, which all in generall are here brought in with him. To come then neerer to the historie, ye haue in all the destructions of Christs enemies, the causes repeated for which they bee destroyed, to the end that it may well appeare, that they haue but their desert. So shall ye finde it here, that is, before Satans condemnation is described, here is set forth how wel he hath deserued such torments. His mischiefes that he hath wrought are briefly rehearsed. But now I will come to the words of the text.

Saint Iohn saith, *And I saw an Angell descending from heauen, hauing the key of the bottomlesse pit, and a great chaine in his hand.* This doth not set foorth Satans finall destruction, but an ancient matter, that is, how he was bound and chained vp in olde time. And therefore there is in this vision preparation shewed for that matter, for heere commeth an Angell from heauen with the key of the bottomles pit, and a great chaine. Here is the key of the prison into which he must be locked vp, and the chaine with which he must there lye bound. Then who is this Angell, and when came he downe thus for to bind him, and to lock him vp in the bottomles pit? This Angell is our Lord Iesus, the great chaine wherewith he doth bind him, is the holy and pure doctrine of the Gospell, the time when he was thus taken and bound with it, was when first Christ preached it, and then his Apostles vnto al nations. And now marke how he is bound. This dragon, as we see is set forth chap. 12. hauing seuen heads and ten hornes, and vpon his heads seuen crownes. He had with his might and with his subtilties seduced and ouercome the nations of the earth, and raigned as Lord and king, yea they worshipped him as God. For all the worship of the heathen nations was the worship of diuels, as Saint Paul teacheth, 1.Cor.10. He did not onely beare sway in all the great & large kingdomes of the world which were heathen, but also wheras the Lord had separated one little corner, euen one nation of the Iewes, and had giuen them his holie ordinances and lawes, whereby they might haue light and not be seduced, euen among them also, he had set in his foote, and seduced euen the most of them. He brought in sundrie sects among them which corrupted and depraued the doctrine of Moses, and the Prophets. What a prince was Satan now? how did he range ouer the worlde? But now commeth a chaine for him. Christ doth preach, & sendeth forth his disciples with power, & saith, I saw Satan fall down fr̅o heauen like lightning, Luk.10. 18. Hee now beginneth to fall downe from his dignitie and great magnificence. Afterward when the Lord was ascended, and had sent downe the holy Ghost vpon his Apostles, and they preached not onely in Iudea, but also among the heathen nations, & great multitudes had their eies opened, & turned from idolatrie to worship the true and liuing God, then was there a great chaine put vpon him, and he was bound. The light did now shine so cleere, that he could not seduce as he had done. For that is the binding of Satan, when he is so restrained by the light of the Gospel, that he cannot seduce men vnto false worship. And marke, that although he be the great mightie dragon, euen that old craftie serpent, yet he cannot winde out neither by might, nor yet by any sleight, but that this angel doth catch him and chaine him vp. They vse to chaine vp such fell things as will do harme when they runne loose. And because Satan of all other is the most mischieuous, he must be chained vp. And besides all this, he must be shut vp in prison, which is in the bottomlesse pit, and the doore locked and sealed vp, euen to shew that hee must bee strongly restrained or else hee will abroad, he is to set vpon all mischiefe. Also the sealing doth teach, that God hath decreed with an vnchangeable purpose, that he shall not be let loose vntill the time be expired. And the time is set that he should be chained for a thousand yeeres. It is not certaine from what yere these thousand are to be begunne, whether from the time that Christ began to preach, and began to bind Satan, or from the time that the Apostles had spread the holy doctrine among the nations, neither is it greatly materiall. For this is the purpose of the holie Ghost to let downe this long time of a thousand yeeres, in which Satan should lye bound, not to tye vs precisely to that number of a iust thousand, as to say, neither one yere or two more or lesse, but though it were some few more, yet the ful number is set downe onely: Satan should for a long time be tyed vp. Now if we count the yeeres, this is most certaine, that somewhat more then a thousand yeeres after our Lords passion, there were most horrible wicked Popes, and especially Hildebrand, called Gregorie the seuenth, who was a coniurer and dealt by the diuell. Their owne histories doe plainly shew, that about that time diuers popes came in by the diuell, and Satan was then said to raigne in the popedome. He had before this obtained, that the Bishop of Rome should be esteemed as head of al Bishops, and now looke what he would vtter to the world, hee vttereth it vnder his name, euen as vnder the name of Chrifts vicar, and as one that fitteth in Peters chayre. The world, as we fhall see when we come to the loofing of Satan, was now again seduced. But now arifeth a queftion, was Satan fhut vp in hell for the space of a thousand yeeres? was he not in the world? who then seduced the reprobate in all that time? for howfoeuer great multitudes imbraced the truth, yet far greater did impugne and blafpheme it. And who ftirred vp thofe cruell perfecutions, as he said before in this book vnto one of the Churches, behold Satan fhall caft some of you into prifon? Or who sent thofe horrible routs of heretikes of who we reade, which immediatly after the Apoftles times entered? I anfwere, that we muft not take it that Satan is fhut vp in hell for this time in such sort as that he fhould doe nothing in the world: but he is said to be chained vp in the bottomleffe pit, to signifie that he could not now generally seduce as he had done. He wrought now in the wicked mightily, and with so great rage and wrath, that it is said chap. 12. Woe be to the inhabitants of the earth, and of the sea: for behold, the diuell is come downe vnto you, full of wrath, knowing that he hath but a fhort time. Then make this account that Satan, in these thousand yeeres, was bound one way, but another way he was loofe. He was bound for seducing (as S. Iohn expreffeth it) but he was not bound from other mifchiefes which he wrought in great plentie. After the thousand yeeres expired, Saint Iohn saith, he muft bee let loofe againe, for a little season. This little time, in which the diuell was let loofe, is the time in which the great Antichrift did beare sway. For the comming of Antichrift (as S. Paul teacheth) fhould be, with all efficacie of Satan. There be fifteene hundreth yeeres paft since the Apoftles were taken out of this world, and for these threescore yeres & more, the Gospell hath been preached, so that the very fulnes, and strength of the poperie lafted but foure or fiue hundred yeeres. In that time, Satan deluded the world, and led them into all abominable superftition, Idolatrie, and wicked errors, and with such strong delusion, to beleeue lies, as it is wonderfull to thinke vpon.

In the next words the state of the Church is set foorth, for that thousand yeeres in which the diuel is chained vp. Saint Iohn saith, he saw seates, and there were that sate vpon them, and iudgement was giuen vnto them: and the soules of them that were beheaded for the teftimonie of Iesus, and for the word of God, &c. The Church of God is but one, but yet wee say, the Church militant, and the Church triumphant: for one part is warring vpon the earth and that is militant, the other part hath gotten the victorie ouer the diuell and sinne, and their soules triumph in heauen, and therefore called the Church triumphant. Now the queftion is here, whether S. Iohn doe here set forth the florifhing eftate of the Church triumphant only when he saith, I saw seates, and there were that sate on them, and iudgement was giuen vnto them, &c. Or whether he be to bee vnderftood of both, that is the militant, and triumphant: becaufe that after hee hath said, I saw seates, and there were that sate on them, he addeth that he saw the soules of them that were beheaded for the teftimonie of Iesus. It is vsually taken of interpreters onely for the Church triumphant. That is to say, that S. Iohn in vision saw the soules of the martyrs fitting vpon seats, & exercising iudgement, not as hauing the office of Chrift

deriued.

THE REVELATION. 389

deriued vnto them, who is properly the onely Iudge of both quicke and dead, but as the members ioyned vnto their head: and so they are sayd to liue and to raigne with Christ. This doctrine is according to the words of Christ to his Apostles, Ye shall sit vpon twelue seates, iudging the twelue tribes of Israel. And to that which Saint Paul saith, Know ye not that we shall iudge the Angels? 1.Cor.6.3. So that it may very well be said here, that the soules of the martyrs doe sit vpon seates, and iudge and raigne with Christ. But I take it, that Saint Iohn doth not here alone set forth the state of the Church triumphant, for that time in which Satan was bound, but also sheweth how in those daies the Church militant vpon earth, did flourish and exercise her power: for it seemeth very requisite, that somewhat should bee sayd of the state of the Church in the world, while Satan did lie in his chaine. And the words themselues which Saint Iohn hath set downe, doe diuide the matter in to two parts. I saw (saith he) seates: and there were that sate vpon them, & iudgement was giuen vnto them. And the soules, that is, and I saw the soules of them that were beheaded for the testimonie of Iesus, &c. I take the seates then, & them that sit vpon them, to bee vpon the earth in the Church militant: and that to describe and set forth how the Church exercised her power in the world that thousand yeeres that Satan was bound. The Scribes and Pharisees were sayd to sit in Moses chaire, as wee reade how Christ our Lord speaketh, Matth.23. Euen so all the Apostles, and their successours haue chaires, or seates in the which they exercise iudgement, whilest they doe deliuer forth the pure doctrine, that ruleth and iudgeth among the nations, as it is written Esai.2. These seates were set in many lands, where there were great Churches, which had very famous teachers, that did instruct and guide the flockes, according to the rules of the holy word. Now was iudgement giuen them, now was the power of our Lord Iesus exercised whilest Satan lay bound with his chaine. In this thousand yeeres those Churches did liue and raigne with Christ. For that latter clause, which is, they did liue and raigne, may very well be referred to the former part of the sentence: and not onely to the soules of the martyrs which liue with Christ for euermore. He speaketh then, as I suppose, how the church here vpon earth should liue and raigne with Christ those thousand yetes, in which the dragon was tyed vp from seducing: For all the faithfull doe after a sort liue and raigne with Christ while they be here vpon the earth: seeing that through faith, they ouercome the world, as it is written: 1.Ioh.5. They subdue Satan, and sinne. This is to be obserued against the error of the Chiliastes, or Millenaries. They be both one, for *Chilias* in the Greeke tongue is a thousand, and *Mille* is so many in the Latin. So that *Chiliastes*, or *Millenarij*, are they which from this scripture did gather, that after the ouerthrow of Antichrist, the Lord Iesus would come, and with the faithfull raigne heere a thousand yeeres vpon the earth. And that in this time, that Christ should so raigne as a great and glorious king vpon earth, his subiects should inioy all manner of earthly pleasures and delights. This fond error is confuted by the words that follow in the text, as we shall see afterward.

Cc 3 But

But here may arise some doubt, vpon this that Saint Iohn saith, he saw the soules of them, which refused to worship the beast, and the image of the beast, and that receiued not his marke, in their forehead, nor in their handes. The doubt is this, how he may be said, to see the soules of those, that would not worship the image of the beast, in those thousand yeeres that Satan was bound: seeing the image of the beast was not set vp vntill Satan was loosed. We know this that in, and from the time of the Apostles, the sixt head of the Romane tyrannie was vp, that is the Empire, and that vnder the heathē Emperors many thousands were put to death, for refusing to worship that beast. They would not obey the Romish lawes, which commanded to worship Idols: and so they were put to death. These were indeed in those thousand yeeres. But now the seuenth head of that beast, which is the second beast, the beast with two hornes like a lambe, which without al controuersie is graunted on all partes to bee the great Antichrist, he setteth vp the image of the beast, and causeth the inhabitants of the earth to worship it. He causeth them to receiue the marke, of which he here speaketh. This beast, that setteth vp the Image to be worshipped, raigneth not in those thousand yeeres in which Satan is bound, but is he by whom Satan when he is loosed, doth seduce the nations. How then saith Saint Iohn, that those which were slaine, because they would not worshippe the image of the beast, nor receiue his marke, did liue and raigne with Christ that thousand yeeres? They are slaine for not worshipping the image of the beast, after those thousand yeeres are expired, euen in the daies that Satan againe being let loose, seduceth the nations. It may be answered, that the second beast, the tyrannie of the popes, which is called the false prophet, rose not vp of a sudden, or at once, but by degrees, and was growne to a great height before that full loosing of Satan. We reade how Saint Paul speaketh of it, 2. Thes. 2. How the mysterie of iniquitie did worke euen in his time. If Satan in those daies of the Apostle when the greatest power was for to binde him, did secretly lay the foundations of that wicked apostasie, we may well thinke that the worke was growne to some perfection, before the thousand yeeres were expired: although not to such as at the full loosing and after the loosing of Satan. So then there might be, and was, great tyrannie vsed against the seruants of God before Satans loosing, by the second beast. It may be some wil say, that although those holy seruants of God which were put to death, because they would not worship the image of the beast, were after the thousand yeares, yet Saint Iohn seeth them altogether in vision, with those which were slaine by the heathen Emperors in the former part of those thousand yeares. If wee take it so, how could he say, that they did liue and raigne with Christ, that thousand yeares? I take it therefore, that the words are thus to bee ioyned, that Iohn saw stats, and there were that sate vpon them, and iudgement was giuen vnto them, and they liued and raigned with Christ a thousand yeares, taking it of the Church in earth: and not to ioyn it to the soules which he saw, as to say, that they liued and raigned with Christ a thousand yeers. For that thousand yeeres then, in which Satan was bound from seducing the nations so generally as hee had

done,

done, the Gospell preuailed and conuerted very many vnto God, ruling and iudging, though not in so full measure as in the former times. For in the time of the Apostles, the light of the Gospell was spread farre and neere in the heathen kingdomes, and that with all pure sinceritie. After their daies, abuses and corruptions crept in, and superstition increased and that more and more, but yet so that euen to the full thousand yeeres, the principles and grounds of the holie faith were held in great Churches. So although after sixe hundreth yeeres the cleere sinceritie of the trueth was much dimmed, yet there was a generall power still, and they liued and raigned with Christ which were quickened by the Gospell in all lands. The words which doe follow doe more cleerely carrie the sence this way. For first he expoundeth the matter by the contrarie, when he saith, the rest of the dead liued not, vntill the thousand yeeres were finished. Marke well this saying: for it openeth much, together with that exposition which followeth of it. For indeede the words that follow doe declare in expresse and plaine manner, what life, and what rising from the dead this is to be vnderstood of, which the rest of the dead doe not attaine vnto.

Touching the former, wherein, as I said, he openeth the matter by the contrarie: it is in these words, the rest of the dead liued not vntill these thousand yeeres were finished: here is first euidently shewed that all were dead, and that one part are raised from death in these thousand yeeres, and another part is not raised, who he calleth the rest of the dead. For vnles some were raised from death to life, in those thousand yeeres, and others not raised, how could it bee said, the rest of the dead liued not, &c? or how could he speake of a resurrection? To make this more euident, we must first note the generall estate that all be in by nature, both the elect and the reprobate, and that is, all be dead, for in regard of the elect which are raised vp out of that generall estate, the reprobate are called the rest of the dead. What manner of death this is, the holy Scriptures do euidently set forth. Being all corrupted in Adam, we all die in him as the Apostle teacheth, 1. Cor. 15. And that is to be vnderstood, not onely of this separation of the soule and bodie, but also of a spirituall death in the soule, euen while we liue here. For whosoeuer are separated from God, there is no true life in them. But looke how the diuels may after a sort be said to liue, and yet it is no life indeed, but an euerlasting death: so the soules of men although they haue naturall powers and faculties in them by which they giue life to the bodies, and in that respect are immortall, because those faculties neuer dye, yet so long as they be vnder the dominion of sinne, they be dead touching the spirituall life. And in this state are all, both the elect and the reprobate, the elect herein only differing, that they be raised vp to life in Christ. And you (saith S. Paul) hath he quickned, that were dead in trespasses and sins, Ephes. 2. vers. 1. Also in the same chapter he saith, he made vs aliue together with Christ, when we were dead through trespasses. And in the 4. chapter of the same epistle, he saith, they were strangers from the life of God, vers. 18. All then being by nature (as the same Apostle saith) the children of wrath, now let vs see how the difference of the elect

Cc 4   is

is made from those whom he calleth here the rest of the dead. It is made by Christ, they are raised vp to a spirituall life by him, euen while they liue heere. And our Lord Iesus himselfe setteth foorth this thing very plainly, Iohn 5. verse 25. saying: The time shall come, and now is, when the dead shall heare the voice of the sonne of God, and they that heare it shall liue. Then Christ by his voice raiseth the soule to life, they that are chosen, heare the Gospell and liue by it. But all are not raised, for he saith, the rest of the dead liued not vntill the thousand yeeres were finished. What is that? This it is, in those thousand yeeres, in which the Gospel is preached, and the voice of Christ which raiseth the dead, is sounded forth with great power, there be many which are not raised vp vnto life by it, but doe continue still in their former estate, vnder the power of sinne euen strangers from the life of God. All are not raised from the death of sinne, vnto the life of righteousnesse, at the sound of the Gospell. There were many that heard Christ himselfe preach, many that heard the Apostles, which were not raised to life, but remained still vnder the power of Satan, and were dead in sinne. Many in those thousand yeeres in which the Gospell flourished, and Satan lay bound, were raised from death, and did liue and raigne with Christ, but many more, whom he calleth the rest of the dead, despised the Gospell, and so were not raised to life by it, whom hee calleth the rest of the dead. This thing is fulfilled in all times and in all places where the Gospell is preached: for some doe imbrace it, and by it haue Christ liuing in them: others are neuer the better for it: but the diuell and sinne haue euen as great power ouer them, as before. But here the Chiliastes, of whom I told you before, doe ground their error, because hee saith, vntill the thousand yeeres were finished. For this speech seemeth to import that after the thousand yeeres finished, they shall rise also whom he calleth the rest of the dead. For to say they shall not liue vntill the thousand yeeres bee finished, what is it but to say that they shall then liue? This then they take thus. That the diuell shall bee bound a thousand yeeres, and then shall all the faithfull be raised vp in bodie, and raigne all that thousand yeeres vpon the earth with Christ. And this (say they) is the first resurrection. Then when the thousand yeeres are finished, they take it that all the dead shall liue, and that they call the second resurrection. So they held that there should bee two resurrections of the bodie, the first of the faithfull, and the second of all the dead. We doe beleeue, for the holy Scripture doth so teach, that all the dead both good and bad shall rise with their bodies: but wee are also taught by the word of God, that all shall rise at once, there shall be but one resurrection of the body. The first resurrection therefore (as it is here called) is in the soule, when it is raised from the death of sinne. Of which Saint Paul speaketh, saying, If ye be risen with Christ, seeke those things which are aboue, where Christ sitteth at the right hand of God, Coloss. 3. verse 1. Then to maintaine their opinion, they must shew that there bee three resurrections. For if there bee two of the bodies, then this which Saint Paul doth speake of, maketh the third. Againe, they must proue, which they can neuer, that the resurrection of the bodies of the faithfull, goeth before the resurrection

which

which S. Paul speaketh of to the Colossians, If ye bee risen with Christ: for there resurrection which Iohn here speaketh of is the first. And as I said, if it be of bodies, then is the resurrection of the bodies the first: which is most absurd. Whereupon it must needes follow, that the first resurrection which Saint Iohn here speaketh of, is not of the bodie, but when the soule receiueth the life of Christ. This is the first resurrection, and it is peculiar to the faithfull, the rest of the dead doe not rise at all in this resurrection. But yet the matter is not answered: for that word vntill. For if it be so, that the rest of the dead neuer rise in this kind of resurrection, how should it be said, they liue not vntill the thousand yeeres bee finished? I answere; that for this word vntill, it is both in common speech and in the vsuall phrase of the Scripture, to say a thing was not vntill such a time, which in deede when that time is come, is not neither. As Ioseph tooke Mary, and knew her not vntill shee had brought forth her first borne sonne, Matth. 1. Where we are not to take it, that he knew her after shee had brought forth her first borne. Also where Dauid daunced before the Arke, and Michol despised him for it in her heart; therefore sayth the holy Ghost, Michol the daughter of Saul, had no childe vntill the day of her death, 2. Sam. 6. Shall we rather vpon this, that shee had a child at the day of her death? We say also that such a man was neuer maried vntill his death. No man taketh it thereupon, that after his death or at his death he was maried. So when it is said, that the rest of the dead liued not, vntill the thousand yeeres were finished, it is as much as to say they were neuer raised to that spirituall life. That thousand yeeres was a time in which many were raised to life at the sound of the Gospell: but there were many then not raised. For although Satan were bound so that he could not so seduce the nations as he had done, yet he did harden the hearts, and blind the eyes of the reprobate, so that they imbraced not the life offered. Then we see what this first resurrection is. And now that we may bee moued with the desire of it, euen to labour to haue our part therein, here is the commendation thereof set forth. Blessed and holy (faith Saint Iohn) is he that hath his part in this first resurrection, for on such the second death hath no power, but they shall bee the priests of God, and of Christ, and shall raigne with him a thousand yeres. This is a singular commendation of the first resurrection, that euery one is blessed and holie that hath his part in it. What is greater then true blessednes? And euery one that is raised to life in this first resurrection, is pronounced to be blessed. Then this is a resurrection of none but of blessed ones. And it is to bee marked how he ioyneth these two together, blessed and holie. For there is none raised to life in Christ, but by his spirit. Christ dwelleth in them, and they in him. They walke not after the flesh, but after the spirit, Rom. 8. They bee new creatures which are in Christ, as the holie Apostle plentifully teacheth. If therefore yee doe make account of blessednes, if ye doe make account to haue your part in the first resurrection, labour to bee holy. Seeke to bee found in Christ, that ye may dye vnto sinne, your old man being crucified, and that ye may be raised vp vnto newnes of life, euen vnto true holines. For many may imagine that they haue their part in this first re-

surrection,

surrection, becauſe they profeſſe the Goſpell, and bee deceiued, for except they be rayſed vp from vnder the dominion of ſinne, they be not holy, they be ſtill dead. Then there is a reaſon rendred why theſe are bleſſed, which is in theſe words, for on ſuch the ſecond death hath no power. It is as much as to ſay, they be bleſſed, for they be deliuered from the damnation of hell. For there is the ſecond death, in which the diuels and the reprobate doe dye eternally. So you ſee then, that as there is the firſt and the ſecond reſurrection, ſo is there the firſt and the ſecond death. The firſt death is the ſeparation of the ſoule and bodie, which the elect doe paſſe thorough: the ſecond death is in the torments of hell, into which all thoſe doe enter that doe dye in their ſinnes. And are not they right happie which doe eſcape from hell, ouer whom that death hath no power? And hee teacheth that all that haue their part in the firſt reſurrection, that ſecond death ſhall haue no power ouer them. Here is yet a further reaſon of this alſo rendred. For ſuch as be conſecrated to God and to his Chriſt, and that get the victorie as Kings to raigne with him, how ſhall the ſecond death haue any power ouer them? But Saint Iohn ſheweth how theſe that riſe in the firſt reſurrection are prieſtes to God, and to his Chriſt, and they ſhall raigne with him. And what is that but to be conquerers and Kings? Theſe ouercome, theſe be in the preſence of God, who ſhall pull them downe from thence? But this ſeemeth hard that hee ſaith, they ſhall raigne with him a thouſand yeares. For ſhall they raigne but a thouſand yeares? Shall not the Saints raigne world without ende? Ye muſt note that he ſpeaketh here of the raigne of the faithfull euen vpon earth, for the ſpace of that thouſand yeares, in which Satan is bound: which excludeth not their eternall glorie in the heauens. O beloued, giue your ſelues to God, ſeeke this firſt reſurrection, that yee may be bleſſed for euermore in the heauens.

THE XLIIII. SERMON.
CHAP. XX.

7   *And when the thouſand yeares are expired, Satan ſhall be looſed out of his priſon,*
8   *And ſhall goe out to deceiue the people which are in the foure quarters of the earth, Gog, and Magog, to gather them together to battaile, whoſe number is as the ſand of the ſea.*
9   *And they went vp into the plaine of the earth, and compaſſed the tents of the ſaints about, and the beloued citie; but fire came downe from God out of heauen, and denoured them.*

10   *And*

10 *And the diuell that deceiued them was cast into a lake of fire and brimstone, where the beast and the false prophet shall be tormented day and night for euermore.*

IN the former part of this chapter we had the binding of Satan for a thousand yeares. We had also set forth the flourishing estate of the Church for that time. And now we come to the loosing of Satan out of his prison. He delighteth wholly in mischiefe, his great desire is for to doe all the harme that may be: and therefore it was an exceeding griefe vnto him, when hee was by the cleere light and power of the Gospell tyed vp and restrayned from seducing the nations, in so whole and generall a maner as he had done. And now that he is let loose againe, it is very ioyfull vnto him, and he goeth very roundly to worke.

When the thousand yeares (saith Iohn) are expired, Satan shall be loosed out of his prison. I noted before, that the reckening of this thousand yeeres is not for certaine in what yeere they began. Whether from the time that our Sauiour first preached (for then Satan began to come downe) or from the time that the holy Apostles, after the holy Ghost was sent downe vpon them, with great power published the Gospell, seeing that did more restraine him: or from the time that those blessed Apostles had spread the light of it among the Gentiles, and had founded great Churches in many kingdomes. If it be the purpose of the holy Ghost to leade vs so neerely vnto a time, I suppose this last should bee it: although wee cannot stand vpon any one yeere, as to say this or that yeere after the birth of our Sauiour: but the more the Gospell preuailed, the more Satan was chayned vp. And we may note, that as Satan was by degrees bound vp, so by degrees, hee commeth to be loosed. And as the holy Ghost beginneth the thousand yeeres from the fullest binding of him vp, so he saith, they be expired at his fullest loosing. The holy Apostles were not long taken out of the world, but he gate some scope to seduce, and raised vp foule monsters, to sowe most horrible and abominable heresies, by which many were seduced, but what was this, so long as many thousand thousands in all lands, stoode constant and sincere in the faith of Christ, and could not be driuen from it by any torments? Within foure or fiue hundreth yeeres after Christ, besides the heresies that he had raysed vp, he also had brought into the Church sundry superstitious deuices, which many of the faithfull and true seruants of God were blemished withall. So that hee was now somewhat more loosed. When eyght or nine hundreth yeeres were expired, the sinceritie of the truth, & the puritie of Gods worship was much more dimmed, so that before the thousand yeeres were expired, great corruptions did ouerspread almost all Churches, but yet so as the groundes of the holy faith remained. Things were very dimme in comparison of auncient puritie. The Bishop of Rome was aloft, and vsurped with great tyranny, and spread much euill ouer many nations, so that Sathan had gotten much scope in comparison of that which he had in former times. But as yet he was not fully loosed, the Gospell euen in the middest of many trumperies, yet tooke place in many. Come then downe a little lower, about the yeere of our Lorde, 998. Syluester the second came to bee Pope, who was in league with the diuell. The histories doe shew, that at his death he called for the Cardinals, and confessed all how he had familiarity with the diuel, and how he had giuen himselfe vnto him, so that he might come to that Papall dignitie. What shall we thinke now, when such an one was esteemed to be the head of the Church, Christs Vicar that could not erre, and to haue full power ouer the soules of men? How much did Sathan get loose now? What was it that he would not now seeke to broach? About the yeare of our Lord, 1074. rose vp Hildebrand a most horrible wicked Pope, who had also familiaritie with the diuel, & wrought exceeding much mischiefe. Now the trueth was oppressed, good men were hated and persecuted, idolatrie and all diuelish inuentions were maintained. Satan had now his full scope to seduce the nations with his lying signes and wonders. Now began Antichrist to be in his prime: and many worthie men in those times cried out against the Romish Clergie, for their horrible impieties, affirming Rome to be Babel, euen the seate of the great Antichrist.

Then it followeth, that he shall goe out to deceiue the people, which are in the foure quarters of the earth. In this we haue three things to consider: the first is the industrie of Satan, or his readines to doe mischiefe so soone as euer he getteth loose. The holy Ghost sheweth, that he goeth out to seduce presently: For the diuels doe burne with such hatred against God, and such malice against the felicitie of man, that they be restles in seeking by all meanes to dishonour his most holy name, and to draw men to perdition. Wee must prepare our selues to looke for none other thing at Satans hands. Then the second thing is, that the euill men are seduced and misled by him. They are deceiued, supposing that they be in a good way, when he hath blinded them, and led them into the way of destruction. Which thing is to be well obserued: for it sheweth that all the rabblements that worship the beast, or that doe cleaue to the great Antichrist, thinke they goe right, and that all are awry that ioyne not with them: how else are they seduced by Satan? In the poperie, euen from the highest to the lowest, blindnes is cast vpon them, and they dote vpon the doctrines of diuels. True it is, that the prelates and clergie men seduced the people, being themselues first seduced by Satan. As Saint Paul prophecied of them, saying, But the euill men and deceiuers shall waxe worse and worse, deceiuing, and being deceiued, 2. Timoth. 3. vers. 13. Doth not this mitigate the offence of the great Antichrist and his subiects, that poore foolish men are seduced by subtill diuels? as hauing an intent to doe well (as we see how they boast of their good intents in the poperie) and are beguiled? I answer, that it doth little mitigate their offence, seeing the cause of this seduction is in themselues. Which S. Paul sheweth, dealing about this same matter, and shewing how Antichrist should come by the effectuall power of Satan, 2. Thess. 2. Hee also rendreth this cause why God would send this heauie iudgement vpon the world, namely, that men receiued not the loue of the trueth. God sent the glad tidings of the Gospell to giue light, and

THE REVELATION.

to bring men vnto eternall happines: and they loued darknesse more then light, they loued falsehood, vncleannes and lyes: and therefore Satan in the iuſt iudgement of God is let loose, euen to fill them with such things as they loued and were worthie of.

Then there is the third poynt, which sheweth that Satan being let loose, he seduceth not some few kingdomes, but all nations vpon the foure quarters of the earth. A matter worthie the noting, because the papists doe boast and bragge so much of their multitudes. They doe despise and condemne the true profeſſors of the Gospell, because that for the space of these fiue hundreth yeeres, vntill now of late, they haue been very few, and in al that time also by an vniuersall consent condemned and reputed but as heretikes. Can so many nations swarue, and so long time, and a few others onely hold the trueth? Looke vpon this place, Satan goeth foorth to seduce the people which are in the foure quarters of the earth. Here is an vniuersalitie, heere is a catholike consent in apostasie and departing from the trueth. And if any shall say, he went forth being let loose after the thousand yeeres expired, for to deceiue the people so generally which are in the foure quarters of the earth: but did he therefore preuaile so generally? Might it not be that he attempted so generall a matter, but yet was restrained from his purpose? I answere, that the next words doe euidently shew, that hee failed not of his purpose, but seduced generally the nations of the earth: for otherwise how should it bee sayd, Gog and Magog, to gather them together to battell, whose number is as the sand of the sea?

And they went vp into the plaine of the earth, and compassed the tents of the Saints about, and the beloued citie. These words doe manifestly declare, an innumerable multitude which the diuell seduceth, and gathereth together vnto battell as his souldiers, against the true Church of Christ. Wee see then that Satan is gotten loose out of his prison, and his chaine is off: the light of the Gospel shineth not, but there is palpable darknes, so that he may now perswade almost what he will: and therefore now the multitudes are great which he leadeth away. Here be many things offered to our consideration in this description of the armies of Gog and Magog: as first it is to be considered whether this loosing of Satan to seduce, be the same that is spoken of before, chapt. 13. where the beast with two hornes by his signes & wonders which he wrought, deceiued the inhabitants of the earth. I answere, that it is out of controuersie that the second beast which cōmeth with signes and wonders to seduce, is the great Antichrist. Then further, Antichrists comming is by the effectuall power of Satan, with lying sighes and wonders, 2. Theſſ. 2. Whereupon it must needes bee graunted, that this seducing by Satan here spoken of, is the same with that which is there set forth, chapter 13. onely this excepted, that this of Gog and Magog is more generall. Wee reade there how all nations, kindreds and tongues were made to worship the image of the beast, and to receiue his marke: but that is to be extended no further then to those kingdoms which were subiect to the poperie. And here by these armies of Gog and Magog, are vnderstood all the chiefe enemies of the Church in these last times, since the

loosing of Satan. Here are besides the swarmes of papists, the huge armies of the Turkes: for howsoeuer the Papists are set against the Turkes, and the Turkes against the Papists: yet both against the holy Gospell, and against the true Church: as the Pharisees and Sadduces could not endure each other, but yet were both against Christ. Then we are to consider about the names Gog and Magog, what should bee meant by them. Some doe take it that these names doe signifie couered, and vncouered, and are vsed for to note the two speciall sorts of enemies of the Church, the Papists and the Turkes. For the Pope he commeth vnder the name of Christ, boasting that he is his vicar, and that Christ hath committed all power into his hands, and so he is a couered enemie, he is Gog: for vnder that couering he hath brought in and set vp all his abominations. And the Turke, he openly denieth and impugneth Christ, and so is vncouered, that is Magog. Moreouer, they doe take it, that these names, Gog and Magog, are to note of what countries the chiefe enemies should spring: because in Ezechiel chap.38. and 29. in which the prophecie is set forth against Gog and Magog, they are called the prince and head of Meshech and Tubal. Now Meshech is Arabia, which gaue originall to the Scythians. Mahomet was of Arabia, and the Turkes of Scythia. And Tubal dwelt in Italy, where the Pope hath risen vp. I doe not see how these things can be gainesayd: but for a more full exposition of this matter, we are to looke vpon that prophecie of the Prophet Ezechiel against Gog and Magog. Thus it is, the Lord by his seruant Ezechiel hauing promised two things, that is, the bringing of his people out of the captiuitie of Babel into their owne land, and their instauration by Christ, chap. 37. Least the Iewes should take it that these two should come together, or as it were neere at one instant: that is to say, that so soone as they were returned home from Babel, he would send the Messias: this prophecie of Gog and Magog, is to preuent that error, and to teach them, that after their returne out of Babylon, they should suffer grieuous calamities by many cruell enemies, before the comming of the Messias: and withall, there is set forth what horrible vengeance God would execute vpon those enemies. Those enemies were collected of diuers nations, but serued chiefely vnder the princes of Asia the lesser, of Syria, and of Scythia, in which was the citie of Gog, and the land of Magog, or the citie called the citie of Magog. Gog and Magog then are put for the princes of those countries, which were the chiefe captaines in gathering great and mightie armies vnto battaile against the children of Israel, after they were come out of the captiuitie of Babel. The Lord doth there in one summe, vnder the armies of Gog and Magog, comprehend all the enemies that fought against them from time to time after the captiuitie, vnto the comming of Christ. And now for the application of this vnto the enemies of the Church vnder the Gospell: wee must first note, that through this booke, as it is euident, the speeches and figures of matters are taken out of the lawe and the Prophets. Now when the Lorde would set forth in one summe all the enemies of the Church, which Satan mustereth after the time of his loosing out of prison, before the comming of Christ to iudgement, there is no one place more fit to set forth all these armies, then those armies of Gog and Magog:
and

and therefore the names, euen Gog and Magog, are here brought in, to set forth these huge armies of the Pope and of the Turke, and of all such enemies. Moreouer ye are to note, that the ouerthrow and destruction of all those enemies is so set forth in that prophecie of Ezechiel, that it doth serue also most fitly to declare the vengeance of God almightie against these. Then we see why they be called the armies of Gog and Magog, namely, because those were the great armies of enemies, which fought against the Church in olde time, and which the Lord in his vengeance did destroy.

Let vs in the next place obserue, that he saith they be gathered together vnto battaile. It appeareth in the words that follow, against whom they are assembled for to fight, euen against the Saints. Here is the horrible crueltie of Satan, that he is not content to seduce the nations, and to leade them into error, and from the way of life into the way of destruction: but also euen for to double their condemnation, he setteth them on worke to fight against God, against his trueth, and against his Church. It is an heauie iudgement of God, that men are led from the trueth to beleeue lyes, and from the true worship of God, vnto the worship of diuels: but this is more grieuous that they doe not stay there, but cruelly fight against all that will not forsake the trueth, and ioyne with them. Satan herein doth exceedingly blinde them, and set them in a rage. You knowe how it is, and how it hath been with the papists, that they fight and warre most bitterly against all that will not worship the beast, condemning them to be heretikes, and men not worthie to liue vpon the earth.

The next clause sayth, Whose number is as the sand of the sea. This is wonderfull, how can this be, when all the men that euer liued in the world, put altogether, are nothing comparable to the sand of some little part of the sea shore, in number: how much lesse can this armie bee in number as the sand of the whole sea? We must note that there is a kinde of speech which we doe call *Hyperbole*, which is an excessiue speech, that the holy scripture doth sometime vse, when some exceeding qualitie or quantitie is to be expressed. As in this place, because the multitude which Satan hath seduced to fight against the Church, is such as no man is able for to comprehend, or to reach vnto the number of them in his minde, the holy Ghost sayth, they be in number as the sand of the sea. Here it will be sayd againe: Are the number of the armies of Gog and Magog, that is, of the Papists and Turkes, innumerable to the capacitie of man? I answere, who can doubt of that? Doe but consider in your minde thus: what a multitude of people there be in England, it is enough for a man, if not more then his minde can containe, to see into the number of them in such sort as to comprehend it. Then note that in the poperie, almost all the land were for the Pope, euen a fewe that were scattered being excepted, whom they did persecute. Moreouer, yee must know that the kingdome of England is but a little corner, in comparison of all the great and large kingdomes which were subject to the Pope. Then what is the number in them all, who is able to come nigh to the numbring thereof? And yet we are not come by many

many degrees to the toppe of the matter. For now you must count what multitudes there haue been in all these kingdomes, which haue stood in the defence of the popish religion, and fought against the Gospel, for the space of these fiue hundreth yeeres. Are ye not now come as it were to the sand of the sea? and yet yee are not come nigh the matter. For vnto these ye must now adde al the multitudes of the Turkes for so many hundreth yeeres: for vnder Gog and Magog are contained all that Satan hath seduced in all lands to fight against the truth, euer since he was loosed, and all that he shall seduce to the worlds end. Do but ponder these things in your minde, and see if there be not cause to say, whose number is as the sand of the sea. What extreame folly is it then in the papists to make such brags of their multitudes? Doth that proue them to bee the true Catholike Church? Nay, if ye looke well vpon it, ye shall finde that it doth euidently declare that they be a great part of these armies of Gog and Magog, whose number is as the sand of the sea.

The next words doe also shew the same thing, when he sayth, they went vp into the plaine of the earth. They couer the face of the earth, and not of some one kingdome, but euen of the world. And in that he sayth, they compassed the tents of the Saints about, and the beloued citie, it declareth not onely how small a thing the true Church is in comparison of them, euen as a few tents, or as some citie which they inclose round about: but also that their endeuour is to swallow vp and vtterly to destroy all that professe the holie and pure worship of God. The histories of these latter times doe shew, that wheresoeuer in any countrie where poperie had taken place, there were any that would not worshippe the beast, how furiously they did compasse them about to fight against them. For the tents of the Saints and the beloued citie, were in al lands where any did with pure and sincere faith worship the true God, and condemne the false worship and enormities of the Romish synagogue. Reade what they did to the Waldenses, more then foure hundreth yeeres past: how did they persecute and scatter them? Reade also how they dealt against the Albigenses, more then three hundreth yeres past: where we may see how often they assailed Raymundus the Earle of Tholouse. About those times, and not long after, wee may reade of diuers excellent men, which cried out of the Romish Antichrist, whom they compassed about, and condemned as heretikes. Afterward more then two hundreth yeeres past, in the dayes of Wickliffe and after, here was much stir in England, they compassed the tents of the Saints about. What a stirre kept the Popes and their armies against that famous Church of the Bohemians, how did they compasse them about? But what followeth? Fire (saith S. Iohn) came downe from God out of heauen and deuoured them. Now he commeth to set foorth the destruction of the armies of Gog and Magog, and of their chiefe captaine also which seduced the. He beginneth with the armies, and sheweth how they are consumed with fire from heauen. It might bee said: What shall become of the tents of the Saints? what shall become of the beloued citie, when all these innumerable multitudes doe compasse them about? To answere

this,

this, here is shewed that the Lord God from heauen dooth miraculously destroy these armies, and deliuer his Church. For that is meant when hee saith, that fire came downe from God out of heauen and deuoured them. It will be demanded: when was this? or where was this seene? I answere, that ye must vnderstand, that this is a mysticall speech. The truth of God is compared to fire, and so is his wrath a consuming fire: and who seeth not, that by the liuely word, & by his vengeance he hath already begun to consume and to destroy the popish armies? In the 38. chapter of Ezechiel, the Lord doth threaten a tempest of haile, fire and brimstone vpon the armies of Gog. And accordingly he speaketh in this place of fire comming downe from God from heauen, which doth deuoure them. What way soeuer they bee destroyed, it is the fire of Gods word, and of his wrath from heauen, and wee must acknowledge his miraculous power in preseruing his Church. Let not the multitude of the armies of Gog and Magog discourage vs: for they were farre greater then they bee, and as the Lorde hath begun, so will he vtterly burne them vp, and consume them in his good time.

Thus much for the destruction of these armies: Now touching their chiefe captaine, who hath seduced them, and led them forth vnto battell against the Lord. Shall he escape? No, he shall not escape. He is the chiefe worker of all mischiefe: and therefore it followeth, The diuell which deceiued them, was cast into a lake of fire and brimstone. This is that euerlasting fire, which our Sauiour saith, is prepared for the diuell and his angels. Here shall all the diuels be tormented for their sinnes which they haue committed, euen world without end. And here are also mentioned his chiefe instruments which he hath vsed, the beast and the false prophet, these are ioyned with him in the lake of fire and brimstone: for such as serue the diuell here in the worlde, shall dwell with him for euer in hell, and there take such part as he shall. The beast is all the Heathen Emperours of Rome, with all that ioyned with them in persecuting and murthering the seruants of God. The false prophet is the Popes and popish clergie, with all their adherents, which in these latter daies haue so much corrupted the earth. Seeing this is the end of all Gods enemies, beloued, let vs not feare them, but let vs stand fast in the truth, and constantly renounce all their false worship and abominations: for they shall all downe with most horrible destruction and vengeance, when we shall stand, triumph and reioyce in the Lord for euermore.

Dd   THE.

THE XLV. SERMON.
CHAP. XX.

11. *And I saw a great white throne, and one that sate on it, from whose face fled both the earth and the heauen, and their place was no more found.*

12. *And I saw the dead both small and great stand before God, and the books were opened, and another booke was open, which is the booke of life, and the dead were iudged according to those things which were written in the bookes, according to their deedes.*

13. *And the sea gaue vp her dead, and death and hell gaue vp their dead which were in them, and they were iudged euery man according to his workes.*

14. *And death and hell were cast into the lake of fire: this is the second death.*

15. *And whosoeuer was not written in the the booke of life, was cast into the lake of fire.*

His Scripture (beloued) containeth a description of the last iudgement. Wee haue had the day of iudgement figured diuers times before in this booke, but more darkly, and here more fully, and more cleerely. For that is the manner of handling thinges in this prophecie: first, to make as it were a darke shadow, and then afterward to draw a more liuely picture. Touching the parts of this description, we shall see them seuerally as they come. In the first place the Iudge himselfe is described: for the first verse of this text, doth set foorth the maiestie, the power, the integritie, the seueritie, and terror of the Iudge: for the things which are spoken of his throne, and of the flying away of the earth and the heauen out of his presence, are to set foorth those properties indeede of the iudge himselfe. First then that he sayth, it is a great throne: it is to shew his maiestie and power, with which he shall come from the right hand of God, to iudge the world. The kings and Iudges of the earth, are of great maiestie and power, and accordingly haue high thrones, vpon which they sit in iudgement. But this throne is called great, by a singular height and greatnes which it hath aboue all others. He that sitteth vpon this throne, is the Iudge of the whole world, both of the liuing, and of the dead. This is that throne of his glorie, as he speaketh, Matt. 25. which he shall sit vpon when hee commeth in the clowdes, and all the holy Angels with him.

Then it is sayd to be a white throne. The white colour in the holy scriptures is vsed to represent puritie and glorie. As heere it is to teach vs, that this iudge shall

iudge

iudge vprightly, and doe no man wrong. Among the iudges of the earth iudgement often swarueth and is peruerted diuers waies. And the wisest & the best iudges are vnperfect in knowledge, and so do somtimes misse of the perfect sentence. Againe the respect of persons, either with feare of the mightie, for loue of friends, or hatred of enemies, and such like, doth leade the iudge awry: and sometimes bribes do blind the eyes: so that iudgement is wrested. Against al these the whitenes of this seate is opposed. Here is no spot, but all cleere and pure. Here is no imperfection through ignorance. Here is no respecting of persons through feare, hatred, or loue, nor yet any peruerting of iudgement for reward.

 Now followeth that which declareth the terror of the iudge, in these words, *From whose face fled both the earth & the heauen, and their place was no more found.* Looke what we dread and feare, wee flie from the presence thereof for to hide vs, that we may not appeare in sight: euen so to declare the most terrible maiestie of this iudge, the earth and the heauens are said to flie away from his presence, and as it were to hide themselues, which is expressed in this, that their place was no more found. For to say their place was not found any more, is as much as to say, they did not appeare any more, as we reade chap. 12. where the dragon and his angels were cast down, it is said, their place was not found any more in heauen. Then the earth and the heauen here flying from his face and hiding themselues, doe shew his terror. And beloued note it well, for it is no small terror which is resembled by this. The earth and the heauen are without sence. They be very great and mightie creatures: and they haue not sinned. Now if they tremble, flie, and hide themselues out of his presence, as not able to endure the terrour of his sight: what shall wicked men doe? what shall become of those poore wretches? or how shall they bee able to endure the terrour and seueritie of this iudge? They shall now be at their wittes end, and void of all succour or refuge. For vnto whom shall they flie for helpe? or who shall deliuer them from the most dreadfull vengeance of this iudge? It is not sayd any where else in the Scripture, that the earth and the heauen shal flie from his presence, and appeare no more. Indeed our Sauiour saith, The powers of heauen shall bee moued. Saint Peter saith, that the heauens shall passe away with noise, the elements shal melt with heate, the earth and the things that be therein shall be burnt, 2. Pet. 3. And now that Saint Iohn speaketh more here which was shewed him in vision, namely, that the earth and heauen do flie his presence, it is a mysticall speech, euen as I sayd, to expresse the wonderfull terrour that shall be. It may be said, if flying his presence wil serue, there be others will flie also. I answere, that the earth and the heauens haue not sinned, and therefore they bee permitted in their trembling and terrour to flie and hide themselues, and are not drawne forth before the iudge. But as for the sinners, euen the wicked deuils, and vngodly men, let them flie and hide themselues where they can, they shall bee drawne foorth vnto iudgement and execution. There is no darke corner for any one of them to hide themselues in. Let them goe downe into the bottome of the sea, yet his hand will find them out, and he will draw them forth. This thing would be well considered of, that there shall be such a terrour in the iudge, that the earth and heauen shall flie and hide themselues, that we may now in time learne wisedome and be admonished. For wee see how bold men are now in committing euill, nothing at al regarding this terror of the iudge, which is here set forth. It might enter into their hearts to thinke thus, the Lord will come to iudge the world, wee must all appeare before him to bee iudged according to our deedes, his seueritie and terror will be such, that the heauens and the earth wil flie his presence & hide themselues: what then shall become of vs, what case shall we be in, which doe commit these foule sinnes? O how shall we then tremble and quake, and be euen ouerwhelmed in horror? Where shall we finde any succour, when hee that alone should helpe and succour vs is our great terror? Is it not better for vs now to forsake our vngodly waies, and so studie to please him, that wee may reioyce at his comming? Most vnhappie are they which shall haue this terrible iudge against them. For how shall they be able to endure the fire of his vengeance? Thus I say, men might thinke in their hearts when they heare of such terror of the iudge. But it may then bee obiected, if the heauen and the earth are so afraid at the terror of his presence, not for any offence which they haue committed, but at the wrath wherewith he commeth armed against the foule sinnes which haue bin wrought by men as it were in their sight and view: shall it not then be a most fearfull day vnto all men? Who is so cleere and innocent as that hee may come before this iudge? I answere, that this iudge in all his glorious power and maiestie, shall not be any terror at all to the godly. It is the day of redemption vnto them, they are willed to lift vp their heads and reioyce at it. For all their sins are blotted out, and they shall stand innocent without all spot before this iudge, their redeemer. It shal bee vnto them a day of all ioy and consolation. They are willed to long for the comming of this iudge. Thus much touching the iudge. Now to those who are for to be iudged.

I saw (saith he) the dead both small and great stand before God. Who are they then that stand here to be iudged? Euen all that euer haue liued vpon the earth euer since the beginning of the world, no one excepted. But when Saint Paul teacheth, 1. Cor. 15. that all shall not die, but all shall be changed: and when as we say, he shall iudge both the quicke and the dead, how agreeth it with this, that here are none spoken of but the dead? I answer, that when Saint Iohn saith here, that he saw the dead standing, it doth not exclude the liuing. For he speaketh only of those, of whom there might be doubt. Thus it is, if not any of the dead, that euer died in the world of what death soeuer, shall escape from this iudgement: how shall any of the quick be wanting? It is euident then, that Saint Iohn saw all both the quick and the dead in vision, standing before the iudge. This is a great assemblie, euen the greatest that euer was, or euer shall be. Here again it may be demanded, how this is to be vnderstood, that he saith, he saw the dead both small and great. Is it to be taken of the stature of their bodies, or of worldly degrees that they liued in here in this world? For we see that some doe die very small infants, and some grow vp first and be men of great stature. Likewise we see how there be of all sorts here in this world: Some be kings, princes, and nobles: others bee in low estate, yea very

many.

THE REVELATION. 405

many poore beggers. Now I take it, that Saint Iohn doth not call the dead here small and great in respect of the stature of their bodies, but in regarde of their place and degree in which they liued. There are all both high and lowe, both rich and poore. I speake this because it is a question whether any shall rise in the stature of little infants. It is by some maintained, that all shall rise in a full stature: because at the resurrection all shall be perfect. And looke what age or sicknesse hath taken away shall be restored, and what through want of yeares is wanting, shal be added. Wee are not indeed to be curious about this matter. Now followeth the chiefest matter of all in this iudgement, and that is, after what manner they shall be iudged.

It is expressed in these words, And the books were opened, and an other booke was opened, which is the booke of life, and the dead were iudged of those things which were written in the books, according to their workes. It might be wondred how all this great multitude should be iudged. We see when earthly iudges do sit in indgement what a long time it holdeth to trie and to iudge a few persons: There is so much a doe for prooues and euidence of matters to be giuen. Saint Iohn sheweth that it shall not be so here: but all shall proceede according to the written recordes, which are the bookes. There shall be none other euidence. But what are those bookes, or what writings according to the which iudgement shall be awarded? It is easie to knowe what bookes they are, euen the conscience of euerie one. For this is a wonderfull worke of God, that hee hath giuen vnto euery man a conscience, as it were a book, in which are writte vp al their thoughts, their words, and their deedes. A wicked man hath infinite vaine thoughts and vncleane desires, night and day, they passe away to him, but they bee euery one written vp in the booke of his conscience. A vaine wicked man vttereth in his whole life multitudes of wordes, which are vaine, or lying, filthie, slaunderous, and blasphemous. If hee should lose his life he cannot remember all that he vttereth in one day: but in this booke they are all written vp, and shall come to iudgement. Such a man committeth sins in action innumerable euen as the sand on the sea shore, hee remembreth some of them, the greater part he perceiueth not to be sinnes, or they slip out of his mind, but they be euery one written in this booke of his conscience, and shall bee opened in iudgement. Yea further in the vnbeleeuers there be many things in their thoughtes, wordes, and workes, which seeme to them to be excellent, which yet are abominable before God, which falleth out because they are blind and can neither iudge rightly of the intents of their owne hearts, neither in many things which is good and which is euill. Now in this booke of the conscience, the deepe counsels and intents of the heart are written vp, and at this iudgement shall be disclosed? For how shall iudgement be perfected according to their workes, if the secrets of mens hearts be not laid open? Ye see therefore that the bookes shall bee opened: there shall be euidence vpon record, there shall need no production of witnesses. But will some say, the companie will be great that commeth to bee iudged, when all that haue liued in all ages, and in all countries of the world shall bee raised and come together: and the bookes will be manie and large to be read ouer. Is not here an endlesse worke? How long would it hold one, to reade ouer the thoughtes, the wordes and deedes of one man? I answer, that wee must not conceiue so of these bookes, as that there shall be any standing to reade them. They shall all appeare at once. All the filthie vncleannes of mens hearts shall lie open to the viewe of men and Angels, and their own conscience shall then shew vnto them their deeds, their words, and their wicked thoughts. Then shall their inwards be as it were displayed. We are thus told aforehand, that the bookes shall be opened, that we may beware, and preuent so great a daunger. It is the great kindnes of God to giue vs this warning: and more then starke fooles and mad men we be, if it doe not moue vs to take heed. But how shall we take heed? we cannot auoid our appearance before this iudge. Our bookes must needes be opened when we come there: there is no remedie for this. Very true, but the danger is auoyded, when the bookes are such, as we need not feare or be ashamed to haue them opened, but reioyce. For as the opening of the books shalbe the shame, horror, and vtter confusion of one part, so shall it be to the praise, honour, and glorie of the other part. Such as are foule within, and full of abominable vncleannes, being opened shall stinke and be reiected: When the pure in hart shal see God, and greatly reioyce in his presence. Wherby we may plainely see, that our onely way is to be purged in our heart from an euill conscience. For if the heart be sincere and the conscience pure, the booke will open very faire. But alas, who can attaine to such sinceritie of hart, and to such puritie of conscience? Who (saith Salomon) can say my heart is cleane? I am purged from my sinne. Who is it that is not priuie to himselfe of much vanitie, and great imperfections in this booke of his conscience? God is greater then man, and seeeth farre more perfectly into the heart of man then he himselfe: How then shall he abide his triall? how shall he endure the opening of his secrets? For answere to this we are to consider what Dauid saith, Blessed is the man whose iniquitie is forgiuen, and whose sinne is couered: blessed is the man vnto whom the Lord imputeth not sinne, and in whose spirite there is no guile, Psalm. 32. Where all sin and iniquitie is purged away, there shall bee a faire booke opened, that man need not to feare. What then are we to doe all our life long, but to reforme the booke of our conscience? And this is to be done onely by the holy word of the Lord. There we shall learne the true faith, by which we are incorporate into Christ as members of his mysticall bodie. There is repentance taught, euen how wee shall forsake the euill workes and doe the good. There is the true light to expell all our darkenes, to correct all our errors, and to guide vs in the right way. We are for to looke dayly into this word to find what is amisse, and by the same for to reforme it. If we attain vnto that faith that worketh by loue, happie are we, our heart and conscience shall bee found sincere. For touching all our sinnes, they are washed away and discharged through the pretious bloud of Christ. And the fruites of our faith, euen the workes of loue shall appeare and stand vp to our praise and glorie. These workes indeede are vnperfect and full of spots, but as all other sinnes are blotted out, so the spots of these shalbe washed away, and they shall be found perfect. If we haue but the dead faith, we deceiue our selues, our bookes are not reformed, but all will be foule

foule when they come to bee opened. For then we haue, as we imagine, a right faith, which yet is without repentance. Then wee omitte those dueties which God commandeth, and boldly commit many sinnes which hee hath forbidden, presuming vpon pardon? The heart is hardned daily more and more, and treasureth vp wrath, against the day of wrath. For doe we not all confesse that without repentance, there is no saluation. The conscience is reformed daily by repentance. For as by faith wee haue free pardon of all our sinnes: so by the same are wee dayly purged and sanctified, wee die vnto sinne and liue vnto righteousnesse. He that is in Christ crucified, the death of Christ doth kill sinne in him, for his olde man is crucified with Christ. Againe, he that is graffed to the similitude of his death, shall be also graffed to the similitude of his resurrection. Rom. 6. Then consider for your repentance, without which ye cannot be saued: because your bookes will be foule when they be opened, where that hath not beene. Consider, I say, first, for the reforming of you heart and conscience how sinne doeth die in you. For by nature the minde of every one is ouerspread with vanitie, and with ignorance of God: by nature the heart is full of all euill lusts. There is couetousnesse, there is pride, there is selfe loue, there is enuie, and hatred, there is crueltie, with many filthie vncleane desires. Vntill these things bee blotted out of the booke, and better things put in their place, there is no saluation: For ye see it set downe, that the dead are iudged according to the things, which are written in the Bookes. It shall not auaile a man to crie, Lord, Lord, if naughtie things be written vp in this booke. If thou doe not repent for thy couetousnes, and cast foorth a number of sinnes, which spring from it, thou must needes bee damned. The holy Apostle saith, that couetousensse is idolatrie, for the worldly wan doth set riches in the place of God: and so maketh them an Idoll. If thy heart be set vpon riches, if thou put thy trust in them, as if thy life did consist in the aboundance of them: blot it out of thy booke, put thy trust in the Lord, set thy hearts delight in him: and despise this world. If thou hast gotten goods wrongfully, restore them to the right owners: Doe not flatter thy selfe that thou hast repentance, vnlesse thou feele such a worke: for bee it thou hast gotten wrongfully others goods in time of thine ignorance. Thou diddest therein commit theft. Now thou commest to see, how fowle a sinne thou diddest commit, and the land, the house, or the goods euill gotten remaine still with thee: thou knowest thou holdest them wrongfully, and yet thou doest detaine them: is this repentance? Nay is it not greater theft, then thy former? for at the first thou diddest steale them being ignorant: and now thou withholdest, and so euen stealest them of knowledge. Here is no repentance, but an increase, and an heaping vp of sinne, for yee know the saying of our Sauiour: That hee that knoweth his masters will, and doth it not, shall bee beat with many stripes. Then reforme your bookes, deale vprightly, giue vnto euery man his owne, bee liberall and mercifull to the poore, euen to the widowe, and to the fatherlesse: For vpright dealing, mercie and pitie, are good things to be found written in your bookes: They will make yee glad when they come to bee opened. If ye bee proude, vainglorious,

glorious, and high minded: doe yee not reade, that God resisteth the proude? O what abominable things are written vp against ye, in your conscience? Learne then to knowe the vanitie of your owne mindes, learne to knowe your selues: humble your selues, and become meeke and lowely in heart, for therein God is pleased. Weepe, and lament for the loftie pride of your hearts, which is so abominable before God. And then shall yee not bee afraide to come to the opening of your bookes. Let not the hautie vanitie of your hearts haue her will so much, as to shew it selfe in excesse of apparell. Yee will say, that a purple heart may lie vnder a course mantle: and therefore the garment is not the matter. That is very true, but yet the delight in gorgeous apparell, bewrayeth the pride of the heart. If yee bee giuen to wrath, yee haue then set open (as it were) a wide doore vnto Satan to enter, and to bring in many euils. Wherefore the holy Apostle saith, Be angry but sinne not, let not the sunne goe downe vpon your wrath, giue not place to the diuell, Ephes. 4. If yee doe suffer wrath to indure, Satan worketh hatred, enuie, and cruell words and deeds. So that the booke of the conscience is stuffed with many fowle things. O labour now by repentance to blot them out, and be meeke, patient, and long suffering. What should I mention particulars from vice to vice, this is the summe, search the heart and conscience by the holy word of God, and seeke to roote out all vices which ye shall finde there, and to plant in the vertues which are wanting. If yee be wise, thinke alwaies of this opening of the bookes, and let it be your dailie care and trauaile, still to reforme and to amend. What busines haue wee of that waight, that may draw vs from this thing? Doth it not stand vs greatly vpon to haue our reckening bookes in good order against this iudgement? Is it not then requisite that our whole life, be euen a studie and a labour how we may die well? Beloued to conclude this poynt, let vs not hide our sinnes and our vncleannes, but open and confesse them to the Lord. Let vs be ashamed of them, and bewaile them, with the sorowfull teares of true repentance: for if we doe not, they shall be opened and vncouered vnto our euerlasting shame and confusion: seeing the bookes shall be opened.

Then it followeth, that another booke was opened which is the booke of life. Of this booke the holy scripture speaketh in diuers places, and not onely in the newe Testament, but also in the olde. Moses praieth the Lord to forgiue the sinne of the people, when they had made the golden calfe, and if not (saith he,) Blot me out of the booke which thou hast written, Exod. 32. But what booke is it, will some man say? It is the booke in which their names are written, whom God hath elected vnto eternall life. For out of the whole lumpe of mankind, being all lost in Adam, God chose of his free loue and mercie, a remnant whome hee would redeeme in his sonne: and the names of these are written in this booke: which is here opened, that we may know that the faithfull doe not come to a terrible iudge, but to their Sauiour. But are their names then written indeede in a booke, which shall bee saued? To this I answere, that ye must consider, that the holy scripture in the high matters of God, applieth it selfe vnto our capacitie, and ascribeth vnto God such things as are agreeable vnto men. As wee see when men take the

names

names of great multitudes for any purpose, they write them downe, because they cannot otherwise remember them. Now God needeth no such helpe: but yet to shew that he hath in his counsell determined and decreed whom he will saue, it is said he hath written vp their names in a booke, and that is called the booke of life. This booke shall now bee opened, and so it shall appeare, that so many as the Lord in his vnchangeable counsell hath decreed to bring to life, that he hath redeemed them in his sonne, called and sanctified them by his spirite vnto an holy conuersation, and that now hee will glorifie them. And he saith, that the dead were iudged according to the things that were written in the bookes, according to their workes. The iudgement (as I noted before,) proceedeth according to the euidence which is vpon recorde, euen according to the things which are written in the bookes, and that is according to their deedes. For what are written in the consciences of men but their workes? So that wee vnderstand by workes, not onely outward actions, but also inward thoughts and secret intents. Here is now a matter beyond all reason, how the dead should all rise againe: and therefore Saint Iohn speaketh more particularlie of it. Men haue dyed of sundry kindes of deaths: as some haue beene drowned in the sea: some haue beene slaine in the warres, some haue been burnt to ashes, others haue died in their beddes. In the sea, the fishes haue deuoured them, in the warres the fowles of the ayre haue eaten their flesh, as also the wilde beastes. The ashes of the other haue been scattered who can tell whither? Shall all these arise to iudgement? Saint Iohn answereth, and saith plainely, that the sea gaue vp her dead, and then death rendreth her dead, that is, if they were slaine with the sword in warres, or burnt, or put to any other death and neuer buried, now they rise. Likewise hell or the graue yeeldeth vp the dead, that haue been buried. Then there shall not any one be wanting. For that diuine power which created all of nothing, is able to gather together, and to giue vnto euery one his owne flesh and his owne bones.

And marke how he repeateth it againe: that they were iudged euery man according to his workes. Why is it repeated so often? We may easilie perceiue why it is repeated so often: euen because men are hardly brought to beleeue any such matter. Ye haue many horrible swearers, blasphemers, raylers, and full of filthie ribaldrie, that liue in ryot, in drunkennes, and in abominable whoredomes: tell them of this iudgement day, and of their reckoning, and they laugh. And why? O, say they, God is mercifull, we will aske him forgiuenes. Ye haue others which liue in wrath, in malice, in enuie and debate, whose tongues are giuen to backbite, to lye and to slaunder, and whose whole life almost is nothing else but in seeking how to harme, and how to bee reuenged vpon their enemies, or vpon such as they vniustly hate. Talke with these, and tell them what the Scripture dooth pronounce vpon them, and they will answer, we know that well enough: but we can in one quarter of an houre forgiue all the world. Then haue ye these hautie proude persons, and those which are couetous and worldly minded, so that they doe oppresse and defraude, they spoyle the fatherles and the widow, they bribe, they extort, they

forsweare

forsweare themselues to get goods. Doe but trie these, and tell them, that they must come to iudgement, and that they shall bee iudged euery one according to their deedes, and see what they will say. Shall ye not heare this answere, or some such like? I must liue, I must prouide for my selfe, I will repent for that which I doe amisse, and so I trust God will pardon me. Deale after the like maner with other sorts of grieuous sinners, and yee shall heare them make the like answere: so that we may see plainely, that men are not perswaded that they shall giue an account of their deedes. Then, as I sayd, ye may easily see the cause why this is so often repeated, that they shall euery one be iudged according to their workes: let men therefore be fully assured of this. Let vs not be so foolish as to imagine, that Lord, Lord, and Lord haue mercie vpon vs, will carrie away the matter: but while wee haue time, let vs turne with true repentance from those euill workes, that they may be blotted out. Such as doe sinne presumptuously in hope of pardon, know not what repentance is. He that repenteth, is sorrowfull in his heart for the sinne which he hath committed, and so doth lament and bewaile it, confessing it to the Lord, and crauing pardon for it with teares. Moreouer he doth hate, detest, and loathe the euill, because it is contrarie to the holy will of God, and doth dishonour him. Finally, he doth renounce and forsake the euill and wicked deede. And all this is through the worke of grace, that his olde man is crucified by the power of Christs death. Then on the other side, he doth loue entirely, and from the bottome of his heart, that which is pure and good: he doth euen hunger and thirst after it: hee is glad to performe it in action, and so to bee full of good deedes, whereby he may glorifie God. This is the right way, and behold how farre awry men doe goe from this: and therefore shall be iudged according to their workes: let them crie out neuer so loude, Lord, Lord, and Lord haue mercie vpon vs. It may be here demaunded then, whether this be to be vnderstoode of both parts, or whether the wicked onely shall be iudged according to their workes. Our Sauiour declareth plainely, Matth. 25. that both the good and the bad shall be iudged according to their deedes: as, Come yee blessed of my father, &c. When I was hungrie yee gaue me meate, &c. And, Goe ye cursed, &c. When I was hungrie ye gaue me no meate, &c. For thus it is, the true beleeuer, whose true and liuely faith worketh by charitie, forsaketh sinne, and receiueth pardon, so that no euill of his shall appeare in iudgement: but the good deedes which he doth shall come forth and be rewarded with glorie: And looke how much greater they Be, so much the greater shall his honour, his praise, and his glorie be with God.

 Now on the contrarie part, the wicked man, whose works doe euidently declare that he hath no true faith, shall haue all his deeds set before him: and then according to the greatnes or fowlnes of them, hee shall receiue his damnation: for looke how much greater his offences haue been, so much greater torment shall hee receiue. The neerer hee commeth in sinning to the diuell, the deeper shall hee bee cast with him into horror and miserie in the pit of hell. Would God wee could bee well perswaded of this, that euery one shall bee iudged according to his workes.

Then

THE REVELATION. 411

Then it followeth, that death and hell were cast into the lake of fire, this is the second death: Here is the execution of iudgement vpon the reprobate, in this sentence, and in the next. All the damned shall bee cast into hell, which hee calleth the lake of fire: and so die the second death. This second death is a wofull death, and lasteth for euer and euer. Goe yee cursed (saith Christ) into euerlasting fire, which is prepared for the diuell and his Angels, Matth. 25. But this is a strange maner of speech that hee saith, death and hell shall bee cast into the lake of fire. What is death that hee shall bee cast into eternall fire? Is death any creature that hath sense to suffer torments? Surely death is not any creature, death is not any thing that hath a substance, death hath no sense or feeling either of ioy or sorrowe. How then shall death bee cast into hell? Then further, the lake of fire is hell. How then doth hee say that hell shall bee cast into the lake of fire? Shall hell bee cast into hell? For answere vnto these things yee must vnderstand, that death and hell are here put for the heyres of death and hell: that is, for the reprobate that shall bee damned in hell and there dye for euer. This speech wanteth not his efficacie, but indeede declareth the exceeding miserie of the reprobate, and their cursed estate to bee such in hell, that they are called euen death and hell. O poore wretches that are euen death and hell it selfe. And then finally hee sheweth, that whosoeuer is not found written in the booke of life, shall bee cast into hell. Onely the elect of God which doe obey and honour him, shall escape damnation.

THE XLVI. SERMON.
CHAP. XXI.

1 *And I saw a new heauen and a new earth, for the first heauen and the first earth were passed away, and there was no more sea.*

2 *And I Iohn saw the holy citie new Ierusalem, come downe from God out of heauen, prepared as a bride trimmed for her husband.*

3 *And I heard a great voyce out of heauen, saying, behold the tabernacle of God is with men, and he will dwell with them: and they shall be his people, and God himselfe shall be their God with them.*

4 *And God shall wipe away all teares from their eyes, and there shall be no more death, neither sorrow, neither crying, neither shall there be any more paine, for the first things are passed.*

5 *And he that sate vpon the throne sayd, behold I make all things new: and he said vnto me write, for these words are faithfull and true.*

6 And

6 And he said vnto me, it is done, I am Alpha and Omega, the beginning and the ende: I will giue to him that is a thirst, of the well of the water of life freely.

7 He that ouercommeth shall inherite all things, and I will be his God and he shall be my sonne.

8 But the fearefull and vnbeleeuing, and abominable, and murtherers, and whore-mongers, and sorcerers, and idolaters, and all lyars, shall haue their part in the lake which burneth with fire and brimstone, which is the second death.

IN the former chapter wee had a full description of the generall iudgement, which is one great article of our faith, that Christ shall come to iudge the worlde. Wee had also the resurrection of the dead, which is an other chiefe article of our faith. And moreouer, there is noted the endles torments of the reprobate. But there remayneth vntouched the last article of our beliefe, which is, the life euerlasting, and the description of that commeth now in the last place. In this whole chapter therefore, and in some part of the next, are described and shadowed out the ioyes of heauen, euen that most happie and blessed estate which the faithfull shall dwell in for euermore. This is to moue and to perswade vs vnto true godlines, euen to forsake euill, and to walke constantly in the way of righteousnes. It commeth here as a second argument with the sweetnes thereof to draw and allure, and that with great efficacie. For if neither the grisely torments of hell on the one part, nor the sweete ioyes of heauen on the other, can moue vs to forsake iniquitie, and to follow the way of godlines, wee are more then blockes or stones. What a madnes is it for a man wilfully to cast himselfe into such endles miserie, and wilfully to depriue himselfe of such endlesse ioyes, for a few vaine lustes and pleasures of sinne, that last but for a seasonꝭ Marke well then beloued the purpose of the holy Ghost, and let vs come to the description. And I saw (saith he) a new heauen, and a new earth, for the first heauen and the first earth were passed away, and there was no more sea. The first entrance here is with the restauration of the whole frame of the world. The Lorde God in the beginning made the heauens and the earth, and all their hoast for the vse and seruice of man. So that man was a great king, yea euen as a petty God vpon the earth. When hee sinned, hee cast downe with him all the creatures which were made for his sake, into the bondage of corruption. There is a curse laide vpon the earth, as wee reade Genes. 3. And Saint Paul saith, that the creature is subiect vnto vanitie, Rom. 8. All the whole frame of the heauens and the earth doe wholy incline to glorifie the mightie creator. Then what a vanitie is this which they bee subiect vnto, that now they doe their seruice vnto wicked men which dishonour God? The sunne, the moone and the stars doe giue their light to the wicked. The

cloudes

clowdes drop downe their raine vpon the bad. The earth yeeldeth foorth her increase vnto the vngodly and abominable sinners. They doe not sinne in this, but yet they are subiect vnto corruption: and now at the latter day shall bee purged, deliuered, and restored into a perfect estate and libertie. Hee calleth them new heauens and a new earth then, and saith that the old are passed away, not that the substance of the heauens and the earth that now are shall bee abolished, but their estate shall be altered. Which thing is cleerely proued by the words of Paul, Romanes 8. vers. 21. where he saith, that the creature shall be deliuered from the bondage of corruption, into the glorious libertie of the sonnes of God. Where hee sheweth also that the creature doth grone for this. Then, as I said, it is euident that the heauens and the earth shall not bee abolished but renewed. This doctrine of the new heauens, and the new earth, the Prophet Esay speaketh of, chapter 65. Likewise Saint Peter, hauing shewed that the heauens being on fire shall be dissolued, and the elements shall melt with heate, addeth by and by, but wee looke for new heauens, and a new earth according to his promise, in which dwelleth righteousnesse, 2. Peter 3. I will not enter here to dispute with what creatures the Lord will furnish the earth withall. For it may bee demaunded, shall there bee beasts, foules and fishes made againe? I leaue it as I sayd, although I take it most agreeable to the perfection of the Lords worke to the prophecie of Esay (though his words touching the beasts may be taken allegorically) chapter 11. And to the doctrine of Psalme the 8. that the earth shall be furnished with beasts. It is certaine that the beasts did agree at the first, and not one deuoure another, neither could they be subiect to corruption and death, but through mans sinne. And as he saith in the Psalme, man shall haue all things subdued vnder him. Which as wee may see is not yet fulfilled but in Iesus, as the holie Ghost sheweth, Hebr. 2. Here doth arise a difficult question, vpon this that he saith there was no more sea. Shall the sea be vtterly abolished? what reason is there that this creature shall faile? hath the sea committed any offence for which it shall faile? I answere, that we are not to take this according to the letter, but wee are to looke how the word sea is vsed in this prophecie. In the fourth chapter there is a sea of glasse before the throne. Also in the chapter 13. the beast with seuen heads ariseth out of the sea. And there is a glassie sea againe, chapter 15. Now in all these places the sea is not to be taken for that great gathering of waters where the ships passe, and where the fishes doe swimme: but indeede for the troublesome and confused estate of this world. The Romane monarchie did rise out of the confused broyles, waues, and tempests that were among the nations, which are euen like vnto a sea. The faithful passe through the broylings of this worlde euen as the children of Israel passed through the red sea. When he saith then, that there was no more sea: it declareth the effect of the restauration, it sheweth that there shall bee no confusion, no broyles, no waues, no turmoiles nor tempests in the new world. There dwelleth, as Peter saith, righteousnes, there shall bee no sinne, nor no sinfull thing, and therefore there shall bee no effect of sinne. All things shall be pure, safe, and calme in the new world. The sea

is

is troublesome, daungerous, and a stop and separation: and to declare that there shall bee no such matter in the new world, it is said, there was no more sea: and yet there shall be this great gathering of the waters, which are called seas.

It followeth: *And I Iohn, saw the holie citie new Ierusalem come downe from God out of heauen, prepared as a bride trimmed for her husband.* The restauration of all things being shewed, he commeth more necrely to declare the blisse of the children of God, for that is the principall. Their habitation with God in the heauens, is compared to the dwelling in a citie: and therefore in vision there is shewed vnto him the holie citie new Ierusalem. Ierusalem vpon the earth was for some respects called the holie citie: for there was the Temple, and signe of Gods presence, there was the speciall place of worship: but yet in that Ierusalem there dwelt many vncleane persons. In this heauenly Ierusalem there shall bee no vncleane thing, all shall be holy and pure indeede. It is also called new Ierusalem, because all old things are gone. The former things were vaine and transitorie, and so waxed old: but this shall flourish for euer. We reade that the Saints shall dwell in heauen, how is it that this citie commeth downe then from God out of heauen? The Saints shall inherit heauen and earth: and this citie commeth downe in vision to be described. We are to note indeed that the builder of this citie is God, as it is sayd Heb. 11. As S. Paul also speaketh, saying: But Ierusalem which is aboue is free, which is the mother of vs all, Galat. 4. vers. 26. And he addeth in a word the glorie of this citie, when hee saith, trimmed as a bride, prepared for her husband. They trimme and decke themselues with the richest iewels that they can. Then the glorie and beautie of this citie is very great, being trimmed as a bride.

In the next place here followeth a great voice from heauen, which proclaimeth the happines of all those which shall enter into and dwell in this heauenly Ierusalem. And the voice beginneth with the fountaine of this happie estate, or as I may speake, with the efficient cause therof, namely, the habitation of God is with men. Wee are assured in the holie Scriptures, that the godly shall dwell with the Lorde for euer. And the voyce saith here, Behold the tabernacle of God is with men, and he will dwell with them. And he addeth further, They shal be his people, and God himselfe shall be their God with them. Consider (beloued) what God is, and what they shall inioy that bee his people, and hee their God, and that dwell with him. The Lord God is an infinit treasurie of all good things: so that this is to be obserued, that such as dwell with God, no good thing can be wanting vnto them, neither can any euill come nigh them. To want no good thing, and to bee free from the feare of all euill, is perfect felicitie, which is a principall poynt: and therefore the voyce saith, Behold the tabernacle of God is with men, &c. Now as the former of these, namely, that they shall inioy all good things, is included in this that God will dwell in them, and they shall be his people, and he their God with them: so the latter, that is to say, that no euill shall come nigh them, is expressed by some particulars, in the next words following.

They shall weepe and lament no more, there shall bee no more death, nor sor-
sow,

row, nor crying, nor paine: all euill then shall bee remoued. The faithfull are here subiect to temptations and doe sinne, which causeth them to weepe and lament with teares. They passe through many afflictions and tribulations, they bee not made of iron or of stone, they doe feele them, and they doe weepe: otherwise how should it bee said, that God will wipe away all teares from their eyes? The teares which they shed shall be wiped away, and they shall neuer weep any more. They shall sinne no more, they shall not feare death any more, there shall be no griefe nor sorrow. O blessed people that shall dwell with such a God. And marke the reason that is rendred, which is partly in these words, that he saith, the first things are passed: and partly in the words that follow, and hee that sate vpon the throne said, Behold I make all things new. The first things, that is, the state in which the world is now, is very grieuous and lamentable. Sinne is committed, for the diuell hath a kingdome, horrible confusion, and afflictions doe follow. But all these former things shall passe away, and the most mightie and holy God maketh all new. Ye see that the words be plaine, which open the reason of the remouing of all euill from the elect of God: and now that we may be out of all doubt, for the certaintie of the matter here is added: And he sayd vnto me, write, for these words are faithfull and true. Saint Iohn is willed to set it downe in writing, that the words are faithfull and true. And againe, it is the eternall and vnchangeable God, which is expressed in this that hee saith, I am Alpha and Omega, the beginning and the end, that confirmeth it with this speech, It is done. Things to come, which are decreed in the counsell of God, are as certaine as if they were past: for the Lord God cannot erre; neither can hee alter and change, neither can any hinder his decree. Looke what he hath determined before the world, he may say long before it come to passe, it is done, for it cannot be altered: and if he say it is done, although we see no likelihood yet we may ground vpon his word, euen as surely, as if wee saw the things fulfilled before our eyes.

Now after he hath thus ratified vnto vs the full certaintie of these things, touching the new heauens, and the new earth, and the holy citie, with the happie estate of those that shall dwell in it, hee addeth certaine promises, which declare on the one part what manner of persons shall enter and dwell in it: and on the other part a threatning shewing who shall bee thrust out, and cast into hell. The first promise is in these words, To him that is a thirst, will I giue of the well of the water of life freely. Here is euerlasting life promised vnder a figuratiue speech, which is, that it shall be giuen vnto men to drinke of the well of the water of life. Men for their vse in this naturall life, doe draw waters out of welles, and fresh springs. Accordingly he speaketh here of the spirituall life which is giuen of God in Christ: The Lord God is the fountaine of liuing waters, and he hath put the life into his sonne, who is the well of the waters of life vnto vs For thus he speaketh of himselfe: If any man thirst, let him come vnto me and drinke: He that beleeueth in me, as saith the Scripture, out of his bellie shall flow riuers of water of life. Ioh.7.vers.37.38. What the waters of life are, the Euangelist sheweth in the next verse of that seuenth chapter, saying, this spake he of the spirit, that they which beleeued in him,

should

should receiue. It is then a spirituall and an heauenly life which is here promised. And ye must obserue, that it is giuen freely. If it were by mans desert, how should it be said, I will giue him of the well of the water of life freely? Is that giuen freely, which men doe earne, and may challenge as their due? Indeed the holy Scriptures somtimes vse this phrase, that men are to buy those spiritual things. As in Esay 55. All that thirst are called to the waters, they are willed to come and buy. But it is added, that they may buy without siluer, and without any price: they buy for nothing. True it is, that he which forsaketh, and is readie to loose all earthly pleasures and commodities to attaine to the ioyes of heauen, may after a sort be sayd to buy them. Yet neuerthelesse, the Lord giueth them freely: eternall life is the gift of God.

Now the chiefe thing that wee are to marke dooth yet remaine, and that is to whom the Lorde will giue to drinke of the well of the water of life, which is expressed in one word, to him that is a thirst. The Lord promiseth to giue the waters of life: but to no one, but to such as be a thirst. The meaning of this is plaine, that there shall not any be partaker of this heauenly blessing, but such as doe earnestlie couet and seeke after it. When a man is in a great heate, and sore a thirst, ye know what a vehement desire hee hath of somewhat to quench his thirst. And so the Lord to expresse the vehement desire of heauenly and spirituall things which is in the faithfull, he calleth it thirst. Ye know how our Sauiour speaketh, Mat. 5. Blessed are they which hunger and thirst after righteousnes, for they shall be satisfied. The Lord God offreth exceeding great and precious things: such as do not thirst after them, are despisers, and doe set light by them, and no despiser shall be partaker of the heauenly glory. Ye know the parable of the king that maried his sonne, and sent foorth to call them that were bidden, and how they being addicted to their worldly cares and pleasures, set light and made excuses, Matth. 22. Luk. 14. which men neuer taste of that supper. Also ye know what the Virgin Mary sayth in her song: He hath filled the hungrie with good things, & the rich he sent away emptie. Who are those rich, but all they that are full within themselues, and doe not feele their wants? Then is it euident (beloued) that the first steppe vnto true blessednes, is to know and to feele our miserie. For before such time as wee feele our wretchednes, euen what wee are subiect vnto through our sinnes, wee cannot couet remedie. For who seeketh remedie for that euill which he doth not feele nor feare? If wee come indeede for to see and to feele how cursed wee are in our vncleannes, and withall to know that the Lord hath giuen a remedie, we shall vehemently thirst after the same, euen as after liuing waters for to refresh vs. Will not a wise man then enquire how he may know his miserie, and so be brought to thirst after the liuing waters? Surely (as I sayd) it is the first steppe. We are in our selues full of all vncleannes, and such as doth make vs lothsome and abominable before the Lord God: but we are so blind that we doe not perceiue so much, but swell in pride, as if we were very excellent, and despise the saluation of God. He therefore that will know himselfe, must come to the word of God: for by that he shall see what he is. There is cleere light, there is puritie and cleannes required: there a man

shall

shall finde out all the foule sores and deformities of the soule, and all the spirituall diseases of bodie and minde. There he shall finde, that except he haue remedie, he is vnder the curse and wrath of God, and vtterly forlorne. If hee once taste how sweete the Lord is, by that liuely worde, hee will thirst still exceedingly for more. For assure your selues, that the more a man tasteth the waters of life, the more he is a thirst: and therefore the Lord doth not say, I will giue to him that was a thirst, and hath now his thirst quenched, but to him that is a thirst. If any shall demaund and say, how can that be, that the more a man tasteth of those waters of life, the more he shall thirst? or if it be so, what benefit is it to taste, when the tasting doth not quench but increase thirst? I answere, that the waters of life are so exceeding sweete and comfortable, that whosoeuer hath once tasted some drop of them, his soule is inflamed and rauished with the desire of more, and so he thirsteth more vehemently. He that neuer tasted any droppe of them, knoweth not of any such thing, and so neuer thirsteth. And this is the reason why some men doe vehemently couet to reade the holy Scriptures, and to heare them expounded, seeking daily to quench a thirst which is in them. And others there bee which haue no delight at all in the word of God, as hauing no thirst to be quenched: they read not, they despise to heare sermons, they haue no meditation. If they did know themselues what exceeding miserie they be in, and did but feele some refreshing by the word, they would doe the same thing which now they esteeme to be follie and madnes in others. They laugh, they scoffe, and mocke at those whom they see to frequent holy exercises of religion. And it may be they will say, what are they the neerer for all their running, if their thirst be not quenched, but daily more and more by their hearing increased? I answer, that the more the thirst increaseth in men while they liue here, the more they be blessed: not that the very thirsting it selfe is a matter of blessednes: but because the promise is, that the thirstie shall be satisfied. The Lord God doth giue some droppes now of those sweete waters vnto the thirstie soules: which although they inflame their thirst, yet they be comforted exceedingly by them, and refreshed, in as much as they be assured by them, that they shall come to the full well of those waters of life where they shall be fully satisfied. Marke well then beloued, who they be that shall be saued, euen those that be a thirst: they haue tasted, and they seeke daily for more. Examine thine owne estate: doest thou not thirst? If thou doe not, thine estate is very bad. Thou knowest not thy miserie, thou despisest the graces of God: thou shalt neuer drinke of the well of the water of life, vntill such time as thou doest thirst. What should I stand here to speake of the miserie of these times, in which the cleere light of the Gospell doth shine, shewing the fountaine of the waters of life, and calling vpon men to come to them, and the multitude are not a thirst? Few there be which thirst indeede, and they be had in derision, and much hated. Doe ye not see there be many which neuer reade ouer so much as the new Testament in their life, nor once in the weeke, care either to reade or to heare so much as one chapter of the Bible? If the word of the Lord be preached euen by their doores, the least busines, and euen the meanest pleasure doth keepe them backe from hearing. Is the promise of life made vnto such?

Then followeth the other promise in these words: He that ouercommeth shall inherit all things, and I will be his God, and he shall be my sonne. Here is againe a promise of very great glorie and dignitie: for what greater glorie then to inherit all things, and to be the sonnes of God? If God be our God and we his sonnes, they be great things which we shall possesse in the kingdome of heauen. Then as yee consider the height and greatnes of the glorie here promised, so marke to whom it is promised, which is expressed in these words; hee that ouercommeth. For least we might take it, that because the Lord giueth eternall life freely, that nothing is required on our part, but that we may be idle, slouthfull, and negligent, he sheweth that none shall inherit that glorie, but conquerors. We are in a battaile, if we fight valiantly, and ouercome our enemies, wee shall be crowned: but if we be ouercome and led away captiue, as prisoners taken in the warres, how can we be saued? We haue a corrupt nature full of sinne and sinfull lusts, and the diuell worketh in it very strongly: and if we doe not subdue it, and vanquish Satan, we are taken as prisoners and held captiue. If we doe obtaine the true faith, we shall bee armed with the power of our Lorde to resist the diuell; so that hee shall not blinde the eyes of our mindes, nor harden our hearts, neither shall any euill lust that is in vs, haue dominion ouer vs, but we shall get the victorie ouer them all. This is a most glorious victorie, when we ouercome our owne corruption, and the power of Satan which worketh in it. O beloued, such goodly things are difficult, thinke not that they can be obtained at ease. The lusts and pleasures of sinne are wonderfull sweete and delectable vnto nature, it is a hard worke to deny them. It is euen as much as if a man should indure the digging out of his right eye, or the cutting off of his right hand. Satan also is marueilous subtile and craftie: wee haue no safetie but continually to flye vnto the Lord our God for succour. Wee must stand, and we must get the victorie through his power, and wee must begge grace of him continually to that ende. For marke now what shall become of all those which are ouercome, which the next verse declareth in these words: But the fearefull, and vnbeleeuing, and the abominable, and murtherers, and whoremongers, and sorcerers, and idolaters, and all liars, shall haue their part in the lake which burneth with fire and brimstone, which is the second death. All these sorts of people are conquered by Satan, and by their owne lusts, and are led away captiue into euerlasting woe and perdition. It may be demaunded; are these all the sorts which are ouercome? are there not many other wicked persons which are ouercome of the world, and of the prince of the world, and by him led away vnto hell? Here is no mention of proud persons, of couetous, nor of blasphemers, hee speaketh not of traytors and rebels, nor of such as disobey and dishonor their parents: here is not any word of theeues, of vsurers, extortioners, and irreligious persons: nor of many other. I answere, that it is not the minde and purpose of the holy Ghost, to name particularly all sorts of wicked persons which are vanquished by sinne and Satan, and led away captiue to hell: but naming some, all the rest are vnderstood: as if it were added, all these and such like. Moreouer, we may note that some of the particulars expressed be very large, and may containe many: as

namely,

THE REVELATION.

namely, vnbeleeuers, and abominable reach farre, they may include all manner of vngodly men. But a little to the words: he speaketh of the glorie of conquerors, and of the endles miserie of those which are conquered. And because that fearefull persons are not fit for warre, but are easily ouercome, he beginneth with them among the captiues. The fearefull are they which feare men more then God, contrarie to that precept of our Sauiour, Matth. 10. Feare not them that kill the bodie, but are not able to kill the soule: but feare him rather which is able to destroy both soule and bodie in hell. The holy religion and worship of God is hated and persecuted in the world: and ye haue many which will professe it no further, then they may go safe and free from the hatred and displeasure of men. These feare nian about God, they be ouercome by Satan, and led to hell. All vnbeleeuers want power to ouercome the world, and are held captiue. Through vnbeleefe they are not sanctified, but despise God and his trueth, they be couetous, they be proude, they be full of most foule abominations, and lothsomely doe stinke in the sight of God. All malitious hatefull persons are mutherers: such as be led with vncleane lusts be adulterers: witches and sorcerers there be of sundrie sorts: the superstitious idolaters which worship with mans inuentions, that receiue the very doctrines of diuels, and so indeede worship diuels, are ioyned with them: all that slaunder or deceiue with falsehood and lyes come in among them, and are led together as prisoners into the lake that burneth with fire and brimstone, which is the second death. Beloued, if it be so, as I hope ye doubt not, let vs fight valiantly to get the victorie, that we may escape from the danger of this lake of fire and brimstone, and reigne as conquerors in eternall glorie. There is no one of vs but shall be tempted vnto many sinnes: but let ys resist manfully, our labour therein shall be blessed. Thus much for this time.

THE XLVII. SERMON.
CHAP. XXI.

9 *And there came vnto me one of the seuen Angels, which had the seuen vials full of the seuen last plagues, and talked with me, saying, come I will shew thee the bride, the Lambes wife.*

10 *And he caried me away in the spirit vnto a great and an high mountaine, and he shewed me that great citie, that holy Ierusalem discending out of heauen from God.*

11 *Hauing the glory of God; and her shining was like vnto a stone most precious, as a Iasper stone, cleere as Christall.*

12 *And had a great wall on high, and had twelue gates, and at the gates twelue Angels,*

Angels, and the names written, which are the twelue tribes of the children of Israel.

13. On the East part there were three gates, and on the Northside three gates, on the Southside three gates, and on the West side three gates.

14. And the wall of the citie had twelue foundations, and in them the names of the Lambes twelue Apostles.

15. And he that talked with me had a golden reed, to measure the citie withall, and the gates thereof and the wall thereof.

16. And the citie lay foure square, and the length of it is as large as the breadth of it, and he measured the citie with the reed twelue thousand furlongs, and the length, and the breadth, and the height of it are equall.

17. And he measured the wall thereof, an hundreth fortie and foure cubites, by the measure of man, that is, of the Angell.

18. And the building of the wall of it was of Iasper, and the citie was pure gold, like vnto cleere glasse.

19. And the foundations of the wall of the citie were garnished with all maner of precious stones: the first foundation was Iasper: the second of Saphire: the third of a Chalcedonie: the fourth of an Emeraud.

20. The fift of a Sardonix: the sixt of a Sardius: the seuenth of a Chrysolite: the eyght of a Beryll: the ninth of a Topaze: the tenth of a Chrysoprasus: the eleuenth of a Iacinth: the twelfth an Amethyst.

21. And the twelue gates were twelue pearles, and euery gate is of a pearle, and the streete of the citie is pure gold like shining glasse.

22. And I saw no temple therein, for the Lord God Almightie and the Lambe in it: are the temple of it.

23. And this city hath no neede of the Sunne, neither of the Moone to shine for the glory of God did light it, and the Lambe is the light of it.

24. And the people which are saued shall walke in the light of it: and the kings of the earth shall bring their honour and glory vnto it.

25. And the gates of it shall not be shut by day, for there shall be no night there.

26. And the glorie and honour of the Gentiles shall be brought vnto it.

27. And there shall enter into it, no vncleane thing, neither whatsoeuer worketh abomination, or lies: but they which are written in the Lambes booke of life.

The holy scriptures, beloued, doe set forth that the godly shall dwell with the Lord as it were in a citie: As yee may reade, Hebr. 11. that Abraham, Isaac, and Iaakob dwelled in tents, in the land of promise as in a strange land, and looked for a citie that hath foundations, whose builder and framer is God. Saint Paule also saith, that our *Politeuma* is in the heauens, Phil. 3. which is translated our conuersation, but it is as much as to say, our freedome in a citie. Now as this heauenly habitation is called a citie:

THE REVELATION.

so here it is shewed in vision shadowed foorth and described, to bee a wonderfull goodly citie, most rich and precious, and euery way commodious. It is the minde and purpose of the holy Ghost thus to set it forth, that we may striue to enter into it. For men will striue to attaine vnto rich and precious things. And verily we are more then blockes and stones, if we be not moued with the glorie of this citie, yea euen inflamed, and rauished with the loue of it. But I will come to the wordes, which becausethey tend all vnto one generall purpose, which I haue noted, I will not stand largely vpon them.

First, here is noted who sheweth him this vision, when he saith, It was one of the seuen Angels which had the seuen vials, full of the seuen last plagues, that said vnto him, come I will shew thee the bride the lambes wife. In the 17. chapter he telleth that one of those seuen Angels shewed him the false whorish Church great Babylon: and here one of them, whether the same or not, it is not much materiall for to enquire, doth shew him the true Church the spouse of Christ indeed. There Iohn sayth, hee was caryed into the wildernes, for that whore layeth all wast: and here he is caryed vp into an high mountaine, and there seeth this holy citie: for that place is fit for the beholding of the whole proportion, & they must indeed ascend vp from the earth in heauenly contemplation, that will take the viewe of it aright. And then in a word he setteth forth the great glory of this citie, when hee sayth, hauing the glory of God. What tongue is able to expresse the great glory of almightie God?

And then there is shewed, that this citie shall flourish and continue in her excellent beautie for euer: when he sayth, her shining was like to a stone most precious, to a Iasper cleere as christall. The Iasper is of a greene colour, but the Iasper is not transparent, and therefore vnto it is added that which is in the chrystall, that is cleere quite through. Then both these together, the greenenes of the Iasper, and the through cleerenes of the chrystall, as if they did concurre in some stone most precious, doe declare the shining of this citie. This is a greenenes that flourisheth for euer. Ye haue goodly greene things here in the world, but they wither in time, it shall not be so here in the heauenly Ierusalem.

The next thing is, That it hath a great wall and high. What the vse of a wall is in a citie, ye doe know well enough. It is for defence and safetie of the inhabitants, by keeping out enemies. The wall then is the strength of the citie. This citie, this holy Ierusalem, shall not be assaulted by any enemies, for Satan and his companies shall be shut vp in hell: but yet it is said to haue a great high wall, to represent the strength and safetie of it. No danger can approch vnto those which dwell in it. He saith further, that it hath twelue gates, and twelue Angels at the twelue gates. This is commendable in a citie, that there is hard accesse for the enemies, and easie and commodious passage in and out for the citizens. That same is noted in this citie. The wall doth defend by keeping out enemies, the gates are for the friends to enter in by. And as in kings courts and cities, there be keepers of the gates, to see who enter: so here are twelue Angels at euery gate one, to declare that there shall be no entrance in at these gates for any, but the true citizens. And those are they which

Ee 3 are

are noted in the next wordes, and the names written, which are the names of the twelue tribes of Israell. There is none which shall be saued but Israell, and therefore here are the names of the twelue tribes of Israel. Not that all are Israel (as the Apostle speaketh) which are of Israel. All are not the children of God, which are the children of Abraham after the flesh. Againe, all the true beleeuers of the Gentiles, though they bee not the children of Abraham after the flesh, yet are they his children by faith, and are as it were incorporate into the tribes of Israell. All the faithfull then, euen all the true worshippers of God, both of the Iewes and Gentiles, are included within the names of the twelue tribes of Israel, and are written vp as the freemen of this citie. So that all these doe come and are suffered to passe, and to enter by the gates into the citie.

It is added, that there were on the East part three gates, and on the Northside three gates, on the Southside three gates, and on the Westside three gates. We are taught that the Lord hath his chosen and faithfull seruants in all quarters of the worlde, and will gather them from the East, from the West, from the North, and from the South, into the kingdome of heauen. Now that which the scripture vttereth touching that point by plaine speeches in sundrie places, here is figured out by the gates. For these gates on all parts are to shew, that out of all quarters of the earth, the redeemed shall bee gathered, and enter into blisse. It is all one then, of what kingdome or people a man bee, so that he feare God, and worke righteousnes, the passage lieth open to him into this citie. There shal not any one faile, wander or loose his way, but all shall meete through these gates.

He addeth further, that the wall of the citie had twelue foundations, & in them the names of the lambes twelue Apostles. How is this to be taken? hath the church more foundations then one? Doth not the holy Apostle Saint Paul teach that there is no foundation of the Church but Iesus Christ? 1. Cor. 3. How then are the twelue Apostles here set as twelue foundations? To this I answere, that Saint Paule teacheth how this is to be vnderstood, when he saith, that we are built vpon the foundation of the Apostles and prophets, Iesus Christ being the head corner stone. Thus it is, the doctrine of the Apostles and Prophets doth lay Iesus Christ the only foundation of the Church. Heere are therefore vnder the names of the Apostles, to bee vnderstood all the prophets, in as much as they all teach but one and the same doctrine. This must needs be so, because the holy Apostles were in the last times chosen by Christ when he walked vpon the earth; but the Church was before, euen from the beginning of the worlde, and had prophets which did instruct her. The prophets then being first, why are the Apostles named for all? The reason is, that the doctrine of the Apostles touching Christ is more cleere, the the doctrine of the Prophets. Moreouer, yee may see that the number of twelue is much vsed in this prophecie.

It followeth, he that talked with me had a golden reed to measure the city withall, and the gates thereof, and the wall thereof. It is one great d.scommoditie in a citie, if it be so that the inhabitants be scanted for roome: for then one doth annoy an other. In this heauenly citie, there shall bee no such annoyance, but roome enough

nough for all to dwell most commodiously. Now to represent this, the citie must be measured, that the largenes thereof may bee knowne. And for that cause the Angell hath a golden reede to measure withall. It was the maner in some countries where those great reedes did growe, to vse them for measuring poles, because they were very light and fit for such a purpose. Therefore the measuring pole here is called a reede, notwithstanding he saith it was of gold. All things are so precious about this citie, that the very measuring rod is of pure gold, which it is to be measured withall.

And then it is said, that the citie lay fouresquare, and the length of it is as large as the breadth of it. This setteth forth the situation and proportion of the citie by a square figure: in which the length and breadth are all one. If ye be desirous to know what is signified hereby, marke but a little. A round thing may bee rolled and moued out of the place more easilie then a square. That which standeth square standeth fast and vnmoueable. When hee saith therefore that this citie lay foure square, it represents, that it standeth fast for euer and euer. The strongest built cities that euer haue been vpon the earth, haue come to ruine and decay: but the heauenly habitations are durable. It is one great and speciall comfort, for all the godly to know, that their habitation is so surely founded by their Lord God almightie, that it cannot be moued. This is it which is spoken in the Epistle to the Hebrewes, chapter 12. verse 28. Wherefore receiuing a kingdome that cannot bee shaken, let vs haue grace, whereby we may so serue God, that we may please him. Then the citie is measured, and it is twelue thousand furlongs. This is a very large citie if ye count the miles. Eight furlongs are a mile, so that the whole commeth to a thousand and fiue hundreth miles. And then it seemeth euident that he measured but one square, because the foure squares were equall. Then if one square were 12. thousand furlongs, the whole is foure times so much, and then the compasse about of the whole citie is sixe thousand miles. Here may a question be moued, because it is euident by the word of our Sauiour Christ, that the multitude of the damned doth farre exceede the multitude of those that shall be saued. For he saith, the way is streight, and the gate narrow which leadeth vnto life, and fewe there be that finde it. But the way is broad and the gate wide that leadeth vnto destruction, and many walke in it. If this be so, how commeth it that hell is described to be so farre lesse then heauen? For Chapter the 14. the great wine fatte of the wrath of God (which is hell) is troden, and he saith blood came out by the space of a thousand and fiue hundreth furlongs. Here is a great difference. I answer that the multitudes in hell are cast in together on heapes, as clusters of grapes into the wine presse, and shall not haue large and commodious dwelling, but be there as it were pressed together: But in heauen the citizens shall haue large and commodious dwelling, there shall bee no streightnes: there shall be no annoyance, the citie is capable of them all.

But now ye are to obserue, that it is not the purpose of the holy Ghost to set forth the iust, and full compasse of the heauenly Ierusalem (for it is vnmeasurable to our capacitie) but by this great measure, he giueth vs as it were some taste of the largenes thereof. And this number of twelue thousand is vsed, becaufe in this booke all is as yee may fee by twelues. That number is chofen, becaufe of the twelue tribes of Ifrael. The citie being of fo wonderfull a breadth and length, this is wonderfull that he faith, the length, the breadth, and the height of it are equall. Here is a moft diuine workemanfhip, here is a large roome for habitation, wee muft not thinke of this citie after any earthly maner. For how can any thing bee built fo high, but by the almightie power of God? The wall then is meafured, and found to bee an hundreth fortie and foure Cubites. Concerning the length of the wall thofe twelue thoufand furlongs, fet it foorth. And touching the height, he fayd it was equall with the length: then this is to bee taken of the thickenes of the wall. The number of the Cubites doth arife of twelue times twelue. And this is to declare the inuincible ftrength of the wall. What can pearce through this wall. What can bring any danger vnto the inhabitants of this citie. They are protected with fuch a power of God, that they fhall dwell fafe for euer.

In the next place hee fetteth forth the rich and precious ftuffe that the citie is made of: beginning with the wall faying: the building of the wall was of Iafper. Then hee addeth, that the citie was of pure golde. Then next hee fheweth that the twelue foundations were garnifhed with all maner of precious ftones, and hee rehearfeth twelue fortes of thofe precious ftones, for euerie foundation one. Then hee commeth to the gates, and faith that the twelue gates were twelue pearles, euery gate one pearle. And laftly he faith, that the ftreet of the citie is pure golde, like vnto fhining glaffe. Here is a wonderfull rich and precious thing if yee confider well of it. For firft, what is more glorious in the earth, then the greene flourifhing colour of the Iafper, fhining through like cleere Chryftall? And fuch is the wall thereof. What is there among men more rich then golde, precious ftones and pearles? And then note, how the meaneft partes in the citie, as the foundations of the walles, the gates, and the ftreetes are of thefe rich things. If in a citie, the walles, the ftreetes, and the gates bee of very rich and coftlie things; wee looke for more excellent things in mens chambers: So if the meaneft partes of this citie, as the very ftreete bee of pure golde that fhineth thorough like glaffe, which is a wonderfull glorious thing; the gates of pearles, and the foundations of precious ftones; what fhall we thinke to bee the glorie, and the riches of the chiefe parts? But what fhall we fay, or how is this to bee taken, fhall there bee golde, and pearle and precious ftones indeede? Nay we are not to conceiue fo of the heauenly citie. But the holy Ghoft would giue vs as it were a fhadowe of the glorie and riches of heauen, and for the fame purpofe chufeth the richeft and the moft precious things that bee in the earth. Wee may not take it that the glorie fhall bee no greater, nor the riches, then are here defcribed, but as I fayd, that thefe things are to make fome fhadowe and refemblance of thofe heauenly ioyes, riches, and glorie. For to fpeake the trueth, there is nothing vnder heauen which is comparable to thefe glorious things which the elect fhall poffeffe in the kingdome of God: but thefe are the richeft and the

good-

THE REVELATION. 425

goodliest things which come into our knowledge, and therefore the description is made by them. Moreouer, they be such things as men doe naturally couet and desire to possesse. What a great desire is there of a little golde, of a few small pearles and precious stones? Here is all golde, pearle and precious stone; and not onely so, but such pure golde as shineth through the cleere glasse. This being, as I said, but a shadowe, taken from such things as we be acquainted withall, and which wee couet to possesse, and comming many degrees short of the things which they doe here resemble, may yet greatly moue our mindes with the glory and riches thereof: How much more then ought wee to bee moued with the things themselues which these doe represent, which are incomparable? I may speake thus, and that boldly, if the beautie, the riches, the glorie, and the ioyes of this citie doe not as it were rauish and inflame our minds with the loue of it, and raise vp in our hearts a studie to attaine vnto it, wee are very blockes. Shall men rise early in the morning, toyle and labour all the daye long, fare hardly, and goe late to bed, passe ouer large seas into farre countries, and through many dangers, for to get a little golde, or a fewe small pearles, which yet they shall possesse but for a fewe dayes? And shall we vse no labour, nor diligence, nor care to attaine to this heauenly citie, where all the meanest things, as it were the pauement of the streete, are of pure shining golde, goodly rich pearles, and precious stones of very great glorie? I pray you thinke vpon the glorie of this citie, and in comparison of it, despise all the vaine and transitorie things of this life. How foolish are they and madde, nay worse then madde, which for a few pleasures and vaine delights which last but for a season, depriue themselues of so great glorie? For they that are giuen to the world, commit such sinnes, and are ouerwhelmed in such filthines, that they are shut out of this heauenly citie.

Then Saint Iohn addeth, I saw no Temple therein: for the Lord God and the Lambe are the Temple of it. Ierusalem vpon the earth had the temple in it, builded by Salomon, which was the speciall place of Gods worship. There was the signe of Gods presence, there were the sacrifices, there was the lawe taught. But this heauenly Ierusalem hath no temple: for there shall bee no neede of any place to come vnto for instruction, there shall neede no Sacraments or signes of Gods presence, for the glorified shall beholde the Lord God present, and shall inioy his presence, and shall see and know him perfectly, so that they shall neede no more any teaching. When I say they shall see and knowe the Lord God perfectly, I meane so farre as the creature is capable of the sight and knowledge of the creator. For we may not take it that any of the creatures, either among men or Angels, can beholde or know God in the fulnes or perfection of his glorie: seeing the Lorde God is infinite, and incomprehensible. We must needes confesse that a creature then cannot see into the fulnesse of his glorie. For can any creature reach so farre as to comprehend that which is incomprehensible? Can a creature see into the depth of that which is infinite? The Lorde will reueale himselfe so farre as shall bee a full sufficiencie for the happines of the creature. Otherwise as Saint Paul saith, God dwelleth in light that none can come vnto. This great inui-

sible:

sible God is the temple of that heauenly citie, and the Lambe: for the Lambe is of equall maiestie, power and glory with the father. There is none that is the Temple but God, but the Lambe is the Temple, whereby it is manifest that the Lambe is God. Moreouer, the father doeth manifest himselfe in his sonne, the elect are reconciled to God by Christ, and therefore he saith that the Lorde God and the Lambe are the Temple thereof. We shall knowe God, and we shall beholde him in Christ, and through Christ we shall dwell with him for euer. O beloued, is not here happie dwelling? Haue we not great cause to long after this heauenly habitation, and euen with impatient desire, to waite when this glorie shall be reuealed.

In the next place hee commendeth the light and the brightnes of this citie, which is such, and so great, that he saith it needeth not the sunne nor the moone to shine in it. And the reason is rendred, that the glory of God doth light it, and the Lambe is the light of it. The Lord God is the father of lightes, hee hath created the sunne and the moone, they be but dimme sparkes in comparison of his glorie. Where his glorie doth shine, where the glory and light of the Lambe is, what neede is there of the light of the sunne or of the moone? Nay the light of the sunne is so farre inferiour to the brightnesse of God which shineth in that citie, that it is as it were put out. For looke how it is betweene a small candle and the sunne, so is it betweene the sunne and that light of the Lambe Iesus Christ. Set vp a little candle in a darke place, it shineth, and giueth light: But set it vp at noone in the cleere sunne-shine, and where is then the light of your candle? what vse is there of it then? Euen so the sunne in the firmament is a goodly light, and shineth full bright ouer the world: but if the brightnes of God which lightneth this citie should shine forth, the light of the sunne should become as nothing. Moreouer yee knowe what our Sauiour saith in the Gospell, that the righteous shall shine as the sunne in the kingdome of their father. If euery one of Gods elect shall be as bright as the sunne (as it cannot be denied vnlesse we will gaine-say our Lord) what neede shall there be of the sunne to giue light to them? Hee addeth, that the people which are saued shall walke in the light of it. This is a most ioyfull light which is prepared for all the chosen of God, they shall walke in it. The wicked shall be in darkenes and in horror, euen the deepe gulfe of hell. What difference there shall bee, you can easilie conceiue. Men doe a little perceiue how vncomfortable darkenes is, and how ioyfull and cheerefull a thing the light is: and at the lighting of a candle will say, God send vs the light of heauen: And it were very well if we had the care to walke as the children of light. For alas the wishing is little, vnlesse we endeuour most earnestly to attaine to the true faith, sound knowledge of God, and sincere repentance. Most certaine it is, that if we walke in darkenes here, committing the workes of darkenes, euen the wicked deedes of the flesh, wee shall neuer enter into this light, but as children of darkenes, bee cast into the darke pitte. The kings of the earth shall bring their honour and glorie vnto it. This is harder to be vnderstoode. Shall kings adde glorie to this citie? or shall any earthly glorie be added to that heauenlie? I

answer

answere that we may not so take it. They that come to dwell in this citie, doe not bring their glory with them, and so as it were adde glory to the citie, neither is there any earthly pompe or magnificence which can increase the glory thereof: but they finde their glory there, and the citie doth bestowe it vpon them. Then must we consider how the words may be taken. And that is, that there haue been great and glorious kings in the earth which are saued, as Dauid and Salomon with many other both in the times of the lawe and vnder the Gospell. All these are said to bring their glory to this citie, when they doe here as it were lay it downe. For they lay it down after a sort, when as they receiue so great a glory in this citie, that the glory which they had as kinges vpon the earth is vanished and gone. For what is the glory which king Salomon had, to the glory of the least of Gods children in the kingdome of heauen? He saith the gates of it shall not be shut by day, for there shall be no night there. They vse to shut vp the gates of cities by night to keepe out enemies, and the gates of the cities are not shut by day, vnles it be for the feare of enemies that do besiege or ly in waite. Here shall be no feare of any inuasion, and therefore he saith the gates shall neuer be shut. For when he saith, the gates shall not bee shut by day, it is as much as to say, the gates shall neuer bee shut for the day lasteth euer, which he declareth in the next words, when he saith there shall be no night there. The sun compasseth about here, and so there commeth a shadow of the earth which maketh a night: for our night is no more but the shadow of the earth. But in the heauenly Ierusalem the Lord God is the light and the lambe, and with him there is no variablenes nor shadow by turning, Iam. 1. He sheweth further that all the glory of the Gentils shall be brought vnto it. As I said before, be the glory of the Gentils and kingdoms neuer so great, yet there it shall be laid downe. And then followeth a terrible sentence, that no vncleane thing shall enter into it, neither whatsoeuer worketh abomination or lies. This is diuers times rehearsed because vngodly men doe sooth and flatter themselues, as though they should get to heauen well enough for all their sinnes and abominable vncleannes, and notwithstanding all their falshood and lies. They are very much deceiued. And marke how he addeth, but they which are written in the lambes booke of life. This sheweth plainely that the elect of God are sanctified, purged and clensed from al filthy abominations and lies. Therefore if we will haue assurance that we be Gods chosen, and that we shal enter into this citie, we must be purged in our hearts from an euil conscience, and we must lead an holy life. The Lord graunt vs that grace, Amen.

THE.

THE XLVIII. SERMON.
CHAP. XXII.

1. *And he shewed me a pure riuer of water of life, cleare as chryſtall, proceeding out of the throne of God, and of the lambe.*
2. *In middeſt of the ſtreet of it, and of either ſide of the riuer was the tree of life, which bare twelue maner of fruits, and gaue fruit euery moneth: and the leaues of the wood ſerued to heale the Gentiles.*
3. *And there ſhall be no more curſe, but the ſeate of God and of the lambe ſhall be in it, and his ſeruants ſhall ſerue him.*
4. *And they ſhall ſee his face, and his name ſhall be written in their foreheads.*
5. *And there ſhall be no night, and they neede no candle, neither the light of the ſunne: for the Lorde God giueth them light, and they ſhall raigne for euermore.*
6. *And he ſaid vnto me, theſe ſayings are faithfull and true, and the Lord God of the holy prophets ſent his Angell, to ſhew vnto his ſeruants the things which muſt ſhortly be fulfilled.*
7. *Behold I come ſhortly, happie is he that keepeth the wordes of this propheſie.*
8. *I am Iohn which ſaw theſe things and heard them: and when I had heard and ſeene, I fell downe to worſhip before the feet of the Angel which ſhewed me thoſe things.*
9. *But he ſaid vnto me, ſee thou do it not, for I am thy fellow ſeruant, and the fellow ſeruant of thy brethren the prophets, and of them which keepe the ſayings of this booke: worſhip God.*

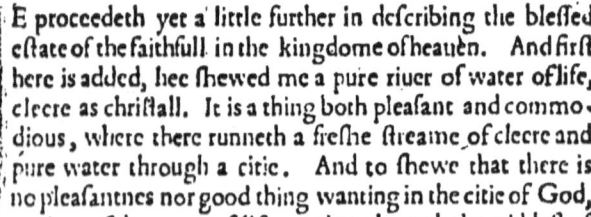

HE proceedeth yet a little further in deſcribing the bleſſed eſtate of the faithfull in the kingdome of heauen. And firſt here is added, hee ſhewed me a pure riuer of water of life, cleere as chriſtall. It is a thing both pleaſant and commodious, where there runneth a freſhe ſtreame of cleere and pure water through a citie. And to ſhewe that there is no pleaſantnes nor good thing wanting in the citie of God, Saint Iohn ſeeth a pure riuer of the water of life running through the middeſt of the ſtreet thereof. Here are two great things repreſented by this riuer; the one is the ouerflowing abundance of life which the godly ſhall haue in heauen; and the other is the perpetuity of the ſame life. The firſt is euident in this, that there ſhall not onely be life, but an ouerflowing ſtreame of life. The inhabitants ſhall drinke

drinke as of the streame of a full riuer. There shall be then no scarcity of the spirituall life, which ouerfloweth in this maner. The true life is sweete and precious, and here it is in great abundance. The second poynt is, that this abundant life shall be perpetuall, which is represented by this that they be liuing waters, or running waters that flow from the fountaine. A standing water drieth vp and diminisheth if it be much drawne, and no supply made: but waters that doe flow from a freshe spring doe continue. What would it helpe to inioy abundance of life for a time, and then the same to faile? What a griefe would ensue? But the elect are assured, that the heauenly life shall neuer faile nor diminish. They shall liue in perfect ioyes for euer, euen world without end: for this sweet and pleasant riuer shall neuer drie vp. And it is to be obserued that he addeth in the next wordes, namely that this pure riuer which is cleere as chrystall, proceedeth out of the throne of God, and of the lambe. For this noteth the fountaine or spring head from whence this riuer floweth: and that is the Lord God himselfe. God is the author and fountaine of life: this riuer therefore floweth forth from his throne. And verely here is the cause, both of that abundance, and of the perpetuitie of heauenly life. For the Lorde God is a bottomles, and an infinite fountaine of life which can neuer bee diminished. He continueth the same for euer and euer, giuing life in all abundance to his chosen. Yee see therefore that the streame of these most pure waters doe flow out of the throne of God. And it is also well to be obserued, that he saith, and of the lambe. The lambe Iesus Christ hath the same throne with the father, being eternall God with him, and the father giueth life through his sonne vnto the world. Hee saith *I am the bread of life that came downe from heauen* Iohn 6. No man can haue any part of true life from God, but through the mediation of Iesus Christ. And therefore yee see that this pure riuer of the waters of life proceedeth out of the throne of God, and of the lambe. So many then as with true faith beleeue in the Lorde Iesus, this riuer of the water of life shall flow plentifully vnto them. Then hee saith further, in the middest of the street of it, and on either side of the riuer was the tree of life. There was in paradise a tree of life which was a sacrament vnto our first parents, that continuing in obedience they should liue. So here is the tree of life in the open street of this citie, and euen on both sides of that riuer watered by the same: which figureth that spirituall foode of eternall life, which all the blessed company of heauen shall receiue in Christ Iesu. *And the trees bare new fruite twelue times in the yeere, euery moneth new:* which doth signifie that the fruites of life shall bee alwaies delightsome. Wee see that if men haue their fill of sweete things, it breedeth a kinde of loathing, if they haue not still change and fresh added. Wherefore to teach vs that men shall inioy the most precious and sweet fruits of life without all such fulnes as breedeth any loathing, it is said that the trees doe beare fruit euery moneth. What a ioyfull thing is this? Trie it who will, they shall finde it most certaine that the great abundance of the sweetest things worketh as I said a loathing. But here where the sweetnes of the fruits far excelleth all the pleasantest delights that be vpon the earth, there

shall.

certaine and out of al controuersy, that there shal be no infirmity, neither sicknes, paine nor sore. How then will yee say is this to be vnderstood? I answere, that the arte of healing doth consist of two parts, the one is preseruatiue, which doth preuent all diseases, remouing or destroying the causes of them: the other is restoratiue, that is where the disease is come, and the health impaired, to remoue the disease, and to restore the health. Now albeit there be no infirmities in the kingdome of heauen and so no vse of this second part, yet through the Lord Iesus the tree of life the saued are preserued and kept from all diseases and griefes, so that this declareth a most blessed life, not subiect vnto griefes. It followeth, *and there shall be no more curse.* Adam sinned in the earthly paradise, and so brought a curse vpon himselfe and vpon all his posteritie, and he was thrust forth of paradise. But here shall be no curse, here shall be no casting forth nor separating of any one, that shall once enter. It were a more heauie case if the state were such that any might fall from it. If a man should rise vp vnto great wealth and honor, and then fall quite from it, would it not greeue him more then if he had neuer knowen it? In like maner, if a man should attaine vnto the blessed life and glorie of the heauens, and then haue a curse light vpon him to be cast forth, it would be more torment and sorowe vnto him, then if he had neuer beene partaker thereof. Wherefore the holy Ghost, taketh away all feare and doubt of any such matter, and sayth, there shall be no more curse. They shall remaine in that blessed estate for euer without any feare of danger. Here be reasons added to confirme this, as first that the seate of God and of the lambe, shalbe in it. Where the blessed God sitteth and raigneth reconciled to his people through the lambe, what curse can there approch? but in this holy Ierusalem shalbe the seate of the liuing God, he shall raigne for euermore in it, no euil shall then annoy. This is through God doth raigne in his sonne Iesus Christ, and therefore he sayth the seate of God and of the lambe. It followeth, *and his seruants shall serue him.* This confirmeth the matter, where the kingdome of God is set vp, this effect followeth, that his people obey him: for where God raigneth, those must needs serue and obey him in whome he raigneth. Now then in the holy Ierusalem where the seate of God is, and so his seruants obey him, there can be no sinne committed, and so there can be no curse. For where there is no sinne, there is no curse. It is then to be noted, that when he sayth, that his seruants shal serue him, that the seruice shalbe perfect, euen as the seruice of the holy Angels is. They do wholy and altogether delight in obeying and glorifiyng God: So shall the faythfull also when they bee vnburdened of this corruption. This seruice of the Lord shall bee no base thing nor any bondage: but a most honorable and glori-
·ous

ous freedom, for the seruice of our God (as we vse to say) is perfect freedom. Sinne and corruption, euen the vanitie of our owne mindes doth nowe hold vs so vnder, that we can not serue him perfectly, but we shalbe set free from the yoake thereof and then, as I said, our seruice shalbe perfect. Then when the seruice and the obedience is perfect, so that there shalbe no spot of sinne, all daunger and feare of curse, or separation is remoued.

He sayth further, they shall see his face, and his name shalbe written in their foreheads. These bee great priuileges, and such as accompany true blessednes, and are farre remoued from curse. Our Sauiour saith, blessed are the pure in hart for they shall see God, Math. 5. To bee in Gods presence, and to bee able to behold him with ioy and comfort, as the holy Angels do behold him, is so perfect and so high an estate, that well it may bee brought in as a reason to shewe, that in that heauenly citie there can be none subiect to the feare of any curse, especially when they shall beare his name in their foreheads as his peculiar. The wicked in some sort shall see and behold the glorie of the Lorde God: but not with any ioy therein, but with extreame horror and torment. For then shall they perceiue what a glorious diuine maiestie they haue dispised. O beloued, here is a waightie matter, euen this, that wee (if we be wise) endeuour with all the might and power that we can to be pure in heart, that so wee may attaine to this high blessing, to see God. Wee are full of impure things, and our hearts fraught with euill desires of the flesh, seeke to haue them purged out, and to be replenished with the heauenly gifts and graces of the holy spirit. And nowe hee concludeth the description of the heauenly ioyes, with this sentence, there shalbee no night, and they neede no candle, nor the light of the sunne: for the Lorde God giueth them light, and they shall raigne for euermore. These wordes containe great and high matters, and haue no difficulty in them. The glorious light of heauen is set forth, that there shalbe no night, no neede of a candle, nor the light of the sunne: because the Lorde God who in brightnes infinitely exceedeth all lights shall shine vpon them and lighten them with his glorie. Here is againe the light of heauen. And the other clause addeth, and they shall raigne for euermore. It hath beene shewed before what a life they should liue, and howe they should serue God without all feare of danger, and nowe in a worde hee toucheth the glorie and honor of their life: they shall raigne for euermore. Who raigne but kings? They be then all as greate and honorable kings. What shall not all this quicken and stir vp our spirites? Shall not all this moue vs to seeke after the true knowledge of God, and after spirituall thinges? If this I say can not moue vs to the feare and seruice of God, what are we? Howe dull and howe senseles may it be thought wee are? I beseech ye reade ouer sometimes by your selues the description of the heauenly glorie which is in the former chapter and in the beginning of this. The wordes are plaine and cleare. Ye shall euen at the first sight behold the richest, the pleasantest, and the most glorious thinge that euer yee heard of. Let the loue, and desire of it possesse your heartes. If ye will seeke, it is set before yee, God hath promised to giue it, vnto all that longe after it. Hitherto therte we haue had the description of the heauenly Ierusalem, to declare the happines and glorie that the saints of God shall liue in for euer.

Now we come to the conclusion of this prophecie. It is a generall conclusion, consisting of diuers poynts, whereof I haue read the first vnto yee, which is to set forth, to confirme and to ratifie the authoritie of this booke. And ye shall see that here are foure things brought for the same. The first is the affirmation of the Angel in these words, and he said vnto me, these sayings are faithfull and true. In the second, we haue the authoritie of the high God, the God of the holy prophets which sent his Angell to shew to his seruants, things that must shortly be fulfilled. Then next the Lord Iesus is brought in, who saith he will come shortly, and therfore pronounceth them blessed, which keepe the words of this prophecie. And lastly, Saint Iohn testifieth, that hee heard and sawe them. But let vs come to euery poynt particularly.

First, that the Angell affirmeth, saying, these words are faithfull and true: it may be sayd, what needeth this asseueration, who doubteth of them? Doe not all that professe the name of our Lord Iesu Christ acknowledge that this prophecie is the vndoubted word of God? I confesse men doe in some sort acknowledge, that the wordes of this booke are faithfull and true: but if we looke narrowly to the matter, we shall find that men doe not beleeue them to be faithfull and true. He saith, that the bookes shalbe opened, the bookes of mens conscience, and that men shall be iudged according to their deedes. This booke doth also plentifully shew, what horrible torments of hell are prepared for wicked deedes. Doe men thinke yee beleeue this? Would they then commit whoredomes, theftes, and periuries? would they liue in malice, in enuie, and hatred? would they despise God, and liue in all wicked wayes? would they lie and slaunder, and commit all filthie abominations? I will tell yee how they doe beleeue. We know say they, that all men shall come to iudgement. We know these things are euill which we doe. We know that hell is prepared for sinners, but God is mercifull, and we will crie God mercy. Doth this booke say, that men may commit all manner of wicked deeds, and then if they crie God mercie they shall be saued? No, it sayth euery man shal be iudged according to his deedes. And doth not Christ tell vs, that not euery one that sayth Lord, Lord, shall enter into the kingdome of heauen, but hee that doth the will of my father which is in heauen. Yea but shall not a sinner if he repent be pardoned? Doth not the word of God make plentifull promises that way? There is no doubt but that whosoeuer hath true repentance, he shalbe saued. But we must vnderstand that repentance is not in mans power, it is the gift of God. For thus it is, where there is not the spirite of God, where there is not the true faith which that spirite worketh, there is not, nor there cannot bee any true repentance. Then further, this is most certaine, that where sinne doth raigne, and a man is giuen ouer vnto filthie vices, there is not in that man the grace of God, there is not the true faith. His deeds doe declare that he is void of the feare of God, his workes do shew that he hath no true faith. Then you know that the prayer of such a man cannot bee acceptable, for the Scripture saith, his prayer is abominable to the Lord. This man hath com-
mitted

mitted heapes of abominable sinnes, lyeth sicke, and feareth the torments of hell, and for the same doth tremble and quake. Yea he weepeth and cryeth God mercie, what is he the better if his prayer be abominable? He hath no hope but in this, that he will crie God mercie, and what is he the better if his prayer be not heard? The Lord sheweth plainlie, & threatneth, that he will not heare the prayers of such wicked men, Esay 1. and Prouerb. 1. When a man hath prouoked the Lord God to wrath, shall he by and by at his pleasure haue the spirit of God and true faith? Shall he at pleasure be regenerate in the new and spirituall birth? for without that no man can be saued, Iohn 3. Beloued, let not men presumptuously commit wickednes vpon this hope that they will crie God mercie: but let them beleeue the wordes of this booke, that men for their vngodly deedes, in which they haue despised God shall be cast into the torments of hell. And let all that will deale wiselie seeke speedily for true repentance, and see if they can obtaine it. The multitude of the wicked damned soules, which are now in hell, some for pride, couetousnes, and extortion, some for drunkennes gluttonie, and lecherie, others for hatred, malice, and such like, did all know that the things were euill which they committed, and presumed vpon this, we will crie God mercie at our end. Surely if it were so, that when men haue committed all wicked deeds, they might by and by wash away all with a few wordes, the way to heauen should be a broad way and easie to find, quite contrarie to that which our Sauiour hath taught. Therefore beloued, know ye for certaintie, that the wordes of this prophecie be faithfull and true in euery part: and so in this, that they which leade an holie life shall be partakers of the ioyes of heauen, and they that commit wicked deeds shall for the same, be cast into the torments of hell. The most gracious Lorde make vs wise to beleeue these things, that we be not seduced. For then vndoubtedly wee shall eschew the foule vices which we see dayly committed euen with contempt of God: and wee shall be studious of good workes, that wee may enter into that holy citie, and haue our part in that blessed fellowship. Come then to the second which is the authoritie of the God of the holy prophets.

The summe of the matter cometh to this in effect, that this prophecie is of equall authoritie with the Prophecies of the prophets which were of olde, and shall as certainly in euery matter contained therein be accomplished in the time, as they were in theirs. The bookes of Moses, and of the other prophets which prophecied of things to come, are iustly helde in most high and sacred authoritie, as the vndoubted word of God. Then is this booke to bee held in the same account, in as much as the same God euen the God of those holy prophets, is the author of it: for he sent his Angell to shew the things which are vttered in it. Then touching that one point, namely that this booke is to stand equall with the olde prophecies, in as much as that same God of those holy prophets sent his Angell now in this, I need to speake no further.

The other point is, that as the Prophecies of those old prophets were al fulfilled in their time, so shall euery thing in this. In Esay, in Ieremie, in Ezechiel, in Daniel, and in the rest, ye shall find many things which the Lord shewed by them long

Ff time

time before they should come to passe. And among other matters there was foreshewed, how the people of Israell should go into captiuitie, how long they should continue, & what great calamities should come vpon them after their returne out of captiuitie, by diuers wicked tyrants. Ye shall find, that there was not one word that fell to the ground of all those things which the Lord spake by those his holy seruants, but that indeede euery thing was fulfilled in their season. Euen so, concerning this booke, there be many things foreshewed in it, and they shall all be fulfilled. As our Sauiour said, Heauen and earth shall passe, but one title or iote of the law shall not passe, vntill all be fulfilled, Math. 5. So assure your selues, this prophecie comming from the same God, no one iote of it shall passe vnfulfilled. He that can looke into the times that are past, since this prophecie was giuen, shal find that all things haue fallen out agreable to the prophecie of this booke. And we may assure our selues that the things which remaine, shall vndoubtedly come to passe. Ioyne this booke then to the other prophecies of the scripture, both in authoritie vndoubted and sacred, and also for the certaintie of the fulfilling the words of it.

This latter may leade vs to the former. For true it is, that the authoritie of this booke was in old time called into question by some: but if there were none other thing to perswade vs, touching the authoritie thereof, this might suffice, that euery thing hath fallen out from time to time, euen as this prophecie did foreshew. It is our great negligence, that we doe not cleerly see so much. Well, then to conclude this second poynt, the authoritie of this prophecie is equal with the prophecies that were of old in the time of the lawe, and shall as certainly be fulfilled as they were. Then in the third place the Lord Iesus is brought in to ratifie it, saying, behold I come shotly, blessed is he that keepeth the words of this prophecie. This as ye see consisteth of two branches, the one, that Christ saith he wil come shortly; the other, how well it shall go with them which keepe the words of this prophecie. But what doth the comming of Christ serue to the matter in hand? It toucheth the matter most neerely: For at his comming the full accomplishment shall be of all things that are here written. At his comming men shal find indeed, that the words of this booke are true. Then shal ye see the kingdom of the great Antichrist fully cast down, & ye ful measure of Gods wrath poured forth vpon al his enimies: then shall ye find, y^t al wicked men shalbe destroyed in hel as this book describeth. The glory of the church shall then be reuealed, so that wee shall then bee brought to the perfect sight, that they be blessed which keepe the words of this prophecie. It is but a little while before this shall come to passe, for he saith, behold I come shortly. Well then, let vs stand fast for a little time, and all controuersies shall bee decided. Here is striuing and contending, here is cauilling and much deprauing of the word of God, and all to leade the people into error and superstition, and to make them imbrace the doctrine of the great Antichrist: but let men learne to know the doctrine of this prophecie, and to stand in it, and they shall find and feele at the comming of Christ, that they are therein blessed, What an encouragement ought this to be vnto vs? Is there any thing to bee preferred before true blessednes? It is sayd in the beginning of this booke, Blessed is he that readeth, and blessed are they that heare the words of this prophecie, and keepe the things which are written in it: for the time is at hande: And here in the conclusion the Lord Iesus pronounceth the same thing againe. Shall we then beleeue the popish companie which affirme that this book is not to be medled withal? Nay let vs know that the authority of it is sacred and holy, and not onely that (for so much the papists do confesse) but also that it is a right profitable booke for all the seruants of God to bee exercised in: which shall euidently appeare at the comming of Christ. Seeing then beloued, that this is confirmed vnto vs double, let it stirre and moue our minds vnto the doubling of our care and diligence. This ought to be, for why doth the Lord else repeate it againe? Doubtlesse we are dull, slow, and negligent, otherwise these spurres should not be added: and it will be to our great condemnation if we bee not moued the more hereby. For it is the great kindnes of our Lord to shew vs wherein our safetie and blessednes consisteth, and how great a sinne is it then, to despise or neglect such kindnes?

In the fourth place S. Iohn setteth himselfe as a witnes, saying, I am Iohn which saw these things and heard them. His testimonie is of great waight, though he be but a man: for he is such a man as is firmly to be beleeued in all that hee speaketh. He is an Apostle, an instrument of the holy Ghost, and so guided by the spirit, that he speaketh and vttereth nothing that is his owne. He was well knowen to the Churches to be one of Christs Apostles, his authoritie among all the faithfull was throughly knowne and approued. For ye must consider, that looke what an Apostle did vtter, he did vtter it but as the instrument of that spirit which cannot erre. When he saith therefore, I am Iohn which saw these things, and heard them: hee giueth vs to vnderstand, that he was both an eye and an eare witnes. He bringeth not matters which he hath receiued by vncertaine report. He deliuereth this booke to the churches, they which receiue it at his hands do know him to be a most faithfull seruant of the Lord, euen a great Apostle, which deliuereth not any thing but that which he receiueth of the Lord, and he testifieth that he saw and heard all the things which he hath writtē in this book. And the faithfulnes of this holy man doth shew it selfe also euen in this, that he for the good of the Church spareth not to report his owne fault. For he telleth how he fell downe againe to worship the Angell, and how the Angell chargeth him not to do it, rendring reasons wherefore he might not. We had the like before in the 19. chapter, where I handled the matter, so that I need not but touch the matters here. It is to bee wondred at that so great an Apostle, so richly replenished with the spirite of God should faile in such a matter, and especially the second time, when he had been once before forbidden. But we must consider, that the vision shewed vnto him were so maruelous, and the glory of the Angel so great, that for the time he forgetteth himselfe. Hee tooke it that he must shew some reuerence in worship towards the Angell, and goeth beyond that which is due to any creature, euen to bestow vpon a seruant, a creature, some part of that diuine worship, which belongeth peculiarly to the Lord the creator. For that is manifest by this, that the Angell hauing shewed reason why hee might not doe it vnto him, as namely being his fellow seruant, and the fellow seruant of all true beleeuers, he willeth him to doe it vnto God. For the Lord God is alone to be worshipped with diuine worship: and the worship of Angels, of saints, vtterly by this forbidden. In the poperie they worship Angels and saints, yea they worship Images, and rotten bones and reliques, and because this place is so direct and manifest against them, they seeke all shifts and cauils to auoyde. And whereas Saint Iohn telleth plainly, that it was one of the seuen Angels which had the seuen vials full of the seuen last plagues, which came vnto him chapt. 17. and said, come I will shew thee the damnation of the great whore, whom he chapt. 19. fel downe to worship: and likewise whereas he saith chap. 21. ver. 9. there came one of those seuen Angels which had the seuen vials ful of the seuen last plagues, and said, come, I will shew thee the bride the lambes wife, whom he is about to worship, chap. 22. The Iesuites cauil and say, that S. Iohn tooke this Angel to be Christ, so meant to worship him with the highest worship. For they would make the blind beleeue, that there is a diuine worship to be giuen to creatures, which if Iohn had not passed beyond taking it to be Christ whom he worshipped, he should not haue been reprooued. Their other cauill, that it may bee the Angell doth refuse it not as vnlawfull, but because he will not take it at the hands of so great a person as Iohn, is most foolish. This is euident, that albeit the holy Apostles touching the deliuerie of Gods word, did it so perfectly, that Saint Paul is bolde to say, if an Angel from heauen preach vnto you any other Gospell besides that I haue preached, let him be accursed, Galath. 1. yet were they not so farre sanctified as in their deeds in obeying the same doctrine to be as perfect as the Angels. For the Angel reproueth Iohn with none other doctrine, but with that which hee knew. Wee are taught hereby how easie the fall is vnto the worship of excellent creatures, and how necessarie a thing it is to craue of the Lord God to sanctifie and guide vs so with his spirit, that we may obey the doctrine which we know. For who did better know then Saint Iohn, that God onely is to be worshipped with diuine worship? Who did vnderstand better then he, that Angels are but seruants of God, and that it is not lawfull to giue to them any part of the worship which is due to their Lord?

THE

THE XLIX. SERMON.
CHAP. XXII.

10 *And he sayd vnto me, Seale not the words of the prophecie of this booke: for the time is at hand.*

11 *He that is vniust, let him be vniust still: and he that is filthie, let him be filthie still: and he that is iust, let him be iust still: and he that is holy, let him be holy still.*

12 *And behold I come quickly: and my reward is with me, that I may giue vnto euery one as his worke shall be.*

13 *I am Alpha and Omega, the beginning and the end, the first and the last.*

14 *Blessed are they which keepe his commandements: that their part may be in the tree of life: and that they may enter in by the gates into the citie.*

15 *For without shall bee dogges, and enchanters, and whoremongers, and murtherers, and Idolaters, and whosoeuer loueth and maketh lyes.*

OME part of the generall conclusion of this booke I handled the last time: and now wee come vnto some other. And the first thing here is a commaundement, in which John is willed that hee should not seale vp the words of the prophecie of this booke: and a reason is rendred, becaufe the time is at hand. Where first to enquire here what should be meant by this not sealing, or that he willeth that the booke should remaine, or the words in the booke should remaine vnsealed. We know there be two speciall vses of sealing: the one is, when a seale is set to for to confirme and ratifie a writing: the other is, when a writing is sealed vp, so that it can not, nor may not be read nor knowne. Touching the former of these, we may not take it that the words of this prophecie must be vnsealed in that sense: for they be ratified, and ratified againe. Then it must be taken in the latter, that is to say, seale them not vp, let them be open for all men to reade, to heare, and to know. This is the plaine meaning: and touching this ye shall reade in diuers places of holy scripture: The Lord sayth, Esay. 29. vers. 11. that the vision should be as the words of a booke sealed vp, which they deliuered vnto one that can reade, saying, reade this I pray thee: then he shall say, I cannot; for it is sealed. The Prophet Daniel heard some thing vttered by the Angell which hee did not vnderstand, and sayd: O my Lord, what shall be the end of these things? And he sayd, Goe thy way Daniel, for these things are shut vp and sealed vntill the time determined, Daniel. 12. Ye see also before in this prophecie chap. 4. the booke sealed with seuen seales. The things are sealed vp and secret, and as the seales are opened, they be opened, reuealed and made knowne. In the tenth chapter of this prophecie, there is an Angel commeth downe from heauen with a little booke open in his hand: and he cryed with a loude voyce as when a lyon roreth: and when he had cryed, seuen thunders vttered their voyces. And when the thunders (sayth S. Iohn) had vttered their voyces, I was about to write: but I heard a voyce from heauen saying vnto me, Seale vp the things which the seuen thunders haue spoken, and write them not. Iohn had receiued a commandement at the first to write the things that he sawe: and therefore when he had heard the most dreadfull iudgements of God denounced against the enemies by terrible thunders, he was about to write what the thunders spake, so that the things might be read and knowne: but the Lord willeth him for to seale them vp, they shall not be knowne vntill the time appoynted doe come. Thus you may perceiue what is meant by sealing vp words; that is, what they cannot be vnderstood. And so (as I sayd before) when hee willeth that the wordes of this prophecie shall not be sealed vp, it is euident that he meaneth, they shall be read and knowne. This maketh flat against all those which affirme, that the words of this booke are so darke that they cannot bee vnderstood. For by their affirmation the wordes are sealed vp: but the Lord sayth, they be open and not sealed. Shall not we rather giue credit to the word of the Lord, then to men? If any shal replie and say, we feele and finde, that the words of this booke are hard to bee vnderstood. I answere that the fault is in our selues: we are so negligent and careles. For if we did with that reuerent care which ought to bee in vs, search after the knowledge of the things reuealed in this booke, we should finde that they be not sealed vp, but lye open for to be knowne. The Iesuites doe affirme, that it is very little that can in this booke be noted, in respect. The trueth is, they care not how little: for it painteth out their kingdome: but whatsoeuer they would beare men in hand, because they would not haue men see how fully the papisme is described in this booke to be the Antichristianisme: yet let vs hearken to the worde of the Lord, which sayth to Iohn, Seale not vp the words of the prophecie of this booke. Then the reason is added: for the time is at hand. This is as much as if hee should say, there is some present vse of the words of this booke, therefore they must not be sealed vp. Matters prophecied in this Reuelation, did beginne to be fulfilled euen presently after they were shewed to S. Iohn. There were great persecutions and afflictions vpon the Church, and grieuous calamities vpon the world. The mysterie of iniquitie, (as S. Paul sayth) did euen then beginne to worke. It was then time that the faithful should haue this booke in the hands euen open and vnsealed, that they might be instructed and armed against all assaults. They be therefore no friends, but enemies to the Church of God, they bee not for Christ, but for Antichrist, which would haue the words of this prophecie kept from the hands of the people, and lie as it were buried. And for your part (beloued, be not discouraged, as if the things vttered in it were so darke and mystical, as that you should not bee able to attaine

to

to the knowledge and vnderstanding of them: but giue your diligence with reuerend care of minde, and you shall finde that true which is here spoken, that the words of this prophecie are not sealed. To those indeede which haue no loue of the trueth, nor any desire to know the waies of God, but loue darknes and delight in the vanities of their owne minde, all the whole worde of God almost, is as a book sealed vp. Euery thing almost is hard and doubtfull vnto them. They are worthy that the light it selfe should be darknes vnto them, and euen that by which they stumble and fall, and are broken.

Thus much touching that one part of the conclusion of this prophecie, wherein he is willed not to seale vp the words thereof. Now let vs proceed vnto the next, which is in these words: He that is vniust, let him be vniust still: and he that is filthie, let him be filthie still: and he that is iust, let him be iust still: and he that is holie, let him be holie still: and behold I come quickly, &c. One part of these words is easie to bee vnderstood, when he sayth, hee that is iust, let him be iust still, and he that is holy, let him bee holy still: but how is the other part to bee taken, he that is vniust, let him be vniust still: he that is filthie, let him be filthie still? Doth the holy Scripture allow, or encourage, or giue leaue to men to be vniust, or filthie? because he saith, let him be filthie still? In other places the holy word of God calleth vpon men that bee filthie and vniust, to turne from the euill wayes: and here he sayth, let them bee filthie and vniust still. I answere, here is no allowance, here is no encouragement, here is no leaue graunted vnto wicked men to continue in their euill waies: but in very deede a very terrible threatning, if ye take all the words together, and marke well the manner of the phrase. For taking the words, as I sayd together, it must be thus: he that is filthie, let him be filthie still, I will come shortly and giue to euery one, or reward euery one as his workes shall be. That is, I will execute iudgement, I will powre foorth wrath and vengeance vpon such persons. Doe ye not see that here followeth (as we vse to say in our prouerbe) a sower sawce to their sweete meate? The Lord threatneth, as if hee should say, they that are in their banquet, and take their delight in their filthie lusts and pleasures of sinne, and by no meanes will bee restrained, let them alone, I will marre all their mirth ere it be long: for I will come and rewarde them according to their filthines in the torments of hell. Then ye may see that this threatning is but in a manner of phrase, as when we see one in an euill race obstinately bent and setled to goe forward, and will giue eare to no holesome counsell, wee will say, let him goe on, he will smart for it in the end. We haue the like manner of speech in Ecclesiast. chap. 11. where Salomon speaketh thus: Reioyce young man in thy youth, and let thy heart cheere thee in the dayes of thy youth, and walke in the wayes of thine heart, and in the sight of thine eyes: but know that for al these things God will bring thee to iudgement. A man would thinke that Salomon did encourage youth vnto all vain delights and pleasures: as yee haue many men which vse to say, that youth will bee merie, and thinke that no kinde of wantones, ryot, or lasciuious dealing is to bee reproued in them. Nay, ye shall haue many euen angry when they heare one finde fault with such dealings in young persons: and they say, they would haue youth deale like youth, it becommeth them to follow all maner of sports and pleasures. Such men as be of that opinion, could like well of these words of Salomon, when he willeth the youth to walke in all pleasures and delights: but the latter part doth pinch and bite them, where hee willeth them to knowe for certaintie, that for all those things, God will bring them to iudgement. If there were no Iudge to call men vnto their account; if there were no vengeance to be executed vpon sinners; if there were no torments in hell prepared for euill doers, it were the wisest way, with the Epicure, euen to follow all the carnall pleasures which a man could deuise: but when it is so that the end of them is so bitter, men were best to renounce them. Thus may you see, that he doth not allow nor giue leaue vnto men to commit sinne, when he sayth, he that is vniust, let him be vniust still, and he that is filthie, let him be filthie still: but contrariwise, by that phrase or maner of speaking, and by shewing that they shall come to iudgement, threatneth the euill doers. Men are bold and presumptuous now, euen to despise all holesome admonitions which the holy Ghost giueth in the word of God, and to heape vp all maner of sinnes and transgression: neuer looking to heare more of them, when they be once done and past: and readie they are for to plucke out his throte that shall rebuke and admonish them. Let them goe on, saith the Lord, they shall shortly come to their account, and receiue their desert.

Then touching the other part of the words, he that is iust, let him be iust still: and he that is holy, let him be holy still: There is a promise included, yea, a great promise, euen to incourage and strengthen the godly constantly to proceede in their godlines. It is but a little while, let them stand fast and continue to the ende which walke in the way of righteousnes and true holinesse, they shall haue their reward. For I come quickly, and my reward is with me, that I may giue euery man, as his worke shall bee. O beloued marke well, how that which is a most terrible and seuere threatning to the wicked, is the most comfortable and ioyfull promise that may bee to the godly. Christ will come and giue rewarde: a fearefull thing to him that hath committed those euill deeds whose rewarde by iust desert, is eternall fire in hell. Christ will come and giue reward, a most cheerfull thing to him that hath feared the Lord, and renouncing the way of wickednes, hath shewed the fruits of a true and liuely faith, euen all those holy workes which God hath prepared for his seruants to walke in, and which of his free mercie he hath promised to reward with eternall glorie. Is it not a good thing then for vs to studie dailie to please God, and to stand fast in the same, when there shall ere it be long be such a difference? Is it not much better for vs, that the comming of Christ should be a promise vnto vs, rather then a threatning. For as I sayd, that Christ doth tell vs he will come quickly and reward euery man as his worke shall be, is a grieuous threatning to the vngodly, and a comfortable promise to the righteous. And when he sayd he that is filthie, let him be filthie still, it is to confirme the righteous in their righteousnes, that they be not drawne awrie by their example. Let the wicked be wicked still, be not you like them. We know what a force there is in example for to draw men from good to euill: and especially where

we

THE REVELATION.

we see the multitude goe as it were whole with on consent, and no harme to follow. Yee shall heare many vtter such like speeches as these: I see my betters, my equals, and my inferiours doe these things, and shall I walke alone? shall I be one that men shall point, as one that will be singular? If God punish with damnation such as doe these things, there are but a few that shall escape from hell. Againſt such vaine thoughts, the holy ghoſt doth arme the godly, and sheweth that howsoeuer the multitudes of wicked persons perswade themselues that there is no harme, yet is it farre otherwise, for they shall ere it be long haue the wrath of GOD in a full measure powred foorth vpon them. Our Sauiour Chriſt as ye know telleth in the Goſpell, how the wicked shall flatter themselues and say peace and all is well, and euen ſuddenly, when they shall thinke that they be ſafe, ſhall deſtruction come vpon them, euen like a net that is ſpred ouer. For by ſuch a compariſon the holy ſcripture doth ſet forth the things vnto vs. When a net is layd for birdes the ſharp is made, the baite is ſpread, a birde commeth alone, ſitteth looking vpon it but is afraid. Afterward ſhe ſeeth many other birds flocke into it, and then ſhee is boldened and goeth in among them, ſo many doe harten each other: the fouler ſeeth his time and ſuddenly ſpreadeth the net ouer them, and they are caught. Euen ſo here be the allurementes of ſinne, as ſweet baites, the Lord GOD doth threaten, ſome man is fraid at the firſt, and doeth ſome what refraine, vntill hee ſeeth the multitude flocking in, and no harme to follow, but whatſoeuer iudgement the Lorde denounceth they laugh and deride it, hee alſo waxeth bold. But Chriſt will come, and at the laſt they ſhall all haue, as it were a net ſpred ouer them. And this is the reaſon why the Lord ſaith here, he that is vniuſt, let him be vniuſt ſtill, he that is filthy let him be filthy ſtill, behold I come quickly, let the iuſt and holy not bee moued with their boldnes, and ſo led to commit ſinne, but let them goe on till their time doe come. Salomon in Eccleſiaſtes Chap. 9. handleth this matter, and ſheweth that the heart of the children of men is full in them to doe euill, becauſe all commeth alike to all. A godly man proſpereth, a wicked man proſpereth: A wicked man doeth fall into aduerſitie and affliction, and a godly man is alſo afflicted. There appeareth no difference almoſt at all in outward things. How merrie, how pleaſant and full of delights, are many filthy men? and how they abound in all riches and wealth? which maketh them exceeding proud both againſt God and man, as the Prophet teacheth Pſal. 73. and how this doth weaken many touching the way of godlines who ſeeth not, that hath any ſight at all? Is it not then very needfull that the faithfull ſhould be armed with this. Let them goe on, let them be filthie, ſtand you faſt in the right way of godlines and be not discouraged, I will ſhortly come to iudgement, and they ſhall haue their reward euen according as their workes haue beene. Let me here ſpeake thus much vnto yee, and iudge in your ſelues whether it bee the counſell of man or the counſell of the holy ghoſt. If it bee but the counſell of man, deſpiſe it as vaine: but if yee cannot denie but that it is the moſt wholeſome aduiſe which the ſpirit of the Lorde giueth, then take heede how you ſet light by it. Hee willeth him that is entred into a good

way

way to stand fast and to continue. We see many that haue made some shew, so that there was great hope of them, but they are fallen backe, and returned euen as a dog to his vomite, and as the sow that was washed, to the wallowing in the myre 2. Pet. 2. It had been better for them if they had neuer knowne the truth, then so to turne from the holy commandement. It is but a little while, but he that commeth will come and will not tarrie. Can wee not hold out for a little time? I know it is hard, our nature is so vaine, wee are so corrupt, so light and so inconstant: and the temptations and allurements bee so many and so forcible: but seeing the end will be so good to the iust, and so grieuous to the wicked, stand fast. If it were but to escape the damnation of hell, it should bee of waight enough to moue vs: then how much more that continuing in the true feare of God, and glorifying him with good works, wee shall be partakers of the ioyes of heauen? The glory is exceeding great which is set before vs, if wee can striue to enter. And if it were so that man should but lose that glorie through their euill life, it were a great matter; but when beside that losse, they goe also into hell, euen into a gulfe of endles miseries, what a madnes is it? I leaue it to your consideration, wishing euery man to thinke vpon these words, He that is vniust, let him be vniust still: He that is filthie, let him be filthie still: He that is iust, let him be iust still: He that is holy, let him be holy still. And beholde I come quickly, and my rewarde is with me, to giue vnto euery one as his worke shall bee. If yee would but thinke vpon these things, it might make you carefull and warie, but because wee let slippe out of our minde the day of iudgement, and make account that our sinnes passe away euen as they bee committed, and shall neuer bee called into question, wee are bold not onely to neglect those holy and iust deedes which the Lord hath appointed vs to walke in, by which wee should glorifie the name of his sonne Iesus Christ which we do professe, and adorne the holy Gospell: but also wee doe fall into sundry offences whereby wee dishonour the Lord and our profession. Well, wee are much called vpon and put in minde in the holy scriptures touching these matters, and I pray you let it moove vs seriously to lay faster hold of the way of truth and righteousnes. Shall wicked & vngodly men be more constant in their vngodlines then wee in the feare of the Lord? They serue the deuill, they serue their lustes, their reward is in hell: we are to serue the Lord in holinesse, and to be rewarded with glory in heauen: shall they be more forward and constant in the seruice of that their Lord the deuil, then we in the seruice of our gracious God? let it shame vs, for of such a thing we ought to be ashamed indeed. And moreouer if they be so forward for such a reward as is bestowed in hell, shall we be slacke for the reward which is in heauen? Againe, let euery one of vs make this account, that if we will be aduised by the holy ghost and follow his counsell, when he sayth, he that is holy, let him be holy still: we must not continue weake, but we must grow vp in Christ and become strong men. For what is the cause that many fall and that so grieuously, but that they contented themselues in their weake estate, & did not labour to growe vp and to become strong? They professed the Gospel, and neuer consider, how farre the power of it had proceeded in them. They tooke some

delight,

THE REVELATION.

delight, and rested therein: but they should haue seene how it did subdue pride, selfe loue, vaine glory, with a number of suchlike euill and filthie affections which are deeply rooted in mans nature. For beloued when hee saith, hee that is holy, let him be holy still, it aduertiseth vs to gather strength that we may stand euen in the greatest temptations. If a man be giuen to anger, and doe not in time seeke to subdue it, yee know what the holy Apostle teacheth: he shall giue place to the deuill, and so the deuill entring leadeth him into many sinnes. I might here enter into many particulars, but know that except ye striue to subdue in all, ye hazard your selues: for looke wherein yee be weake, the temptation will come there at one time or another; and when men are fallen, it is no easie rising againe. Herein therefore we ought alwaies to be more then fearefull, least there should remaine any secret corrupt roote in our heart. The Lord purge our hearts from all those euill desires which we are by nature so stuffed and fraught withall, and fill vs with the graces of his spirit, that we may be strong and constant in true godlines, euen to the end. And thus much for this point of the conclusion. Let vs proceed to the next.

I am Alpha and Omega, the beginning and the ende, the first and the last. This is added as a ratification of the former words. They be not the wordes of a man, that either is not able to performe that which he speaketh, or else may alter and chaunge his minde, when he sayeth he will come and giue vnto euery one as his worke shall be: but they be the words of him that is eternall, almightie, and vnchangeable. And therefore he sayth, I am Alpha and Omega. Alpha is the first of the Greeke letters, and Omega is the last. Wherefore he expoundeth it saying, the first and the last, the beginning and the ende. In the first Chapter of this Prophecie, the Lord sayd, I am Alpha and Omega, the first and the last. Whereby you see it euident that he is eternall God, equall with the father. How is he else the beginning and the ende? How is he otherwise the first and the last? Then may ye see why it is here added againe, euen as I sayd, for confirmation. When we heare of great reward promised at the comming of our Lord, vnto all those which walke in the trueth, it doeth not so much moue vs, or affect vs as it ought to doe, and why? euen because we doe not giue so firme credite thereunto as we ought. We doe not throughly way and consider that the promise is made by him that is Alpha and Omega, euen the first and the last, who is almightie and vnchangeable. Also when the threatning is vttered against the euill doers, that hee will recompence vnto them vengeance for al their euill deeds, it is despised, and neglected, euen as if it came but from a mortall man. Therefore we are here assured, that there shall no iote fall to the ground of the terrible vengeance denounced against the wicked, in as much as it proceedeth not from a mortall man, but from him that is Alpha and Omega.

And herein because we are dull, marke how the promise and the threatning are againe repeated. First, the promise in these words, Blessed are they that keepe his commandements, that their part may be in the tree of life, and that they may enter in by the gates into the citie. Touching the tree of life, ye heard of it before, where

he

he speaketh of the riuer that runneth through the citie. Also we haue seene what a priuiledge it is to be admitted to enter into that heauenly Ierusalem. And here we learne againe who shall enter, and so who shall bee blessed, euen all that walke in the feare of God, and keepe his commandements. We are generally of the minde that a few words shal carry away the matter, as if men for saying Lord, Lord, shuld enter into the kingdom of heauen, but we are stil and often admonished and told, that none shall enter but such as doe the will of God. Is it not then our part first to be studious to learne to know the commandements, the ordinances and wayes of the Lord our God? For if we doe not know them, how shall we walke in them? Can a man walke in those waies which he doth not know nor vnderstand? Or shal a man bee thought to haue any loue or desire to walke in that way, which he seeketh not to know?

Then secondly, when we doe vnderstand the commaundement of God, it is our dutie to put them in practise, or els we are neuer the better: nay we are in worse case then before: for you know what our Sauiour saith in the Gospell, the seruant that knoweth his masters will and doeth it not, shall be beaten with many stripes. And Saint Iames handleth this point in the first chapter of his Epistle, where hauing shewed what benefite wee receiue by the word of trueth, namely, that we are begotten by it, he by and by exhorteth men to be swift to heare. And then further he willeth, that we should be doers of the word, and not hearers onely, deceiuing our selues. And then by a similitude of one that beholdeth his face in a glasse, and by and by goeth his way and forgetteth what manner of one hee is, hee teacheth what a vaine thing it is to be hearers of the worde of God onely, and not doers. Afterward he telleth what a blessed thing it is for a man to be both a very diligent student in the law of God, and also a doer of the same. Let vs then receiue admonition. Let vs become wise vnto saluation: for they that do this which is here taught, become wise vnto saluation: they shall haue their part in the tree of life, they shall enter in by the gates into the citie. And surely there is no greater follie and madnes, then for men to content and satisfie themselues with a bare hearing of the word of God preached. Doth not our Sauiour say, Blessed are they that heare the word of God and keepe it? What doth he meane by keeping of it? Is it that they keepe it in memorie, to dispute and talke of it, and no more? Nay they are not said to keepe it, which doe not in deeds performe it. And the Lord saith; whosoeuer doth the will of my father which is in heauen; he is my brother, sister & mother, Math. 12. vers. 50. Let no man then any longer be deceiued about this point, but know that onely such as doe the will of God shall be blessed for euermore.

Then followeth the threatning, For without shall be dogs and enchanters, and whoremongers, and murderers, and idolaters, and whosoeuer loueth and maketh lies. Here are the companie that shall not enter into the holy citie but shall be without, they shall be in hell. As the one part who keepe the commandements of God are blessed, so these filthie persons are accursed. But let vs now looke vpon the wordes, he beginneth with dogges. What are these dogges? Shall dogges goe to hell? Beloued, ye may not take it that hee meaneth these beastes which are called
dogs

dogs. It may seeme a very hard and a very vncharitable speech to call men dogges: but when the holy Ghost doth it, we may be bold. This ye may note, that they be wonderfull abominable and vile in the sight of the Lord, whom he calleth dogs. How be they degenerate, how haue they forgotten themselues, which are turned from men into dogs? But let vs see who they bee whom the holy scripture calleth dogs.

  First, the vnskilfull and couetous priests are called dumbe dogs, and greedie dogs, Esay 56. So foule a sinne it is to haue the charge ouer the Lords people, and not faithfully to feed and guide them. Saint Paul (speaking of the false Apostles, which corrupted the simplicitie of the Gospell) willeth the Philippians to beware of dogs, to beware of euill workmen, Philip. 3. Our Sauiour Christ giueth this precept, Giue not holy things to dogs, and cast not your pearles before swine, least they tread them vnder their feete, and the other turne againe and rent you, Matth. 7. verse 6. where ye are to note that there bee some men who when the Gospell is preached vnto them are not moued with wrath, but onely as it were neglect and despise the same, who are likned therefore vnto swine, and they are called swine which tread in the mire pearles, and so these tread vnder feete the heauenly pearles of the Gospell. Others there bee who when the Gospell is preached, are moued with rage and furie, because they cannot abide the pure doctrine. These flie vpon those that preach it. They rend and teare them. They be called dogs. These in old time murdered the holy prophets that spake in the name of the Lord. These haue put the Saints and Martyrs of Christ to death. These doe daily barke at the ministers and professors of the Gospell. Vnder a Christian prince where the holy word of God is set forth, these dogs do in some sort (at the least many of them) conforme themselues to the outward profession of it: and because the light of Gods trueth doth conuince them, they dare not for shame find fault with that, but say they reuerence it, when as indeed they abhorre it in their hearts, and seeke to finde faultes with those that doe publish it. How filthie and abominable these dogs are before the Lord, who is able to declare? Ye may reade what our Sauiour saith to his Apostles when he sent them forth at the first, how it should bee easier for Sodome and Gomorrha in the day of iudgement, then for those which should refuse to heare their doctrine, Math. 10. Then how horrible is the sinne, not onely to refuse, but also to be moued with wrath, euen to hate and persecute those that doe preach it? Yee shall see many of these vncleane and prophane men in all places, which euen gnash their teeth, that they cannot like dogs runne vpon those that reproue their euill works, and like dogs rend and teare them. As these doe now vtter many hard and slaunderous speeches, and many reproches against the ministers of the Gospel, so would they if time did serue, persecute them euen to the death. They be like dogs that are chained vp so long as the Gospell is maintained by the Christian prince. Here are ioyned with those dogs first inchaunters, then whoremongers, then murderers, then idolaters, and lastly, whosoeuer loueth & maketh lies. There be sundry sortes of inchaunters, coniurers, witches, and such as deele by the deuill, and by diuelish art. And how foule and monstrous a thing it is for men to deale and to be in

league

league with deuils, which are the sworne enemies of God, ye may easily consider. Whoredome is little or no euill in the sight of many. They esteeme it as a matter to laugh at, and many are come to that impudencie, that they can euen glorie and boast of it: But how abominable a thing it is before God, is seene by this, that the whoremongers are here associate with dogges and enchaunters, and the rest here named. Then also come in murderers, who are all those, as Saint Iohn plainely sheweth in his Epistle, that doe liue in hatred. The superstitious Idolaters perswade themselues in their blinde deuotion, and in their good intentes (as they call them) that they be very holy persons: and you may see here, that they bee euen as holy as murderets, whoremongers, witches and dogges with whom they be here associate. Meruaile not at it, for the idolater forsaketh the truth and the worship of the true God, and worshippeth deuils. Last of all he nameth an other very bond kind of people, and that is, whosoeuer loueth and maketh lies. This extendeth very large, for there be they that doe make lies in Gods matters, vttering false doctrine, and those which doe loue the same. And there be that do raise and vtter all manner of lies, vntruthes, and slaunders in mens matters. These are abominable. Let vs beware wee be not found among the number of such, for ye see there is no place for them within the holy citie: but they shall be without.

THE

THE L. SERMON.
CHAP. XXII.

16 *I Iesus sent mine Angel to testifie vnto ye these things in the Churches: I am the roote and the generation of Dauid, the bright morning starre.*

17 *And the spirit and the bride say come: and he that heareth let him say come. And he that is a thirst let him come. And hee that will let him take of the waters of life freely.*

18 *And I testifie vnto euery man that heareth the words of this prophecie: if any shall adde vnto these things, God will adde vnto him the plagues that are written in this booke.*

19 *And if any shall take away from the words of the prophecie of this booke, God will take away his part out of the booke of life, and out of the holy citie, and from the things which are wirtten in this booke.*

20 *He that testifieth these things saith, surely I come quickly, Amen, euen so, come Lord Iesus.*

21 *The grace of our Lord Iesus Christ be with ye all. Amen.*

WE are now come to the last part of the conclusion of this booke, wherein there be yet diuers pointes to handle. And first of all the authoritie of it is againe ratified from the person of him that is the author of it. For as yee see, the Lorde Iesus himselfe affirmeth, saying, I Iesus sent mine Angell to testifie these thinges vnto yee in the Churches. Looke what dignitie and authoritie hee is of, from whome the booke commeth, and accordingly esteeme the dignitie and authoritie of the same.

And if ye will consider the dignitie of the Lord Iesus the king of glorie, marke what he sayth of himselfe in the words that follow: I am the roote and the generation of Dauid, the bright morning starre. Here is the excellencie of Christ contained in these few words. The first part of them seemeth to bee drawne from the

Prophet

sell and power, the spirit of knowledge and of the feare of the Lord. And there it is shewed what great things hee shall doe: yea there is described the goodly reſtauration of all things by him. So that when he sayth, I am the roote and generation of Dauid, he leadeth vs to the consideration of all those great and excellent things, euen the things which are in the restauration made by him. All was cast downe, all was lost and fallen into vtter ruine, he as a most mightie redeemer restoreth them againe. In a worde then, whatsoeuer blessing God bestoweth vpon the world in his sonne, wee are led to the consideration of it in these words; I am the roote and the generation of Dauid. Moreouer, the Lorde Iesus (as hee saith in the Gospell of Iohn) is the light of the world: and therefore he saith here, I am the bright morning starre. But when as the holy Scripture calleth our Sauiour Christ the sonne of righteousnes, doth not this diminish of his glorie that he calleth him selfe the morning starre? For albeit the morning starre is bright and goodly, yet what is it to the Sunne? When the Sunne riseth, the light of that starre dooth giue place. To this I answer, that our Lord Iesus being called the bright morning starre, it doth not exclude the other, but he is also the Sunne. He is the morning starre, and he is the Sunne that ariseth with the full light. But seeing it is the purpose of the Lord to set forth the glorie of the riches and heauenly treasures which he bringeth vnto vs, why doth he rather choose the lesser then the greater? for the starre, as I sayd, is lesser then the Sunne. To this it may bee answered, that it is to shew that euen the very beginning of all light vnto vs is from Iesus Christ. We are couered vnder the night of spirituall darknes: he riseth vnto vs as the morning starre, very bright and comfortable, and proceedeth euen to be the full light of that cleere and blessed day that shall shine for euer, where there shall be no night. Then ye see that this Reuelation commeth from a person of most high dignitie, excellencie and glorie, and full of all pretious things: and so wee ought to esteeme of it. For comming from him (as he sayth, I Iesus sent mine Angell, &c.) wee must knowe that there be very good things in it, and such as doe neerely concerne vs. The Angell is but the seruant and messenger to testifie the things. Now vpon these words that our Lord saith, he is the roote and the generation of Dauid, and the bright morning starre, the spirit and the bride say, come. This spirit is the holy Ghost. The bride ye know is the Lambes wife, euen the Church. She hearing of these excellent things in Christ the redeemer and restorer, is inflamed and euen rauished with the desire of his comming, that she may haue the full fruition of them: For all the excellencie of those precious things in Christ are for her. And least we should thinke that this her earnest desire proceeded but from some humaine passion, when she

craueth

THE REVELATION.   449

craueth of him to come, here is expressed that the spirit also with her sayth, come. Her request and earnest desire then of the comming of Christ is good. But here will arise a doubt, how this is to be vnderstood that the holy Ghost dooth pray for the comming of Christ? We know that he is God equall with the Father and the Sonne. How then can he be said to make this request? Can we say that God doth pray? Indeede vpon this and such like places some haue wickedly held, that the holy Ghost is a creature, and not eternall God. But marke, I will shew you how it is to be taken. It is the same thing which S. Paul teacheth, Rom. 8. Wee know not (saith he) how to pray as wee ought: but the spirit himselfe maketh request for vs with gronings, which cannot be expressed. And he that searcheth the harts knoweth what the meaning is of the spirit: for he maketh intercession for the Saints according to God. Now beloued, looke how that place of Saint Paul is to be vnderstood, and so must we vnderstand this of S. Iohn. When he saith, that the spirit maketh request for vs with grones: we may not take it that the holy Ghost is subiect vnto any griefe or passion: but hee worketh those gronings in the hearts of the faithfull. He maketh them, or he teacheth them to pray with most vehement desires, euen with sighs and gronings that cannot bee expressed: and therefore he is sayd to pray with gronings. Euen so it is the spirit that instructeth and teacheth, and inflameth the Church with the vehement desire of the comming of Christ: and therefore he sayth, the spirit and the bride say, come. As S. Paul sayth then that the spirit maketh request according to God: so wee are to take it here, when hee saith, the spirit, and the bride say come, that the Church directed and taught by the holy Ghost, most vehemently longeth and prayeth for the comming of Christ, and that her prayer and desire herein is according to God. The bride verely could not pray thus but by ye holy Ghost, she could not haue that desire of heauenly things, but euen with the children of this world set her affections here below: and therefore to note who directeth her to this heauenly motion, it is sayd, the spirit and the bride say, come.

And let him that heareth say come. It is a thing indeede peculiar to the bride to loue the comming of Christ: in as much as she only hath the spirit which worketh that desire. And now to teach how excellent a thing it is, Saint Iohn dooth wish euery one that heareth to say come. It is as much as if he should stirre vs vp to couet aboue all other things to bee one of the children of the Church, to bee instructed and guided by that spirit which inflameth the heart, to crye come Lord Iesus. Here is a speciall thing to bee noted, and that is, that the Church and all her children doe waite for, and vehemently desire the comming of Christ vnto iudgement. If we feele no such desire in vs; is it not an argument against vs that wee bee not led by that spirit? Either we are in loue with the things of this world, and could be content euen to be seated in them for euer, not thirsting after heauenly things: or els our conscience doth so accuse vs, that we are afraide when wee heare of his comming. What an excellent thing is it to bee led by such a spirit, that dooth so purge the heart and reforme the conscience, that the comming of the Lord Iesus

vnto

vnto iudgement, which shal be most terrible and dreadfull vnto others, vnto them is most ioyfull and longed for? Is not here a wonderfull difference betweene the faithfull & the children of this world? Let euery man therefore make this account, that if he doe not long for the comming of the Lorde vnto iudgement, hee is not right, all is not well with him. For if he be a child of the Church endued with true faith, if he be led by the spirit of God, if he look for his part in those heauēly things: how can he but crie out in the feruent desire of his soule, Come Lord Iesus, come quickly. I pray you therefore, let euery one looke vnto their owne heart, and see what desire there is of this comming. If it be feeble and weake, seeke to be quickned with more abundance of the holy Ghost: seeke to haue the liuely hope of the partaking of those things which shall bee manifest and bestowed at his comming. There bee many things done here to the dishonor of God, and defacing of his trueth. We be here subiect vnto a thousand calamities. The things be wonderfull great which are layd vp in Christ to bee bestowed at his comming: shall wee not long for them? Then let him that heareth, say come. Doe ye heare that Iesus is the roote and generation of Dauid: euen he that shall make the glorious restauration? Doe ye heare that he is the bright morning starre, and that by him wee shall dwell in glorious light: and will ye not say come? Will ye not long for the time when these things shall be shewed forth?

Then he addeth: *And he that is a thirst, let him come.* Ye heard before that the promise is made to those that be a thirst. They be blessed that do thirst for the waters of life: for they shall come to the fountaine and drinke their fill. But such as be not a thirst, woe bee to them, they despise and set light by heauenly things, the fountaine shall be shut vp against them. They bee not worthie to be partakers of so precious things, which esteeme them so lightly. Woe bee to those then which care not for hearing the Gospell: if they had euer tasted how sweete the Lord is, they would runne after it: but alas they haue not tasted. They loue their owne wayes, and they shall be filled with their owne inuentions. They thirst after gold, and siluer, after houses and lands. They delight in gay garmēts. They couet earthly delights and pleasures, euen to fill themselues from day to day: and these things they shall abound in. But what are they the better? for all these shall vanish and come to nought. He that is a thirst for the waters of life, he that earnestly desireth those heauenly blessings which are bestowed in Christ, shall bee happie and blessed with the Lord God in heauen for euer.

Then there is added further: *And he that will, let him take of the waters of life freely.* Here is a very large offer: that whosoeuer will, shall take of the waters of life. It may be sayd, who is it that would not be saued? Men indeed loue to walke in wicked waies, and take pleasure in those sinnes which bring damnation both to the soule and to the bodie: but they doe not loue damnation, they could bee content to escape that, and willingly they would be saued: how then is it said here, let him that will, take of the waters of life freely? As I sayd, is not this a very large offer? is not here a very wide gate set open into heauen? Surely here is no more then

then that he saith before, hee will giue to him that is a thirst of the waters of life freely, chap. 21. for he that thirsteth hath a will: and he that thirsteth not, hath not a will. For this ye must know, that the will is not here put for euery light desire, or for euery wish that a man doth wish in his heart, when, as I said before, he walketh in the way of destruction, and committeth the things that deserue damnation, and yet would bee saued: But he is sayd to will, that loueth the way of the trueth, the way of godlines, the way that leadeth vnto saluation, and chooseth it and setteth himselfe in it. And how may this man be sayd to will and to choose? but euen when he imbraceth the holy doctrine of the Gospell, and by the same tasteth of the waters of life. They that will not loue, and delight in that pure doctrine, are sayd not to will. There is no way to drinke of the waters of life, but by drinking in that doctrine, which they will not. Then he that will, is he that imbraceth the pure word of the Lord, and filleth his soule therewith. True it is that men haue not this will of themselues: for man is wholly ouerspread in his minde with vanitie. There is a desire (as I sayd before) or a kinde of will in man, by which he coueteth to be free from calamities and miseries, and to inioy good and happie things: but to haue a will to hate that which is vncleane and filthie, to loue that which is pure and good, and to delight in the doctrine of the Lord, is farre from nature, and indeede is giuen onely by God. Make an end (sayth the holy Apostle) of your saluation with feare and trembling: for it is God that worketh in you both the will and the deede, euen of his good pleasure, Philip. 2. vers. 13. The spirit and the bride say come: euen the holy bride could not say come, but as the spirit instructeth and moueth her: how then can we haue any right will in vs, but that which the same spirit frameth? Indeede it is a firme will in the wicked that they will not take of the waters of life. They are carried naturally and of their owne accord to will and to choose that euill day, and they doe euen willingly despise the holy things of the Lord. Mans heart is corrupt and vaine, it cannot change it selfe, it cannot denye it selfe, it is inclined to that which is like it selfe: it hateth the contrary. Wherefore where vaine things and corrupt doe offer themselues, it apprehendeth them, loueth them, willeth them, chuseth them, and delighteth in them. When holy things are propounded, they be disagreeing, it hateth them, it despiseth them, it reiecteth them, it will none of them, vntill such time as the holy spirit of the Lord doe work and frame that will by changing it. Whereby ye may know, that when hee saith, he that will, let him take of the waters of life freely, the wicked refuse them of their owne corrupt will, and the godly doe chuse them being taught by his spirit. He that willeth then, euen he that is a thirst for the waters of life, let him giue all the praise to God, who hath endued him with that grace, and let him know, that were it not for the grace of God, hee should neuer haue had any will to come to those waters. And let such a man also daily begge of the Lord, that he may haue his will more and more reformed, euen to make choise of those things which indeede are most holy and precious.

And I testifie vnto euery man that heareth the words of the prophecie, if any ny man shall adde vnto these things, God will adde vnto him the plagues that are written in this booke. And if any man shall take away from the words of the prophecie of this booke, God will take away his part, &c. Here is another ratification of the high and sacred authoritie of this booke: which is by a commination very sharpe and terrible. It is for adding or diminishing. God dooth commaund by Moses, that they should adde nothing to the wordes which hee did commaund them, neither take any thing from them. And great presumption it is for any man to take vpon him such a matter. What is it indeede but for one to take vpon him to bee wiser then GOD? For either there is somewhat wanting which argueth an imperfection, or else there is somewhat superfluous, why else should it bee taken away? Doubtles it cannot bee but with exceeding wicked pride of mans heart and iniurie to the authoritie of the most high God, when any take vppon them either to adde to, or to diminish from his word. In this place therefore here is a sore threatning to such as shall any way presume, that is, either to adde or to diminish: which commendeth the booke as perfect and absolute, and such as commeth with the high authoritie of God. For the adding, he dooth threaten the adding of the plagues written in this booke: which are verie great. For besides diuerse and sundrie other plagues, yee haue seene the plague of hell diuerse times set foorth, and after moe waies then one. It is the great winepresse of the wrath of God which wee call hell. It is called the lake of fire and brimstone, in which the diuell and all the wicked shall bee tormented for euer. Hee that addeth, shall haue this great plague added vnto him. Likewise ye haue seene a goodly description of the ioyes of heauen, euen the glorie and felicitie of that holie citie. Ye haue heard also of the Lambes booke of life: he that taketh away any thing from the words of the prophecie of this booke, hee shall haue no name written in that booke, nor any part in that holie citie. To bee depriued of life and glorie, and not onely that, but also to bee cast into endles torments, might make men afraide how to bee so bolde with the word of the Lord. It may bee demaunded, what should bee the cause that here are so many things heaped vp for the confirmation of the authoritie of this booke. Surely there is some speciall cause, for the holie Ghost doth not vse to deale so much in a matter, and so earnestly, but vpon great cause. Ye may easily gather what the cause is. This booke as ye haue seene painteth out the kingdome of Antichrist and all Satans cunning and sleight: and for that cause Satan hath laboured especially to bring downe the authoritie and credit of this booke. He by some meanes in olde time preuailed thus farre, that euen among some Churches of true Christians, the authoritie and truth of it was doubted of. The holy Ghost did foresee this practise of Satan, and addeth the more for the confirmation thereof: for it was needfull. If the booke should neuer in speciall sort be impugned, there needed not any such speciall confirmation. Now by the singular goodnes of God, there is no question, nor controuersie, nor doubt concerning the authoritie of this booke. The papists themselues doe acknowledge it to bee the sacred and vndoubted word of God.

THE REVELATION. 453

God. In deede of all scriptures they cannot endure that it should bee medled withall. They say it is so darke that it cannot be vnderstoode. They holde that little in comparison can bee noted in it, which indeede is almost to deny the authoritie thereof. For to make it without vse, is to make the authoritie of it to no purpose. And what doe they but make it without vse almost, if little can be noted in it? But blessed be God, it is so cleere, that as many as haue their eyes opened, both of learned and vnlearned, may see their kingdome described in it. Now let it here bee considered, whether wee or the papists may more rightly bee charged to adde to the worde of God. We holde strictly that the bookes of the Apostles and Prophets, euen the bookes of the olde and newe Testament, which the churches since the Apostles time haue receiued for canonicall, are the perfect worde of God, and none other. Wee holde that the Lorde in these bookes hath deliuered his whole counsels and will, touching the faith and obedience which hee requireth of man. Wee holde indeede, that the worship of God is so perfectly set forth in those writings of the Apostles and Prophets, that all matters of religion are to bee ruled by that written word. We doe maintaine, that whatsoeuer is added as a matter of religion, the same is wicked and abominable. Wee holde that all they which dare take vpon them to dispense with any part of the holy word, are cursed. Wee holde indeede that the word of God written, is absolutely perfect, and all controuersies to bee decided by it. Our aduersaries take vpon them to maintaine that besides the written word, there bee also vnwritten verities, which are kept by tradition. They adde to the holy Scriptures sundrie bookes, which they take vpon them to make Canonicall: which bookes were neuer written by any Prophets or Apostles. They say that the holy Scriptures are doubtfull and vncertaine, and not sufficient to decide and to determine all controuersies in religion. They maintaine that the authoritie of the holy scripture in respect of men, dependeth vpon their church. They holde the decretall epistles of their Popes, and Canons of generall Councels in some equalitie with the written word of God: in as much as they maintaine them to be free from all error. In all these things, doe they not adde nor take away? I suppose there is no man of vnderstanding, which will not confesse that they doe both adde and diminish. What an impudencie is it then in them, vpon this place to charge vs? We being so cleere, and standing so firme for the whole scriptures, and for nothing but scripture, and they themselues so guiltie many waies. Let them alone, the threatning here vttered against such as adde or diminish, must needes come vpon them. Touching the cauill of those of the familie of loue, it is not worth the answering. Some of them saye, that such as expounde doe adde to the holy scriptures: but interpretation, and the true application of the word of GOD, is no adding. Then Saint Iohn addeth, hee that testifieth these things saith, Beholde I come quickely. This is to stirre vp the mindes of the faithfull to watch for his comming. For wee are dull, and thinke the comming of the Lorde farre off. The reason is, that wee cannot rightly measure time. For if wee could see, it should appeare that a thousand yeeres is euen almost as nothing: for what is it to eternitie, which after many thousand thousand yeeres, commeth not any neerer to an end: for where there is no end, the end commeth not neere. Men thinke the time of their life here a great long time, and very madly for a few pleasures of sinne cast away themselues for euer. We should remember that the end of the world is euen come vpon vs, and that the Lord will come quickly, and so prepare our selues for his comming. The Lord saith he will come quickly, and Saint Iohn crieth out with great zeale, Amen, euen so, come Lord Iesus. This desire of his comming ought wee all to haue, if we be led by that same spirit that Saint Iohn was. Then he concludeth this holy booke with the last part of the conclusion, that is, by wishing all spirituall blessings vpon them, which he expresseth in these words: The grace of our Lord Iesus Christ be with ye all, Amen. The Lord bring his prayer vpon vs.

FINIS.

www.ingramcontent.com/pod-product-compliance
Lightning Source LLC
Chambersburg PA
CBHW022104300426
44117CB00007B/575